# COLLINS
# ESSENTIAL
# ATLAS
## OF THE WORLD

HarperCollinsPublishers

# ESSENTIAL ATLAS OF THE WORLD

# CONTENTS

## THE WORLD

Collins Essential Atlas of the World
First published 1998
Reprinted 1998, 1999

Copyright ©HarperCollinsPublishers Ltd 1998

Maps © Bartholomew Ltd 1998

Collins
An Imprint of HarperCollinsPublishers
77-85 Fulham Palace Road
London W6 8JB

Printed in Singapore

ISBN 0 00 448611 0

Cover/title page photo : Wayne Lawler; Ecoscene/Corbis

MH10217 Imp 03

## EUROPE

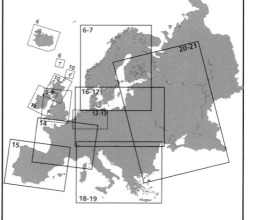

## ASIA

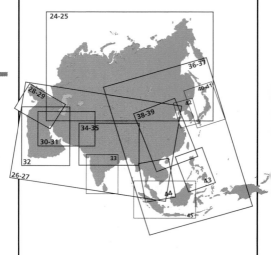

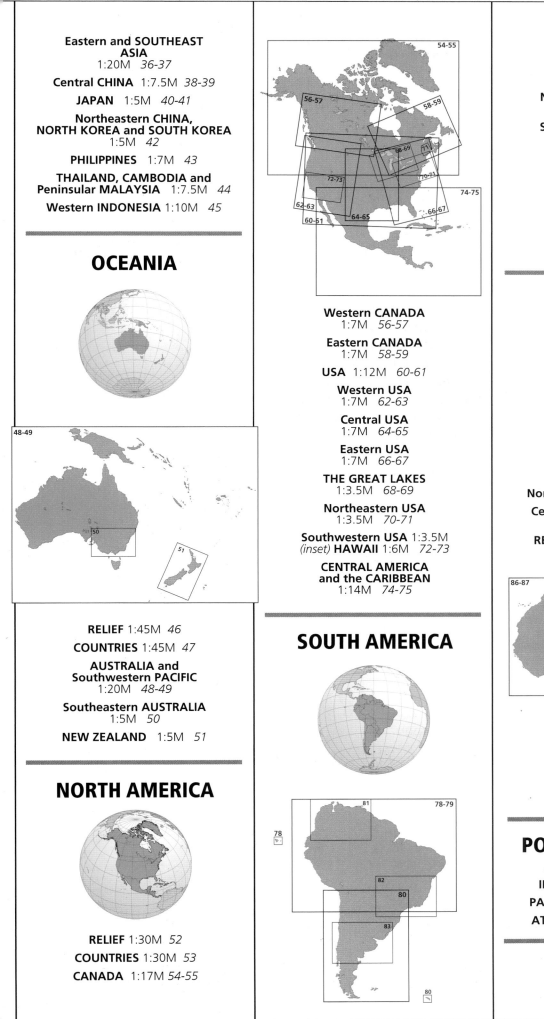

# NATIONS OF THE WORLD

| COUNTRY | AREA | | POPULATION | | | CITY | LANGUAGES | RELIGIONS | CURRENCY |
|---|---|---|---|---|---|---|---|---|---|
| | | | TOTAL | DENSITY PER | | CAPITAL | | | |
| | sq ml | sq km | | sq ml | sq km | | | | |
| ALBANIA | 11 100 | 28 748 | 3 414 000 | 308 | 119 | Tirana | Albanian | Muslim, Orthodox, Roman Catholic | Lek |
| ANDORRA | 180 | 465 | 65 000 | 362 | 140 | Andorra la Vella | Catalan, Spanish, French | Roman Catholic | Fr franc, Sp pese |
| AUSTRIA | 32 377 | 83 855 | 8 031 000 | 248 | 96 | Vienna | German, Serbo-Croat | Roman Catholic, Protestant | Schilling |
| AZORES | 868 | 2 247 | 237 800 | 274 | 106 | Ponta Delgada | Turkish Portuguese | Roman Catholic, Protestant | Port. escudo |
| BELARUS | 80 155 | 207 600 | 10 355 000 | 129 | 50 | Minsk | Belorussian, Russian, Ukrainian | Orthodox, Roman Catholic | Rouble |
| BELGIUM | 11 784 | 30 520 | 10 080 000 | 855 | 330 | Brussels | Dutch (Flemish), French, German | Roman Catholic, Protestant | Franc |
| BOSNIA-HERZEGOVINA | 19 741 | 51 130 | 4 459 000 | 226 | 87 | Sarajevo | Serbo-Croat | Muslim, Orthodox, Roman Catholic, Protestant | Dinar |
| BULGARIA | 42 855 | 110 994 | 8 443 000 | 197 | 76 | Sofia | Bulgarian, Turkish | Orthodox, Muslim | Lev |
| CHANNEL ISLANDS | 75 | 195 | 149 000 | 1987 | 764 | St Helier, St Peter Port | English, French | Protestant, Roman Catholic | Pound |
| CROATIA | 21 829 | 56 538 | 4 777 000 | 219 | 84 | Zagreb | Serbo-Croat | Roman Catholic, Orthodox, Muslim | Kuna |
| CZECH REPUBLIC | 30 450 | 78 864 | 10 336 000 | 339 | 131 | Prague | Czech, Moravian, Slovak | Roman Catholic, Protestant | Koruna |
| DENMARK | 16 631 | 43 075 | 5 205 000 | 313 | 121 | Copenhagen | Danish | Protestant, Roman Catholic | Krone |
| ESTONIA | 17 452 | 45 200 | 1 499 000 | 86 | 33 | Tallinn | Estonian, Russian | Protestant, Orthodox | Kroon |
| FAROE ISLANDS | 540 | 1 399 | 47 000 | 87 | 34 | Tórshavn | Danish, Faeroese | Protestant | Danish krone |
| FINLAND | 130 559 | 338 145 | 5 088 000 | 39 | 15 | Helsinki | Finnish, Swedish | Protestant, Orthodox | Markka |
| FRANCE | 210 026 | 543 965 | 58 375 000 | 278 | 107 | Paris | French, French dialects, Arabic, German (Alsatian) | Roman Catholic, Protestant, Muslim | Franc |
| GERMANY | 138 174 | 357 868 | 81 912 000 | 593 | 229 | Berlin | German | Protestant, Roman Catholic, | Mark |
| GIBRALTAR | 3 | 7 | 28 000 | 11157 | 4308 | Gibraltar | English, Spanish | Roman Catholic, Protestant, | Pound |
| GREECE | 50 949 | 131 957 | 10 426 000 | 205 | 79 | Athens | Greek | Greek Orthodox | Drachma |
| HUNGARY | 35 919 | 93 030 | 10 261 000 | 286 | 110 | Budapest | Hungarian | Roman Catholic, Protestant | Forint |
| ICELAND | 39 699 | 102 820 | 266 000 | 7 | 3 | Reykjavik | Icelandic | Protestant, Roman Catholic | Króna |
| ISLE OF MAN | 221 | 572 | 73 000 | 331 | 128 | Douglas | English | Protestant, Roman Catholic | Pound |
| ITALY | 116 311 | 301 245 | 57 193 000 | 492 | 190 | Rome | Italian, Italian dialects | Roman Catholic | Lira |
| LATVIA | 24 595 | 63 700 | 2 548 000 | 104 | 40 | Rīga | Latvian, Russian | Protestant, Roman Catholic, Orthodox | Lat |
| LIECHTENSTEIN | 62 | 160 | 31 000 | 502 | 194 | Vaduz | German | Roman Catholic, Protestant | Swiss franc |
| LITHUANIA | 25 174 | 65 200 | 3 721 000 | 148 | 57 | Vilnius | Lithuanian, Russian, Polish | Roman Catholic, Protestant, Orthodox | Litas |
| LUXEMBOURG | 998 | 2 586 | 404 000 | 405 | 156 | Luxembourg | Letzeburgish, Portuguese | Roman Catholic, Protestant | Franc |
| MACEDONIA, Former Yugoslavian Republic of | 9 928 | 25 713 | 2 142 000 | 216 | 83 | Skopje | Macedonian | Orthodox, Muslim, Roman Catholic | Denar |
| MADEIRA | 307 | 794 | 253 000 | 825 | 319 | Funchal | Portuguese | Roman Catholic, Protestant | Port. escudo |
| MALTA | 122 | 316 | 373 000 | 3057 | 1180 | Valletta | Maltese, English | Roman Catholic | Lira |
| MOLDOVA | 13 012 | 33 700 | 4 350 000 | 334 | 129 | Chişinău | Romanian, Russian, Ukrainian | Moldovan, Orthodox, | Leu |
| MONACO | 1 | 2 | 32 821 | 32821 | 16410 | Monaco | French, Monegasque, Italian | Roman Catholic | French franc |
| NETHERLANDS | 16 033 | 41 526 | 15 517 000 | 968 | 374 | Amsterdam | Dutch, Frisian | Roman Catholic, Protestant | Guilder |
| NORWAY | 125 050 | 323 878 | 4 325 000 | 35 | 13 | Oslo | Norwegian | Protestant, Roman Catholic | Krone |
| POLAND | 120 728 | 312 683 | 38 544 000 | 319 | 123 | Warsaw | Polish, German | Roman Catholic, Orthodox | Zæoty |
| PORTUGAL | 34 340 | 88 940 | 9 902 000 | 288 | 111 | Lisbon | Portuguese | Roman Catholic, Protestant | Escudo |
| REPUBLIC OF IRELAND | 27 136 | 70 282 | 3 571 000 | 132 | 51 | Dublin | English, Irish | Roman Catholic, Protestant | Punt |
| ROMANIA | 91 699 | 237 500 | 22 731 000 | 248 | 96 | Bucharest | Romanian | Orthodox | Leu |
| RUSSIAN FEDERATION | 6 592 849 | 17 075 400 | 147 739 000 | 22 | 9 | Moscow | Russian, Tatar, Ukrainian, local languages | Orthodox, Muslim, other Christian, Jewish | Rouble |
| RUSSIAN FEDERATION (in Europe) | 1 527 343 | 3 955 800 | 105 984 000 | 69 | 27 | | | | |
| SAN MARINO | 24 | 61 | 25 000 | 1061 | 410 | San Marino | Italian | Roman Catholic | Ital. lira |
| SLOVAKIA | 18 933 | 49 035 | 5 347 000 | 282 | 109 | Bratislava | Slovak, Hungarian, Czech | Roman Catholic, Protestant | Koruna |
| SLOVENIA | 7 819 | 20 251 | 1 989 000 | 254 | 98 | Ljubljana | Slovene, Serbo-Croat | Roman Catholic, Protestant | Tólar |
| SPAIN | 194 897 | 504 782 | 39 143 000 | 201 | 78 | Madrid | Spanish, Catalan, Galician, Basque | Roman Catholic | Peseta |
| SWEDEN | 173 732 | 449 964 | 8 781 000 | 51 | 20 | Stockholm | Swedish | Protestant, Roman Catholic | Krona |
| SWITZERLAND | 15 943 | 41 293 | 6 995 000 | 439 | 169 | Bern | German, French, Italian, Romansch | Roman Catholic, Protestant | Franc |
| UNITED KINGDOM | 94 241 | 244 082 | 58 144 000 | 617 | 238 | London | English, South Indian languages, Welsh, Gaelic | Protestant, Roman Catholic, Muslim | Pound |
| UKRAINE | 233 090 | 603 700 | 51 910 000 | 223 | 86 | Kiev | Ukrainian, Russian, regional languages | Orthodox, Roman Catholic | Karbovanets |
| VATICAN CITY | | 0.44 | 1000 | | 2273 | | Italian | Roman Catholic | Ital. lira |
| YUGOSLAVIA | 39 449 | 102 173 | 10 516 000 | 267 | 103 | Belgrade | Serbo-Croat, Albanian, Hungarian | Serbian and Montenegrin Orthodox, Muslim | Dinar |

| COUNTRY | AREA | | POPULATION | | | CITY | LANGUAGES | RELIGIONS | CURRENCY |
|---|---|---|---|---|---|---|---|---|---|
| | | | TOTAL | DENSITY PER | | CAPITAL | | | |
| | sq ml | sq km | | sq ml | sq km | | | | |
| AFGHANISTAN | 251 825 | 652 225 | 18 879 000 | 75 | 29 | Kābul | Dari, Pushtu, Uzbek | Sunni & Shi'a Muslim | Afghani |
| ARMENIA | 11 506 | 29 800 | 3 548 000 | 308 | 119 | Yerevan | Armenian, Azeri, Russian | Orthodox, Roman Catholic, Muslim | Dram |
| AZERBAIJAN | 33 436 | 86 600 | 7 472 000 | 223 | 86 | Baku | Azeri, Armenian, Russian, | Shi'a & Sunni Muslim, | Manat |
| BAHRAIN | 267 | 691 | 599 000 | 2244 | 867 | Al Manāma | Arabic, English | Shi'a & Sunni Muslim, Christian | Dinar |
| BANGLADESH | 55 598 | 143 998 | 120 073 000 | 2160 | 834 | Dhaka | Bengali | Muslim, Hindu | Taka |
| BHUTAN | 18 000 | 46 620 | 1 614 000 | 90 | 35 | Thimphu | Dzongkha, Nepali, Assamese | Buddhist, Hindu, Muslim | Ngultrum |
| BRUNEI | 2 226 | 5 765 | 280 000 | 126 | 49 | Bandar Seri Begawan | Malay, English, Chinese | Muslim, Buddhist, Christian | Dollar (ringgit) |
| CAMBODIA | 69 884 | 181 000 | 9 568 000 | 137 | 53 | Phnum Penh | Khmer | Buddhist, Muslim | Riel |
| CHINA | 3 691 899 | 9 560 900 | 1 232 083 000 | 334 | 129 | Beijing | Chinese, regional languages | Confucian, Taoist, Buddhist | Yuan |
| CYPRUS | 3 572 | 9 251 | 726 000 | 203 | 78 | Nicosia | Greek, Turkish, English | Greek Orthodox, Muslim | Pound |
| GEORGIA | 26 911 | 69 700 | 5 450 000 | 203 | 78 | T'bilisi | Georgian, Russian, Armenian | Orthodox, Muslim | Lari |
| INDIA | 1 269 219 | 3 287 263 | 944 580 000 | 744 | 287 | New Delhi | Hindi, English, regional languages | Hindu, Muslim, Sikh, Christian | Rupee |
| INDONESIA | 741 102 | 1 919 445 | 196 813 000 | 266 | 103 | Jakarta | Indonesian, local languages | Muslim, Protestant, Roman Catholic | Rupiah |
| IRAN | 636 296 | 1 648 000 | 61 128 000 | 96 | 37 | Tehrān | Farsi, Azeri, Kurdish | Shi'a & Sunni Muslim | Rial |
| IRAQ | 169 235 | 438 317 | 19 925 000 | 118 | 45 | Baghdād | Arabic, Kurdish | Shi'a & Sunni Muslim | Dinar |
| ISRAEL | 8 019 | 20 770 | 5 399 000 | 673 | 260 | Jerusalem | Hebrew, Arabic | Jewish, Muslim, Christian | Shekel |
| JAPAN | 145 841 | 377 727 | 125 761 000 | 862 | 333 | Tōkyō | Japanese | Shintoist, Buddhist | Yen |
| JORDAN | 34 443 | 89 206 | 5 198 000 | 151 | 58 | 'Ammān | Arabic | Sunni & Shi'a Muslim | Dinar |
| KAZAKSTAN | 1 049 155 | 2 717 300 | 17 027 000 | 16 | 6 | Almaty | Kazakh, Russian | Muslim, Orthodox, Protestant | Tanga |
| KUWAIT | 6 880 | 17 818 | 1 620 000 | 235 | 91 | Kuwait | Arabic | Sunni & Shi'a Muslim, Christian | Dinar |
| KYRGYZSTAN | 76 641 | 198 500 | 4 473 000 | 58 | 23 | Bishkek | Kirghiz, Russian, Uzbek | Muslim, Orthodox | Som |
| LAOS | 91 429 | 236 800 | 4 742 000 | 52 | 20 | Vientiane | Lao, local languages | Buddhist, traditional beliefs | Kip |
| LEBANON | 4 036 | 10 452 | 2 915 000 | 722 | 279 | Beirut | Arabic, French, Armenian | Shi'a & Sunni Muslim, Protestant, Roman Catholic | Pound |
| MACAU | 7 | 17 | 440 000 | 62857 | 25882 | Macau | Chinese, Portuguese | Buddhist | Pataca |
| MALAYSIA | 128 559 | 332 965 | 20 097 000 | 156 | 60 | Kuala Lumpur | Malay, English, Chinese, | Muslim, Buddhist, Roman Catholic, Christian, trad. beliefs | Ringgit |
| MALDIVES | 115 | 298 | 263 015 | 2287 | 883 | Male | Divehi (Maldivian) | Muslim | Rufiyaa |
| MONGOLIA | 604 250 | 1 565 000 | 2 363 000 | 4 | 2 | Ulaanbaatar | Khalka (Mongolian), Kazakh | Buddhist, Muslim, traditional beliefs | Tugrik |
| MYANMAR | 261 228 | 676 577 | 43 922 000 | 168 | 65 | Yangon | Burmese, Shan, Karen | Buddhist, Muslim, Protestant, | Kyat |
| NEPAL | 56 827 | 147 181 | 21 360 000 | 376 | 145 | Kathmandu | Nepali, Maithili, Bhojpuri | Hindu, Buddhist | Rupee |
| NORTH KOREA | 46 540 | 120 538 | 23 483 000 | 505 | 195 | P'yŏngyang | Korean | Trad. beliefs, Chondoist | Won |
| OMAN | 105 000 | 271 950 | 2 096 000 | 20 | 8 | Muscat | Arabic, Baluchi | Muslim | Rial |
| PAKISTAN | 310 403 | 803 940 | 134 146 000 | 432 | 167 | Islamabad | Urdu, Punjabi, Sindhi, Pushtu | Muslim, Christian, Hindu | Rupee |
| PALAU | 192 | 497 | 17 000 | 89 | 34 | Koror | Palauan, English | Roman Catholic, Protestant | US dollar |
| PHILIPPINES | 115 831 | 300 000 | 71 899 000 | 621 | 240 | Manila | Filipino, Cebuano, local languages | Roman Catholic, Aglipayan, Muslim | Peso |
| QATAR | 4 416 | 11 437 | 593 000 | 134 | 52 | Doha | Arabic, Indian lang. | Muslim, Christian | Riyal |
| RUSSIAN FEDERATION | 6 592 849 | 17 075 400 | 147 739 000 | 22 | 9 | Moscow | Russian, Tatar, Ukrainian, local languages | Orthodox, other Christian, Muslim, Jewish | Rouble |
| RUSSIAN FEDERATION (in Asia) | 5 065 506 | 13 119 600 | 41 755 000 | 8 | 3 | | | | |
| SAUDI ARABIA | 849 425 | 2 200 000 | 17 451 000 | 21 | 8 | Riyadh | Arabic | Sunni & Shi'a Muslim | Riyal |
| SINGAPORE | 247 | 639 | 3 044 000 | 12324 | 4764 | Singapore | Chinese, English, Malay, Tamil | Buddhist, Taoist, Muslim, Christian | Dollar |
| SOUTH KOREA | 38 330 | 99 274 | 45 547 000 | 1188 | 450 | Seoul | Korean | Buddhist, Protestant, Roman Catholic | Won |
| SRI LANKA | 25 332 | 65 610 | 17 865 000 | 705 | 272 | Colombo | Sinhalese, Tamil, English | Buddhist, Hindu, Muslim | Rupee |
| SYRIA | 71 498 | 185 180 | 13 844 000 | 194 | 75 | Damascus | Arabic, Kurdish | Muslim, Christian | Pound |
| TAIWAN | 13 969 | 36 179 | 21 212 000 | 1518 | 586 | T'ai-pei | Chinese, local languages | Buddhist, Taoist, Confucian, | Dollar |
| TAJIKISTAN | 55 251 | 143 100 | 5 933 000 | 107 | 41 | Dushanbe | Tajik, Uzbek, Russian | Muslim | Rouble |
| THAILAND | 198 115 | 513 115 | 60 003 000 | 303 | 117 | Bangkok | Thai, Lao, Chinese | Buddhist, Muslim | Baht |
| TURKEY | 300 948 | 779 452 | 62 697 000 | 208 | 80 | Ankara | Turkish, Kurdish | Sunni & Shi'a Muslim | Lira |
| TURKMENISTAN | 188 456 | 488 100 | 4 010 000 | 21 | 8 | Ashgabat | Turkmen, Russian | Muslim | Manat |
| UNITED ARAB EMIRATES | 30 000 | 77 700 | 1 861 000 | 62 | 24 | Abu Dhabi | Arabic | Sunni & Shi'a Muslim, Christian | Dirham |
| UZBEKISTAN | 172 742 | 447 400 | 22 633 000 | 131 | 51 | Tashkent | Uzbek, Russian, Tajik, Kazakh | Muslim, Orthodox | Som |
| VIETNAM | 127 246 | 329 565 | 75 181 000 | 591 | 228 | Ha Nôi | Vietnamese | Buddhist, Roman Catholic | Dong |
| YEMEN | 203 850 | 527 968 | 12 672 000 | 62 | 24 | Şan'ā | Arabic | Sunni & Shi'a Muslim | Dinar, rial |

| COUNTRY | AREA | | POPULATION | | | CITY | LANGUAGES | RELIGIONS | CURRENCY |
|---|---|---|---|---|---|---|---|---|---|
| | | | TOTAL | DENSITY PER | | CAPITAL | | | |
| | sq ml | sq km | | sq ml | sq km | | | | |
| AMERICAN SAMOA | 76 | 197 | 55 000 | 723 | 279 | Pago Pago | Samoan, English | Protestant, Roman Catholic | US dollar |
| AUSTRALIA | 2 966 153 | 7 682 300 | 17 838 000 | 6 | 2 | Canberra | English, Aboriginal languages | Protestant, Roman Catholic, Aboriginal beliefs | Dollar |
| FIJI | 7 077 | 18 330 | 784 000 | 111 | 43 | Suva | English, Fijian, Hindi | Christian, Hindu, Muslim | Dollar |
| FRENCH POLYNESIA | 1 261 | 3 265 | 215 000 | 171 | 66 | Papeete | French, Polynesian languages | Protestant, Roman Catholic, | Pacific franc |
| GUAM | 209 | 541 | 146 000 | 699 | 270 | Agana | Chamorro, English | Roman Catholic | US dollar |
| KIRIBATI | 277 | 717 | 77 000 | 278 | 107 | Bairiki | I-Kiribati (Gilbertese), English | Roman Catholic, Protestant | Austr. dollar |
| MARSHALL ISLANDS | 70 | 181 | 54 000 | 773 | 298 | Dalap-Uliga-Darrit | Marshallese, English | Protestant, Roman Catholic | US dollar |
| FED. STATES OF MICRONESIA | 271 | 701 | 104 000 | 384 | 148 | Palikir | English, Trukese, Pohnpeian, local languages | Protestant, Roman Catholic | US dollar |
| NAURU | 8 | 21 | 11 000 | 1357 | 524 | Yaren | Nauruan, Gilbertese, English | Protestant, Roman Catholic | Austr. dollar |
| NEW CALEDONIA | 7 358 | 19 058 | 184 000 | 25 | 10 | Nouméa | French, local languages | Roman Catholic, Protestant | Pacific franc |
| NEW ZEALAND | 104 454 | 270 534 | 3 493 000 | 33 | 13 | Wellington | English, Maori | Protestant, Roman Catholic | Dollar |
| NORTH. MARIANA IS. | 184 | 477 | 47 000 | 255 | 99 | Saipan | English, Chamorro, Tagalog | Roman Catholic, Protestant | US dollar |
| PAPUA NEW GUINEA | 178 704 | 462 840 | 3 997 000 | 22 | 9 | Port Moresby | English, Tok Pisin | Protestant, Roman Catholic | Kina |
| SOLOMON ISLANDS | 10 954 | 28 370 | 366 000 | 33 | 13 | Honiara | English, Pidgin | Protestant, Roman Catholic | Dollar |
| TONGA | 289 | 748 | 98 000 | 339 | 131 | Nuku'alofa | Tongan, English | Protestant, Roman Catholic, Mormon | Pa'anga |
| TUVALU | 10 | 25 | 10 000 | 1000 | 400 | Fongafale | Tuvaluan, English | Protestant | Dollar |
| VANUATU | 4 707 | 12 190 | 165 000 | 35 | 14 | Port Vila | English, Bislama, French | Protestant, Roman Catholic | Vatu |
| WALLIS AND FUTUNA | 106 | 274 | 14 000 | 132 | 51 | Mata-Utu | French, Polynesian | Roman Catholic | Pacific franc |
| WESTERN SAMOA | 1 093 | 2 831 | 164 000 | 150 | 58 | Apia | Samoan, English | Protestant, Roman Catholic | Tala |

# ECONOMIC GROUPS

## EUROPEAN UNION (EU)

Originally the European Economic Community, founded by the Treaty of Rome in 1957, signed by Belgium, France, West Germany, Italy, Luxembourg and the Netherlands. Denmark, the Republic of Ireland and the United Kingdom joined in 1973; Greece in 1981 and Spain and Portugal in 1986. The objectives, under the Treaty of Rome, are to lay the foundations of an ever closer union among the peoples of Europe, and to ensure economic and social progress.
*Headquarters* : Brussels, Belgium

## EUROPEAN ECONOMIC AREA (EEA)

On 1 January 1994 the EU nations and the EFTA nations formed the European Economic Area, the World's largest multi-lateral trading area.

## ASSOCIATION OF SOUTH EAST ASIAN NATIONS (ASEAN)

Established in 1967, the objectives of ASEAN are to promote economic, political and social co-operation. The founder members were Indonesia, Malaysia, the Philippines, Singapore and Thailand; Brunei joined in 1984 and Vietnam in 1995. Cambodia, Laos and Myanmar have applied for membership.
*Headquarters* : Jakarta, Indonesia

## ASIA PACIFIC ECONOMIC CO-OPERATION FORUM (APEC)

Formed in 1989 to promote trade and economic co-operation, with the long term aim of the creation of a Pacific free trade area. The original members were Australia, Brunei, Canada, Indonesia, Japan, Malaysia, New Zealand, the Philippines, Singapore, South Korea, Thailand and U.S.A.. China, Hong Kong and Taiwan joined in 1991, Mexico and Papua New Guinea in 1993, and Chile in 1994.
*Headquarters* : Singapore

## CARIBBEAN COMMUNITY (CARICOM)

CARICOM was established in 1973. The original members were Barbados, Guyana, Jamaica and Trinidad and Tobago; in May 1974, Belize, Dominica, Grenada, Montserrat, St Lucia, and St Vincent joined followed by Antigua and St Kitts-Nevis in August 1974, the Bahamas in 1984 and Surinam in 1995. The objectives of CARICOM are to foster co-operation, co-ordinate foreign policy, and to formulate and carry out common policies on health, education and culture, communications and industrial relations.
*Headquarters* : Georgetown, Guyana

## MERCADO COMMUN DEL SUR (Southern Common Market MERCOSUR)

Established by a treaty signed in Paraguay in 1991 by Argentina, Brazil, Paraguay and Uruguay, Mercosur's objective is to establish a regional common market.
*Headquarters* : Mercosur's headquarters rotate between member states' capitals.

## NORTH AMERICAN FREE TRADE AREA (NAFTA)

NAFTA grew out of a 1988 free trade agreement between U.S.A. and Canada, which was extended to include Mexico in 1992. The accord came into force in January 1994.

## ORGANISATION FOR ECONOMIC CO-OPERATION AND DEVELOPMENT (OECD)

Established in 1961, the OECD's objective is to promote economic and social welfare throughout the OECD area. It does this by assisting member governments in the formulation and co-ordination of policies to meet this objective; it also aims to stimulate and harmonise members' efforts in favour of developing countries.
*Headquarters* : Paris, France

## ORGANIZATION OF PETROLEUM EXPORTING COUNTRIES (OPEC)

Established in 1960 to co-ordinate the price and supply policies of oil-producing states, and to provide member countries with economic and technical aid. Member countries are Algeria, Ecuador, Gabon, Indonesia, Iran, Iraq, Kuwait, Libya, Nigeria, Qatar, Saudi Arabia, U.A.E., and Venezuela.
*Headquarters* : Vienna, Austria

## SOUTHERN AFRICAN DEVELOPMENT COMMUNITY (SADC)

The founder members of SADC were Angola, Botswana, Lesotho, Malawi, Mozambique, Swaziland, Tanzania, Zambia and Zimbabwe. Namibia joined in 1990, South Africa in 1994 and Mauritius in 1995. The objectives are deeper economic co-operation and integration and the promotion of political and social values, human rights and the alleviation of poverty.
*Headquarters* : Gaborone, Botswana

| COUNTRY | AREA | | POPULATION | | | CITY | LANGUAGES | RELIGIONS | CURRENCY |
| | | | TOTAL | DENSITY PER | | CAPITAL | | | |
| | sq ml | sq km | | sq ml | sq km | | | | |
| --- | --- | --- | --- | --- | --- | --- | --- | --- | --- |
| ANGUILLA | 60 | 155 | 8 000 | 134 | 52 | The Valley | English | Protestant, Roman Catholic | E. Carib. dollar |
| ANTIGUA & BARBUDA | 171 | 442 | 65 000 | 381 | 147 | St John's | English, Creole | Protestant, Roman Catholic | E. Carib. dollar |
| BAHAMAS | 5 382 | 13 939 | 272 000 | 51 | 20 | Nassau | English, Creole, French Creole | Protestant, Roman Catholic | Dollar |
| BARBADOS | 166 | 430 | 264 000 | 1590 | 614 | Bridgetown | English, Creole (Bajan) | Protestant, Roman Catholic | Dollar |
| BELIZE | 8 867 | 22 965 | 211 000 | 24 | 9 | Belmopan | English, Creole, Spanish, Mayan | Roman Catholic, Protestant | Dollar |
| BERMUDA | 21 | 54 | 64 000 | 3048 | 1185 | Hamilton | English | Protestant, Roman Catholic | Dollar |
| CANADA | 3 849 674 | 9 970 610 | 29 251 000 | 8 | 3 | Ottawa | English, French, Amerindian languages, Inuktitut (Eskimo) | Roman Catholic, Protestant | Dollar |
| CAYMAN ISLANDS | 100 | 259 | 31 000 | 310 | 120 | George Town | English | Protestant, Roman Catholic | Dollar |
| COSTA RICA | 19 730 | 51 100 | 3 071 000 | 156 | 60 | San José | Spanish | Roman Catholic, Protestant | Colón |
| CUBA | 42 803 | 110 860 | 10 960 000 | 256 | 99 | Havana | Spanish | Roman Catholic, Protestant | Peso |
| DOMINICA | 290 | 750 | 71 000 | 245 | 95 | Roseau | English, French Creole | Roman Catholic, Protestant | E. Carib. dollar, |
| DOMINICAN REPUBLIC | 18 704 | 48 442 | 7 769 000 | 415 | 160 | Santo Domingo | Spanish, French Creole | Roman Catholic, Protestant | Peso |
| EL SALVADOR | 8 124 | 21 041 | 5 641 000 | 694 | 268 | San Salvador | Spanish | Roman Catholic, Protestant | Colón |
| GREENLAND | 840 004 | 2 175 600 | 55 000 | | | Nuuk | Greenlandic, Danish | Protestant | Danish krone |
| GRENADA | 146 | 378 | 92 000 | 630 | 243 | St George's | English, Creole | Roman Catholic, Protestant | E. Carib. dollar |
| GUADELOUPE | 687 | 1 780 | 421 000 | 613 | 237 | Basse Terre | French, French Creole | Roman Catholic | French franc |
| GUATEMALA | 42 043 | 108 890 | 10 322 000 | 246 | 95 | Guatemala | Spanish, Mayan languages | Roman Catholic, Protestant | Quetzal |
| HAITI | 10 714 | 27 750 | 7 041 000 | 657 | 254 | Port-au-Prince | French, French Creole | Roman Catholic, Protestant | Gourde |
| HONDURAS | 43 277 | 112 088 | 5 770 000 | 133 | 51 | Tegucigalpa | Spanish, Amerindian languages | Roman Catholic, Protestant | Lempira |
| JAMAICA | 4 244 | 10 991 | 2 429 000 | 572 | 221 | Kingston | English, Creole | Protestant, Roman Catholic | Dollar |
| MARTINIQUE | 417 | 1 079 | 375 000 | 900 | 348 | Fort-de-France | French, French Creole | Roman Catholic | French franc |
| MEXICO | 761 604 | 1 972 545 | 96 578 000 | 127 | 49 | México | Spanish, Amerindian languages | Roman Catholic | Peso |
| MONTSERRAT | 39 | 100 | 11 000 | 285 | 110 | Plymouth | English | Protestant, Roman Catholic | E. Carib. dollar |
| NICARAGUA | 50 193 | 130 000 | 4 401 000 | 88 | 34 | Managua | Spanish, Amerindian languages | Roman Catholic, Protestant | Córdoba |
| PANAMA | 29 762 | 77 082 | 2 583 000 | 87 | 34 | Panamá | Spanish, English Creole, Amerindian languages | Roman Catholic | Balboa |
| PUERTO RICO | 3 515 | 9 104 | 3 736 000 | 1063 | 410 | San Juan | Spanish, English | Roman Catholic, Protestant | US dollar |
| ST KITTS & NEVIS | 101 | 261 | 41 000 | 407 | 157 | Basseterre | English, Creole | Protestant, Roman Catholic | E. Carib. dollar |
| ST LUCIA | 238 | 616 | 141 000 | 593 | 229 | Castries | English, French Creole | Roman Catholic, Protestant | E. Carib. dollar |
| ST VINCENT & THE GRENADINES | 150 | 389 | 111 000 | 739 | 285 | Kingstown | English, Creole | Protestant, Roman Catholic | E. Carib. dollar |
| TURKS & CAICOS ISLANDS | 166 | 430 | 14 000 | 84 | 33 | Cockburn Town | English | Protestant | US dollar |
| USA | 3 787 425 | 9 809 386 | 266 557 000 | 70 | 27 | Washington | English, Spanish, Amerindian languages | Protestant, Roman Catholic | Dollar |
| VIRGIN ISLANDS (UK) | 59 | 153 | 18 000 | 305 | 118 | Road Town | English | Protestant, Roman Catholic | US dollar |
| VIRGIN ISLANDS (USA) | 136 | 352 | 104 000 | 765 | 295 | Charlotte Amalie | English, Spanish | Protestant, Roman Catholic | US dollar |

# INTERNATIONAL ORGANIZATIONS

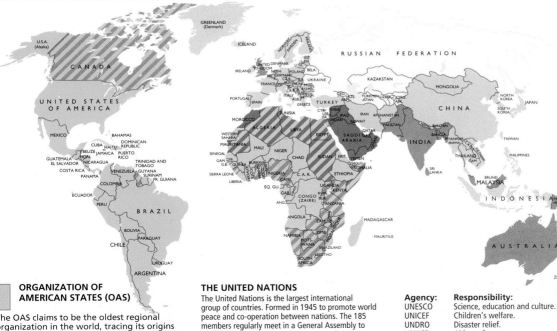

### ARAB LEAGUE

Founded in 1945 in Cairo, by Egypt, Syria, Iraq, Lebanon, Jordan, Saudi Arabia and Yemen. The membership has been extended to include 14 other countries in the region.
*Headquarters* : Cairo, Egypt

### THE COMMONWEALTH

The status and relationship of members of the Commonwealth, which grew out of the British Empire was defined in 1926 and enshrined in the 1931 Statute of Westminster. There are 53 members of the Commonwealth.

### COMMONWEALTH OF INDEPENDENT STATES (CIS)

Established by the Minsk agreement and the Alma-Ata Declaration in 1991 following the collapse of the U.S.S.R..
*Headquarters* : Minsk, Belarus

### ORGANIZATION OF AMERICAN STATES (OAS)

The OAS claims to be the oldest regional organization in the world, tracing its origins back to 1826. The charter of the present OAS came into force in 1951. There are 34 member states spread throughout North and South America.
*Headquarters* : Washington, U.S.A.

### THE UNITED NATIONS

The United Nations is the largest international group of countries. Formed in 1945 to promote world peace and co-operation between nations. The 185 members regularly meet in a General Assembly to settle disputes and agree on common policies to world problems. The work of the United Nations is carried out through its various agencies which include:

*Headquarters* : New York, U.S.A.

| Agency: | Responsibility: |
| --- | --- |
| UNESCO | Science, education and culture. |
| UNICEF | Children's welfare. |
| UNDRO | Disaster relief. |
| UNHCR | Aid to refugees. |
| WHO | Health. |
| FAO | Food & agriculture. |
| UNEP | Environment. |
| UNDP | Development programme. |

### ORGANIZATION OF AFRICAN UNITY (OAU)

The OAU grew out of the Union of Africa states which was founded in 1961. All continental African countries are members together with Cape Verde, the Comoros, Sao Tome and Principe, and Seychelles.
*Headquarters* : Addis Ababa, Ethiopia

© Collins

# NATIONS OF THE WORLD

# SOUTH AMERICA

| COUNTRY | AREA | | POPULATION | | | CITY | LANGUAGES | RELIGIONS | CURRENCY |
|---|---|---|---|---|---|---|---|---|---|
| | | | TOTAL | DENSITY PER | | CAPITAL | | | |
| | sq ml | sq km | | sq ml | sq km | | | | |
| ARGENTINA | 1 068 302 | 2 766 889 | 34 180 000 | 32 | 12 | Buenos Aires | Spanish, Amerindian languages | Roman Catholic | Peso |
| ARUBA | 75 | 193 | 69 000 | 926 | 358 | Oranjestad | Dutch, Papiamento, | Roman Catholic, Protestant | Florin |
| BOLIVIA | 424 164 | 1 098 581 | 7 237 000 | 17 | 7 | La Paz | Spanish, Quechua, Aymara | Roman Catholic | Boliviano |
| BRAZIL | 3 286 488 | 8 511 965 | 157 872 000 | 48 | 19 | Brasília | Portuguese, Italian, Amerindian languages | Roman Catholic | Real |
| CHILE | 292 258 | 756 945 | 13 994 000 | 48 | 18 | Santiago | Spanish, Amerindian languages | Roman Catholic | Peso |
| COLOMBIA | 440 831 | 1 141 748 | 34 520 000 | 78 | 30 | Bogotá | Spanish, Amerindian languages | Roman Catholic | Peso |
| ECUADOR | 105 037 | 272 045 | 11 221 000 | 107 | 41 | Quito | Spanish, Amerindian languages | Roman Catholic | Sucre |
| FALKLAND ISLANDS | 4 699 | 12 170 | 2 000 | | | Stanley | English | Protestant, Roman Catholic | Pound |
| FRENCH GUIANA | 34 749 | 90 000 | 141 000 | 4 | 2 | Cayenne | French, French Creole | Roman Catholic, Protestant | French franc |
| GUYANA | 83 000 | 214 969 | 825 000 | 10 | 4 | Georgetown | English, Creole, Hindi, Amerindian languages | Protestant, Hindu, Roman Catholic, Sunni Muslim | Dollar |
| NETH. ANTILLES | 283 | 732 | 158 206 | 560 | 216 | Willemstad | Dutch, Papiamento | Roman Catholic, Protestant | Guilder |
| PARAGUAY | 157 048 | 406 752 | 4 700 000 | 30 | 12 | Asunción | Spanish, Guaraní | Roman Catholic | Guaraní |
| PERU | 496 225 | 1 285 216 | 23 088 000 | 47 | 18 | Lima | Spanish, Quechua | Roman Catholic | Sol |
| SURINAME | 63 251 | 163 820 | 418 000 | 7 | 3 | Paramaribo | Dutch, Surinamese | Hindu, Roman Catholic, Protestant, Muslim | Guilder |
| TRINIDAD AND TOBAGO | 1 981 | 5 130 | 1 250 000 | 631 | 244 | Port Of Spain | English, Creole, Hindi | Roman Catholic, Hindu, Protestant | Dollar |
| URUGUAY | 68 037 | 176 215 | 3 167 000 | 47 | 18 | Montevideo | Spanish | Roman Catholic, Protestant | Peso |
| VENEZUELA | 352 144 | 912 050 | 21 177 000 | 60 | 23 | Caracas | Spanish, Amerindian languages | Roman Catholic | Bolívar |

# AFRICA

| COUNTRY | AREA | | POPULATION | | | CITY | LANGUAGES | RELIGIONS | CURRENCY |
|---|---|---|---|---|---|---|---|---|---|
| | | | TOTAL | DENSITY PER | | CAPITAL | | | |
| | sq ml | sq km | | sq ml | sq km | | | | |
| ALGERIA | 919 595 | 2 381 741 | 27 561 000 | 30 | 12 | Algiers | Arabic, French, Berber | Muslim | Dinar |
| ANGOLA | 481 354 | 1 246 700 | 10 674 000 | 22 | 9 | Luanda | Portuguese | Roman Catholic, Protestant, traditional beliefs | Kwanza |
| BENIN | 43 483 | 112 620 | 5 387 000 | 124 | 48 | Porto Novo | French, local languages | Trad. beliefs, Roman Catholic | CFA franc |
| BOTSWANA | 224 468 | 581 370 | 1 443 000 | 6 | 2 | Gaborone | English, Setswana | Traditional beliefs, Protestant, Roman Catholic | Pula |
| BURKINA | 105 869 | 274 200 | 9 889 000 | 93 | 36 | Ouagadougou | French, local languages | Traditional beliefs, Muslim, Roman Catholic | CFA franc |
| BURUNDI | 10 747 | 27 835 | 6 134 000 | 571 | 220 | Bujumbura | Kirundi, French | Roman Catholic, Protestant | Franc |
| CAMEROON | 183 569 | 475 442 | 12 871 000 | 70 | 27 | Yaoundé | French, English | Trad. beliefs, Roman Catholic, Muslim, Protestant | CFA franc |
| CAPE VERDE | 1 557 | 4 033 | 381 000 | 245 | 94 | Praia | Portuguese | Roman Catholic | Escudo |
| CENTRAL AFRICAN REPUBLIC | 240 324 | 622 436 | 3 235 000 | 13 | 5 | Bangui | French, Sango | Protestant, Roman Catholic, traditional beliefs | CFA franc |
| CHAD | 495 755 | 1 284 000 | 6 214 000 | 13 | 5 | Ndjamena | Arabic, French | Muslim, traditional beliefs, Roman Catholic | CFA franc |
| COMOROS | 719 | 1 862 | 630 000 | 876 | 338 | Moroni | Comorian, French, Arabic | Muslim | Franc |
| CONGO | 132 047 | 342 000 | 2 516 000 | 19 | 7 | Brazzaville | French, local languages | Roman Catholic, Protestant | CFA franc |
| CONGO (ZAIRE) | 905 568 | 2 345 410 | 42 552 000 | 47 | 18 | Kinshasa | French, local languages | Roman Catholic, Protestant | Zaïre |
| CÔTE D'IVOIRE | 124 504 | 322 463 | 13 695 000 | 110 | 42 | Yamoussoukro | French, local languages | Traditional beliefs, Muslim, Roman Catholic | CFA franc |
| DJIBOUTI | 8 958 | 23 200 | 566 000 | 63 | 24 | Djibouti | French, Arabic | Muslim | Franc |
| EGYPT | 386 199 | 1 000 250 | 60 603 000 | 157 | 61 | Cairo | Arabic, French | Muslim, Coptic Christian | Pound |
| EQUATORIAL GUINEA | 10 831 | 28 051 | 389 000 | 36 | 14 | Malabo | Spanish | Roman Catholic | CFA franc |
| ERITREA | 45 328 | 117 400 | 3 437 000 | 76 | 29 | Asmara | Tigrinya, Arabic, Tigre, English | Muslim, Coptic Christian | Ethiopian birr |
| ETHIOPIA | 437 794 | 1 133 880 | 58 506 000 | 134 | 52 | Addis Ababa | Amharic, local languages | Ethiopian Orthodox, Muslim, traditional beliefs | Birr |
| GABON | 103 347 | 267 667 | 1 283 000 | 12 | 5 | Libreville | French, local languages | Roman Catholic, Protestant | CFA franc |
| GAMBIA | 4 361 | 11 295 | 1 081 000 | 248 | 96 | Banjul | English | Muslim | Dalasi |
| GHANA | 92 100 | 238 537 | 16 944 000 | 184 | 71 | Accra | English, local languages | Protestant, Roman Catholic, Muslim, traditional beliefs | Cedi |
| GUINEA | 94 926 | 245 857 | 6 501 000 | 68 | 26 | Conakry | French, local languages | Muslim | Franc |
| GUINEA-BISSAU | 13 948 | 36 125 | 1 050 000 | 75 | 29 | Bissau | Portuguese, local languages | Traditional beliefs, Muslim | Peso |
| KENYA | 224 961 | 582 646 | 29 292 000 | 130 | 50 | Nairobi | Swahili, English | Roman Catholic, Protestant, traditional beliefs | Shilling |
| LESOTHO | 11 720 | 30 355 | 1 996 000 | 170 | 66 | Maseru | Sesotho, English | Roman Catholic, Protestant | Loti |
| LIBERIA | 43 000 | 111 369 | 2 700 000 | 63 | 24 | Monrovia | English, local languages | Muslim, Christian | Dollar |
| LIBYA | 679 362 | 1 759 540 | 4 899 000 | 7 | 3 | Tripoli | Arabic, Berber | Muslim | Dinar |
| MADAGASCAR | 226 658 | 587 041 | 14 303 000 | 63 | 24 | Antananarivo | Malagasy, French | Traditional beliefs, Roman Catholic, Protestant | Franc |

| COUNTRY | AREA | | POPULATION | | | CITY | LANGUAGES | RELIGIONS | CURRENCY |
|---|---|---|---|---|---|---|---|---|---|
| | | | TOTAL | DENSITY PER | | CAPITAL | | | |
| | sq ml | sq km | | sq ml | sq km | | | | |
| MALAWI | 45 747 | 118 484 | 9 461 000 | 207 | 80 | Lilongwe | English, Chichewa | Protestant, Roman Catholic, traditional beliefs, Muslim | Kwacha |
| MALI | 478 821 | 1 240 140 | 10 462 000 | 22 | 8 | Bamako | French, local languages | Muslim, traditional beliefs | CFA franc |
| MAURITANIA | 397 955 | 1 030 700 | 2 211 000 | 6 | 2 | Nouakchott | Arabic, local languages | Muslim | Ouguiya |
| MAURITIUS | 788 | 2 040 | 1 134 000 | 1439 | 556 | Port Louis | English | Hindu, Roman Catholic, Muslim | Rupee |
| MOROCCO | 172 414 | 446 550 | 26 590 000 | 154 | 60 | Rabat | Arabic | Muslim | Dirham |
| MOZAMBIQUE | 308 642 | 799 380 | 16 614 000 | 54 | 21 | Maputo | Portuguese, local languages | Traditional beliefs,Roman Catholic, Muslim | Metical |
| NAMIBIA | 318 261 | 824 292 | 1 500 000 | 5 | 2 | Windhoek | English, Afrikaans, German, Ovambo | Protestant, Roman Catholic | Dollar |
| NIGER | 489 191 | 1 267 000 | 8 846 000 | 18 | 7 | Niamey | French, local languages | Muslim, traditional beliefs | CFA franc |
| NIGERIA | 356 669 | 923 768 | 115 020 000 | 322 | 126 | Abuja | English, Hausa, Yoruba, Ibo, Fulani | Muslim, Protestant, Roman Catholic, traditional beliefs | Naira |
| RÉUNION | 985 | 2 551 | 644 000 | 654 | 252 | St-Denis | French | Roman Catholic | French franc |
| RWANDA | 10 169 | 26 338 | 7 750 000 | 762 | 294 | Kigali | Kinyarwanda, French | Roman Catholic, traditional beliefs | Franc |
| SÃO TOMÉ AND PRÍNCIPE | 372 | 964 | 125 000 | 336 | 130 | São Tomé | Portuguese | Roman Catholic, Protestant | Dobra |
| SENEGAL | 75 954 | 196 720 | 8 102 000 | 107 | 41 | Dakar | French, local languages | Muslim | CFA franc |
| SEYCHELLES | 176 | 455 | 74 000 | 421 | 163 | Victoria | Seychellois, English | Roman Catholic, Protestant | Rupee |
| SIERRA LEONE | 27 699 | 71 740 | 4 402 000 | 159 | 61 | Freetown | English, local languages | Traditional beliefs, Muslim | Leone |
| SOMALIA | 246 201 | 637 657 | 9 077 000 | 37 | 14 | Mogadishu | Somali, Arabic | Muslim | Shilling |
| SOUTH AFRICA | 470 689 | 1 219 080 | 40 436 000 | 86 | 33 | Pretoria/Cape Town | Afrikaans, English, local languages | Protestant, Roman Catholic | Rand |
| SUDAN | 967 500 | 2 505 813 | 28 947 000 | 30 | 12 | Khartoum | Arabic, local languages | Muslim, traditional beliefs | Dinar |
| SWAZILAND | 6 704 | 17 364 | 879 000 | 131 | 51 | Mbabane | Swazi, English | Protestant, Roman Catholic, traditional beliefs | Emalangeni |
| TANZANIA | 364 900 | 945 087 | 28 846 000 | 79 | 31 | Dodoma | Swahili, English, local languages | Christian, Muslim, traditional beliefs | Shilling |
| TOGO | 21 925 | 56 785 | 3 928 000 | 179 | 69 | Lomé | French, local languages | Traditional beliefs, Roman Catholic, Muslim | CFA franc |
| TUNISIA | 63 379 | 164 150 | 8 814 000 | 139 | 54 | Tunis | Arabic | Muslim | Dinar |
| UGANDA | 93 065 | 241 038 | 20 621 000 | 222 | 86 | Kampala | English, Swahili | Roman Catholic, Protestant | Shilling |
| ZAMBIA | 290 586 | 752 614 | 9 196 000 | 32 | 12 | Lusaka | English, local languages | Christian, traditional beliefs | Kwacha |
| ZIMBABWE | 150 873 | 390 759 | 11 150 000 | 74 | 29 | Harare | English, Shona, Ndebele | Protestant, Roman Catholic, traditional beliefs | Dollar |

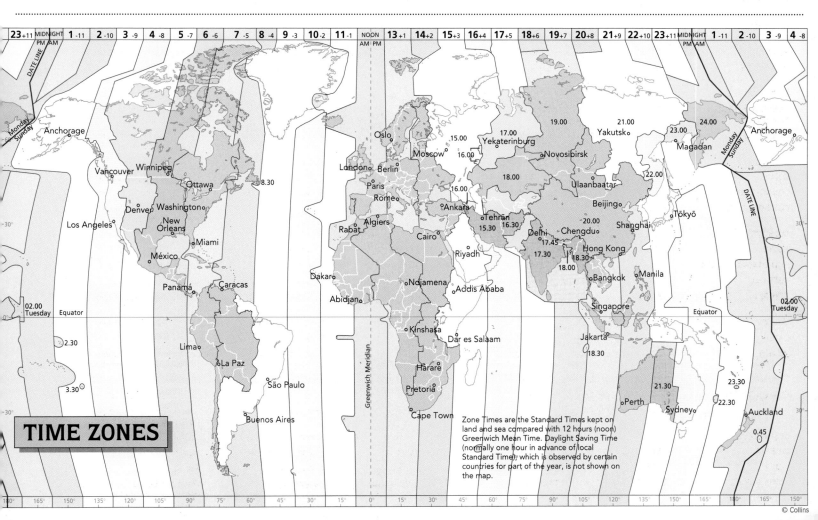

# TIME ZONES

Zone Times are the Standard Times kept on land and sea compared with 12 hours (noon) Greenwich Mean Time. Daylight Saving Time (normally one hour in advance of local Standard Time), which is observed by certain countries for part of the year, is not shown on the map.

© Collins

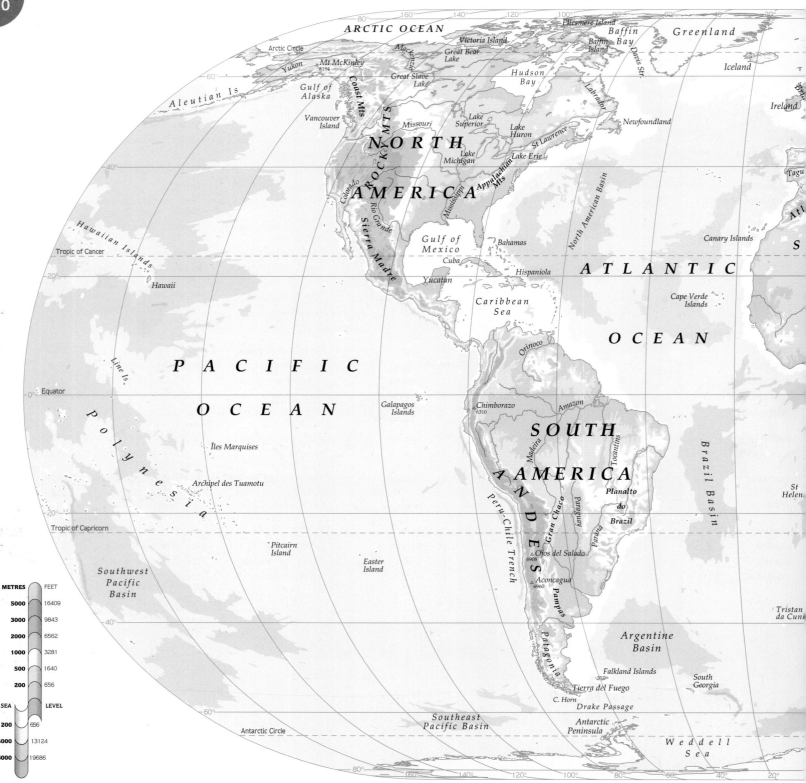

# PHYSICAL FEATURES

## WORLD EXTREMES

### Highest Mountain
| | | |
|---|---|---|
| 8 848 m | MT EVEREST (Asia) | 29 028 ft |

### Largest Inland Water Area
| | | |
|---|---|---|
| 371 000 sq km | CASPIAN SEA (Asia) | 143 205 sq mls |

### Largest Island
| | | |
|---|---|---|
| 2 175 600 sq km | GREENLAND (N. America) | 839 780 sq mls |

### Longest River
| | | |
|---|---|---|
| 6 695 km | NILE (Africa) | 4 160 mls |

### Largest Drainage Basin
| | | |
|---|---|---|
| 7 050 000 sq km | AMAZON (S. America) | 2 721 000 sq mls |

### Deepest Water
| | | |
|---|---|---|
| 11 022 m | MARIANAS TRENCH | 36 161 ft |
| | (Pacific Ocean) | |

## CONTINENTS and OCEANS

| sq km | | sq miles |
|---|---|---|
| 45 036 492 | ASIA | 17 388 590 |
| 30 343 578 | AFRICA | 11 715 655 |
| 25 680 331 | NORTH AMERICA | 9 529 076 |
| 17 815 420 | SOUTH AMERICA | 6 878 534 |
| 13 340 000 | ANTARCTICA | 5 150 574 |
| 9 908 599 | EUROPE | 3 825 710 |
| 8 504 241 | OCEANIA | 3 283 487 |
| | | |
| 165 384 000 | PACIFIC OCEAN | 63 838 000 |
| 82 217 000 | ATLANTIC OCEAN | 31 736 000 |
| 73 481 000 | INDIAN OCEAN | 28 364 000 |
| 14 056 000 | ARCTIC OCEAN | 5 426 000 |

## MOUNTAINS

| metres | | feet |
|---|---|---|
| 8 848 | MT EVEREST (Nepal/China) | 29 028 |
| 8 611 | K2 (India/China) | 28 251 |
| 8 598 | KANGCHENJUNGA (Nepal/India) | 28 210 |
| 6 960 | ACONCAGUA (Argentina) | 22 834 |
| 6 908 | OJOS DEL SALADO (Arg./Chile) | 22 664 |
| 6 310 | CHIMBORAZO (Ecuador) | 20 703 |
| 6 194 | MT MCKINLEY (USA) | 20 321 |
| 5 895 | KILIMANJARO (Tanzania) | 19 340 |
| 5 642 | ELBRUS (Russian Federation) | 18 510 |
| 5 199 | KIRINYAGA (Kenya) | 17 057 |
| 5 030 | PUNCAK JAYA (Indonesia) | 16 503 |
| 4 808 | MONT BLANC (France/Italy) | 15 774 |

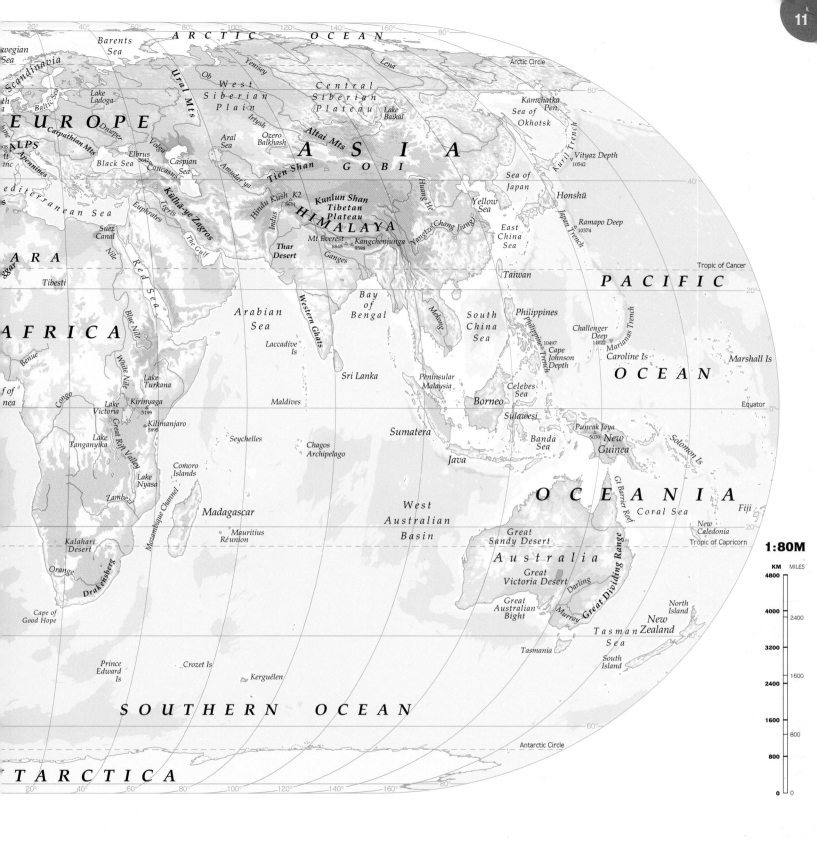

1:80M

| KM | MILES |
|---|---|
| 4800 | |
| 4000 | 2400 |
| 3200 | 1600 |
| 2400 | 800 |
| 1600 | |
| 800 | |
| 0 | 0 |

| ISLANDS | | |
|---|---|---|
| **sq km** | | **sq miles** |
| 2 175 600 | GREENLAND (N. America) | 839 780 |
| 808 510 | NEW GUINEA (Asia/Oceania) | 312 085 |
| 757 050 | BORNEO (Asia) | 292 220 |
| 594 180 | MADAGASCAR (Africa) | 229 355 |
| 524 100 | SUMATERA (Asia) | 202 300 |
| 476 070 | BAFFIN ISLAND (N. America) | 183 760 |
| 230 455 | HONSHŪ (Asia) | 88 955 |
| 229 870 | GREAT BRITAIN (Europe) | 88 730 |
| 212 690 | ELLESMERE ISLAND (N. America) | 82 100 |
| 212 200 | VICTORIA ISLAND (N. America) | 81 190 |
| 189 040 | SULAWESI (Asia) | 72 970 |
| 150 460 | SOUTH ISLAND (Oceania) | 58 080 |

| LAKES | | |
|---|---|---|
| **sq km** | | **sq miles** |
| 371 000 | CASPIAN SEA (Asia) | 143 205 |
| 83 270 | LAKE SUPERIOR (N. America) | 32 140 |
| 68 800 | LAKE VICTORIA (Africa) | 26 560 |
| 60 700 | LAKE HURON (N. America) | 23 430 |
| 58 020 | LAKE MICHIGAN (N. America) | 22 395 |
| 33 640 | ARAL SEA (Asia) | 12 985 |
| 32 900 | LAKE TANGANYIKA (Africa) | 12 700 |
| 31 790 | GREAT BEAR LAKE (N. America) | 12 270 |
| 30 500 | LAKE BAIKAL (Asia) | 11 775 |
| 28 440 | GREAT SLAVE LAKE (N. America) | 10 980 |
| 25 680 | LAKE ERIE (N. America) | 9 915 |
| 22 490 | LAKE NYASA (Africa) | 8 680 |

| RIVERS | | |
|---|---|---|
| **kilometres** | | **miles** |
| 6 695 | NILE (Africa) | 4 160 |
| 6 516 | AMAZON (S. America) | 4 048 |
| 6 380 | YANGTZE (Chang Jiang) (Asia) | 3 964 |
| 6 020 | MISSISSIPPI-MISSOURI (N. America) | 3 740 |
| 5 570 | OB-IRTYSH (Asia) | 3 461 |
| 5 464 | HUANG HE (Asia) | 3 395 |
| 4 667 | CONGO (Africa) | 2 900 |
| 4 425 | MEKONG (Asia) | 2 749 |
| 4 416 | AMUR (Asia) | 2 744 |
| 4 400 | LENA (Asia) | 2 734 |
| 4 250 | MACKENZIE (N. America) | 2 640 |
| 4 090 | YENISEY (Asia) | 2 541 |

### ICE CAP

Areas of permanent ice cap around the north and south poles. The intense cold, dry weather and the ice cover render these regions almost lifeless. In Antarctica, tiny patches of land free of ice have a cover of mosses and lichens which provide shelter for some insects and mites.

### TUNDRA and MOUNTAIN

Sub-arctic areas or mountain tops which are usually frozen. Tundra vegetation is characterized by mosses, lichens, rushes, grasses and flowering herbs; animals include the arctic fox and reindeer. Mountain vegetation is also characterized by mosses and lichens, and by low growing birch and willow.

### TAIGA (NORTHERN FOREST)

Found only in the high latitudes of the northern hemisphere where winters are long and very cold, and summers are short. The characteristic vegetation is coniferous trees, including spruce and fir; animals include beavers, squirrels and deer.

### MIXED and DECIDUOUS FOREST

Typical of both temperate mid-latitude and eastern subtropical regions. The vegetation is a mixture of broadleaf and coniferous trees, including oak, beech and maple. Humankind has had a major impact on these regions, and in many areas little natural vegetation remains.

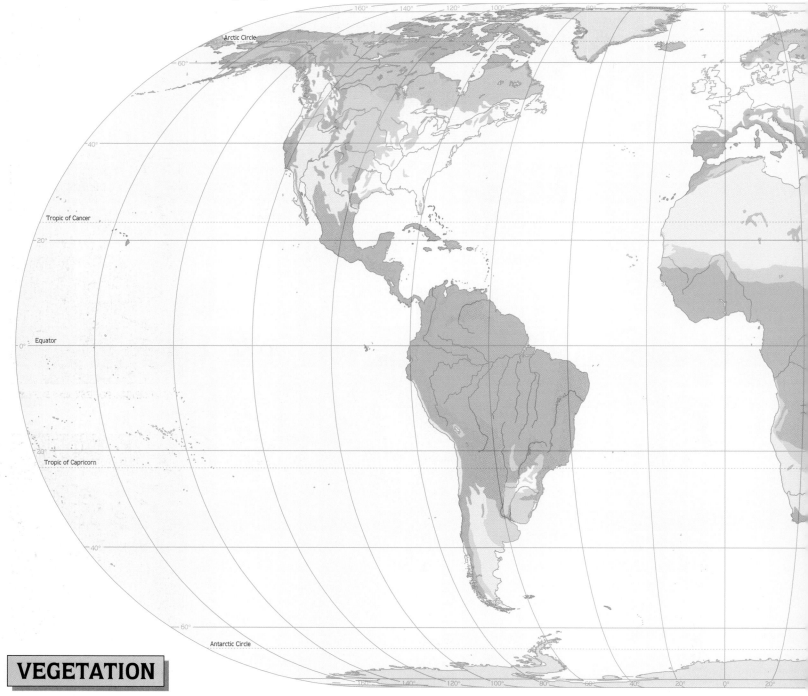

## VEGETATION

ICE CAP

TUNDRA and MOUNTAIN

TAIGA (NORTHERN FOREST)

MIXED and DECIDUOUS FOREST

### MEDITERRANEAN SCRUB
Long, hot, dry summers and short, warm, wet winters characterize these areas. A variety of herbaceous plants grow beneath shrub thickets with pine, oak and gorse.

### GRASSLAND
Areas of long grasslands (prairies) and short grasslands (steppe) in both the northern and southern hemispheres. These grasslands have hot summers, cold winters and moderate rainfall.

### SAVANNA
Tropical grasslands with a short rainy season; areas of grassland are interspersed with thorn bushes and deciduous trees such as acacia and eucalyptus.

### DESERT
Little vegetation grows in the very hot, dry climate of desert areas. The few shrubs, grasses and cacti have adapted by storing water when it is available.

### RAINFOREST
Dense evergreen forests found in areas of high rainfall and continuous high temperatures. Up to three tree layers grow above a variable shrub layer: high trees, the tree canopy and the open canopy.

### DRY TROPICAL FOREST and SCRUB
Low to medium size semi-deciduous trees and thorny scrub with thick bark and long roots characterize the forest areas; in the scrub areas the trees are replaced by shrubs, bushes and succulents.

**DRY TROPICAL FOREST and SCRUB**

**DESERT**

**MEDITERRANEAN SCRUB**

**GRASSLAND**

**SAVANNA**

**RAINFOREST**

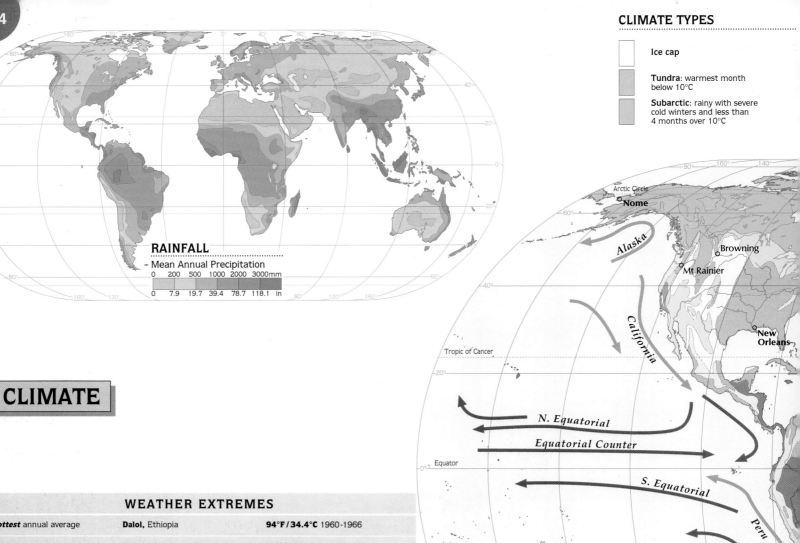

### RAINFALL
Mean Annual Precipitation

| 0 | 200 | 500 | 1000 | 2000 | 3000mm |
|---|---|---|---|---|---|
| 0 | 7.9 | 19.7 | 39.4 | 78.7 | 118.1 in |

### CLIMATE TYPES

- **Ice cap**
- **Tundra:** warmest month below 10°C
- **Subarctic:** rainy with severe cold winters and less than 4 months over 10°C

# CLIMATE

## WEATHER EXTREMES

| | | |
|---|---|---|
| *Hottest* annual average | **Dalol**, Ethiopia | **94°F / 34.4°C** 1960-1966 |
| *Coldest* annual average | **Pole of Inaccessibility**, Antarctica | **-72°F / -57.8°C** |
| *Hottest* location | **Al 'Azīzīyah**, Libya | **136°F / 57.8°C** 13 September 1992 |
| *Coldest* location | **Vostok Station**, Antarctica | **-128.6°F / -89.2°C** 21 July 1983 |
| *Highest* annual average rainfall | **Meghalaya**, India | **467.5in / 11 874.5mm** |
| *Greatest* measured annual rainfall | **Cherrapunji**, India | **1 041.75in / 26 461.7mm** 1 August 1860 - 31 July 1861 |
| *Greatest* 24hr rainfall | **Chilaos, Réunion**, Indian Ocean | **73.5in / 1 869.9mm** 15 March 1952 |
| *Driest* location | **Atacama Desert**, Chile | **0.003in / 0.08mm** (annual rainfall) |
| *Greatest* 24hr temperature change | **Browning**, USA | **100°F / 55.6°C** (From 44°F/6.7°C to -56°F/-49°C) 23-24 January 1916 |
| *Greatest* annual snowfall | **Mt Rainier**, USA | **1 224.5in / 31 102mm** 19 February 1971 - 8 February 1972 |
| *Largest* hailstone | **Gopalganj**, Bangladesh | **2.25lbs / 1.02kg** 14 April 1986 |
| *Highest* measured wind gust | **Mt Washington**, USA | **231mph / 372kph** 12 April 1934 |

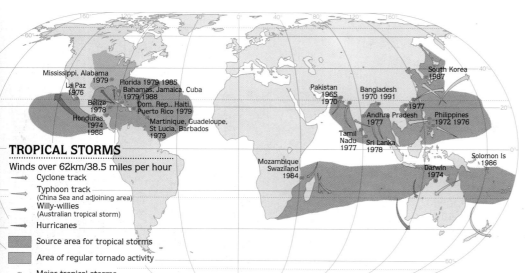

## TROPICAL STORMS

Winds over 62km/38.5 miles per hour

→ Cyclone track

→ Typhoon track (China Sea and adjoining area)

→ Willy-willies (Australian tropical storm)

→ Hurricanes

■ Source area for tropical storms

■ Area of regular tornado activity

• Major tropical storms

## CLIMATE GRAPHS

The graphs show the average monthly temperature and the average monthly rainfall; the colour relates to the Climate Type shown on the map and key above.

The climate stations are shown on the map in bold type; the names in light type on the map show the locations of the Weather Extremes on the chart on the left.

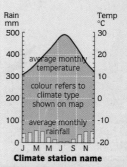

**Continental cool summer:** rainy with warmest month below 22°C

**Continental warm summer:** with warmest month above 20°C

**Temperate:** rainy with mild winters and coolest month above 0°C

**Humid subtropical:** coolest month above 0°C and warmest month above 22°C

**Mediterranean:** rainy with mild wet winters and dry summers

**Steppe:** semi-arid, dry

**Desert**

**Savanna:** rainy tropical climate

**Rain forest:** rainy tropical climate, constantly wet throughout the year

→ Warm Currents

→ Cold Currents

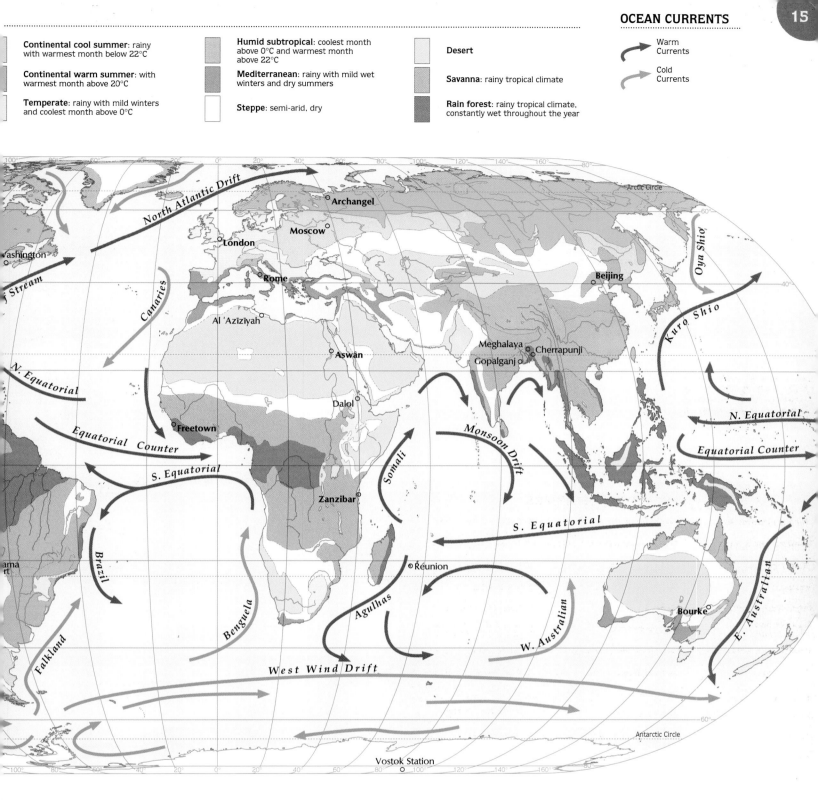

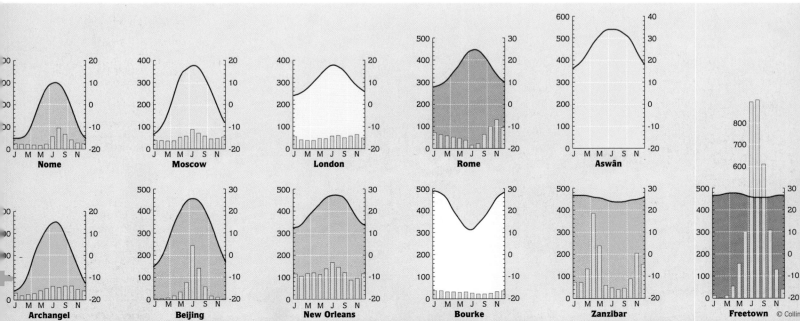

Nome    Moscow    London    Rome    Aswân

Archangel    Beijing    New Orleans    Bourke    Zanzibar    Freetown

© Collins

## WORLD POPULATION RANKINGS

| Rank | Mid 1996 population | | Population density 1996 (persons per square kilometre) | |
|------|---------------------|---|---------------------------------------------|---|
| 1 | CHINA | 1 232 083 000 | MACAU | 25882.4 |
| 2 | INDIA | 944 580 000 | MONACO | 16410.3 |
| 3 | U.S.A. | 266 557 000 | SINGAPORE | 4763.7 |
| 4 | INDONESIA | 196 813 000 | GIBRALTAR | 4307.7 |
| 5 | BRAZIL | 157 872 000 | VATICAN CITY | 2272.7 |
| 6 | RUSSIAN FEDERATION | 147 739 000 | BERMUDA | 1185.2 |
| 7 | PAKISTAN | 134 146 000 | MALTA | 1180.4 |
| 8 | JAPAN | 125 761 000 | MALDIVES | 882.6 |
| 9 | BANGLADESH | 120 073 000 | BAHRAIN | 866.9 |
| 10 | NIGERIA | 115 020 000 | BANGLADESH | 833.9 |
| 11 | MEXICO | 96 578 000 | CHANNEL ISLANDS | 764.1 |
| 12 | GERMANY | 81 912 000 | BARBADOS | 607.0 |
| 13 | VIETNAM | 75 181 000 | TAIWAN | 586.3 |
| 14 | PHILIPPINES | 71 899 000 | MAURITIUS | 555.9 |
| 15 | TURKEY | 62 697 000 | NAURU | 523.8 |
| 16 | IRAN | 61 128 000 | SOUTH KOREA | 458.8 |
| 17 | EGYPT | 60 603 000 | PUERTO RICO | 410.4 |
| 18 | THAILAND | 60 003 000 | SAN MARINO | 409.8 |
| 19 | ETHIOPIA | 58 506 000 | TUVALU | 400.0 |
| 20 | FRANCE | 58 375 000 | NETHERLANDS | 373.7 |

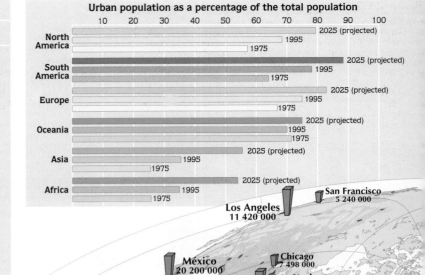

Urban population as a percentage of the total population

# POPULATION PATTERNS

THE WORLD'S POPULATION in mid-1996 totalled 5.8 billion, over half of which live in six countries: China, India, USA, Indonesia, Brazil and the Russian Federation. 80% of the world's population live in developing countries - 95% of people added to the world total are born in the developing world.

The total is still rising, but there are signs that worldwide growth is slowly coming under control. Growth rates and fertility rates are declining, although there are great regional variations which still cause concern. The average annual growth rate in the developed world is 0.4% per annum, whilst in the less developed world it is 1.8%, reaching as high as 2.8% in Africa. Developed regions also have lower fertility rates - an average of 1.7 children per woman, below the 'replacement level' target of 2. In the developing world the rate is 3.4 and can reach 5.6 in the poorest countries.

Until growth is brought under tighter control, the developing world in particular will continue to face enormous problems of supporting a rising population.

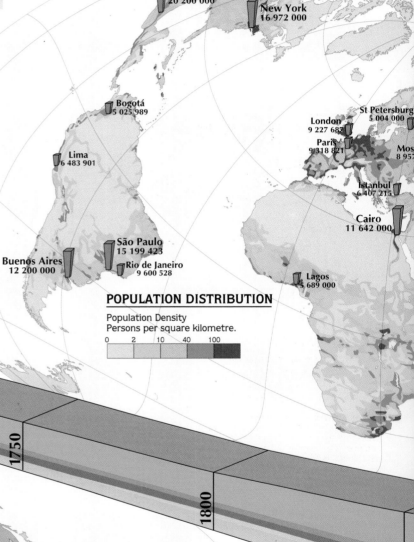

## POPULATION DISTRIBUTION

Population Density
Persons per square kilometre.

0   2   10   40   100

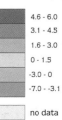

### Population change

Average annual population change 1990-1995 (%)

- 4.6 - 6.0
- 3.1 - 4.5
- 1.6 - 3.0
- 0 - 1.5
- -3.0 - 0
- -7.0 - -3.1
- no data

Countries named are those with the 10 greatest population increases between 1995 and 1996

# RBANIZATION

e of the dominant themes of world population is that of urbanization - the ovement of people from the countryside to towns and cities. In 1995 43% the world's population lived in urban areas and the number of urban ellers is expected to double between 1990 and 2025 to over 5 billion.

he degree of urbanization varies between regions. The populations of rope, North America and South America are over 70% urban compared only 30-35% in Africa and Asia. It is the developing regions, however, t are experiencing the fastest growth of urban populations. Urban wth rates reach over 7% per year in some of the poorest countries of e world, including Burkina and Mozambique.

ne side effect of urbanization is that fertility rates tend to decrease a country's population becomes more urbanized. Decreasing fertility es are a crucial factor in controlling population growth. It seems nic that increased urbanization, with all its problems, may imately help the overall situation

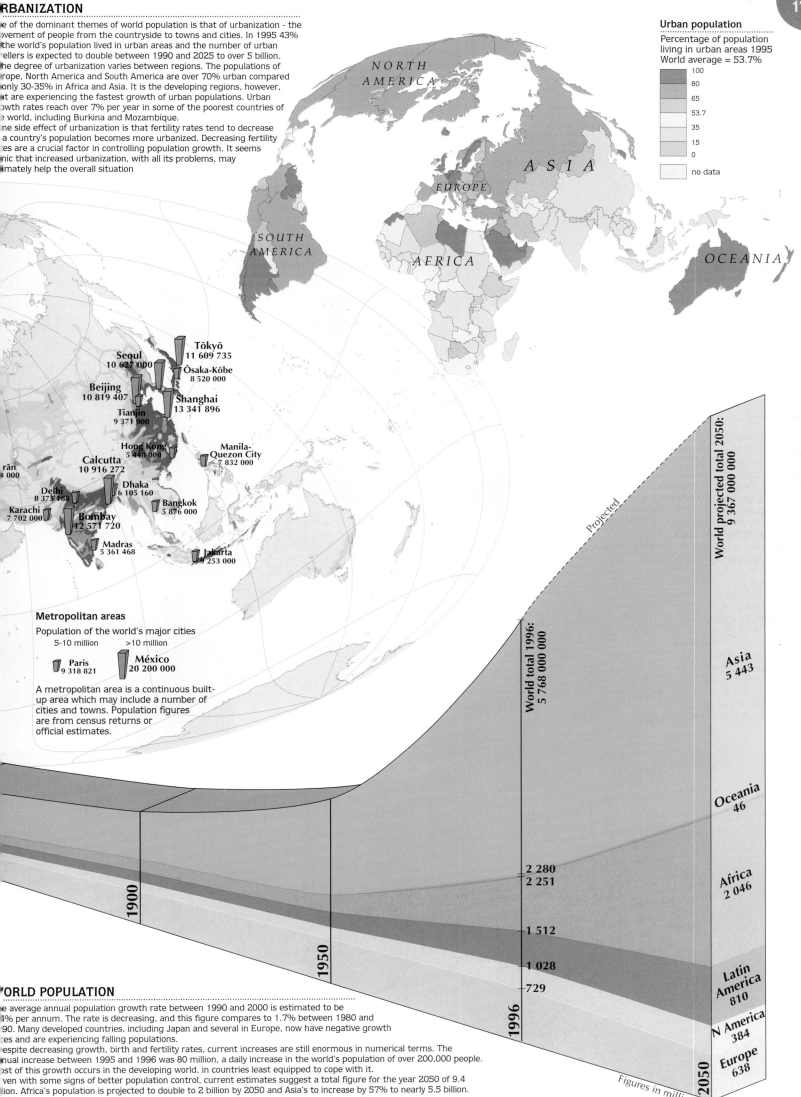

## Urban population

Percentage of population living in urban areas 1995
World average = 53.7%

100
80
65
53.7
35
15
0

no data

**NORTH AMERICA**

**ASIA**

**EUROPE**

**SOUTH AMERICA**

**AFRICA**

**OCEANIA**

Tōkyō
11 609 735

Seoul
10 627 000

Ōsaka-Kōbe
8 520 000

Beijing
10 819 407

Tianjin
9 371 000

Shanghai
13 341 896

rān
000

Hong Kong
5 448 000

Manila-
Quezon City
7 832 000

Calcutta
10 916 272

Delhi
8 375 188

Dhaka
6 105 160

Karachi
7 702 000

Bombay
12 571 720

Bangkok
5 876 000

Madras
5 361 468

Jakarta
9 253 000

### Metropolitan areas

Population of the world's major cities

5-10 million    >10 million

Paris
9 318 821

México
20 200 000

A metropolitan area is a continuous built-up area which may include a number of cities and towns. Population figures are from census returns or official estimates.

## ORLD POPULATION

e average annual population growth rate between 1990 and 2000 is estimated to be 4% per annum. The rate is decreasing, and this figure compares to 1.7% between 1980 and 90. Many developed countries, including Japan and several in Europe, now have negative growth es and are experiencing falling fertility.

espite decreasing growth, birth and fertility rates, current increases are still enormous in numerical terms. The nual increase between 1995 and 1996 was 80 million, a daily increase in the world's population of over 200,000 people. st of this growth occurs in the developing world, in countries least equipped to cope with it.

ven with some signs of better population control, current estimates suggest a total figure for the year 2050 of 9.4 ion. Africa's population is projected to double to 2 billion by 2050 and Asia's to increase by 57% to nearly 5.5 billion.

World projected total 2050:
9 367 000 000

Projected

World total 1996:
5 768 000 000

1900

1950

1996

2050

2 280
2 251

1 512

1 028
729

Asia
5 443

Oceania
46

Africa
2 046

Latin America
810

N America
384

Europe
638

Figures in millions

© Collins

## Health Indicators
### (Selected Countries)

| Life Expectancy 1995 | Country | Infant Mortality Rate 1995 |
|---|---|---|
| 80 | Japan | 4 |
| 79 | Sweden | 4 |
| 79 | Iceland | 5 |
| 78 | Switzerland | 6 |
| 78 | Canada | 6 |
| 78 | Netherlands | 6 |
| 78 | Italy | 7 |
| 78 | Australia | 7 |
| 78 | Spain | 8 |
| 77 | U.K. | 6 |
| 48 | Somalia | 125 |
| 47 | Mali | 117 |
| 47 | Mozambique | 158 |
| 46 | Gambia | 80 |
| 46 | Guinea | 128 |
| 45 | Guinea-Bissau | 134 |
| 45 | Malawi | 138 |
| 45 | Afghanistan | 165 |
| 44 | Uganda | 111 |
| 40 | Sierra Leone | 164 |

**Infant mortality**
Deaths before first birthday per 1000 live births 1995

- 0-9
- 10-49
- 50-99
- 100-149
- >149
- no data

# A HEALTHY WORLD?

**STANDARDS OF HEALTH** vary widely throughout the world. Richer countries enjoy higher standards than poorer countries and there are similar inequalities within countries. Great progress is being made in all aspects of health and there have been significant improvements in the two main indicators of health levels over the last few decades. The world average life expectancy increased from 48 to 65 years between 1955 and 1995; and infant mortality rates have fallen - deaths among children under five declined from 19 million in 1960 to 11 million in 1996. Longer life and a greater chance of survival do not necessarily mean a healthy life. There is still a need to ensure a freedom from additional years of ill-health and poverty - quality of life is as important as quantity.

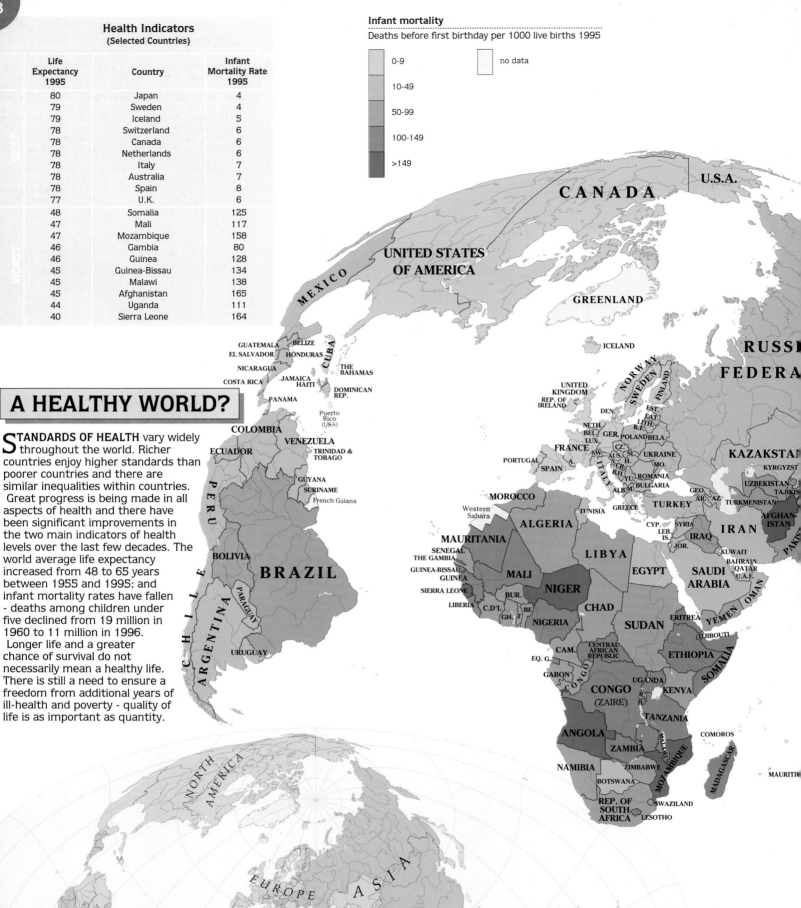

**Life expectancy**
Number of years a new born child can expect to survive

- <50
- 50-59
- 60-69
- 70-79
- >79
- no data

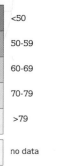

# CAUSES OF DEATH

The dominant causes of death in the developing world are infectious and parasitic diseases, in particular lower respiratory infection, tuberculosis, diarrhoeal diseases and malaria. By contrast, people in the richer, developed countries suffer more from circulatory diseases and cancers - illnesses generally occurring later in life and often associated with life-style.

This pattern is gradually changing. As living standards and life expectancy increase throughout the world there is a corresponding increase in the risks from diseases prevalent in the developed world. This provides the developing world with the 'double burden' of coping with existing high rates of infectious diseases and increasing rates of chronic illness.

Patterns in causes of death again reflect relative wealth. Infectious and parasitic diseases are the easiest to prevent and eradicate but, despite great successes in the eradication of smallpox and the imminent demise of polio, the resources are so often lacking in the areas suffering most.

**Developed countries**

Total deaths 1996: 12 million

**Developing countries**

Total deaths 1996: 40 million

# HEALTH PROVISION

Easy access to appropriate health services are taken for granted in the developed world where 100% access for the population can often be assumed. In developing countries, however, such access is often far more limited, as the graph below shows. Social and economic conditions in a country can greatly influence the chances of a healthy life.

The provision of conditions for good health, including trained personnel, medical facilities and equipment as well as those of safe water, food and sanitation, obviously costs money. Some countries are in a much better position to meet these costs than others. This is reflected in the overall differences in standards of health between the developed and developing world. The richer countries not only enjoy better health, but also spend proportionately more of their Gross National Product on health provision. The poorer countries of the world are spending a smaller proportion of much less money on vital facilities.

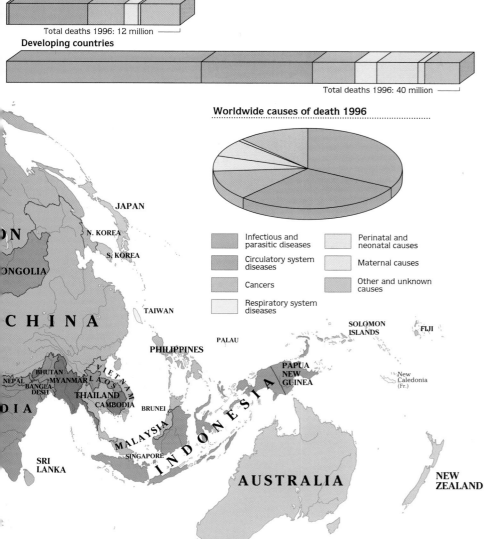

### Worldwide causes of death 1996

- Infectious and parasitic diseases
- Circulatory system diseases
- Cancers
- Respiratory system diseases
- Perinatal and neonatal causes
- Maternal causes
- Other and unknown causes

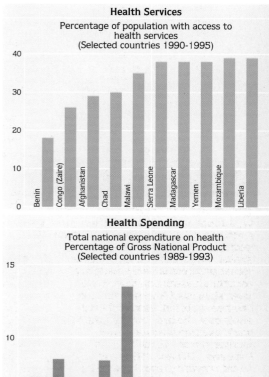

**Health Services**
Percentage of population with access to health services
(Selected countries 1990-1995)

**Health Spending**
Total national expenditure on health
Percentage of Gross National Product
(Selected countries 1989-1993)

### Access to safe water
Percentage of population with reasonable access to sufficient safe water 1995

- 0-20
- 21-40
- 41-75
- 76-90
- 91-100
- no data

© Collins

# MEASURING THE WORLD'S WEALTH

A commonly used measure of wealth is Gross National Product (GNP). This is the total value of goods and services produced by a country in any one year, including income from investments abroad. If the total GNP figure is divided by the country's population, the average wealth per person is provided as GNP per capita.

GNP per capita statistics provide only an average figure and give no indication of the relative distribution of wealth within the country. They show neither the great inequalities which can exist, nor the relative numbers of people living in poverty. Also, GNP is usually based on valuations in US$ and not in local currencies. Purchasing Power Parity (PPP), measured in International Dollars, is another means of measuring individual wealth which uses local exchange rates and takes account of cost of living differences between countries (see table below).

No method provides a perfect picture of the world's complex ecomomy, but whichever method is used clear patterns of wealth and poverty - the rich and poor of the world - emerge.

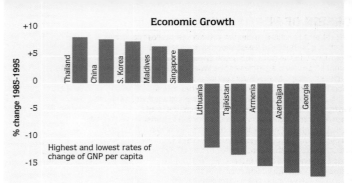

**Economic Growth**

% change 1985-1995

Highest and lowest rates of change of GNP per capita

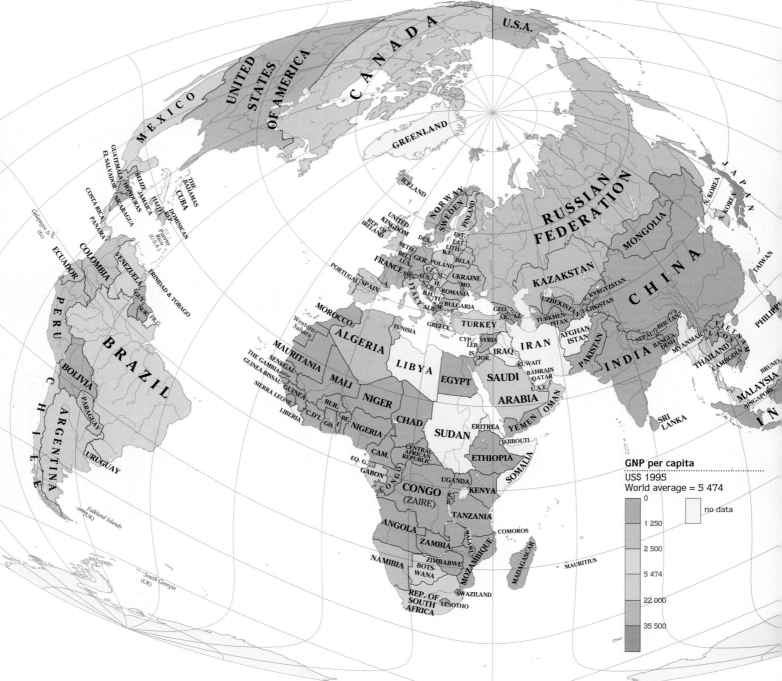

**GNP per capita**

US$ 1995
World average = 5 474

| | |
|---|---|
| 0 | no data |
| 1 250 | |
| 2 500 | |
| 5 474 | |
| 22 000 | |
| 35 500 | |

| Rank | GROSS NATIONAL PRODUCT (GNP) (US$ Millions 1995) | GNP PER CAPITA (US$ 1995) | PURCHASING POWER PARITY(PPP) ($ International 1995) | EXTERNAL DEBT (% of GNP 1995) Low- and middle-income economies | Rank |
|---|---|---|---|---|---|
| 1 | U.S.A. (7 100 007) | LUXEMBOURG (41 210) | LUXEMBOURG (37 930) | NICARAGUA (520) | 1 |
| 2 | JAPAN (4 963 587) | SWITZERLAND (40 630) | U.S.A. (26 980) | MOZAMBIQUE (333) | 2 |
| 3 | GERMANY (2 252 343) | JAPAN (39 640) | SWITZERLAND (25 860) | CONGO (325) | 3 |
| 4 | FRANCE (1 451 051) | NORWAY (31 250) | KUWAIT (23 790) | ANGOLA (260) | 4 |
| 5 | UNITED KINGDOM (1 094 734) | DENMARK (29 890) | SINGAPORE (22 770) | GUINEA-BISSAU (235) | 5 |
| 6 | ITALY (1 088 085) | GERMANY (27 510) | JAPAN (22 110) | CÔTE D'IVOIRE (185) | 6 |
| 7 | CHINA (744 890) | U.S.A. (26 980) | NORWAY (21 940) | MAURITANIA (166) | 7 |
| 8 | BRAZIL (579 787) | AUSTRIA (26 890) | BELGIUM (21 660) | TANZANIA (148) | 8 |
| 9 | CANADA (573 695) | SINGAPORE (26 730) | AUSTRIA (21 250) | ZAMBIA (139) | 9 |
| 10 | SPAIN (532 347) | FRANCE (24 990) | DENMARK (21 230) | VIETNAM (138) | 10 |
| 10 | COMOROS (237) | YEMEN (260) | NIGER (750) | KYRGYZSTAN (15) | 10 |
| 9 | DOMINICA (218) | GUINEA-BISSAU (250) | CHAD (700) | ARMENIA (14) | 9 |
| 8 | MICRONESIA (215) | HAITI (250) | MADAGASCAR (640) | BOTSWANA (13) | 8 |
| 7 | ST KITTS & NEVIS (212) | MALI (250) | TANZANIA (640) | UKRAINE (10) | 7 |
| 6 | VANUATU (202) | BANGLADESH (240) | BURUNDI (240) | LITHUANIA (9) | 6 |
| 5 | WESTERN SAMOA (184) | UGANDA (240) | SIERRA LEONE (580) | AZERBAIJAN (8) | 5 |
| 4 | TONGA (170) | VIETNAM (240) | MALI (550) | LATVIA (7) | 4 |
| 3 | EQUATORIAL GUINEA (152) | BURKINA (230) | RWANDA (540) | UZBEKISTAN (7) | 3 |
| 2 | KIRIBATI (73) | MADAGASCAR (230) | CONGO (ZAIRE) (490) | BELARUS (6) | 2 |
| 1 | SÃO TOMÉ & PRÍNCIPE (45) | NIGER (220) | ETHIOPIA (450) | CONGO (6) | 1 |

HIGHEST

LOWEST

# FOREIGN DEBT

A critical problem facing many of the world's poorest countries is that of foreign debt. To assist them in development programmes in the past, many countries borrowed huge amounts from such agencies as the World Bank. Changes in the world's economy have created conditions in which it is virtually impossible for these countries to repay their loans.

The total amount of debt need not be a problem if the country can make its payments (or 'service' the debt), through income from its own exports. Problems arise where the debt service ratio (total debt service as a percentage of exports of goods and services) is high. A country with a debt service ratio of 50% needs to spend half of its income on debt repayments - money which could otherwise be spent on developing the country's economy as a whole.

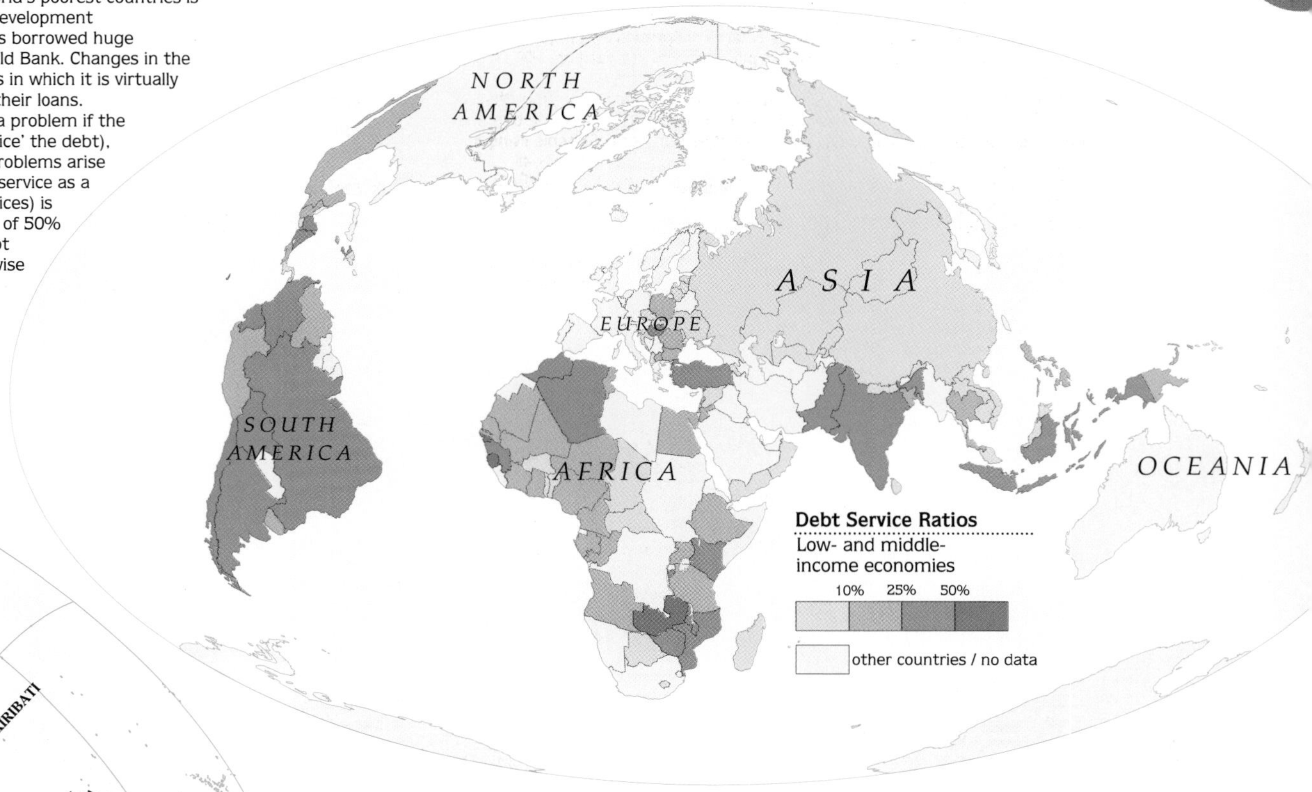

NORTH AMERICA

EUROPE

ASIA

SOUTH AMERICA

AFRICA

OCEANIA

### Debt Service Ratios
Low- and middle-income economies

10%  25%  50%

other countries / no data

KIRIBATI

Northern Mariana Islands (U.S.A.)

MARSHALL ISLANDS

Hawaiian Islands (U.S.A.)

FED. STATES OF MICRONESIA

TUVALU

W. SAMOA

PALAU

SOLOMON ISLANDS

FIJI  TONGA

VANUATU

New Caledonia (Fr.)

...NESIA

PAPUA NEW GUINEA

AUSTRALIA

NEW ZEALAND

# THE WORLD'S WEALTH

### Regional distribution of wealth

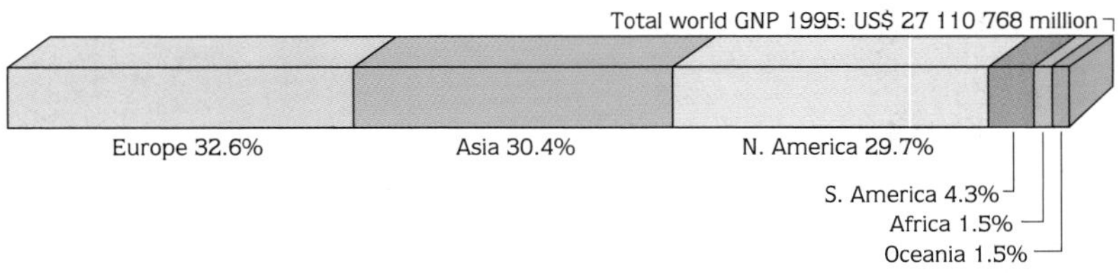

Total world GNP 1995: US$ 27 110 768 million

Europe 32.6%    Asia 30.4%    N. America 29.7%

S. America 4.3%
Africa 1.5%
Oceania 1.5%

## OVERSEAS AID

Overseas Aid is the provision of funds or services at non-commercial rates for developmental purposes. The flow is from rich countries to poor countries, with the major donors generally being those countries with the highest GNP. Aid can either be Official Development Assistance (ODA) provided by governments, or Voluntary Aid from private donations usually through non-governmental organizations (NGOs) such as Oxfam.

An important group of donor countries is the Development Assistance Committee (DAC) of the Organization for Economic Co-operation and Development (OECD). The DAC recommends that its members should donate 0.7% of their GNP in aid. Most fall well short of this figure.

It is not always the poorest countries which receive the aid on offer. Political considerations are often a factor, with donor countries choosing carefully which countries they support.

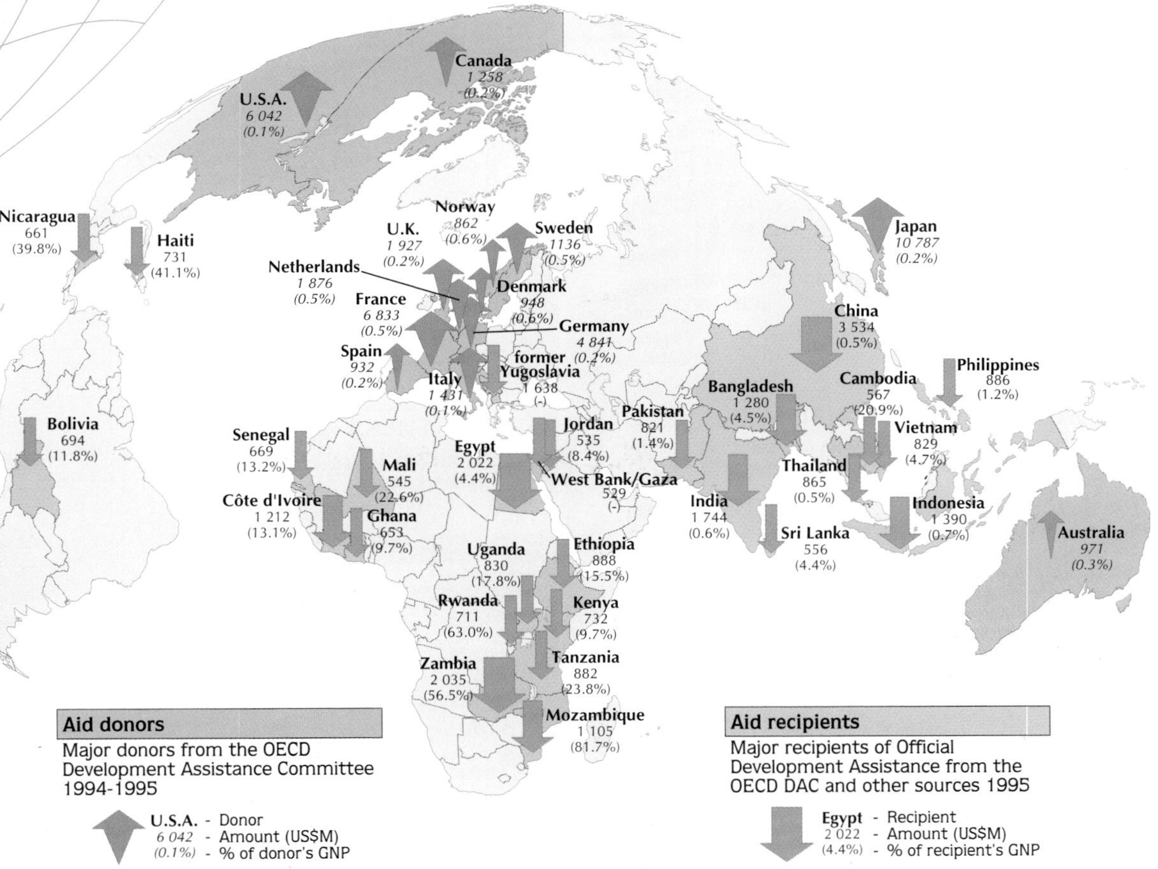

Canada
1 258
(0.2%)

U.S.A.
6 042
(0.1%)

Nicaragua
661
(39.8%)

Haiti
731
(41.1%)

Norway
862
(0.6%)

U.K.
1 927
(0.2%)

Sweden
1136
(0.5%)

Japan
10 787
(0.2%)

Netherlands
1 876
(0.5%)

Denmark
948
(0.6%)

France
6 833
(0.5%)

Germany
4 841
(0.2%)

China
3 534
(0.5%)

Spain
932
(0.2%)

former Yugoslavia
1 638
(-)

Italy
1 431
(0.1%)

Philippines
886
(1.2%)

Bolivia
694
(11.8%)

Senegal
669
(13.2%)

Egypt
2 022
(4.4%)

Jordan
535
(8.4%)

Pakistan
821
(1.4%)

Bangladesh
1 280
(4.5%)

Cambodia
567
(20.9%)

Vietnam
829
(4.7%)

Côte d'Ivoire
1 212
(13.1%)

Mali
545
(22.6%)

Ghana
653
(9.7%)

West Bank/Gaza
529
(-)

Thailand
865
(0.5%)

India
1 744
(0.6%)

Indonesia
1 390
(0.7%)

Uganda
830
(17.8%)

Ethiopia
888
(15.5%)

Sri Lanka
556
(4.4%)

Australia
971
(0.3%)

Rwanda
711
(63.0%)

Kenya
732
(9.7%)

Zambia
2 035
(56.5%)

Tanzania
882
(23.8%)

Mozambique
1 105
(81.7%)

### Aid donors
Major donors from the OECD Development Assistance Committee 1994-1995

U.S.A. - Donor
6 042 - Amount (US$M)
(0.1%) - % of donor's GNP

### Aid recipients
Major recipients of Official Development Assistance from the OECD DAC and other sources 1995

Egypt - Recipient
2 022 - Amount (US$M)
(4.4%) - % of recipient's GNP

© Collins

## INTERNATIONAL TRAVEL

All parts of the world are experiencing steady growth in air travel and tourism. Worldwide, airline traffic for passengers and freight grew by 7% in 1995 and the rise is expected to continue at a similar rate into the next century. Rates of growth vary between regions, with the dominant region being East Asia and the Pacific which is expected to sustain a growth rate in passenger traffic of approximately 12%.

New international airports have recently been completed in Denver, USA and Macau; and Hong Kong's new Chek Lap Kok airport is due to open in 1998 - further indicators of the strength of the aviation business.

Healthy economic conditions, particularly in the developed world, have encouraged recent increases in international tourism. Both tourist arrivals and receipts increased significantly in 1995 with the fastest-growing region again being that of East Asia and the Pacific.

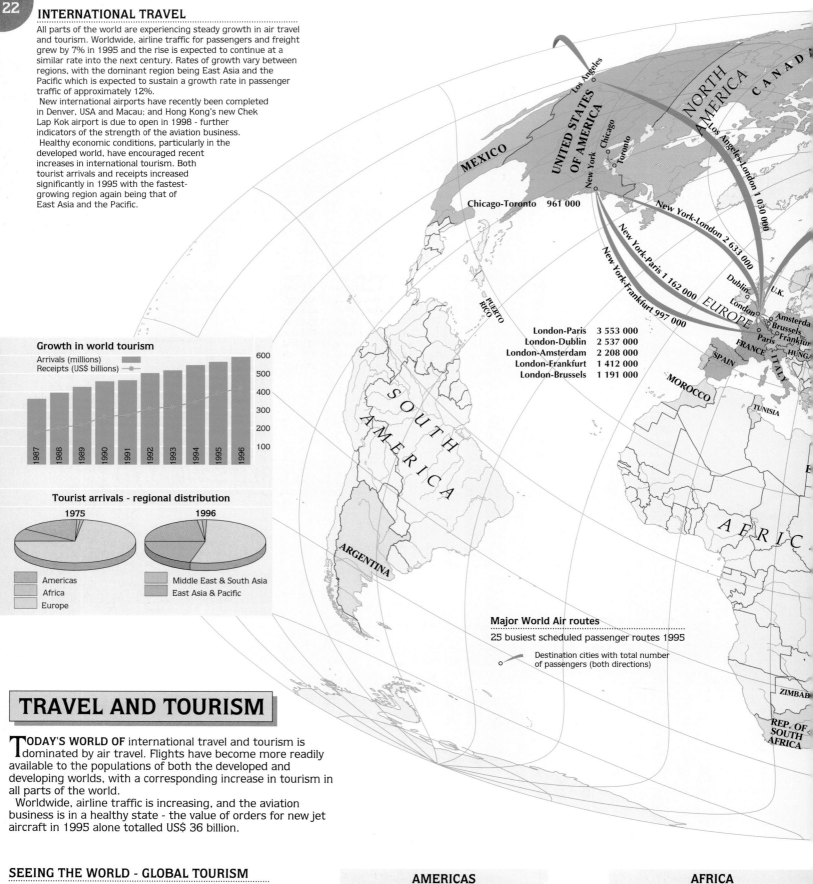

Chicago-Toronto    961 000

New York-London 2 633 000
New York-Paris 1 162 000
New York-Frankfurt 997 000
Los Angeles-London 1 030 000

London-Paris      3 553 000
London-Dublin     2 537 000
London-Amsterdam  2 208 000
London-Frankfurt  1 412 000
London-Brussels   1 191 000

### Growth in world tourism

Arrivals (millions)
Receipts (US$ billions)

1987 1988 1989 1990 1991 1992 1993 1994 1995 1996

### Tourist arrivals - regional distribution

1975          1996

Americas
Africa
Europe

Middle East & South Asia
East Asia & Pacific

### Major World Air routes

25 busiest scheduled passenger routes 1995

Destination cities with total number of passengers (both directions)

# TRAVEL AND TOURISM

**T**ODAY'S WORLD OF international travel and tourism is dominated by air travel. Flights have become more readily available to the populations of both the developed and developing worlds, with a corresponding increase in tourism in all parts of the world.

Worldwide, airline traffic is increasing, and the aviation business is in a healthy state - the value of orders for new jet aircraft in 1995 alone totalled US$ 36 billion.

## SEEING THE WORLD - GLOBAL TOURISM

In 1996 worldwide tourist arrivals and receipts from tourism increased by 4.5% and 7.6% respectively. Growth is expected to continue, largely because of increasing numbers of short-duration overseas visits by travellers from the developed world. Foreign travel from within the developing regions is also increasing steadily.

Europe is the dominant region in terms of arrivals and receipts, but its relative share is decreasing. Its market share has fallen by over 10% since 1975, compared with a corresponding rise of 11.3% in the East Asia and Pacific region. This shift reflects an overall increase in long-haul flights, from Europe in particular, to tourist destinations such as China (including Hong Kong), Malaysia and Thailand.

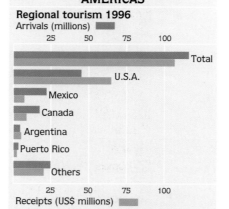

### AMERICAS
**Regional tourism 1996**

Arrivals (millions)

25    50    75    100

Total
U.S.A.
Mexico
Canada
Argentina
Puerto Rico
Others

25    50    75    100

Receipts (US$ millions)

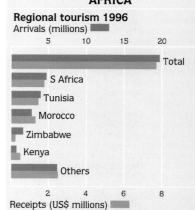

### AFRICA
**Regional tourism 1996**

Arrivals (millions)

5    10    15    20

Total
S Africa
Tunisia
Morocco
Zimbabwe
Kenya
Others

2    4    6    8

Receipts (US$ millions)

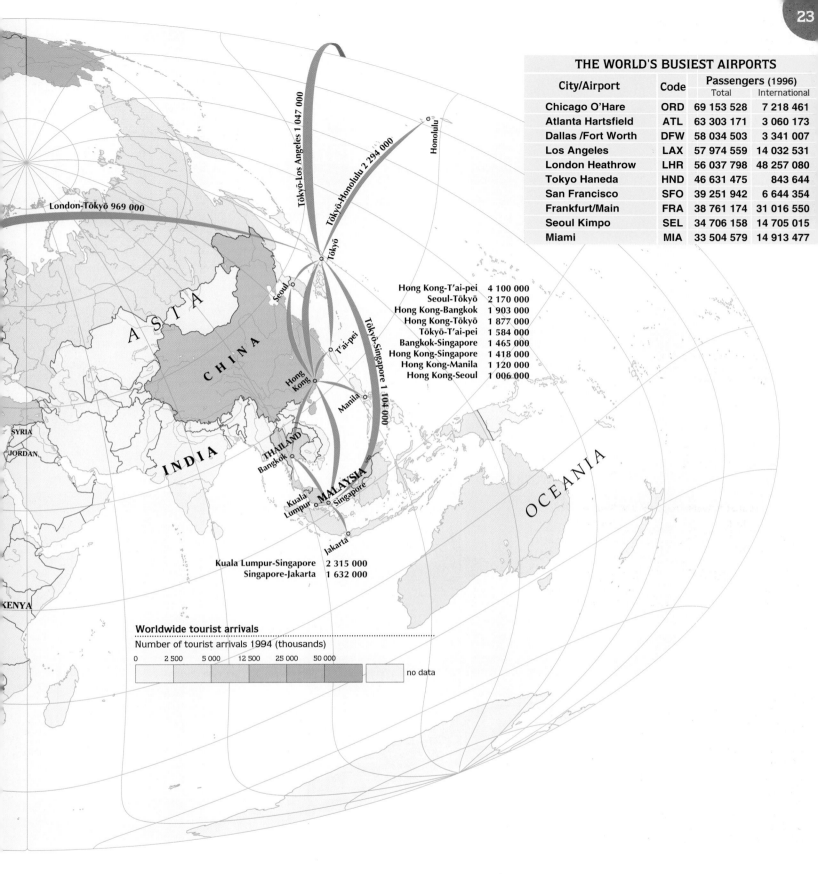

## THE WORLD'S BUSIEST AIRPORTS

| City/Airport | Code | Passengers (1996) Total | International |
|---|---|---|---|
| Chicago O'Hare | ORD | 69 153 528 | 7 218 461 |
| Atlanta Hartsfield | ATL | 63 303 171 | 3 060 173 |
| Dallas /Fort Worth | DFW | 58 034 503 | 3 341 007 |
| Los Angeles | LAX | 57 974 559 | 14 032 531 |
| London Heathrow | LHR | 56 037 798 | 48 257 080 |
| Tokyo Haneda | HND | 46 631 475 | 843 644 |
| San Francisco | SFO | 39 251 942 | 6 644 354 |
| Frankfurt/Main | FRA | 38 761 174 | 31 016 550 |
| Seoul Kimpo | SEL | 34 706 158 | 14 705 015 |
| Miami | MIA | 33 504 579 | 14 913 477 |

Tōkyō-Los Angeles 1 047 000

Tōkyō-Honolulu 2 294 000

London-Tōkyō 969 000

Tōkyō-Singapore 1 104 000

Honolulu

Tōkyō

Seoul

ASIA

CHINA

T'ai-pei

Hong Kong

Manila

SYRIA

JORDAN

INDIA

THAILAND

Bangkok

Kuala Lumpur

MALAYSIA

Singapore

Jakarta

KENYA

OCEANIA

Hong Kong-T'ai-pei 4 100 000
Seoul-Tōkyō 2 170 000
Hong Kong-Bangkok 1 903 000
Hong Kong-Tōkyō 1 877 000
Tōkyō-T'ai-pei 1 584 000
Bangkok-Singapore 1 465 000
Hong Kong-Singapore 1 418 000
Hong Kong-Manila 1 120 000
Hong Kong-Seoul 1 006 000

Kuala Lumpur-Singapore 2 315 000
Singapore-Jakarta 1 632 000

### Worldwide tourist arrivals
Number of tourist arrivals 1994 (thousands)

| 0 | 2 500 | 5 000 | 12 500 | 25 000 | 50 000 | no data |

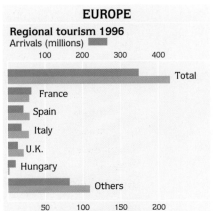

## EUROPE
### Regional tourism 1996
Arrivals (millions)

| 100 | 200 | 300 | 400 |

- Total
- France
- Spain
- Italy
- U.K.
- Hungary
- Others

| 50 | 100 | 150 | 200 |

Receipts (US$ millions)

## MIDDLE EAST & SOUTH ASIA
### Regional tourism 1996
Arrivals (millions)

| 5 | 10 | 15 | 20 |

- Total
- GCC*
- Egypt
- India
- Jordan
- Syria
- Others

| 5 | 10 | 15 |

Receipts (US$ millions)
*GCC - Gulf Co-operation Council

## EAST ASIA & PACIFIC
### Regional tourism 1996
Arrivals (millions)

| 25 | 50 | 75 | 100 |

- Total
- China
- Hong Kong
- Malaysia
- Thailand
- Singapore
- Others

| 25 | 50 | 75 | 100 |

Receipts (US$ millions)

© Collins

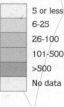

## COMMUNICATIONS TECHNOLOGY

**Satellite transmission basics**

Satellites are used by earth stations to receive and amplify information which is in the form of high-powered, high-frequency signals, and retransmit it back to stations in another part of the world.

Fibre-optic cables have been developed to overcome the limited capacity of the copper wires traditionally used for communication. Information is encoded into beams of laser light and sent down fine fibres of coated glass which can carry signals over large distances with little loss of quality.

Improving cost:capacity ratios have meant that fibre-optic cables are overtaking satellites in the transmission of point-to-point communications (e.g. telephone calls) but satellites remain the prime carrier of point-to-multi point signals (e.g. television broadcasts).

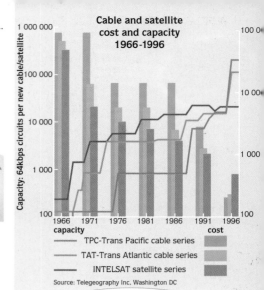

**Cable and satellite cost and capacity 1966-1996**

Capacity: 64kbps circuits per new cable/satellite

- —— TPC-Trans Pacific cable series
- —— TAT-Trans Atlantic cable series
- —— INTELSAT satellite series

Source: Telegeography Inc. Washington DC

# GLOBAL TELECOMMUNICATIONS

**D**EVELOPMENTS IN TECHNOLOGY have improved the speed and extent of voice, image and text communication to a level previously unimaginable, now making possible almost instant connection between people throughout the world by means of telephone, television, facsimile, and personal computer.

## MAJOR FIBRE-OPTIC SUBMARINE NETWORKS

## AND COMMUNICATIONS SATELLITE POSITIONS

**Cable capacity in gigabits per second**

- —— 1-5 gb    1gb per second=80 000 calls (approximately)
- —— 10-20 gb    Pecked lines show cables under construction
- —— 40-80 gb

**Satellite ownership**
(shows major international communications satellites transmitting to fixed terminals 1997)

- ◆ IS 512   INTELSAT
- ◆ PAS-5   PANAMSAT
- ◆ ORION1   ORION

## TELEPHONE DENSITY 1995

Wireline telephones per 1 000 people

- 5 or less
- 6-25
- 26-100
- 101-500
- >500
- No data

# WORLD COMMUNICATIONS EQUIPMENT

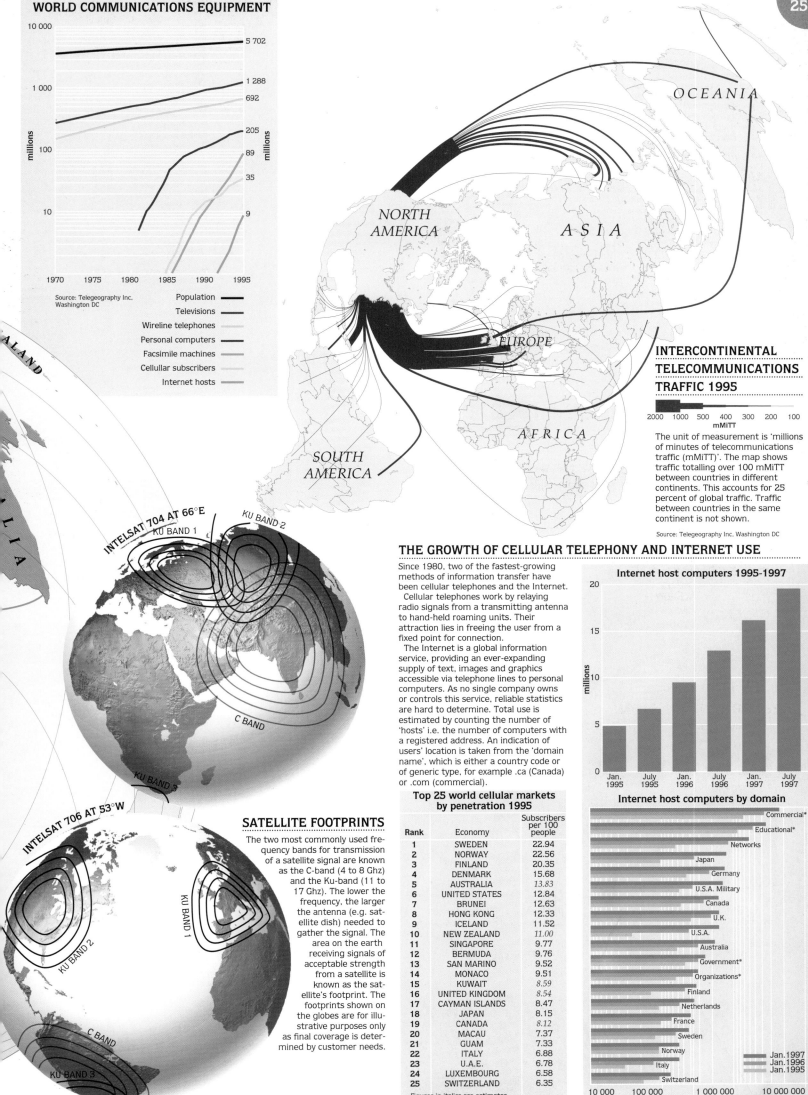

millions

| | |
|---|---|
| 10 000 | |
| 1 000 | 5 702 |
| 100 | 1 288 |
| | 692 |
| | 205 |
| 10 | 89 |
| | 35 |
| | 9 |

1970  1975  1980  1985  1990  1995

Source: Telegeography Inc,
Washington DC

Population ━━━
Televisions ━━━
Wireline telephones ━━━
Personal computers ━━━
Facsimile machines ━━━
Cellular subscribers ━━━
Internet hosts ━━━

## INTERCONTINENTAL TELECOMMUNICATIONS TRAFFIC 1995

2000 1000 500 400 300 200 100
mMiTT

The unit of measurement is 'millions of minutes of telecommunications traffic (mMiTT)'. The map shows traffic totalling over 100 mMiTT between countries in different continents. This accounts for 25 percent of global traffic. Traffic between countries in the same continent is not shown.

Source: Telegeography Inc, Washington DC

## SATELLITE FOOTPRINTS

INTELSAT 704 AT 66°E
KU BAND 1
KU BAND 2
C BAND
KU BAND 3
INTELSAT 706 AT 53°W
KU BAND 1
KU BAND 2
C BAND
KU BAND 3

The two most commonly used frequency bands for transmission of a satellite signal are known as the C-band (4 to 8 Ghz) and the Ku-band (11 to 17 Ghz). The lower the frequency, the larger the antenna (e.g. satellite dish) needed to gather the signal. The area on the earth receiving signals of acceptable strength from a satellite is known as the satellite's footprint. The footprints shown on the globes are for illustrative purposes only as final coverage is determined by customer needs.

## THE GROWTH OF CELLULAR TELEPHONY AND INTERNET USE

Since 1980, two of the fastest-growing methods of information transfer have been cellular telephones and the Internet.

Cellular telephones work by relaying radio signals from a transmitting antenna to hand-held roaming units. Their attraction lies in freeing the user from a fixed point for connection.

The Internet is a global information service, providing an ever-expanding supply of text, images and graphics accessible via telephone lines to personal computers. As no single company owns or controls this service, reliable statistics are hard to determine. Total use is estimated by counting the number of 'hosts' i.e. the number of computers with a registered address. An indication of users' location is taken from the 'domain name', which is either a country code or of generic type, for example .ca (Canada) or .com (commercial).

### Internet host computers 1995-1997

millions

| | |
|---|---|
| 20 | |
| 15 | |
| 10 | |
| 5 | |
| 0 | |

Jan. 1995  July 1995  Jan. 1996  July 1996  Jan. 1997  July 1997

### Top 25 world cellular markets by penetration 1995

| Rank | Economy | Subscribers per 100 people |
|---|---|---|
| 1 | SWEDEN | 22.94 |
| 2 | NORWAY | 22.56 |
| 3 | FINLAND | 20.35 |
| 4 | DENMARK | 15.68 |
| 5 | AUSTRALIA | 13.83 |
| 6 | UNITED STATES | 12.84 |
| 7 | BRUNEI | 12.63 |
| 8 | HONG KONG | 12.33 |
| 9 | ICELAND | 11.52 |
| 10 | NEW ZEALAND | 11.00 |
| 11 | SINGAPORE | 9.77 |
| 12 | BERMUDA | 9.76 |
| 13 | SAN MARINO | 9.52 |
| 14 | MONACO | 9.51 |
| 15 | KUWAIT | 8.59 |
| 16 | UNITED KINGDOM | 8.54 |
| 17 | CAYMAN ISLANDS | 8.47 |
| 18 | JAPAN | 8.15 |
| 19 | CANADA | 8.12 |
| 20 | MACAU | 7.37 |
| 21 | GUAM | 7.33 |
| 22 | ITALY | 6.88 |
| 23 | U.A.E. | 6.78 |
| 24 | LUXEMBOURG | 6.58 |
| 25 | SWITZERLAND | 6.35 |

Figures in italics are estimates
Source: Telegeography Inc, Washington DC

### Internet host computers by domain

Commercial*
Educational*
Networks
Japan
Germany
U.S.A. Military
Canada
U.K.
U.S.A.
Australia
Government*
Organizations*
Finland
Netherlands
France
Sweden
Norway
Italy
Switzerland

10 000   100 000   1 000 000   10 000 000
*majority in U.S.A.                Source: Network Wizards

Jan.1997
Jan.1996
Jan.1995

© Collins

# OUTBREAK OF THE FIRST WORLD WAR 1914

In 1912 the desire for independence and territory motivated the people in the Balkan peninsula to go to war, first with their Ottoman rulers, and then amongst themselves. These actions had repercussions for the other European powers who saw their security threatened by the instability of the frontier area between three great empires. By this time, Europe had divided itself into two alliance blocs, the Central Powers (Germany, Austria-Hungary, Italy) and the Entente Powers (France, Russia, Britain) whose opposing interests prevented them resolving the Balkan dispute.

The crisis in the Balkans intensified the growing rivalry between the old dynastic empires of Russia and Austria-Hungary, into which their respective allies were inextricably drawn. The turning point came in June 1914 when Austria blamed Serbia for the assassination of the heir to their throne, Franz Ferdinand, and Russia pledged to defend their Balkan ally in the event of war. These actions triggered the wider system of alliances, whose members had considerably reinforced their armies, and so by August the major states of Europe found themselves at war.

- mobilizations, with date
- ultimata issued, with date
- declarations of war, with date
- Entente Powers at outbreak of war
- joined Entente Powers during war, with date
- Central Powers at outbreak of war
- joined Central Powers during war, with date
- frontiers 1914

North Sea · SWEDEN · DENMARK · Copenhagen · RUSSIAN EMPIRE · Riga · Mosco · UNITED KINGDOM · 29 July · 4 Aug: to Germany · 4 Aug: against Germany · 12 Aug: against Austria-Hungary · London · GERMAN EMPIRE · Berlin · Warsaw · 26 July · 31 July: to Russia · 31 July · NETHERLANDS · BELGIUM Brussels · LUX. · Paris · 1 Aug. · FRANCE · 1 Aug: against Russia · 3 Aug: against Belgium and France · Vienna · AUSTRO-HUNGARIAN EMPIRE · 23 July: to Serbia · 25 July · SWITZ. · 4 Aug: against Germany · 13 Aug: against Austria-Hungary · 28 July: against Serbia · 5 Aug: against Russia · ROMANIA · 28 Aug. 1916 · Black Sea · 9 Mar. 1916 · PORTUGAL · Lisbon · Madrid · ANDORRA · SPAIN · ITALY · 25 May 1915 · Rome · Corsica · MONTENEGRO · 25 July · 5 Aug: against Austria-Hungary · 11 Aug: against Germany · Belgrade · Bucharest · SERBIA · Sofia · BULGARIA · 5 Oct. 1915 · Constantinop (Istanbul) · Gibraltar British · Sardinia · Mediterranean Sea · Sicily · ALBANIA · GREECE · 29 June 1917 · Athens · Dodecanese Italian · OTTOMAN EMPIRE · 30 Oct. 1914

---

# CENTURY OF CHANGE I 1900-1934

## COLLAPSE OF CENTRAL POWERS 1918

By September 1918, facing an advancing Allied army in the west, mutinies in the army and navy, and public calls for economic and political change, the Central Powers disunited in the hope of securing a separate peace and better treatment. In the Austro-Hungarian Empire the diverse ethnic groups called for independence, leading to the states of Czechoslovakia and Yugoslavia. Following armistice agreements in November, Austria and Hungary declared themselves republics. Germany followed suit, so that, coupled with revolution in the Russian Empire, by the end of the year three major European empires had disintegrated.

- USSR, determined by Treaty of Brest-Litovsk, March
- controlled by Entente Powers, 30 Sept.
- limit of Central Powers' control, 30 Sept.
- lost by Central Powers before armistices
- evacuated by Central Powers under armistices of 3-11 Nov.
- ceded to former nationalities of Austro-Hungarian empire by 6 Dec.
- Austria, declared independent 12 Nov.
- Hungary, declared independent 16 Nov.
- controlled by Czechoslovakia 31 Dec.
- ★ declaration of independence
- ▲ overthrow of monarchy

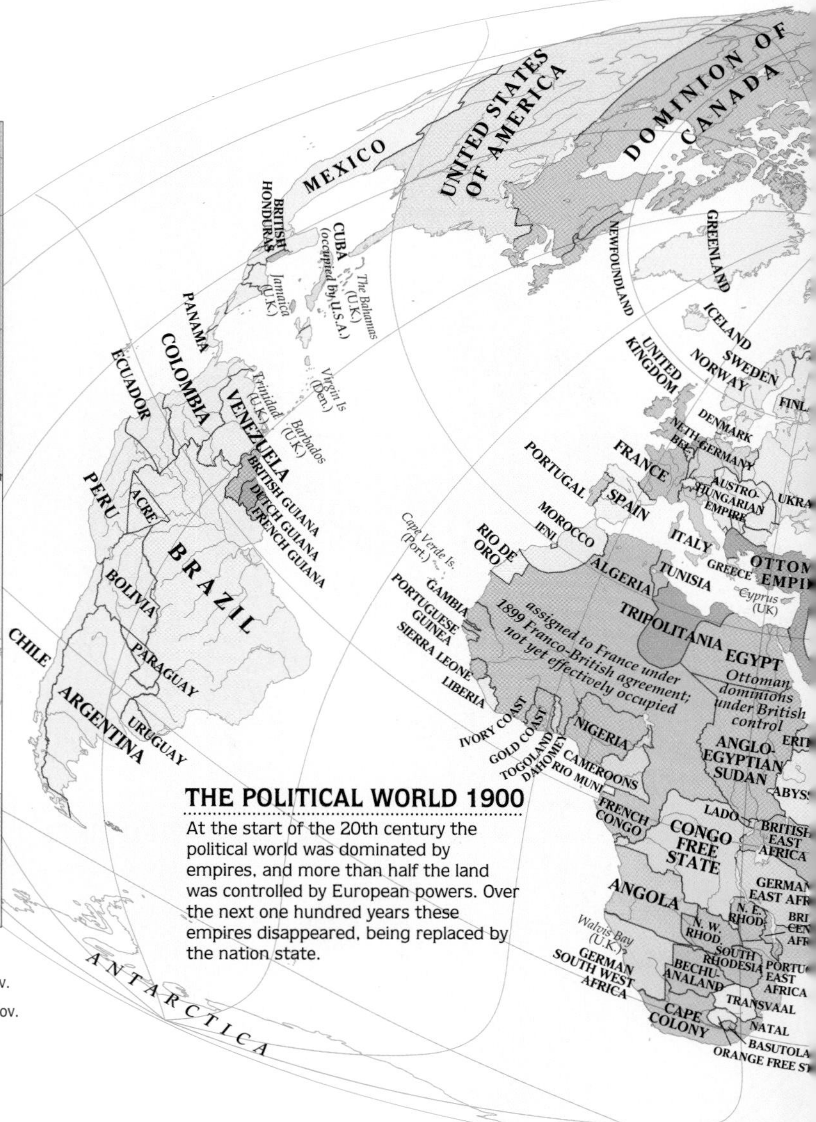

FINLAND independent 6 Dec. 1917 · Helsingfors (Helsinki) · Petrograd (St Petersburg) · ESTONIA · U.S.S.R. · Riga · LATVIA · Moscow · LITHUANIA · Vilna · Minsk · U.K. · NETHERLANDS · BELGIUM Brussels · Cologne · Frankfurt · LUX. · Paris · FRANCE · GERMAN EMPIRE · Berlin · Warsaw ★ · POLAND · Prague ★ · BOHEMIA · Cracow (Kraków) · Lemberg · UKRAINE · occupied by Romania, 11 Nov. · Munich · LIECH. · AUSTRO-HUNGARIAN · Vienna ▲ · Budapest ▲ · BUKOVINA · SWITZ. · EMPIRE · Odessa · Trieste · Laibach · Gyulafehérvár · BESSARABIA · annexed by Romania, April · Zagreb · CROATIA-SLAVONIA · ROMANIA · ITALY · BOSNIA-HERZEGOVINA · Sarajevo · Belgrade · Bucharest · Black Sea · MONACO SAN MARINO · DALMATIA · SERBIA · BULGARIA · Rome · MONTE-NEGRO · Sofia · Constantinople (Istanbul) · Tirana · Skopje · ALBANIA · Salonica · OTTOMAN EMPIRE · GREECE · Mudros

## THE POLITICAL WORLD 1900

At the start of the 20th century the political world was dominated by empires, and more than half the land was controlled by European powers. Over the next one hundred years these empires disappeared, being replaced by the nation state.

DOMINION OF CANADA · UNITED STATES OF AMERICA · MEXICO · BRITISH HONDURAS · CUBA (occupied by U.S.A.) · The Bahamas (U.K.) · Jamaica (U.K.) · PANAMA · COLOMBIA · VENEZUELA · Trinidad (U.K.) · Barbados (U.K.) · BRITISH GUIANA · DUTCH GUIANA · FRENCH GUIANA · ECUADOR · PERU · BRAZIL · ACRE · BOLIVIA · PARAGUAY · CHILE · ARGENTINA · URUGUAY · ANTARCTICA · GREENLAND · ICELAND · NORWAY · SWEDEN · FINL · UNITED KINGDOM · DENMARK · NETHERLANDS · GERMANY · AUSTRO-HUNGARIAN EMPIRE · FRANCE · PORTUGAL · SPAIN · ITALY · GREECE · OTTOMAN EMPIRE · Cape Verde Is. (Port.) · RIO DE ORO · MOROCCO · IFNI · ALGERIA · TUNISIA · TRIPOLITANIA · EGYPT · 1899 Franco-British agreement; not yet effectively occupied · assigned to France under Franco-British agreement · Cyprus (UK) · Ottoman dominions under British control · PORTUGUESE GUINEA · GAMBIA · SIERRA LEONE · LIBERIA · IVORY COAST · GOLD COAST · TOGOLAND · DAHOMEY · NIGERIA · CAMEROONS · RIO MUNI · FRENCH CONGO · CONGO FREE STATE · ANGOLA · ANGLO-EGYPTIAN SUDAN · ABYS · ERI · BRITISH EAST AFRICA · GERMAN EAST AFRICA · N.W. RHOD. · N.E. RHOD. · PORTU EAST AFR · BRI · SOUTH RHODESIA · BECHU ANALAND · GERMAN SOUTH WEST AFRICA · Walvis Bay (U.K.) · CAPE COLONY · TRANSVAAL · NATAL · BASUTOLA · ORANGE FREE ST

---

*Timeline at bottom:*

1900 – Planck evolves quantum theory (Germany)
1901 – Commonwealth of Australia proclaimed
1902 – End of Boer War between British and established settlers for control of South Africa · USA gain control of Panama Canal
1903 – First air flight by Wright brothers, USA
1905 – Norway becomes independent from Sweden · Einstein evolves theory of relativity (Germany)
1907 – New Zealand achieves dominion status
1908 – Bulgaria achieves independence · Austria annexes Bosnia and Herzegovina · Young Turk revolution – Ottoman sultan deposed
1910 – Mexican revolution begins · Japan annexes Korea · Formation of Union of South Africa
1911 – Chinese Revolution – rise to power of Warlords
1912 – Start of Balkan Wars against Ottoman Empire
1913 – Henry Ford develops conveyor belt system for production of Model T vehicle
1914 – Start of First World War · Panama Canal opens
1915 – Italy breaks alliance with Austria and joins Entente Powers in First World War
1917 – Russian Revolution – first socialist state established · Balfour Declaration – politician committing Britain to provide an independent Jewish state in the Palestine region · USA enters First World War · First use of massed tanks in warfare (Cambrai, France)
1918 – End of First World War · USA President Wilson announces "Fourteen Points" favoured nationalism in Europe
1919 – Paris treaties redraw map of Europe · USA refuse to ratify · First transatlantic flight by Alcock and Brown, UK
1920 – League of Nati... · Britain refuse to rat...

## CLINE OF THE OTTOMAN EMPIRE

Ottoman Empire was the dominant force in the Balkans, dle East and North Africa, and its decline from 1800 was a duct of the corrupt nature of the ruling family, the economic religious interests of the Christian European imperial powers, the desire for independence by various nationalist groups. wing a revolution in 1908 the sultan was deposed, and by the t of the First World War the Ottomans had lost all control in th Africa, and the Balkan Wars had limited their territory in ope to a strip of land around Constantinople. After the War the -Turkish territories in the Empire were divided between the ors, and the remaining land ame the republic of key in 1923, wing a war of pendence.

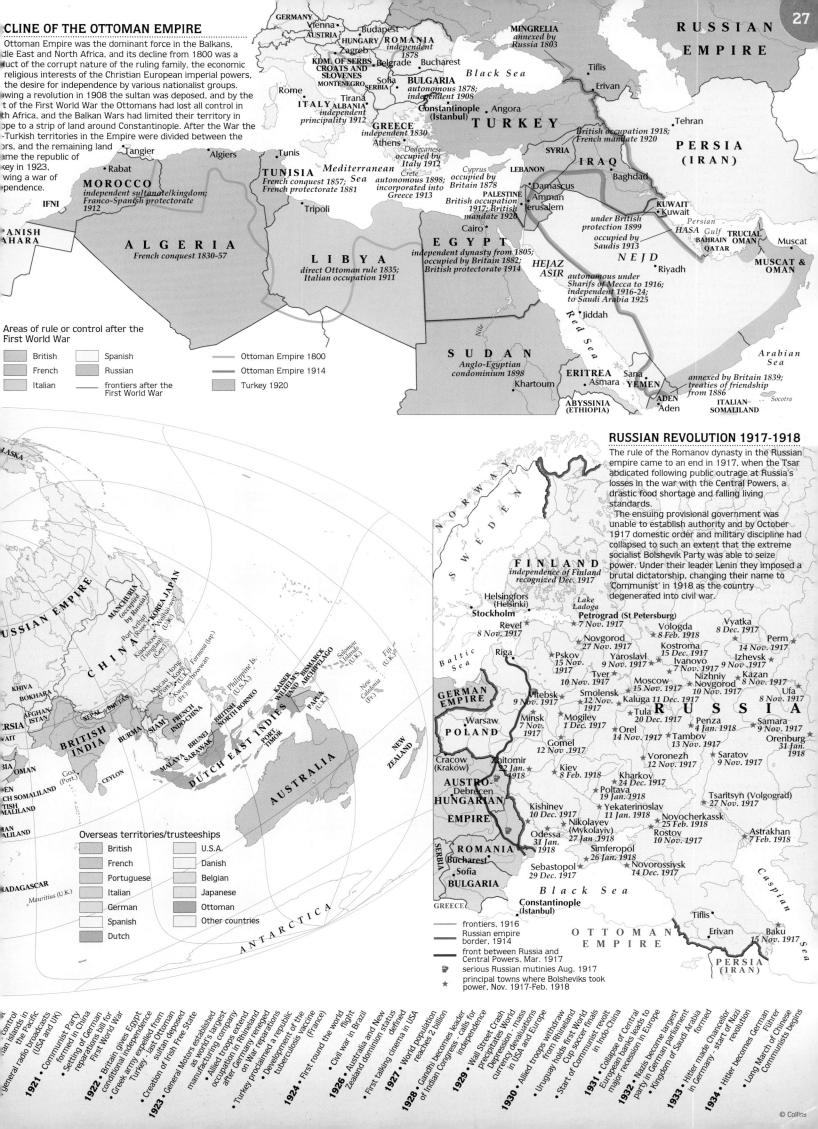

**Areas of rule or control after the First World War**

- British
- French
- Italian
- Spanish
- Russian
- Ottoman Empire 1800
- Ottoman Empire 1914
- frontiers after the First World War
- Turkey 1920

## RUSSIAN REVOLUTION 1917-1918

The rule of the Romanov dynasty in the Russian empire came to an end in 1917, when the Tsar abdicated following public outrage at Russia's losses in the war with the Central Powers, a drastic food shortage and falling living standards.

The ensuing provisional government was unable to establish authority and by October 1917 domestic order and military discipline had collapsed to such an extent that the extreme socialist Bolshevik Party was able to seize power. Under their leader Lenin they imposed a brutal dictatorship, changing their name to 'Communist' in 1918 as the country degenerated into civil war.

**Overseas territories/trusteeships**

- British
- French
- Portuguese
- Italian
- German
- Spanish
- Dutch
- U.S.A.
- Danish
- Belgian
- Japanese
- Ottoman
- Other countries

- frontiers, 1916
- Russian empire border, 1914
- front between Russia and Central Powers, Mar. 1917
- serious Russian mutinies Aug. 1917
- principal towns where Bolsheviks took power, Nov. 1917-Feb. 1918

© Collins

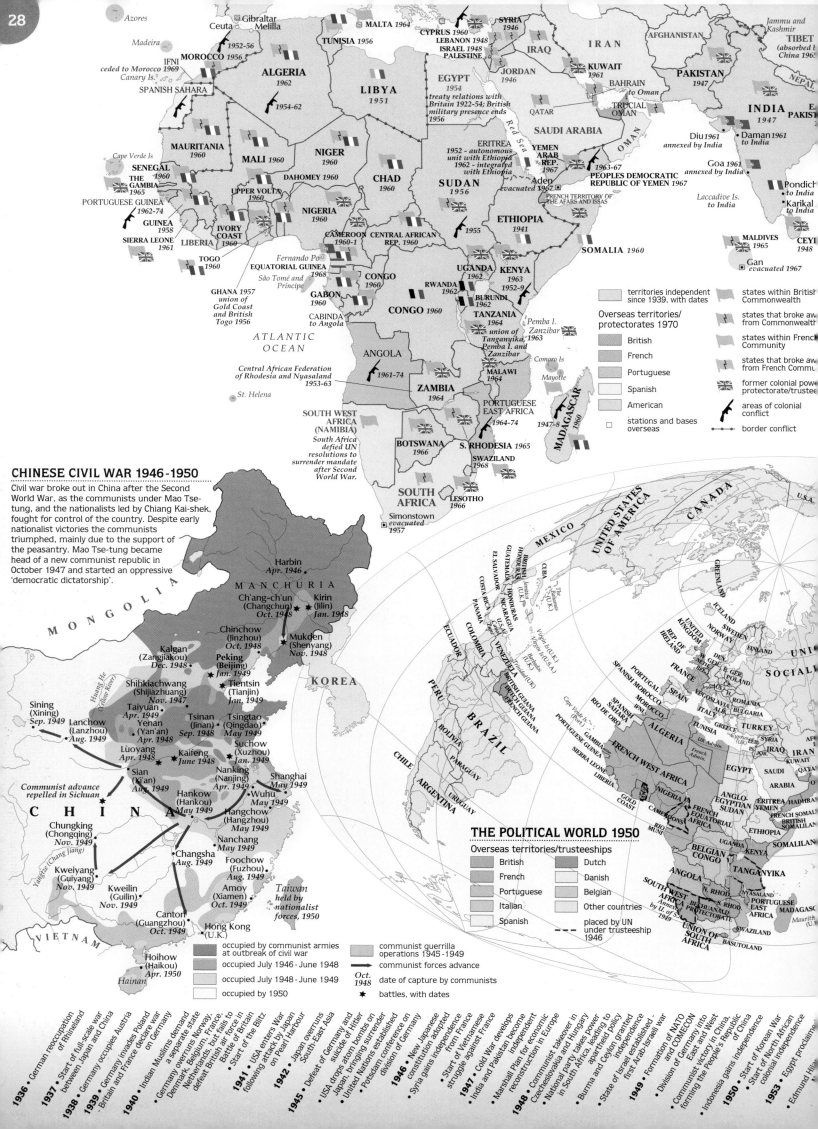

## Africa and Middle East map labels

Azores · Gibraltar · Ceuta · Melilla · MALTA 1964 · CYPRUS 1960 · SYRIA 1946 · Jammu and Kashmir · AFGHANISTAN · TIBET (absorbed by China 1965)

Madeira · TUNISIA 1956 · LEBANON 1948 · ISRAEL 1948 · PALESTINE · IRAQ · IRAN

IFNI · MOROCCO 1956 · 1952-56 · ALGERIA 1962 · LIBYA 1951 · EGYPT · JORDAN 1946 · KUWAIT 1961 · BAHRAIN to Oman · QATAR · TRUCIAL OMAN · PAKISTAN 1947 · NEPAL

ceded to Morocco 1969 · Canary Is. · SPANISH SAHARA · 1954-62

treaty relations with Britain 1922-54; British military presence ends 1956

SAUDI ARABIA · OMAN · INDIA 1947 · E. PAKIST

Cape Verde Is · MAURITANIA 1960 · MALI 1960 · NIGER 1960 · CHAD 1960 · SUDAN 1956 · ERITREA 1952 - autonomous unit with Ethiopia 1962 - integrated with Ethiopia · YEMEN ARAB REP. · Aden evacuated 1967 · PEOPLES DEMOCRATIC REPUBLIC OF YEMEN 1967 · FRENCH TERRITORY OF THE AFARS AND ISSAS · 1963-67 · Diu 1961 annexed by India · Daman 1961 to India · Goa 1961 annexed by India · Laccadive Is. to India · Pondich to India · Karikal to India

SENEGAL 1960 · THE GAMBIA 1965 · DAHOMEY 1960 · UPPER VOLTA 1960 · NIGERIA 1960 · CENTRAL AFRICAN REP. 1960 · ETHIOPIA 1941 · 1955 · SOMALIA 1960 · MALDIVES 1965 · CEYL 1948

PORTUGUESE GUINEA 1962-74 · GUINEA 1958 · IVORY COAST 1960 · LIBERIA · TOGO 1960 · CAMEROON 1960-1 · UGANDA 1962 · KENYA 1963 · 1952-9 · Gan evacuated 1967

SIERRA LEONE 1961 · Fernando Po · EQUATORIAL GUINEA 1968 · São Tomé and Príncipe · GHANA 1957 union of Gold Coast and British Togo 1956 · GABON 1960 · CONGO 1960 · RWANDA 1962 · BURUNDI 1962 · TANZANIA 1964 union of Tanganyika, Pemba I. and Zanzibar · Pemba I. Zanzibar 1963 · Comoro Is

CABINDA to Angola · CONGO 1960 · MALAWI 1964 · Mayotte

ATLANTIC OCEAN · Cape Verde Is · St. Helena · Central African Federation of Rhodesia and Nyasaland 1953-63 · ANGOLA 1961-74 · ZAMBIA 1964 · PORTUGUESE EAST AFRICA 1964-74 · MADAGASCAR 1947-8 1960

SOUTH WEST AFRICA (NAMIBIA) South Africa defied UN resolutions to surrender mandate after Second World War. · BOTSWANA 1966 · S. RHODESIA 1965 · SWAZILAND 1968 · LESOTHO 1966

SOUTH AFRICA · Simonstown evacuated 1957

### Legend (Africa map)

- territories independent since 1939, with dates

**Overseas territories/protectorates 1970**
- British
- French
- Portuguese
- Spanish
- American
- □ stations and bases overseas

- states within British Commonwealth
- states that broke away from Commonwealth
- states within French Community
- states that broke away from French Commu
- former colonial power protectorate/trustee
- areas of colonial conflict
- border conflict

---

## CHINESE CIVIL WAR 1946-1950

Civil war broke out in China after the Second World War, as the communists under Mao Tse-tung, and the nationalists led by Chiang Kai-shek, fought for control of the country. Despite early nationalist victories the communists triumphed, mainly due to the support of the peasantry. Mao Tse-tung became head of a new communist republic in October 1947 and started an oppressive 'democratic dictatorship'.

### China map labels

MONGOLIA · MANCHURIA · Harbin Apr. 1946 · Ch'ang-ch'un (Changchun) Oct. 1948 · Kirin (Jilin) Jan. 1948 · Chinchow (Jinzhou) Oct. 1948 · Mukden (Shenyang) Nov. 1948 · Kalgan (Zangjiakou) Dec. 1948 · Peking (Beijing) Jan. 1949 · Tientsin (Tianjin) Jan. 1949 · KOREA · Shihkiachwang (Shijiazhuang) Nov. 1947 · Sining (Xining) Sep. 1949 · Taiyuan Apr. 1949 · Yenan (Yan'an) Apr. 1948 · Tsinan (Jinan) Sep. 1948 · Tsingtao (Qingdao) May 1949 · Lanchow (Lanzhou) Aug. 1949 · Lùoyang Apr. 1948 · Kaifeng June 1948 · Suchow (Xuzhou) Jan. 1949 · Huang He (Yellow River) · Sian (Xi'an) Aug. 1949 · Nanking (Nanjing) Apr. 1949 · Shanghai May 1949 · Communist advance repelled in Sichuan · C H I N A · Hankow (Hankou) May 1949 · Wuhu May 1949 · Hangchow (Hangzhou) May 1949 · Chungking (Chongqing) Nov. 1949 · Nanchang May 1949 · Kweiyang (Guiyang) Nov. 1949 · Changsha Aug. 1949 · Foochow (Fuzhou) Aug. 1949 · Yangtze (Chang Jiang) · Kweilin (Guilin) Nov. 1949 · Amoy (Xiamen) Oct. 1949 · Taiwan held by nationalist forces, 1950 · Canton (Guangzhou) Oct. 1949 · Hong Kong (U.K.) · VIETNAM · Hoihow (Haikou) Apr. 1950 · Hainan

### Legend (China map)

- occupied by communist armies at outbreak of civil war
- occupied July 1946 - June 1948
- occupied July 1948 - June 1949
- occupied by 1950
- communist guerrilla operations 1945-1949
- → communist forces advance
- Oct. 1948 date of capture by communists
- ★ battles, with dates

---

## THE POLITICAL WORLD 1950

### World map labels

UNITED STATES OF AMERICA · CANADA · U.S.A. · GREENLAND · ICELAND · UNITED KINGDOM · REP. OF IRELAND · NORWAY · SWEDEN · FINLAND · UNIO SOCIALI

MEXICO · British Honduras (U.K.) · GUATEMALA · HONDURAS · EL SALVADOR · NICARAGUA · COSTA RICA · PANAMA · Panama Canal · Jamaica (U.K.) · The Bahamas (U.K.) · CUBA

ECUADOR · COLOMBIA · VENEZUELA · BRITISH GUIANA · DUTCH GUIANA · FRENCH GUIANA · Virgin Is (U.K.) · Virgin Is (U.S.A.) · Barbados (U.K.) · Trinidad (U.K.)

PERU · BRAZIL · BOLIVIA · Cape Verde Is (Port.) · PORTUGAL · SPAIN · W. GER. · E. GER. · POLAND · DEN. · NETH. · BEL. · FRANCE · ITALY · YUGOSLAVIA · ROMANIA · BULGARIA · SPANISH MOROCCO · IFNI · RIO DE ORO · SPANISH SAHARA · ALGERIA · TUNISIA · GREECE · TURKEY · UK Admin. · Cyprus (UK) · SYRIA · IRAQ · IRAN · JOR. · KUWAIT · QATAR

CHILE · ARGENTINA · PARAGUAY · URUGUAY · GAMBIA · PORTUGUESE GUINEA · SIERRA LEONE · LIBERIA · GOLD COAST · French Admin. · FRENCH WEST AFRICA · NIGERIA · CAMEROONS · RIO MUNI · FRENCH EQUATORIAL AFRICA · EGYPT · ANGLO-EGYPTIAN SUDAN · ERITREA/HADHRA · YEMEN · SAUDI ARABIA · FRENCH SOMALI · BRITISH SOMALILAN

UGANDA · KENYA · BELGIAN CONGO · TANGANYIKA · SOMALILAN · ETHIOPIA · ANGOLA · SOUTH WEST AFRICA Annexed by U. of S. 1949 · N. RHOD. · S. RHOD. · NYASALAND · PORTUGUESE EAST AFRICA · MADAGAS · BECHUANALAND PROTECTORATE · UNION OF SOUTH AFRICA · BASUTOLAND · SWAZILAND · Mauriti (U.

### Legend (Political World 1950)

**Overseas territories/trusteeships**
- British
- French
- Portuguese
- Italian
- Spanish
- Dutch
- Danish
- Belgian
- Other countries
- — — placed by UN under trusteeship 1946

---

1936 • German reoccupation of Rhineland
1937 • Start of full-scale war between Japan and China
1938 • Germany occupies Austria
1939 • Germany invades Poland - Britain and France declare war on Germany
1940 • Indian Muslims demand a separate state • Germany overruns Norway, Denmark, Belgium, France, Netherlands, but fails to defeat British air force in Battle of Britain • Start of the Blitz
1941 • USA enters War following attack by Japan on Pearl Harbour
1942 • Japan overruns South-East Asia
1945 • Defeat of Germany and suicide of Hitler • USA drops atom bombs on Japan, bringing surrender • United Nations established
1946 • New Japanese constitution adopted • Syria gains independence • Start of Vietnamese struggle against France
1947 • Start of Cold War • India and Pakistan become independent • Marshall Plan for economic reconstruction in Europe
1948 • Communist takeover in Czechoslovakia and Hungary • National party takes power in South Africa, leading to apartheid policy • Burma and Ceylon granted independence • State of Israel established - first Arab-Israeli war
1949 • Formation of NATO and COMECON • Division of Germany into East and West • Communist victory in China, forming the People's Republic of China
1950 • Indonesia gains independence • Start of Korean War • Start of North African colonial independence
1953 • Egypt proclaime · Edmund Hil

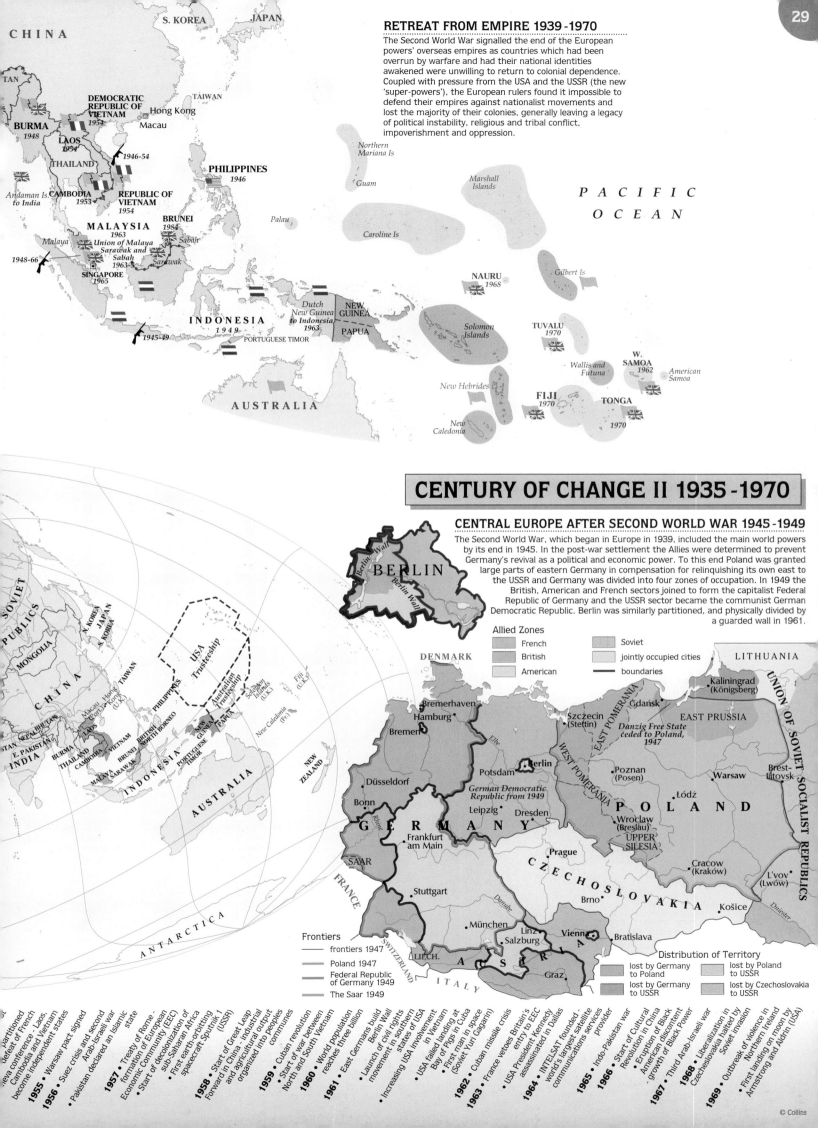

## RETREAT FROM EMPIRE 1939-1970

The Second World War signalled the end of the European powers' overseas empires as countries which had been overrun by warfare and had their national identities awakened were unwilling to return to colonial dependence. Coupled with pressure from the USA and the USSR (the new 'super-powers'), the European rulers found it impossible to defend their empires against nationalist movements and lost the majority of their colonies, generally leaving a legacy of political instability, religious and tribal conflict, impoverishment and oppression.

### Map labels (top):

CHINA
S. KOREA
JAPAN
TAIWAN
Hong Kong
Macau
DEMOCRATIC REPUBLIC OF VIETNAM 1954
BURMA 1948
LAOS 1954
THAILAND
1946-54
PHILIPPINES 1946
Andaman Is. to India
CAMBODIA 1953
REPUBLIC OF VIETNAM 1954
MALAYSIA 1963
BRUNEI 1984
Sabah
Malaya
Union of Malaya Sarawak and Sabah 1963-5
Sarawak
1948-66
SINGAPORE 1965
INDONESIA 1949
1945-49
Dutch New Guinea to Indonesia 1963
NEW GUINEA
PAPUA
PORTUGUESE TIMOR
AUSTRALIA

Northern Mariana Is
Guam
Marshall Islands
Palau
Caroline Is
NAURU 1968
Gilbert Is
Solomon Islands
TUVALU 1970
Wallis and Futuna
W. SAMOA 1962
American Samoa
New Hebrides
FIJI 1970
TONGA 1970
New Caledonia

PACIFIC OCEAN

# CENTURY OF CHANGE II 1935-1970

## CENTRAL EUROPE AFTER SECOND WORLD WAR 1945-1949

The Second World War, which began in Europe in 1939, included the main world powers by its end in 1945. In the post-war settlement the Allies were determined to prevent Germany's revival as a political and economic power. To this end Poland was granted large parts of eastern Germany in compensation for relinquishing its own east to the USSR and Germany was divided into four zones of occupation. In 1949 the British, American and French sectors joined to form the capitalist Federal Republic of Germany and the USSR sector became the communist German Democratic Republic. Berlin was similarly partitioned, and physically divided by a guarded wall in 1961.

**BERLIN** — Berlin Wall

**Allied Zones**
- French
- British
- American
- Soviet
- jointly occupied cities
- boundaries

### Map labels (Central Europe):

DENMARK
LITHUANIA
Bremerhaven
Hamburg
Bremen
Kaliningrad (Königsberg)
Szczecin (Stettin)
Gdańsk
EAST PRUSSIA
EAST POMERANIA
WEST POMERANIA
Danzig Free State ceded to Poland, 1947
Berlin
Potsdam
Brest-Litovsk
Poznan (Posen)
Warsaw
Düsseldorf
German Democratic Republic from 1949
GERMANY
Bonn
Leipzig
Łódź
POLAND
Dresden
Wrocław (Breslau)
UPPER SILESIA
Frankfurt am Main
Cracow (Kraków)
L'vov (Lwów)
UNION OF SOVIET SOCIALIST REPUBLICS
SAAR
Prague
CZECHOSLOVAKIA
Stuttgart
Brno
Košice
München
Linz
Salzburg
Vienna
Bratislava
AUSTRIA
SWITZERLAND
LIECH.
ITALY
Graz

**Frontiers**
- frontiers 1947
- Poland 1947
- Federal Republic of Germany 1949
- The Saar 1949

**Distribution of Territory**
- lost by Germany to Poland
- lost by Germany to USSR
- lost by Poland to USSR
- lost by Czechoslovakia to USSR

### Globe map labels:

SOVIET REPUBLICS
MONGOLIA
N. KOREA
JAPAN
S. KOREA
CHINA
TAIWAN
NEPAL
BHUTAN
INDIA
E. PAKISTAN
BURMA
THAILAND
CAMBODIA
VIETNAM
LAOS
Macau (Port.)
Hong Kong (U.K.)
PHILIPPINES
USA Trusteeship
Fiji (U.K.)
MALAYA
SINGAPORE
BRUNEI
BRITISH NORTH BORNEO
SARAWAK
INDONESIA
PORTUGUESE TIMOR
NEW GUINEA
PAPUA
Australian Trusteeship
Solomon Islands (U.K.)
New Caledonia (Fr.)
NEW ZEALAND
AUSTRALIA
ANTARCTICA

### Timeline (bottom):

- partitioned ... defeat of French ... Cambodia and Laos, become independent states ... eva conference - Laos, Cambodia and Vietnam
- **1955** • Warsaw pact signed
- **1956** • Suez crisis and second Arab-Israeli war • Pakistan declared an Islamic state
- **1957** • Treaty of Rome - formation of European Economic Community (EEC) • Start of decolonization of sub-Saharan Africa • First earth-orbiting spacecraft Sputnik 1 (USSR)
- **1958** • Start of Great Leap Forward in China - industrial and agricultural output organized into peoples communes
- **1959** • Cuban revolution • Start of war between North and South Vietnam
- **1960** • World population reaches three billion
- **1961** • East Germans build Berlin Wall • Launch of civil rights movement in southern states of USA • Increasing USA involvement in Vietnam • USA failed landing at Bay of Pigs in Cuba • First man in space (Soviet Yuri Gagarin)
- **1962** • Cuban missile crisis
- **1963** • France vetoes Britain's entry to EEC • USA President Kennedy assassinated in Dallas
- **1964** • INTELSAT founded - world's largest satellite communications provider
- **1965** • Indo-Pakistan war
- **1966** • Start of Cultural Revolution in China • Eruption of Black American discontent - growth of Black Power
- **1967** • Third Arab-Israeli war
- **1968** • Liberalization in Czechoslovakia halted by Soviet invasion
- **1969** • Outbreak of violence in Northern Ireland • First landing on moon by Armstrong and Aldrin (USA)

© Collins

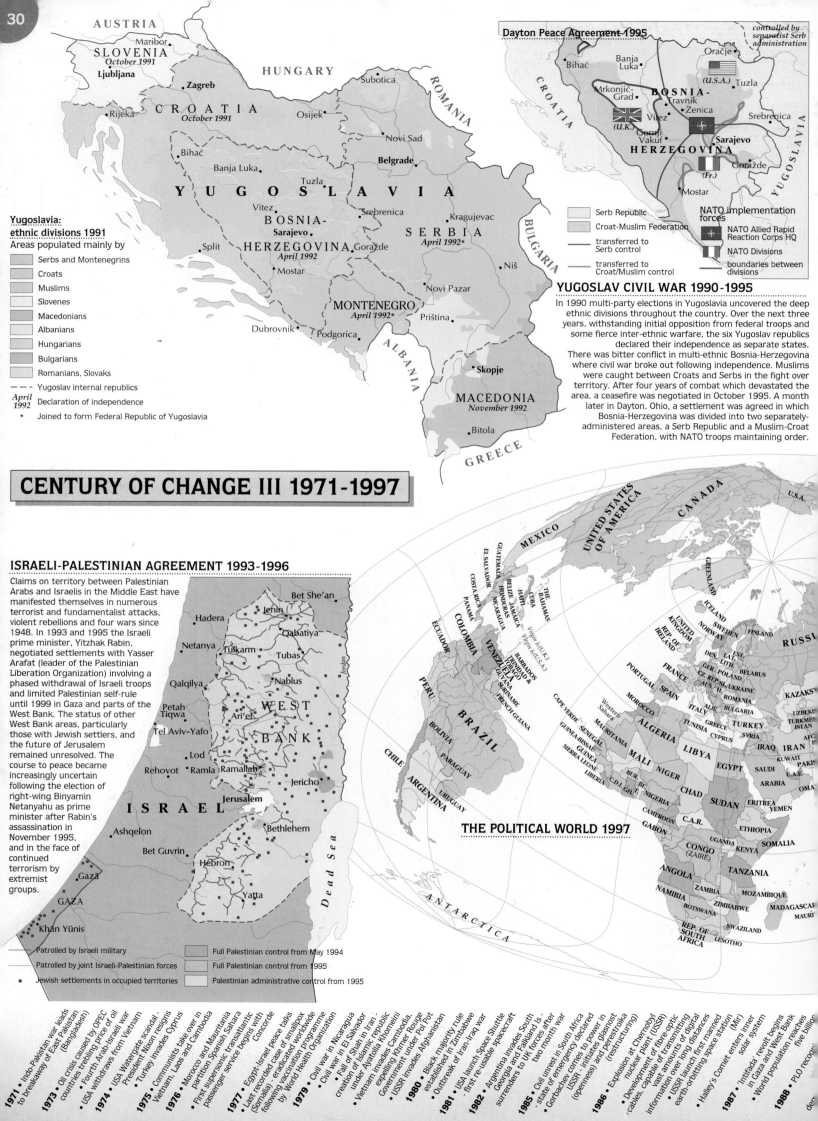

## Yugoslavia: ethnic divisions 1991

Areas populated mainly by

- Serbs and Montenegrins
- Croats
- Muslims
- Slovenes
- Macedonians
- Albanians
- Hungarians
- Bulgarians
- Romanians, Slovaks

– – – Yugoslav internal republics

*April 1992* Declaration of independence

\* Joined to form Federal Republic of Yugoslavia

**Dayton Peace Agreement 1995**

*controlled by separatist Serb administration*

- Serb Republic
- Croat-Muslim Federation
- ─── transferred to Serb control
- ─── transferred to Croat/Muslim control

**NATO implementation forces**

- NATO Allied Rapid Reaction Corps HQ
- NATO Divisions
- boundaries between divisions

## YUGOSLAV CIVIL WAR 1990-1995

In 1990 multi-party elections in Yugoslavia uncovered the deep ethnic divisions throughout the country. Over the next three years, withstanding initial opposition from federal troops and some fierce inter-ethnic warfare, the six Yugoslav republics declared their independence as separate states. There was bitter conflict in multi-ethnic Bosnia-Herzegovina where civil war broke out following independence. Muslims were caught between Croats and Serbs in the fight over territory. After four years of combat which devastated the area, a ceasefire was negotiated in October 1995. A month later in Dayton, Ohio, a settlement was agreed in which Bosnia-Herzegovina was divided into two separately-administered areas, a Serb Republic and a Muslim-Croat Federation, with NATO troops maintaining order.

# CENTURY OF CHANGE III 1971-1997

## ISRAELI-PALESTINIAN AGREEMENT 1993-1996

Claims on territory between Palestinian Arabs and Israelis in the Middle East have manifested themselves in numerous terrorist and fundamentalist attacks, violent rebellions and four wars since 1948. In 1993 and 1995 the Israeli prime minister, Yitzhak Rabin, negotiated settlements with Yasser Arafat (leader of the Palestinian Liberation Organization) involving a phased withdrawal of Israeli troops and limited Palestinian self-rule until 1999 in Gaza and parts of the West Bank. The status of other West Bank areas, particularly those with Jewish settlers, and the future of Jerusalem remained unresolved. The course to peace became increasingly uncertain following the election of right-wing Binyamin Netanyahu as prime minister after Rabin's assassination in November 1995, and in the face of continued terrorism by extremist groups.

- ─── Patrolled by Israeli military
- ─── Patrolled by joint Israeli-Palestinian forces
- ■ Jewish settlements in occupied territories
- Full Palestinian control from May 1994
- Full Palestinian control from 1995
- Palestinian administrative control from 1995

## THE POLITICAL WORLD 1997

- 1971 • Indo-Pakistan war leads to breakaway of East Pakistan (Bangladesh)
- 1973 • Oil crisis caused by OPEC countries trebling price of oil • Fourth Arab-Israeli war
- 1974 • USA withdraws from Vietnam • USA Watergate scandal - President Nixon resigns
- 1975 • Communists take over in Vietnam, Laos and Cambodia • Turkey invades Cyprus
- 1976 • Moroco and Mauritania partition Spanish Sahara • First supersonic transatlantic passenger service begins with Concorde
- 1977 • Egypt-Israel peace talks • Last recorded case of smallpox (Somalia) - eradicated worldwide following vaccination programme by World Health Organization
- 1979 • Civil war in Nicaragua • Civil war in El Salvador • Fall of Shah in Iran - creation of Islamic republic under Ayatolla Khomeini • Vietnam invades Cambodia, expelling Khmer Rouge Government under Pol Pot • USSR invades Afghanistan
- 1980 • Black majority rule established in Zimbabwe • Outbreak of Iran-Iraq war
- 1981 • USA launch Space Shuttle - first re-usable spacecraft
- 1982 • Argentina invades South Georgia and Falkland Is - surrenders to UK forces after two month war
- 1985 • Civil unrest in South Africa - state of emergency declared • Gorbachev comes to power in USSR - initiates glasnost (openness) and perestroika (restructuring)
- 1986 • Explosion at Chernobyl nuclear plant (USSR) • Development of fibre-optic cables capable of transmitting vast amounts of digital information over long distances
- 1987 • USSR launch first manned earth-orbiting space station (Mir) • Halley's Comet enters inner solar system
- 1988 • 'Intifada' revolt begins in Gaza and West Bank • World population reaches five billion • PLO recog

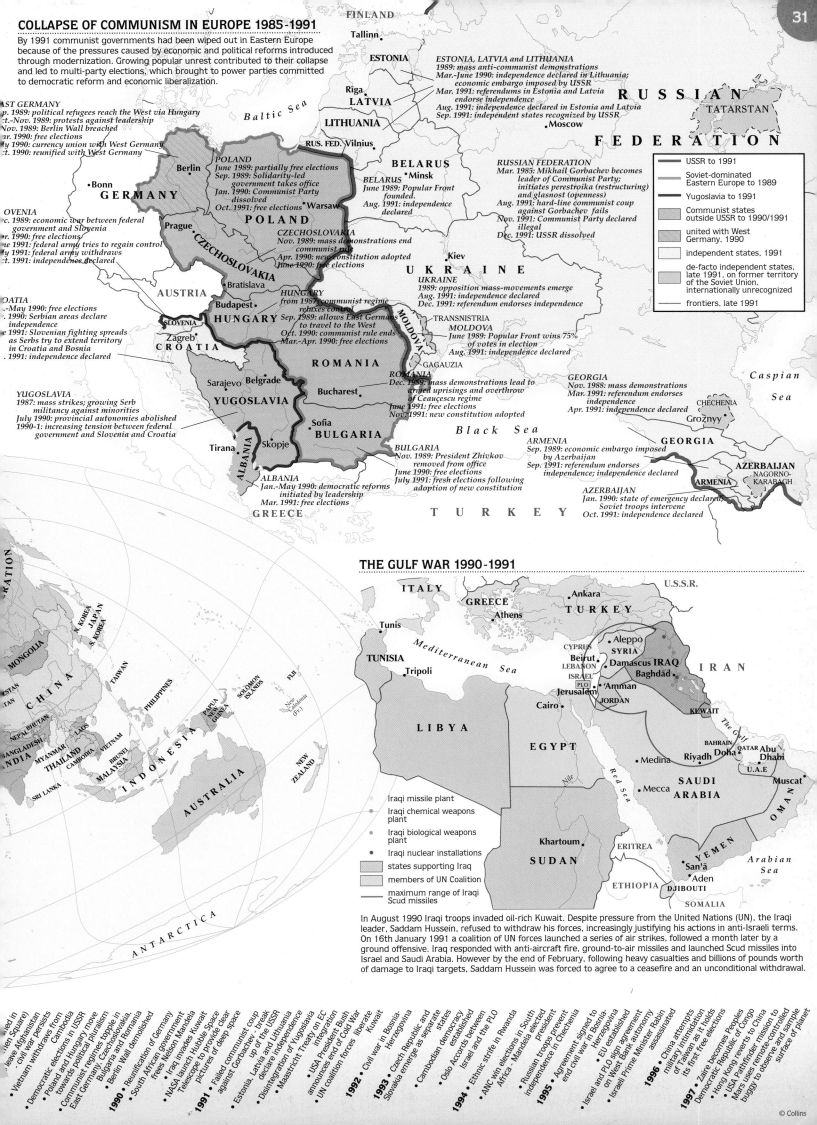

# COLLAPSE OF COMMUNISM IN EUROPE 1985-1991

By 1991 communist governments had been wiped out in Eastern Europe because of the pressures caused by economic and political reforms introduced through modernization. Growing popular unrest contributed to their collapse and led to multi-party elections, which brought to power parties committed to democratic reform and economic liberalization.

**AST GERMANY**
*p. 1989: political refugees reach the West via Hungary*
*t.-Nov. 1989: protests against leadership*
*Nov. 1989: Berlin Wall breached*
*ar. 1990: free elections*
*ly 1990: currency union with West Germany*
*ct. 1990: reunified with West Germany*

**OVENIA**
*c. 1989: economic war between federal government and Slovenia*
*r. 1990: free elections*
*ne 1991: federal army tries to regain control*
*ly 1991: federal army withdraws*
*ct. 1991: independence declared*

**OATIA**
*.–May 1990: free elections*
*. 1990: Serbian areas declare independence*
*e 1991: Slovenian fighting spreads as Serbs try to extend territory in Croatia and Bosnia*
*. 1991: independence declared*

**YUGOSLAVIA**
*1987: mass strikes; growing Serb militancy against minorities*
*July 1990: provincial autonomies abolished*
*1990-1: increasing tension between federal government and Slovenia and Croatia*

**ESTONIA, LATVIA and LITHUANIA**
*1989: mass anti-communist demonstrations*
*Mar.-June 1990: independence declared in Lithuania; economic embargo imposed by USSR*
*Mar. 1991: referendums in Estonia and Latvia endorse independence*
*Aug. 1991: independence declared in Estonia and Latvia*
*Sep. 1991: independent states recognized by USSR*

**POLAND**
*June 1989: partially free elections*
*Sep. 1989: Solidarity-led government takes office*
*Jan. 1990: Communist Party dissolved*
*Oct. 1991: free elections*

**BELARUS**
*June 1989: Popular Front founded.*
*Aug. 1991: independence declared*

**RUSSIAN FEDERATION**
*Mar. 1985: Mikhail Gorbachev becomes leader of Communist Party; initiates perestroika (restructuring) and glasnost (openness)*
*Aug. 1991: hard-line communist coup against Gorbachev fails*
*Nov. 1991: Communist Party declared illegal*
*Dec. 1991: USSR dissolved*

**CZECHOSLOVAKIA**
*Nov. 1989: mass demonstrations end communist rule*
*Apr. 1990: new constitution adopted*
*June 1990: free elections*

**UKRAINE**
*1989: opposition mass-movements emerge*
*Aug. 1991: independence declared*
*Dec. 1991: referendum endorses independence*

**HUNGARY**
*from 1987: communist regime relaxes control*
*Sep. 1989: allows East Germans to travel to the West*
*Oct. 1990: communist rule ends*
*Mar.-Apr. 1990: free elections*

**TRANSNISTRIA**
**MOLDOVA**
*June 1989: Popular Front wins 75% of votes in election*
*Aug. 1991: independence declared*

**GAGAUZIA**

**ROMANIA**
*Dec. 1989: mass demonstrations lead to armed uprisings and overthrow of Ceaucescu regime*
*June 1991: free elections*
*Nov. 1991: new constitution adopted*

**GEORGIA**
*Nov. 1988: mass demonstrations*
*Mar. 1991: referendum endorses independence*
*Apr. 1991: independence declared*

**BULGARIA**
*Nov. 1989: President Zhivkov removed from office*
*June 1990: free elections*
*July 1991: fresh elections following adoption of new constitution*

**ARMENIA**
*Sep. 1989: economic embargo imposed by Azerbaijan*
*Sep. 1991: referendum endorses independence; independence declared*

**ALBANIA**
*Jan.-May 1990: democratic reforms initiated by leadership*
*Mar. 1991: free elections*

**AZERBAIJAN**
*Jan. 1990: state of emergency declared; Soviet troops intervene*
*Oct. 1991: independence declared*

### Legend
- USSR to 1991
- Soviet-dominated Eastern Europe to 1989
- Yugoslavia to 1991
- Communist states outside USSR to 1990/1991
- united with West Germany, 1990
- independent states, 1991
- de-facto independent states, late 1991, on former territory of the Soviet Union, internationally unrecognized
- frontiers, late 1991

---

# THE GULF WAR 1990-1991

### Legend
- Iraqi missile plant
- Iraqi chemical weapons plant
- Iraqi biological weapons plant
- Iraqi nuclear installations
- states supporting Iraq
- members of UN Coalition
- maximum range of Iraqi Scud missiles

In August 1990 Iraqi troops invaded oil-rich Kuwait. Despite pressure from the United Nations (UN), the Iraqi leader, Saddam Hussein, refused to withdraw his forces, increasingly justifying his actions in anti-Israeli terms. On 16th January 1991 a coalition of UN forces launched a series of air strikes, followed a month later by a ground offensive. Iraq responded with anti-aircraft fire, ground-to-air missiles and launched Scud missiles into Israel and Saudi Arabia. However by the end of February, following heavy casualties and billions of pounds worth of damage to Iraqi targets, Saddam Hussein was forced to agree to a ceasefire and an unconditional withdrawal.

© Collins

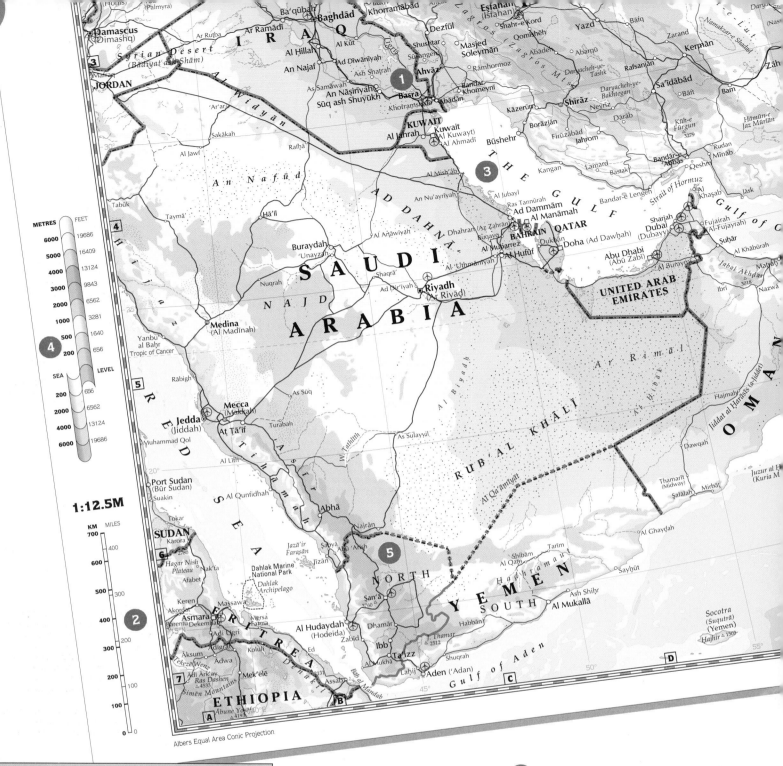

METRES / FEET

6000 / 19686
5000 / 16409
4000 / 13124
3000 / 9843
2000 / 6562
1000 / 3281
500 / 1640
200 / 656

SEA LEVEL

200 / 656
2000 / 6562
4000 / 13124
6000 / 19686

**1:12.5M**

KM / MILES

700 / 400
600
500 / 300
400 / 200
300
200 / 100
100

0 / 0

Albers Equal Area Conic Projection

# HOW TO USE THE ATLAS

**T**HIS SECTION HELPS the reader to interpret the reference maps in the Atlas of the World. It explains the main features shown on the mapping and the policies adopted in deciding what to show and how to show it.

The databases used to create the maps provide the freedom to select the best map coverage for each part of the world. Maps are arranged on a continental basis, with each continent being introduced by maps of the political situation and the main physical features. Maps of Antarctica and the world's oceans complete the extensive worldwide coverage.

## ① SYMBOLS & GENERALIZATION

Maps show information by using signs, or symbols, which are designed to reflect the features on the earth that they represent. Symbols can be in the form of points - such as those used to show towns and airports; lines - used to represent roads and rivers; or areas - lakes, marsh. Variation in size, shape and colour of these types of symbol allow a great range of information to be shown. The symbols used in

this atlas are explained in the panel to the right.

Not all information can be shown, and much has to be generalized to be clearly shown on the maps. This generalization takes the form of selection - the inclusion of some features and the omission of others of less importance; and simplification - where lines are smoothed, areas combined, or symbols displaced slightly to add clarity. This is done in such a way that the overall character of the area mapped is retained. The degree of generalization varies, and is determined largely by the scale at which the map is drawn.

## ② SCALE

Scale is the relationship between the size of an area shown on the map and the actual size of the area on the ground. It determines the amount of detail shown on a map - larger scales show more, smaller scales show less - and can be used to measure the distance between two points, though the projection of the map must also be taken into account when measuring distances.

Scale is shown in two ways. The representative fraction (1:12.5M on the extract above) tells us that a distance of 1 mm on the map actually measures 12,500,000 mm (or 12.5 kilometres) on the ground. The linear scale, or scale bar, converts this into easily measurable units.

## ③ GEOGRAPHICAL NAMES

The spelling of place names on maps is a complex problem for the cartographer. There is no single standard way of spelling names or of converting them from one alphabet, or symbol set, to another. Changes in official languages also have to be taken into account when creating maps and databases, and policies need to be established for the spelling of names on

individual atlases and maps. Such policies must take account of the local official position, international conventions or

# SYMBOLS

## Relief

| METRES | | FEET |
|---|---|---|
| 6000 | | 19686 |
| 5000 | | 16409 |
| 4000 | | 13124 |
| 3000 | | 9843 |
| 2000 | | 6562 |
| 1000 | | 3281 |
| 500 | | 1640 |
| 200 | | 656 |
| SEA | | LEVEL |
| 200 | | 656 |
| 2000 | | 6562 |
| 4000 | | 13124 |
| 6000 | | 19686 |

Additional bathymetric contour layers are shown at scales greater than 1:2m. These are labelled on an individual basis.

213 △ Summit
*height in metres*

## Boundaries

- ▪▪▪ International
- ▫▪▫▪ International disputed
- ●●●●● Ceasefire line
- ▬▬▬ Main administrative (U.K.)
- ▬▬▬ Main administrative
- ▬ ▬ Main administrative through water

## Styles of Lettering

| Country name | **FRANCE** | Island | *Gran Canaria* |
| | **BARBADOS** | Lake | *LAKE ERIE* |
| Main administrative name | HESSEN | Mountain | *ANDES* |
| Area name | *ARTOIS* | River | *Zambezi* |

## Settlements

| POPULATION | NATIONAL CAPITAL | ADMINISTRATIVE CAPITAL | CITY OR TOWN |
|---|---|---|---|
| Over 5 million | ▣ **Beijing** | ◉ **Tianjin** | ◉ **New York** |
| 1 to 5 million | ▣ **Seoul** | ◉ **Lagos** | ◉ **Barranquilla** |
| 500000 to 1 million | ▣ **Bangui** | ◎ **Douala** | ◎ **Memphis** |
| 100000 to 500000 | ▢ Wellington | ○ Mansa | ○ Mara |
| 50000 to 100000 | ▢ Port of Spain | ○ Lubango | ○ Arecibo |
| 10000 to 50000 | ▫ Malabo | ○ Chinhoyi | ○ El Tigre |
| Less than 10000 | ▫ Roseau | ○ Áti | ○ Soledad |

☐ Urban area

## Communications

- ═══ Motorway
- ┅┅┅ Motorway tunnel

Motorways are classified separately at scales greater than 1:5 million. At smaller scales motorways are classified with main roads.

- ─── Main road
- ──── Main road under construction
- ┄┄┄ Main road tunnel
- ─── Other road
- ──── Other road under construction
- ┄┄┄ Other road tunnel
- ─ ─ ─ Track
- ┼┼┼ Main railway
- ─┼─┼─ Main railway under construction
- ┄┼┄ Main railway tunnel
- ─── Other railway
- ──── Other railway under construction
- ┄┄┄ Other railway tunnel
- ⊕ Main airport
- ✈ Other airport

## Physical Features

- Freshwater lake
- Seasonal freshwater lake
- Saltwater lake *or* Lagoon
- Seasonal saltwater lake
- Dry salt lake *or* Salt pan
- Marsh
- River
- ─┼─ Waterfall
- ─┼─ Dam *or* Barrage
- ─ ─ ─ Seasonal river *or* Wadi
- Canal
- ┅┅┅ Flood dyke
- Reef
- ▲ Volcano
- Lava field
- Sandy desert
- Rocky desert
- ◡ Oasis
- ┅┅┅ Escarpment
- ⩎ 923 Mountain pass *height in metres*
- Ice cap or Glacier

## Other Features

- ┄┄┄ National park
- ┅┅┅ Reserve
- ∿∿∿ Ancient wall
- ∴ Historic or Tourist site

---

traditions, and the purpose of the atlas or map. The policy in this atlas is to use local name forms which are officially recognized by the governments of the countries concerned. However, English conventional name forms are used for the most well-known places. In these cases, the local form is included in brackets on the map and also appears as a cross-reference in the index. Examples of this policy on the above names extract include:

| ENGLISH FORM | LOCAL FORM |
|---|---|
| **Kuwait** | **Al Kuwayt** |
| **Riyadh** | **Ar Riyāḏ** |
| **Doha** | **Ad Dawḥah** |

Other examples in the atlas include:

| | |
|---|---|
| **Moscow** | **Moskva** |
| **Vienna** | **Wien** |
| **Crete** | **Kriti** |
| **Serbia** | **Srbija** |

All country names and those for international features appear in their English forms. Other alternative names, such as well-known historical names or those in other languages, may also be included in brackets and as index cross-references.

## 4 REPRESENTATION OF RELIEF

One important element of mapping the earth is the depiction of relief - the 'shape' of the land. This presents a problem to the cartographer who has to show the earth's three-dimensional surface on the two-dimensional page. The maps in this atlas use two main methods of relief representation.

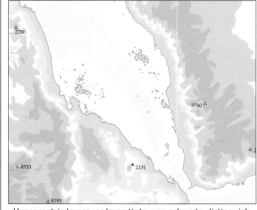

Hypsometric layers, or layer tints, use colour to distinguish areas which lie in specific altitude or relief bands. The colours give an immediate impression of the height and shape of the land and are indicated on the altitude bar in the margin of each map. The height of the land at selected points is shown by summit symbols or spot heights which indicate the height at that point in metres above sea level. On the maps of the oceans, small dots show the depth of the ocean below sea level in metres.

A third method of relief depiction is used on the maps of the oceans and Antarctica - hill or relief shading simulates the effect of a light shining across the landscape, providing an impression of the shape of the land.

## 5 BOUNDARIES

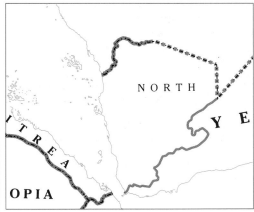

The status of nations and their boundaries are shown in this atlas as they are in reality at the time of going to press, as far as can be ascertained. Where international boundaries are the subject of dispute. the aim is to take a strictly neutral viewpoint, based on advice from expert consultants.

Every attempt is made to show where territorial disputes exist and their depiction varies accordingly, as illustrated on the above extract. Generally, prominence is given to the 'de facto' situation - that existing on the ground.

© Collins

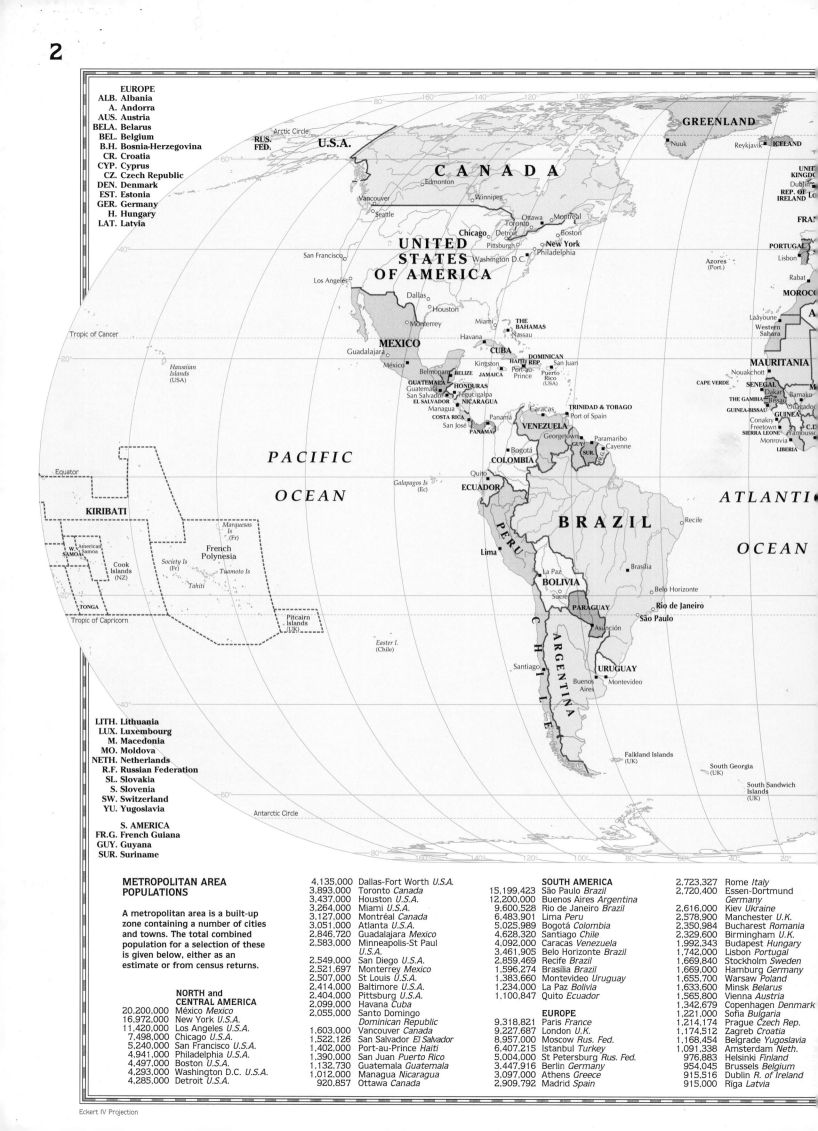

**2**

EUROPE
ALB. Albania
A. Andorra
AUS. Austria
BELA. Belarus
BEL. Belgium
B.H. Bosnia-Herzegovina
CR. Croatia
CYP. Cyprus
CZ. Czech Republic
DEN. Denmark
EST. Estonia
GER. Germany
H. Hungary
LAT. Latvia

LITH. Lithuania
LUX. Luxembourg
M. Macedonia
MO. Moldova
NETH. Netherlands
R.F. Russian Federation
SL. Slovakia
S. Slovenia
SW. Switzerland
YU. Yugoslavia

S. AMERICA
FR.G. French Guiana
GUY. Guyana
SUR. Suriname

Eckert IV Projection

## METROPOLITAN AREA POPULATIONS

A metropolitan area is a built-up zone containing a number of cities and towns. The total combined population for a selection of these is given below, either as an estimate or from census returns.

**NORTH and CENTRAL AMERICA**

| | |
|---|---|
| 20,200,000 | México *Mexico* |
| 16,972,000 | New York *U.S.A.* |
| 11,420,000 | Los Angeles *U.S.A.* |
| 7,498,000 | Chicago *U.S.A.* |
| 5,240,000 | San Francisco *U.S.A.* |
| 4,941,000 | Philadelphia *U.S.A.* |
| 4,497,000 | Boston *U.S.A.* |
| 4,293,000 | Washington D.C. *U.S.A.* |
| 4,285,000 | Detroit *U.S.A.* |
| 4,135,000 | Dallas-Fort Worth *U.S.A.* |
| 3,893,000 | Toronto *Canada* |
| 3,437,000 | Houston *U.S.A.* |
| 3,264,000 | Miami *U.S.A.* |
| 3,127,000 | Montréal *Canada* |
| 3,051,000 | Atlanta *U.S.A.* |
| 2,846,720 | Guadalajara *Mexico* |
| 2,583,000 | Minneapolis-St Paul *U.S.A.* |
| 2,549,000 | San Diego *U.S.A.* |
| 2,521,697 | Monterrey *Mexico* |
| 2,507,000 | St Louis *U.S.A.* |
| 2,414,000 | Baltimore *U.S.A.* |
| 2,404,000 | Pittsburg *U.S.A.* |
| 2,099,000 | Havana *Cuba* |
| 2,055,000 | Santo Domingo *Dominican Republic* |
| 1,603,000 | Vancouver *Canada* |
| 1,522,126 | San Salvador *El Salvador* |
| 1,402,000 | Port-au-Prince *Haiti* |
| 1,390,000 | San Juan *Puerto Rico* |
| 1,132,730 | Guatemala *Guatemala* |
| 1,012,000 | Managua *Nicaragua* |
| 920,857 | Ottawa *Canada* |

**SOUTH AMERICA**

| | |
|---|---|
| 15,199,423 | São Paulo *Brazil* |
| 12,200,000 | Buenos Aires *Argentina* |
| 9,600,528 | Rio de Janeiro *Brazil* |
| 6,483,901 | Lima *Peru* |
| 5,025,989 | Bogotá *Colombia* |
| 4,628,320 | Santiago *Chile* |
| 4,092,000 | Caracas *Venezuela* |
| 3,461,905 | Belo Horizonte *Brazil* |
| 2,859,469 | Recife *Brazil* |
| 1,596,274 | Brasília *Brazil* |
| 1,383,660 | Montevideo *Uruguay* |
| 1,234,000 | La Paz *Bolivia* |
| 1,100,847 | Quito *Ecuador* |

**EUROPE**

| | |
|---|---|
| 9,318,821 | Paris *France* |
| 9,227,687 | London *U.K.* |
| 8,957,000 | Moscow *Rus. Fed.* |
| 6,407,215 | Istanbul *Turkey* |
| 5,004,000 | St Petersburg *Rus. Fed.* |
| 3,447,916 | Berlin *Germany* |
| 3,097,000 | Athens *Greece* |
| 2,909,792 | Madrid *Spain* |
| 2,723,327 | Rome *Italy* |
| 2,720,400 | Essen-Dortmund *Germany* |
| 2,616,000 | Kiev *Ukraine* |
| 2,578,900 | Manchester *U.K.* |
| 2,350,984 | Bucharest *Romania* |
| 2,329,600 | Birmingham *U.K.* |
| 1,992,343 | Budapest *Hungary* |
| 1,742,000 | Lisbon *Portugal* |
| 1,669,840 | Stockholm *Sweden* |
| 1,669,000 | Hamburg *Germany* |
| 1,655,700 | Warsaw *Poland* |
| 1,633,600 | Minsk *Belarus* |
| 1,565,800 | Vienna *Austria* |
| 1,342,679 | Copenhagen *Denmark* |
| 1,221,000 | Sofia *Bulgaria* |
| 1,214,174 | Prague *Czech Rep.* |
| 1,174,512 | Zagreb *Croatia* |
| 1,168,454 | Belgrade *Yugoslavia* |
| 1,091,338 | Amsterdam *Neth.* |
| 976,883 | Helsinki *Finland* |
| 954,045 | Brussels *Belgium* |
| 915,516 | Dublin *R. of Ireland* |
| 915,000 | Rīga *Latvia* |

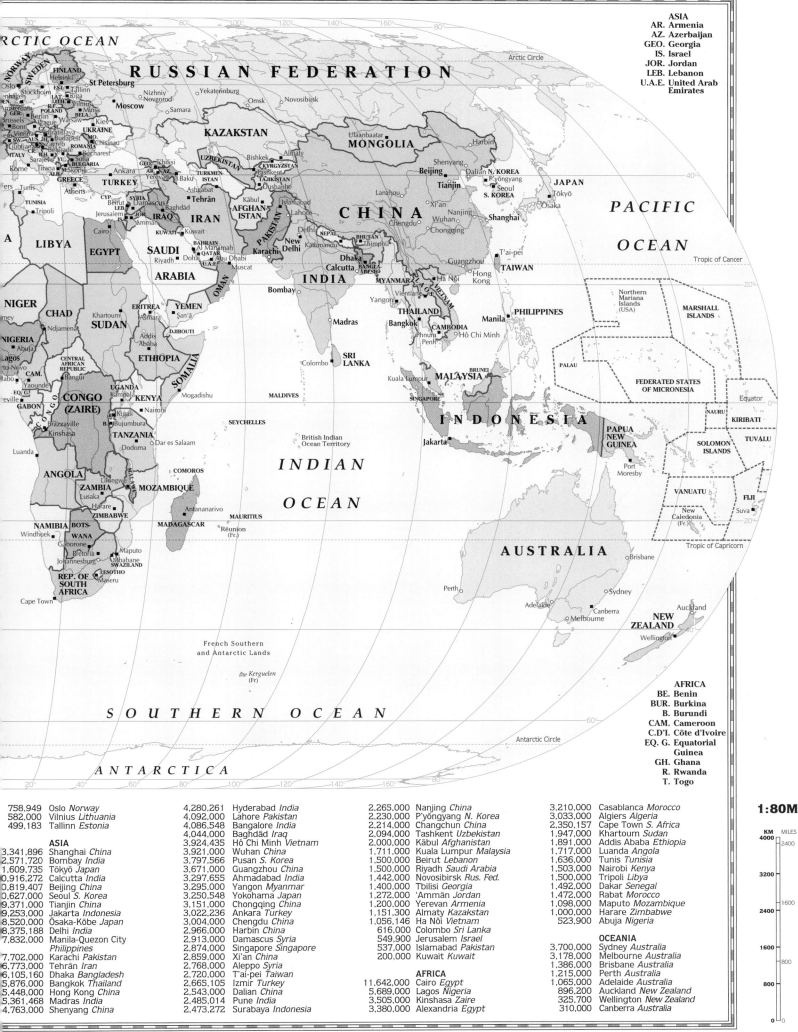

ASIA
AR. Armenia
AZ. Azerbaijan
GEO. Georgia
IS. Israel
JOR. Jordan
LEB. Lebanon
U.A.E. United Arab Emirates

AFRICA
BE. Benin
BUR. Burkina
B. Burundi
CAM. Cameroon
C.D'I. Côte d'Ivoire
EQ. G. Equatorial Guinea
GH. Ghana
R. Rwanda
T. Togo

1:80M

| KM | MILES |
|---|---|
| 4000 | 2400 |
| 3200 | 1600 |
| 2400 | 800 |
| 1600 | 800 |
| 800 | |
| 0 | 0 |

758,949 Oslo *Norway*
582,000 Vilnius *Lithuania*
499,183 Tallinn *Estonia*

**ASIA**
3,341,896 Shanghai *China*
2,571,720 Bombay *India*
1,609,735 Tōkyō *Japan*
0,916,272 Calcutta *India*
0,819,407 Beijing *China*
0,627,000 Seoul *S. Korea*
9,371,000 Tianjin *China*
9,253,000 Jakarta *Indonesia*
8,520,000 Ōsaka-Kōbe *Japan*
8,375,188 Delhi *India*
7,832,000 Manila-Quezon City *Philippines*
7,702,000 Karachi *Pakistan*
6,773,000 Tehrān *Iran*
6,105,160 Dhaka *Bangladesh*
5,876,000 Bangkok *Thailand*
5,448,000 Hong Kong *China*
5,361,468 Madras *India*
4,763,000 Shenyang *China*

4,280,261 Hyderabad *India*
4,092,000 Lahore *Pakistan*
4,086,548 Bangalore *India*
4,044,000 Baghdad *Iraq*
3,924,435 Hô Chi Minh *Vietnam*
3,921,000 Wuhan *China*
3,797,566 Pusan *S. Korea*
3,671,000 Guangzhou *China*
3,297,655 Ahmadabad *India*
3,295,000 Yangon *Myanmar*
3,250,548 Yokohama *Japan*
3,151,000 Chongqing *China*
3,022,236 Ankara *Turkey*
3,004,000 Chengdu *China*
2,966,000 Harbin *China*
2,913,000 Damascus *Syria*
2,874,000 Singapore *Singapore*
2,859,000 Xi'an *China*
2,768,000 Aleppo *Syria*
2,720,000 T'ai-pei *Taiwan*
2,665,105 Izmir *Turkey*
2,543,000 Dalian *China*
2,485,014 Pune *India*
2,473,272 Surabaya *Indonesia*

2,265,000 Nanjing *China*
2,230,000 P'yŏngyang *N. Korea*
2,214,000 Changchun *China*
2,094,000 Tashkent *Uzbekistan*
2,000,000 Kābul *Afghanistan*
1,711,000 Kuala Lumpur *Malaysia*
1,500,000 Beirut *Lebanon*
1,500,000 Riyadh *Saudi Arabia*
1,442,000 Novosibirsk *Rus. Fed.*
1,400,000 Tbilisi *Georgia*
1,272,000 'Ammān *Jordan*
1,200,000 Yerevan *Armenia*
1,151,300 Almaty *Kazakstan*
1,056,146 Ha Nôi *Vietnam*
616,000 Colombo *Sri Lanka*
549,900 Jerusalem *Israel*
537,000 Islamabad *Pakistan*
200,000 Kuwait *Kuwait*

**AFRICA**
11,642,000 Cairo *Egypt*
5,689,000 Lagos *Nigeria*
3,505,000 Kinshasa *Zaire*
3,380,000 Alexandria *Egypt*

3,210,000 Casablanca *Morocco*
3,033,000 Algiers *Algeria*
2,350,157 Cape Town *S. Africa*
1,947,000 Khartoum *Sudan*
1,891,000 Addis Ababa *Ethiopia*
1,717,000 Luanda *Angola*
1,636,000 Tunis *Tunisia*
1,503,000 Nairobi *Kenya*
1,500,000 Tripoli *Libya*
1,492,000 Dakar *Senegal*
1,472,000 Rabat *Morocco*
1,098,000 Maputo *Mozambique*
1,000,000 Harare *Zimbabwe*
523,900 Abuja *Nigeria*

**OCEANIA**
3,700,000 Sydney *Australia*
3,178,000 Melbourne *Australia*
1,386,000 Brisbane *Australia*
1,215,000 Perth *Australia*
1,065,000 Adelaide *Australia*
896,200 Auckland *New Zealand*
325,700 Wellington *New Zealand*
310,000 Canberra *Australia*

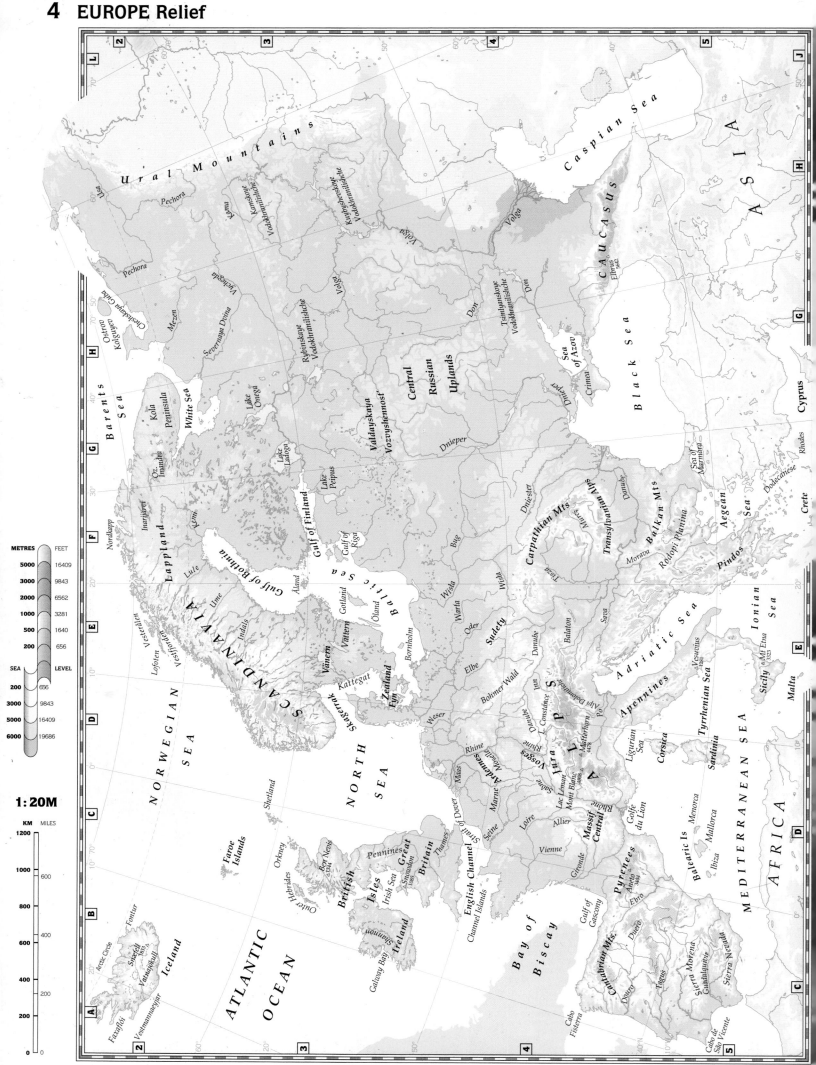

METRES | FEET
5000 | 16409
3000 | 9843
2000 | 6562
1000 | 3281
500 | 1640
200 | 656

SEA | LEVEL
200 | 656
3000 | 9843
5000 | 16409
6000 | 19686

**1:20M**

KM | MILES
1200 |
1000 | 600
800 |
600 | 400
400 |
200 | 200
0 | 0

Albers Equal Area Conic Projection

© Collins

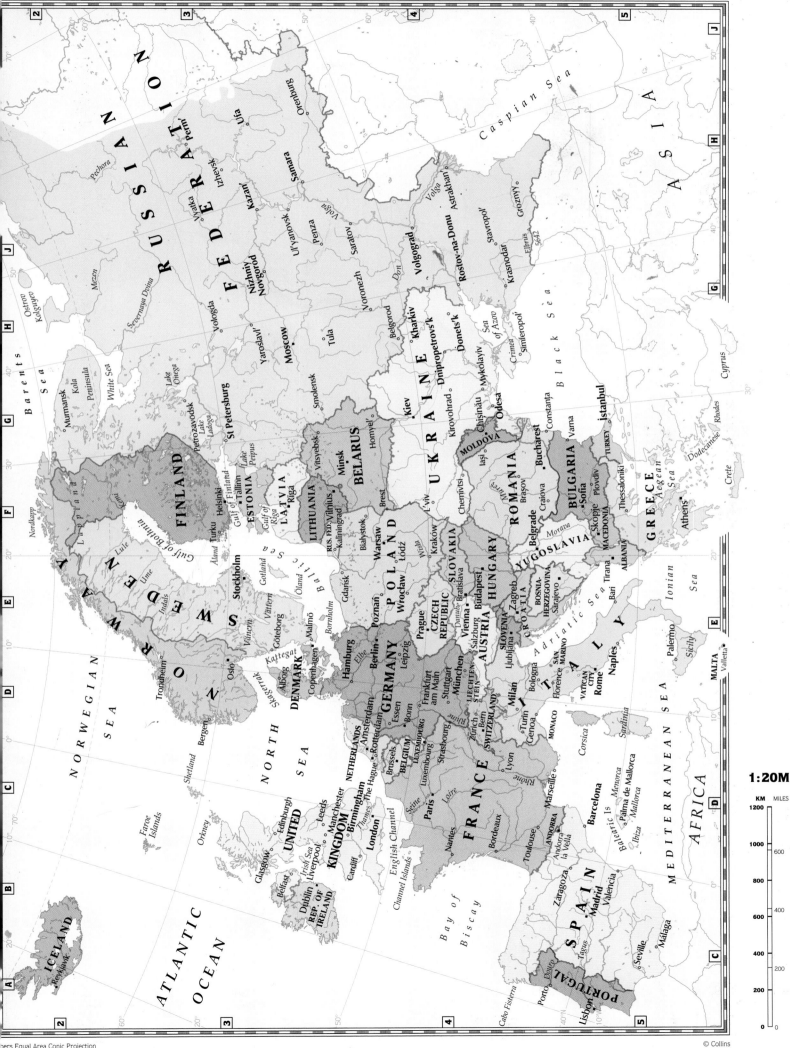

**1:20M**

KM | MILES
1200
1000 | 600
800 | 
600 | 400
400 | 
200 | 200
0 | 0

© Collins

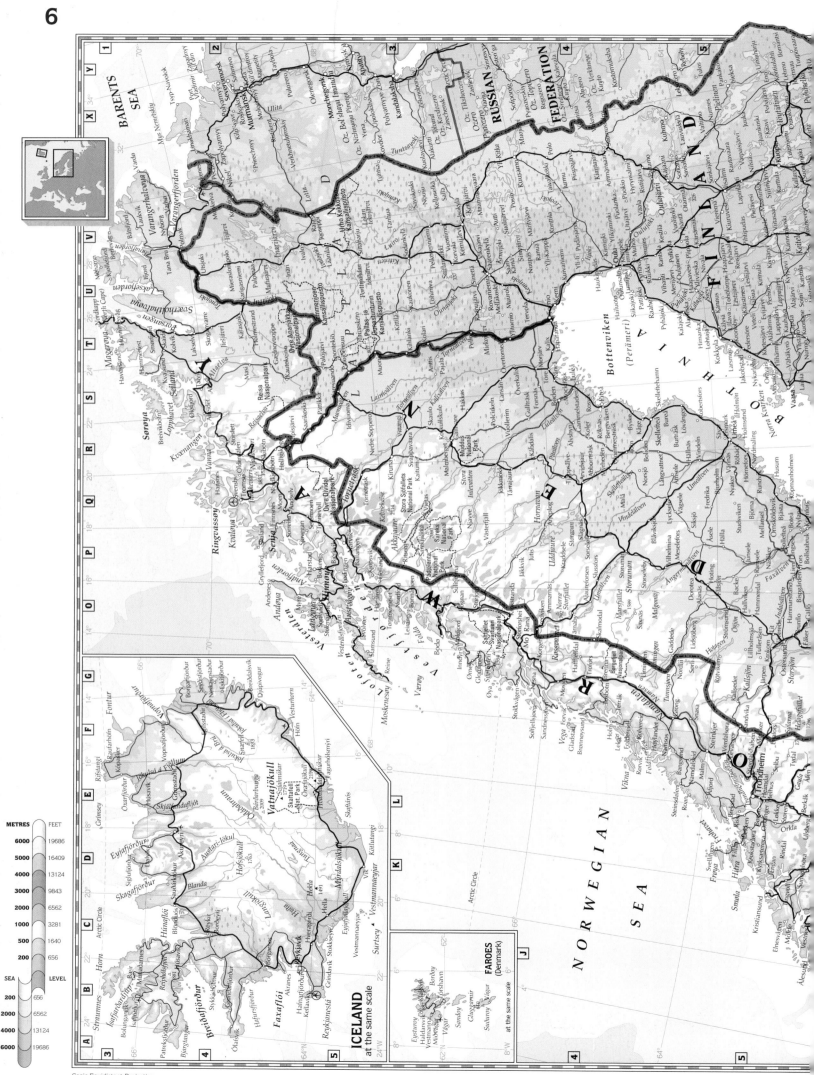

**6**

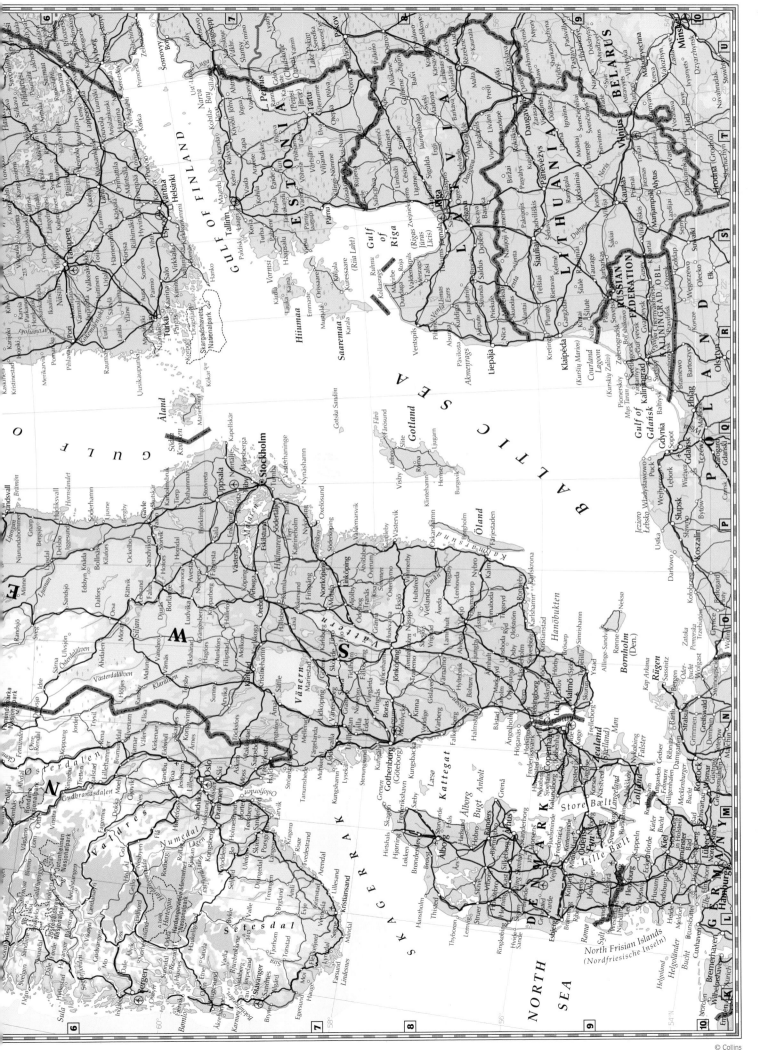

1:5M

KM    MILES

250

200

150

100

50

0

© Collins

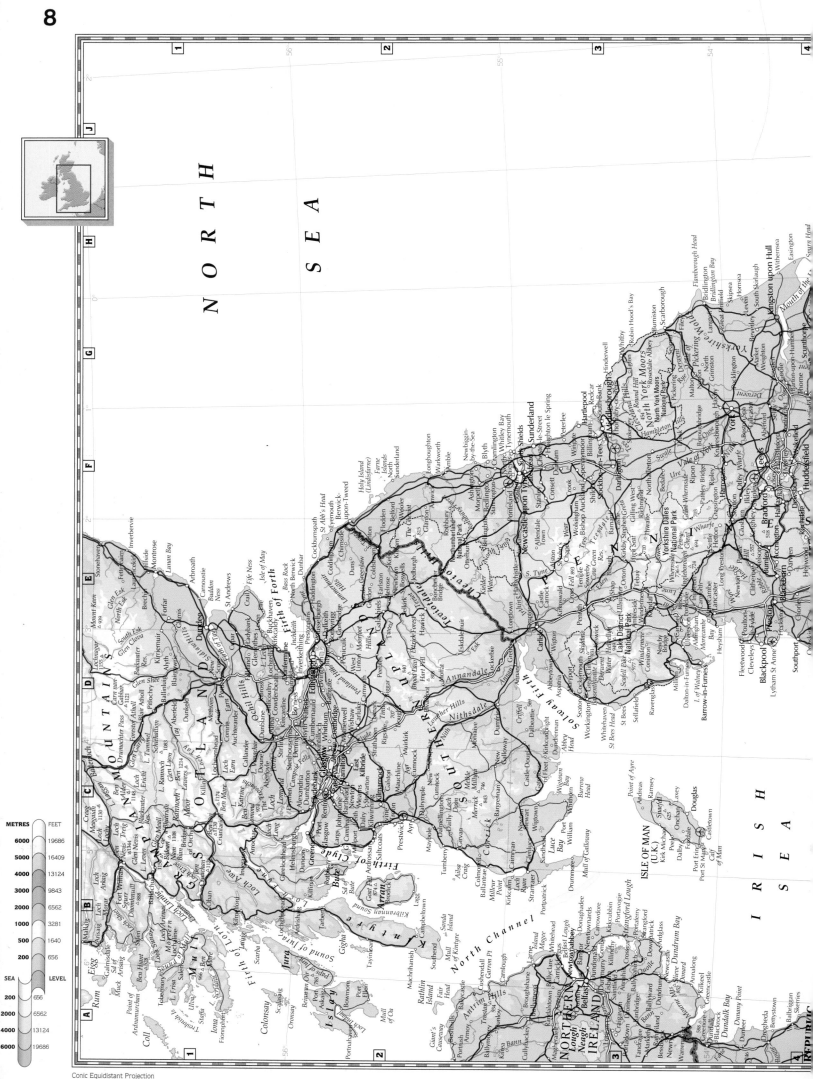

Conic Equidistant Projection

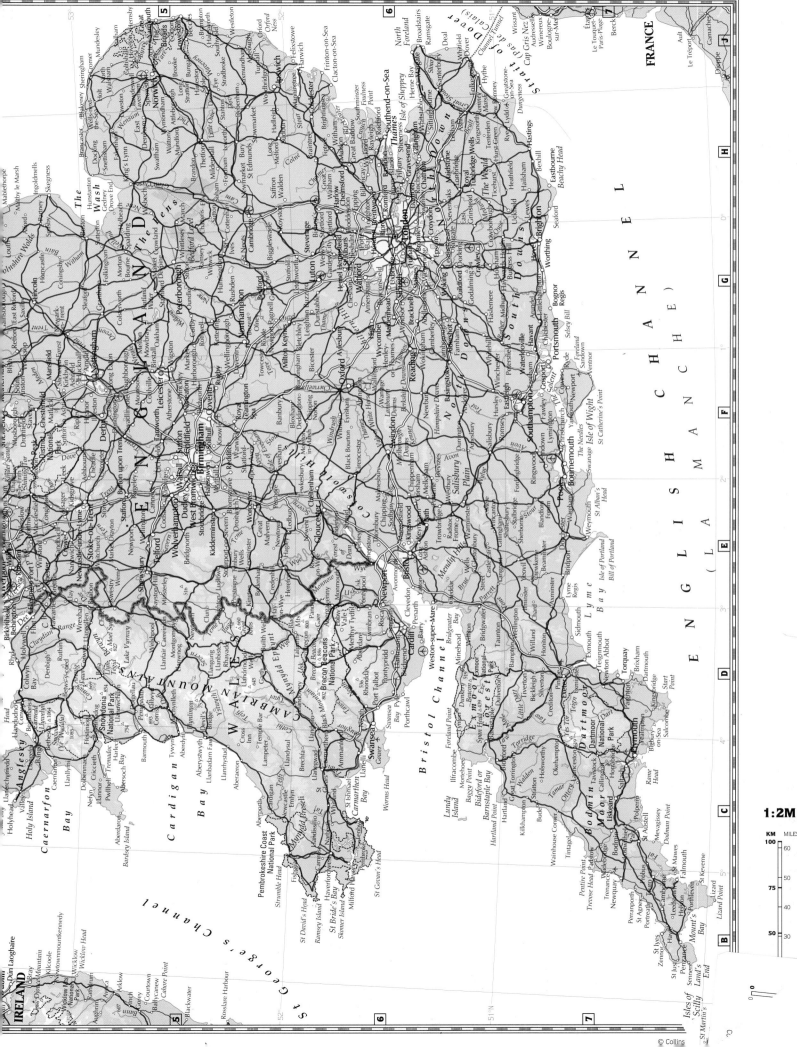

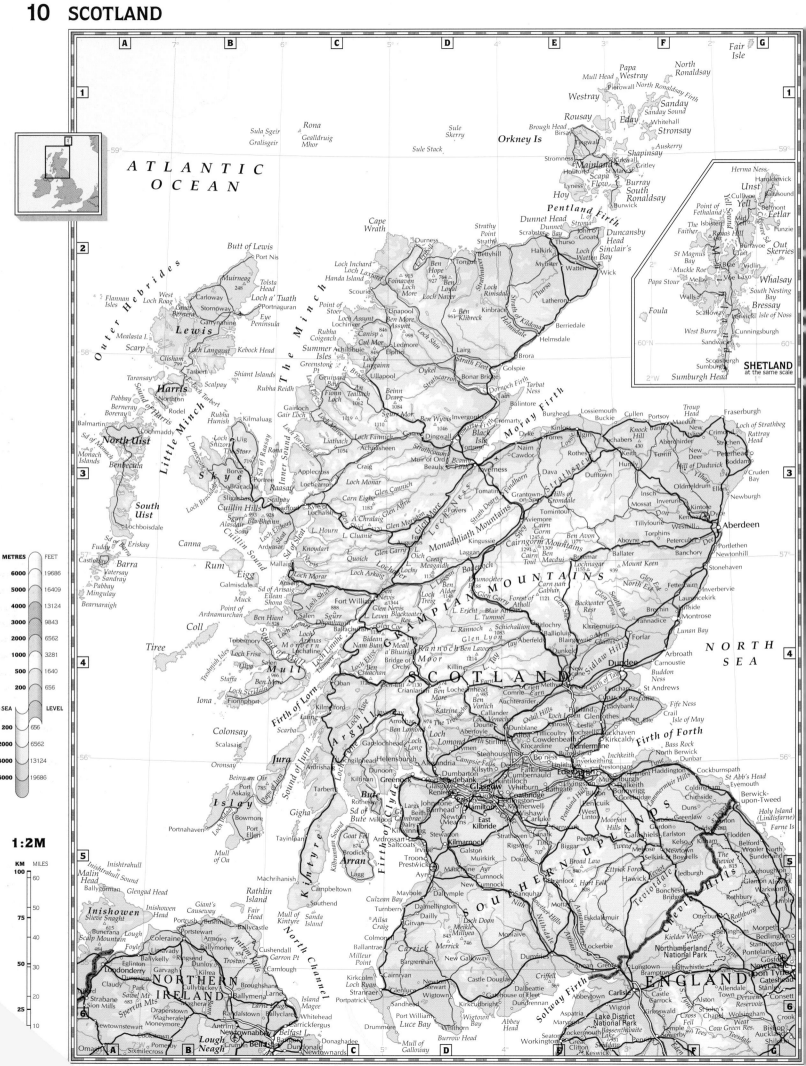

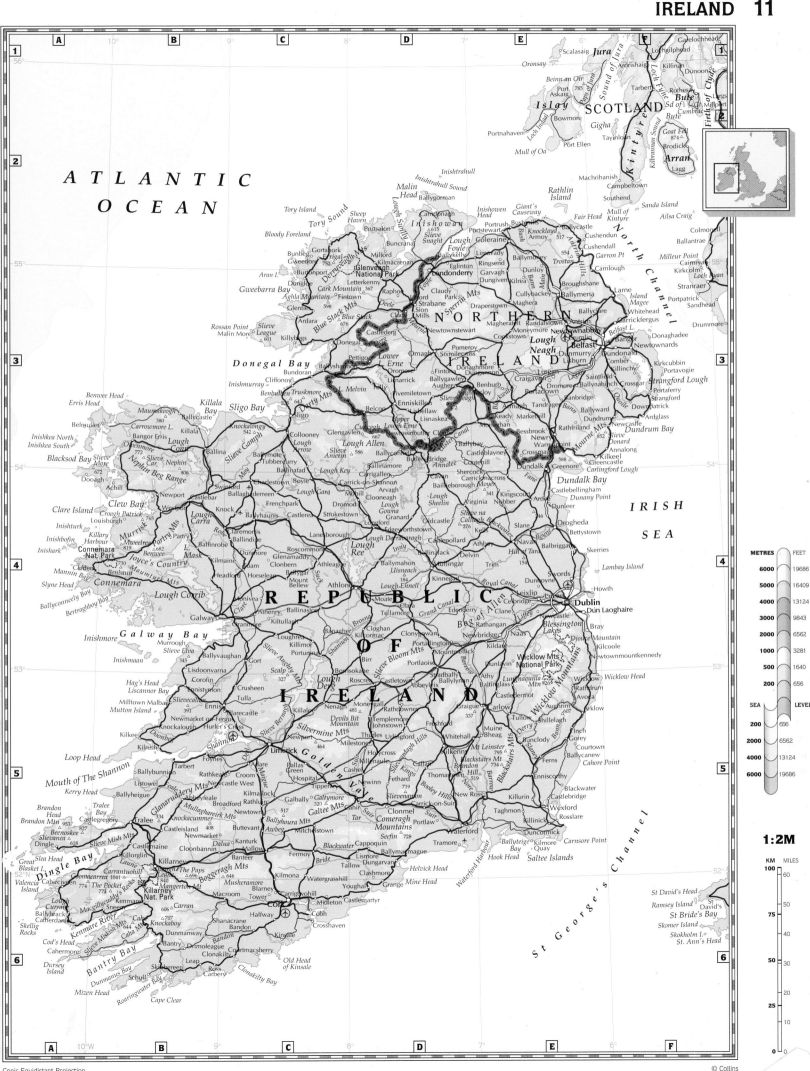

Conic Equidistant Projection

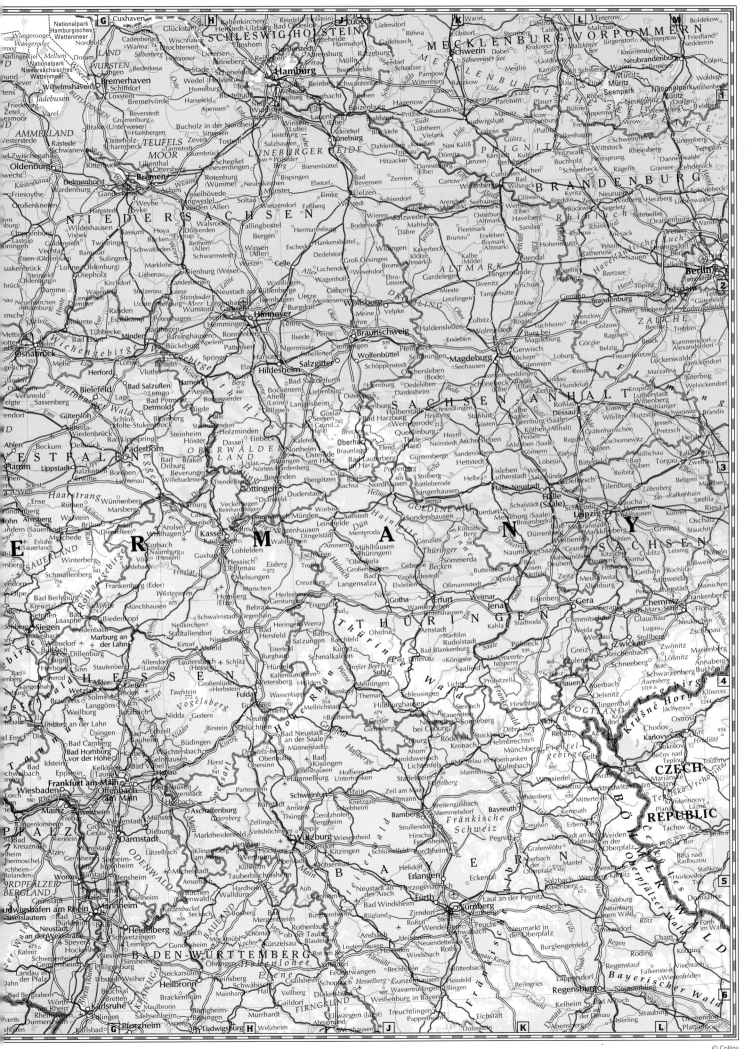

1:2M

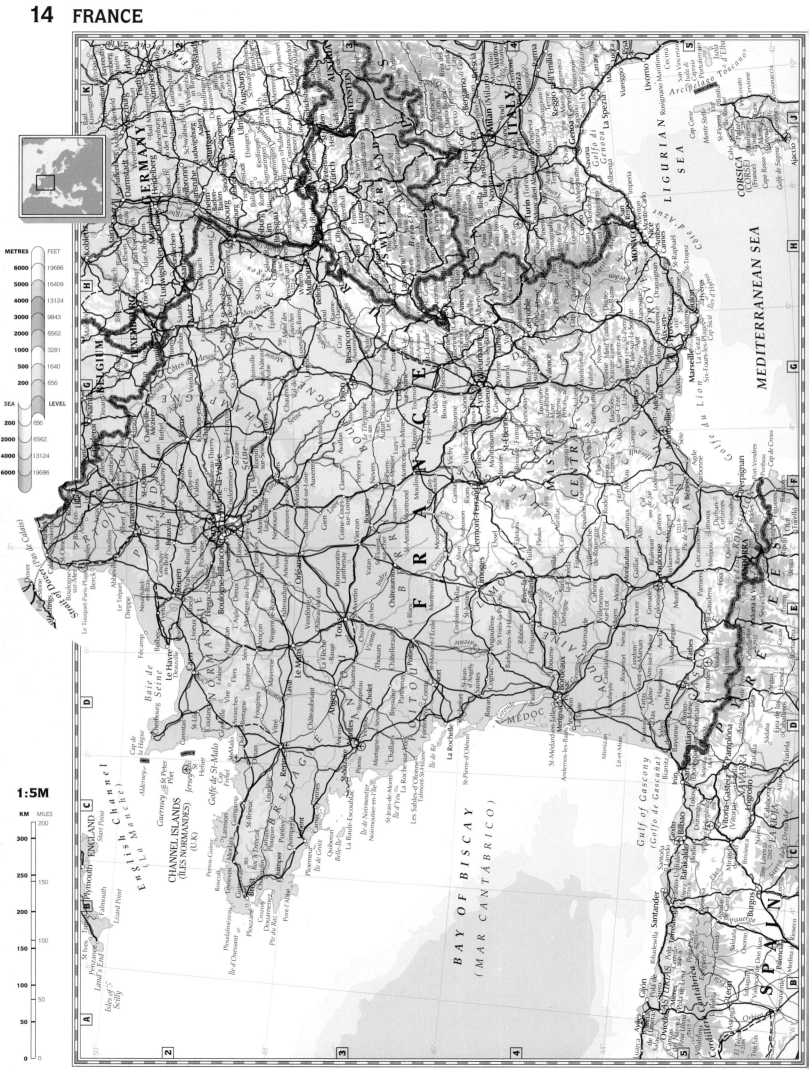

**METRES** **FEET**

| 6000 | 19686 |
| 5000 | 16409 |
| 4000 | 13124 |
| 3000 | 9843 |
| 2000 | 6562 |
| 1000 | 3281 |
| 500 | 1640 |
| 200 | 656 |

**SEA** **LEVEL**

| 200 | 656 |
| 2000 | 6562 |
| 4000 | 13124 |
| 6000 | 19686 |

1:5M

KM   MILES

Conic Equidistant Projection

© Collins

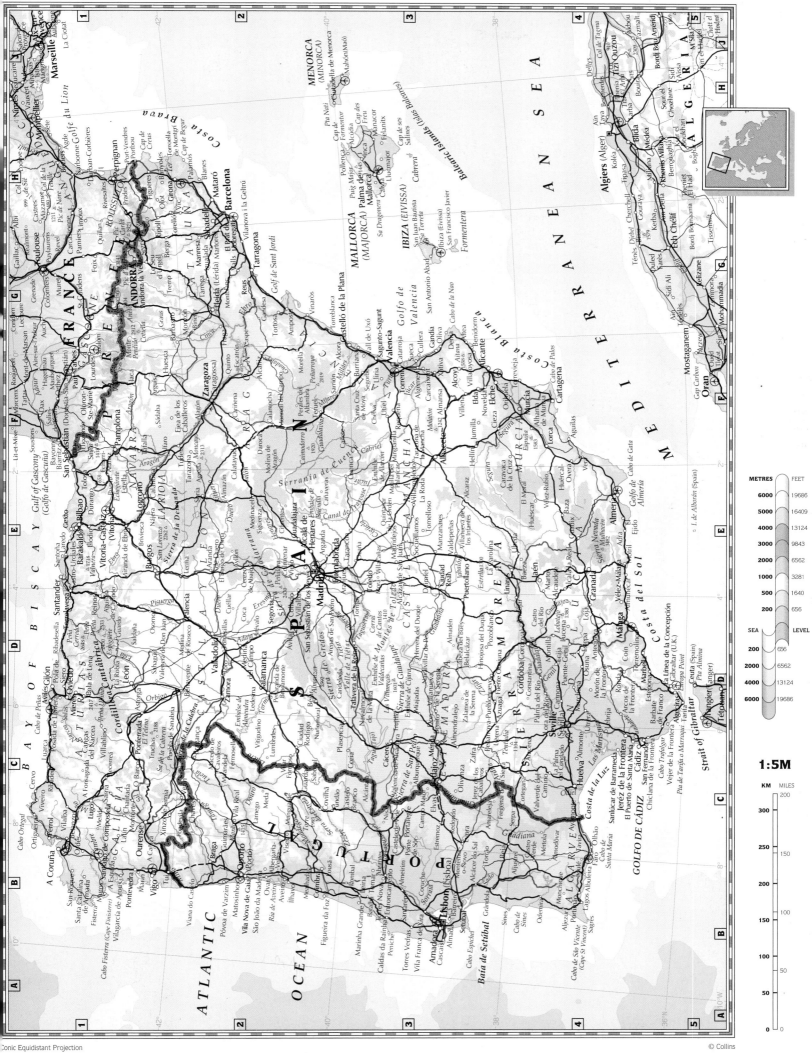

1:5M

© Collins

METRES   FEET
6000   19686
5000   16409
4000   13124
3000   9843
2000   6562
1000   3281
500   1640
200   656
SEA   LEVEL
200   656
2000   6562
4000   13124
6000   19686

Conic Equidistant Projection

1:5M

Conic Equidistant Projection

1:5M

KM    MILES
250   150

200

150   100

100

50

50

0

© Collins

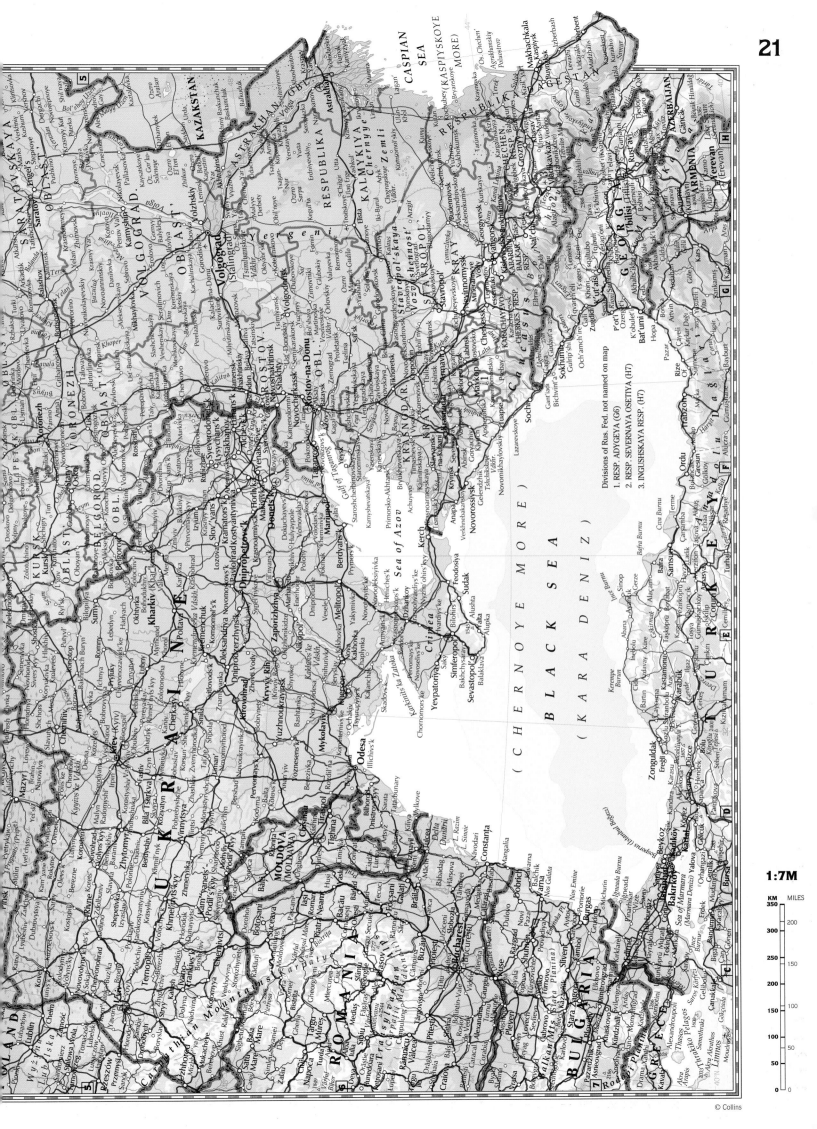

CASPIAN SEA (KASPIYSKOYE MORE)

KAZAKSTAN

SARATOVSKAYA OBLAST

ASTRAKHAN. OBL.

VOLGOGRAD OBLAST

RESPUBLIKA KALMYKIYA Chernyye Zemli

Yergeni

Volgograd (Stalingrad)

Saratov

Engel's

VORONEZH OBLAST

LIPETK OBL.

KURSK OBLAST

Kursk

BELGOROD OBL.

Voronezh

Belgorod

ROSTOV. OBL.

Rostov-na-Donu

Shakhty

Novoshakhtinsk

STAVROPOL'SKAYA KRAY

Stavropol'

KARACHAYEVO-CHERKES. RESP.

KABARDIN-BALKAR. RESP.

CHECHEN. RESP.

Groznyy

RESPUBLIKA DAGESTAN

Makhachkala

Kaspiysk

Derbent

Caucasus Kavkaz

Caucasus

GEORGIA

T'bilisi (Tbilisi)

ARMENIA

Yerevan (Erevan)

AZERBAIJAN

Gäncä

UKRAINE

Kharkiv (Khar'kov)

Dnipropetrovs'k

Donets'k

Makiyivka

Zaporizhzhya

Kryvyy Rih

Mariupol'

Sea of Azov

Kirovohrad

Mykolayiv

Kiev (Kyiv)

Odesa

Illichivs'k

Simferopol'

Sevastopol'

Yalta

Feodosiya

Sudak

Crimea

Kerch

Novorossiysk

Sochi

Sokhumi

Bat'umi

P'ot'i

Och'amch'ire

Rize

Trabzon

Ordu

Samsun

BLACK SEA

CHERNOYE MORE

(KARA DENIZ)

Divisions of Rus. Fed. not named on map

1. RESP. ADYGEYA (G6)
2. RESP. SEVERNAYA OSETIYA (H7)
3. INGUSHSKAYA RESP. (H7)

Zonguldak

Ereğli

MOLDOVA (MOLDAWA)

Chişinău

Tighina

ROMANIA

Bucharest

Constanţa

Iaşi

Galaţi

Brăila

Ploieşti

Piteşti

Craiova

Carpathian Mountains

Transylvanian Alps

BULGARIA

Varna

Burgas

Ruse

Pleven

Sofia

Plovdiv

Bursa

Istanbul

Sea of Marmara (Marmara Denizi)

Bosporus (İstanbul Boğazı)

GREECE

TURKEY

Yalova

Bakırköy

1:7M

KM 350 300 250 200 150 100 50 0

MILES 200 150 100 50 0

© Collins

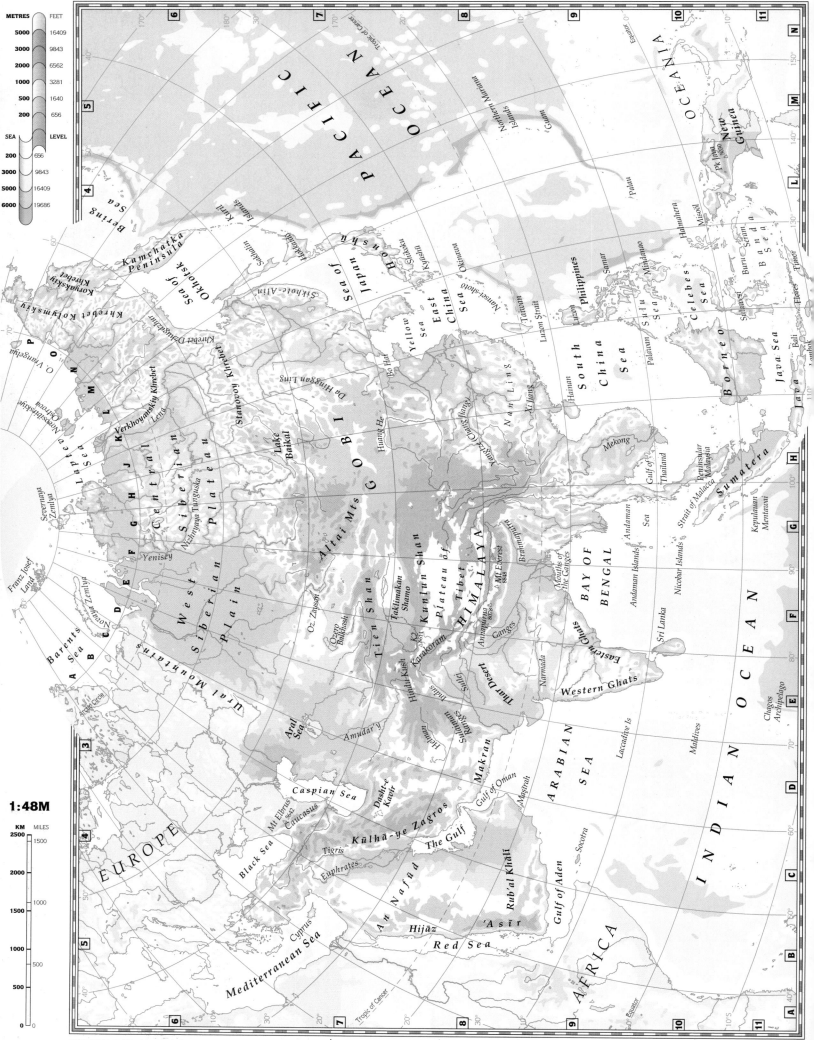

METRES   FEET
5000     16409
3000     9843
2000     6562
1000     3281
500      1640
200      656

SEA      LEVEL
200      656
3000     9843
5000     16409
6000     19686

1:48M

KM   MILES
2500  1500
      1000
2000
1500   500
1000
500

0     0

Lambert Azimuthal Equal Area Projection

© Collins

PACIFIC OCEAN

Tropic of Cancer

Northern Mariana Islands

Guam

OCEANIA

New Guinea

Pk Jaya 5030

Palau

Halmahera

Misoöl

Buru   Seran   Banda Sea

Philippines

Samar

Luzon

Mindanao

Luzon Strait

Sulawesi

Sulu Sea

Celebes Sea

Borneo

Nansei-shotō

Taiwan

Hainan

South China Sea

Nan Ling

Xi Jiang

Palawan

Peninsular Malaysia

Strait of Malacca

Sumatera

Kepulauan Mentawai

Java Sea

Bali   Flores Sea   Timor

Lombok

Java

Mekong

Gulf of Thailand

Andaman Sea

Andaman Islands

Nicobar Islands

BAY OF BENGAL

Mouths of the Ganges

Brahmaputra

Ganges

Eastern Ghats

Western Ghats

Sri Lanka

Narmada

Thar Desert

Mt Everest 8848

HIMALAYA

Plateau of Tibet

Kunlun Shan

Karakoram

K2 8611

Annapurna 8078

Indus

Sutlej

Taklimakan Shamo

Tien Shan

Hindu Kush

Laccadive Is

Maldives

Chagos Archipelago

INDIAN OCEAN

ARABIAN SEA

Makran

Gulf of Oman

Masirah

The Gulf

Dasht-e Kavir

Kūlhā-ye Zagros

Tigris

Euphrates

Caspian Sea

Mt Elbrus 5642

Caucasus

Black Sea

Cyprus

Mediterranean Sea

EUROPE

An Nafūd

Hijāz

Red Sea

'Asīr

Rub'al Khālī

Gulf of Aden

Socotra

AFRICA

Tropic of Cancer

Equator

GOBI

Da Hinggan Ling

Huang He

Bo Hai

Yellow Sea

East China Sea

Sea of Japan

Honshū

Hokkaidō

Shikoku

Kyūshū

Okinawa

Yangtze (Chang Jiang)

Altai Mts

Lake Baikal

Sikhote-Alin

Sea of Okhotsk

Sakhalin

Kuril Islands

Kamchatka Peninsula

Koryakskiy Khrebet

Khrebet Kolymskiy

Khrebet Dzhugdzhur

Stanovoy Khrebet

Nizhnyaya Tunguska

Central Siberian Plateau

Lena

Verkhoyansky Khrebet

West Siberian Plain

Yenisey

Ural Mountains

Aral Sea

Amudar'y

Oz. Zaysan

Ozero Balkhash

Plotomtains

Helmand

Sulaiman Ranges

P O L A R

O. Vrangelya

Vostochno-Sibirskoye More

Novosibirskiye Ostrova

Laptev Sea

Severnaya Zemlya

Barents Sea

Novaya Zemlya

Franz Josef Land

Arctic Circle

Bering Sea

Tropic of Cancer

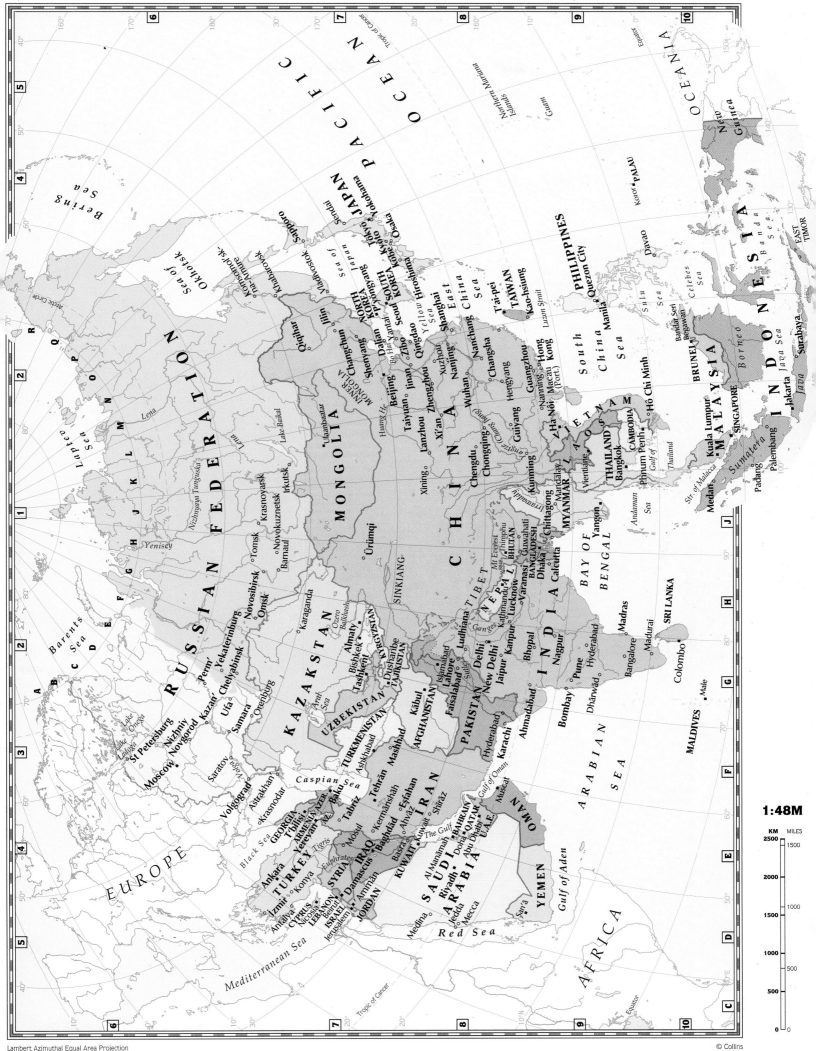

1:48M

Lambert Azimuthal Equal Area Projection

© Collins

Conic Equidistant Projection

**1:21M**

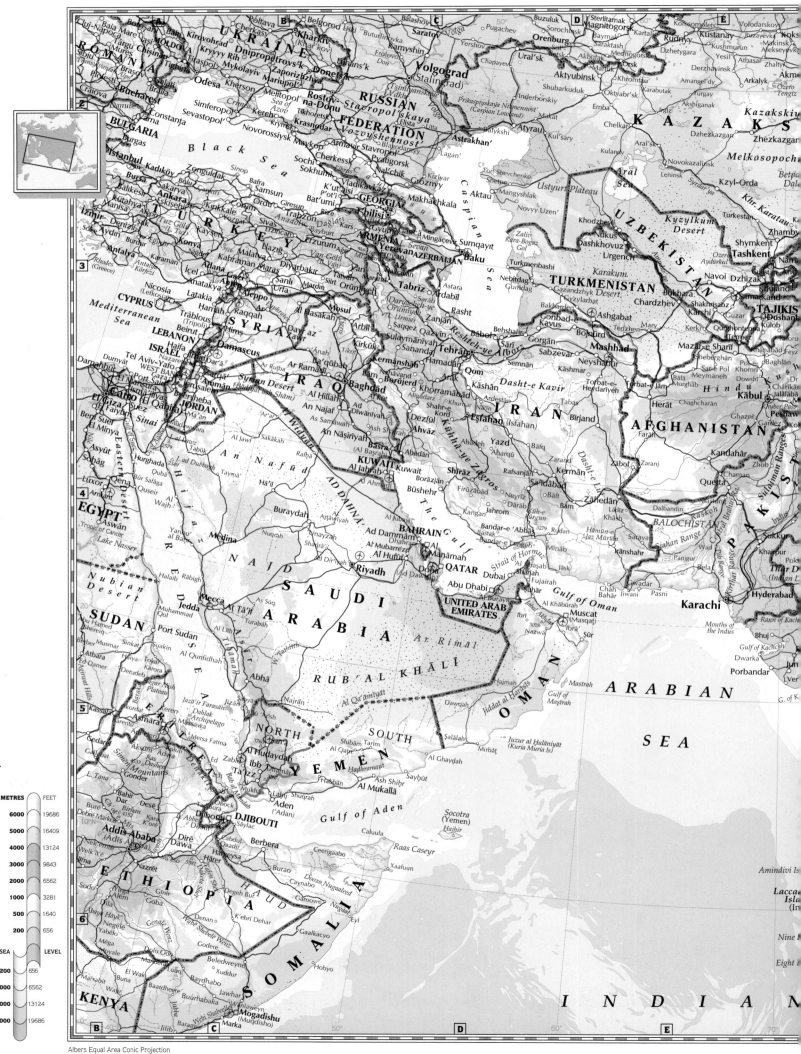

Albers Equal Area Conic Projection

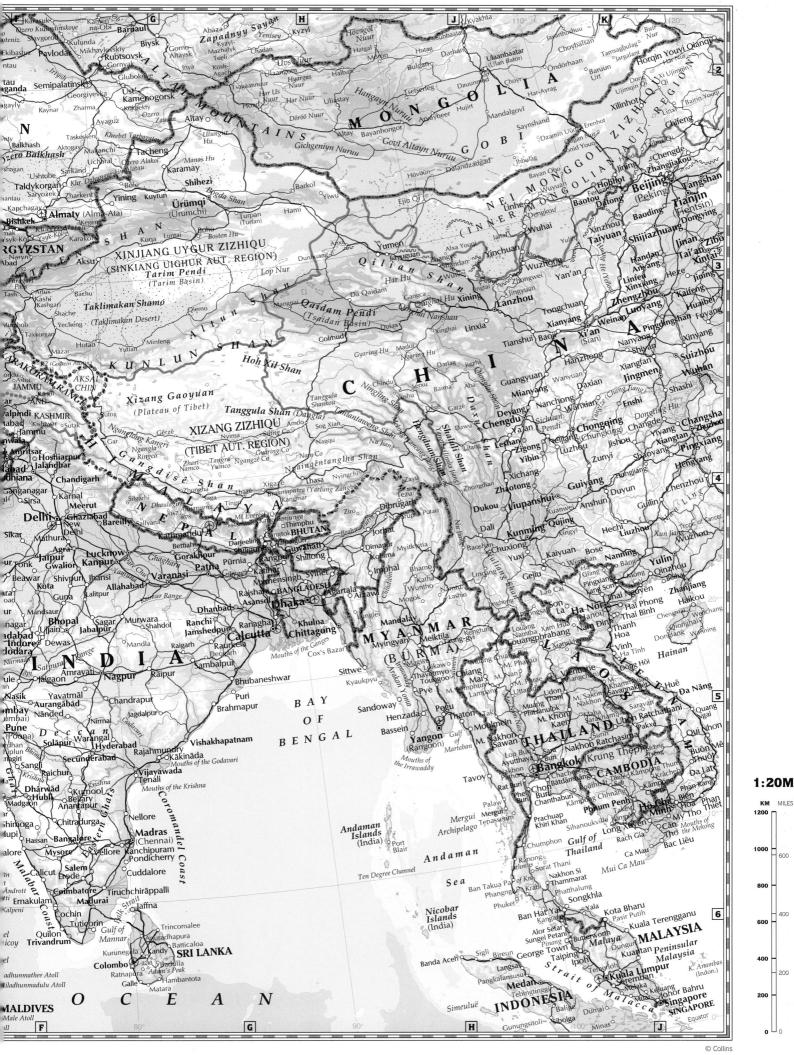

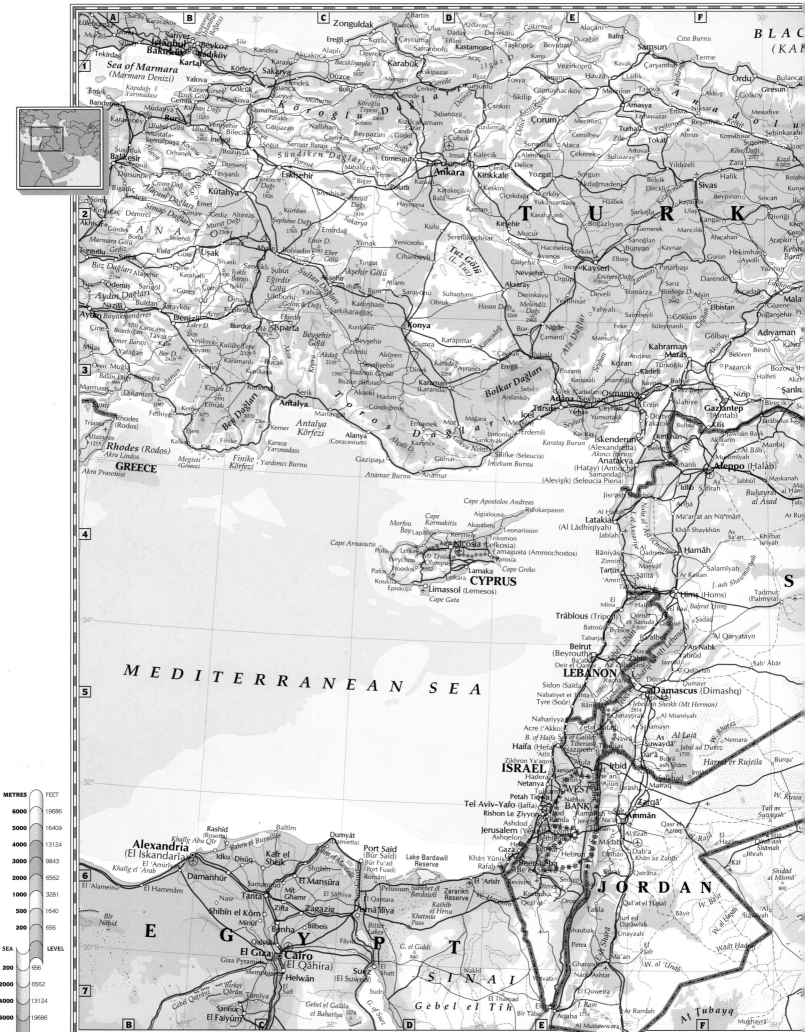

Conic Equidistant Projection

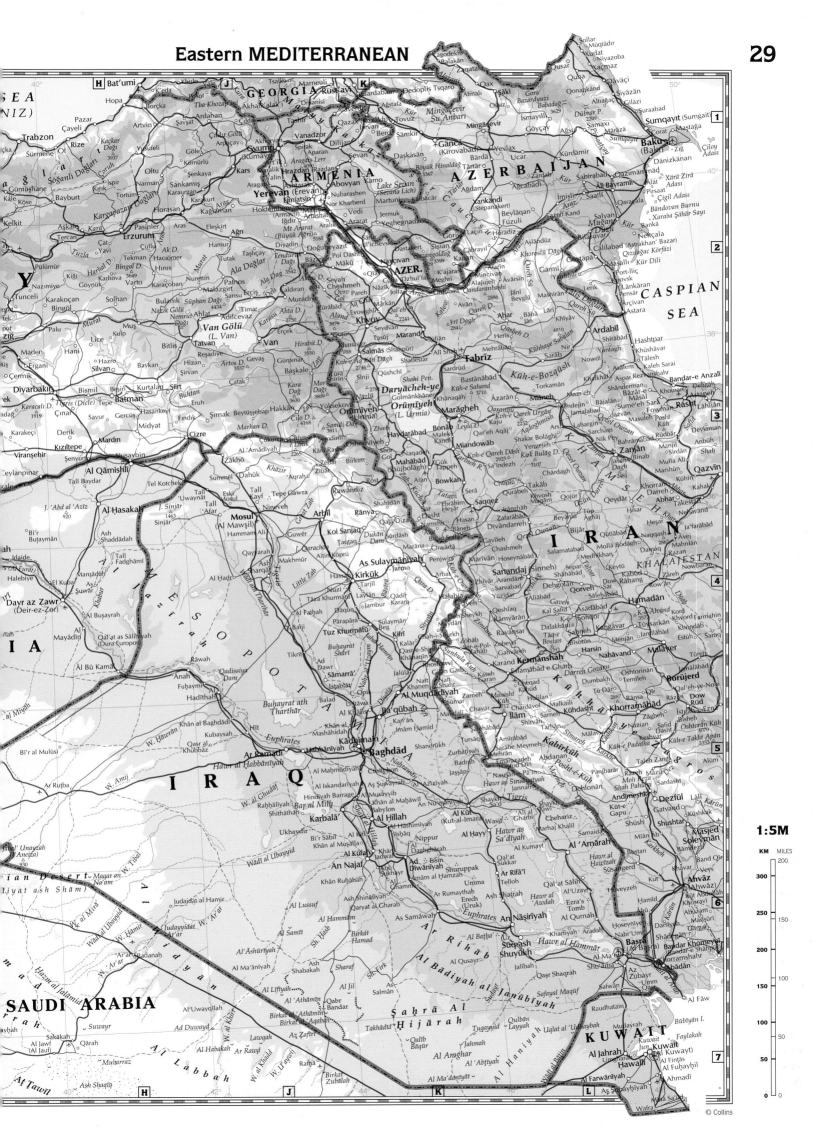

1:5M

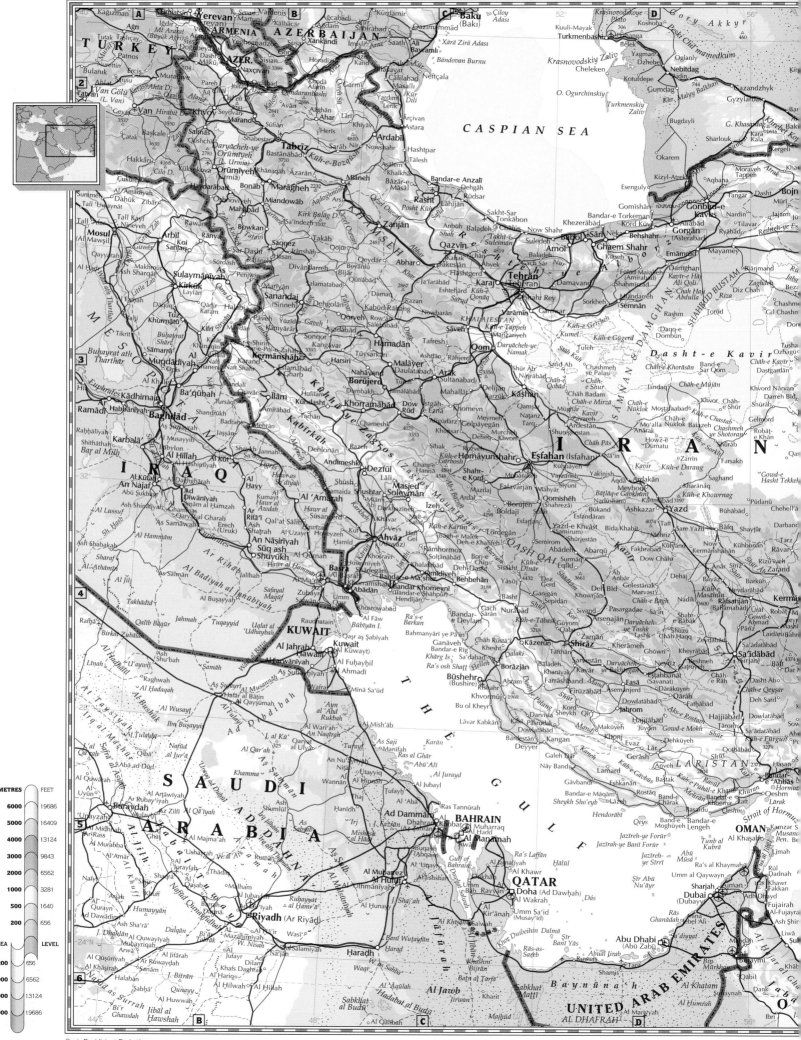

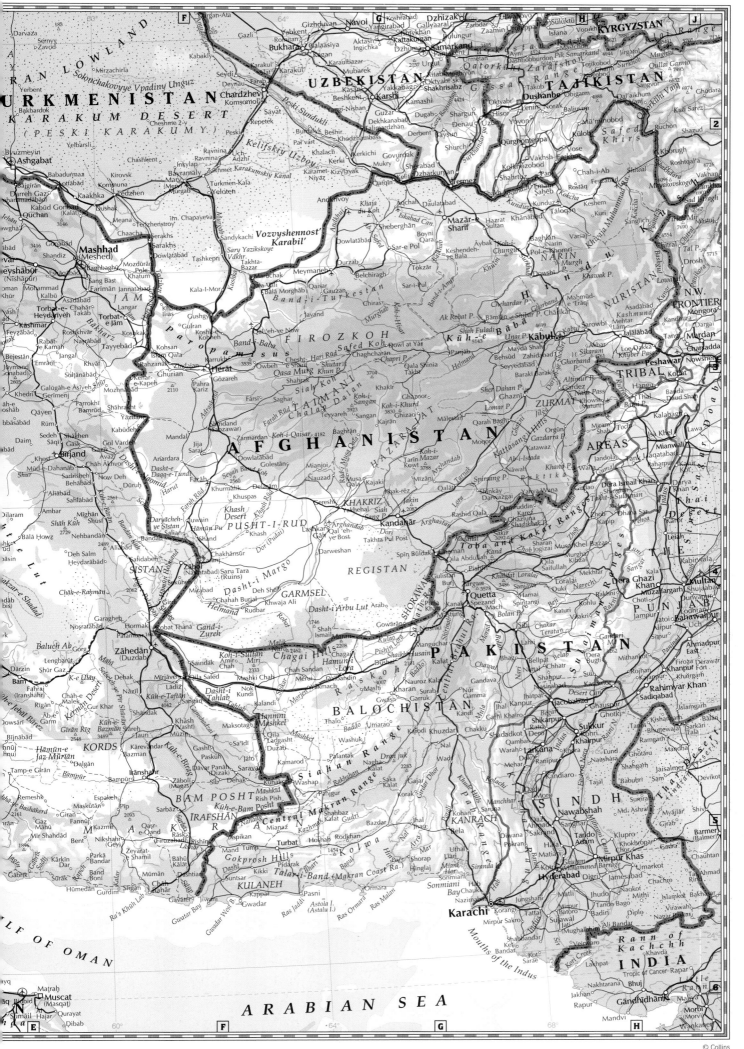

1:7M

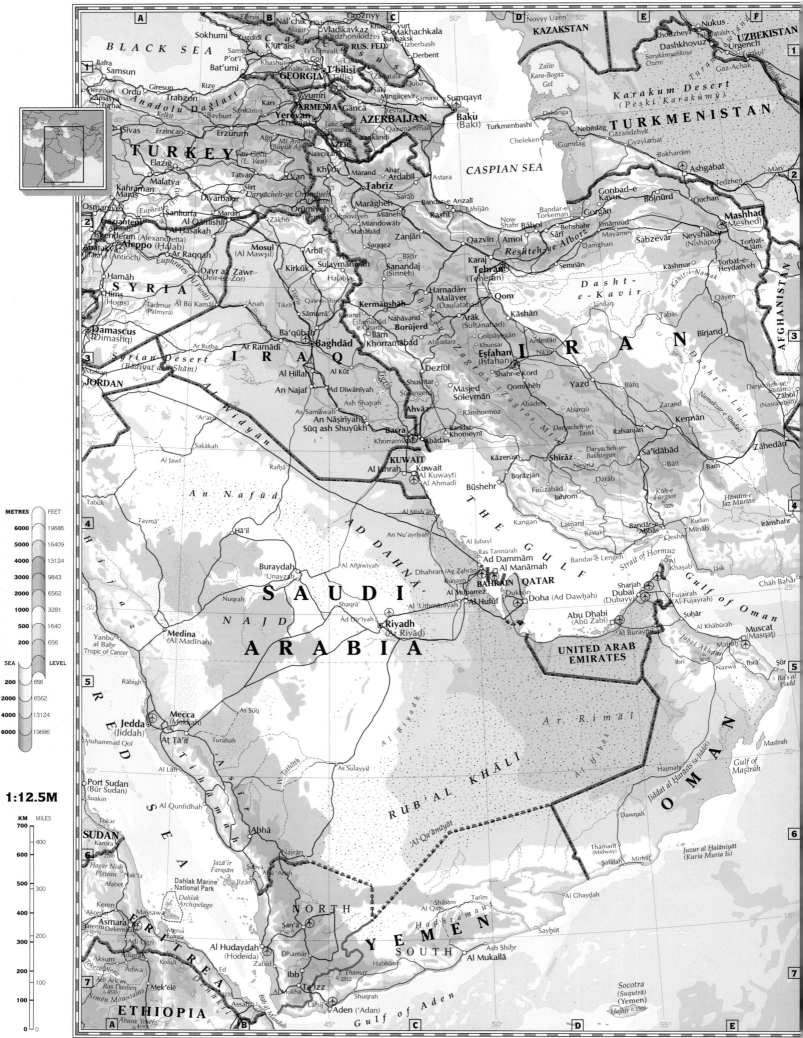

1:12.5M

Albers Equal Area Conic Projection

© Coll

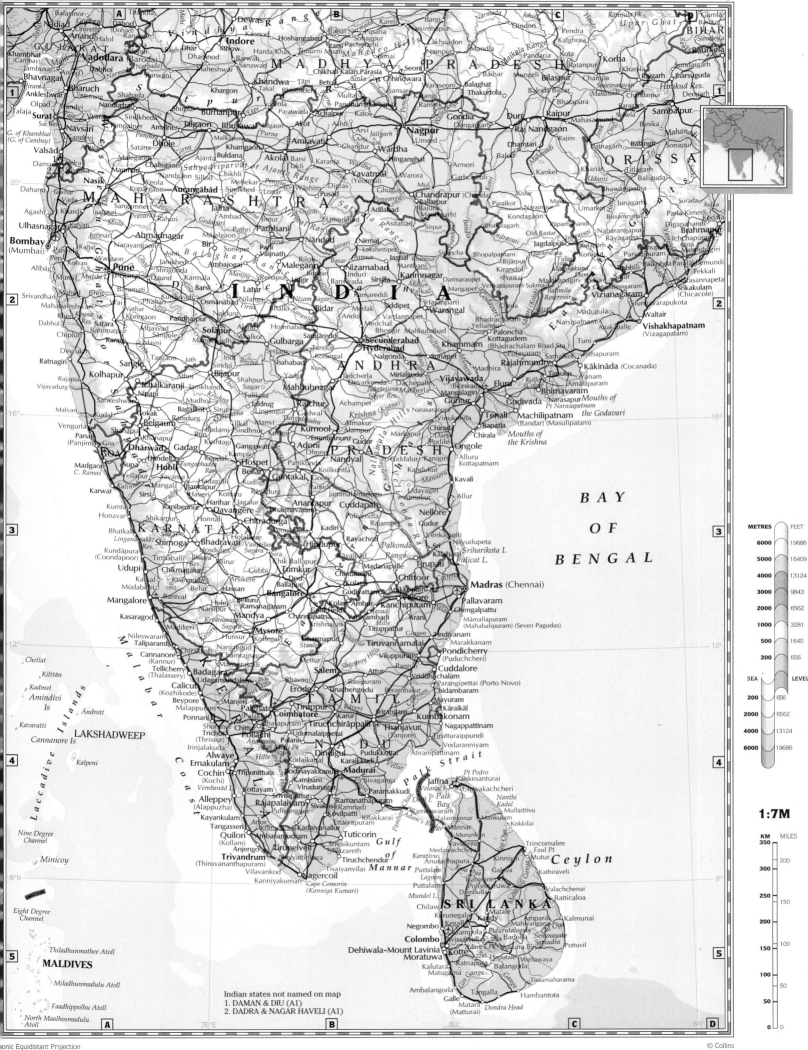

Conic Equidistant Projection

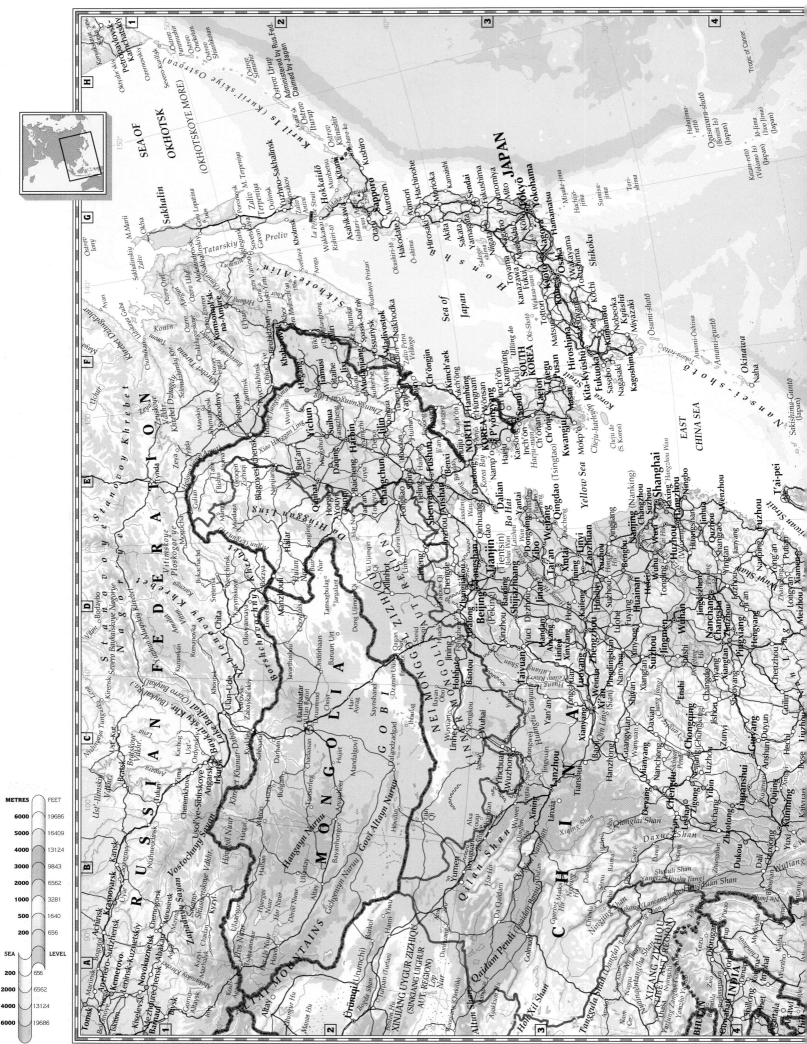

Conic Equidistant Projection

1:20M

KM    MILES
1200

1000          600

800

600          400

400          200

200

0

© Collins

METRES FEET
6000 19686
5000 16409
4000 13124
3000 9843
2000 6562
1000 3281
500 1640
200 656

SEA LEVEL

200 656
2000 6562
4000 13124
6000 19686

Conic Equidistant Projection

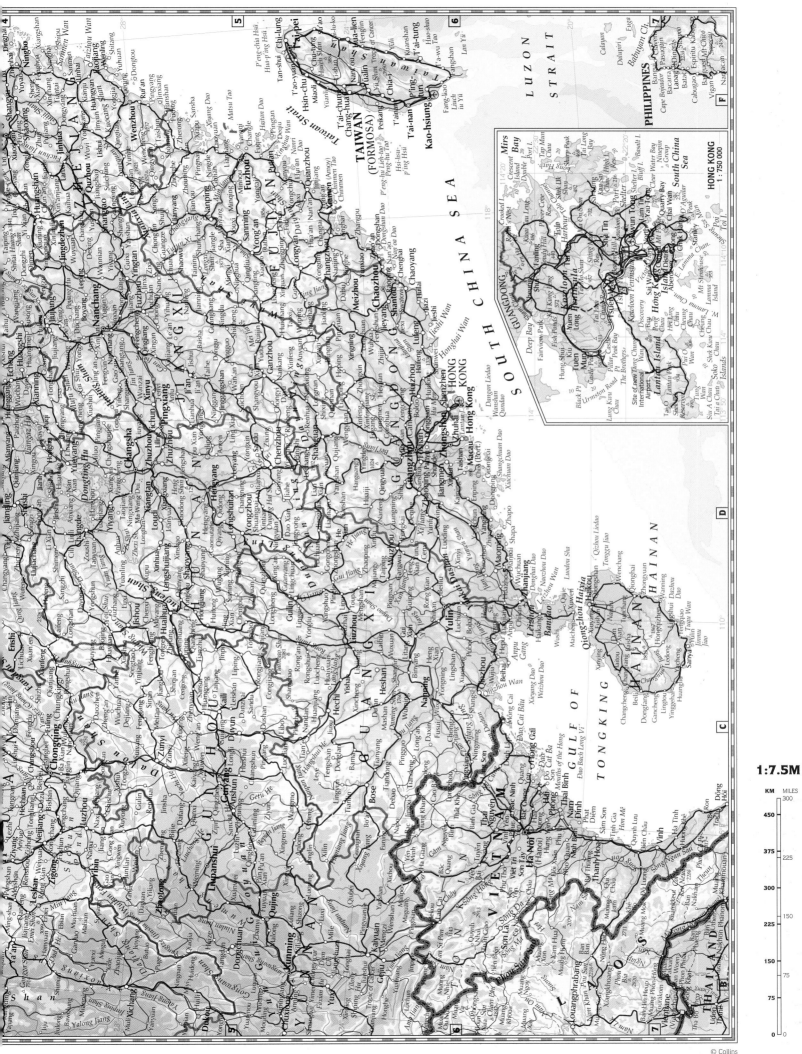

1:7.5M

METRES FEET
6000 19686
5000 16409
4000 13124
3000 9843
2000 6562
1000 3281
500 1640
200 656

SEA LEVEL

200 656
2000 6562
4000 13124
6000 19686

Conic Equidistant Projection

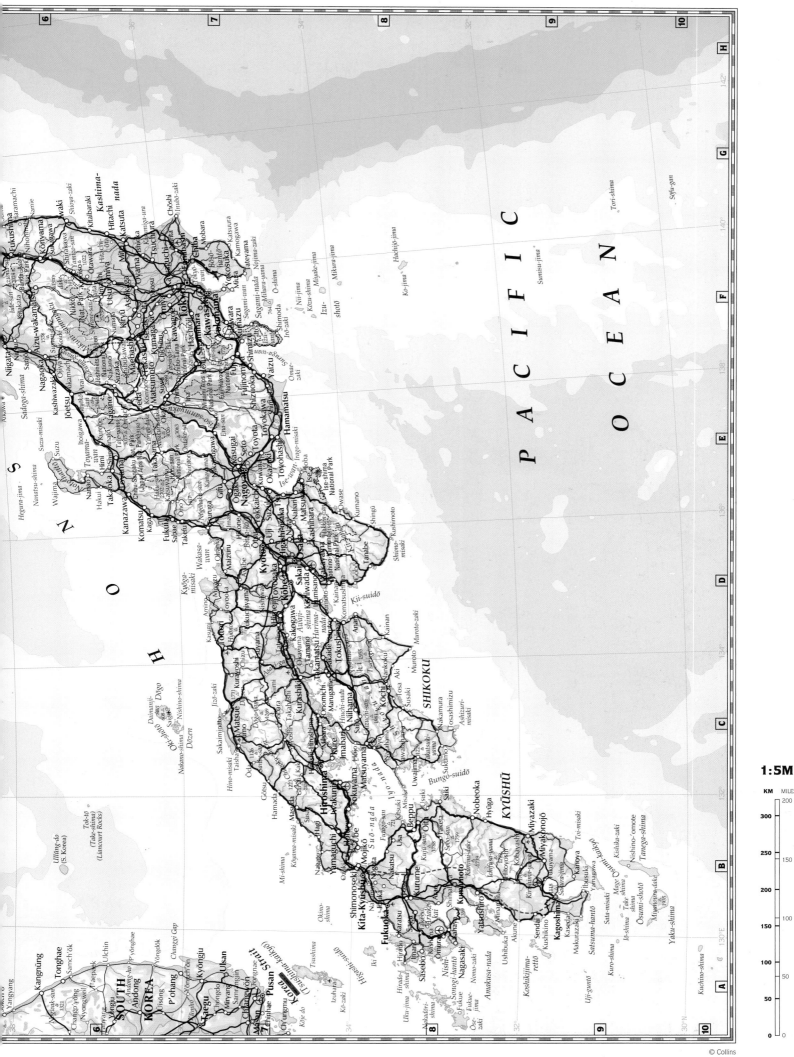

PACIFIC

OCEAN

SHIKOKU

KYŪSHŪ

HONSHŪ

SOUTH
KOREA

**1:5M**

KM MILES

© Collins

Conic Equidistant Projection

© Collin

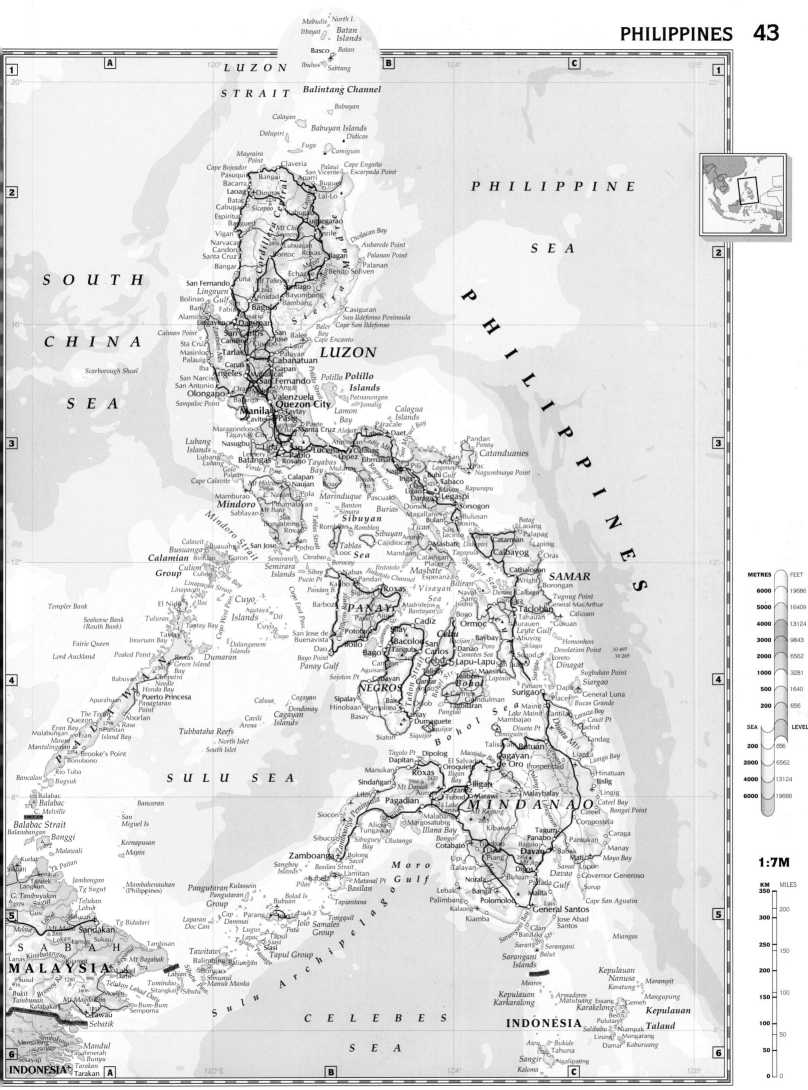

Mabudis  North I.
Itbayat  Batan
Basco  Islands
Ibuhos  Batan
Sabtang

LUZON

STRAIT  Balintang Channel

Calayan  Babuyan

Dalupiri  Babuyan Islands

Fuga  Didicas
Camiguin

Mayraira
Point
Cape Bojeador  Claveria  Palaui  Cape Engaño
Pasuquin  San Vicente  Escarpada Point
Bacarra  Buguey
Laoag  Dingras  Lal-Lo
Batac  Sicapoo  Aparri  Abulug
Cabugao  Espiritu
Bangued  Bangui  Tuguegarao  Divilacan Bay
Vigan  Mt Chico  Ilagan  Aubarede Point
Narvacan  Lubuagan  Roxas  Palanan Point
Santa Cruz  Bontoc  Echague  Palanan
Bangar  Tuao  Santiago  Benito Soliven
San Fernando  Trinidad  Bayombong
Bolinao  Baguio  Bambang  Casiguran
Bani  Fabian  Cape San Ildefonso Peninsula
Alaminos  Rosario  Baler  Cape San Ildefonso
Lingayen  Dagupan  San Jose  Baler
Caiman Point  Camiling  Bay
San Carlos  Laur  Cape Encanto
Masinloc  Tarlac  Palayan
Palauig  Capas  Cabanatuan
Iba  Gapan  LUZON
San Narciso  Angeles  Polillo  Polillo
San Antonio  San Fernando  Islands
Olongapo  Valenzuela  Patnanongan
Manila  Quezon City  Jomalig
Cavite  Pasig  Lamon
Maragondon  Paete  Bay  Calagua
Tagaytay City  Santa Cruz  Alabat  Islands
Nasugbu  San  Lucena  Pandan  Panay
Lemery  Pablo  Lopez  Catanduanes
Batangas  Rosario  Tayabas  San  Virac
Lubang  Bay  Andres  Nagumbuaya Point
Cape Calavite  Roxas  Mt  Lagonoy
Mt Halcon  Calapan  Naga  Pili  Rapurapu
Mamburao  Naujan  Iriga  Mayon  Tabaco
Pola  Oas  Legaspi
Mindoro  Mt Baco  Daraga  Sorsogon
Sablayan  Bongabong  Donsol  Bulusan
Roxas  Magallanes  Irosin
San Jose  San Pedro  Sibuyan  Bulan  Batag
Calawit  Masbate  San  Laoang
Busuanga  Romblon  Jacinto  Palapag
Calamian  Culion  Tablas  Ticao  Catarman  Lapinig
Group  Coron  Sibuyan  Masbate  Tagapula  Oras
Culion  Sea  Cajidiocan  Placer  Calbayog
Semirara  Borocay  Jintotolo Channel  SAMAR
Islands  Mandaon  Wright  Catbalogan
El Nido  Cuyo  Nabas  Jintotolo  Esperanza  Borongan
Iloc  Islands  Pandan  Visayas  Biliran  Daram  Calbiga
Templer Bank  Agutaya  Kalibo  Naval  Isidro
Seahorse Bank  Barbaza  Madridejos  Leyte  Calicoan
(Routh Bank)  Cuyo  PANAY  Bantayan  Bogo  Tacloban
Tuluran  Passi  Ajuy  Cadiz  Ormoc  Guiuan
Fairie Queen  Dumaran  San Jose de  Silay  San  Baybay
Lord Auckland  Buenavista  Bacolod  Carlos  Leyte Gulf  Homonhon
Roxas  Dao  Iloilo  Danao  Poro  Silago  Desolation Point
Peaked Point  Pototan  Bago  Tangub  Cebu  Camotes Sea
PALAWAN  Dumaran  Bayo Point  Canlaon  Cebu  Dinagat
Apurahuan  Panay Gulf  Lapu-Lapu  Loreto
Puerto Princesa  Sipalay  NEGROS  Talisay  Maasin  Surigao
Aborlan  Bais  Talibon  Surigao  Siargao
The Teeth  Sipalay  Carcar  Bohol  Mainit  General Luna
Quezon  Hinobaan  Argao  Carmen  Dapa  Bucas Grande
Eran  Basay  Tanjay  Oslob  Tagbilaran  Lake Mainit  Cantilan
Malabungan  Dumaguete  Jimenez  Placer  Cauit Pt
Mount  Pamplona  Siquijor  Pangao  Mambajao  Dinagat Mts  Madrid
Mantalingajan  Siaton  Siquijor  Camiguin  Tandag
Brooke's Point  Tagolo Pt  Talisayan  Butuan  Lianga
Bonobono  Dipolog  Cagayan  Lianga Bay
Rio Tuba  Dapitan  El Salvador  de Oro  Prosperidad  Hinatuan
Bugsuk  Manukan  Iligan  Bislig
Sindangan  Mt Dapiak  Zamboanga  Lingig
Balabac  Mindanao  Ozamiz  Malaybalay  Cateel Bay
C. Melville  Liloy  Pagadian  Iligan  Marawi  Bangai Point
Balabac Strait  Siocon  Tubod  Cateel
Balambangan  Alicia  Lake  Compostela
Banggi  Tungawan  Lanao  Mt Ragang  Kibawe  Caraga
Malawali  Margosatubig  MINDANAO  Pantukan  Manay
Keenapusan  Illana Bay  Cotabato  Baguio  Babak
Kudat  Mapin  Bongo  Tagum  Mati
Senaja  Zamboanga  Sacol  Upi  Panabo  Mayo Bay
Langkon  Pangutaran  Basilan Strait  Talayan  Davao  Lupon  Governor Generoso
G. Tambuyukon  Pangutaran  Isabela  Moro  Norala  Davao  Surup
Gusi  Group  Lamitan  Gulf  Banga  Malita  Cape San Agustin
Kulassein  Matanal Pt  Lebak  Polomoloc
Mambahenauhan  Basilan  General Santos
Telukan  (Philippines)  Bolod Is  Palimbang  Jose Abad
Cap  Bubuan  Tapiantana  Kalaong  Santos
Parang  Jolo  Samales  Kiamba
Doc Can  Dammai  Group  Glan
SABAH  Lugus  Tapul  Batulaki
Jolo  Siasi  Tongquil  Sarangani
MALAYSIA  Tawitawi  Balimbing  Pata  Sarangani  Miangas
Tandek  Tapaan Passage  Tapul Group  Islands  Balut
Simunul  Manuk Manka
Tumindao  Bongao  Kepulauan
Sibutu Pass  Nanusa  Marampit
Sibutu  Karatung
INDONESIA  Kepulauan  Mangupung
Karkaralong  Essang  Gemeh
Tawau  Meares  Armadores  Matutuang  Karakelong
Sebatik  Pulutan  Beo
CELEBES  Salibabu  Niampak  Kepulauan
INDONESIA  Awu  Bukide  Liruñg  Mangarang  Talaud
Sangir  Tahuna  Mangaran
Kaloma  Ngalipaeng  Damar  Kauburang

SOUTH  CHINA  SEA

Scarborough Shoal

PHILIPPINE  SEA

PHILIPPINES

VISAYAN  SEA

SULU  SEA

Tubbataha Reefs
North Islet
South Islet

Cuyo
Calusa
Cavili
Arena
Cagayan
Islands
Dondonay
Islands

Bohol Sea

Moro
Gulf

Sarangani
Bay

MALAYSIA

INDONESIA

1:7M

| METRES | FEET |
|--------|------|
| 6000 | 19686 |
| 5000 | 16409 |
| 4000 | 13124 |
| 3000 | 9843 |
| 2000 | 6562 |
| 1000 | 3281 |
| 500 | 1640 |
| 200 | 656 |
| SEA | LEVEL |
| 200 | 656 |
| 2000 | 6562 |
| 4000 | 13124 |
| 6000 | 19686 |

| KM | MILES |
|-----|-------|
| 350 |  |
| 300 | 200 |
| 250 | 150 |
| 200 |  |
| 150 | 100 |
| 100 |  |
| 50 | 50 |
| 0 | 0 |

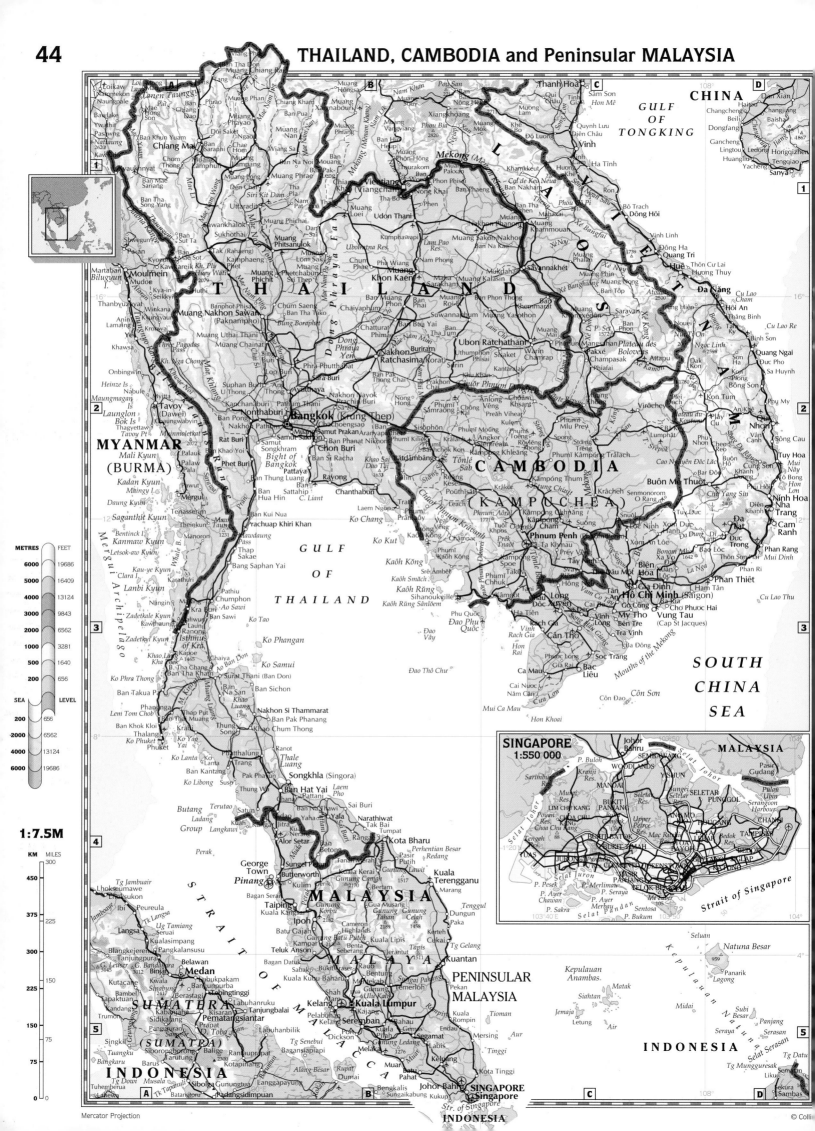

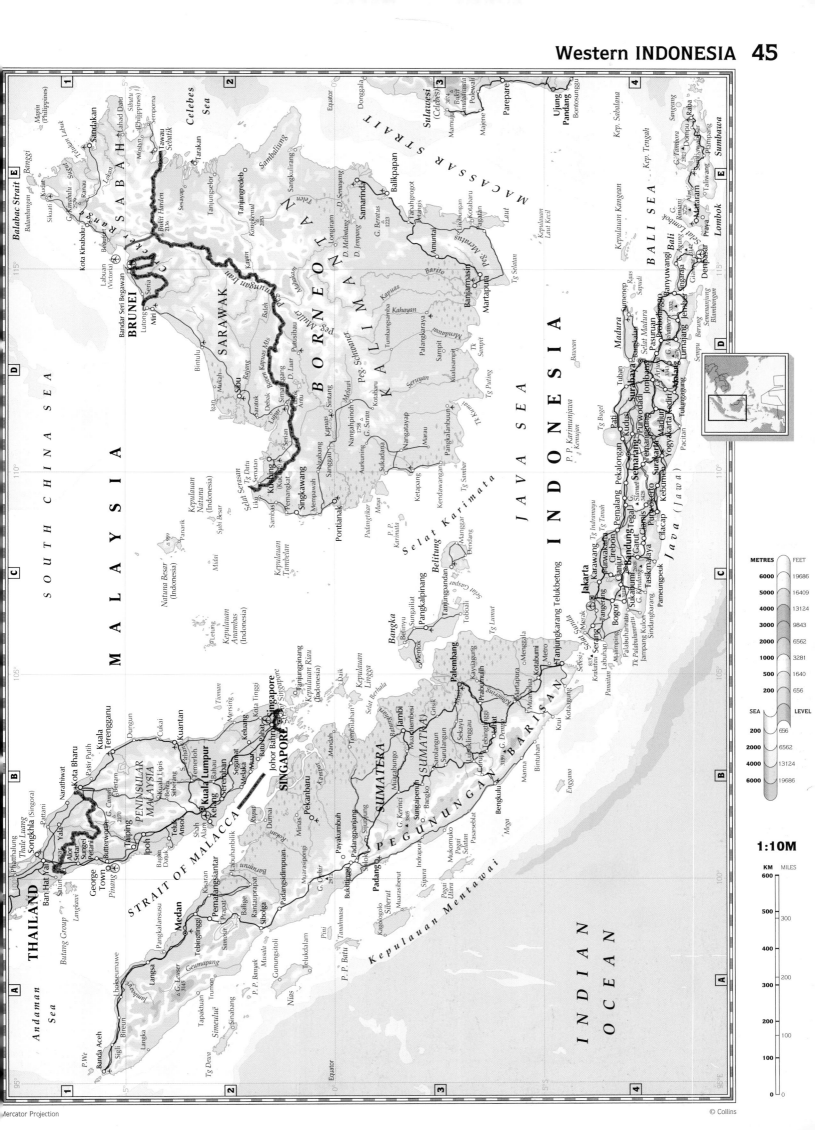

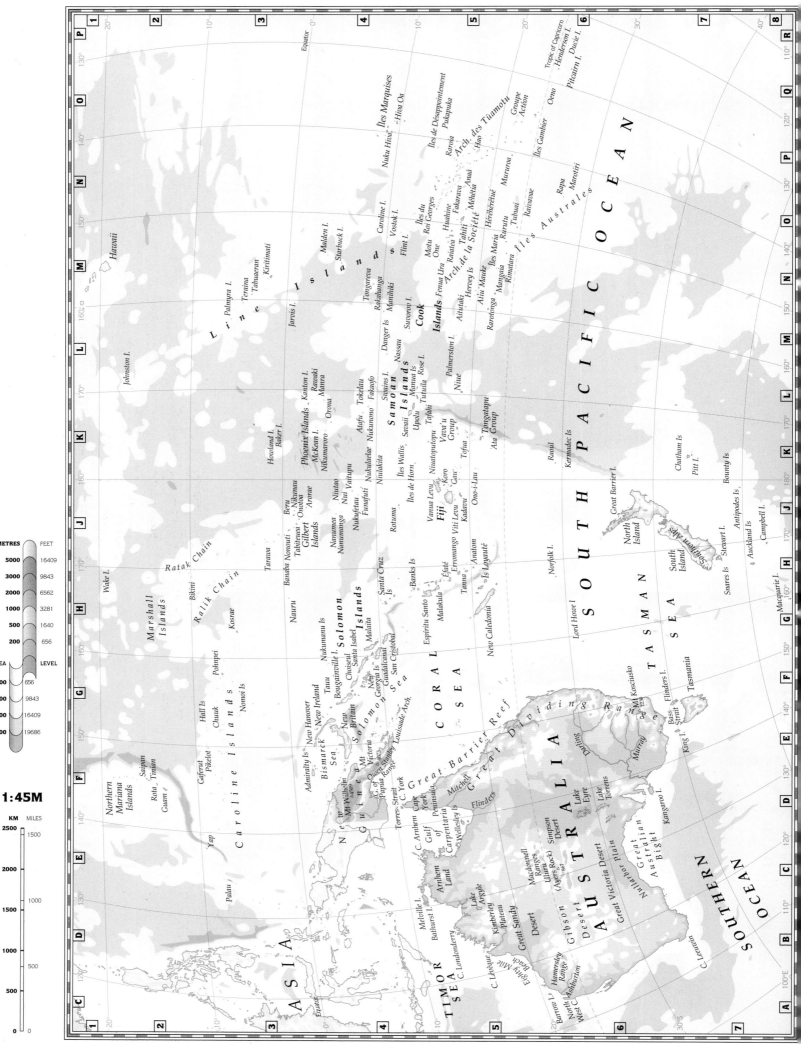

METRES / FEET

| 5000 | 16409 |
| 3000 | 9843 |
| 2000 | 6562 |
| 1000 | 3281 |
| 500 | 1640 |
| 200 | 656 |

SEA / LEVEL

| 200 | 656 |
| 3000 | 9843 |
| 5000 | 16409 |
| 6000 | 19686 |

1:45M

KM / MILES

2500 / 1500
2000
1500 / 1000
1000
500 / 500
0 / 0

Lambert Azimuthal Equal Area Projection

© Collin

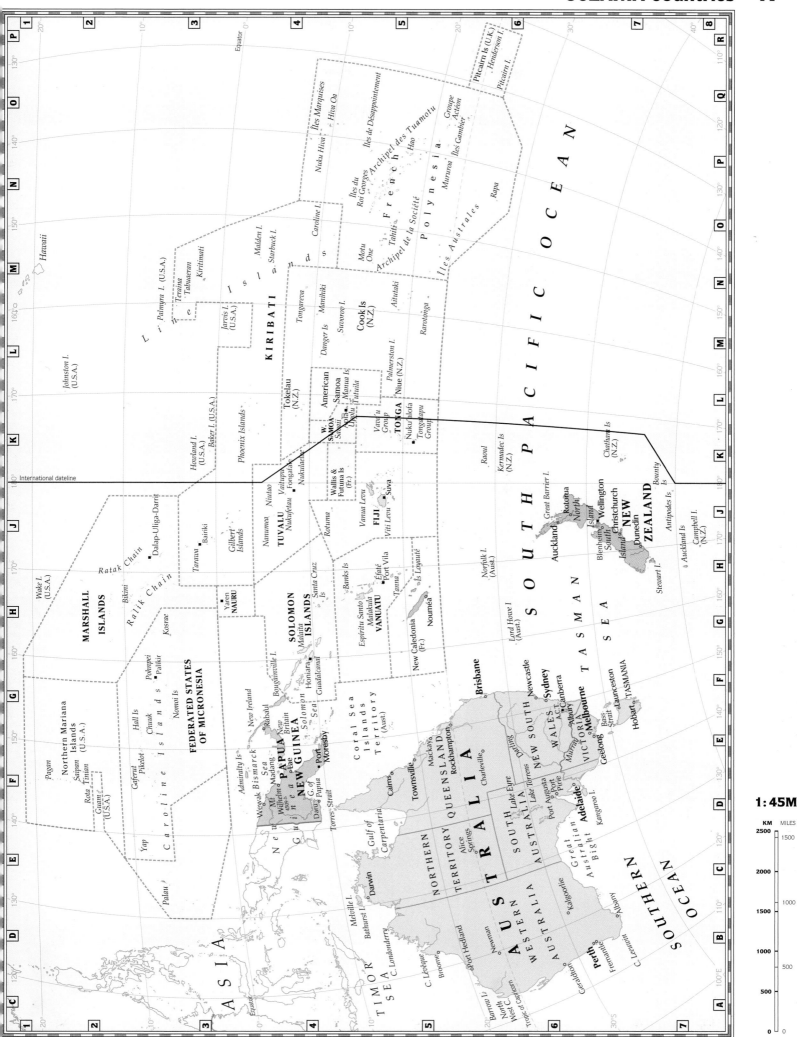

1:45M

KM    MILES
2500  1500

2000

1500  1000

1000

500   500

0     0

Lambert Azimuthal Equal Area Projection

© Collins

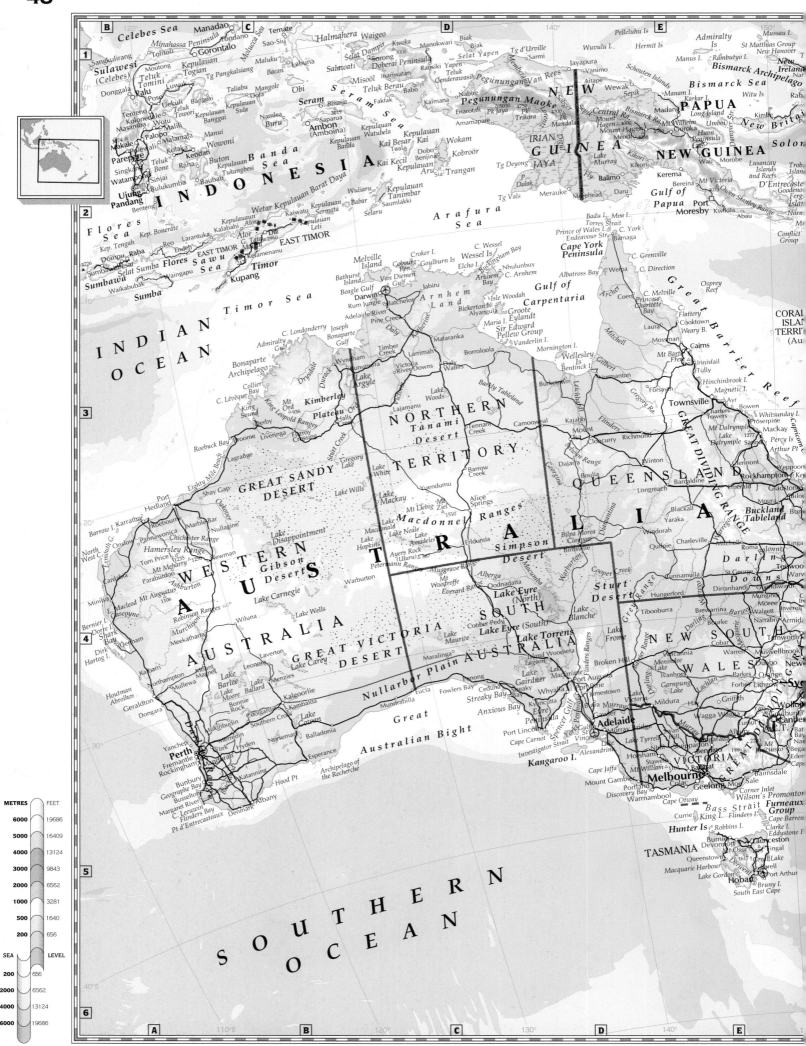

**METRES** **FEET**
6000 — 19686
5000 — 16409
4000 — 13124
3000 — 9843
2000 — 6562
1000 — 3281
500 — 1640
200 — 656

SEA — LEVEL

200 — 656
2000 — 6562
4000 — 13124
6000 — 19686

Lambert Azimuthal Equal Area Projection

**SOLOMON ISLANDS**

Bougainville Island
Arawa
Choiseul
Treasury
Vella Lavella
Kolombangara
New Georgia Is (Solomon Is)
Rendova
Russell Is
Honiara
Guadalcanal
Santa Isabel
Buala
Malu'u
Malaita
Maramasike
Avuavu
Ulawa I.
Kirakira
San Cristobal
Rennell
Florida Is
Stewart Is

Nuguria Is
Kilinailau Is
Tauu (Mortlock Is)
Nukumanu Is
Ontong Java Atoll
Roncador Reef
Indispensable Reefs

**NAURU**
Yaren
Banaba (Kiribati)

**Gilbert Islands (Kiribati)**
Aranuka
Nonouti
Tabiteuea
Beru
Nikunau
Onotoa
Tamana
Arorae
Kingsmill Group

**KIRIBATI**
Equator
Phoenix Islands
McKean Island
Nikumaroro
Orona (Kiribati)
Kanton Island
Manra

Howland Island (U.S.A.)
Baker Island (U.S.A.)

**TUVALU**
Nanumea
Niutao
Nanumanga
Nui
Nukufetau
Vaitupu
Fongafale
Funafuti
Nukulaelae
Niulakita

Atafu
Nukunono
Fakaofo
**TOKELAU (N.Z.)**

**Santa Cruz Islands (Solomon Is)**
Duff Is
Swallow Is
Nupani
Ndeni
Utupua
Vanikoro Is
Cherry Island
Tikopia
Mitre Island
San Ana

**CORAL SEA**

**VANUATU**
Torres Islands
Uréparapara
Vanua Lava
Banks Islands
Santa María I.
Espíritu Santo
Tabwémasana 1879
Aoba
Maëwo
Malo
Pentecost I.
Norsup
Ambrym
Malakula
Épi
Émaé
Shepherd Is
Éfaté
Port Vila
Erromango
Tanna
Aniwa
Futuna
Anatom (Vanuatu)

Rotuma (Fiji)

**WALLIS AND FUTUNA IS (Fr.)**
Îles Wallis
Îles de Horn

**WESTERN SAMOA**
Savaii
Apia
Upolu
Tutuila (U.S.A.)

Îles Chesterfield (New Caledonia)
Récifs d'Entrecasteaux
I. de Sable
Grand Passage
Îles Bélep
Grand Récif de Cook
Récif des Français
Koumac
**NEW CALEDONIA (NOUVELLE CALÉDONIE) (Fr.)**
Ouvéa
Lifou
Tadine
Nouméa
Yaté
Maré
I. des Pins
Grand Récif du Sud

**FIJI**
Yasawa Group
Great Sea Reef
Labasa
**Vanua Levu**
Bligh Water
Lautoka
Tomaniivi 1323
Koro
Koro Sea
**Viti Levu**
Suva
Ovalau
Gau
Bega
Kadavu Passage
Moala
Kadavu
Lakeba
Matuku

Niuatoputopu (Tonga)
Tafahi (Tonga)

Vava'u Group
Tofua
**TONGA**
Ono-i-Lau (Fiji)
Ata (Tonga)
Nuku'alofa
Tongatapu Group

**NIUE (N.Z.)**

Hunter I. (Fr.)
Conway Reef (Fiji)

Horizon Depth •10882

Tropic of Capricorn

Norfolk Island (Aust.)

**SOUTH PACIFIC OCEAN**

Raoul
Kermadec Is (N.Z.)

Lord Howe Island (Aust.)

**TASMAN SEA**

Three Kings Is
Cape Maria van Diemen
North Cape
Whangarei
Kaipara Harbour
Great Barrier Island
Takapuna
**Auckland**
Manukau
Tauranga
Bay of Plenty
Hamilton
**NORTH ISLAND**
East Cape
Tokoroa
Hikurangi
Gisborne
North Taranaki Bight
New Plymouth
Mt Ruapehu
Lake Taupo
Mt Egmont (Mt Taranaki)
Wairoa
Mahia Peninsula
South Taranaki Bight
Napier
Cape Farewell
Wanganui
Hawke Bay
Hastings
Karamea Bight
Nelson
Palmerston North
Westport
Blenheim
Masterton
Greymouth
Lower Hutt
Hokitika
**Wellington**
Cook Strait
Cape Palliser

**NEW ZEALAND**

Mt Cook (Mt Aoraki)
Pegasus Bay
Mt Aspiring
**Southern Alps**
Lake Pukaki
**Christchurch**
Banks Peninsula
Mt Christina
Lake Tekapo
Timaru
**Canterbury Bight**
Lake Te Anau
Lake Wanaka
Oamaru
Resolution Island
Lake Wakatipu
**SOUTH ISLAND**
Cape Providence
Otago Peninsula
Foveaux Strait
**Dunedin**
**Invercargill**
**Stewart Island**
South West Cape
Snares Is

Chatham Islands (N.Z.)
Pitt I.

Bounty Islands

Auckland Is

**1:20M**

KM  MILES
800
1200
600
1000
800  400
600
400  200
200
0

© Collins

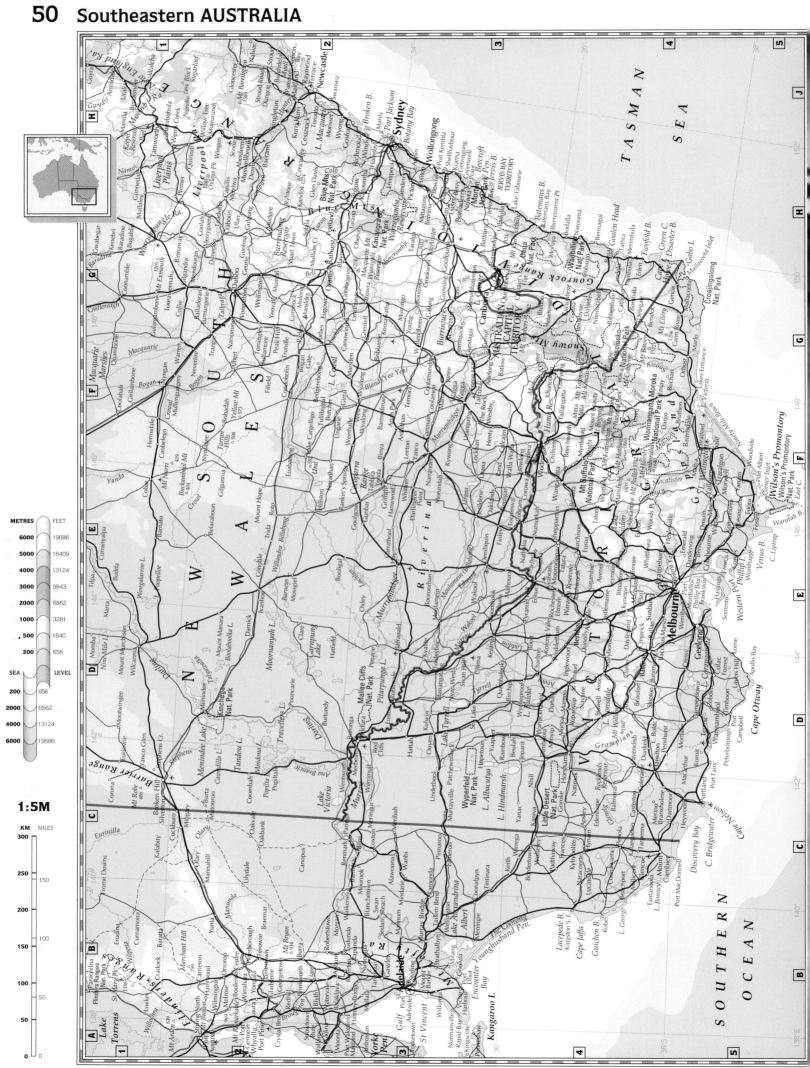

TASMAN
SEA

NORTH ISLAND

SOUTH ISLAND

SOUTH PACIFIC
OCEAN

Canterbury
Bight

Foveaux Strait

METRES    FEET
6000      19686
5000      16409
4000      13124
3000      9843
2000      6562
1000      3281
500       1640
200       656

SEA       LEVEL
200       656
2000      6562
4000      13124
6000      19686

1:5M

KM    MILES
            200
300
            150
250
200       100
150
            50
100

50

0

# NORTH AMERICA Relief

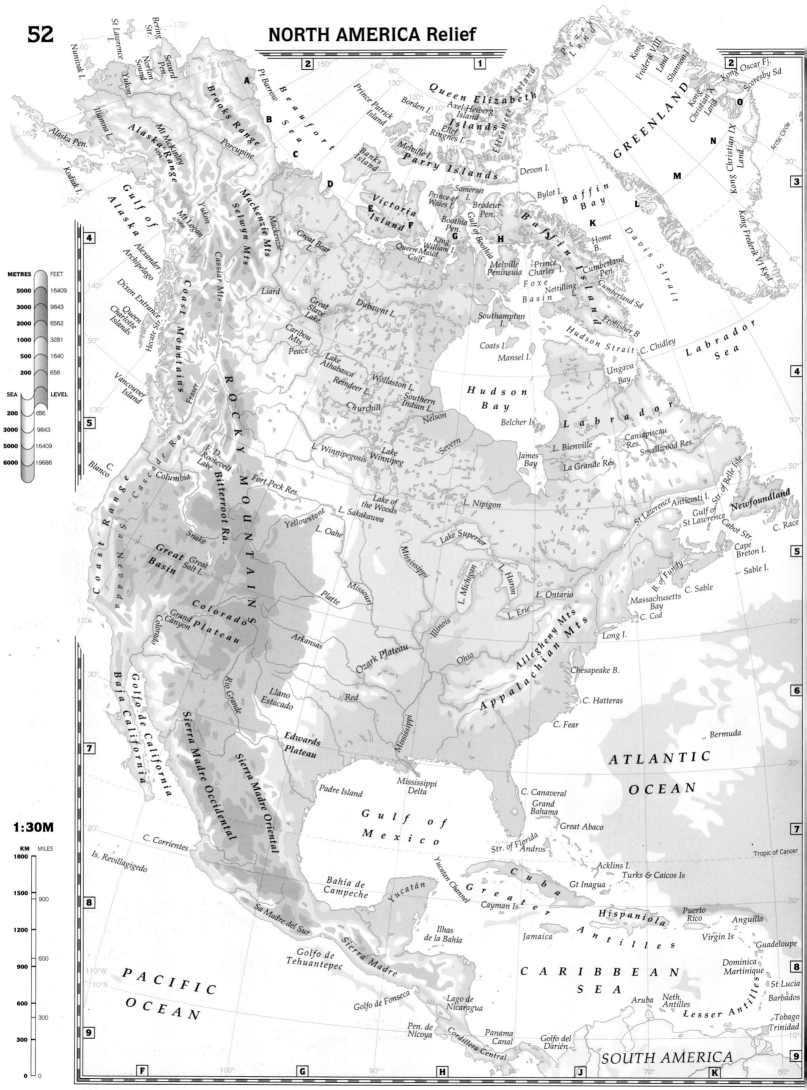

© Collins

1:30M

Chamberlin Trimetric Projection

| METRES | | FEET |
|---|---|---|
| 6000 | | 19686 |
| 5000 | | 16409 |
| 4000 | | 13124 |
| 3000 | | 9843 |
| 2000 | | 6562 |
| 1000 | | 3281 |
| 500 | | 1640 |
| 200 | | 656 |
| SEA | | LEVEL |
| 200 | | 656 |
| 2000 | | 6562 |
| 4000 | | 13124 |
| 6000 | | 19686 |

ARCTIC OCEAN

BEAUFORT SEA

PACIFIC OCEAN

GULF OF ALASKA

U. S. A.

A L A S K A

RUS. FED.

YUKON TERRITORY

BRITISH COLUMBIA

NORTHWEST TE

ALBERTA

SASKATCHEWAN

WASHINGTON

OREGON

IDAHO

MONTANA

NORTH DAKO

SOUTH DAKOT

NEBRASKA

WYOMING

NEVADA

UTAH

CALIFORNIA

C A N

U.

Bering Strait

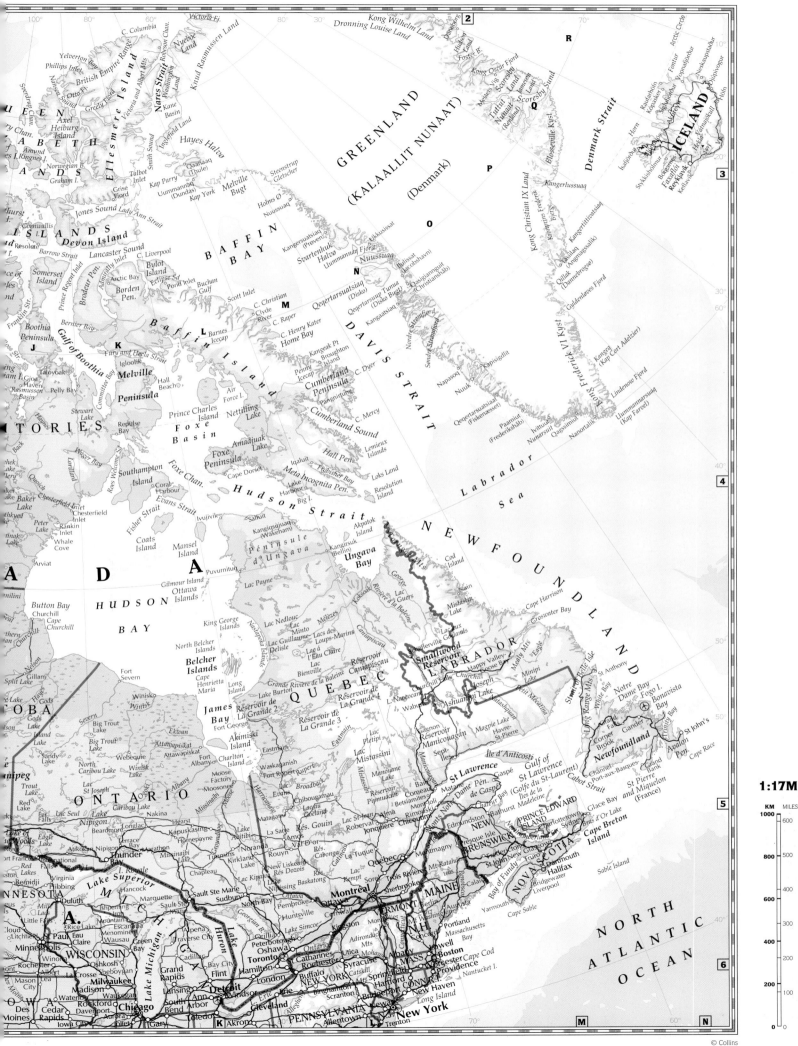

Transverse Mercator Projection

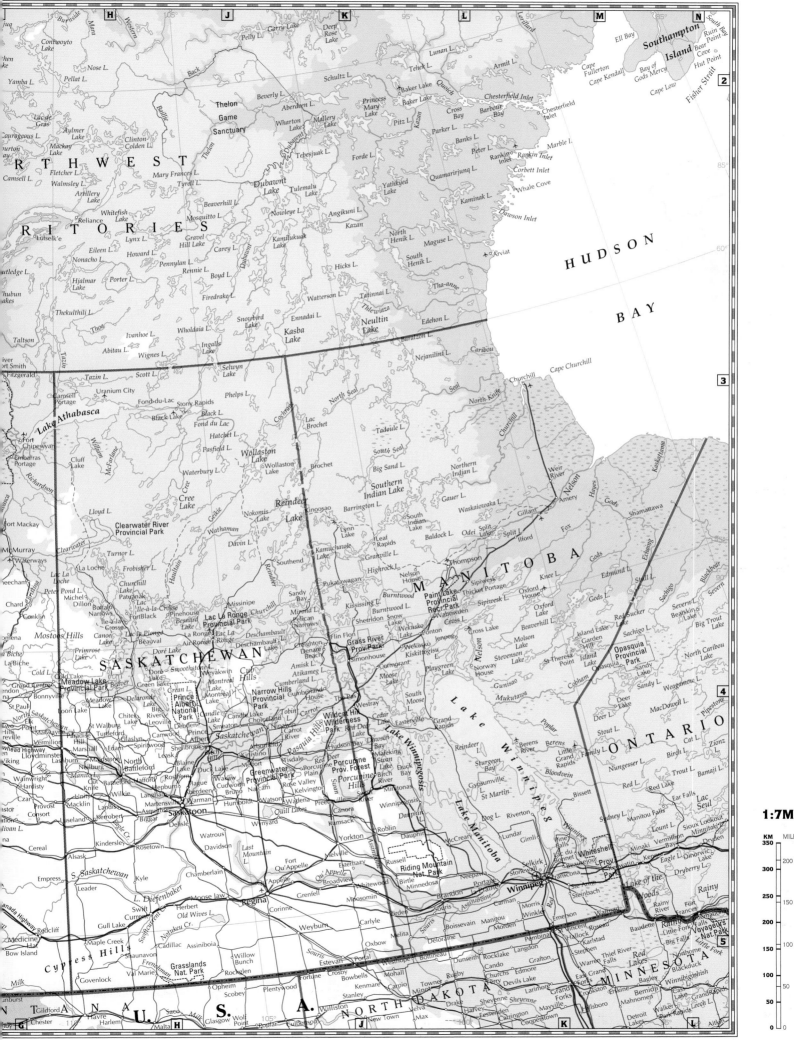

1:7M

KM MILES
350
300
250
200
150
100
50
0

© Collins

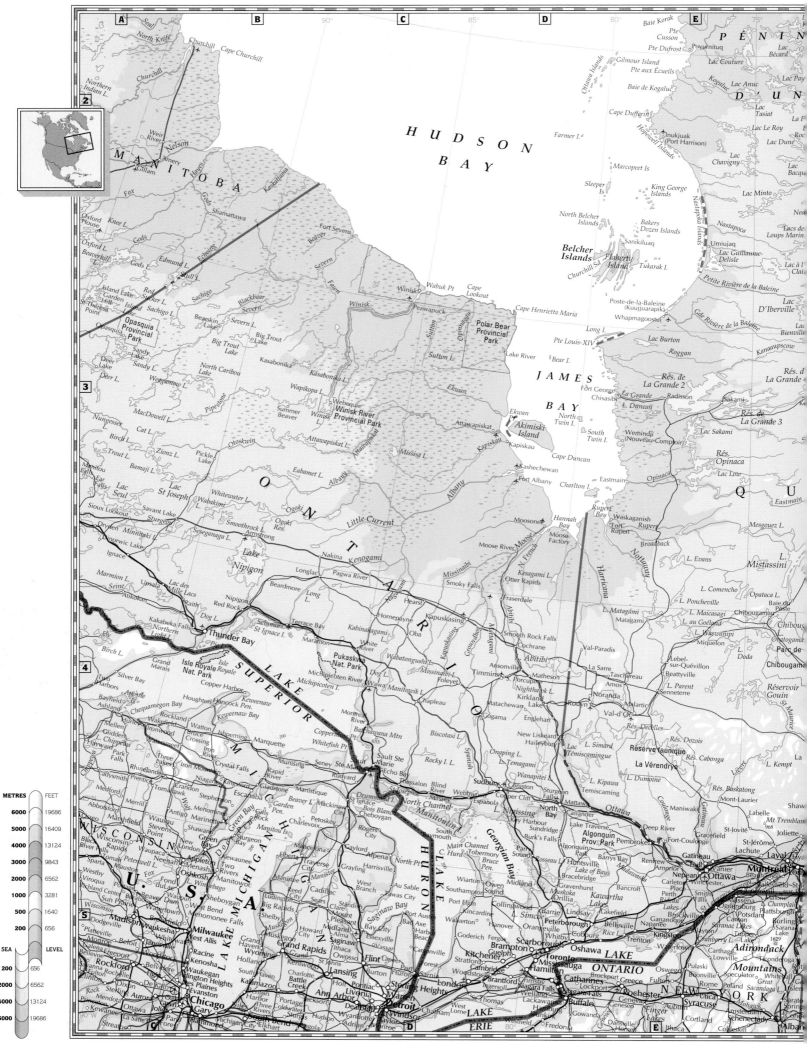

Transverse Mercator Projection

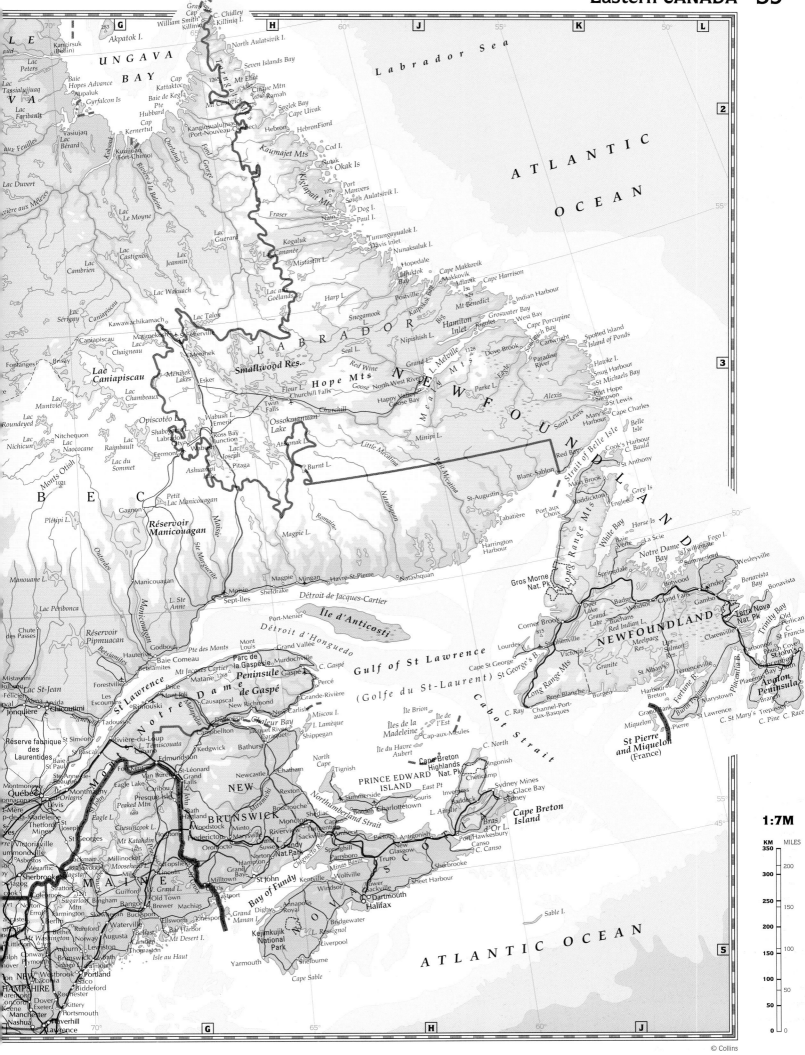

**1:7M**

Lambert Conformal Conic Projection

© Collins

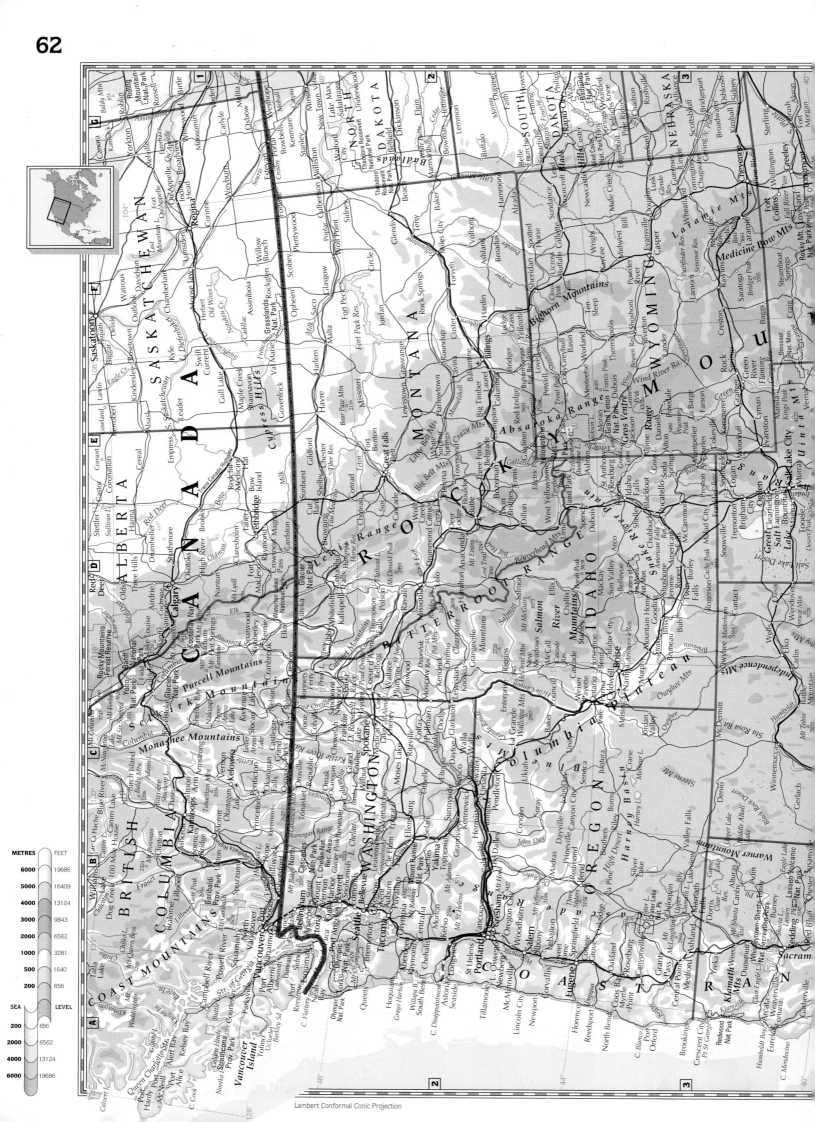

Lambert Conformal Conic Projection

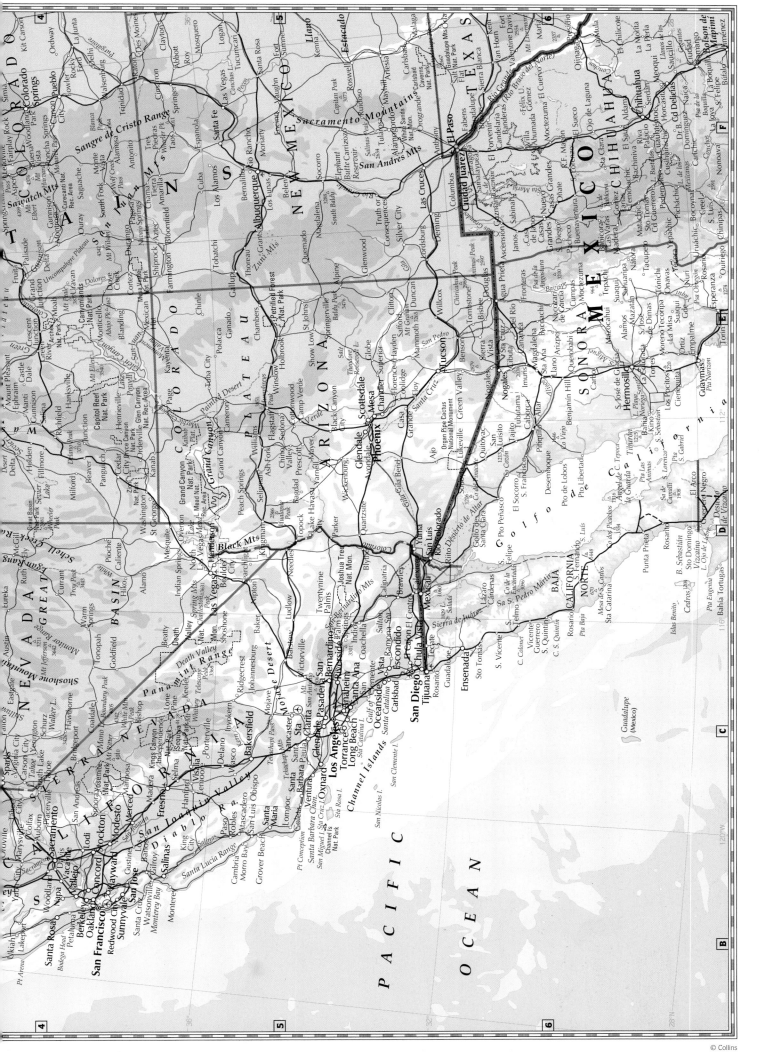

**1:7M**

KM / MILES
350 / 200
300 / 
250 / 150
200 / 100
150 / 
100 / 50
50 / 
0 / 0

© Collins

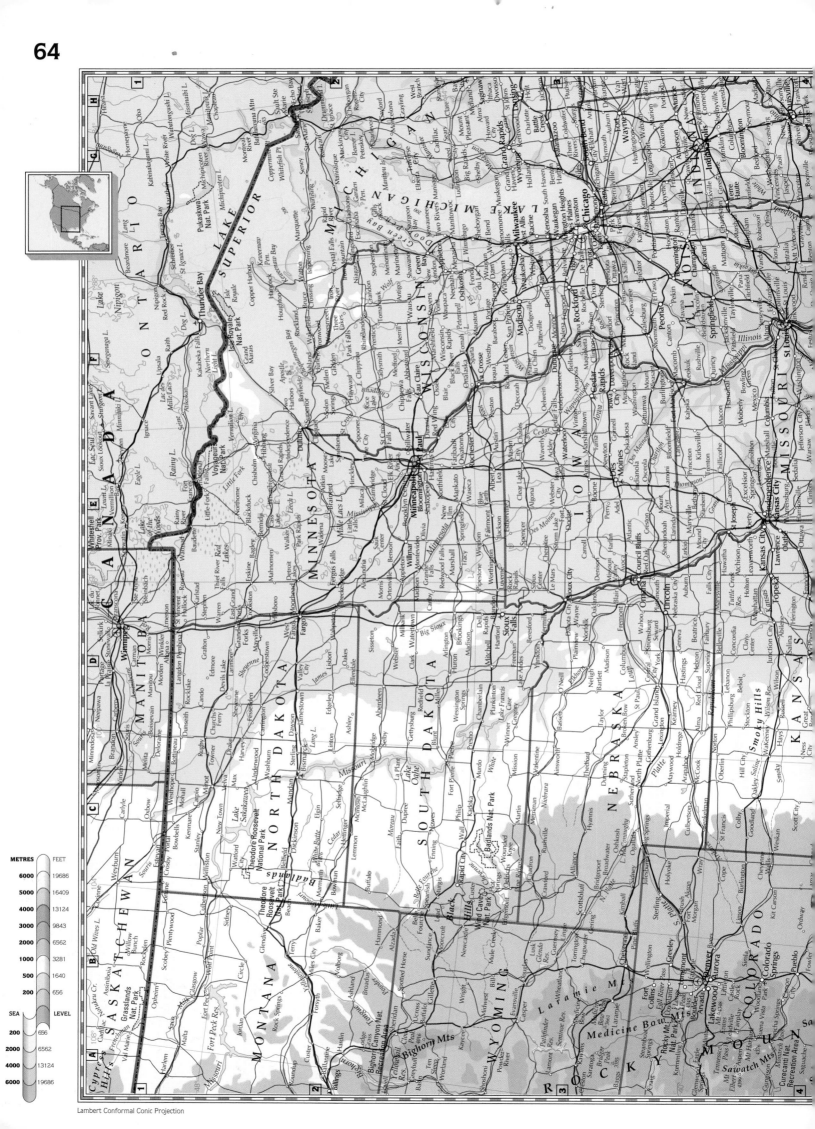

Lambert Conformal Conic Projection

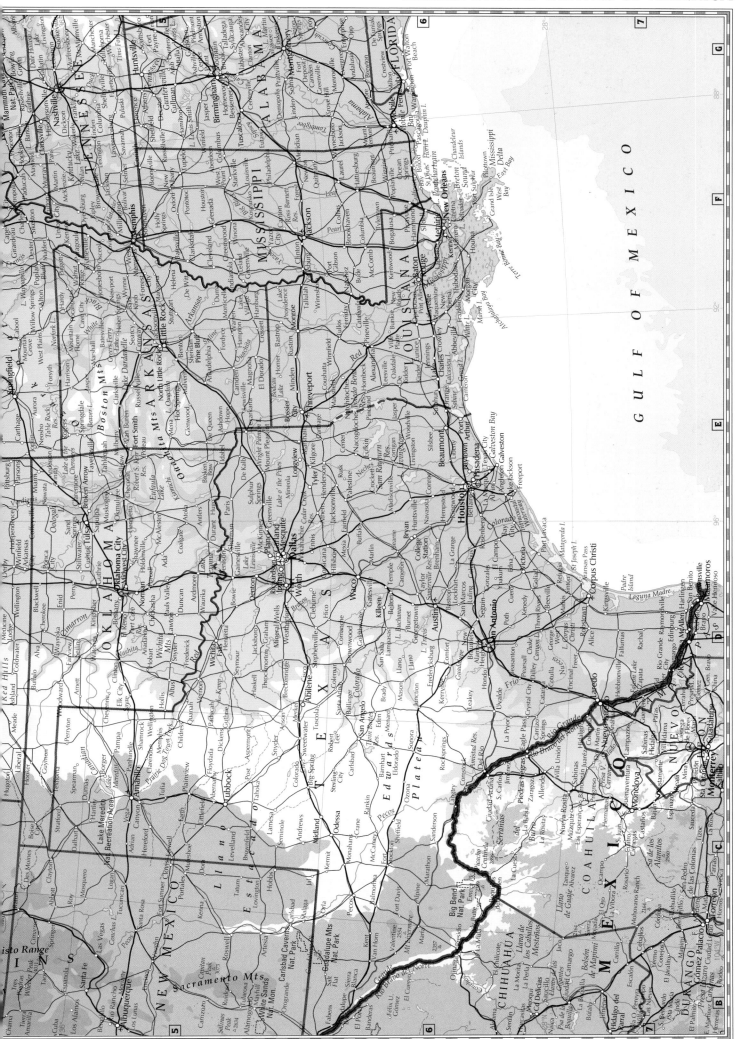

**1:7M**

| KM | MILES |
|---|---|
| 350 | |
| | 200 |
| 300 | |
| 250 | 150 |
| 200 | |
| | 100 |
| 150 | |
| 100 | 50 |
| 50 | |
| 0 | 0 |

Lambert Conformal Conic Projection

1:7M

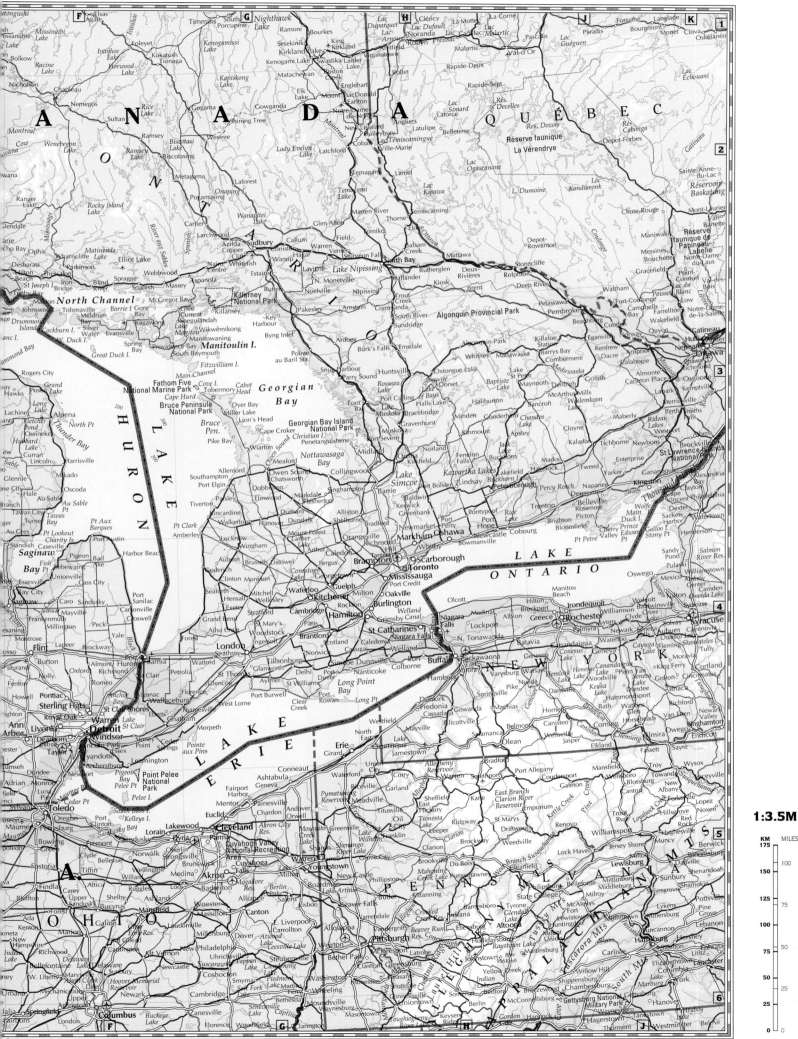

© Collins

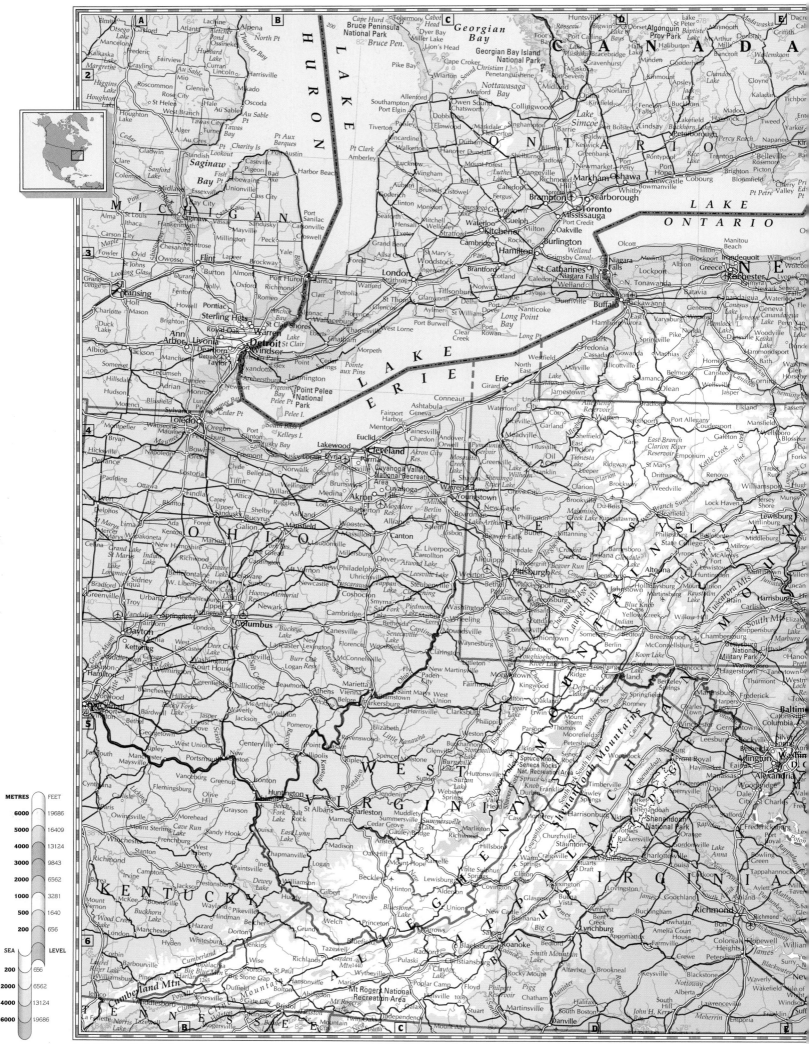

Lambert Conformal Conic Projection

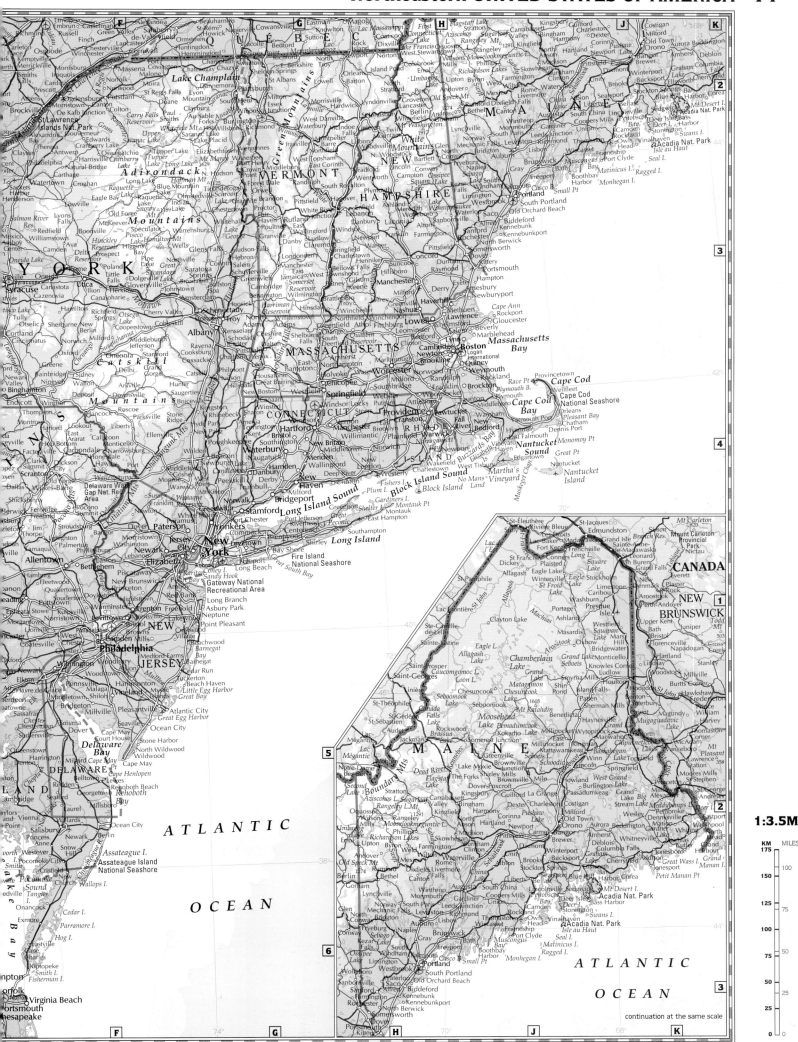

1:3.5M

KM 175 MILES
150 100
125 75
100
75 50
50
25
25
0

continuation at the same scale

© Collins

Lambert Conformal Conic Projection

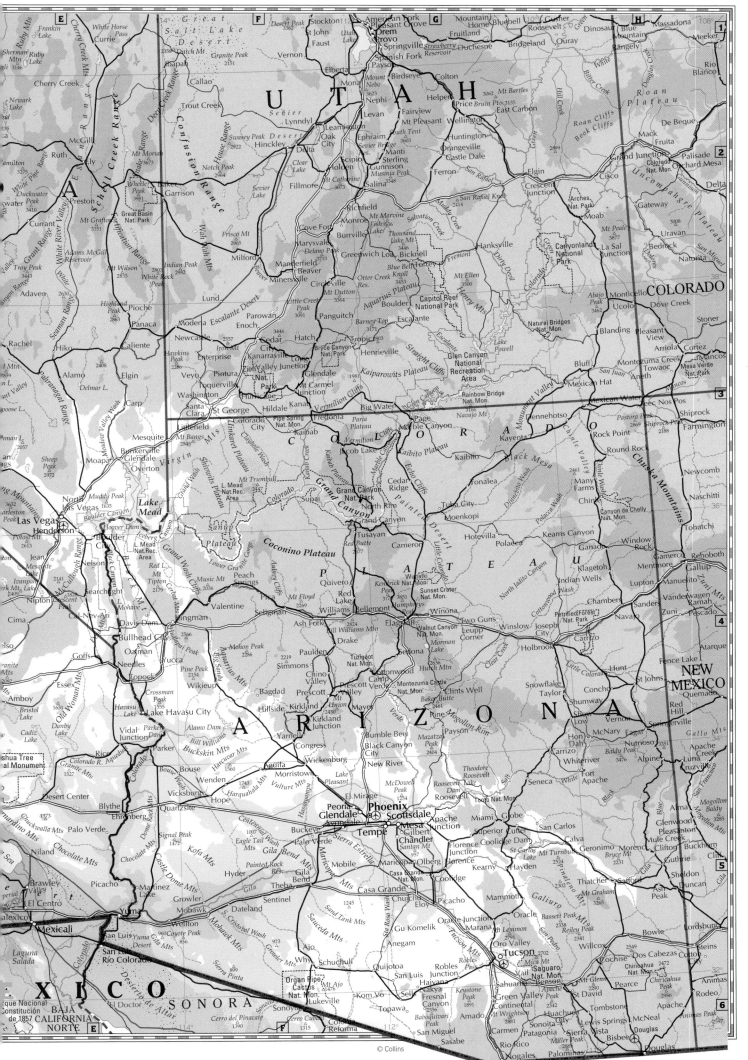

1:3.5M

KM    MILES
175   —
      — 100
150   —
125   — 75
100   —
      — 50
75    —
50    — 25
25    —
0     — 0

© Collins

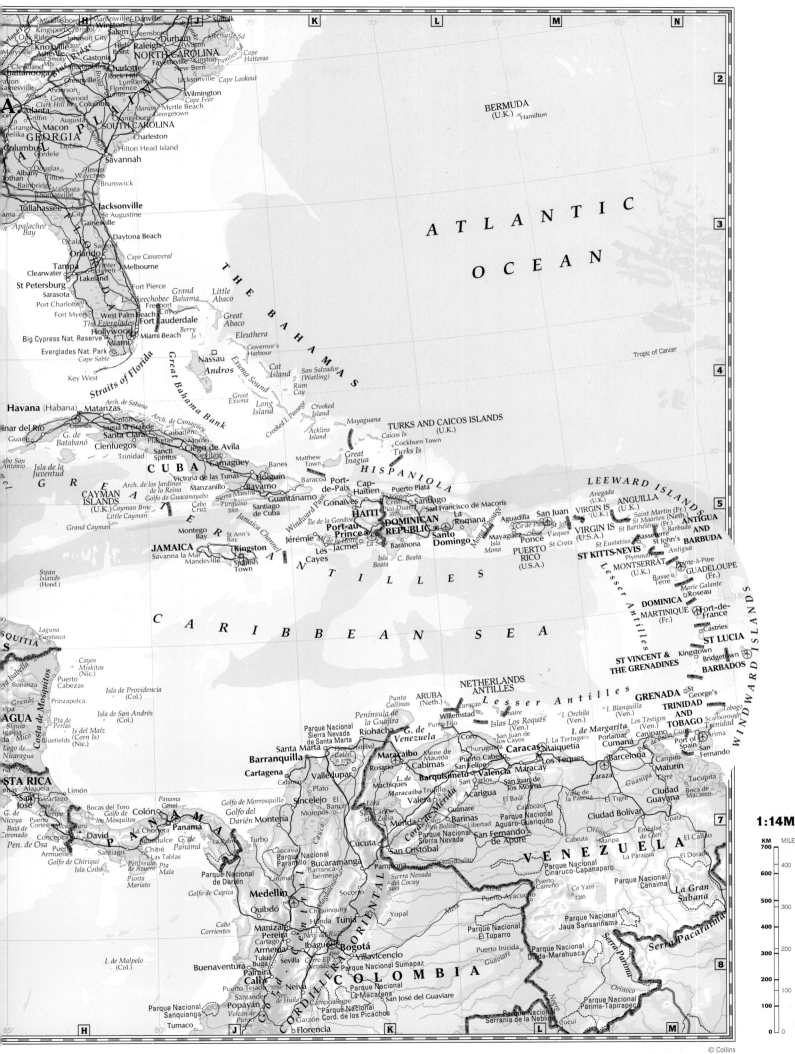

ATLANTIC OCEAN

BERMUDA
(U.K.)  ●Hamilton

Tropic of Cancer

THE BAHAMAS

TURKS AND CAICOS ISLANDS
(U.K.)
Cockburn Town
Turks Is

HISPANIOLA

LEEWARD ISLANDS

ANGUILLA (U.K.)
Anegada (U.K.)
Saint Martin (Fr.)
St Maarten (Neth.)
VIRGIN IS (U.K.)
VIRGIN IS (U.S.A.)
St Barthélémy (Fr.)
Barbuda
ANTIGUA AND BARBUDA
Antigua
St John's
St Eustatius (Neth.)
Basseterre
ST KITTS-NEVIS
MONTSERRAT (U.K.)
Plymouth
GUADELOUPE (Fr.)
Pointe-à-Pitre
Basse-Terre
Marie Galante
Roseau
DOMINICA
MARTINIQUE (Fr.)
Fort-de-France
Castries
ST LUCIA
ST VINCENT & THE GRENADINES
Kingstown
Bridgetown
BARBADOS
GRENADA
St George's
TRINIDAD AND TOBAGO
Scarborough
Tobago
Trinidad
Port of Spain

Lesser Antilles

WINDWARD ISLANDS

CUBA

Havana (Habana)  Matanzas
Pinar del Río
Guane
Arch. de Sabana
Colón
Santa Clara
Sagua la Grande
G. de Batabanó
Cienfuegos
Cabo San Antonio
Isla de la Juventud
Placetas
Trinidad
Sancti Spíritus
Ciego de Ávila
Morón
Arch. de Camagüey
Camagüey
Nuevitas
Victoria de las Tunas
Banes
Holguín
Bayamo
Manzanillo
Golfo de Guacanayabo
Baracoa
Guantánamo
Santiago de Cuba
Sierra Maestra
Turquino 2005
Cabo Cruz

CAYMAN ISLANDS (U.K.)
Cayman Brac
Little Cayman
Grand Cayman

Port-de-Paix
Cap-Haïtien
Gonaïves
Monte Cristi
Pico Duarte 3175
Santiago
San Francisco de Macorís
Puerto Plata
HAITI
Port-au-Prince
DOMINICAN REPUBLIC
Santo Domingo
La Romana
Barahona
Isla Beata
C. Beata
Île de la Gonâve
Jérémie
La Selle
Jacmel
Les Cayes
Mayagüez
Aguadilla
Ponce
PUERTO RICO (U.S.A.)
San Juan
Isla Mona
Mona Passage
Ca de Punta
St John
St Croix
Vieques

JAMAICA
Montego Bay
Savanna la Mar
Mandeville
Kingston
Spanish Town
St Ann's Bay

Windward Passage
Jamaica Channel

GREATER ANTILLES

CARIBBEAN SEA

NETHERLANDS ANTILLES
ARUBA (Neth.)
Curaçao
Bonaire
Willemstad
Lesser Antilles

Punta Gallinas
Península de la Guajira
Ríohacha
G. de Venezuela
Punto Fijo
Coro
Islas Los Roques (Ven.)
I. Orchila (Ven.)
I. Blanquilla (Ven.)
I. de Margarita
Porlamar
Los Testigos (Ven.)
La Tortuga (Ven.)
San Juan de los Cayos
Churuguara
Mene de Mauroa
Cabimas
Maracaibo
L. de Maracaibo
Rosario
San Felipe
Puerto Cabello
Barquisimeto
Maracay
Valencia
Caracas
Maiquetía
Los Teques
Barcelona
Cumaná
Carúpano
Güiria
Maturín
Caripito
Boca de Macareo

VENEZUELA

Santa Marta
Sierra Nevada de Santa Marta
Pico Cristóbal Colón 5775
Parque Nacional Sierra Nevada de Santa Marta
Barranquilla
Cartagena
Calamar
Valledupar
Plato
Sincelejo
El Banco
Mompós
Montería
Golfo de Morrosquillo

Trujillo
Valera
Barinas
San Fernando de Apure
Valle de la Pascua
El Tigre
Ciudad Guayana
Ciudad Bolívar
Upata
El Callao
El Dorado
La Paragua

MISQUITIA
Laguna Caratasca
Cayos Miskitos
Isla de Providencia (Col.)
Isla de San Andrés (Col.)
Puerto Cabezas
Prinzapolka
Pta de Perlas
Is del Maíz (Corn Is) (Nic.)
Bluefields
Costa de Mosquitos
Lago de Nicaragua

AGUA
Siquia
Mico
Rama
Grande

COSTA RICA
San José
Cartago
Alajuela
Limón
G. de Nicoya
Pen. de Osa
Golfo de Chiriquí
Isla Coiba (Col.)
I. de Malpelo (Col.)

PANAMA
David
Santiago
Chitré
Las Tablas
Colón
Panamá
Panama Canal
Bocas del Toro
La Chorrera
Golfo de los Mosquitos
Golfo del Darién
Golfo de Panamá
Punta Mariato
Península de Azuero
Pta Mala

COLOMBIA

Turbo
La Palma
Cabo Corrientes
Quibdó
Medellín
Manizales
Pereira
Cartago
Armenia
Tuluá
Buga
Palmira
Cali
Buenaventura
Popayán
Tumaco
Parque Nacional de Darién
Parque Nacional Paramillo
Bucaramanga
Barrancabermeja
Yarumal
Caucasia
Socorro
Tunja
Honda
Ibagué
Bogotá
Villavicencio
Neiva
Florencia
Cúcuta
San Cristóbal
Pamplona
San Fernando
Puerto Carreño
Puerto Ayacucho
San José del Guaviare
Puerto Inírida

Serra Pacaraima
La Gran Sabana
Serra Parima

1:14M

KM 700 | MILES
600 | 400
500 | 300
400 | 200
300
200 | 100
100
0 | 0

© Collins

NORTH
AMERICA

CARIBBEAN SEA

ATLANTIC

OCEAN

Punta
Gallinas

Golfo
del
Darién

G. de
Venezuela

Isla de
Margarita

Cabo Corrientes

L. de
Maracaibo

Orinoco
Delta

Waini Point

I. de Malpelo

Cordillera Occidental
Cordillera Central
Cordillera Oriental

Llanos

Mela

Guaviare

Orinoco

Cerro Yavi
2285

La Gran
Sabana

Sa Pacaraima

Essequibo

Moroni

Pointe Isère

Cabo Orange

Ilha de Maracá

Cotopaxi
5896

Chimborazo
6310

Caquetá

Putumayo

Japurá

Amazon

Marañón

Golfo de
Guayaquil

Ucayali

Juruá

Negro

Branco

Represa
de Balbina

Amazon

Tapajós

Iriri

Mouths of
the Amazon

I. de
Marajó

Tocantins

Equator

Baía de São Marcos

Ponta do
Calcanhar

S  E  L  V  A  S

Purús

Madeira

Xingu

Teles Pires

Arinos

Represa
Tucuruí

Tocantins

Parnaíba

ANDES

Cordillera Central

Nevado de
Huascaran
6768

Cordillera Oriental

Bahía de
Pisco

Cordillera Occidental

Beni

Guaporé

Lago de
San Luis

San Miguel

Juruena

Araguaia

Tocantins

São Francisco

Chapada Diamantina

Cabo Santo
Antônio

Lago Titicaca

Yungas

Altiplano

L. de
Poopó

Bañados
del
Izozog

Velhas

Ponta da Baleia

Pta Tetas

Desierto de Atacama

Gran Chaco

Pilcomayo

Teuco

Paranaíba

Grande

Paraná

Paranapanema

Cabo de
São Tomé

Tropic of Capricorn

Islas de los
Desventurados

Pta Ballena

Pta Morro

Cerro Bonete
6872

Iguaçu
Falls

Uruguay

Ilha de
São Sebastião

Juan Fernandez
Islands

Aconcagua
6960

Salinas
Grandes

Desaguadero

Salado

Sierras de Córdoba

Paraná

PAMPAS

Lagoa dos Patos

Lagoa Mirim

Río de la Plata

PACIFIC

Colorado

Rio de la Plata

ATLANTIC

OCEAN

Pta Galera

Negro

Bahía Blanca

OCEAN

Golfo San Matías

Península Valdés

Isla de
Chiloé

Patagonia

Archipiélago de
los Chonos

Golfo de  San Jorge

Golfo de Penas

Pta Medanosa

L. San Martín

L.
Argentino

Bahía
Grande

Falkland Islands

West
Falkland

East
Falkland

South Georgia

Est. de
Magallanes

Tierra del
Fuego

I. de los
Estados

Cape Horn

METRES | FEET
5000 | 16409
3000 | 9843
2000 | 6562
1000 | 3281
500 | 1640
200 | 656

SEA | LEVEL
200 | 656
3000 | 9843
5000 | 16409
6000 | 19686

1:30M

KM | MILES
1800
1500 | 900
1200
900 | 600
600 | 300
300
0 | 0

Sinusoidal Projection

© Colli

NORTH
AMERICA

*CARIBBEAN SEA*

**Barranquilla**
Cartagena ○
**Maracaibo**
**Valencia** ○ **Caracas** Cumaná ○
Monteria ○ **Barquisimeto**

*I. de Malpelo*
(Col.)

**Medellín** ○
Manizales ○ **Bogotá** ■
Buenaventura ○ **Cali** ○

**COLOMBIA**

Florencia ○

*Orinoco* Ciudad Guayana ○

**VENEZUELA**

*Orinoco*

**G U Y A N A**
Georgetown ●
Paramaribo ■
**SURINAME** FRENCH
GUIANA
Cayenne ○

Boa Vista ○

*ATLANTIC*

*OCEAN*

Portoviejo ○ **Quito** ■
**ECUADOR**
**Guayaquil** ○ Cuenca ○
Iquitos ○
*Marañón*
Piura ○
Chiclayo ○
Trujillo ○ Pucallpa ○

**PERU**

Callao ○ **Lima** ■
Ica ○ Ayacucho ○
Arequipa ○ Juliaca ○
*Lago Titicaca*
**La Paz** ■
Arica ○ Cochabamba ○
Iquique ○ **Sucre** ■
Potosí ○
Calama ○ Tarija ○
Antofagasta ○

*Negro*
*Amazon*
*Amazon*
**Manaus** ○
Itaituba ○
*Purus*
**B**
Pôrto Velho ○
Rio Branco ○ Ariquemes ○

*Mouths of
the Amazon*
Equator
**Belém** ○
São Luís ○
Altamira ○
Parnaíba ○
Bacabal ○ **Fortaleza**
Maraba ○ Codó ○ **Teresina** ○
Imperatriz ○ Natal
Araguaína ○ João
Pessoa
**Recife**
Maceió ○

**R A Z I L**

Trinidad ○
Cáceres ○ Cuiabá ○
**BOLIVIA**
Santa Cruz ○

*São Francisco*
**Brasília** ■
**Goiânia** ○
Espinosa ○
Teófilo
Otôni ○
**Salvador**

Aracaju ○

Uberaba ○ Vitória ○
Campo Grande ○ Aracatuba ○ **Belo Horizonte** ○
Dourados ○ Campos ○
**PARAGUAY** Campinas ○ **Nova
Iguaçu**
San Salvador Campinas ○ **São Paulo** **Rio de Janeiro** Tropic of Capricorn
de Jujuy San Pedro ○ Santos ○
**Asunción** ■ **Curitiba** ○
San Miguel Foz do Iguaçu ○
de Tucumán ○ Florianopolis ○
Catamarca ○ Corrientes ○ Posadas ○
Santa Maria ○
La Serena ○ **Córdoba** ○ Uruguaiana ○ **Porto
Alegre**
San Juan ○ Santa Fé ○ Tacuarembó ○
Valparaíso ○ Mendoza ○ Paraná ○ Rio Grande ○
*Aconcagua* **URUGUAY**
6960
**Santiago** ■ Rosario ○ Rocha ○
**Buenos Aires** ■
Talca ○ La Plata ○ **Montevideo** ■
Concepción ○ Santa Rosa ○
Temuco ○ Bahía Blanca ○ Mar del Plata ○
Neuquén ○

**C**
**H**
**I**
**L**
**E**

**A**
**R**
**G**
**E**
**N**
**T**
**I**
**N**
**A**

*Islas de los
Desventurados*
(Chile)

*Juan Fernandez
Islands*
(Chile)

*P A C I F I C*

*O C E A N*

*ATLANTIC*

*OCEAN*

Puerto Montt ○
*Isla de
Chiloé*
Esquel ○
*Archipiélago de
los Chonos*
Cochrane ○
Viedma ○
Rawson ○

*Patagonia*

Comodoro
Rivadavia ○
Deseado ○
*Pta Medanosa*

Puerto Natales ○
Río Gallegos ○
Punta Arenas ○
*Est. de
Magallanes*
*Tierra del
Fuego*
Ushuaia ○

*Cape Horn*

Falkland Islands
(U.K.)
Stanley ○

South Georgia (U.K.)

**1:30M**

KM  MILES
1800

1500  900

1200

900  600

600

300  300

0  0

Sinusoidal Projection

© Collins

GALAPAGOS IS
(Ecuador)
at the same scale

Lambert Azimuthal Equal Area Projection

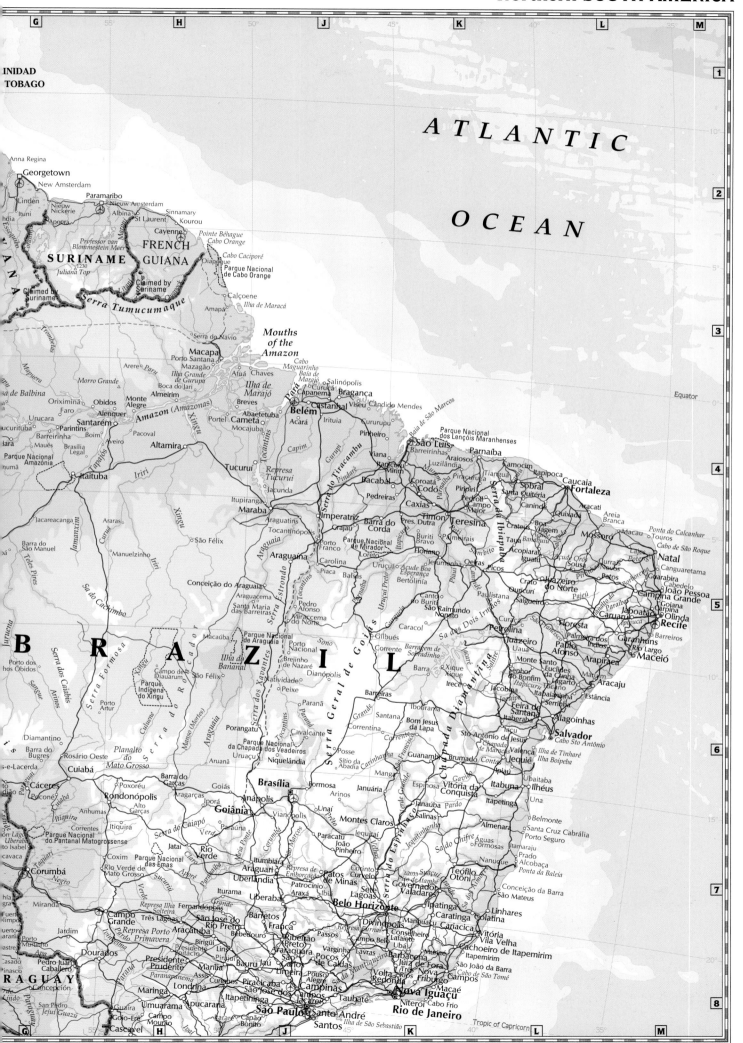

ATLANTIC

OCEAN

1:15M

| KM | MILES |
|---|---|
| | 600 |
| 900 | |
| | 450 |
| 750 | |
| | 300 |
| 600 | |
| | |
| 450 | |
| | 150 |
| 300 | |
| 150 | |
| 0 | 0 |

© Collins

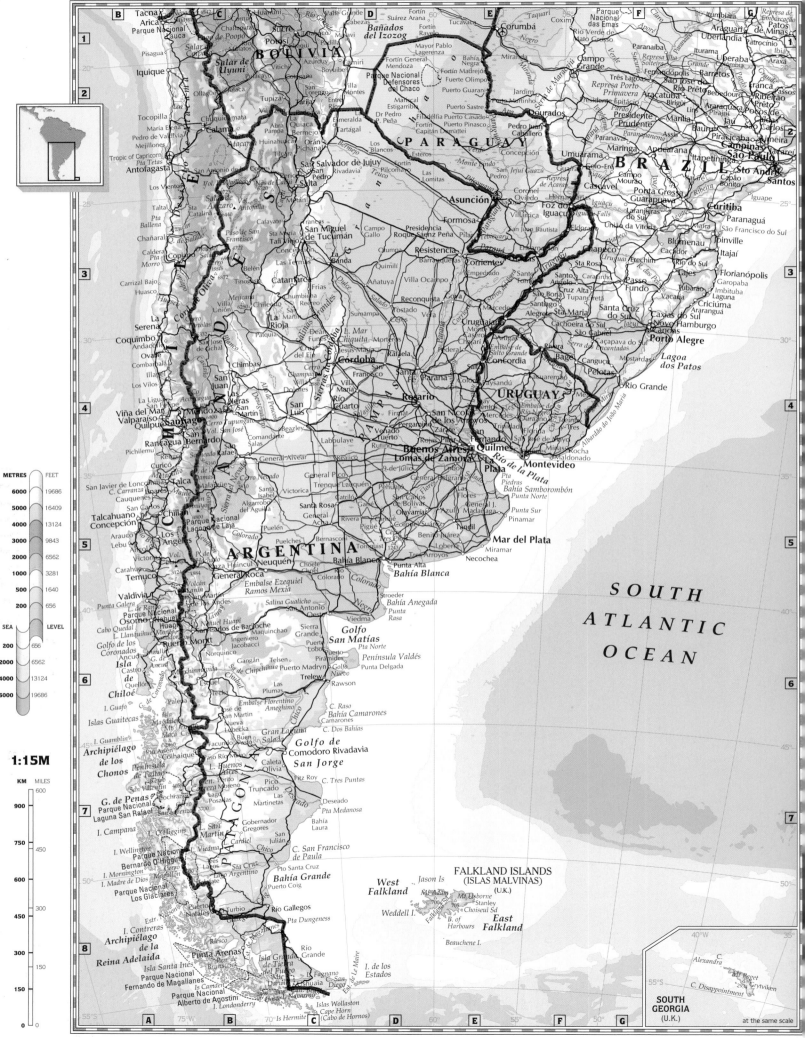

Lambert Azimuthal Equal Area Projection

© Collins

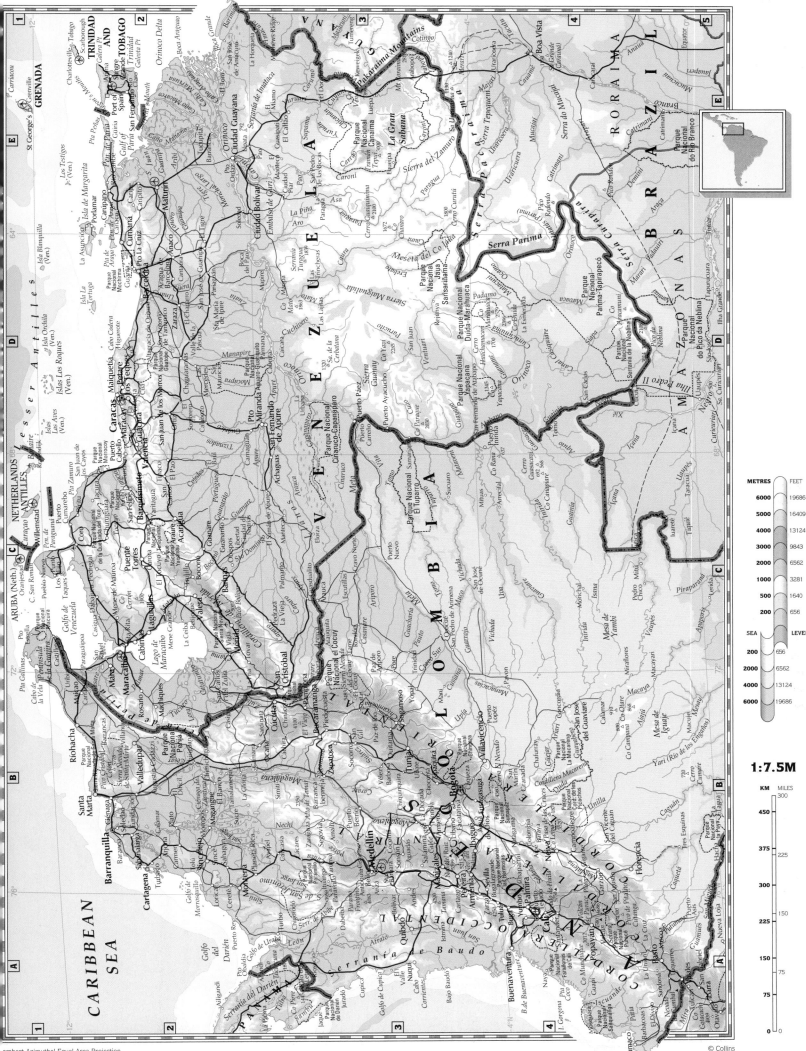

© Collins

1:7.5M

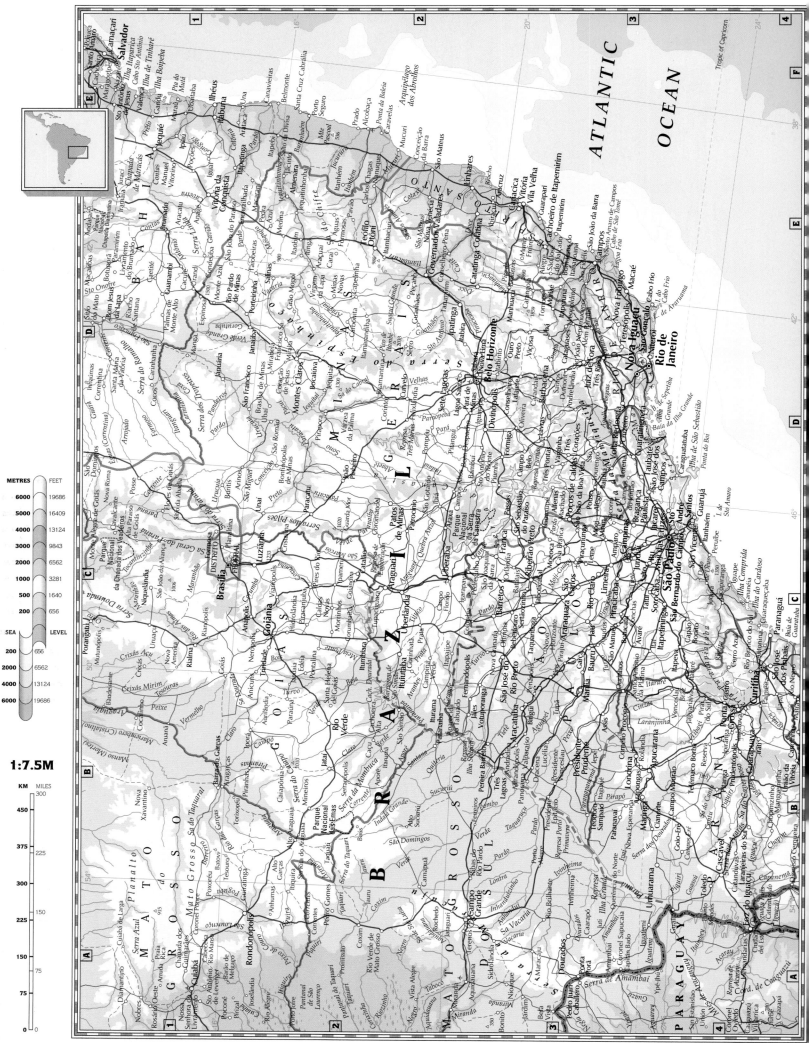

1:7.5M

Lambert Azimuthal Equal Area Projection

© Collins

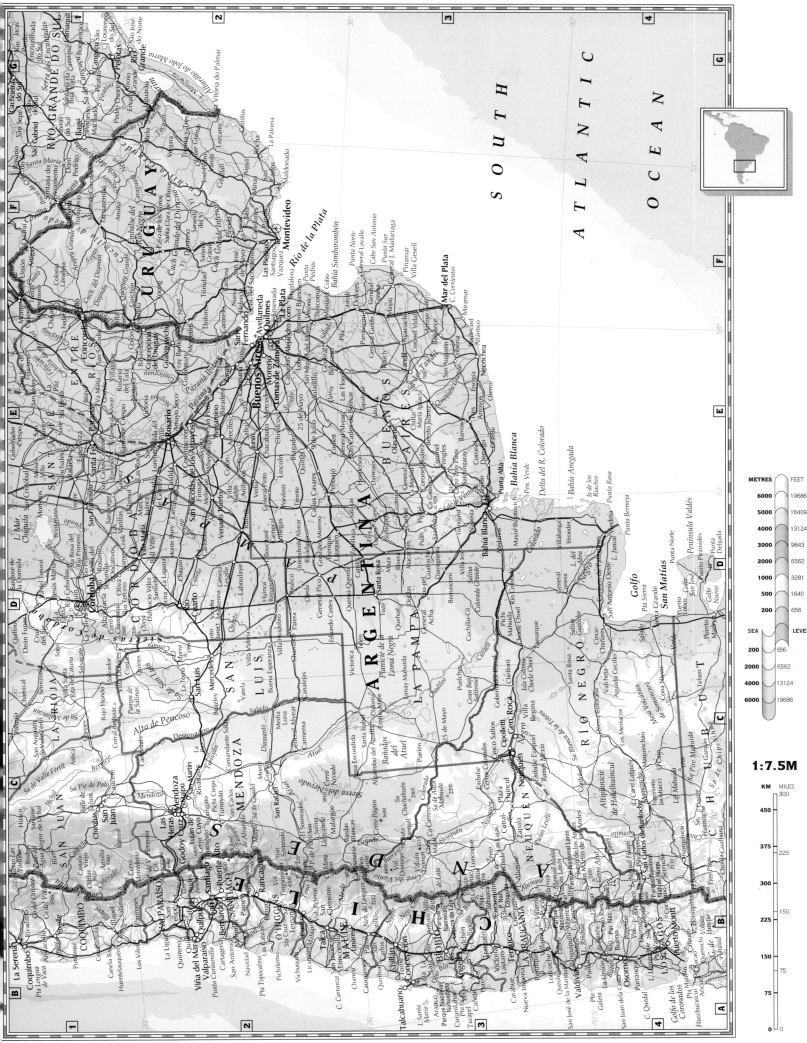

1:7.5M

| METRES | | FEET |
|---|---|---|
| 6000 | | 19686 |
| 5000 | | 16409 |
| 4000 | | 13124 |
| 3000 | | 9843 |
| 2000 | | 6562 |
| 1000 | | 3281 |
| 500 | | 1640 |
| 200 | | 656 |
| SEA | | LEVEL |
| 200 | | 656 |
| 2000 | | 6562 |
| 4000 | | 13124 |
| 6000 | | 19686 |

| KM | MILES |
|---|---|
| | 300 |
| 450 | |
| | 225 |
| 375 | |
| 300 | 150 |
| 225 | |
| | 75 |
| 150 | |
| 75 | |
| 0 | 0 |

Lambert Azimuthal Equal Area Projection

© Collins

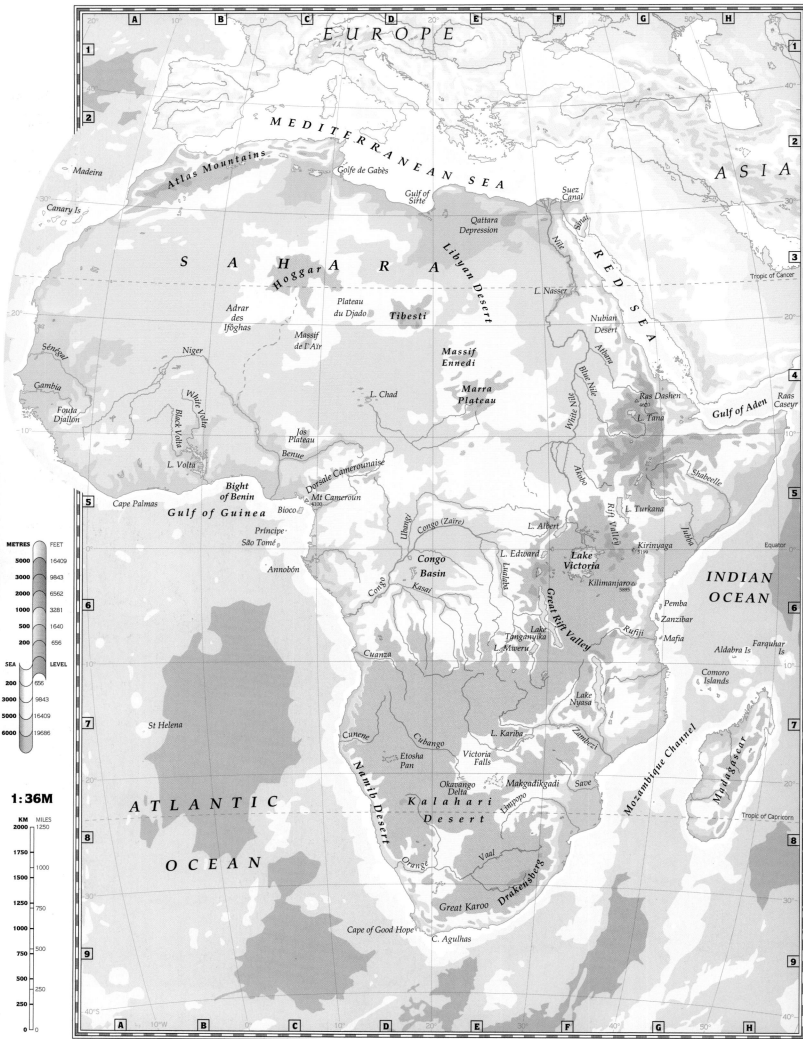

**METRES** **FEET**
5000 — 16409
3000 — 9843
2000 — 6562
1000 — 3281
500 — 1640
200 — 656

**SEA** **LEVEL**
200 — 656
3000 — 9843
5000 — 16409
6000 — 19686

**1 : 36M**

**KM** **MILES**
2000 — 1250
1750 — 
1500 — 1000
1250 — 750
1000 — 
750 — 500
500 — 250
250 — 
0 — 0

Lambert Azimuthal Equal Area Projection

© Collir

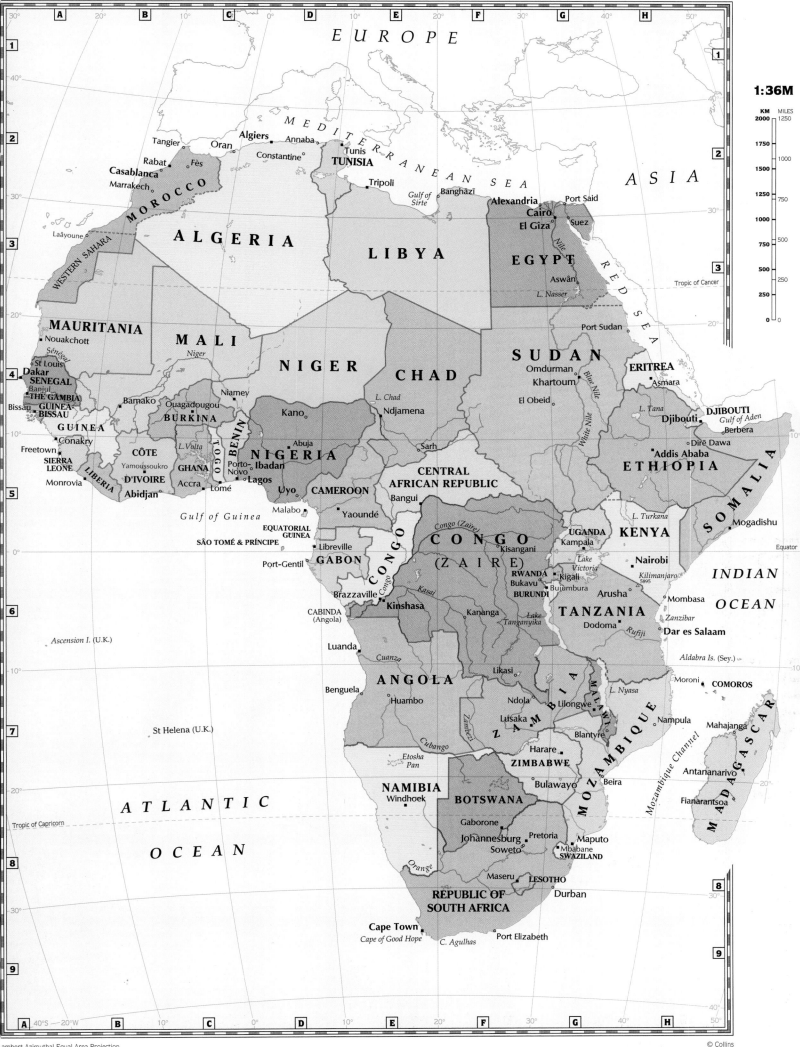

1:36M

KM MILES
2000 — 1250
1750
— 1000
1500
1250 — 750
1000
750 — 500
500 — 250
250
0 — 0

EUROPE

ASIA

MEDITERRANEAN SEA

Tangier  Oran  Algiers  Annaba
Rabat  Fès  Constantine  Tunis
Casablanca  TUNISIA
Marrakech  Tripoli  Banghāzī  Gulf of Sirte
MOROCCO  Alexandria  Port Said
Cairo  Suez
El Gîza
Laâyoune
WESTERN SAHARA  ALGERIA  LIBYA  EGYPT
RED SEA
Aswân  Tropic of Cancer
L. Nasser

MAURITANIA  MALI
Nouakchott  Niger
Sénégal  NIGER  CHAD  SUDAN  Port Sudan  ERITREA
St Louis  SENEGAL  Bamako  Niamey  L. Chad  Omdurman  Asmara
Dakar  THE GAMBIA  Ouagadougou  Kano  Ndjamena  Khartoum  Blue Nile  L. Tana
Banjul  GUINEA-  BURKINA  El Obeid  DJIBOUTI
Bissau  BISSAU  BENIN  Abuja  Djibouti  Gulf of Aden
GUINEA  TOGO  NIGERIA  Sarh  Berbera
Freetown  Conakry  CÔTE  L.Volta  Ibadan  CENTRAL  White Nile  Dirē Dawa
SIERRA  Yamoussoukro  GHANA  Porto-  Lagos  AFRICAN REPUBLIC  Addis Ababa  ETHIOPIA
LEONE  LIBERIA  D'IVOIRE  Novo  Uyo  CAMEROON  Bangui
Monrovia  Abidjan  Accra  Lomé  Malabo  Yaoundé  SOMALIA
Gulf of Guinea  EQUATORIAL  L. Turkana  KENYA
GUINEA  CONGO  Congo (Zaire)  UGANDA  Mogadishu
SÃO TOMÉ & PRÍNCIPE  Libreville  Kisangani  Kampala  Equator
Equator  GABON  CONGO  Lake  Nairobi
Port-Gentil  (ZAIRE)  Victoria  INDIAN
Congo  RWANDA  Kigali  Kilimanjaro  OCEAN
Brazzaville  Bukavu  5895
CABINDA  Kinshasa  BURUNDI  Bujumbura  Arusha
(Angola)  Kasai  Kananga  Lake  TANZANIA  Mombasa
Luanda  Tanganyika  Dodoma  Zanzibar  Dar es Salaam
Ascension I. (U.K.)  Cuanza  Rufiji  Aldabra Is. (Sey.)
ANGOLA  Likasi  Moroni  COMOROS
St Helena (U.K.)  Benguela  L. Nyasa  Nampula  Mahajanga
Huambo  Ndola  Lilongwe  MADAGASCAR
ZAMBIA  MALAWI  Antananarivo
Cubango  Lusaka  Blantyre  MOZAMBIQUE
Etosha  Zambezi  Harare  Mozambique Channel
Pan  ZIMBABWE  Beira  Fianarantsoa
NAMIBIA  Bulawayo
Windhoek  BOTSWANA
ATLANTIC  Gaborone
Tropic of Capricorn  Johannesburg  Pretoria  Maputo
OCEAN  Soweto  Mbabane  SWAZILAND
Orange  Maseru  LESOTHO
REPUBLIC OF  Durban
SOUTH AFRICA
Cape Town
Cape of Good Hope  C. Agulhas  Port Elizabeth

Lambert Azimuthal Equal Area Projection

© Collins

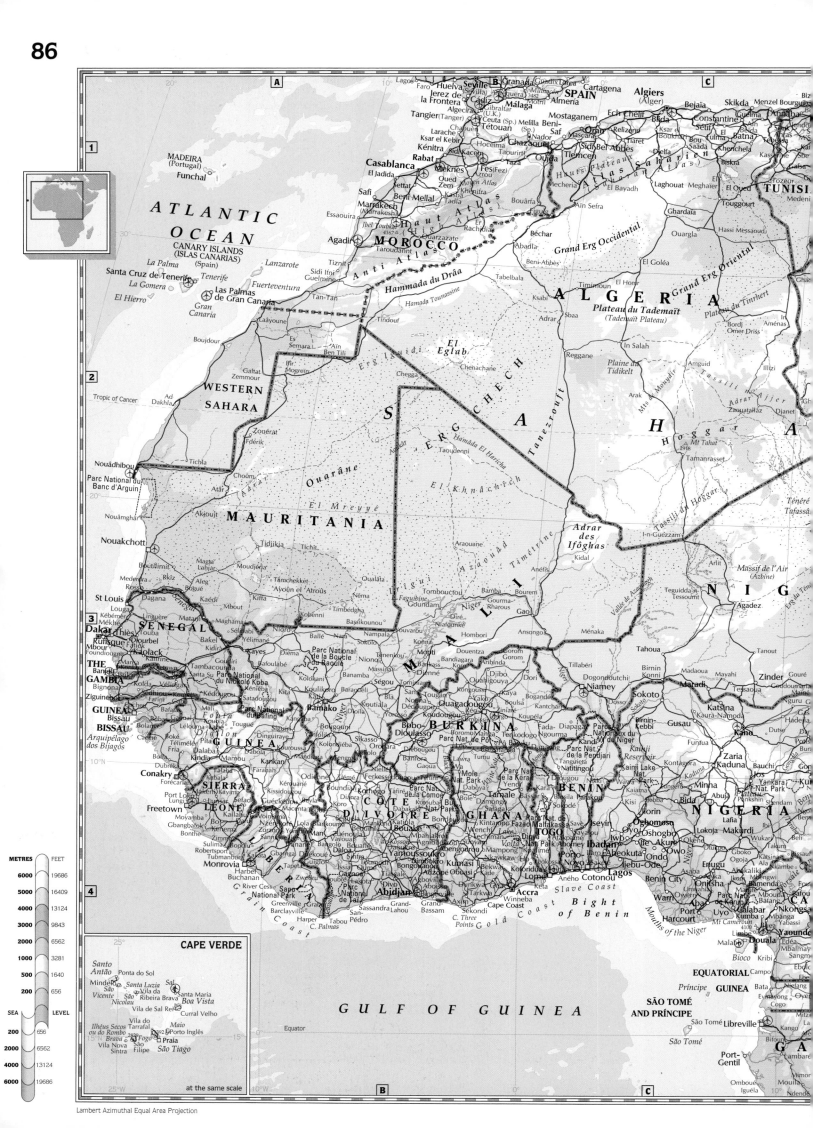

ATLANTIC OCEAN

MADEIRA (Portugal)
Funchal

CANARY ISLANDS (ISLAS CANARIAS) (Spain)
La Palma
Santa Cruz de Tenerife
La Gomera    Tenerife
El Hierro    Gran Canaria
Las Palmas de Gran Canaria
Lanzarote
Fuerteventura

SPAIN
Huelva  Seville (Sevilla)  Granada  Guadix  Lorca  Cartagena
Faro  Jerez de la Frontera  Antequera  Motril  Almería
Algeciras  Cádiz  Málaga
Gibraltar (U.K.)  Ceuta (Sp.)
Tangier (Tanger)  Tétouan  Melilla (Sp.)
Larache  Ksar el Kebir  Nador
Kénitra  Chauen  Taourirt
Rabat  Meknes  Fes (Fez)  Taza  Oujda
Casablanca  El Jadida  Oued Zem  Kasba Tadla  Khenifra
Safi  Beni Mellal  Bouârfa
Essaouira  Marrakech (Marrakesh)
Agadir  Jbel Toubkal 4167  Ouarzazate  Er Rachidia
Taroudannt  Tiznit  Guelmine  Tan-Tan
Sidi Ifni
Laâyoune

ALGIERS (Alger)  Bejaïa  Skikda  Menzel Bourguiba  Bizerte
Mostaganem  Ech Cheliff  Blida  Constantine  Guelma  Annaba
Oran  Relizane  Tiaret  Bou Saâda  Sétif  Batna  Khenchela
Sidi Bel Abbès  Boukhari  El Eulma  Kasserine  Gafsa
Tlemcen  Delfa  Biskra  Tébessa
TUNISIA  Medenine
Hauts Plateaux  Atlas Saharien (Saharan Atlas)
Mecheria  El Bayadh  Laghouat  Meghaïer  El Oued  Touggourt
Aïn Sefra  Ghardaïa  Ouargla  Hassi Messaoud
Béchar  Grand Erg Occidental  El Goléa  Ghadamès
Abadla  Beni-Abbès  Ksabi  Timimoun  In Salah  Grand Erg Oriental
Bordj Omer Driss  In Aménas  Illizi

ALGERIA
Plateau du Tademaït (Tademaït Plateau)
Plaine du Tidikelt
Adrar  Reggane  Arak  Amguid
Tabelbala  Chenachane  Aoulef  Tassili n' Ajjer  Djanet
Tindouf  Taoudenni
El Eglab
Erg Iguidi
Erg Chech  S  A  H  A  R  A
El Khnâchîch
Tanezrouft  Hoggar  Mt Tahat 2918
Mts de Mouydir  Tamanrasset  Hoggar  Tassili du Hoggar
I-n-Guezzam  Adrar des Ifôghas
In Salah

WESTERN SAHARA
Tropic of Cancer
Ad Dakhla
Boujdour
Es Semara  Aïn Ben Tili
Bir Mogrein
Galtat Zemmour

MAURITANIA
Nouâdhibou
Parc National du Banc d'Arguin
Nouâmghar
Akjoujt
Nouakchott
Boutilimit
Atâr  Choûm  Tichla
Tidjikja  Tichît
El Mreyyé  Araouane
Ouarâne  Hamâda El Haricha
Oualâta  El Djouf
Néma  Tombouctou
Kidal  Anéfis  Vallée de Azaouagh

NIGER
Arlit
Massif de l'Aïr (Azbine)
Ténéré
Tafassâsset
Agadez
Teguidda-n-Tessoumt

MALI
Aguelhok  Kidal
Bamba  Bourem  Gao
Gourma Rharous  Ménaka
Niger  Ansongo
Gourma
Goundam  Diré  Niafounké  Hombori
Nampala  Douentza  Gossi  Gorom Gorom
Nioro  Sokolo  Mopti  Bandiagara  Dori  Tillabéri
Nara  Niono  Ké-Macina  Djenné  Ouahigouya  Dogondoutchi  Niamey
Nioro  Diéma  Nampala  Massina  Ségou  San  Tominian  Yako  Bogandé  Kantchari  Dosso
Bassikounou  Banamba  Koutiala  Tougan  Boulsa  Kaya  Koupéla
Balé  Sikasso  Dédougou  Ouagadougou  Koudougou  Fada-Ngourma  Diapaga
Bafoulabé  Kita  Kati  Dioïla  Yorosso  Bobo-Dioulasso  Boromo  Manga  Tenkodogo  Kandi
Kayes  Bamako  Koulikoro  Bougouni  San  Koutiala
Diamou  Kolokani  Banfora  Gaoua  Tumu  Diébougou

SENEGAL
St Louis  Dagana  Richard-Toll
Louga  Matam
Kébémèr  Linguère  Ouro Sogui
Mékhé  Bakel
Dakar  Thiès  Diourbel  Maghama
Rufisque  Fatick  Kaolack  Kaffrine  Sélibabi  Yélimané
Mbour  Foundiougne  Kidira  Diéma
Fatick  Birkelane  Nioro  Kayes

THE GAMBIA
Banjul  Brikama
Bignona  Kolda  Vélingara
Ziguinchor  Kédougou  Satadougou

GUINEA-BISSAU
Bissau
Arquipélago dos Bijagós
Bafatá  Gabú
Bolama  Boké

GUINEA
Fria  Boffa  Télimélé  Pita  Labé  Koundara  Mali
Dubréka  Dalaba  Dabola  Tougué  Siguiri
Conakry  Kindia  Mamou  Dinguiraye
Forécariah  Faranah  Kouroussa  Kankan
Kissidougou  Dabola  Kérouané  Mandiana  Siguiri
Guéckédou  Macenta  Kissidougou  Beyla  Odienné

SIERRA LEONE
Port Loko  Lungi  Makeni  Kabala
Freetown  Koidu  Kailahun
Moyamba  Bo  Kenema
Bonthe  Sefadu  Pendembu

LIBERIA
Robertsport  Gbarnga  Voinjama  Ganta  Nzérékoré  Man
Monrovia  Bopolu  Tubmanburg  Sanniquellie  Danané  Touba
Harbel  Buchanan  Zwedru  Bangolo  Guiglo  Duékoué
River Cess  Sapo National Park  Tapeta  Zuénoula
Greenville  Grand Cess  Toulépleu  Daloa
Barclayville  Sassandra  Gagnoa
Harper  Tabou  C. Palmas  San-Pédro  Issia  Divo

CÔTE D'IVOIRE
Séguéla  Mankono  Katiola  Bouaké  Dabakala
Vavoua  Béoumi  Sakassou  M'bahiakro  Bondoukou
Bouaflé  Yamoussoukro  Dimbokro  Abengourou  Agnibilékrou
Sinfra  Oumé  Toumodi  Bongouanou  Abengourou
Gagnoa  Lakota  Adzopé  Aboisso
Tiassalé  Agboville  Bonoua  Grand-Bassam
Abidjan  Dabou  Jacqueville  Grand-Lahou  Axim

BURKINA
Ouahigouya  Djibo  Dori
Ouagadougou  Ziniaré  Koupéla  Bogandé  Kantchari
Koudougou  Tenkodogo  Fada-Ngourma  Diapaga
Bobo-Dioulasso  Boromo  Manga  Pô  Léo  Gaoua
Banfora  Orodara  Diébougou  Parc Nat. de Pô  Parc National du W du Niger
Parc Nat. de la Comoé
Parc Nat. de la Kéran  Parc Nat. de la Pendjari

GHANA
Bolgatanga  Bawku  Navrongo  Gambaga
Wa  Tumu  Walewale  Yendi
Lawra  Bole  Tamale  Bassila
Wenchi  Techiman  Salaga  Kete Krachi  Kpalimé  Atakpamé
Kintampo  Fazao Malfakassa Nat. Park  Sokodé
Sunyani  Mampong  Yeji  Nkwanta  Kara  Bassar
Berekum  Kumasi  Kpandu  Hohoe  Sokodé
Dunkwa  Obuasi  Ho  Kpalimé  Atakpamé
Bekwai  Nkawkaw  Koforidua  Aného  Anfoega
Tarkwa  Kade  Akim Oda  Keta  Lomé
Sekondi  Cape Coast  Accra  Tema  Cotonou
C. Three Points  Gold Coast

TOGO
Mango  Dapaong  Sansanné-Mango
Kara  Niamtougou  Bassar  Kandé
Sokodé  Sotouboua  Atakpamé  Badou
Kpalimé  Notsé  Tabligbo  Aného  Lomé

BENIN
Malanville  Kandi  Banikoara  Parc Nat. du W du Niger
Parc Nat. de la Pendjari  Natitingou  Kouandé  Nikki
Tanguiéta  Djougou  Parakou  Bembèrèkè
Bassila  Savè  Savalou  Dassa-Zoumé
Abomey  Bohicon  Kétou  Pobè
Lokossa  Allada  Porto-Novo  Sakété
Ouidah  Cotonou

NIGERIA
Sokoto  Gusau  Katsina  Kaura-Namoda  Daura  Kano
Argungu  Birnin Kebbi  Funtua  Zaria  Hadejia
Kontagora  Kaduna  Bauchi  Jos  Gombe
Kaiama  Jebba  Minna  Abuja  Plateau Nat. Park  Yankari Nat. Park
Kainji Lake  Kainji Nat. Park  Lafia  Makurdi  Wukari
New Bussa  Ilorin  Keffi  Lokoja  Ogbomosho  Oshogbo  Iwo
Iseyin  Oyo  Ife  Akure  Owo  Kabba  Idah  Ankpa  Enugu
Abeokuta  Ibadan  Ijebu-Ode  Ondo  Benin City  Asaba  Onitsha  Awka  Abakaliki
Lagos  Ado-Ekiti  Sapele  Warri  Aba  Owerri  Umuahia
Badagry  Epe  Ughelli  Port Harcourt  Uyo  Calabar
Mouths of the Niger  Bonny

Slave Coast  Bight of Benin

EQUATORIAL GUINEA
Bata  Mbini
Príncipe  Bioco

SÃO TOMÉ AND PRÍNCIPE
São Tomé

GABON
Libreville  Kango
Port-Gentil  Lambaréné  Ndjolé  Oyem  Bitam
Edéa  Kribi  Ebolowa  Mbalmayo
Yaoundé  Eséka  Akonolinga  Bertoua
Douala  Mbanga  Nkongsamba  Bafia  Bafang
Mt Cameroon 4100  Limbe  Bamenda  Foumban
Bangangté  Bafoussam  Dschang  Mamfé
Kumba  Tiko  Buea

GULF OF GUINEA

Equator

CAPE VERDE
Santo Antão  Ponta do Sol  Sal
Mindelo  Santa Luzia  Vila da
São Vicente  São Nicolau  Ribeira Brava  Boa Vista
Santa Maria
Vila de Sal Rei
Curral Velho
Ilhéus Secos ou do Rombo  Tarrafal  Maio
Brava  Fogo 2829  Porto Inglês
Vila Nova  São Filipe  Praia  São Tiago
Sintra

at the same scale

Lambert Azimuthal Equal Area Projection

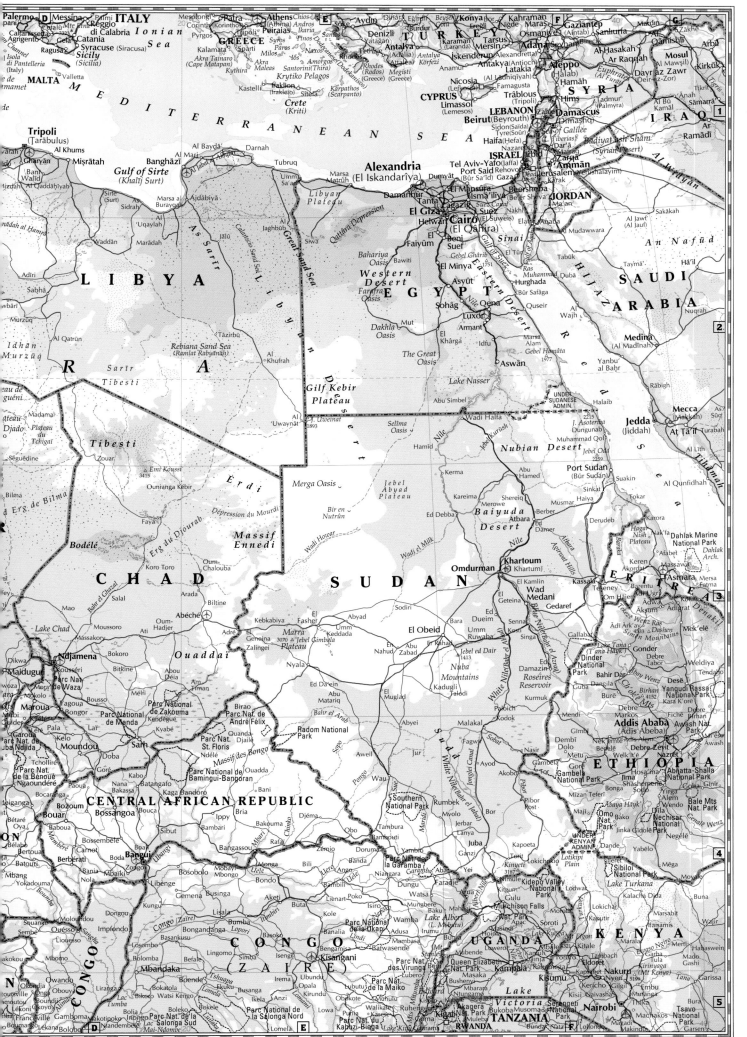

© Collins

1:16M

| KM | MILES |
|---|---|
| 1000 | 600 |
| | 500 |
| 800 | 400 |
| 600 | 300 |
| 400 | 200 |
| 200 | 100 |
| 0 | 0 |

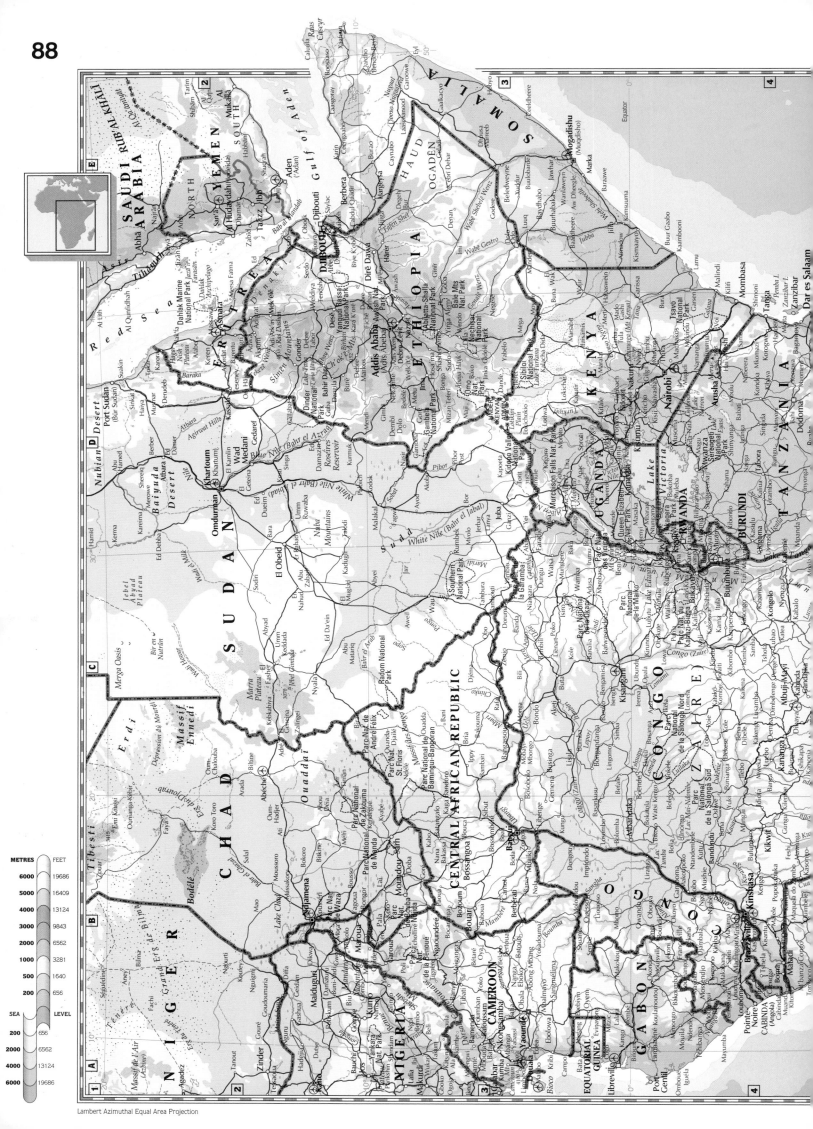

Lambert Azimuthal Equal Area Projection

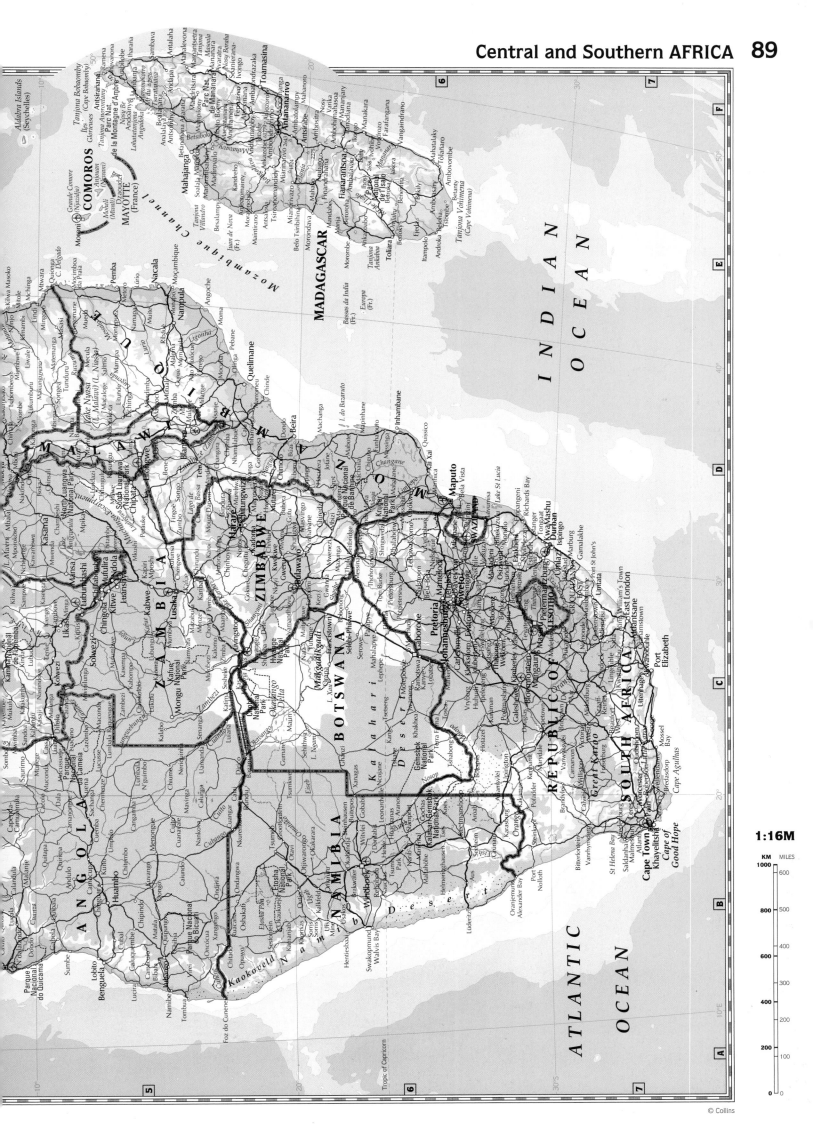

ATLANTIC

OCEAN

| METRES | | FEET |
|--------|--|------|
| 6000 | | 19686 |
| 5000 | | 16409 |
| 4000 | | 13124 |
| 3000 | | 9843 |
| 2000 | | 6562 |
| 1000 | | 3281 |
| 500 | | 1640 |
| 200 | | 656 |
| SEA | | LEVEL |
| 200 | | 656 |
| 2000 | | 6562 |
| 4000 | | 13124 |
| 6000 | | 19686 |

Lambert Azimuthal Equal Area Projection

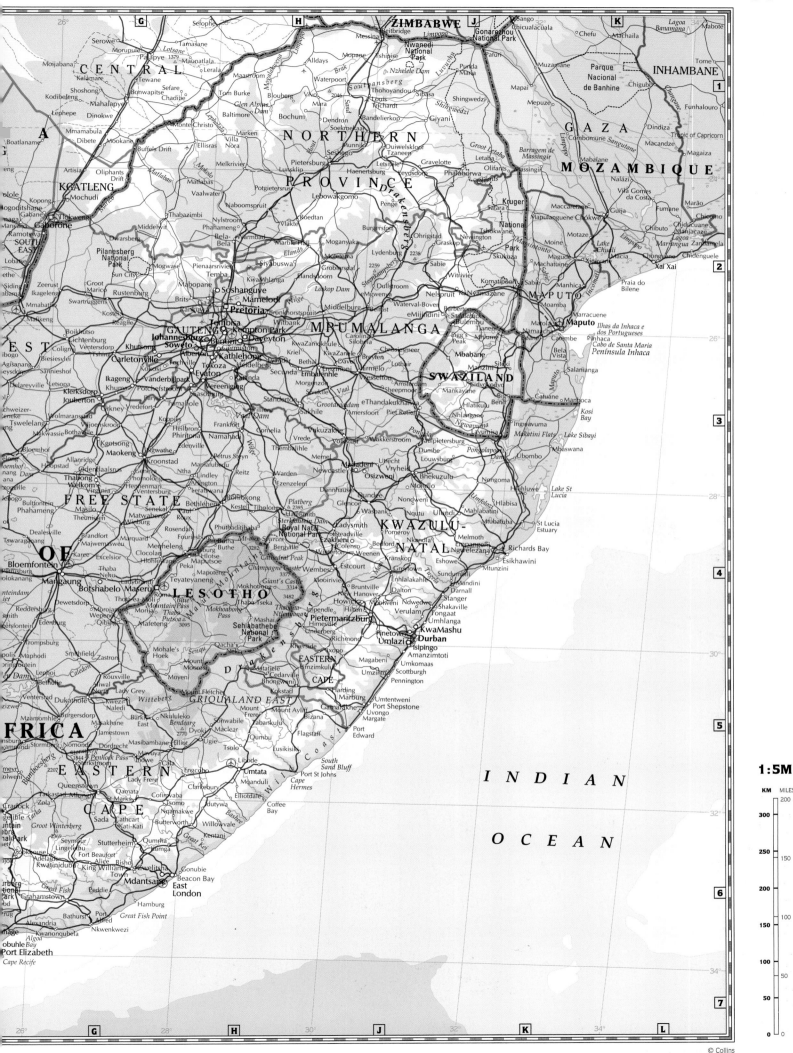

1:5M

KM MILES
300
250
200
150
100
50
0

200
150
100
50
0

© Collins

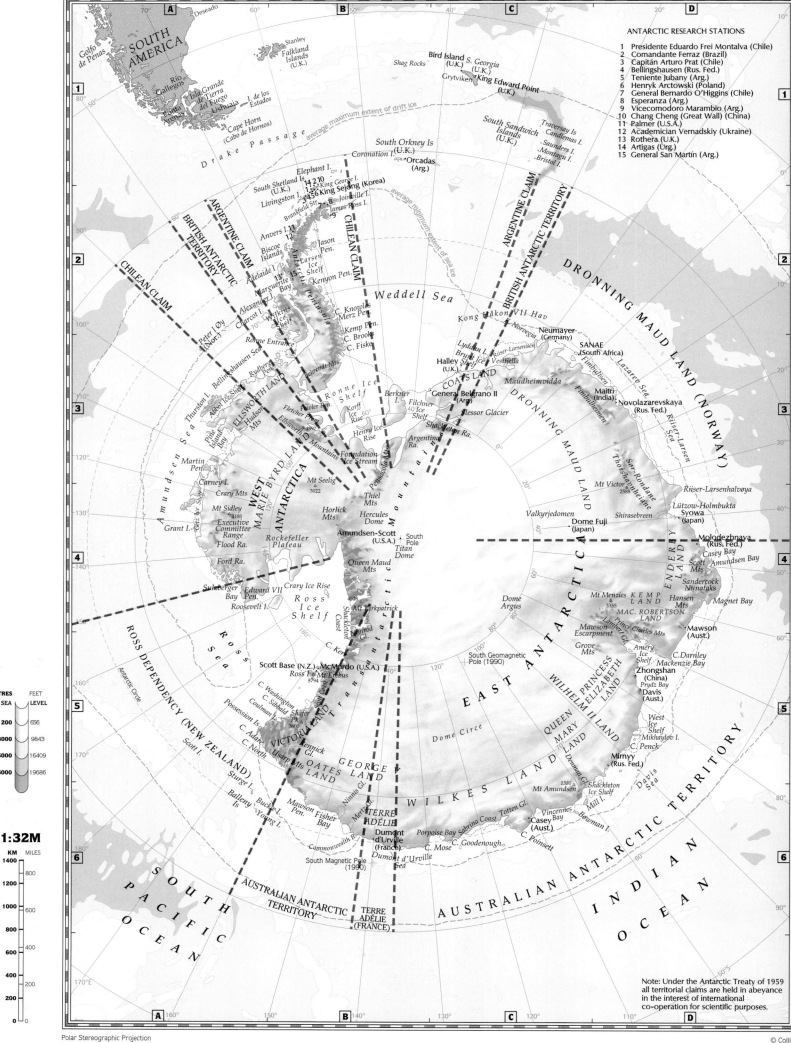

ANTARCTIC RESEARCH STATIONS

1 Presidente Eduardo Frei Montalva (Chile)
2 Comandante Ferraz (Brazil)
3 Capitán Arturo Prat (Chile)
4 Bellingshausen (Rus. Fed.)
5 Teniente Jubany (Arg.)
6 Henryk Arctowski (Poland)
7 General Bernardo O'Higgins (Chile)
8 Esperanza (Arg.)
9 Vicecomodoro Marambio (Arg.)
10 Chang Cheng (Great Wall) (China)
11 Palmer (U.S.A.)
12 Academician Vernadskiy (Ukraine)
13 Rothera (U.K.)
14 Artigas (Urg.)
15 General San Martín (Arg.)

Note: Under the Antarctic Treaty of 1959 all territorial claims are held in abeyance in the interest of international co-operation for scientific purposes.

1:32M

| METRES | FEET |
| --- | --- |
| SEA | LEVEL |
| 200 | 656 |
| 3000 | 9843 |
| 5000 | 16409 |
| 6000 | 19686 |

| KM | MILES |
| --- | --- |
| 1400 | 800 |
| 1200 | |
| 1000 | 600 |
| 800 | 400 |
| 600 | |
| 400 | 200 |
| 200 | |
| 0 | 0 |

Polar Stereographic Projection

© Collins

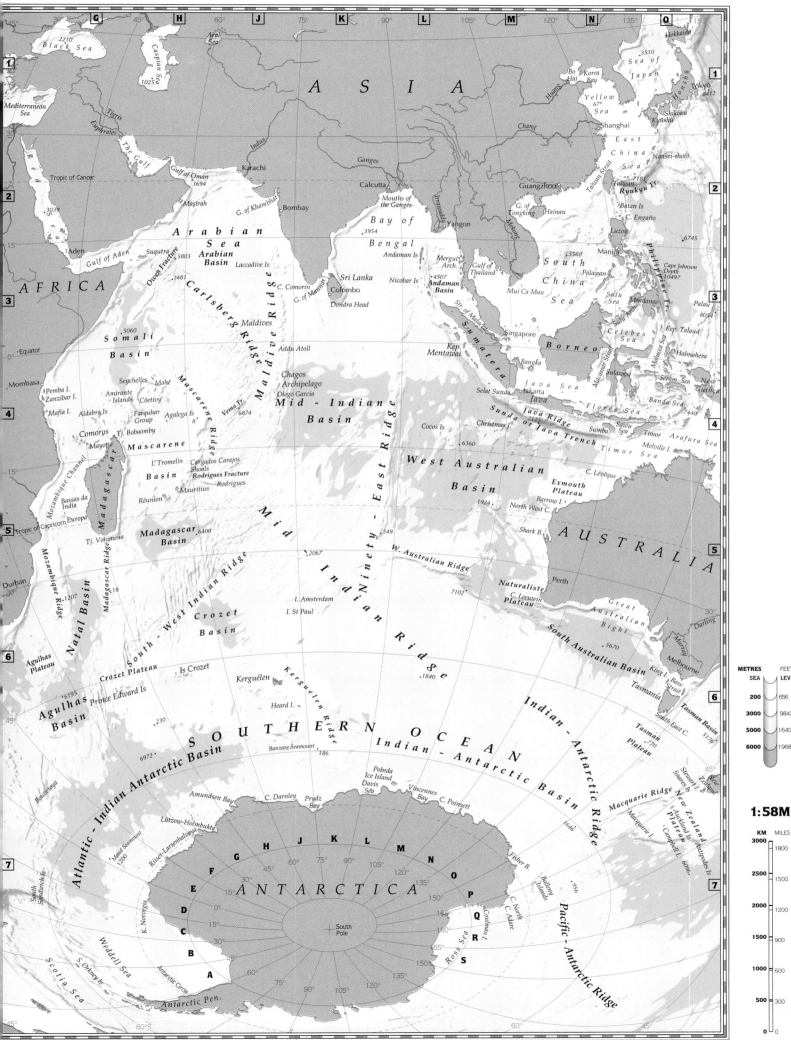

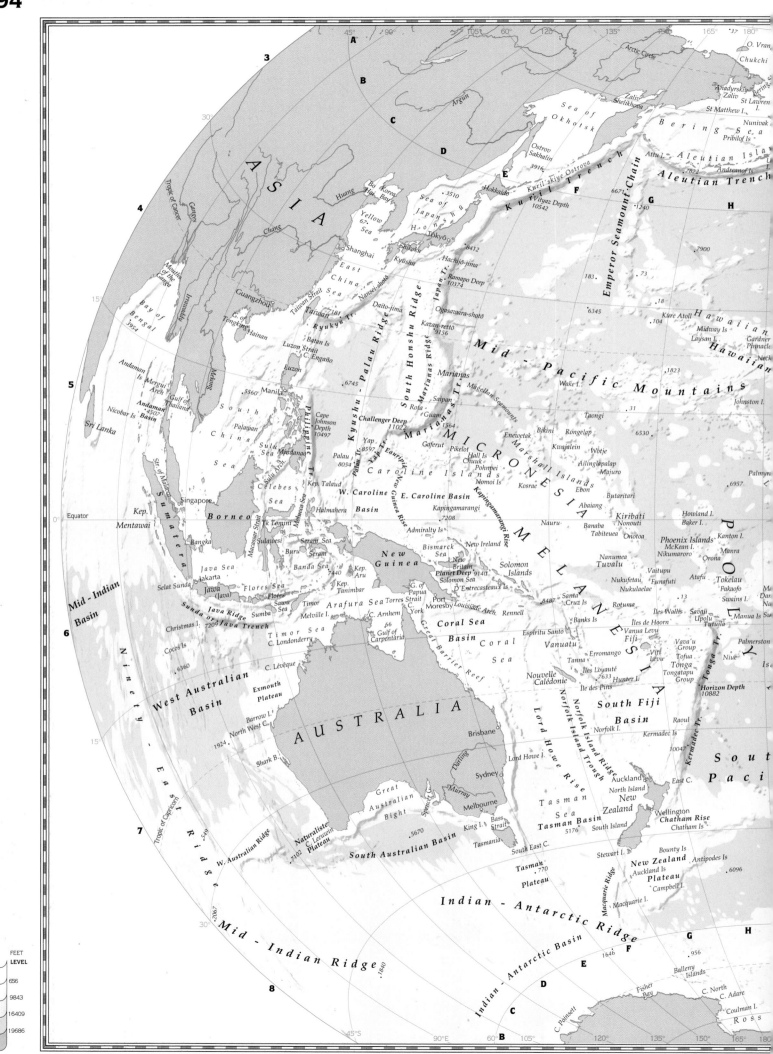

A B C D E F G H

**ASIA**

Arctic Circle

O. Vran
Chukchi

Anadyrskiy
Zaliv
Zaliv
Shelikhova
St Lawren
St Matthew I.
Nunivak

Argun

Sea of
Okhotsk
*Bering Sea*
Pribilof Is

Ostrov
Sakhalin
.3916

Atatu Aleutian Isla
.7822 Andreanof Is

**Aleutian Trench**

Tropic of Cancer

Ganges

Huang
Bo Korea
Hai Bay
Yellow
67 Sea

Sea
of
Japan sha
.3510
Hokkaido
Kuril'skiye Ostrova
Vityaz Depth
10542

Kuril Trench

.6671

.1240

Emperor Seamount Chain

Chang

Honshu

Tokyo

.8412

Ramapo Deep
10374

Japan Tr.

.183 .73

.7900

Shanghai

East
China
Sea

Kyushu

Shikoku

Hachijo-jima

Mouths
of the
Ganges

Irrawaddy

Bay
of
Bengal
.3954

Guangzhou

G. of
Tongking

Hainan

Taiwan Strait

Taiwan

Nansei-shoto

Daito-jima

Ogasawara-shoto

.6345

Kure Atoll *Hawaiian*
.104 Midway Is
Laysan I. Gardner
Pinnacle
Neck

**Mid - Pacific Mountains**

*Hawaiian*

Mekong

Andaman
Is Mergui
Arch
Gulf of
Thailand

.7181

Batan Is
Luzon Strait
C. Engaño

Luzon

Ryukyu Tr.

South Honshu Ridge

Kazan-retto
.9156

.1823

Wake I.

Marianas

Magellan Seamounts

Johnston I.

Nicobar Is

**Andaman
Basin**
.4507

Manila
.5560

Cape
Johnson
Depth
10497

Saipan
Rota

Guam

.1564

.31

Taongi

.6530

Sri Lanka

South

Palawan

Philippine Tr.

Challenger Deep 11022

**Marianas Tr.**

**MICRONESIA**

Bikini Rongelap

Eniwetak

Enewetak

Sumatera

Equator

Kep.

Singapore

China

Sulu
Arch.

Str. of Malacca

Sea

Mindanao

Celebes
Sea

Yap. Tr.
.8597
Palau
8054

Yap Eauripik
Palau Tr.

Gaferut
Pikelot

Hall Is
Chuuk

**Caroline Islands**

Pohnpei
Kosrae

Kwajalein Wotje

Ailinglapalap
Majuro

**Marshall Islands**

Ebon

.6957 Palmyra

Butaritari

Mentawai

Bangka

Borneo

Sulawesi

Tk Tomini

Moluccca
Sea

Halmahera

W. Caroline
Basin

New Guinea Rise

E. Caroline Basin

Kapingamarangi

Nomoi Is

Kapingamarangi Rise

Abaiang

Nauru

Kiribati
Nonouti

Banaba Tabiteuea

Howland I.
Baker I.

Kanton I.

Buru
Seram

Seram Sea

.7208

Admiralty Is

**MELANESIA**

Onotoa

Phoenix Islands
McKean I.
Nikumaroro

Manra

Orona

Java Sea

Jakarta

Banda Sea

Kep.
Aru

New
Guinea

Bismarck
Sea New Ireland

New
Britain
Planet Deep .9140
Solomon Sea

Solomon
Islands

Nanumea

Tuvalu

Nanumea

Nukufetau Funafuti

Vaitupu
Atafu
Tokelau

Nukulaelae

Pakaofo
Swains I.

Jawa
(Java)

Flores Sea

Flores

Kep.
Tanimbar
.7440

D'Entrecasteaux Is

.8487

Santa
Cruz Is

Rotuma

.13

Iles Wallis
Savaii
Upolu

Manu'a
Tutuila

**Mid - Indian
Basin**

Selat Sunda

Java Ridge

Sumba

Sawu
Sea

Timor

Port
Moresby

G. of
Papua

Arafura Sea

Torres Strait

Louisiade Arch.

Rennell

Banks Is

Iles de Hoorn

Vanua Levu

Palmerston

Christmas I. 7209

Sunda or Java Trench

Melville I.

C. Arnhem

C. York

Gulf of
Carpentaria

**Coral Sea
Basin**

Great Barrier Reef

Espiritu Santo

Vanuatu

Viti
Levu

Tanna

Fiji

Niue

Cocos Is

Timor Sea

Timor

C. Londonderry

Vanuatu

Coral
Sea

Erromango
Iles Loyauté

Vava'u
Group
Tofua

**Ninety - East Ridge**

.6360

C. Lévêque

Tanna

Nouvelle
Calédonie

.7633
Île des Pins

Hunter I.

Tonga
Tongatapu
Group

**Horizon Depth**
10882

**West Australian
Basin**

Exmouth
Plateau

Barrow I.
North West C.

.1924

**AUSTRALIA**

Lord Howe Rise

Norfolk Island Ridge

Norfolk Island Trough

Norfolk I.

**South Fiji
Basin**

Kermadec Is

Raoul

.10047

Kermadec Tr.

**Sou
Paci**

Shark B.

Brisbane

Lord Howe I.

Darling

Sydney

Auckland

North Island

New
Zealand

East C.

Great
Australian
Bight

Murray

Melbourne

Naturaliste
C. Leeuwin
Plateau .7102

Spencer
G.

King I.

Bass
Strait

Tasman
Sea

Tasman Basin
5176

South Island

Wellington

**Chatham Rise**
Chatham Is

.549

W. Australian Ridge

.5670

South Australian Basin

Tasmania

South East C.

**Tasman
Plateau**

.770

Stewart I.

**New Zealand
Plateau**
Auckland Is

Bounty Is

Antipodes Is

.6096

Campbell I.

**Indian - Antarctic Ridge**

Macquarie Ridge

Macquarie I.

**Mid - Indian Ridge**
.1840

.2907

**Indian - Antarctic Basin**

.1646

.956

Balleny
Islands

Fisher
Bay

C. North

C. Adare

Coulman I.

Ross

C. Poinsett

Equator 0°

15°

30°

45°

60°

90°E

105°

120°

135°

150°

165°

180°

METRES FEET
SEA LEVEL

| METRES | | FEET |
|---|---|---|
| **SEA** | | **LEVEL** |
| 200 | | 656 |
| 3000 | | 9843 |
| 5000 | | 16409 |
| 6000 | | 19686 |

Lambert Azimuthal Equal Area Projection

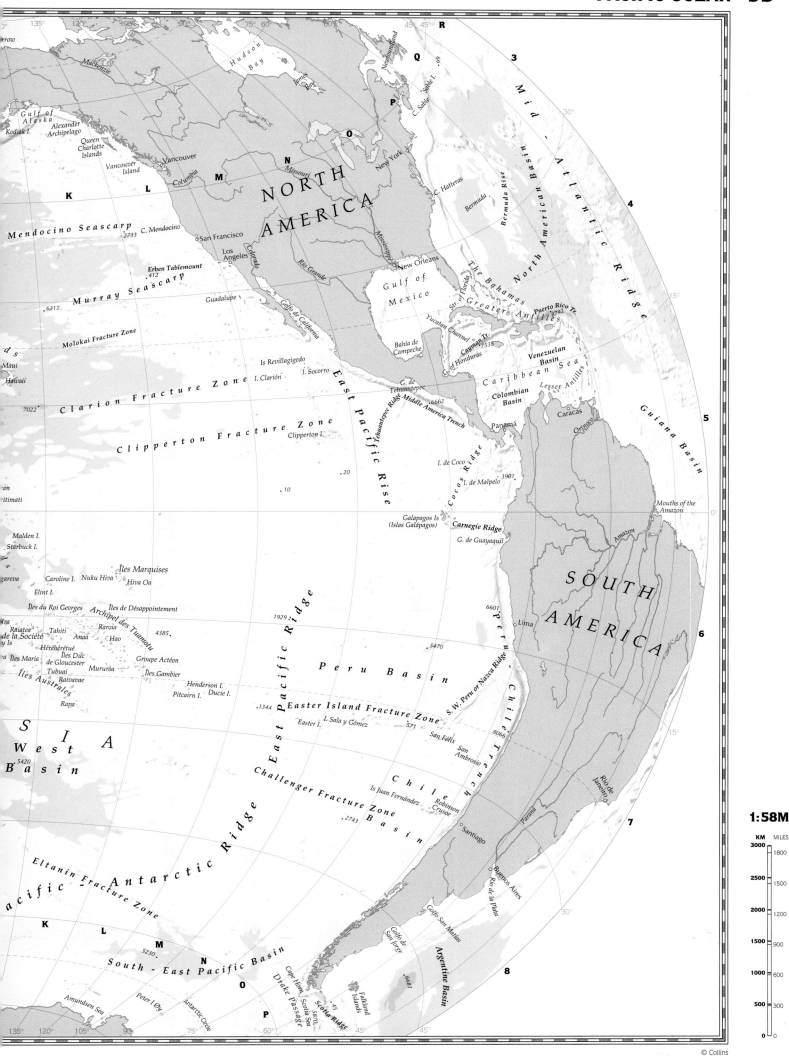

**1:58M**

KM MILES
3000 — 1800
2500 — 1500
2000 — 1200
1500 — 900
1000 — 600
500 — 300
0 — 0

© Collins

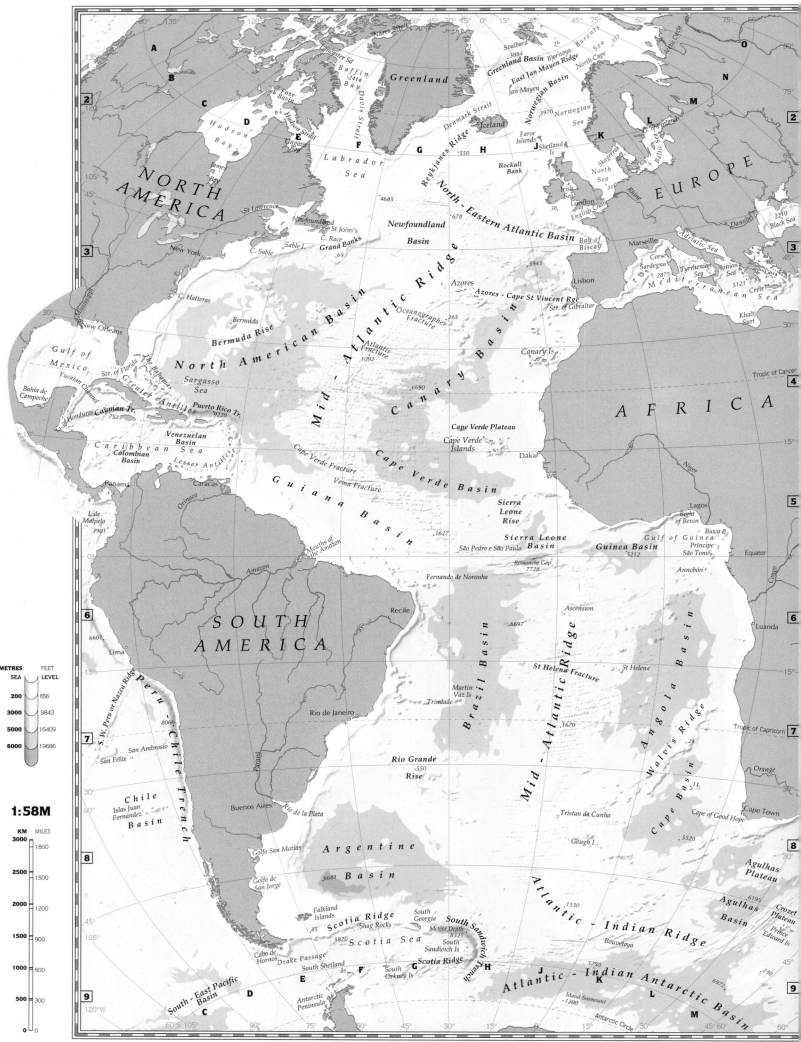

METRES SEA LEVEL / FEET LEVEL

| METRES SEA | FEET LEVEL |
|---|---|
| 200 | 656 |
| 3000 | 9843 |
| 5000 | 16409 |
| 6000 | 19686 |

**1:58M**

| KM | MILES |
|---|---|
| 3000 | 1800 |
| 2500 | 1500 |
| 2000 | 1200 |
| 1500 | 900 |
| 1000 | 600 |
| 500 | 300 |
| 0 | 0 |

Lambert Azimuthal Equal Area Projection

© Co

THE INDEX includes the names on the maps in the ATLAS. The names are generally indexed to the largest scale map on which they appear, and can be located using the grid reference letters and numbers around the map frame. Names on insets have a symbol: ▫, followed by the inset number.

Abbreviations used to describe features in the index and on the maps are explained below.

## ABBREVIATIONS AND GLOSSARY

A. Alp Alpen Alpi *alp*
Alt *upper*
A.C.T. Australian Capital Territory
Afgh. Afghanistan
Afr. Africa African
Aig. Aiguille *peak*
AK Alaska
AL Alabama
Alg. Algeria
Alta Alberta
Ant. Antarctica
AR Arkansas
Arch. Archipelago
Arg. Argentina
Arr. Arrecife *reef*
Atl. Atlantic
Austr. Australia
AZ Arizona
Azer. Azerbaijan

B. Bad *spa*
Ban *village*
Bay
Bangla. Bangladesh
B.C. British Columbia
Bg Berg *mountain*
Bge. Barragem *reservoir*
Bgt Bight Bugt *bay*
Bj Burj *hills*
Bol. Bolivia
Bos.-Herz. Bosnia Herzegovina
Br. Burun Burnu *point, cape*
Bt Bukit *bay*
Bü. Büyük *big*
Bulg. Bulgaria

C. Cape
Col *high pass*
Ç. Çay *river*
CA California
Cabo Cabeço *summit*
Can. Canada
Canal Canale *canal*
Cañon Canyon *canyon*
C.A.R. Central African Republic
Cat. Cataract
Catena *mountains*
Cd Ciudad *town city*
Ch. Chaung *stream*
Chott *salt lake, marsh*
Chan. Channel
Che Chaîne *mountain chain*
Cma Cima *summit*
Cno Corno *peak*
Co Cerro *hill, peak*
CO Colorado
Co. County
Col. Colombia
Cord. Cordillera *mountain chain*
Cr. Creek
CT Connecticut
Cuch. Cuchilla *mountain chain*
Czo Cozzo *mountain*

D. Da *big, river*
Dag Dagh Daği *mountain*
Dağlari *mountains*
-d. -dake *peak*
DC District of Columbia
DE Delaware
Des. Desert
Div. Division
Dj. Djebel *mountain*
Dom. Rep. Dominican Republic

Eil. Eiland *island*
Eilanden *islands*
Emb. Embalse *reservoir*
Eng. England
Equat. Equatorial
Escarp. Escarpment

Est. Estuary
Eth. Ethiopia
Etg Etang *lake, lagoon*

F. Firth
Fin. Finland
Fj. Fjell *mountain*
Fjord Fjördur *fjord*
Fl. Fleuve *river*
FL Florida
Fr. Guiana French Guiana

G. Gebel *mountain*
Göl Gölö Göl *lake*
G. Golfe Golfo Gulf *gulf, bay*
Góra *mountain*
Gunung *mountain*
-g. -gawa *river*
GA Georgia
Gd Grand *big*
Gde Grande *big*
Geb. Gebergte *mountain range*
Gebirge *mountains*
Gl. Glacier
Ger. Germany
Gr. Graben *trench, ditch*
Gross Grosse Grande *big*
Grp Group
Gt Great Groot Groote *big*
Gy Góry Gory *mountains*

H. Hawr *lake*
Hill Hills
Hoch *high*
Hora *mountain*
Hory *mountains*
Halv. Halvøy *peninsula*
Harb. Harbour
Hd Head Headland
Hg. Hegység *mountains*
Hgts Heights
HI Hawaii
Ht Haut *high*
Hte Haute *high*

I. Île Ilha Insel Isla
Island Isle *island, isle*
Isola Isole *island*
IA Iowa
ID Idaho
IL Illinois
IN Indiana
In. Inlet
Indon. Indonesia
Is Islas Îles Ilhas
Islands Isles *islands, isles*
Isr. Israel
Isth. Isthmus

J. Jabal Jebel *mountain*
Jibāl *mountains*
Jrvi Jaure Jezero
Jezioro *lake*
Jökull *glacier*

K. Kaap Kap Kapp *cape*
Kaikyō *strait*
Kato Káto *lower*
Kiang *river or stream*
Ko *island, lake, inlet*
Koh Küh Kühha *island*
Kolpos *gulf*
Kopf *hill*
Kuala *estuary*
Kyst *coast*
Küçük *small*
Kan. Kanal Kanaal *canal*
Kazak. Kazakhstan
Kep. Kepulauan *archipelago, islands*
Kg Kampong *village*
Khr Khrebet *mountain range*
Kl. Klein Kleine *small*
Kör. Körfez Körfezi *bay, gulf*
KS Kansas
KY Kentucky
Kyrg. Kyrgyzstan

L. Lac Lago Lake
Liqen Loch Lough *lake, loch*
Lam *stream*
LA Louisiana
Lag. Lagoon Laguna
Lagôa *lagoon*
Lith. Lithuania
Lux. Luxembourg

M. Mae *river*
Me *great, chief, mother*
Meer *lake, sea*
Muang *kingdom, province, town*
Muong *town*
Mys *cape*
Maloye *small*
MA Massachusetts
Madag. Madagascar
Man. Manitoba
Maur. Mauritania
MD Maryland
ME Maine
Mex. Mexico
Mf Massif *mountains, upland*
Mgna Montagna *mountain*
Mgne Montagne *mountain*
Mgnes Montagnes *mountains*
MI Michigan
MN Minnesota
MO Missouri
Mon. Monasterio Monastery *monastery*
Monument *monument*
Moz. Mozambique
MS Mississippi
Mt Mont Mount *mountain*
Mt. Mountain
MT Montana
Mte Monte *mountain*
Mtes Montes *mountains*
Mti Monti Munţi *mountains*
Mtii Munţii *mountains*
Mth Mouth
Mths Mouths
Mtn Mountain
Mts Monts Mountains

N. Nam *south(ern), river*
Neu Ny *new*
Nevado *peak*
Nudo *mountain*
Noord Nord Nörre
Nörre North *north(ern)*
Nos *spit, point*
Nac. Nacional *national*
Nat. National
N.B. New Brunswick
NC North Carolina
ND North Dakota
NE Nebraska
Neth. Netherlands
Neth. Ant. Netherlands Antilles
Nfld Newfoundland
NH New Hampshire
Nic. Nicaragua
Nizh. Nizhneye Nizhniy
Nizhnyaya *lower*
Nizm. Nizmennost' *lowland*
NJ New Jersey
NM New Mexico
N.O. Noord Oost Nord Ost *northeast*
Nov. Novyy Novaya
Noviye Novoye *new*
N.S. Nova Scotia
N.S.W. New South Wales
N.T. Northern Territory
NV Nevada
Nva Nueva *new*
N.W.T. Northwest Territories
NY New York
N.Z. New Zealand

O. Oost Ost *east*
Ostrov *island*
Ø Østre *east*
Ob. Ober *upper, higher*
Oc. Ocean
Ode Oude *old*
Ogl. Oglat *well*
OH Ohio
OK Oklahoma
Ont. Ontario
Or. Óri Óros Ori *north(ern)*
Oros *mountain*
OR Oregon
Orm. Ormos *bay*
O-va Ostrova *islands*

Ot Olet *mountain*
Öv. Över Övre *upper*
Oz. Ozero *lake*
Ozera *lakes*
P. Pass
Pic Pico Piz *peak*
Pou *mountain*
Pulau *island*
PA Pennsylvania
Pac. Pacific
Pak. Pakistan
Para. Paraguay
Pass. Passage
Peg. Pegunungan *mountain range*
P.E.I. Prince Edward Island
Pen. Peninsula Penisola *peninsula*
Per. Pereval *pass*
Phil. Philippines
Phn. Phnom *hill, mountain*
Pgio Poggio *hill*
Pl. Planina Planinski *mountain(s)*
Pla Playa *beach*
Plat. Plateau
Plosk. Ploskogor'ye *plateau*
P.N.G. Papua New Guinea
Pno Pantano *reservoir, swamp*
Pol. Poland
Por. Porog *rapids*
Port. Portugal
P-ov Poluostrov *peninsula*
P.P. Pulau-pulau *islands*
Pr. Proliv *strait*
Przylądek *cape*
Presq. Presqu'île *peninsula*
Prom. Promontory
Prov. Province Provincial
Psa Presa *dam*
Pso Passo *dam*
Pt Point
Pont *bridge*
Petit *small*
Pta Ponta Punta *cape, point*
Puerta *narrow pass*
Pte Pointe *cape, point*
Ponte Puente *bridge*
Pto Porto Puerto *harbour, port*
Pzo Pizzo *mountain peak, mountain*

Qld. Queensland
Que. Quebec

R. Reshteh *mountain range*
Rūd River *river*
Ra. Range
Rca Rocca *rock, fortress*
Reg. Region
Rep. Republic
Res. Reserve
Resr Reservoir
Resp. Respublika *republic*
Rf Reef
Rge Ridge
RI Rhode Island
Riba Ribeira *coast, bottom of the river valley*
Rte Route
Rus. Fed. Russian Federation

S. Salar Salina *salt pan*
San São *saint*
See *lake*
Seto *strait, channel*
Sjö *lake*
Sör Süd Sud Syd South *south(ern)*
Sa Serra Sierra *mountain range*
S.A. South Australia
Sab. Sabkhat *salt flat*
Sask. Saskatchewan
S. Arabia Saudi Arabia
SC South Carolina
Sc. Scoglio *rock, reef*
Sd Sound Sund *sound*
SD South Dakota
Seb. Sebjet Sebkhat Sebkra *salt flat*
Serr. Serrania *mountain range*
Sev. Severnaya Severnyy *north(ern)*
Sh. Sha'ib *watercourse*
Shaţţ *river (-mouth)*
Shima *island*
Shankou *pass*

Si Sidi *lord, master*
Sing. Singapore
Sk. Shuiku *reservoir*
Skt Sankt *saint*
Smt Seamount
Snra Senhora *Mrs, lady*
Snro Senhoro *Mr, gentleman*
Sp. Spain Spanish
Spitze *peak*
Sr Sönder Sonder *southern*
Sr. Sredniy Srednyaya *middle*
St Saint Sint
Staryy *old*
St. Stor Store *big*
Stung *river*
Sta Santa *saint*
Ste Sainte *saint*
Store *big*
Sto Santo *saint*
Str. Strait Stretta *strait*
Sv. Sväty Sveti *holy, saint*
Switz. Switzerland

T. Tal *valley*
Tall Tell *hill*
Tepe Tepesi *hill, peak*
Tajik. Tajikistan
Tanz. Tanzania
Tas. Tasmania
Terr. Territory
Tg Tanjung Tanjong *cape, point*
Thai. Thailand
Tk Teluk *bay*
Tmt Tablemount
TN Tennessee
Tr. Trench Trough
Tre Torre *tower, fortress*
Tte Teniente *lieutenant*
Turk. Turkmenistan
TX Texas

U.A.E. United Arab Emirates
Ug Ujung *point, cape*
U.K. United Kingdom
Ukr. Ukraine
Unt. Unter *lower*
Upr Upper
Uru. Uruguay
U.S.A. United States of America
UT Utah
Uzbek. Uzbekistan

V. Val Valle Valley *valley*
Väster Vest Vester *west(ern)*
Vatn *lake*
Ville *town*
Va Vila *small town*
VA Virginia
Venez. Venezuela
Vic. Victoria
Volc. Volcán Volcan
Volcano *volcano*
Vdkhr. Vodokhranilishche *reservoir*
Vdskh. Vodoskhovshche Vodaskhovishcha *reservoir*
Vel. Velikiy Velikaya Velikiye *big*
Verkh. Verkhniy Verkhneye Verkhne *upper*
Verkhnyaya *upper*
Vost. Vostochnyy *eastern*
Vozv. Vozvyshennost' *hills, upland*
VT Vermont

W. Wadi *watercourse*
Wald *forest*
Wan *bay*
Water *water*
WA Washington
W.A. Western Australia
Wr Wester
WV West Virginia
WY Wyoming

-y -yama *mountain*
Y.T. Yukon Territory
Yt. Ytre Ytter Ytri *outer*
Yugo. Yugoslavia
Yuzh. Yuzhnaya Yuzhno Yuzhnyy *southern*

Zal. Zaliv *bay*
Zap. Zapadnyy Zapadnaya Zapadno Zapadnoye *western*
Zem. Zemlya *land*

# A


12 E4 Aachen Ger.
16 E6 Aalen Ger.
12 C4 Aalst Belgium
12 C4 Aarschot Belgium
38 A3 Aba China
88 D3 Aba Congo(Zaire)
86 C4 Aba Nigeria
30 B5 Abā ad Dūd S. Arabia
30 C4 Ābādān Iran
30 D4 Ābādeh Iran
86 B1 Abadla Alg.
82 D2 Abaeté r. Brazil
79 J4 Abaetetuba Brazil
38 E1 Abag Qi China
94 G5 Abaiang i. Pac. Oc.
63 E4 Abajo Pk summit U.S.A.
86 C4 Abakaliki Nigeria
36 B1 Abakan Rus. Fed.
36 A1 Abakanskiy Khrebet mts Rus. Fed.
21 E7 Abana Turkey
30 D4 Āb Anbār Iran
78 D6 Abancay Peru
30 D4 Abarqū Iran
40 J2 Abashiri Japan
40 J2 Abashiri-wan b. Japan
48 E3 Abau P.N.G.
88 D3 Ābaya Hāyk' l. Eth.
Ābay Wenz r. see Blue Nile
24 L4 Abaza Rus. Fed.
31 E3 Abbāsābād Iran
18 C4 Abbasanta Sardinia Italy
68 C2 Abbaye, Pt pt U.S.A.
88 E2 Abbe, L. l. Eth.
14 E1 Abbeville France
65 E6 Abbeville LA U.S.A.
67 D5 Abbeville SC U.S.A.
11 B5 Abbeyfeale Rep. of Ireland
10 E6 Abbey Head hd U.K.
11 D5 Abbeyleix Rep. of Ireland
8 D3 Abbeytown U.K.
6 Q4 Abborrträsk Sweden
92 A3 Abbot Ice Shelf ice feature Ant.
56 E5 Abbotsford Can.
68 B3 Abbotsford U.S.A.
63 F4 Abbott U.S.A.
34 C2 Abbottabad Pak.
29 H3 'Abd al 'Azīz, J. h. Syria
29 L5 Abdanan Iran
87 E3 Abéché Chad
31 E4 Āb-e Garm Iran
51 D4 Abel Tasman National Park N.Z.
86 B4 Abengourou Côte d'Ivoire
7 L9 Åbenrå Denmark
13 K6 Abensberg Ger.
86 C4 Abeokuta Nigeria
9 C5 Aberaeron U.K.
10 F3 Aberchirder U.K.
50 G2 Abercrombie r. Austr.
9 D6 Aberdare U.K.
9 C5 Aberdaron U.K.
50 H2 Aberdeen Austr.
57 H4 Aberdeen Can.
39 □ Aberdeen H.K. China
90 F6 Aberdeen S. Africa
10 F3 Aberdeen U.K.
71 E5 Aberdeen MD U.S.A.
65 F5 Aberdeen MS U.S.A.
64 D2 Aberdeen SD U.S.A.
62 B2 Aberdeen WA U.S.A.
57 J2 Aberdeen Lake l. Can.
9 C5 Aberdyfi U.K.
10 E4 Aberfeldy U.K.
8 F4 Aberford U.K.
10 D4 Aberfoyle U.K.
9 D6 Abergavenny U.K.
65 C5 Abernathy U.S.A.
9 C5 Aberporth U.K.
9 C5 Abersoch U.K.
9 C5 Aberystwyth U.K.
32 B6 Abhā S. Arabia
30 C2 Abhar Iran
30 C2 Abhar r. Iran
Abiad, Bahr el r. see White Nile
30 C3 Ab-i-Bazuft r. Iran
81 A2 Abibe, Serranía de mts Col.
86 B4 Abidjan Côte d'Ivoire
31 H3 Ab-i-Istada l. Afgh.
88 D3 Abijatta-Shalla National Park Eth.
30 E3 Ab-i-Kavir salt flat Iran
64 D4 Abilene KS U.S.A.
65 D5 Abilene TX U.S.A.
9 F6 Abingdon U.K.
68 B5 Abingdon IL U.S.A.
70 C6 Abingdon VA U.S.A.
21 F6 Abinsk Rus. Fed.
31 G2 Ab-i-Safed r. Afgh.
78 C5 Abiseo, Parque Nacional nat. park Peru
57 H2 Abitau Lake l. Can.
58 D4 Abitibi r. Can.
58 E4 Abitibi, Lake l. Can.
86 B4 Aboisso Côte d'Ivoire
86 C4 Abomey Benin
35 C3 Abonar India
87 D4 Abong Mbang Cameroon
43 A4 Aborlan Phil.
87 D3 Abou Déia Chad
29 K1 Abovyan Armenia
10 F3 Aboyne U.K.
83 D4 Abra, L. del l. Arg.
15 B3 Abrantes Port.
80 C2 Abra Pampa Arg.
82 E2 Abrolhos, Arquipélago dos is Brazil
62 E2 Absaroka Range mts U.S.A.
13 H6 Abtsgmünd Ger.
30 C5 Abū 'Alī i. S. Arabia
30 D5 Abual Jirab i. U.A.E.
32 B6 Abū 'Arīsh S. Arabia
32 D5 Abu Dhabi U.A.E.
87 F3 Abu Hamed Sudan
86 C4 Abuja Nigeria
87 E3 Abu Matariq Sudan
30 D5 Abū Mūsá i. U.A.E.
78 E5 Abunã Brazil
78 E6 Abunã r. Bol.
32 A7 Ābune Yosēf mt Eth.
28 C6 Abu Qīr, Khalīg b. Egypt
27 F4 Abu Road India
87 F2 Abu Simbel Egypt
29 K6 Abū Şukhayr Iraq
51 C5 Abut Head hd N.Z.
43 C4 Abuyog Phil.
87 E3 Abu Zabad Sudan
Abū Zabī see Abu Dhabi
29 M6 Abūzam Iran
87 E3 Abyad Sudan
87 E4 Abyei Sudan
30 C2 Ābyek Iran
71 J2 Acadia Nat. Park U.S.A.
74 D4 Acambaro Mex.
81 A2 Acandí Col.
15 B1 A Cañiza Spain
74 C4 Acaponeta Mex.
74 E5 Acapulco Mex.
79 J4 Acará Brazil
79 K4 Acaraú r. Brazil
82 A4 Acaray r. Para.
80 E3 Acaray, Represa de resr Para.
81 C2 Acarigua Venez.
74 F5 Acayucán Mex.
86 B4 Accra Ghana
8 E4 Accrington U.K.
81 C3 Achaguas Venez.
34 D5 Achalpur India
33 B2 Achampet India
25 T3 Achayvayam Rus. Fed.
42 D1 Acheng China
12 A4 Achicourt France
11 B4 Achill Rep. of Ireland
11 A4 Achill Island i. Rep. of Ireland
10 C2 Achiltibuie U.K.
13 H1 Achim Ger.
36 B1 Achinsk Rus. Fed.
10 C3 Achnasheen U.K.
10 C3 A'Chralaig mt U.K.
21 F6 Achuyevo Rus. Fed.
28 B3 Acıgöl l. Turkey
28 B3 Acıpayam Turkey
18 F6 Acireale Sicily Italy
64 E3 Ackley U.S.A.
75 K4 Acklins Island i. Bahamas
9 J5 Acle U.K.
83 B2 Aconcagua r. Chile
79 L5 Acopiara Brazil
15 B1 A Coruña Spain
18 C2 Acqui Terme Italy
28 E5 Acre Israel
18 G5 Acri Italy
16 J7 Ács Hungary
46 O6 Actéon, Groupe is Fr. Polynesia Pac. Oc.
70 B4 Ada OH U.S.A.
65 D5 Ada OK U.S.A.
15 D2 Adaja r. Spain
50 G4 Adaminaby Austr.
80 E8 Adam, Mt h. Falkland Is
71 G3 Adams MA U.S.A.
68 C4 Adams WV U.S.A.
33 B4 Adam's Bridge rf India/Sri Lanka
56 F4 Adams L. l. Can.
73 E2 Adams McGill Reservoir U.S.A.
62 B2 Adams, Mt mt U.S.A.
56 C3 Adams Mt. mt U.S.A.
72 B2 Adams Peak mt U.S.A.
33 C5 Adam's Pk Sri Lanka
'Adan see Aden
28 E3 Adana Turkey
11 C5 Adare Rep. of Ireland
92 A5 Adare, C. c. Ant.
73 E2 Adaven U.S.A.
32 C5 Ad Dahnā' des. S. Arabia
86 A2 Ad Dakhla Western Sahara
32 D4 Ad Dammām S. Arabia
30 B5 Ad Dawādimī S. Arabia
Ad Dawḥah see Doha
29 J4 Ad Dawr Iraq
30 B5 Ad Dibdibah plain S. Arabia
30 B6 Ad Dilam S. Arabia
32 C5 Ad Dir'īyah S. Arabia
88 D3 Addis Ababa Eth.
71 K2 Addison U.S.A.
29 K6 Ad Dīwānīyah Iraq
9 G6 Addlestone U.K.
93 J4 Addu Atoll atoll Maldives
29 J6 Ad Duwayd well S. Arabia
67 D6 Adel GA U.S.A.
64 E3 Adel IA U.S.A.
50 B3 Adelaide Austr.
67 E7 Adelaide Bahamas
91 G6 Adelaide S. Africa
92 B2 Adelaide I i. Ant.
48 D3 Adelaide River Austr.
72 D4 Adelanto U.S.A.
50 G3 Adelong Austr.
32 C7 Aden Yemen
12 E4 Adenau Ger.
13 J1 Adendorf Ger.
32 C7 Aden, Gulf of g. Somalia/Yemen
30 D5 Adh Dhayd U.A.E.
37 F7 Adi i. Indon.
88 D2 Ādī Ārk'ay Eth.
88 D2 Ādīgrat Eth.
34 D6 Adilabad India
29 J2 Adilcevaz Turkey
62 B3 Adin U.S.A.
87 D2 Adīrī Libya
71 F2 Adirondack Mountains U.S.A.
Ādīs Ābeba see Addis Ababa
88 D3 Ādīs Alem Eth.
88 D2 Adi Ugri Eritrea
28 G3 Adıyaman Turkey
17 N7 Adjud Romania
59 J3 Adlatok Islands is Can.
48 C3 Admiralty Gulf b. Austr.
55 K2 Admiralty Inlet in. Can.
56 C3 Admiralty Island i. U.S.A.
56 C3 Admiralty Island Nat. Monument res. U.S.A.
48 E2 Admiralty Islands is P.N.G.
33 B3 Adoni India
13 L4 Adorf Ger.
13 G3 Adorf (Diemelsee) Ger.
14 D5 Adour r. France
15 E4 Adra Spain
18 F6 Adrano Sicily Italy
86 B2 Adrar Alg.
86 A2 Adrar mts Alg.
86 C3 Adrar des Ifôghas reg. Mali
86 A2 Adrar Maur
31 F3 Adraskand r. Afgh.
87 E3 Adré Chad
69 E5 Adrian MI U.S.A.
65 C5 Adrian TX U.S.A.
18 E2 Adriatic Sea sea Europe
33 B4 Adur India
88 C3 Adusa Congo(Zaire)
88 D2 Ādwa Eth.
25 P3 Adycha r. Rus. Fed.
21 F6 Adygeya, Respublika div. Rus. Fed.
21 F6 Adygeysk Rus. Fed.
21 H6 Adyk Rus. Fed.
86 B4 Adzopé Côte d'Ivoire
19 L5 Aegean Sea sea Greece/Turkey
13 H2 Aerzen Ger.
15 B1 A Estrada Spain
88 D2 Afabet Eritrea
29 K3 Afan Iran
23 F6 Afghanistan country Asia
6 M5 Åfjord Norway
88 E3 Afmadow Somalia
54 C4 Afognak I. i. U.S.A.
15 C1 A Fonsagrada Spain
28 F3 'Afrīn r. Syria/Turkey
28 F2 Afşin Turkey
12 D2 Afsluitdijk barrage Neth.
62 E3 Afton U.S.A.
79 H4 Afuá Brazil
28 E5 'Afula Israel
28 C2 Afyon Turkey
13 L4 Aga Ger.
86 C3 Agadez Niger
86 B1 Agadir Morocco
27 F2 Agadyr' Kazak.
93 H4 Agalega Islands is Mauritius
35 G5 Agartala India
34 C6 Agashi India
69 F2 Agate Can.
19 M6 Agathonisi i. Greece
86 B4 Agboville Côte d'Ivoire
29 L1 Ağcabädi Azer.
29 L2 Ağdam Azer.
14 F5 Agde France
14 E4 Agen France
90 C4 Aggeneys S. Africa
12 F4 Agger r. Ger.
34 D1 Aghil Pass China
11 C3 Aghla Mountain h. Rep. of Ireland
19 L7 Agia Vervara Greece
28 G2 Ağın Turkey
19 K6 Agios Dimitrios Greece
19 L5 Agios Efstratios i. Greece
19 M5 Agios Fokas, Akra pt Greece
19 K5 Agios Konstantinos Greece
19 L7 Agios Nikolaos Greece
19 K4 Agiou Orous, Kolpos b. Greece
87 F3 Agirwat Hills h. Sudan
91 F3 Agisanang S. Africa
86 B4 Agnibilékrou Côte d'Ivoire
19 L2 Agnita Romania
38 A2 Agong China
34 D4 Agra India
21 H7 Agrakhanskiy Poluostrov pen. Rus. Fed.
15 F2 Agreda Spain
29 J2 Ağrı Turkey
19 K7 Agria Gramvousa i. Greece
18 E6 Agrigento Sicily Italy
19 J5 Agrinio Greece
83 B3 Agrio r. Arg.
18 F4 Agropoli Italy
29 K1 Ağstafa Azer.
29 M1 Ağsu Azer.
81 B3 Aguadas Col.
81 B3 Agua de Dios Col.
75 L5 Aguadilla Puerto Rico
83 D4 Aguado Cecilio Arg.
75 H7 Aguadulce Panama
83 C3 Agua Escondida Arg.
74 D4 Aguanaval r. Mex.
83 C1 Agua Negra, Paso del pass Arg./Chile
82 B3 Aguapeí r. Brazil
74 C2 Agua Prieta Mex.
82 A3 Aguaray Guazú r. Para.
81 D2 Aguaro-Guariquito, Parque Nacional nat. park Venez.
74 D4 Aguascalientes Mex.
82 E2 Águas Formosas Brazil
82 C3 Agudos Brazil
73 F5 Aguila U.S.A.
15 D1 Aguilar de Campóo Spain
15 F4 Águilas Spain
43 B4 Aguisan Phil.
93 F7 Agulhas Basin sea feature Ind. Ocean
90 D7 Agulhas, Cape c. S. Africa
82 D3 Agulhas Negras mt Brazil
93 F6 Agulhas Plateau sea feature Ind. Ocean
45 E4 Agung, G. volc. Indon.
43 C4 Agusan r. Phil.
43 B4 Agutaya Phil.
30 B2 Ahar Iran
51 C5 Ahaura N.Z.
12 F2 Ahaus Ger.
51 E3 Ahimanawa Ra. mts N.Z.
51 D1 Ahipara N.Z.
51 D1 Ahipara Bay b. N.Z.
54 B4 Ahklun Mts mts U.S.A.
29 J2 Ahlat Turkey
13 F3 Ahlen Ger.
34 C5 Ahmadabad India
30 E4 Ahmadī Iran
33 A2 Ahmadnagar India
34 B3 Ahmadpur East Pak.
13 J4 Ahorn Ger.
30 C4 Ahram Iran
13 J1 Ahrensburg Ger.
29 J2 Ahta D. mt Turkey
6 T5 Ähtäri Fin.
7 U7 Ahtme Estonia
29 M6 Āhū Iran
14 F3 Ahun France
51 B6 Ahuriri r. N.Z.
30 C4 Ahvāz Iran
34 C5 Ahwa India
Ahwāz see Ahvāz
42 C3 Ai r. China
90 B3 Ai-Ais Namibia
38 D1 Aibag Gol r. China
30 D2 Aidin Turkm.
72 □1 Aiea U.S.A.
28 E4 Aigialousa Cyprus
19 K6 Aigina i. Greece
19 K5 Aigio Greece
14 H4 Aigle de Chambeyron mt France
83 F2 Aiguá Uru.
41 F5 Aikawa Japan
67 D5 Aiken U.S.A.
81 A2 Ailigandi Panama
94 G5 Ailinglapalap i. Pac. Oc.
12 A5 Ailly-sur-Noye France
69 G4 Ailsa Craig Can.
10 C5 Ailsa Craig i. U.K.
82 E2 Aimorés, Sa dos h. Brazil
86 C1 Aïn Beïda Alg.
86 B2 'Aïn Ben Tili Maur.
15 H4 Aïn Defla Alg.
15 H5 Aïn el Hadjel Alg.
86 B1 Aïn Sefra Alg.
59 H4 Ainslie, Lake l. Can.
64 D3 Ainsworth U.S.A.
Aintab see Gaziantep
15 H4 Aïn Taya Alg.
15 G5 Aïn Tédélès Alg.
81 B4 Aipe Col.
44 C5 Air i. Indon.
56 G4 Airdrie Can.
10 E5 Airdrie U.K.
12 D6 Aire r. France
14 D5 Aire-sur-l'Adour France
55 L3 Air Force I. i. Can.
38 D1 Airgin Sum China
86 C3 Aïr, Massif de l' mts Niger
57 H3 Air Ronge Can.
80 B7 Aisén, Pto Chile
38 F2 Ai Shan h. China
56 B2 Aishihik Can.
56 B2 Aishihik Lake l. Can.
14 G2 Aisne r. France
15 F3 Aitana mt Spain
48 E2 Aitape P.N.G.
64 E2 Aitkin U.S.A.
46 M5 Aitutaki i. Cook Is Pac. Oc.
17 L7 Aiud Romania
14 G5 Aix-en-Provence France
14 G4 Aix-les-Bains France
56 D3 Aiyansh Can.
35 F5 Aiyar Res. resr India
35 H5 Aizawl India
7 T8 Aizkraukle Latvia
7 R8 Aizpute Latvia
41 F6 Aizu-wakamatsu Japan
18 C4 Ajaccio Corsica France
81 B4 Ajajú r. Col.
33 A1 Ajanta India
Ajanta Range h. see Sahyadriparvat Range
6 O4 Ajaureforsen Sweden
51 D5 Ajax, Mt mt N.Z.
87 E1 Ajdābiyā Libya
a-Jiddét gravel area see Jiddat al Ḥarāsīs
40 G4 Ajigasawa Japan
28 E5 'Ajlūn Jordan
30 D5 Ajman U.A.E.
34 C4 Ajmer India
73 F5 Ajo U.S.A.
73 F5 Ajo, Mt mt U.S.A.
43 B4 Ajuy Phil.
40 H3 Akabira Japan
88 D4 Akagera National Park Rwanda
33 B2 Akalkot India
40 J3 Akan National Park Japan
28 D4 Akanthou Cyprus
51 D5 Akaroa N.Z.
55 D5 Akaroa Har in. N.Z.
35 H4 Akas reg. India
31 H3 Akbar Afgh.
35 E4 Akbarpur India
15 J4 Akbou Alg.
24 G4 Akbulak Rus. Fed.
28 F2 Akçadağ Turkey
29 G3 Akçakale Turkey
28 C1 Akçakoca Turkey
28 D3 Akçali D. mt Turkey
28 C3 Ak D. mt Turkey
29 H2 Ak D. mts Turkey
28 C3 Akdağ mt Turkey
28 E2 Akdağmadeni Turkey
7 Q7 Åkersberga Sweden
12 C2 Akersloot Neth.
88 C3 Aketi Congo(Zaire)
29 J1 Akhalk'alak'i Georgia
21 G7 Akhalts'ikhe Georgia
35 G5 Akhaura Bangl.
32 E5 Akhḍar, Jabal mts Oman
28 A2 Akhisar Turkey
28 F3 Akhtarīn Syria
21 H5 Akhtubinsk Rus. Fed.
29 J1 Akhuryan Armenia
41 C8 Aki Japan
58 D3 Akimiski Island i. Can.
28 E3 Akıncı Burun pt Turkey
28 G1 Akıncılar Turkey
40 G5 Akita Japan
86 A3 Akjoujt Maur.
6 P3 Akkajaure l. Sweden
40 J3 Akkeshi Japan
'Akko see Acre
28 F1 Akkuş Turkey
30 D1 Akkyr, Gory h. Turkm.
34 D4 Aklera India
7 R8 Akmeņrags pt Latvia
34 D1 Akmeqit China
26 F1 Akmola Kazak.
41 D7 Akō Japan
87 F4 Akobo Sudan
34 D5 Akola India
88 D2 Akordat Eritrea
28 D3 Akören Turkey
34 D5 Akot India
55 M3 Akpatok Island i. Que. Can.
59 G1 Akpatok Island i. Can.
6 B4 Akranes Iceland
21 C7 Akrathos, Akra pt Greece
7 J7 Åkrehamne Norway
31 G3 Ak Robat Pass Afgh.
62 G3 Akron CO U.S.A.
70 C4 Akron OH U.S.A.
70 C4 Akron City Reservoir U.S.A.
34 D2 Aksai Chin terr. China/India
28 E2 Aksaray Turkey
21 F6 Aksay Rus. Fed.
34 D2 Aksayqin Hu l. China/Jammu and Kashmir
28 C2 Akşehir Turkey
28 C2 Akşehir Gölü l. Turkey
28 C3 Akseki Turkey
30 D4 Aks-e Rostam r. Iran
26 E2 Akshiganak Kazak.
27 G2 Aksu China
28 C3 Aksu r. Turkey
88 D2 Āksum Eth.
35 F1 Aktag mt China
29 K2 Aktas D. mt Turkey
31 G2 Aktash Uzbek.
26 D2 Aktau Kazak.
27 F2 Aktogay Kazak.
17 O4 Aktsyabrski Belarus
26 D1 Aktyubinsk Kazak.
41 B8 Akune Japan
86 C4 Akure Nigeria
6 D4 Akureyri Iceland
35 G1 Akxokesay China
Akyab see Sittwe
28 G3 Akziyaret Turkey
7 L6 Ål Norway
30 C5 Al 'Abā S. Arabia
67 C5 Alabama div. U.S.A.
67 C6 Alabama r. U.S.A.
67 C5 Alabaster U.S.A.
43 B3 Alabat i. Phil.
29 K7 Al 'Abţīyah well Iraq
28 E1 Alaca Turkey
28 F2 Alacahan Turkey
28 E1 Alaçam Turkey
28 B2 Alaçam Dağları mts Turkey
29 J2 Ala Dag mt Turkey
28 E3 Ala Dağlar mts Turkey
29 J2 Ala Dağlar mts Turkey
21 H7 Alagir Rus. Fed.
79 L6 Alagoinhas Brazil
15 F2 Alagón Spain
43 C5 Alah r. Phil.
6 S5 Alahärmä Fin.
29 L7 Al Aḥmadī Kuwait
31 H2 Alai Range mts Asia
6 S5 Alajärvi Fin.
75 H6 Alajuela Costa Rica
29 L2 Alajujeh Iran
34 D3 Alaknanda r. India
27 G2 Alakol', Ozero l. Kazak.
6 W3 Alakurtti Rus. Fed.
78 F4 Alalaú r. Brazil
29 J3 Al 'Amādīyah Iraq
30 B5 Al'Amār S. Arabia
29 L6 Al 'Amārah Iraq
35 H3 Alamdo China
29 K7 Al Amghar waterhole Iraq
43 A2 Alaminos Phil.
65 C7 Alamitos, Sa de los mt Mex.
73 E3 Alamo U.S.A.
73 F4 Alamo Dam dam U.S.A.
63 F5 Alamogordo U.S.A.
65 D6 Alamo Heights U.S.A.
63 E6 Alamos Mex.
60 E6 Alamos Mex.
63 F4 Alamosa U.S.A.
33 B3 Alampur India
6 O4 Alanäs Sweden
33 B2 Åland India
7 Q6 Åland is Fin.
13 K1 Aland r. Ger.
30 B2 Aland r. Iran
44 B5 Alang Besar i. Indon.
68 E3 Alanson U.S.A.
28 D3 Alanya Turkey
28 C1 Alaplı Turkey
Alappuzha see Alleppey
30 C6 Al 'Āqūlah well S. Arabia
15 E3 Alarcón, Embalse de resr Spain
32 C4 Al Arţāwīyah S. Arabia
45 E4 Alas Indon.
28 B2 Alaşehir Turkey
29 J6 Al 'Āshūrīyah well Iraq
54 D3 Alaska div. U.S.A.
54 D4 Alaska, Gulf of g. U.S.A.
56 B3 Alaska Highway Can./U.S.A.
54 B4 Alaska Peninsula U.S.A.
54 D3 Alaska Range mts U.S.A.
29 M2 Älät Azer.
31 F2 Alat Uzbek.
29 J6 Al 'Athāmīn h. Iraq
20 H4 Alatyr' Rus. Fed.
20 H4 Alatyr' r. Rus. Fed.
78 C4 Alausí Ecuador
29 K1 Alaverdi Armenia
6 T4 Alavieska Fin.
6 S5 Alavus Fin.
50 C3 Alawoona Austr.
29 L1 Alazani r. Azer./Georgia
29 K5 Al 'Azīzīyah Iraq
18 C2 Alba Italy
28 F3 Al Bāb Syria
15 F3 Albacete Spain
50 C3 Albacutya, L. l. Austr.
29 K6 Al Bādiyah al Janūbīyah h. Iraq
19 K1 Alba Iulia Romania
58 F3 Albanel, L. l. Can.
5 E4 Albania country Europe
48 B5 Albany Austr.
67 C6 Albany GA U.S.A.
68 E5 Albany IN U.S.A.
66 C4 Albany KY U.S.A.
71 G3 Albany NY U.S.A.
62 B2 Albany OR U.S.A.
58 C3 Albany r. Can.
83 G2 Albardão do João Maria coastal area Brazil
30 B5 Al Barrah S. Arabia
Al Başrah see Basra
29 K6 Al Baṭḥa' marsh Iraq
29 L7 Al Bāṭin, Wādī watercourse Asia
48 E3 Albatross Bay b. Austr.
87 E1 Al Bayḍā' Libya
78 □ Albemarle, Pta pt Galapagos Is Ecuador
67 E5 Albemarle Sd chan. U.S.A.
18 C2 Albenga Italy
15 D3 Alberche r. Spain
48 D4 Alberga watercourse Austr.
15 B2 Albergaria-a-Velha Port.
50 F2 Albert Austr.
14 F2 Albert France
70 E6 Alberta U.S.A.
56 F4 Alberta div. Can.
56 F4 Alberta, Mt mt Can.
90 D7 Albertinia S. Africa
12 D4 Albert Kanaal canal Belgium
50 B3 Albert, Lake l. Austr.
88 D3 Albert, Lake l. Congo(Zaire)/Uganda
64 E3 Albert Lea U.S.A.
88 D3 Albert Nile r. Sudan/Uganda
80 B8 Alberto de Agostini, Parque Nacional nat. park Chile
91 H3 Alberton S. Africa
14 H4 Albertville France
12 E6 Albestroff France
14 F5 Albi France
79 H2 Albina Suriname
72 A2 Albion CA U.S.A.
71 J2 Albion ME U.S.A.
68 E4 Albion MI U.S.A.
70 D3 Albion NY U.S.A.
15 E5 Alborán, Isla de i. Spain
7 L8 Ålborg Denmark
7 M8 Ålborg Bugt b. Denmark
56 F4 Albreda Can.
30 C5 Al Budayyi Bahrain
30 C6 Al Budū', Sabkhat salt pan S. Arabia
15 B4 Albufeira Port.
29 H4 Āl Bū Kamāl Syria
63 F5 Albuquerque U.S.A.
32 E5 Al Buraymī Oman
15 C3 Alburquerque Spain
50 F4 Albury Austr.
29 H4 Al Buşayrah Syria
28 G7 Al Busayţā' plain S. Arabia
30 B4 Al Buşayyah Iraq
30 B4 Al Bushūk well S. Arabia
15 B3 Alcácer do Sal Port.
15 E2 Alcalá de Henares Spain
15 E4 Alcalá la Real Spain
18 E6 Alcamo Sicily Italy
15 F2 Alcañiz Spain
15 C3 Alcántara Spain
15 E3 Alcaraz Spain
15 D4 Alcaudete Spain
15 E3 Alcázar de San Juan Spain
21 F5 Alchevs'k Ukr.
83 D2 Alcira Arg.
82 E2 Alcobaça Brazil
15 F2 Alcora Spain
83 E2 Alcorta Arg.
15 F3 Alcoy Spain
15 H3 Alcúdia Spain
89 E4 Aldabra Islands is Seychelles
29 K5 Al Daghghārah Iraq
25 O4 Aldan Rus. Fed.
25 P3 Aldan r. Rus. Fed.
9 J5 Aldeburgh U.K.
51 F2 Aldermen Is, The is N.Z.
14 D2 Alderney i. Channel Is U.K.
72 B4 Alder Peak summit U.S.A.
9 G6 Aldershot U.K.
70 C6 Alderson U.S.A.
30 D6 Al Dhafrah reg. U.A.E.
8 D3 Aldingham U.K.
9 F5 Aldridge U.K.
68 B5 Aledo U.S.A.
86 A3 Aleg Maur.
82 E3 Alegre Brazil
80 E3 Alegrete Brazil
83 E2 Alejandro Korn Arg.
20 F2 Alekhovshchina Rus. Fed.
20 F3 Aleksandrov Rus. Fed.
21 J5 Aleksandrov Gay Rus. Fed.
21 H6 Aleksandrovskoye Rus. Fed.
25 Q4 Aleksandrovsk-Sakhalinskiy Rus. Fed.
26 F1 Alekseyevka Kazak.
21 F5 Alekseyevka Belgorod. Obl. Rus. Fed.
21 F5 Alekseyevka Belgorod. Obl. Rus. Fed.
21 G5 Alekseyevskaya Rus. Fed.
20 F4 Aleksin Rus. Fed.
19 J3 Aleksinac Yugo.
74 E5 Alemán, Presa Miguel resr Mex.
88 B4 Alèmbé Gabon
28 E1 Alembeyli Turkey
82 D3 Além Paraíba Brazil
6 M5 Ålen Norway
14 E2 Alençon France
79 H4 Alenquer Brazil
72 □2 Alenuihaha Channel U.S.A.
28 F3 Aleppo Syria
78 D6 Alerta Peru
56 D4 Alert Bay Can.
14 G4 Alès France
17 L7 Aleşd Romania
18 C2 Alessandria Italy
6 K5 Ålesund Norway
53 A4 Aleutian Islands is U.S.A.

54 C4 Aleutian Range *mts* U.S.A.
94 H2 Aleutian Trench *sea feature* Pac. Oc.
25 R4 Alevina, Mys *c.* Rus. Fed.
Alevişik *see* Samandağı
71 K2 Alexander U.S.A.
56 B3 Alexander Archipelago *is* U.S.A.
90 B4 Alexander Bay S. Africa
90 B4 Alexander Bay *b.* Namibia/S. Africa
67 C5 Alexander City U.S.A.
92 A2 Alexander I. *i.* Ant.
50 E4 Alexandra Austr.
51 B6 Alexandra N.Z.
80 □ Alexandra, C. *c.* Atl. Ocean
19 K4 Alexandreia Greece
Alexandretta *see* İskenderun
71 F2 Alexandria Can.
87 E1 Alexandria Egypt
19 L3 Alexandria Romania
91 G6 Alexandria S. Africa
10 D5 Alexandria U.K.
68 E5 Alexandria *IN* U.S.A.
65 E6 Alexandria *LA* U.S.A.
64 E2 Alexandria *MN* U.S.A.
70 E5 Alexandria *VA* U.S.A.
71 F2 Alexandria Bay U.S.A.
50 B3 Alexandrina, L. *l.* Austr.
19 L4 Alexandroupoli Greece
68 B5 Alexis U.S.A.
59 J3 Alexis *r.* Can.
56 E4 Alexis Creek Can.
24 K4 Aleysk Rus. Fed.
12 F4 Alf Ger.
15 F1 Alfaro Spain
29 L7 Al Farwānīyah Kuwait
29 J4 Al Fatḩah Iraq
29 M7 Al Fāw Iraq
13 H3 Alfeld (Leine) Ger.
82 D3 Alfenas Brazil
29 M7 Al Finṭās Kuwait
17 K7 Alföld *plain* Hungary
9 H4 Alford U.K.
71 F2 Alfred Can.
71 H3 Alfred U.S.A.
29 M7 Al Fuḩayḩīl Kuwait
Al-Fujayrah *see* Fujairah
30 B4 Al Fulayi *watercourse* S. Arabia
Al Furāt *r. see* Euphrates
7 J7 Algård Norway
83 C3 Algarrobo del Aguilla Arg.
15 B4 Algarve *reg.* Port.
20 G4 Algasovo Rus. Fed.
15 D4 Algeciras Spain
15 F3 Algemesí Spain
Alger *see* Algiers
69 E3 Alger U.S.A.
85 C3 Algeria *country* Africa
13 H2 Algermissen Ger.
29 K6 Al Ghammas Iraq
30 B5 Al Ghāţ S. Arabia
32 D6 Al Ghayḑah Yemen
18 C4 Alghero *Sardinia* Italy
86 C1 Algiers Alg.
91 F6 Algoa Bay *b.* S. Africa
68 D3 Algoma U.S.A.
64 E3 Algona U.S.A.
69 F4 Algonac U.S.A.
69 H3 Algonquin Park Can.
69 H3 Algonquin Provincial Park *res.* Can.
29 J7 Al Habakah *well* S. Arabia
30 B4 Al Ḩadaqah *well* S. Arabia
30 C5 Al Ḩadd Bahrain
30 A4 Al Hadhālīl *plat.* S. Arabia
29 J4 Al Ḩadīthah Iraq
29 J4 Al Ḩaḑr Iraq
28 F4 Al Ḩaffah Syria
30 B5 Al Ḩā'ir S. Arabia
31 E6 Al Hajar Oman
30 E5 Al Ḩajar al Gharbī *mts* Oman
29 G6 Al Hamad *reg.* Jordan/S. Arabia
87 D2 Al Ḩamādah al Ḩamrā' *plat.* Libya
15 F4 Alhama de Murcia Spain
29 J6 Al Hammām *well* Iraq
29 K7 Al Haniyah *esc.* Iraq
30 B6 Al Hariq S. Arabia
29 G6 Al Ḩarrah *reg.* S. Arabia
29 H3 Al Ḩasakah Syria
29 K5 Al Hāshimīyah Iraq
29 L5 Al Ḩayy Iraq
29 K5 Al Ḩillah Iraq
30 B6 Al Ḩillah S. Arabia
30 B6 Al Ḩilwah S. Arabia
30 C5 Al Ḩinnāh S. Arabia
86 B1 Al Hoceima Morocco
32 B7 Al Hudaydah Yemen
32 C4 Al Hufūf S. Arabia
30 D6 Al Ḩumrah *reg.* U.A.E.
30 C5 Al Ḩunayy S. Arabia
30 B6 Al Huwwah S. Arabia
30 D2 'Alīābād Iran
30 E3 'Alīābād Iran
31 E3 'Alīābād Iran
29 L4 'Alīābād Iran
19 M5 Aliağa Turkey
19 K4 Aliakmonas *r.* Greece
29 L5 'Alī al Gharbī Iraq
33 A2 Alībāg India
34 B4 Ali Bandar Pak.
29 M2 Äli Bayramlı Azer.
15 F3 Alicante Spain
91 G6 Alice S. Africa
65 D7 Alice U.S.A.
56 D3 Alice Arm Can.
48 D4 Alice Springs Austr.
67 E7 Alice Town Bahamas
43 B5 Alicia Phil.
34 D4 Aligarh India
30 C3 Alīgūdarz Iran
88 B4 Alima *r.* Congo
7 N8 Alingsås Sweden
28 B2 Aliova *r.* Turkey
34 B3 Alipur Pak.
35 G4 Alipur Duar India
70 C4 Aliquippa U.S.A.
88 E2 Ali Sabieh Djibouti
28 F6 'Al 'Īsāwīyah S. Arabia
29 K2 Alī Shah Iran
29 K5 Al Iskandarīyah Iraq
63 E6 Alisos *r.* Mex.
19 L5 Aliveri Greece
91 G5 Aliwal North S. Africa
56 G4 Alix Can.
87 E1 Al Jabal al Akhḑar *mts* Libya
30 C5 Al Jāfūrah *des.* S. Arabia
87 E2 Al Jaghbūb Libya
29 L7 Al Jahrah Kuwait
30 C5 Al Jamalīyah Qatar
30 C6 Al Jawb *reg.* S. Arabia
32 A4 Al Jawf S. Arabia
87 D1 Al Jawsh Libya
29 G3 Al Jazīrah *reg.* Iraq/Syria
15 B4 Aljezur Port.
30 C5 Al Jībān *reg.* S. Arabia
30 B6 Al Jifārah S. Arabia
29 J6 Al Jil *well* Iraq
30 B5 Al Jilh *esc.* S. Arabia
30 C5 Al Jishshah S. Arabia
28 E6 Al Jīzah Jordan
32 C4 Al Jubayl S. Arabia
30 B5 Al Jubaylah S. Arabia
30 B5 Al Jufayr S. Arabia
30 C5 Al Jurayd *i.* S. Arabia
30 B5 Al Jurayfah S. Arabia
15 B4 Aljustrel Port.
32 E5 Al Khābūrah Oman
29 K5 Al Khāliș Iraq
32 E4 Al Khaşab Oman
30 A6 Al Khāşirah S. Arabia
30 D6 Al Khatam *reg.* U.A.E.
30 C5 Al Khawr Qatar
30 C5 Al Khīşah *well* S. Arabia
30 C5 Al Khobar S. Arabia
30 B5 Al Khuff *reg.* S. Arabia
87 E2 Al Khufrah Libya
87 D1 Al Khums Libya
29 K5 Al Kifl Iraq
30 C5 Al Kir'ānah Qatar
12 C2 Alkmaar Neth.
29 K5 Al Kūfah Iraq
29 L5 Al Kumayt Iraq
29 K5 Al Kūt Iraq
Al Kuwayt *see* Kuwait
29 H7 Al Labbah *plain* S. Arabia
Al Lādhiqīyah *see* Latakia
71 J1 Allagash *ME* U.S.A.
71 J1 Allagash *r. ME* U.S.A.
71 J1 Allagash Lake *l.* U.S.A.
35 E4 Allahabad India
28 F5 Al Lajā *lava* Syria
25 P3 Allakh-Yun' Rus. Fed.
91 G3 Allanridge S. Africa
91 H1 Alldays S. Africa
68 E4 Allegan U.S.A.
70 D4 Allegheny *r.* U.S.A.
70 C6 Allegheny Mountains U.S.A.
70 D4 Allegheny Reservoir U.S.A.
67 D5 Allendale U.S.A.
8 E3 Allendale Town U.K.
13 G4 Allendorf (Lumda) Ger.
69 G3 Allenford Can.
11 C3 Allen, Lough *l.* Rep. of Ireland
71 F4 Allentown U.S.A.
33 B4 Alleppey India
13 J2 Aller *r.* Ger.
64 C3 Alliance *NE* U.S.A.
70 C4 Alliance *OH* U.S.A.
29 J6 Al Līfīyah *well* Iraq
7 O9 Allinge-Sandvig Denmark
69 H3 Alliston Can.
32 B5 Al Līth S. Arabia
10 E4 Alloa U.K.
33 C3 Allur India
33 C3 Alluru Kottapatnam India
29 J6 Al Lussuf *well* Iraq
59 F4 Alma Can.
68 E4 Alma *MI* U.S.A.
64 D3 Alma *NE* U.S.A.
73 H5 Alma *NM* U.S.A.
29 J6 Al Ma'ānīyah Iraq
15 B3 Almada Port.
29 K7 Al Ma'danīyāt *well* Iraq
15 D3 Almadén Spain
Al Madīnah *see* Medina
29 K5 Al Maḩmūdīyah Iraq
30 B5 Al Majma'ah S. Arabia
29 L1 Almalı Azer.
30 C5 Al Malsūnīyah *reg.* S. Arabia
30 C5 Al Manāmah Bahrain
72 B1 Almanor, Lake *l.* U.S.A.
15 F3 Almansa Spain
15 D2 Almanzor *mt* Spain
29 L6 Al Ma'qil Iraq
30 D6 Al Mariyyah U.A.E.
87 E1 Al Marj Libya
82 C1 Almas, Rio das *r.* Brazil
27 F2 Almaty Kazak.
Al Mawşil *see* Mosul
29 H4 Al Mayādīn Syria
30 B5 Al Mazāḩimīyah S. Arabia
15 E2 Almazán Spain
25 N3 Almaznyy Rus. Fed.
79 H4 Almeirim Brazil
15 B3 Almeirim Port.
12 E2 Almelo Neth.
82 E2 Almenara Brazil
15 C2 Almendra, Embalse de *resr* Spain
15 C3 Almendralejo Spain
12 D2 Almere Neth.
15 E4 Almería Spain
15 E4 Almería, Golfo de *b.* Spain
24 G4 Al'met'yevsk Rus. Fed.
7 O8 Älmhult Sweden
30 B5 Al Midhnab S. Arabia
15 D5 Almina, Pta *pt* Morocco
32 C4 Al Mish'āb S. Arabia
28 F5 Al Mismīyah Syria
15 B4 Almodôvar Port.
69 F4 Almont U.S.A.
69 J3 Almonte Can.
15 C4 Almonte Spain
32 C4 Al Mubarrez S. Arabia
28 E7 Al Mudawwara Jordan
30 C5 Al Muharraq Bahrain
32 C7 Al Mukallā Yemen
32 B7 Al Mukhā Yemen
15 E4 Almuñécar Spain
29 K5 Al Muqdādīyah Iraq
30 B5 Al Murabba S. Arabia
28 F1 Almus Turkey
30 B4 Al Musannāh *ridge* S. Arabia
29 K5 Al Musayyib Iraq
19 L7 Almyrou, Ormos *b.* Greece
72 □1 Alna Haina U.S.A.
8 F2 Alnwick U.K.
35 H5 Alon Myanmar
35 H3 Along India
19 K5 Alonnisos *i.* Greece
37 E7 Alor *i.* Indon.
37 E7 Alor, Kepulauan *is* Indon.
45 B1 Alor Setar Malaysia
Alost *see* Aalst
34 C5 Alot India
6 W4 Alozero Rus. Fed.
72 C4 Alpaugh U.S.A.
12 E3 Alpen Ger.
69 F3 Alpena U.S.A.
18 D1 Alpi Dolomitiche *mts* Italy
73 H5 Alpine *AZ* U.S.A.
65 C6 Alpine *TX* U.S.A.
62 E3 Alpine *WY* U.S.A.
4 D4 Alps *mts* Europe
32 C6 Al Qa'āmīyāt *reg.* S. Arabia
87 D1 Al Qaddāḩīyah Libya
28 F4 Al Qadmūs Syria
30 B5 Al Qā'īyah *well* S. Arabia
30 C6 Al Qalībah S. Arabia
29 H3 Al Qāmishlī Syria
30 B5 Al Qar'ah *well* S. Arabia
28 F4 Al Qaryatayn Syria
30 B5 Al Qaşab S. Arabia
32 C6 Al Qaţn Yemen
87 D2 Al Qaţrūn Libya
30 B4 Al Qayşūmah S. Arabia
28 E5 Al Qunayţirah Syria
32 B6 Al Qunfidhah S. Arabia
30 A5 Al Qurayn S. Arabia
29 L6 Al Qurnah Iraq
29 K6 Al Qusayr Iraq
30 B6 Al Qūşūrīyah S. Arabia
28 F5 Al Quţayfah Syria
30 A5 Al Quwārah S. Arabia
30 B5 Al Quwayīyah S. Arabia
14 H2 Alsace *reg.* France
9 E4 Alsager U.K.
29 J6 Al Samīt *well* Iraq
57 H4 Alsask Can.
13 H4 Alsfeld Ger.
13 K3 Alsleben (Saale) Ger.
8 E3 Alston U.K.
7 R8 Alsunga Latvia
6 S2 Alta Norway
6 S2 Altaelva *r.* Norway
83 D1 Alta Gracia Arg.
81 D2 Altagracía de Orituco Venez.
22 F5 Altai Mountains China/Mongolia
67 D6 Altamaha *r.* U.S.A.
79 H4 Altamira Brazil
51 B6 Alta, Mt *mt* N.Z.
18 G4 Altamura Italy
82 C1 Alta Paraiso de Goiás Brazil
70 D6 Altavista U.S.A.
27 G2 Altay China
36 B2 Altay Mongolia
15 F3 Altea Spain
6 S1 Alteidet Norway
12 E4 Altenahr Ger.
12 F2 Altenberge Ger.
13 L4 Altenburg Ger.
12 F4 Altenkirchen (Westerwald) Ger.
35 H1 Altenqoke China
13 M1 Altentreptow Ger.
29 M1 Altıağaç Azer.
31 H3 Altimur Pass Afgh.
29 K4 Altin Köprü Iraq
19 M5 Altınoluk Turkey
28 C2 Altıntaş Turkey
78 E7 Altiplano *plain* Bol.
13 K2 Altmark *reg.* Ger.
13 J5 Altmühl *r.* Ger.
82 B2 Alto Araguaia Brazil
83 C2 Alto de Pencoso *h.* Arg.
81 B3 Alto de Tamar *mt* Col.
82 B2 Alto Garças Brazil
89 D5 Alto Molócuè Moz.
66 B4 Alton *IL* U.S.A.
65 F4 Alton *MO* U.S.A.
71 H3 Alton *NH* U.S.A.
64 D1 Altona Can.
70 D4 Altoona U.S.A.
82 B2 Alto Sucuriú Brazil
16 F6 Altötting Ger.
9 E4 Altrincham U.K.
13 L1 Alt Schwerin Ger.
36 A3 Altun Shan *mts* China
62 B3 Alturas U.S.A.
65 D5 Altus U.S.A.
28 G1 Alucra Turkey
7 U8 Alūksne Latvia
29 M5 Alūm Iran
70 B4 Alum Creek Lake *l.* U.S.A.
83 B3 Aluminé *r.* Arg.
83 B3 Aluminé, L. *l.* Arg.
21 E6 Alupka Ukr.
87 D1 Al 'Uqaylah Libya
30 C5 Al 'Uqayr S. Arabia
21 E6 Alushta Ukr.
29 K4 'Alut Iran
32 C4 Al 'Uthmānīyah S. Arabia
87 E2 Al 'Uwaynāt Libya
29 J6 Al 'Uwayqīlah S. Arabia
30 A5 Al 'Uyūn S. Arabia
29 L6 Al 'Uzayr Iraq
65 D4 Alva U.S.A.
83 C2 Alvarado, P. de *pass* Chile
78 F4 Alvarães Brazil
7 M5 Alvdal Norway
7 O6 Älvdalen Sweden
7 O8 Alvesta Sweden
7 K6 Ålvik Norway
65 E6 Alvin U.S.A.
6 R4 Älvsbyn Sweden
26 B4 Al Wajh S. Arabia
30 C5 Al Wakrah Qatar
30 C5 Al Wannān S. Arabia
34 D4 Alwar India
30 B5 Al Warī'ah S. Arabia
33 B4 Alwaye India
29 H5 Al Widyān *plat.* Iraq/S. Arabia
30 B4 'Al Wusayţ *well* S. Arabia
38 A2 Alxa Youqi China
38 B2 Alxa Zuoqi China
48 D3 Alyangula Austr.
10 E4 Alyth U.K.
7 T9 Alytus Lith.
62 F2 Alzada U.S.A.
12 E5 Alzette *r.* Lux.
13 G5 Alzey Ger.
81 E3 Amacuro *r.* Guyana/Venez.
48 D4 Amadeus, Lake *salt flat* Austr.
55 L3 Amadjuak Lake *l.* Can.
73 G6 Amado U.S.A.
15 B3 Amadora Port.
41 A8 Amakusa-nada *b.* Japan
7 N7 Åmal Sweden
33 C2 Amalapuram India
36 D1 Amalat *r.* Rus. Fed.
81 B3 Amalfi Col.
91 F3 Amalia S. Africa
19 J6 Amaliada Greece
34 C5 Amalner India
37 F7 Amamapare Indon.
82 A3 Amambaí Brazil
82 A3 Amambaí *r.* Brazil
82 A3 Amambaí, Serra de *h.* Brazil/Para.
36 E4 Amami-guntō *is* Japan
36 E4 Amami-Ōshima *i.* Japan
26 E1 Amangel'dy Kazak.
18 G5 Amantea Italy
91 J5 Amanzimtoti S. Africa
79 H3 Amapá Brazil
15 C3 Amareleja Port.
72 D3 Amargosa Desert U.S.A.
72 D3 Amargosa Range *mts* U.S.A.
72 D3 Amargosa Valley U.S.A.
65 C5 Amarillo U.S.A.
18 F3 Amaro, Monte *mt* Italy
34 E4 Amarpatan India
28 E1 Amasya Turkey
12 D4 Amay Belgium
79 H4 Amazon *r.* S. America
81 D4 Amazonas *div.* Brazil
Amazonas *r. see* Amazon
79 G4 Amazónia, Parque Nacional *nat. park* Brazil
79 J3 Amazon, Mouths of the *est.* Brazil
34 C6 Ambad India
33 B2 Ambajogai India
34 D3 Ambala India
33 C5 Ambalangoda Sri Lanka
89 E6 Ambalavao Madag.
89 E5 Ambanja Madag.
31 E4 Ambar Iran
25 S3 Ambarchik Rus. Fed.
33 B4 Ambasamudram India
78 C4 Ambato Ecuador
89 E5 Ambato Boeny Madag.
89 E6 Ambato Finandrahana Madag.
89 E5 Ambatolampy Madag.
89 E5 Ambatomainty Madag.
89 E5 Ambatondrazaka Madag.
13 K5 Amberg Ger.
74 G5 Ambergris Cay *i.* Belize
14 G4 Ambérieu-en-Bugey France
69 G3 Amberley Can.
35 E5 Ambikapur India
89 E5 Ambilobe Madag.
56 C3 Ambition, Mt *mt* Can.
8 F2 Amble U.K.
8 E3 Ambleside U.K.
12 D4 Amblève *r.* Belgium
89 E6 Amboasary Madag.
89 E5 Ambohidratrimo Madag.
89 E6 Ambohimahasoa Madag.
Amboina *see* Ambon
37 E7 Ambon Indon.
37 E7 Ambon *i.* Indon.
89 E6 Ambositra Madag.
89 E6 Ambovombe Madag.
73 E4 Amboy *CA* U.S.A.
68 C5 Amboy *IL* U.S.A.
71 F3 Amboy Center U.S.A.
89 B4 Ambriz Angola
49 G3 Ambrym *i.* Vanuatu
33 B3 Ambur India
35 G2 Amdo China
12 D1 Ameland *i.* Neth.
70 E6 Amelia Court House U.S.A.
71 G4 Amenia U.S.A.
63 D3 American Falls U.S.A.
62 D3 American Falls Res. *resr* U.S.A.
73 G1 American Fork U.S.A.
47 K5 American Samoa *terr.* Pac. Oc.
67 C5 Americus U.S.A.
12 D2 Amersfoort Neth.
91 H3 Amersfoort S. Africa
9 G6 Amersham U.K.
57 L3 Amery Can.
92 D5 Amery Ice Shelf *ice feature* Ant.
64 E3 Ames U.S.A.
9 F6 Amesbury U.K.
71 H3 Amesbury U.S.A.
35 E4 Amethi India
19 K5 Amfissa Greece
25 P3 Amga Rus. Fed.
36 F2 Amgu Rus. Fed.
86 C2 Amguid Alg.
36 F1 Amgun' *r.* Rus. Fed.
59 H4 Amherst Can.
71 G3 Amherst *MA* U.S.A.
71 J2 Amherst *ME* U.S.A.
70 D6 Amherst *VA* U.S.A.
69 F4 Amherstburg Can.
18 D3 Amiata, Monte *mt* Italy
14 F2 Amiens France
29 H5 Amij, Wādī *watercourse* Iraq
33 A4 Amindivi Islands *is* India
41 D7 Amino Japan
90 C1 Aminuis Namibia
30 B3 Amīrābād Iran
Amirabad *see* Fūlād Maïalleh
93 H4 Amirante Islands *is* Seychelles
31 F4 Amir Chah Pak.
57 J4 Amisk L. *l.* Can.
65 C6 Amistad Res. *resr* Mex./U.S.A.
34 D5 Amla *Madhya Pradesh* India
34 D5 Amla *Madhya Pradesh* India
7 L7 Åmli Norway
9 C4 Amlwch U.K.
28 E6 'Ammān Jordan
9 D6 Ammanford U.K.
6 V4 Ämmänsaari Fin.
6 P4 Ammarnäs Sweden
14 F4 Ammerland *reg.* Ger.
13 J3 Ammern Ger.
16 E7 Ammersee *l.* Ger.
Ammochostos *see* Famagusta
42 D4 Amnyong-dan *hd* N. Korea
34 C5 Amod India
39 B6 Amo Jiang *r.* China
30 D2 Amol Iran
13 H5 Amorbach Ger.
19 L6 Amorgos *i.* Greece
58 E4 Amos Can.
Amoy *see* Xiamen
33 C5 Amparai India
82 C3 Amparo Brazil
16 E6 Amper *r.* Ger.
15 G2 Amposta Spain
34 D5 Amravati India
34 B5 Amreli India
34 B4 Amri Pak.
28 F4 'Amrit Syria
34 C3 Amritsar India
34 D3 Amroha India
6 Q4 Åmsele Sweden
12 C2 Amstelveen Neth.
12 C2 Amsterdam Neth.
91 J3 Amsterdam S. Africa
71 F3 Amsterdam U.S.A.
93 K6 Amsterdam, Île *i.* Ind. Ocean
16 G6 Amstetten Austria
87 E3 Am Timan Chad
31 F1 Amudar'ya *r.* Turkm./Uzbek.
55 J2 Amund Ringnes I. Can.
54 F2 Amundsen Bay *b.* Ant.
92 B4 Amundsen Gl. *gl.* Ant.
54 F2 Amundsen Gulf *g.* Can.
92 C5 Amundsen, Mt *mt* Ant.
92 B4 Amundsen-Scott *U.S.A. Base* Ant.
92 A3 Amundsen Sea *sea* Ant.
45 E3 Amuntai Indon.
Amur *r. see* Heilong Jiang
25 P4 Amursk Rus. Fed.
21 F6 Amvrosiyivka Ukr.
68 E1 Amyot Can.
35 H6 An Myanmar
46 N5 Anaa *i. Fr. Polynesia* Pac. Oc.
37 E7 Anabanua Indon.
25 N2 Anabar *r.* Rus. Fed.
25 N2 Anabarskiy Zaliv *b.* Rus. Fed.
50 C2 Ana Branch *r.* Austr.
72 C4 Anacapa Is *is* U.S.A.
81 D2 Anaco Venez.
62 D2 Anaconda U.S.A.
62 B1 Anacortes U.S.A.
65 D5 Anadarko U.S.A.
28 F1 Anadolu Dağları *mts* Turkey
25 T3 Anadyr' *r.* Rus. Fed.
25 U3 Anadyrskiy Zaliv *b.* Rus. Fed.
19 L6 Anafi *i.* Greece
82 E1 Anagé Brazil
29 H4 'Ānah Iraq
72 D5 Anaheim U.S.A.
56 D4 Anahim Lake Can.
65 C7 Anáhuac Mex.
33 B4 Anaimalai Hills *mts* India
33 B4 Anai Mudi Pk *mt* India
33 C2 Anakapalle India
89 E5 Analalava Madag.
78 F4 Anamã Brazil
45 C2 Anambas, Kepulauan *is* Indon.
68 B4 Anamosa U.S.A.
28 D3 Anamur Turkey
28 D3 Anamur Burnu *pt* Turkey
41 D8 Anan Japan
34 C5 Anand India
35 F5 Anandapur India
35 F5 Anandpur *r.* India
33 B3 Anantapur India
34 C2 Anantnag Jammu and Kashmir
21 D6 Anan'yiv Ukr.
21 F6 Anapa Rus. Fed.
82 C2 Anápolis Brazil
30 D4 Anār Iran
30 D3 Anārak Iran
30 C3 Anarbar *r.* Iran
31 F3 Anardara Afgh.
28 D2 Anatolia *reg.* Turkey
49 G4 Anatom *i.* Vanuatu
80 D3 Añatuya Arg.
81 E4 Anauá *r.* Brazil
30 C2 Anbūh Iran
42 D4 Anbyon N. Korea
14 D3 Ancenis France
54 D3 Anchorage U.S.A.
69 F4 Anchor Bay *b.* U.S.A.
18 E3 Ancona Italy
80 B6 Ancud Chile
83 B4 Ancud, Golfo de *g.* Chile
83 B1 Andacollo Chile
35 F5 Andal India
6 K5 Åndalsnes Norway
15 D4 Andalucía *div.* Spain
65 G6 Andalusia U.S.A.
93 L3 Andaman Basin *sea feature* Ind. Ocean
27 H5 Andaman Islands Andaman and Nicobar Is
45 A1 Andaman Sea *sea* Asia
89 E5 Andapa Madag.
82 E1 Andaraí Brazil
6 P2 Andenes Norway
12 D4 Andenne Belgium
12 C4 Anderlecht Belgium
14 D4 Andernos-les-Bains France
54 D3 Anderson *AK* U.S.A.
68 E5 Anderson *IN* U.S.A.
65 E4 Anderson *MO* U.S.A.
67 D5 Anderson *SC* U.S.A.
54 F3 Anderson *r. N.W.T.* Can.
81 B3 Andes Col.
76 C6 Andes *mts* S. America
64 D3 Andes, Lake U.S.A.
6 P2 Andfjorden *chan.* Norway
33 B2 Andhra Pradesh *div.* India
89 E5 Andilamena Madag.
89 E5 Andilanatoby Madag.
30 C3 Andīmeshk Iran
28 F3 Andırın Turkey
21 H7 Andiyskoye Koysu *r.* Rus. Fed.
26 F2 Andizhan Uzbek.
31 G2 Andkhui *r.* Afgh.
31 G2 Andkhvoy Afgh.
89 E5 Andoany Madag.
78 C4 Andoas Peru
33 B2 Andol India
42 E5 Andong S. Korea
42 E5 Andong-ho *l.* S. Korea
5 D4 Andorra *country* Europe
15 G1 Andorra la Vella Andorra
9 F6 Andover U.K.
71 H2 Andover *ME* U.S.A.
70 C4 Andover *OH* U.S.A.
6 O2 Andøya *i.* Norway
82 B3 Andradina Brazil
20 E3 Andreapol' Rus. Fed.
8 C3 Andreas U.K.
88 C3 André Félix, Parc National de *nat. park* C.A.R.
82 D3 Andrelândia Brazil
65 C5 Andrews U.S.A.
18 G4 Andria Italy
89 E6 Androka Madag.
67 E7 Andros *i.* Bahamas
19 L6 Andros *i.* Greece
71 H2 Androscoggin *r.* U.S.A.
67 E7 Andros Town Bahamas
33 A4 Āndrott *i.* India
21 D5 Andrushivka Ukr.
6 Q2 Andselv Norway
15 D3 Andújar Spain
89 B5 Andulo Angola
86 C3 Anéfis Mali
75 M5 Anegada *i.* Virgin Is
83 D4 Anegada, Bahía *b.* Arg.
73 F5 Anegam U.S.A.
86 C4 Anécho Togo
'Aneiza, Jabal *h. see* 'Unayzah, Jabal
73 H3 Aneth U.S.A.
15 G1 Aneto *mt* Spain
87 D3 Aney Niger
39 E5 Anfu China
89 E5 Angadoka, Lohatanjona *hd* Madag.
36 B1 Angara *r.* Rus. Fed.
36 C1 Angarsk Rus. Fed.
43 B3 Angat Phil.
7 O5 Ånge Sweden
74 B3 Angel de la Guarda *i.* Mex.
43 B3 Angeles Phil.
7 N8 Ängelholm Sweden
72 B2 Angels Camp U.S.A.
6 P4 Ångermanälven *r.* Sweden
14 D3 Angers France
57 K2 Angikuni Lake *l.* Can.
44 B2 Angkor Cambodia
9 C4 Anglesey *i.* U.K.
65 E6 Angleton U.S.A.
69 H2 Angliers Can.
Angmagssalik *see* Tasiilaq
44 □ Ang Mo Kio Sing.
88 C3 Ango Congo(Zaire)
89 D5 Angoche Moz.
31 E5 Angohrān Iran
83 B3 Angol Chile
68 E5 Angola U.S.A.
85 E7 Angola *country* Africa
96 K7 Angola Basin *sea feature* Atl. Ocean
74 F5 Angostura, Presa de la *resr* Mex.
14 E4 Angoulême France
24 J5 Angren Uzbek.
44 B2 Ang Thong Thai.
53 K8 Anguilla *terr.* Caribbean Sea
38 E1 Anguli Nur *l.* China
38 E2 Anguo China
82 A3 Anhanduí *r.* Brazil
7 M8 Anholt *i.* Denmark
39 D4 Anhua China
38 E3 Anhui *div.* China
82 A2 Anhumas Brazil
42 D5 Anhŭng S. Korea
82 C2 Anicuns Brazil
20 G3 Anikovo Rus. Fed.
73 H6 Animas U.S.A.
73 H6 Animas Peak *summit* U.S.A.
44 A2 Anin Myanmar
40 H1 Aniva Rus. Fed.
40 H1 Aniva, Mys *c.* Rus. Fed.
36 G2 Aniva, Zaliv *b.* Rus. Fed.
49 G3 Aniwa *i.* Vanuatu
12 B5 Anizy-le-Château France
7 U6 Anjalankoski Fin.
33 B4 Anjengo India
39 F4 Anji China
34 D5 Anji India
31 E3 Anjoman Iran
14 D3 Anjou *reg.* France
89 E5 Anjouan *i.* Comoros
89 E5 Anjozorobe Madag.
42 C4 Anjŭ N. Korea

89 E6 Ankaboa, Tanjona *pt* Madag.
38 C3 Ankang China
28 D2 Ankara Turkey
89 E6 Ankazoabo Madag.
89 E5 Ankazobe Madag.
44 D2 An Khê Vietnam
34 C5 Ankleshwar India
39 B5 Anlong China
44 C2 Ânlong Vêng Cambodia
38 D4 Anlu China
42 D5 Anmyŏn Do *i.* S. Korea
21 G5 Anna Rus. Fed.
86 C1 Annaba Alg.
13 M4 Annaberg-Buchholtz Ger.
28 F4 An Nabk Syria
32 B4 An Nafūd *des.* S. Arabia
8 A3 Annahilt U.K.
29 K6 An Najaf Iraq
70 E5 Anna, Lake *l.* U.S.A.
11 D3 Annalee *r.* Rep. of Ireland
11 F3 Annalong U.K.
10 E6 Annan *Scot.* U.K.
10 E6 Annan *r.* U.K.
10 E5 Annandale *v.* U.K.
70 E5 Annapolis U.S.A.
59 G5 Annapolis Royal Can.
35 E3 Annapurna *mt* Nepal
30 C5 An Naqīrah *well* S. Arabia
69 F4 Ann Arbor U.S.A.
79 G2 Anna Regina Guyana
29 L6 An Nāṣirīyah Iraq
71 H3 Ann, Cape *hd* U.S.A.
14 H4 Annecy France
14 H3 Annemasse France
12 E1 Annen Neth.
56 C4 Annette I. *i.* U.S.A.
39 B5 Anning China
67 C5 Anniston U.S.A.
84 C6 Annobón *i.* Equatorial Guinea
14 G4 Annonay France
32 C4 An Nu'ayrīyah S. Arabia
29 K5 An Nu'mānīyah Iraq
62 E4 Anoka U.S.A.
89 E5 Anorontany, Tanjona *hd* Madag.
19 L7 Ano Viannos Greece
39 D6 Anpu China
39 C6 Anpu Gang *b.* China
39 E4 Anqing China
38 F2 Anqiu China
39 D5 Anren China
12 D4 Ans Belgium
38 C2 Ansai China
28 F4 Ansariye, J. el *mts* Syria
13 J5 Ansbach Ger.
42 B3 Anshan China
39 B5 Anshun China
83 C1 Ansilta *mt* Arg.
83 F1 Ansina Uru.
64 D3 Ansley U.S.A.
65 D5 Anson U.S.A.
86 C3 Ansongo Mali
58 D4 Ansonville Can.
70 C5 Ansted U.S.A.
34 D4 Anta India
78 D6 Antabamba Peru
28 F3 Antakya Turkey
89 F5 Antalaha Madag.
28 C3 Antalya Turkey
28 C3 Antalya Körfezi *g.* Turkey
89 E5 Antananarivo Madag.
92 B2 Antarctic Peninsula Ant.
10 C3 An Teallach *mt* U.K.
72 D2 Antelope Range *mts* U.S.A.
15 D4 Antequera Spain
63 F5 Anthony U.S.A.
86 B2 Anti Atlas *mts* Morocco
14 H5 Antibes France
59 H4 Anticosti, Île d' *i.* Can.
68 C3 Antigo U.S.A.
59 H4 Antigonish Can.
74 F6 Antigua Guatemala
75 M5 Antigua *i.* Antigua
53 K8 Antigua and Barbuda *country* Caribbean Sea
74 E4 Antiguo-Morelos Mex.
19 K7 Antikythira *i.* Greece
19 K7 Antikythiro, Steno *chan.* Greece
Anti Lebanon *mts see* Sharqi, Jebel esh
Antioch *see* Antakya
72 B3 Antioch *CA* U.S.A.
68 C4 Antioch *IL* U.S.A.
81 B3 Antioquia Col.
46 J8 Antipodes Islands *is* N.Z.
19 L5 Antipsara *i.* Greece
65 E5 Antlers U.S.A.
80 B2 Antofagasta Chile
80 C3 Antofalla, Vol. *volc.* Arg.
12 B4 Antoing Belgium
82 C4 Antonina Brazil
82 E1 Antônio *r.* Brazil
72 B3 Antonio *r.* U.S.A.
63 F4 Antonito U.S.A.
11 E3 Antrim U.K.
11 E2 Antrim Hills *h.* U.K.
89 E5 Antsalova Madag.
89 E5 Antsirabe Madag.
89 E5 Antsirañana Madag.
89 E5 Antsohihy Madag.
6 S3 Anttis Sweden
7 U6 Anttola Fin.
42 E2 Antu China
83 B3 Antuco Chile
83 B3 Antuco, Volcán *volc.* Chile
12 C3 Antwerp Belgium
71 F2 Antwerp U.S.A.
Antwerpen *see* Antwerp
40 C3 Anuchino Rus. Fed.
58 E2 Anuc, Lac *l.* Can.
35 F5 Anugul India
42 D6 Anŭi S. Korea
34 C3 Anupgarh India
33 C4 Anuradhapura Sri Lanka
30 D5 Anveh Iran
Anvers *see* Antwerp
92 B2 Anvers I. *i.* Ant.
39 F5 Anxi *Fujian* China
36 B2 Anxi *Gansu* China
38 B4 An Xian China
39 D4 Anxiang China
38 E2 Anxin China
48 D5 Anxious Bay *b.* Austr.
38 E2 Anyang China
42 D5 Anyang S. Korea
19 L6 Anydro *i.* Greece
36 B3 A'nyêmaqên Shan *mts* China
39 E4 Anyi China
39 E5 Anyuan China
39 B4 Anyue China
25 S3 Anyuysk Rus. Fed.
81 B3 Anzá Col.
38 D2 Anze China
36 A1 Anzhero-Sudzhensk Rus. Fed.
88 C4 Anzi Congo(Zaire)
18 E4 Anzio Italy
49 G3 Aoba *i.* Vanuatu
44 A3 Ao Ban Don *b.* Thai.
38 F1 Aohan Qi China
40 G4 Aomori Japan
34 D3 Aonla India
Aoraki, Mt *mt see* Cook, Mt
51 D4 Aorere *r.* N.Z.
44 A3 Ao Sawi *b.* Thai.
18 B2 Aosta Italy
86 B2 Aoukâr *reg.* Mali/Maur.
79 G8 Apa *r.* Brazil
88 D3 Apac Uganda
73 H6 Apache U.S.A.
73 H5 Apache Creek U.S.A.
73 G5 Apache Junction U.S.A.
73 G6 Apache Peak *summit* U.S.A.
67 C6 Apalachee Bay *b.* U.S.A.
67 C6 Apalachicola U.S.A.
81 C4 Apaporis *r.* Col.
29 K1 Aparan Armenia
82 B3 Aparecida do Tabuado Brazil
43 B2 Aparri Phil.
6 X3 Apatity Rus. Fed.
74 D5 Apatzingán Mex.
7 U8 Ape Latvia
12 D2 Apeldoorn Neth.
13 H2 Apelern Ger.
13 H1 Apensen Ger.
34 E3 Api *mt* Nepal
49 J3 Apia Western Samoa
51 E3 Apiti N.Z.
79 G2 Apoera Suriname
13 K3 Apolda Ger.
50 D5 Apollo Bay Austr.
78 E6 Apolo Bol.
43 C5 Apo, Mt *volc.* Phil.
67 D6 Apopka, L. *l.* U.S.A.
82 B2 Aporé Brazil
82 B2 Aporé *r.* Brazil
66 B2 Apostle Islands *is* U.S.A.
68 B2 Apostle Islands National Lakeshore *res.* U.S.A.
28 E4 Apostolos Andreas, Cape *c.* Cyprus
70 B6 Appalachia U.S.A.
70 C6 Appalachian Mountains U.S.A.
18 E3 Appennino Abruzzese *mts* Italy
18 D2 Appennino Tosco-Emiliano *mts* Italy
18 E3 Appennino Umbro-Marchigiano *mts* Italy
50 H3 Appin Austr.
12 E1 Appingedam Neth.
10 C3 Applecross U.K.
64 D2 Appleton *MN* U.S.A.
68 C3 Appleton *WV* U.S.A.
72 D4 Apple Valley U.S.A.
70 D6 Appomattox U.S.A.
18 E4 Aprilia Italy
21 F6 Apsheronsk Rus. Fed.
50 C4 Apsley Austr.
69 H3 Apsley Can.
14 G5 Apt France
82 B3 Apucarana Brazil
43 A4 Apurahuan Phil.
81 D3 Apure *r.* Venez.
78 D6 Apurimac *r.* Peru
28 E7 'Aqaba Jordan
26 B4 Aqaba, Gulf of *g.* Asia
30 D2 Aqbana Iran
31 G2 Āqchah Afgh.
30 B2 Aq Chai *r.* Iran
30 D3 Āqdā Iran
30 B2 Aqdoghmish *r.* Iran
29 K3 Āq Kān Dāgh, Kūh-e *mt* Iran
29 J3 'Aqrah Iraq
73 F4 Aquarius Mts *mts* U.S.A.
73 G3 Aquarius Plateau *plat.* U.S.A.
18 G4 Aquaviva delle Fonti Italy
82 A3 Aquidauana Brazil
82 A2 Aquidauana *r.* Brazil
81 D4 Aquio *r.* Col.
14 D4 Aquitaine *reg.* France
35 F4 Ara India
31 G4 Arab Afgh.
67 C5 Arab U.S.A.
31 E3 'Arabābād Iran
87 E3 Arab, Bahr el *watercourse* Sudan
93 J3 Arabian Basin *sea feature* Ind. Ocean
22 D8 Arabian Sea *sea* Ind. Ocean
81 E3 Arabopó Venez.
81 E3 Arabopó *r.* Venez.
28 D1 Araç Turkey
81 E4 Araça *r.* Brazil
79 L6 Aracaju Brazil
81 D4 Aracamuni, Co *summit* Venez.
82 A4 Aracanguy, Mtes de *h.* Para.
79 L4 Aracati Brazil
82 E1 Aracatu Brazil
82 B3 Araçatuba Brazil
15 C4 Aracena Spain
82 E2 Aracruz Brazil
82 D2 Araçuaí Brazil
82 D2 Araçuaí *r.* Brazil
19 J1 Arad Romania
87 E3 Arada Chad
29 L6 Aradah Iraq
82 D2 Arafura Sea *sea* Austr./Indon.
82 B1 Aragarças Brazil
29 J1 Aragats Armenia
29 K1 Aragats Lerr *mt* Armenia
15 F2 Aragón *div.* Spain
15 F1 Aragón *r.* Spain
79 J5 Araguacema Brazil
81 D2 Aragua de Barcelona Venez.
79 J5 Araguaia *r.* Brazil
79 H6 Araguaia, Parque Nacional de *nat. park* Brazil
79 J5 Araguaína Brazil
82 C2 Araguari Brazil
82 C2 Araguari *r.* *Minas Gerais* Brazil
79 J5 Araguatins Brazil
21 H7 Aragvi *r.* Georgia
41 F6 Arai Japan
79 K4 Araiosos Brazil
86 C2 Arak Alg.
30 C3 Arāk Iran
35 H5 Arakan Yoma *mts* Myanmar
33 B3 Arakkonam India
29 K2 Aralık Turkey
26 E2 Aral Sea *l.* Kazak./Uzbek.
26 E2 Aral'sk Kazak.
Aral'skoye More *salt l. see* Aral Sea
21 J5 Aralsor, Ozero *l.* Kazak.
30 B5 Aramah *plat.* S. Arabia
34 D6 Aran *r.* India
15 E2 Aranda de Duero Spain
29 L4 Arandān Iran
19 J2 Aranđelovac Yugo.
33 B3 Arani India
11 C3 Aran Island *i.* Rep. of Ireland
11 B4 Aran Islands *is* Rep. of Ireland
15 E2 Aranjuez Spain
89 B6 Aranos Namibia
65 D7 Aransas Pass U.S.A.
82 B2 Arantes *r.* Brazil
49 H1 Aranuka *i.* Gilbert Is
41 B8 Arao Japan
86 B3 Araouane Mali
64 D3 Arapahoe U.S.A.
81 E4 Arapari *r.* Brazil
83 F1 Arapey Grande *r.* Uru.
79 L5 Arapiraca Brazil
19 L4 Arapis, Akra *pt* Greece
28 G2 Arapkir Turkey
82 B3 Arapongas Brazil
35 F4 A Rapti Doon *r.* Nepal
32 B3 'Ar'ar S. Arabia
80 G3 Araranguá Brazil
82 C3 Araraquara Brazil
79 H5 Araras Brazil
82 B4 Araras, Serra das *mts* Brazil
29 K2 Ararat Armenia
50 D4 Ararat Austr.
29 K2 Ararat, Mt *mt* Turkey
35 F4 Araria India
82 D3 Araruama, Lago de *lag.* Brazil
29 J6 'Ar'ar, W. *watercourse* Iraq/S. Arabia
29 J2 Aras Turkey
29 J1 Aras *r.* Turkey
82 E1 Arataca Brazil
81 C3 Arauca Col.
81 C3 Arauca *r.* Venez.
83 B3 Arauco Chile
81 C3 Arauquita Col.
81 C2 Araure Venez.
34 C4 Aravalli Range *mts* India
7 T7 Aravete Estonia
49 F2 Arawa P.N.G.
82 C2 Araxá Brazil
81 D2 Araya, Pen. de *pen.* Venez.
81 D2 Araya, Pta de *pt* Venez.
28 C2 Arayıt Dağı *mt* Turkey
29 M2 Araz *r.* Asia
29 K4 Arbat Iraq
20 J3 Arbazh Rus. Fed.
29 K3 Arbīl Iraq
7 O7 Arboga Sweden
57 J4 Arborfield Can.
10 F4 Arbroath U.K.
72 A2 Arbuckle U.S.A.
31 F4 Arbu Lut, Dasht-e *des.* Afgh.
14 D4 Arcachon France
67 D7 Arcadia U.S.A.
62 A3 Arcata U.S.A.
72 D2 Arc Dome *summit* U.S.A.
20 G1 Archangel Rus. Fed.
48 E3 Archer *r.* Austr.
73 H2 Arches Nat. Park U.S.A.
30 E2 Archman Turkm.
29 M2 Ärçivan Azer.
62 D3 Arco U.S.A.
15 D4 Arcos de la Frontera Spain
55 K2 Arctic Bay Can.
54 C3 Arctic Plains U.S.A.
54 E3 Arctic Red *r.* Can.
92 B2 Arctowski *Poland Base* Ant.
30 C2 Ardabīl Iran
29 J1 Ardahan Turkey
30 D3 Ardakān Iran
30 C4 Ardal Iran
7 K6 Årdalstangen Norway
11 C3 Ardara Rep. of Ireland
19 L4 Ardas *r.* Bulg.
20 H4 Ardatov *Mordov.* Rus. Fed.
20 G4 Ardatov *Nizheg.* Rus. Fed.
69 G3 Ardbeg Can.
11 E4 Ardee Rep. of Ireland
50 A2 Arden, Mount *h.* Austr.
12 D5 Ardennes *reg.* Belgium
12 C5 Ardennes, Canal des *canal* France
30 D3 Ardestān Iran
11 F3 Ardglass U.K.
15 C3 Ardila *r.* Port.
50 F3 Ardlethan Austr.
65 D5 Ardmore U.S.A.
10 B4 Ardnamurchan, Point of *pt* U.K.
10 C4 Ardrishaig U.K.
50 A3 Ardrossan Austr.
10 D5 Ardrossan U.K.
10 C3 Ardvasar U.K.
83 E2 Areco *r.* Arg.
79 L4 Areia Branca Brazil
43 B4 Aremberg *h.* Ger.
43 B4 Arena *rf* Phil.
72 A2 Arena, Pt *pt* U.S.A.
15 D2 Arenas de San Pedro Spain
7 L7 Arendal Norway
13 K2 Arendsee (Altmark) Ger.
9 D5 Arenig Fawr *h.* U.K.
19 K6 Areopoli Greece
78 D7 Arequipa Peru
79 H4 Arere Brazil
15 D2 Arévalo Spain
18 D3 Arezzo Italy
28 G6 'Arfajah *well* S. Arabia
38 D1 Argalant Mongolia
15 E2 Arganda Spain
43 B4 Argao Phil.
18 D2 Argenta Italy
14 D2 Argentan France
18 D3 Argentario, Monte *h.* Italy
18 B2 Argentera, Cima dell' *mt* Italy
12 F5 Argenthal Ger.
77 D7 Argentina *country* S. America
92 B3 Argentina Ra. *mts* Ant.
96 F8 Argentine Basin *sea feature* Atl. Ocean
80 B8 Argentino, Lago *l.* Arg.
19 L2 Argeș *r.* Romania
31 G4 Arghandab *r.* Afgh.
31 G4 Arghastan *r.* Afgh.
28 C2 Argıthanı Turkey
19 K6 Argolikos Kolpos *b.* Greece
19 K6 Argos Greece
19 J5 Argostoli Greece
15 F1 Arguís Spain
21 H7 Argun Rus. Fed.
36 E1 Argun' *r.* China/Rus. Fed.
34 D4 Argus Range *mts* U.S.A.
68 C4 Argyle U.S.A.
48 C3 Argyle, Lake *l.* Austr.
10 C4 Argyll *reg.* U.K.
7 M8 Århus Denmark
51 E3 Aria N.Z.
50 F3 Ariah Park Austr.
41 B6 Ariake-kai *b.* Japan
89 B6 Ariamsvlei Namibia
18 F4 Ariano Irpino Italy
81 B4 Ariari *r.* Col.
83 D2 Arias Arg.
27 F6 Ari Atoll Maldives
81 E2 Aribí *r.* Venez.
86 B3 Aribinda Burkina
80 B1 Arica Chile
10 C4 Arienas, Loch *l.* U.K.
28 F4 Arīḩā Syria
62 G4 Arikaree *r.* U.S.A.
81 E2 Arima Trinidad and Tobago
82 C1 Arinos Brazil
79 G6 Arinos *r.* Brazil
81 C3 Ariporo *r.* Col.
78 F5 Aripuanã Brazil
78 F5 Aripuanã *r.* Brazil
78 F5 Ariquemes Brazil
82 B2 Ariranhá *r.* Brazil
90 B1 Aris Namibia
10 C4 Arisaig U.K.
10 C4 Arisaig, Sound of *chan.* U.K.
56 D4 Aristazabal I. *i.* Can.
73 G4 Arizona *div.* U.S.A.
60 D5 Arizpe Mex.
30 B5 'Arjah S. Arabia
6 P3 Arjeplog Sweden
81 B2 Arjona Col.
45 D4 Arjuna, G. *volc.* Indon.
21 G5 Arkadak Rus. Fed.
65 E5 Arkadelphia U.S.A.
10 C4 Arkaig, Loch *l.* U.K.
26 E1 Arkalyk Kazak.
65 E5 Arkansas *div.* U.S.A.
65 F5 Arkansas *r.* U.S.A.
65 D4 Arkansas City U.S.A.
35 G1 Arkatag Shan *mts* China
Arkhangel'sk *see* Archangel
20 G2 Arkhangel'skaya Oblast' *div.* Rus. Fed.
20 F4 Arkhangel'skoye Rus. Fed.
40 C3 Arkhipovka Rus. Fed.
11 E5 Arklow Rep. of Ireland
19 M6 Arkoi *i.* Greece
16 F3 Arkona, Kap *hd* Ger.
24 K2 Arkticheskogo Instituta, Ostrova *is* Rus. Fed.
71 F3 Arkville U.S.A.
14 G5 Arles France
91 G4 Arlington S. Africa
62 B2 Arlington *OR* U.S.A.
64 D2 Arlington *SD* U.S.A.
70 E5 Arlington *VA* U.S.A.
68 D4 Arlington Heights U.S.A.
86 C3 Arlit Niger
12 D5 Arlon Belgium
43 C5 Armadores *i.* Indon.
11 E3 Armagh U.K.
87 F2 Armant Egypt
21 G6 Armavir Rus. Fed.
81 B3 Armenia Col.
23 D5 Armenia *country* Asia
81 B3 Armero Col.
50 H1 Armidale Austr.
57 L2 Armit Lake *l.* Can.
34 E5 Armori India
56 B3 Armour, Mt *mt* Can./U.S.A.
11 E2 Armoy U.K.
56 F4 Armstrong *B.C.* Can.
58 C3 Armstrong *Ont.* Can.
40 E1 Armu *r.* Rus. Fed.
33 B2 Armur India
21 E6 Armyans'k Ukr.
28 D4 Arnaoutis, Cape *c.* Cyprus
59 F1 Arnaud *r.* Can.
7 M6 Årnes Norway
65 D4 Arnett U.S.A.
12 D3 Arnhem Neth.
48 D3 Arnhem Bay *b.* Austr.
48 D3 Arnhem, C. *c.* Austr.
48 D3 Arnhem Land *reg.* Austr.
18 D3 Arno *r.* Italy
9 F4 Arnold U.K.
68 D2 Arnold U.S.A.
69 H1 Arnoux, Lac *l.* Can.
69 J3 Arnprior Can.
13 G3 Arnsberg Ger.
13 J4 Arnstadt Ger.
69 H3 Arnstein Can.
13 H5 Arnstein Ger.
69 H1 Arntfield Can.
81 E3 Aro *r.* Venez.
89 B6 Aroab Namibia
13 H3 Arolsen Ger.
18 C2 Arona Italy
71 K1 Aroostook Can.
71 J1 Aroostook *r.* Can./U.S.A.
49 H2 Arorae *i.* Kiribati
43 B3 Aroroy Phil.
21 G7 Arpa *r.* Armenia/Turkey
29 J1 Arpaçay Turkey
31 G5 Arra *r.* Pak.
29 J5 Ar Ramādī Iraq
28 E7 Ar Ramlah Jordan
10 C5 Arran *i.* U.K.
29 G4 Ar Raqqah Syria
14 F1 Arras France
30 A5 Ar-Rass S. Arabia
28 F4 Ar Rastan Syria
29 J7 Ar Rawḍ *well* S. Arabia
30 C5 Ar Rayyān Qatar
81 C4 Arrecifal Col.
83 E2 Arrecifes Arg.
74 F5 Arriaga Mex.
83 E2 Arribeños Arg.
29 L6 Ar Rifā'ī Iraq
29 K6 Ar Rihāb *salt flat* Iraq
32 D5 Ar Rimāl *reg.* S. Arabia
73 H3 Arriola U.S.A.
Ar Riyāḍ *see* Riyadh
10 D4 Arrochar U.K.
83 G2 Arroio Grande Brazil
82 D1 Arrojado *r.* Brazil
68 B1 Arrow Lake *l.* Can.
11 C3 Arrow, Lough *l.* Rep. of Ireland
62 D3 Arrowrock Res. *resr* U.S.A.
51 C5 Arrowsmith, Mt *mt* N.Z.
72 B4 Arroyo Grande U.S.A.
83 F3 Arroyo Grande *r.* Arg.
83 E2 Arroyo Seco Arg.
30 B5 Ar Rubay'iyah S. Arabia
82 A1 Arruda Brazil
29 K6 Ar Rumaythah Iraq
28 G4 Ar Ruṣāfah Syria
31 E6 Ar Rustāq Oman
29 H5 Ar Ruṭba Iraq
30 B6 Ar Ruwayḍah S. Arabia
7 L8 Års Denmark
30 B2 Ars Iran
30 D4 Arsenajān Iran
40 C2 Arsen'yev Rus. Fed.
33 B3 Arsikere India
20 J3 Arsk Rus. Fed.
28 E3 Arslanköy Turkey
19 J5 Arta Greece
29 K2 Artashat Armenia
40 C3 Artem Rus. Fed.
21 F5 Artemivs'k Ukr.
40 C3 Artemovskiy Rus. Fed.
14 E2 Artenay France
63 F5 Artesia U.S.A.
69 G4 Arthur Can.
70 C4 Arthur, Lake *l.* U.S.A.
48 F4 Arthur Pt *pt* Austr.
51 C5 Arthur's Pass N.Z.
51 C5 Arthur's Pass National Park N.Z.
67 F7 Arthur's Town Bahamas
83 F1 Artigas Uru.
92 B1 Artigas *Uru. Base* Ant.
29 J1 Art'ik Armenia
57 H2 Artillery Lake *l.* Can.
91 G2 Artisia Botswana
14 F1 Artois *reg.* France
12 A4 Artois, Collines d' *h.* France
29 J2 Artos D. *mt* Turkey
28 F1 Artova Turkey
21 D6 Artsyz Ukr.
27 F3 Artux China
29 H1 Artvin Turkey
88 D3 Arua Uganda
82 B1 Aruanã Brazil
53 J8 Aruba *terr.* Caribbean Sea
37 F7 Aru, Kepulauan *is* Indon.
78 F4 Arumã Brazil
35 F4 Arun *r.* Nepal
35 H3 Arunachal Pradesh *div.* India
9 G7 Arundel U.K.
88 D4 Arusha Tanz.
64 B4 Arvada U.S.A.
11 D4 Arvagh Rep. of Ireland
36 C2 Arvayheer Mongolia
34 D5 Arvi India
57 L2 Arviat Can.
59 F4 Arvida Can.
6 Q4 Arvidsjaur Sweden
7 N7 Arvika Sweden
72 C4 Arvin U.S.A.
30 B6 Arwā' S. Arabia
25 O2 Ary Rus. Fed.
20 G4 Arzamas Rus. Fed.
13 L4 Arzberg Ger.
15 F5 Arzew Alg.
21 H6 Arzgir Rus. Fed.
13 L4 Aš Czech Rep.
81 E3 Asa *r.* Venez.
86 C4 Asaba Nigeria
31 H3 Asadābād Afgh.
30 C3 Asadābād Iran
31 E3 Asadābād Iran
28 G3 Asad, Buḩayrat al *resr* Syria
44 A5 Asahan *r.* Indon.
40 H3 Asahi-dake *volc.* Japan
41 C7 Asahi-gawa *r.* Japan
40 H3 Asahikawa Japan
30 C2 Asālem Iran
42 D5 Asan Man *b.* S. Korea
35 F5 Asansol India
12 F4 Asbach Ger.
59 F4 Asbestos Can.
90 E4 Asbestos Mountains S. Africa
71 F4 Asbury Park U.S.A.
18 F4 Ascea Italy
78 F7 Ascensión Bol.
74 G5 Ascensión, B. de la *b.* Mex.
85 B6 Ascension Island *i.* Atlantic Ocean
13 H5 Aschaffenburg Ger.
12 F3 Ascheberg Ger.
13 K3 Aschersleben Ger.
18 E3 Ascoli Piceno Italy
7 O8 Åseda Sweden
6 P4 Åsele Sweden
30 D4 Asemānjerd Iran
9 E6 Ashbourne U.K.
51 C5 Ashburton N.Z.
48 B4 Ashburton *watercourse* Austr.
68 D1 Ashburton Bay *b.* Can.
56 E4 Ashcroft Can.
28 E6 Ashdod Israel
65 E5 Ashdown U.S.A.
67 E5 Asheboro U.S.A.
67 D5 Asheville U.S.A.
9 H6 Ashford U.K.
73 F4 Ash Fork U.S.A.
31 E2 Ashgabat Turkm.
40 H3 Ashibetsu Japan
41 F6 Ashikaga Japan
8 F2 Ashington U.K.
20 J3 Ashit *r.* Rus. Fed.
41 C8 Ashizuri-misaki *pt* Japan
30 D4 Ashkazar Iran
65 D4 Ashland *KS* U.S.A.
70 B5 Ashland *KY* U.S.A.
71 J1 Ashland *ME* U.S.A.
62 F2 Ashland *MT* U.S.A.
71 H3 Ashland *NH* U.S.A.
70 B4 Ashland *OH* U.S.A.
62 B3 Ashland *OR* U.S.A.
70 E6 Ashland *VA* U.S.A.
68 B2 Ashland *WV* U.S.A.
64 D2 Ashley U.S.A.
20 C4 Ashmyany Belarus
73 F5 Ash Peak U.S.A.
28 E6 Ashqelon Israel
34 B4 Ashraf, Md. Pak.
29 J6 Ash Shabakah Iraq
29 H3 Ash Shaddādah Syria
29 H7 Ash Shaqīq *well* S. Arabia
30 B5 Ash Sha'rā' S. Arabia
29 J4 Ash Sharqāṭ Iraq
29 L6 Ash Shaṭrah Iraq
32 C7 Ash Shiḩr Yemen
29 K6 Ash Shināfīyah Iraq
30 E5 Ash Shināṣ Oman
30 B4 Ash Shu'bah S. Arabia
30 B5 Ash Shumlūl S. Arabia
70 C4 Ashtabula U.S.A.
29 K1 Ashtarak Armenia
34 D5 Ashti India
33 A2 Ashti India
30 C3 Āshtiān Iran
90 D6 Ashton S. Africa
62 E2 Ashton U.S.A.
8 E4 Ashton-under-Lyne U.K.
55 M4 Ashuanipi Lake *l.* Can.
67 C5 Ashville U.S.A.
33 B2 Asifabad India
35 F6 Āsika India
28 F4 'Āṣī, Nahr al *r.* Asia
18 C4 Asinara, Golfo dell' *b.* *Sardinia* Italy
24 K4 Asino Rus. Fed.
20 D4 Asipovichy Belarus
32 B5 'Asīr *reg.* S. Arabia
29 H2 Aşkale Turkey
7 M7 Asker Norway
7 O7 Askersund Sweden
7 M7 Askim Norway
36 B1 Askiz Rus. Fed.
29 L2 Aşlāndūz Iran
88 D2 Asmara Eritrea
7 O8 Åsnen *l.* Sweden
19 L3 Asenovgrad Bulg.
34 C4 Asop India
29 M3 Aspar Iran
8 D3 Aspatria U.K.
63 F4 Aspen U.S.A.
13 H6 Asperg Ger.
65 C5 Aspermont U.S.A.
51 B6 Aspiring, Mt *mt* N.Z.
57 H4 Asquith Can.
28 F4 As Sa'an Syria
88 E2 Assab Eritrea
30 C5 As Sabsab *well* S. Arabia
28 F3 As Safirah Syria
30 C5 As Saji *well* S. Arabia
30 B5 As Salamiyah S. Arabia
29 K6 As Salmān Iraq
35 H4 Assam *div.* India
29 K6 As Samāwah Iraq
28 F5 Aş Şanamayn Syria
87 E2 As Sarīr *reg.* Libya
71 F5 Assateague I. *i.* U.S.A.
71 F6 Assateague Island National Seashore *res.* U.S.A.
12 E1 Assen Neth.
12 B3 Assenede Belgium
12 D4 Assesse Belgium
35 F5 Assia Hills *h.* India
87 D1 As Sidrah Libya
57 H5 Assiniboia Can.
57 K5 Assiniboine *r.* Can.
56 F4 Assiniboine, Mt *mt* Can.
82 B3 Assis Brazil
18 E3 Assisi Italy
13 G4 Aßlar Ger.
29 L7 Aş Şubayḩīyah Kuwait
30 B4 Aş Şufayrī *well* S. Arabia
29 G4 As Sukhnah Syria
29 K4 As Sulaymānīyah Iraq

# B

18 C2 Biella Italy
17 J6 Bielsko-Biała Pol.
17 L4 Bielsk Podlaski Pol.
13 J1 Bienenbüttel Ger.
44 C3 Biên Hoa Vietnam
Bienne see Biel
58 F2 Bienville, Lac l. Can.
12 C3 Biesbosch, Nationaal Park de nat. park Neth.
91 F3 Biesiesvlei S. Africa
13 H6 Bietigheim-Bissingen Ger.
12 D5 Bièvre Belgium
88 B4 Bifoun Gabon
59 J3 Big r. Can.
72 A2 Big r. U.S.A.
21 C7 Biga Turkey
28 B2 Bigadiç Turkey
19 M5 Biga Yarımadası pen. Turkey
68 D2 Big Bay U.S.A.
68 D3 Big Bay de Noc b. U.S.A.
72 D4 Big Bear Lake U.S.A.
62 E2 Big Belt Mts mts U.S.A.
91 J3 Big Bend Swaziland
65 C6 Big Bend Nat. Park U.S.A.
65 F5 Big Black r. U.S.A.
9 D7 Bigbury-on-Sea U.K.
67 D7 Big Cypress Nat. Preserve res. U.S.A.
68 C3 Big Eau Pleine Reservoir U.S.A.
57 L5 Big Falls U.S.A.
57 H4 Biggar Can.
10 E5 Biggar U.K.
56 B3 Bigger, Mt mt Can.
9 G5 Biggleswade U.K.
62 D2 Big Hole r. U.S.A.
62 F2 Bighorn r. U.S.A.
62 E2 Bighorn Canyon Nat. Recreation Area res. U.S.A.
62 F2 Bighorn Mountains U.S.A.
67 F7 Bight, The Bahamas
55 L3 Big Island i. N.W.T. Can.
58 F2 Big Island i. Can.
71 K2 Big Lake l. U.S.A.
86 A3 Bignona Senegal
70 D6 Big Otter r. U.S.A.
72 C3 Big Pine U.S.A.
68 E4 Big Rapids U.S.A.
68 C3 Big Rib r. U.S.A.
57 H4 Big River Can.
68 D3 Big Sable Pt pt U.S.A.
56 C2 Big Salmon r. Can.
57 K3 Big Sand Lake l. Can.
73 F4 Big Sandy r. U.S.A.
64 D2 Big Sioux r. U.S.A.
72 D2 Big Smokey Valley v. U.S.A.
65 C5 Big Spring U.S.A.
64 C3 Big Springs U.S.A.
70 B6 Big Stone Gap U.S.A.
72 B3 Big Sur U.S.A.
62 E2 Big Timber U.S.A.
58 C3 Big Trout Lake Can.
58 C3 Big Trout Lake l. Can.
73 G3 Big Water U.S.A.
69 H3 Bigwin Can.
18 F2 Bihać Bos.-Herz.
35 F4 Bihar div. India
35 F4 Bihar Sharif India
40 J3 Bihoro Japan
17 L7 Bihor, Vârful mt Romania
86 A3 Bijagós, Arquipélago dos is Guinea-Bissau
34 C4 Bijainagar India
33 A2 Bijapur India
30 B3 Bījār Iran
33 C2 Bijarpur India
19 H2 Bijeljina Bos.-Herz.
19 H3 Bijelo Polje Yugo.
39 B5 Bijie China
31 E5 Bījnābād Iran
35 G4 Bijni India
34 D3 Bijnor India
34 B3 Bijnot Pak.
34 C3 Bikaner India
36 F2 Bikin Rus. Fed.
40 D1 Bikin r. Rus. Fed.
46 H3 Bikini i. Marshall Islands
88 B4 Bikoro Congo(Zaire)
38 B3 Bikou China
34 C4 Bilara India
35 E5 Bilaspur India
29 M2 Biläsuvar Azer.
21 D5 Bila Tserkva Ukr.
44 A2 Bilauktaung Range mts Myanmar/Thai.
15 E1 Bilbao Spain
28 C6 Bilbeis Egypt
19 H3 Bileća Bos.-Herz.
28 B1 Bilecik Turkey
17 L5 Biłgoraj Pol.
88 D4 Bilharamulo Tanz.
21 D6 Bilhorod-Dnistrovs'kyy Ukr.
88 C3 Bili Congo(Zaire)
25 S3 Bilibino Rus. Fed.
43 C4 Biliran i. Phil.
42 B4 Biliu r. China
62 F3 Bill U.S.A.
9 H6 Billericay U.K.
8 F3 Billingham U.K.
62 E2 Billings U.S.A.
9 E7 Bill of Portland hd U.K.
73 F4 Bill Williams r. U.S.A.
73 F4 Bill Williams Mtn mt U.S.A.
87 D3 Bilma Niger
48 F4 Biloela Austr.
21 E6 Bilohirs'k Ukr.
17 N5 Bilohir"ya Ukr.
33 B2 Biloli India
21 F5 Bilolut's'k Ukr.
21 E5 Bilopillya Ukr.
21 F5 Bilovods'k Ukr.
67 B6 Biloxi U.S.A.
48 D4 Bilpa Morea Claypan salt flat Austr.
10 E5 Bilston U.K.
87 E3 Biltine Chad
44 A1 Bilugyun I. i. Myanmar
20 J4 Bilyarsk Rus. Fed.
21 D6 Bilyayivka Ukr.
12 D4 Bilzen Belgium
50 G3 Bimberi, Mt mt Austr.
67 E7 Bimini Is is Bahamas
29 M3 Binab Iran
34 D4 Bina-Etawa India
37 E7 Binaija, G. mt Indon.
28 F2 Binboğa Daği mt Turkey
34 E4 Bindki India
89 B4 Bindu Congo(Zaire)
89 D5 Bindura Zimbabwe
15 G2 Binefar Spain
38 B2 Bingcaowan China
13 F5 Bingen am Rhein Ger.
86 B4 Bingerville Côte d'Ivoire
71 J2 Bingham U.S.A.
71 F3 Binghamton U.S.A.
29 H2 Bingöl Turkey
29 H2 Bingol D. mt Turkey
39 C6 Binh Gia Vietnam
44 D2 Binh Sơn Vietnam
35 H4 Bini India
35 E5 Binika India
44 A5 Binjai Indon.
30 D5 Bin Mürkhan well U.A.E.
50 G1 Binnaway Austr.
44 C5 Bintan i. Indon.
43 B3 Bintuan Phil.
45 B3 Bintuhan Indon.
45 D2 Bintulu Malaysia
38 C3 Bin Xian China
50 F3 Binya Austr.
39 C6 Binyang China
38 F2 Binzhou China
83 B3 Biobío div. Chile
83 B3 Bío Bío r. Chile
86 C4 Bioco i. Equatorial Guinea
18 F3 Biograd na Moru Croatia
18 G3 Biokovo mts Croatia
33 A2 Bir India
31 F5 Bīrag, Kūh-e mts Iran
29 H5 Bi'r al Mulūsi Iraq
20 F2 Birandozero Rus. Fed.
88 C2 Birao C.A.R.
35 F4 Biratnagar Nepal
29 G3 Bi'r Buṭaymān Syria
56 G3 Birch r. Can.
57 H4 Birch Hills Can.
50 D3 Birchip Austr.
56 F4 Birch Island Can.
58 B3 Birch L. l. Can.
68 B2 Birch Lake l. U.S.A.
56 G3 Birch Mountains h. Can.
57 J4 Birch River Can.
12 D1 Birdaard Neth.
92 C1 Bird Island U.K. Base Ant.
73 G2 Birdseye U.S.A.
48 D4 Birdsville Austr.
28 F3 Birecik Turkey
87 E3 Bir en Nutrûn well Sudan
45 A1 Bireun Indon.
30 B6 Bi'r Ghawdah well S. Arabia
88 D2 Birhan mt Eth.
82 B3 Birigüi Brazil
31 E3 Bīrjand Iran
29 J6 Birkat al 'Aqabah well Iraq
29 J6 Birkat al 'Athāmīn well Iraq
29 K6 Birkāt Hamad well Iraq
30 A4 Birkat Zubālah waterhole S. Arabia
12 F5 Birkenfeld Ger.
9 D4 Birkenhead U.K.
28 C7 Birket Qârûn l. Egypt
29 K3 Bīrkim Iraq
18 F7 Birkirkara Malta
9 F5 Birmingham U.K.
67 C5 Birmingham U.S.A.
86 A2 Bîr Mogreïn Maur.
28 B6 Bi'r Nāḥid oasis Egypt
86 C3 Birnin-Kebbi Nigeria
86 C3 Birnin Konni Niger
36 F2 Birobidzhan Rus. Fed.
11 D4 Birr Rep. of Ireland
29 J5 Bi'r Sābil Iraq
10 E1 Birsay U.K.
9 F5 Birstall U.K.
13 H4 Birstein Ger.
28 E7 Bîr Tâba Egypt
57 J4 Birtle Can.
35 H3 Biru China
33 A3 Birur India
7 T8 Biržai Lith.
73 H6 Bisbee U.S.A.
4 C4 Biscay, Bay of sea France/Spain
67 D7 Biscayne Nat. Park U.S.A.
16 F7 Bischofshofen Austria
92 B2 Biscoe Islands is Ant.
69 F2 Biscotasi Lake l. Can.
69 F2 Biscotasing Can.
39 C4 Bishan China
29 M5 Bīsheh Iran
27 F2 Bishkek Kyrg.
35 F5 Bishnupur India
91 G6 Bisho S. Africa
72 C3 Bishop U.S.A.
8 F3 Bishop Auckland U.K.
9 H6 Bishop's Stortford U.K.
29 G4 Bishrī, Jabal h. Syria
36 E1 Bishui China
86 C1 Biskra Alg.
43 C4 Bislig Phil.
64 C2 Bismarck U.S.A.
48 E2 Bismarck Archipelago is P.N.G.
48 E2 Bismarck Range mts P.N.G.
48 E2 Bismarck Sea sea P.N.G.
13 K2 Bismark (Altmark) Ger.
29 H3 Bismil Turkey
7 L6 Bismo Norway
29 L4 Bīsotūn Iran
6 P5 Bispgården Sweden
13 J1 Bispingen Ger.
15 G4 Bissa, Djebel mt Alg.
33 C2 Bissamcuttak India
86 A3 Bissau Guinea-Bissau
86 D4 Bissaula Nigeria
57 K4 Bissett Can.
56 F3 Bistcho Lake l. Can.
17 M7 Bistriţa Romania
17 N7 Bistriţa r. Romania
12 E5 Bitburg Ger.
12 F5 Bitche France
87 D3 Bitkine Chad
29 J2 Bitlis Turkey
19 J4 Bitola Macedonia
18 G4 Bitonto Italy
30 B6 Bitrān, J. h. S. Arabia
73 H2 Bitter Creek r. U.S.A.
13 L3 Bitterfeld Ger.
90 C5 Bitterfontein S. Africa
28 D6 Bitter Lakes l. Egypt
62 D2 Bitterroot Range mts U.S.A.
13 K2 Bittkau Ger.
21 G5 Bityug r. Rus. Fed.
87 D3 Biu Nigeria
41 D7 Biwa-ko l. Japan
38 D3 Biyang China
34 D5 Biyāvra India
88 E2 Bīye K'obē Eth.
24 K4 Biysk Rus. Fed.
91 H5 Bizana S. Africa
86 C1 Bizerte Tunisia
6 A4 Bjargtangar hd Iceland
6 Q5 Bjästa Sweden
18 G2 Bjelovar Croatia
6 P2 Bjerkvik Norway
7 L8 Bjerringbro Denmark
7 P6 Björklinge Sweden
7 L5 Bjorli Norway
6 Q5 Björna Sweden
Bjørnøya i. see Bear Island
6 Q5 Bjurholm Sweden
86 B3 Bla Mali
10 B3 Bla Bheinn mt U.K.
65 F5 Black r. AR U.S.A.
73 H5 Black r. AZ U.S.A.
69 F4 Black r. MI U.S.A.
68 B3 Black r. WI U.S.A.
48 E4 Blackall Austr.
68 C1 Black Bay b. Can.
58 B3 Blackbear r. Can.
9 F6 Black Bourton U.K.
8 E4 Blackburn U.K.
72 A2 Black Butte summit U.S.A.
72 A2 Black Butte L. l. U.S.A.
73 E4 Black Canyon U.S.A.
73 F4 Black Canyon City U.S.A.
64 E2 Blackduck U.S.A.
56 G4 Blackfalds Can.
62 D3 Blackfoot U.S.A.
62 D2 Black Foot r. U.S.A.
64 C2 Black Hills reg. U.S.A.
10 D3 Black Isle i. U.K.
57 H3 Black Lake Can.
57 H3 Black Lake l. Can.
69 E3 Black Lake l. U.S.A.
73 G3 Black Mesa plat. U.S.A.
9 D6 Black Mountain h. U.K.
72 D4 Black Mt mt U.S.A.
9 D6 Black Mts h. U.K.
73 E4 Black Mts mts AZ U.S.A.
90 C1 Black Nossob watercourse Namibia
39 □ Black Point pt H.K. China
8 D4 Blackpool U.K.
68 B3 Black River Falls U.S.A.
8 A4 Blackrock Rep. of Ireland
62 C3 Black Rock Desert U.S.A.
70 C6 Blacksburg U.S.A.
4 G4 Black Sea sea Asia/Europe
11 A3 Blacksod Bay b. Rep. of Ireland
11 E5 Blackstairs Mountain h. Rep. of Ireland
11 E5 Blackstairs Mountains h. Rep. of Ireland
70 E6 Blackstone U.S.A.
50 H1 Black Sugarloaf mt Austr.
86 B4 Black Volta r. Africa
11 E5 Blackwater Rep. of Ireland
11 E4 Blackwater r. Rep. of Ireland
11 D5 Blackwater r. Rep. of Ireland
11 E3 Blackwater r. Rep. of Ireland/U.K.
9 H6 Blackwater r. U.K.
70 E6 Blackwater r. U.S.A.
56 E2 Blackwater Lake l. Can.
10 D4 Blackwater Reservoir U.K.
65 D4 Blackwell U.S.A.
48 B5 Blackwood r. Austr.
21 G6 Blagodarnyy Rus. Fed.
40 D2 Blagodatnyy Rus. Fed.
19 K3 Blagoevgrad Bulg.
36 E1 Blagoveshchensk Rus. Fed.
64 E4 Blain U.S.A.
62 B1 Blaine U.S.A.
57 H4 Blaine Lake Can.
64 D3 Blair NE U.S.A.
68 B3 Blair WI U.S.A.
10 E4 Blair Atholl U.K.
10 E4 Blairgowrie U.K.
67 C6 Blakely U.S.A.
9 J5 Blakeney U.K.
68 C1 Blake Pt pt U.S.A.
83 E3 Blanca, Bahía b. Arg.
83 C3 Blanca de la Totora, Sa h. Arg.
63 F4 Blanca Peak summit U.S.A.
48 D4 Blanche, L. salt flat Austr.
70 B5 Blanchester U.S.A.
50 B3 Blanchetown Austr.
14 H4 Blanc, Mont mt France/Italy
83 C1 Blanco r. Arg.
78 F6 Blanco r. Bol.
62 A3 Blanco, C. c. U.S.A.
59 J3 Blanc-Sablon Can.
50 F2 Bland r. Austr.
6 D4 Blanda r. Iceland
9 E7 Blandford Forum U.K.
73 H3 Blanding U.S.A.
15 H2 Blanes Spain
68 E2 Blaney Park U.S.A.
44 A5 Blangkejeren Indon.
12 B3 Blankenberge Belgium
12 E4 Blankenheim Ger.
81 D2 Blanquilla, Isla i. Venez.
16 H6 Blansko Czech Rep.
89 D5 Blantyre Malawi
11 C6 Blarney Rep. of Ireland
13 H5 Blaufelden Ger.
6 Q4 Blåviksjön Sweden
50 G2 Blayney Austr.
13 J1 Bleckede Ger.
51 D4 Blenheim N.Z.
12 E3 Blerick Neth.
11 E4 Blessington Lakes l. Rep. of Ireland
9 G5 Bletchley U.K.
86 C1 Blida Alg.
12 F5 Blies r. Ger.
49 H3 Bligh Water b. Fiji
69 F2 Blind River Can.
62 D3 Bliss U.S.A.
69 F5 Blissfield U.S.A.
71 H4 Block I. i. U.S.A.
71 H4 Block Island Sound chan. U.S.A.
91 G4 Bloemfontein S. Africa
91 F3 Bloemhof S. Africa
91 F3 Bloemhof Dam dam S. Africa
13 H3 Blomberg Ger.
6 C4 Blönduós Iceland
71 E5 Bloodsworth I. i. U.S.A.
57 K4 Bloodvein r. Can.
11 C2 Bloody Foreland pt Rep. of Ireland
69 J4 Bloomfield Can.
68 A5 Bloomfield IA U.S.A.
66 C4 Bloomfield IN U.S.A.
63 E4 Bloomfield NM U.S.A.
68 C5 Bloomington IL U.S.A.
66 C4 Bloomington IN U.S.A.
64 E2 Bloomington MN U.S.A.
71 E4 Bloomsburg U.S.A.
70 E4 Blossburg U.S.A.
55 O3 Blosseville Kyst Greenland
91 H1 Blouberg S. Africa
9 F5 Bloxham U.K.
73 H5 Blue r. U.S.A.
73 G1 Bluebell U.S.A.
73 G2 Blue Bell Knoll summit U.S.A.
64 E3 Blue Earth U.S.A.
70 C6 Bluefield U.S.A.
75 H6 Bluefields Nic.
71 J2 Blue Hill U.S.A.
69 H5 Blue Knob h. U.S.A.
73 H1 Blue Mountain U.S.A.
35 H5 Blue Mountain mt India
73 F3 Blue Mountain Lake U.S.A.
91 G4 Blue Mountain Pass Lesotho
50 G2 Blue Mountains N.S.W. Austr.
62 C2 Blue Mountains U.S.A.
50 H2 Blue Mountains Nat. Park Austr.
87 F3 Blue Nile r. Sudan
54 G3 Bluenose Lake l. Can.
67 C5 Blue Ridge U.S.A.
70 D6 Blue Ridge mts U.S.A.
56 F4 Blue River Can.
72 D2 Blue Springs U.S.A.
11 C3 Blue Stack mt Rep. of Ireland
11 C3 Blue Stack Mts h. Rep. of Ireland
70 C6 Bluestone Lake l. U.S.A.
51 B7 Bluff N.Z.
73 H3 Bluff U.S.A.
39 □ Bluff I. i. H.K. China
67 E7 Bluff, The Bahamas
68 E5 Bluffton IN U.S.A.
70 B4 Bluffton OH U.S.A.
80 G3 Blumenau Brazil
64 C2 Blunt U.S.A.
62 B3 Bly U.S.A.
50 B2 Blyth Austr.
8 F2 Blyth Eng. U.K.
9 F4 Blyth Eng. U.K.
73 E5 Blythe U.S.A.
65 F5 Blytheville U.S.A.
7 L7 Bø Norway
86 A4 Bo Sierra Leone
43 B3 Boac Phil.
79 K5 Boa Esperança, Açude resr Brazil
38 D3 Bo'ai Henan China
39 C6 Bo'ai Yunnan China
88 B3 Boali C.A.R.
91 K3 Boane Moz.
70 C4 Boardman U.S.A.
91 F1 Boatlaname Botswana
79 L5 Boa Viagem Brazil
81 E4 Boa Vista Brazil
86 □ Boa Vista i. Cape Verde
50 F2 Bobadah Austr.
39 D6 Bobai China
89 E5 Bobaomby, Tanjona c. Madag.
33 C2 Bobbili India
86 B3 Bobo-Dioulasso Burkina
89 C6 Bobonong Botswana
21 G5 Bobrov Rus. Fed.
21 D5 Bobrovytsya Ukr.
21 E5 Bobrynets' Ukr.
89 E6 Boby mt Madag.
81 E2 Boca Araguao est. Venez.
81 D2 Boca del Pao Venez.
75 M7 Boca de Macareo Venez.
78 E5 Boca do Acre Brazil
79 H4 Boca do Jari Brazil
81 E2 Boca Grande est. Venez.
82 D2 Bocaiúva Brazil
81 C2 Bocanó r. Venez.
88 B3 Bocaranga C.A.R.
67 D7 Boca Raton U.S.A.
75 H7 Bocas del Toro Panama
17 K6 Bochnia Pol.
12 E3 Bocholt Ger.
12 F3 Bochum Ger.
91 H1 Bochum S. Africa
13 J2 Bockenem Ger.
81 C2 Boconó Venez.
88 B3 Boda C.A.R.
50 H4 Bodalla Austr.
36 D1 Bodaybo Rus. Fed.
65 E5 Bodcau Lake l. U.S.A.
10 G3 Boddam U.K.
13 K3 Bode r. Ger.
72 A2 Bodega Head hd U.S.A.
87 D3 Bodélé reg. Chad
6 R4 Boden Sweden
9 E5 Bodenham U.K.
Bodensee l. see Constance, Lake
13 J2 Bodenteich Ger.
13 H3 Bodenwerder Ger.
33 B2 Bodhan India
33 B4 Bodinayakkanur India
9 C7 Bodmin U.K.
9 C7 Bodmin Moor reg. U.K.
6 O3 Bodø Norway
19 M6 Bodrum Turkey
12 C3 Boechout Belgium
88 C4 Boende Congo(Zaire)
86 A3 Boffa Guinea
35 H3 Boga India
65 F6 Bogalusa U.S.A.
50 F1 Bogan r. Austr.
86 B3 Bogandé Burkina
50 F2 Bogan Gate Austr.
20 J3 Bogatye Saby Rus. Fed.
28 E2 Boğazlıyan Turkey
35 F3 Bogcang Zangbo r. China
36 A2 Bogda Shan mts China
11 B5 Boggeragh Mts h. Rep. of Ireland
15 H5 Boghar Alg.
9 G7 Bognor Regis U.K.
43 C4 Bogo Phil.
11 D4 Bog of Allen reg. Rep. of Ireland
20 E4 Bogolyubovo Rus. Fed.
50 F4 Bogong, Mt mt Austr.
40 D2 Bogopol' Rus. Fed.
45 C4 Bogor Indon.
20 G3 Bogorodsk Rus. Fed.
20 J3 Bogorodskoye Rus. Fed.
81 B3 Bogotá Col.
36 A1 Bogotol Rus. Fed.
35 G4 Bogra Bangl.
25 L4 Boguchany Rus. Fed.
21 G5 Boguchar Rus. Fed.
86 A3 Bogué Maur.
38 F2 Bo Hai g. China
42 A4 Bohai Haixia chan. China
14 F2 Bohain-en-Vermandois France
38 E2 Bohai Wan b. China
13 L3 Böhlen Ger.
91 H4 Bohlokong S. Africa
13 L5 Böhmer Wald mts Ger.
13 G2 Bohmte Ger.
21 E5 Bohodukhiv Ukr.
43 C4 Bohol i. Phil.
43 C4 Bohol Sea sea Phil.
43 B4 Bohol Str. chan. Phil.
27 G2 Bohu China
21 D5 Bohuslav Ukr.
71 F4 Boiceville U.S.A.
90 E4 Boichoko S. Africa
91 G3 Boikhutso S. Africa
79 G4 Boim Brazil
35 H5 Boinu r. Myanmar
82 E1 Boipeba, Ilha i. Brazil
82 D4 Boi, Ponta do pt Brazil
82 C2 Bois r. Brazil
69 E3 Bois Blanc I. i. U.S.A.
12 C4 Bois de Chimay woodland Belgium
62 C3 Boise U.S.A.
65 C4 Boise City U.S.A.
57 J5 Boissevain Can.
91 F3 Boitumelong S. Africa
13 J1 Boizenburg Ger.
43 B2 Bojeador, Cape c. Phil.
30 E2 Bojnūrd Iran
35 G1 Bokadaban Feng mt China
35 H4 Bokajan India
35 F5 Bokaro India
88 B4 Bokatola Congo(Zaire)
86 A3 Boké Guinea
88 C4 Bokele Congo(Zaire)
7 J7 Boknafjorden chan. Norway
87 D3 Bokoro Chad
21 G5 Bokovskaya Rus. Fed.
20 E3 Boksitogorsk Rus. Fed.
90 D3 Bokspits Botswana
88 C4 Bolaiti Congo(Zaire)
86 A3 Bolama Guinea-Bissau
34 A3 Bolan r. Pak.
34 A3 Bolan Pass Pak.
14 E2 Bolbec France
30 C4 Boldajī Iran
13 M1 Boldekow Ger.
27 G2 Bole China
86 B4 Bole Ghana
88 B4 Boleko Congo(Zaire)
86 B3 Bolgatanga Ghana
21 D6 Bolhrad Ukr.
40 B2 Boli China
88 B4 Bolia Congo(Zaire)
6 R4 Boliden Sweden
43 A2 Bolinao Phil.
19 L2 Bolintin-Vale Romania
81 A3 Bolívar Col.
78 C5 Bolívar Peru
65 E4 Bolivar MO U.S.A.
67 B5 Bolivar TN U.S.A.
77 D4 Bolivia country S. America
28 E3 Bolkar Dağları mts Turkey
20 F4 Bolkhov Rus. Fed.
69 F1 Bolkow Can.
14 G4 Bollène France
7 P6 Bollnäs Sweden
6 P5 Bollstabruk Sweden
7 N8 Bolmen l. Sweden
21 H7 Bolnisi Georgia
88 B4 Bolobo Congo(Zaire)
43 B5 Bolod Islands is Phil.
18 D2 Bologna Italy
17 P2 Bologovo Rus. Fed.
20 E3 Bologoye Rus. Fed.
91 F4 Bolokanang S. Africa
88 B3 Bolomba Congo(Zaire)
43 B5 Bolong Phil.
24 K4 Bolotnoye Rus. Fed.
44 C2 Bolovens, Plateau des plat. Laos
35 F5 Bolpur India
18 D3 Bolsena, Lago di l. Italy
17 K3 Bol'shakovo Rus. Fed.
6 X3 Bol'shaya Imandra, Oz. l. Rus. Fed.
21 G6 Bol'shaya Martinovka Rus. Fed.
25 M2 Bolshevik, O. i. Rus. Fed.
20 H2 Bol'shiye Chirki Rus. Fed.
25 S3 Bol'shoy Aluy r. Rus. Fed.
40 C3 Bol'shoy Kamen' Rus. Fed.
Bol'shoy Kavkaz mts see Caucasus
21 J5 Bol'shoy Uzen' r. Rus. Fed.
74 D3 Bolson de Mapimí des. Mex.
12 D1 Bolsward Neth.
8 E4 Bolton U.K.
70 B6 Bolton U.S.A.
28 C1 Bolu Turkey
6 B3 Bolungarvík Iceland
39 E6 Boluo China
28 C2 Bolvadin Turkey
18 D1 Bolzano Italy
88 B4 Boma Congo(Zaire)
50 H3 Bomaderry Austr.
50 G4 Bombala Austr.
33 A2 Bombay India
37 F7 Bomberai Peninsula Indon.
78 E5 Bom Comércio Brazil
82 D2 Bom Despacho Brazil
35 H4 Bomdila India
35 H3 Bomi China
82 D1 Bom Jesus da Lapa Brazil
82 E3 Bom Jesus do Itabapoana Brazil
7 J7 Bømlo i. Norway
30 B2 Bonāb Iran
70 E6 Bon Air U.S.A.
75 L6 Bonaire i. Neth. Ant.
75 H6 Bonanza Nic.
48 C3 Bonaparte Archipelago is Austr.
10 D3 Bonar Bridge U.K.
59 K4 Bonavista Can.
59 K4 Bonavista Bay b. Can.
87 D1 Bon, Cap c. Tunisia
10 F5 Bonchester Bridge U.K.
88 C3 Bondo Congo(Zaire)
43 B3 Bondoc Peninsula Phil.
86 B4 Bondoukou Côte d'Ivoire
68 A3 Bone Lake l. U.S.A.
13 F3 Bönen Ger.
37 E7 Bonerate, Kepulauan is Indon.
10 E4 Bo'ness U.K.
37 E7 Bone, Teluk b. Indon.
82 D2 Bonfinópolis de Minas Brazil
88 D3 Bonga Eth.
43 B3 Bongabong Phil.
35 G4 Bongaigaon India
88 C3 Bongandanga Congo(Zaire)
90 E4 Bongani S. Africa
43 A5 Bongao Phil.
35 G3 Bong Co l. China
43 C5 Bongo i. Phil.
89 E5 Bongolava mts Madag.
88 C3 Bongo, Massif des mts C.A.R.
87 D3 Bongor Chad
86 B4 Bongouanou Côte d'Ivoire
44 D2 Bông Sơn Vietnam
12 C3 Bonheiden Belgium
18 C4 Bonifacio Corsica France
18 C4 Bonifacio, Strait of str. France/Italy
Bonin Is is see Ogasawara-shotō
82 A3 Bonito Brazil
12 F4 Bonn Ger.
6 O3 Bonnåsjøen Norway
62 C1 Bonners Ferry U.S.A.
14 H3 Bonneville France
50 C4 Bonney, L. l. Austr.
48 B5 Bonnie Rock Austr.
10 E5 Bonnyrigg U.K.
57 G4 Bonnyville Can.
43 A4 Bonobono Phil.
44 C3 Bonom Mhai mt Vietnam
14 C4 Bonorva Sardinia Italy
90 D7 Bontebok National Park S. Africa
86 A4 Bonthe Sierra Leone
43 B2 Bontoc Phil.
45 E4 Bontosunggu Indon.
91 F6 Bontrug S. Africa
91 G1 Bonwapitse Botswana
73 H2 Book Cliffs cliff U.S.A.
50 D2 Boolaboolka L. l. Austr.
50 B2 Booleroo Centre Austr.
11 D5 Booley Hills h. Rep. of Ireland
50 E2 Booligal Austr.
67 A4 Boone IA U.S.A.
67 D4 Boone NC U.S.A.
70 B6 Boone Lake l. U.S.A.
70 B6 Booneville KY U.S.A.
65 F5 Booneville MS U.S.A.
72 A2 Boonville CA U.S.A.
66 C4 Boonville IN U.S.A.
64 E4 Boonville MO U.S.A.
71 F3 Boonville NY U.S.A.
50 E3 Booroorban Austr.
50 G3 Boorowa Austr.
50 D4 Boort Austr.
88 E2 Boosaaso Somalia
71 J3 Boothbay Harbor U.S.A.
55 J2 Boothia, Gulf of Can.
55 J2 Boothia Peninsula Can.
9 E4 Bootle U.K.
86 A4 Bopolu Liberia
12 F4 Boppard Ger.
83 G1 Boquerião Brazil
60 E6 Boquilla, Presa de la resr Mex.
13 L5 Bor Czech Rep.
87 F4 Bor Sudan
28 E3 Bor Turkey
19 K2 Bor Yugo.
62 D2 Borah Peak summit U.S.A.
7 N8 Borås Sweden
30 C4 Borāzjān Iran
79 G4 Borba Brazil

79 L5 Borborema, Planalto da plat. Brazil
13 G3 Borchen Ger.
92 B5 Borchgrevink Coast coastal area Ant.
29 H1 Borçka Turkey
28 B3 Bor D. mt Turkey
14 D4 Bordeaux France
59 H4 Borden Can.
54 G2 Borden I. i. Can.
55 K2 Borden Peninsula Can.
50 C4 Bordertown Austr.
6 C4 Borðeyri Iceland
15 J4 Bordj Bou Arréridj Alg.
15 G5 Bordj Bounaama Alg.
86 C2 Bordj Omer Driss Alg.
6 □ Borðoy i. Faroe Is
10 A3 Boreray i. U.K.
6 G4 Borgarfjörður Iceland
6 C4 Borgarnes Iceland
6 N4 Børgefjell Nasjonalpark nat. park Norway
65 C5 Borger U.S.A.
7 P8 Borgholm Sweden
18 B2 Borgo San Dalmazzo Italy
18 D3 Borgo San Lorenzo Italy
18 C2 Borgosesia Italy
12 B4 Borinage reg. Belgium
21 G5 Borisoglebsk Rus. Fed.
21 F5 Borisovka Rus. Fed.
20 F3 Borisovo-Sudskoye Rus. Fed.
30 C4 Borj-e Chīn Iran
21 G7 Borjomi Georgia
12 E3 Borken Ger.
6 P2 Borkenes Norway
12 E1 Borkum Ger.
12 E1 Borkum i. Ger.
7 O6 Borlänge Sweden
28 B2 Borlu Turkey
13 L3 Borna Ger.
12 D1 Borndiep chan. Neth.
12 E2 Borne Neth.
45 D2 Borneo i. Asia
7 O9 Bornholm i. Denmark
19 M5 Bornova Turkey
43 B4 Borocay i. Phil.
24 K3 Borodino Rus. Fed.
7 V6 Borodinskoye Rus. Fed.
21 D5 Borodyanka Ukr.
25 P3 Borogontsy Rus. Fed.
20 F3 Borok Rus. Fed.
86 B3 Boromo Burkina
43 C4 Borongan Phil.
8 F3 Boroughbridge U.K.
20 E3 Borovichi Rus. Fed.
20 J3 Borovoy Kirovsk. Rus. Fed.
20 K2 Borovoy Komi Rus. Fed.
20 E1 Borovoy Korel. Rus. Fed.
11 C5 Borrisokane Rep. of Ireland
48 D3 Borroloola Austr.
6 M5 Børsa Norway
17 M7 Borşa Romania
21 C5 Borshchiv Ukr.
36 C2 Borshchovochnyy Khrebet mts Rus. Fed.
30 C4 Borūjen Iran
30 C3 Borūjerd Iran
10 B3 Borve U.K.
21 B5 Boryslav Ukr.
21 D5 Boryspil' Ukr.
21 E5 Borzna Ukr.
36 D1 Borzya Rus. Fed.
18 G2 Bosanska Dubica Bos.-Herz.
18 G2 Bosanska Gradiška Bos.-Herz.
18 G2 Bosanska Krupa Bos.-Herz.
18 G2 Bosanski Novi Bos.-Herz.
18 G2 Bosansko Grahovo Bos.-Herz.
68 B4 Boscobel U.S.A.
39 C6 Bose China
91 F4 Boshof S. Africa
5 E4 Bosnia-Herzegovina country Europe
88 B3 Bosobolo Congo(Zaire)
41 G7 Bōsō-hantō pen. Japan
28 B1 Bosporus str. Turkey
88 B3 Bossangoa C.A.R.
88 B3 Bossembélé C.A.R.
65 E5 Bossier City U.S.A.
90 B2 Bossiesvlei Namibia
35 F1 Bostan China
29 L6 Bostan Iran
36 A2 Bosten Hu l. China
9 G5 Boston U.K.
71 H3 Boston U.S.A.
69 H1 Boston Creek Can.
71 H3 Boston-Logan International airport U.S.A.
65 E5 Boston Mts mts U.S.A.
8 F4 Boston Spa U.K.
68 D5 Boswell U.S.A.
34 B5 Botad India
50 H2 Botany Bay b. Austr.
6 P5 Boteå Sweden
19 L3 Botev mt Bulg.
19 K3 Botevgrad Bulg.
91 G3 Bothaville S. Africa
6 Q6 Bothnia, Gulf of g. Fin./Sweden
21 H5 Botkul', Ozero l. Kazak./Rus. Fed.
17 N7 Botoşani Romania
38 E2 Botou China
44 C1 Bô Trach Vietnam
91 G4 Botshabelo S. Africa
85 F8 Botswana country Africa
18 G5 Botte Donato, Monte mt Italy
6 S4 Bottenviken g. Fin./Sweden
8 G4 Bottesford U.K.
64 C1 Bottineau U.S.A.
12 E3 Bottrop Ger.
82 C3 Botucatu Brazil
82 D1 Botuporã Brazil
59 K4 Botwood Can.
86 B4 Bouaflé Côte d'Ivoire
86 B4 Bouaké Côte d'Ivoire
88 B3 Bouar C.A.R.
86 B1 Bouârfa Morocco
87 D4 Bouba Ndjida, Parc National de nat. park Cameroon
88 B3 Bouca C.A.R.
12 B4 Bouchain France
83 D2 Bouchard, H. Arg.
71 G2 Boucherville Can.
69 K2 Bouchette Can.
86 B3 Boucle du Baoulé, Parc National de la nat. park Mali
59 H4 Bouctouche Can.
49 F2 Bougainville Island i. P.N.G.
86 B3 Bougouni Mali
12 D5 Bouillon Belgium
15 H4 Bouira Alg.
86 A2 Boujdour Western Sahara
62 F3 Boulder CO U.S.A.
62 D2 Boulder MT U.S.A.
73 G3 Boulder UT U.S.A.
73 E3 Boulder Canyon U.S.A.
73 E4 Boulder City U.S.A.
72 D5 Boulevard U.S.A.
83 E3 Boulevard Atlántico Arg.
48 D4 Boulia Austr.
14 F2 Boulogne-Billancourt France
14 E1 Boulogne-sur-Mer France
86 B3 Boulsa Burkina
88 B4 Boumango Gabon
87 D4 Boumba r. Cameroon
15 H4 Boumerdes Alg.
86 B4 Bouna Côte d'Ivoire
71 H2 Boundary Mountains U.S.A.
72 C3 Boundary Peak summit U.S.A.
86 B4 Boundiali Côte d'Ivoire
88 B4 Boundji Congo
44 D1 Boung r. Vietnam
39 A6 Boun Nua Laos
62 E3 Bountiful U.S.A.
49 H6 Bounty Islands is N.Z.
86 B3 Bourem Mali
14 E4 Bourganeuf France
14 G3 Bourg-en-Bresse France
14 F3 Bourges France
71 F2 Bourget Can.
69 K1 Bourgmont Can.
14 G3 Bourgogne reg. France
50 E5 Bourke Austr.
69 G1 Bourkes Can.
9 G5 Bourne U.K.
9 F7 Bournemouth U.K.
12 F2 Bourtanger Moor reg. Ger.
86 C1 Bou Saâda Alg.
18 C6 Bou Salem Tunisia
73 E5 Bouse U.S.A.
73 E5 Bouse Wash r. U.S.A.
87 D3 Bousso Chad
12 B4 Boussu Belgium
86 A3 Boutilimit Maur.
96 K9 Bouvetøya i. Atl. Ocean
12 C5 Bouy France
13 H3 Bovenden Ger.
45 D2 Boven Kapuas Mts mts Malaysia
83 E1 Bovril Arg.
57 G4 Bow r. Can.
64 C1 Bowbells U.S.A.
54 E4 Bowen Austr.
68 B5 Bowen U.S.A.
50 G4 Bowen, Mt mt Austr.
73 H5 Bowie AZ U.S.A.
65 D5 Bowie TX U.S.A.
57 G5 Bow Island Can.
30 B2 Bowkan Iran
66 C4 Bowling Green KY U.S.A.
64 F4 Bowling Green MO U.S.A.
68 B4 Bowling Green OH U.S.A.
70 E5 Bowling Green VA U.S.A.
64 C2 Bowman U.S.A.
92 C6 Bowman I. i. Ant.
54 E4 Bowman, Mt mt Can.
92 B3 Bowman Pen. pen. Ant.
69 H4 Bowmanville Can.
10 B5 Bowmore U.K.
50 H3 Bowral Austr.
56 E4 Bowron r. Can.
56 E4 Bowron Lake Provincial Park res. Can.
13 H5 Boxberg Ger.
38 E3 Bo Xian China
38 F2 Boxing China
12 D3 Boxtel Neth.
28 E1 Boyabat Turkey
39 E4 Boyang China
57 J2 Boyd Lake l. Can.
56 G4 Boyle Can.
11 C4 Boyle Rep. of Ireland
11 E4 Boyne r. Rep. of Ireland
31 G2 Boyni Qara Afgh.
67 D7 Boynton Beach U.S.A.
62 E3 Boysen Res. resr U.S.A.
78 F8 Boyuibe Bol.
29 K1 Böyük Hinaldağ mt Azer.
19 M5 Bozcaada i. Turkey
19 M5 Bozdağ mt Turkey
28 A2 Boz Dağları mts Turkey
28 B3 Bozdoğan Turkey
9 G5 Bozeat U.K.
62 E2 Bozeman U.S.A.
28 D3 Bozkır Turkey
88 B3 Bozoum C.A.R.
28 G3 Bozova Turkey
30 B2 Bozqūsh, Kūh-e mts Iran
28 C2 Bozüyük Turkey
18 B2 Bra Italy
92 B2 Brabant I. i. Ant.
18 G3 Brač i. Croatia
10 B3 Bracadale U.K.
10 B3 Bracadale, Loch b. U.K.
18 E3 Bracciano, Lago di l. Italy
69 H3 Bracebridge Can.
6 O5 Bracke Sweden
13 H5 Brackenheim Ger.
9 G6 Bracknell U.K.
18 G4 Bradano r. Italy
67 D7 Bradenton U.S.A.
69 H3 Bradford Can.
8 F4 Bradford U.K.
70 A4 Bradford OH U.S.A.
70 D4 Bradford PA U.S.A.
71 G3 Bradford VT U.S.A.
65 D6 Brady U.S.A.
56 B3 Brady Gl. gl. U.S.A.
10 □ Brae U.K.
50 B2 Braemar Austr.
10 E3 Braemar U.K.
15 B2 Braga Port.
83 E2 Bragado Arg.
79 J4 Bragança Brazil
15 C2 Bragança Port.
82 C3 Bragança Paulista Brazil
21 D5 Brahin Belarus
13 J1 Brahlstorf Ger.
35 G5 Brahmanbaria Bangl.
35 F5 Brahmani r. India
33 D2 Brahmapur India
35 G4 Brahmaputra r. Asia
19 M2 Brăila Romania
12 B5 Braine France
12 C4 Braine-le-Comte Belgium
64 E2 Brainerd U.S.A.
9 H6 Braintree U.K.
91 H1 Brak r. S. Africa
12 B4 Brakel Belgium
13 H3 Brakel Ger.
13 G1 Brake (Unterweser) Ger.
89 B6 Brakwater Namibia
56 E4 Bralorne Can.
7 L9 Bramming Denmark
7 P5 Brämön i. Sweden
69 H4 Brampton Can.
8 E3 Brampton Eng. U.K.
9 J5 Brampton Eng. U.K.
13 G2 Bramsche Ger.
9 H5 Brancaster U.K.
59 K4 Branch Can.
81 E4 Branco r. Brazil
7 M6 Brandbu Norway
7 L9 Brande Denmark
13 L2 Brandenburg Ger.
13 L2 Brandenburg div. Ger.
91 G4 Brandfort S. Africa
13 M3 Brandis Ger.
57 K5 Brandon Can.
9 H5 Brandon U.K.
64 D3 Brandon SD U.S.A.
71 G3 Brandon VT U.S.A.
11 A5 Brandon Head hd Rep. of Ireland
11 E5 Brandon Hill h. Rep. of Ireland
11 A5 Brandon Mountain mt Rep. of Ireland
90 D5 Brandvlei S. Africa
67 D6 Branford U.S.A.
17 J3 Braniewo Pol.
92 B2 Bransfield Str. str. Ant.
69 G4 Brantford Can.
50 C4 Branxholme Austr.
59 H4 Bras d'Or L. l. Can.
78 E6 Brasileia Brazil
82 C1 Brasília Brazil
82 D2 Brasília de Minas Brazil
79 G4 Brasília Legal Brazil
17 N3 Braslaw Belarus
19 L2 Braşov Romania
43 A5 Brassey Range mts Malaysia
71 J2 Brassua Lake l. U.S.A.
16 H6 Bratislava Slovakia
36 C1 Bratsk Rus. Fed.
36 C1 Bratskoye Vdkhr. resr Rus. Fed.
71 G3 Brattleboro U.S.A.
16 F6 Braunau am Inn Austria
13 G4 Braunfels Ger.
13 J3 Braunlage Ger.
13 K3 Braunsbedra Ger.
13 J2 Braunschweig Ger.
86 □ Brava i. Cape Verde
7 P7 Bråviken in. Sweden
Bravo del Norte, Río r. see Rio Grande r. Mexico/U.S.A.
73 E5 Brawley U.S.A.
11 E4 Bray Rep. of Ireland
56 F4 Brazeau Can.
56 F4 Brazeau r. Can.
77 D3 Brazil country S. America
96 H7 Brazil Basin sea feature Atl. Ocean
65 D5 Brazos r. U.S.A.
88 B4 Brazzaville Congo
19 H2 Brčko Bos.-Herz.
51 A6 Breaksea Sd in. N.Z.
51 E1 Bream Bay b. N.Z.
51 E1 Bream Head hd N.Z.
9 C6 Brechfa U.K.
10 F4 Brechin U.K.
12 C3 Brecht Belgium
64 D2 Breckenridge MN U.S.A.
65 D5 Breckenridge TX U.S.A.
16 H6 Břeclav Czech Rep.
9 D6 Brecon U.K.
9 D6 Brecon Beacons h. U.K.
9 D6 Brecon Beacons National Park U.K.
12 C3 Breda Neth.
90 D7 Bredasdorp S. Africa
50 G3 Bredbo Austr.
13 L2 Breddin Ger.
12 E3 Bredevoort Neth.
6 O3 Bredviken Norway
12 D3 Bree Belgium
70 D5 Breezewood U.S.A.
16 D7 Bregenz Austria
6 B4 Breiðafjörður b. Iceland
6 F4 Breiðdalsvík Iceland
13 G4 Breidenbach Ger.
16 C6 Breisach am Rhein Ger.
13 J1 Breitenfelde Ger.
13 J5 Breitengüßbach Ger.
6 S1 Breivikbotn Norway
79 J6 Brejinho de Nazaré Brazil
6 L5 Brekstad Norway
13 G1 Bremen Ger.
67 C5 Bremen GA U.S.A.
68 D5 Bremen IN U.S.A.
13 G1 Bremerhaven Ger.
62 B2 Bremerton U.S.A.
13 H1 Bremervörde Ger.
12 F4 Bremm Ger.
65 D6 Brenham U.S.A.
6 N4 Brenna Norway
16 E7 Brenner Pass Austria/Italy
69 H2 Brent Can.
18 D2 Brenta r. Italy
9 H6 Brentwood U.K.
72 B3 Brentwood CA U.S.A.
71 G4 Brentwood NY U.S.A.
18 D2 Brescia Italy
18 D1 Bressanone Italy
10 □ Bressay i. U.K.
14 D3 Bressuire France
21 B4 Brest Belarus
14 B2 Brest France
14 C2 Bretagne reg. France
12 A5 Breteuil France
65 F6 Breton Sound b. U.S.A.
51 E1 Brett, Cape c. N.Z.
13 G5 Bretten Ger.
9 E4 Bretton U.K.
67 D5 Brevard U.S.A.
79 H4 Breves Brazil
68 E2 Brevort U.S.A.
48 E4 Brewarrina Austr.
71 J2 Brewer U.S.A.
62 C1 Brewster U.S.A.
65 G6 Brewton U.S.A.
91 H3 Breyten S. Africa
Brezhnev see Naberezhnyye Chelny
17 J6 Brezno Slovakia
18 G2 Brezovo Polje h. Croatia
88 C3 Bria C.A.R.
14 H4 Briançon France
50 F3 Bribbaree Austr.
21 C5 Briceni Moldova
14 H4 Bric Froid mt France/Italy
11 C5 Bride r. Rep. of Ireland
73 G1 Bridgeland U.S.A.
9 D6 Bridgend U.K.
10 D4 Bridge of Orchy U.K.
72 C2 Bridgeport CA U.S.A.
71 G4 Bridgeport CT U.S.A.
64 C3 Bridgeport NE U.S.A.
62 E2 Bridger U.S.A.
62 F3 Bridger Peak summit U.S.A.
71 F5 Bridgeton U.S.A.
75 N6 Bridgetown Barbados
59 H5 Bridgewater Can.
71 K1 Bridgewater U.S.A.
50 C5 Bridgewater, C. hd Austr.
9 E5 Bridgnorth U.K.
71 H2 Bridgton U.S.A.
9 D6 Bridgwater U.K.
9 D6 Bridgwater Bay b. U.K.
8 G3 Bridlington U.K.
8 G3 Bridlington Bay b. U.K.
9 E7 Bridport U.K.
16 C7 Brig Switz.
8 G4 Brigg U.K.
62 D3 Brigham City U.S.A.
50 F4 Bright Austr.
9 J6 Brightlingsea U.K.
69 J3 Brighton Can.
51 C6 Brighton N.Z.
9 G7 Brighton U.K.
69 F4 Brighton U.S.A.
14 H5 Brignoles France
86 A3 Brikama The Gambia
13 G3 Brilon Ger.
18 G4 Brindisi Italy
83 D1 Brinkmann Arg.
50 B2 Brinkworth Austr.
59 H4 Brion, Île i. Can.
14 F4 Brioude France
59 F3 Brisay Can.
49 F4 Brisbane Austr.
71 K1 Bristol Can.
9 E6 Bristol U.K.
71 G4 Bristol CT U.S.A.
71 F4 Bristol PA U.S.A.
70 B6 Bristol TN U.S.A.
54 B4 Bristol Bay b. U.S.A.
9 C6 Bristol Channel est. U.K.
92 C1 Bristol I. i. Atl. Ocean
73 E4 Bristol Lake l. U.S.A.
73 E4 Bristol Mts mts U.S.A.
92 A2 British Antarctic Territory reg. Ant.
56 D3 British Columbia div. Can.
55 K1 British Empire Range mts Can.
3 □ British Indian Ocean Territory terr. Ind. Ocean
91 G2 Brits S. Africa
90 E5 Britstown S. Africa
Brittany reg. see Bretagne
14 E4 Brive-la-Gaillarde France
15 E1 Briviesca Spain
9 D7 Brixham U.K.
16 H6 Brno Czech Rep.
67 D5 Broad r. U.S.A.
71 F3 Broadalbin U.S.A.
58 E3 Broadback r. Can.
50 E4 Broadford Austr.
11 C5 Broadford Rep. of Ireland
10 C3 Broadford U.K.
10 E5 Broad Law h. U.K.
9 J6 Broadstairs U.K.
62 F2 Broadus U.S.A.
57 J4 Broadview Can.
64 C3 Broadwater U.S.A.
51 D1 Broadwood N.Z.
7 S8 Broceni Latvia
57 J3 Brochet Can.
57 J3 Brochet, Lac l. Can.
13 J3 Brocken mt Ger.
54 G2 Brock I. i. Can.
70 E3 Brockport U.S.A.
71 H3 Brockton U.S.A.
69 K3 Brockville Can.
69 F4 Brockway MI U.S.A.
70 D4 Brockway PA U.S.A.
55 K2 Brodeur Peninsula Can.
68 C4 Brodhead U.S.A.
10 C5 Brodick U.K.
17 J4 Brodnica Pol.
21 C5 Brody Ukr.
65 E4 Broken Arrow U.S.A.
50 H2 Broken B. b. Austr.
64 D3 Broken Bow NE U.S.A.
65 E5 Broken Bow OK U.S.A.
50 C1 Broken Hill Austr.
13 J2 Brome Ger.
9 G6 Bromley U.K.
9 E5 Bromsgrove U.K.
7 L8 Brønderslev Denmark
91 H2 Bronkhorstspruit S. Africa
6 N4 Brønnøysund Norway
68 E5 Bronson U.S.A.
9 J5 Brooke U.K.
43 A4 Brooke's Point Phil.
68 C4 Brookfield U.S.A.
65 F6 Brookhaven U.S.A.
62 A3 Brookings OR U.S.A.
64 D2 Brookings SD U.S.A.
71 H3 Brookline U.S.A.
68 A5 Brooklyn IA U.S.A.
68 B5 Brooklyn IL U.S.A.
64 E2 Brooklyn Center U.S.A.
70 D6 Brookneal U.S.A.
57 G4 Brooks Can.
72 A2 Brooks CA U.S.A.
71 J2 Brooks ME U.S.A.
92 B3 Brooks, C. c. Ant.
54 D3 Brooks Range mts U.S.A.
67 D6 Brooksville U.S.A.
70 D4 Brookville U.S.A.
48 C3 Broome Austr.
10 C3 Broom, Loch in. U.K.
10 E2 Brora U.K.
7 O9 Brösarp Sweden
11 D4 Brosna r. Rep. of Ireland
62 B3 Brothers U.S.A.
39 □ Brothers, The is H.K. China
8 E3 Brough U.K.
10 E1 Brough Head hd U.K.
11 E3 Broughshane U.K.
50 B2 Broughton r. Austr.
55 M3 Broughton Island Can.
17 P5 Brovary Ukr.
7 L8 Brovst Denmark
65 C5 Brownfield U.S.A.
62 D1 Browning U.S.A.
50 B2 Brown, Mt mt Austr.
68 D6 Brownsburg U.S.A.
71 F5 Browns Mills U.S.A.
67 B5 Brownsville TN U.S.A.
65 D7 Brownsville TX U.S.A.
71 J2 Brownville U.S.A.
71 J2 Brownville Junction U.S.A.
65 D6 Brownwood U.S.A.
17 O4 Brozha Belarus
14 F1 Bruay-en-Artois France
68 C2 Bruce Crossing U.S.A.
58 D4 Bruce Pen. pen. Can.
69 G3 Bruce Peninsula National Park Can.
13 G5 Bruchsal Ger.
13 L2 Brück Ger.
16 G7 Bruck an der Mur Austria
9 E6 Brue r. U.K.
12 B3 Bruges Belgium
Brugge see Bruges
13 G5 Brühl Baden-Württemberg Ger.
12 E4 Brühl Nordrhein-Westfalen Ger.
73 G2 Bruin Pt summit U.S.A.
35 J3 Bruint India
90 C2 Brukkaros Namibia
68 B2 Brule U.S.A.
12 C5 Brûly Belgium
82 E1 Brumado Brazil
7 M6 Brumunddal Norway
13 K2 Brunau Ger.
62 D3 Bruneau U.S.A.
62 D3 Bruneau r. U.S.A.
23 L9 Brunei country Asia
6 O5 Brunflo Sweden
18 D1 Brunico Italy
51 C5 Brunner, L. l. N.Z.
57 H4 Bruno Can.
16 D4 Brunsbüttel Ger.
67 D6 Brunswick GA U.S.A.
71 J3 Brunswick ME U.S.A.
70 C4 Brunswick OH U.S.A.
80 B8 Brunswick, Península de pen. Chile
16 H6 Bruntál Czech Rep.
92 C3 Brunt Ice Shelf ice feature Ant.
91 J4 Bruntville S. Africa
48 E6 Bruny I. i. Austr.
62 G3 Brush U.S.A.
12 C4 Brussels Belgium
69 G4 Brussels Can.
68 D3 Brussels U.S.A.
17 O5 Brusyliv Ukr.
50 F4 Bruthen Austr.
Bruxelles see Brussels
70 A4 Bryan OH U.S.A.
65 D6 Bryan TX U.S.A.
92 A3 Bryan Coast coastal area Ant.
50 B2 Bryan, Mt h. Austr.
20 E4 Bryansk Rus. Fed.
20 E4 Bryanskaya Oblast' div. Rus. Fed.
21 H6 Bryanskoye Rus. Fed.
73 F3 Bryce Canyon Nat. Park U.S.A.
73 H5 Bryce Mt mt U.S.A.
7 J7 Bryne Norway
21 F6 Bryukhovetskaya Rus. Fed.
17 H5 Brzeg Pol.
49 F2 Buala Solomon Is
86 A3 Buba Guinea-Bissau
29 M7 Būbīyān I. i. Kuwait
43 B5 Bubuan i. Phil.
28 C3 Bucak Turkey
81 B3 Bucaramanga Col.
43 C4 Bucas Grande i. Phil.
50 G4 Buchan Austr.
86 A4 Buchanan Liberia
68 D5 Buchanan MI U.S.A.
70 D6 Buchanan VA U.S.A.
65 D6 Buchanan, L. l. U.S.A.
55 L2 Buchan Gulf b. Can.
59 J4 Buchans Can.
19 M2 Bucharest Romania
13 J1 Büchen Ger.
13 H5 Buchen (Odenwald) Ger.
13 L1 Buchholz Ger.
13 H1 Bucholz in der Nordheide Ger.
72 B4 Buchon, Point pt U.S.A.
17 M7 Bucin, Pasul pass Romania
50 E1 Buckambool Mt h. Austr.
13 H2 Bückeburg Ger.
13 H2 Bücken Ger.
73 F5 Buckeye U.S.A.
70 B5 Buckeye Lake l. U.S.A.
70 C5 Buckhannon U.S.A.
70 C5 Buckhannon r. U.S.A.
10 E4 Buckhaven U.K.
69 H3 Buckhorn Can.
73 H5 Buckhorn U.S.A.
69 H3 Buckhorn Lake l. Can.
70 B6 Buckhorn Lake l. U.S.A.
10 F3 Buckie U.K.
69 K3 Buckingham Can.
9 G5 Buckingham U.K.
70 D6 Buckingham U.S.A.
48 D3 Buckingham Bay b. Austr.
48 E4 Buckland Tableland reg. Austr.
92 A6 Buckle I. i. Ant.
73 F4 Buckskin Mts mts U.S.A.
72 B2 Bucks Mt mt U.S.A.
71 J2 Bucksport U.S.A.
13 L2 Bückwitz Ger.
București see Bucharest
70 B4 Bucyrus U.S.A.
17 P4 Buda-Kashalyova Belarus
17 J7 Budapest Hungary
34 D3 Budaun India
50 E1 Budda Austr.
92 C6 Budd Coast coastal area Ant.
10 F4 Buddon Ness pt U.K.
18 C4 Buddusò Sardinia Italy
9 C7 Bude U.K.
65 F6 Bude U.S.A.
21 H6 Budennovsk Rus. Fed.
13 H4 Büdingen Ger.
34 D5 Budni India
20 E3 Budogoshch' Rus. Fed.
35 H2 Budongquan China
18 C4 Budoni Sardinia Italy
86 C4 Buea Cameroon
72 B4 Buellton U.S.A.
83 D2 Buena Esperanza Arg.
81 A4 Buenaventura Col.
74 C3 Buenaventura Mex.
81 A4 Buenaventure, B. de b. Col.
63 F4 Buena Vista CO U.S.A.
70 D6 Buena Vista VA U.S.A.
15 E2 Buendia, Embalse de resr Spain
83 B4 Bueno r. Chile
83 E2 Buenos Aires Arg.
83 E3 Buenos Aires div. Arg.
80 B7 Buenos Aires, L. l. Arg./Chile
80 C7 Buen Pasto Arg.
70 D3 Buffalo NY U.S.A.
65 D4 Buffalo OK U.S.A.
64 C2 Buffalo SD U.S.A.
65 D6 Buffalo TX U.S.A.
68 B3 Buffalo WI U.S.A.
62 F2 Buffalo WY U.S.A.
56 G3 Buffalo r. Can.
68 B3 Buffalo r. U.S.A.
56 F3 Buffalo Head Hills h. Can.
56 F2 Buffalo Lake l. Can.
50 F4 Buffalo, Mt mt Austr.
57 H3 Buffalo Narrows Can.
90 B4 Buffels watercourse S. Africa
91 G1 Buffels Drift S. Africa
67 D5 Buford U.S.A.
19 L2 Buftea Romania
17 K4 Bug r. Pol.
81 A4 Buga Col.
81 A3 Bugalagrande Col.
50 G1 Bugaldie Austr.
30 D2 Bugdayli Turkm.
45 D4 Bugel, Tanjung pt Indon.
12 C3 Buggenhout Belgium
18 G2 Bugojno Bos.-Herz.
43 A4 Bugsuk i. Phil.
43 B2 Buguey Phil.
30 D4 Būhābād Iran
29 J5 Buḩayrat ath Tharthār l. Iraq
29 K4 Buḩayrat Shārī l. Iraq
89 D5 Buhera Zimbabwe
43 B3 Buhi Phil.
62 D3 Buhl ID U.S.A.
68 A2 Buhl MN U.S.A.
29 J3 Bühtan r. Turkey
17 N7 Buhuşi Romania
9 D5 Builth Wells U.K.
86 B4 Bui National Park Ghana
20 J4 Buinsk Rus. Fed.
29 L4 Bu'in Soflā Iran
36 D2 Buir Nur l. Mongolia
89 B6 Buitepos Namibia
19 J3 Bujanovac Yugo.
88 C4 Bujumbura Burundi
36 D1 Bukachacha Rus. Fed.
30 D4 Būkand Iran
88 C4 Bukavu Congo(Zaire)
31 G2 Bukhara Uzbek.
43 C6 Bukide i. Indon.
44 □ Bukit Batok Sing.
44 B5 Bukit Fraser Malaysia
44 □ Bukit Panjang Sing.
44 □ Bukit Timah Sing.
45 B3 Bukittinggi Indon.
88 D4 Bukoba Tanz.
44 □ Bukum, P. i. Sing.
37 F7 Bula Indon.
20 J4 Bula r. Rus. Fed.
16 D7 Bülach Switz.
50 J2 Bulahdelal Austr.
43 B3 Bulan Phil.
28 G1 Bulancak Turkey
34 D3 Bulandshahr India
29 J2 Bulanık Turkey
89 C6 Bulawayo Zimbabwe
28 F3 Bulbul Syria
28 B2 Buldan Turkey
34 D5 Buldana India
91 J2 Bulembu Swaziland
36 C2 Bulgan Mongolia
38 B1 Bulgan Mongolia
5 F4 Bulgaria country Europe
51 D4 Buller r. N.Z.

50 F4 **Buller, Mt** *mt* Austr.
73 E4 **Bullhead City** U.S.A.
72 D4 **Bullion Mts** *mts* U.S.A.
90 B2 **Büllsport** Namibia
44 □ **Buloh, P.** *i.* Sing.
50 D4 **Buloke, Lake** *l.* Austr.
91 G4 **Bultfontein** S. Africa
43 C5 **Buluan** Phil.
48 C2 **Bulukumba** Indon.
25 O2 **Bulun** Rus. Fed.
88 B4 **Bulungu** *Bandundu* Congo(Zaire)
88 C4 **Bulungu** *Kasai-Occidental* Congo(Zaire)
31 G2 **Bulungur** Uzbek.
43 C3 **Bulusan** Phil.
43 C3 **Bumba** Congo(Zaire)
38 B1 **Bumbat Sum** China
73 F4 **Bumble Bee** U.S.A.
43 A5 **Bum-Bum** *i.* Malaysia
88 B4 **Buna** Congo(Zaire)
88 D3 **Buna** Kenya
88 D4 **Bunazi** Tanz.
11 C2 **Bunbeg** Rep. of Ireland
48 B5 **Bunbury** Austr.
11 E5 **Bunclody** Rep. of Ireland
11 D2 **Buncrana** Rep. of Ireland
88 D4 **Bunda** Tanz.
48 F4 **Bundaberg** Austr.
34 C4 **Bundi** India
11 C3 **Bundoran** Rep. of Ireland
35 F5 **Bundu** India
9 J5 **Bungay** U.K.
44 B2 **Bung Boraphet** *l.* Thai.
50 G3 **Bungendore** Austr.
92 C6 **Bunger Hills** *h.* Ant.
41 C8 **Bungo-suidō** *chan.* Japan
88 D3 **Bunia** Congo(Zaire)
88 C4 **Bunianga** Congo(Zaire)
50 D4 **Buninyong** Austr.
86 D3 **Buni-Yadi** Nigeria
34 C2 **Bunji** Jammu and Kashmir
73 E3 **Bunkerville** U.S.A.
65 E6 **Bunkie** U.S.A.
67 D6 **Bunnell** U.S.A.
28 E2 **Bünyan** Turkey
43 A6 **Bunyu** *i.* Indon.
30 C4 **Bu ol Kheyr** Iran
44 D2 **Buôn Hô** Vietnam
44 D2 **Buôn Mê Thuôt** Vietnam
25 P2 **Buorkhaya, Guba** *b.* Rus. Fed.
32 C4 **Buqayq** S. Arabia
88 D4 **Bura** Kenya
34 E3 **Burang** China
82 E2 **Buranhaém** *r.* Brazil
88 E3 **Burao** Somalia
43 C4 **Burauen** Phil.
32 B4 **Buraydah** S. Arabia
13 G4 **Burbach** Ger.
72 C4 **Burbank** U.S.A.
50 F2 **Burcher** Austr.
31 G2 **Burdalyk** Turkm.
28 C3 **Burdur** Turkey
88 D2 **Burē** Eth.
9 D5 **Bure** *r.* U.K.
6 R4 **Bureå** Sweden
36 F1 **Bureinskiy Khrebet** *mts* Rus. Fed.
28 D6 **Bûr Fu'ad** Egypt
19 M3 **Burgas** Bulg.
67 E5 **Burgaw** U.S.A.
13 K2 **Burg bei Magdeburg** Ger.
13 J5 **Burgbernheim** Ger.
13 J2 **Burgdorf** Ger.
59 J4 **Burgeo** Can.
91 G5 **Burgersdorp** S. Africa
91 J2 **Burgersfort** S. Africa
9 G7 **Burgess Hill** U.K.
13 H4 **Burghaun** Ger.
16 F6 **Burghausen** Ger.
10 E3 **Burghead** U.K.
12 B3 **Burgh-Haamstede** Neth.
18 F6 **Burgio, Serra di** *h. Sicily* Italy
13 L5 **Burglengenfeld** Ger.
15 E1 **Burgos** Spain
13 L4 **Burgstädt** Ger.
7 Q8 **Burgsvik** Sweden
**Burgundy** *reg. see* **Bourgogne**
36 B3 **Burhan Budai Shan** *mts* China
19 M5 **Burhaniye** Turkey
34 D5 **Burhanpur** India
35 E5 **Burhar-Dhanpuri** India
35 F4 **Burhi Gandak** *r.* India
43 B3 **Burias** *i.* Phil.
35 H4 **Buri Dihing** *r.* India
35 E4 **Buri Gandak** *r.* Nepal
59 J4 **Burin Peninsula** Can.
44 B2 **Buriram** Thai.
79 K5 **Buriti Bravo** Brazil
82 C1 **Buritis** Brazil
31 G4 **Burj** Pak.
92 A3 **Burke I.** *i.* Ant.
51 C6 **Burke Pass** N.Z.
48 D3 **Burketown** Austr.
85 C4 **Burkina** *country* Africa
69 H3 **Burk's Falls** Can.
62 D3 **Burley** U.S.A.
69 H4 **Burlington** Can.
64 C4 **Burlington** *CO* U.S.A.
68 B5 **Burlington** *IA* U.S.A.
68 D5 **Burlington** *IN* U.S.A.
71 J2 **Burlington** *ME* U.S.A.
71 G2 **Burlington** *VT* U.S.A.
68 C4 **Burlington** *WV* U.S.A.
**Burma** *country see* **Myanmar**
65 D6 **Burnet** U.S.A.
62 B3 **Burney** U.S.A.
71 J2 **Burnham** U.S.A.
48 E6 **Burnie** Austr.
8 G3 **Burniston** U.K.
8 E4 **Burnley** U.K.
62 C3 **Burns** U.S.A.
57 H1 **Burnside** *r.* Can.
54 F4 **Burns Lake** Can.
70 C5 **Burnsville Lake** *l.* U.S.A.
67 F7 **Burnt Ground** Bahamas
10 E4 **Burntisland** U.K.
59 H3 **Burnt Lake** *l.* Can.
57 K3 **Burntwood** *r.* Can.
57 J3 **Burnt Wood Lake** *l.* Can.
50 D3 **Buronga** Austr.
24 K5 **Burqin** China
28 G5 **Burqu'** Jordan
50 B2 **Burra** Austr.
10 □ **Burravoe** U.K.
10 F2 **Burray** *i.* U.K.
19 J4 **Burrel** Albania
50 G2 **Burrendong Reservoir** Austr.
50 H3 **Burrewarra Pt** *pt* Austr.
15 F3 **Burriana** Spain
50 G3 **Burrinjuck** Austr.
50 G3 **Burrinjuck Reservoir** Austr.
70 B5 **Burr Oak Reservoir** U.S.A.
74 D3 **Burro, Serranías del** *mts* Mex.
10 D6 **Burrow Head** *hd* U.K.
73 G2 **Burrville** U.S.A.
28 B1 **Bursa** Turkey
87 F2 **Bûr Safâga** Egypt
**Bûr Sa'îd** *see* **Port Said**
13 G5 **Bürstadt** Ger.
**Bûr Sudan** *see* **Port Sudan**
50 C2 **Burta** Austr.
68 E3 **Burt Lake** *l.* U.S.A.
69 F4 **Burton** U.S.A.
58 E3 **Burton, Lac** *l.* Can.
11 C3 **Burtonport** Rep. of Ireland
9 F5 **Burton upon Trent** U.K.
6 R4 **Burträsk** Sweden
71 K1 **Burtts Corner** Can.
50 D2 **Burtundy** Austr.
37 E7 **Buru** *i.* Indon.
28 C6 **Burullus, Bahra el** *lag.* Egypt
85 F6 **Burundi** *country* Africa
88 C4 **Bururi** Burundi
56 B2 **Burwash Landing** Can.
10 F2 **Burwick** U.K.
21 E5 **Buryn'** Ukr.
9 H5 **Bury St Edmunds** U.K.
34 C2 **Burzil Pass** Jammu and Kashmir
88 C4 **Busanga** Congo(Zaire)
11 E2 **Bush** *r.* U.K.
30 C4 **Būshehr** Iran
35 E2 **Bushêngcaka** China
88 D4 **Bushenyi** Uganda
**Bushire** *see* **Būshehr**
11 E2 **Bushmills** U.K.
68 B5 **Bushnell** U.S.A.
88 C3 **Businga** Congo(Zaire)
44 □ **Busing, P.** *i.* Sing.
28 F5 **Buşrá ash Shām** Syria
48 B5 **Busselton** Austr.
12 D2 **Bussum** Neth.
65 C7 **Bustamante** Mex.
18 C2 **Busto Arsizio** Italy
43 A3 **Busuanga** Phil.
43 A3 **Busuanga** *i.* Phil.
88 C3 **Buta** Congo(Zaire)
44 A4 **Butang Group** *is* Thai.
83 C3 **Buta Ranquil** Arg.
88 C4 **Butare** Rwanda
94 G5 **Butaritari** *i.* Pac. Oc.
50 A2 **Bute** Austr.
10 C5 **Bute** *i.* U.K.
56 D4 **Butedale** Can.
56 D4 **Bute In.** *in.* Can.
10 C5 **Bute, Sound of** *chan.* U.K.
91 H4 **Butha Buthe** Lesotho
13 G1 **Butjadingen** *reg.* Ger.
68 E5 **Butler** *IN* U.S.A.
70 D4 **Butler** *PA* U.S.A.
11 D3 **Butlers Bridge** Rep. of Ireland
37 E7 **Buton** *i.* Indon.
13 L1 **Bütow** Ger.
62 D2 **Butte** U.S.A.
13 K3 **Buttelstedt** Ger.
72 B1 **Butte Meadows** U.S.A.
45 B1 **Butterworth** Malaysia
91 H6 **Butterworth** S. Africa
11 C5 **Buttevant** Rep. of Ireland
56 D5 **Buttle L.** *l.* Can.
10 B2 **Butt of Lewis** *hd* U.K.
55 J4 **Button Bay** *b.* Can.
72 C4 **Buttonwillow** U.S.A.
43 C4 **Butuan** Phil.
39 B5 **Butuo** China
21 G5 **Buturlinovka** Rus. Fed.
35 E4 **Butwal** Nepal
13 G4 **Butzbach** Ger.
88 E3 **Buulobarde** Somalia
88 E4 **Buur Gaabo** Somalia
88 E3 **Buurhabaka** Somalia
35 F4 **Buxar** India
13 H1 **Buxtehude** Ger.
9 F4 **Buxton** U.K.
20 G3 **Buy** Rus. Fed.
68 A1 **Buyck** U.S.A.
21 H7 **Buynaksk** Rus. Fed.
**Büyük Ağri** *mt see* **Ararat, Mt**
28 A3 **Büyükmenderes** *r.* Turkey
42 B3 **Buyun Shan** *mt* China
12 C5 **Buzancy** France
19 M2 **Buzău** Romania
89 D5 **Búzi** Moz.
24 G4 **Buzuluk** Rus. Fed.
21 G5 **Buzuluk** *r.* Rus. Fed.
71 H4 **Buzzards Bay** *b.* U.S.A.
35 G4 **Byakar** Bhutan
19 L3 **Byala** Bulg.
19 K3 **Byala Slatina** Bulg.
17 O4 **Byalynichy** Belarus
54 H2 **Byam Martin I.** *i.* Can.
20 D4 **Byarezina** *r.* Belarus
20 C4 **Byaroza** Belarus
28 E4 **Byblos** Lebanon
16 J4 **Bydgoszcz** Pol.
20 D4 **Byerazino** Belarus
62 F4 **Byers** U.S.A.
17 O3 **Byeshankovichy** Belarus
7 K7 **Bygland** Norway
20 D4 **Bykhaw** Belarus
7 K7 **Bykle** Norway
55 L2 **Bylot Island** *i.* Can.
69 G3 **Byng Inlet** Can.
92 B5 **Byrd Gl.** *gl.* Ant.
7 K6 **Byrkjelo** Norway
68 C4 **Byron** *IL* U.S.A.
71 H2 **Byron** *ME* U.S.A.
49 F4 **Byron Bay** Austr.
25 M2 **Byrranga, Gory** *mts* Rus. Fed.
6 R4 **Byske** Sweden
25 P3 **Bytantay** *r.* Rus. Fed.
17 J5 **Bytom** Pol.
16 H3 **Bytów** Pol.
31 E2 **Byuzmeyin** Turkm.


# C


80 E3 **Caacupé** Para.
82 A4 **Caagazú, Cordillera de** *h.* Para.
82 A4 **Caaguazú** Para.
82 A3 **Caarapó** Brazil
82 A4 **Caazapá** Para.
78 C6 **Caballas** Peru
78 D4 **Caballococha** Peru
43 B3 **Cabanatuan** Phil.
59 G4 **Cabano** Can.
88 E2 **Cabdul Qaadir** Somalia
82 A1 **Cabeceira Rio Manso** Brazil
79 M5 **Cabedelo** Brazil
15 D3 **Cabeza del Buey** Spain
78 F7 **Cabezas** Bol.
83 E3 **Cabildo** Arg.
81 C2 **Cabimas** Venez.
88 B4 **Cabinda** Angola
88 B4 **Cabinda** *div.* Angola
62 C1 **Cabinet Mts** *mts* U.S.A.
81 B3 **Cable Way** *pass* Col.
82 D3 **Cabo Frio** Brazil
82 E3 **Cabo Frio, Ilha do** *i.* Brazil
58 E4 **Cabonga, Réservoir** *resr* Can.
65 E4 **Cabool** U.S.A.
49 F4 **Caboolture** Austr.
79 H3 **Cabo Orange, Parque Nacional de** *nat. park* Brazil
78 C4 **Cabo Pantoja** Peru
74 B2 **Caborca** Mex.
69 G3 **Cabot Head** *pt* Can.
59 J4 **Cabot Strait** *str.* Can.
82 D2 **Cabral, Serra do** *mts* Brazil
29 L2 **Cäbrayıl** Azer.
15 H3 **Cabrera** *i.* Spain
15 C1 **Cabrera, Sierra de la** *mts* Spain
15 F3 **Cabriel** *r.* Spain
81 D3 **Cabruta** Venez.
43 B2 **Cabugao** Phil.
80 F3 **Caçador** Brazil
19 J3 **Čačak** Yugo.
83 G1 **Caçapava do Sul** Brazil
70 D5 **Cacapon** *r.* U.S.A.
81 B3 **Cácares** Col.
18 C4 **Caccia, Capo** *pt Sardinia* Italy
79 G7 **Cáceres** Brazil
15 C3 **Cáceres** Spain
62 D3 **Cache Peak** *summit* U.S.A.
86 A3 **Cacheu** Guinea-Bissau
80 C3 **Cachi** *r.* Arg.
79 H5 **Cachimbo, Serra do** *h.* Brazil
81 B3 **Cáchira** Col.
82 E1 **Cachoeira** Brazil
82 B2 **Cachoeira Alta** Brazil
83 G1 **Cachoeira do Sul** Brazil
82 E3 **Cachoeiro de Itapemirim** Brazil
86 A3 **Cacine** Guinea-Bissau
79 H3 **Caciporé, Cabo** *pt* Brazil
89 B5 **Cacolo** Angola
88 B4 **Caconda** Angola
73 G5 **Cactus Range** *mts* U.S.A.
82 B2 **Caçu** Brazil
82 D1 **Caculé** Brazil
17 J6 **Čadca** Slovakia
13 H1 **Cadenberge** Ger.
43 B3 **Cadig Mountains** Phil.
69 H1 **Cadillac** *Que.* Can.
57 H5 **Cadillac** *Sask.* Can.
68 E3 **Cadillac** U.S.A.
43 B4 **Cadiz** Phil.
15 C4 **Cádiz** Spain
15 C4 **Cádiz, Golfo de** *g.* Spain
73 E4 **Cadiz Lake** *l.* U.S.A.
14 D2 **Caen** France
9 C4 **Caernarfon** U.K.
9 C4 **Caernarfon Bay** *b.* U.K.
9 D6 **Caerphilly** U.K.
70 B5 **Caesar Creek Lake** *l.* U.S.A.
28 E5 **Caesarea** Israel
82 D1 **Caetité** Brazil
80 C3 **Cafayate** Arg.
43 B4 **Cagayan** *i.* Phil.
82 B2 **Cagayan** *r.* Phil.
43 C4 **Cagayan de Oro** Phil.
43 B4 **Cagayan Islands** *is* Phil.
18 E3 **Cagli** Italy
18 C5 **Cagliari** *Sardinia* Italy
18 C5 **Cagliari, Golfo di** *b. Sardinia* Italy
81 B4 **Caguán** *r.* Col.
11 B6 **Caha** *h.* Rep. of Ireland
67 C5 **Cahaba** *r.* U.S.A.
11 B6 **Caha Mts** *h.* Rep. of Ireland
11 A6 **Cahermore** Rep. of Ireland
11 D5 **Cahir** Rep. of Ireland
11 A6 **Cahirciveen** Rep. of Ireland
89 D5 **Cahora Bassa, Lago de** *resr* Moz.
11 E5 **Cahore Point** *pt* Rep. of Ireland
14 E4 **Cahors** France
78 C5 **Cahuapanas** Peru
21 D6 **Cahul** Moldova
89 D5 **Caia** Moz.
79 G6 **Caiabis, Serra dos** *h.* Brazil
89 C5 **Caianda** Angola
82 B2 **Caiapó** *r.* Brazil
82 B2 **Caiapônia** Brazil
82 B2 **Caiapó, Serra do** *mts* Brazil
75 J4 **Caibarién** Cuba
44 C3 **Cai Be** Vietnam
81 D3 **Caicara** Venez.
75 K4 **Caicos Is** *is* Turks and Caicos Is
83 B1 **Caimanes** Chile
43 A3 **Caiman Point** *pt* Phil.
15 F2 **Caimodorro** *mt* Spain
44 C3 **Cai Nước** Vietnam
10 E3 **Cairn Gorm** *mt* U.K.
10 E3 **Cairngorm Mountains** U.K.
10 C6 **Cairnryan** U.K.
48 E3 **Cairns** Austr.
10 E3 **Cairn Toul** *mt* U.K.
87 F1 **Cairo** Egypt
67 C6 **Cairo** U.S.A.
18 C2 **Cairo Montenotte** Italy
89 B5 **Caiundo** Angola
78 C5 **Cajamarca** Peru
43 B3 **Cajidiocan** Phil.
18 G1 **Čakovec** Croatia
28 B2 **Çal** Turkey
91 G5 **Cala** S. Africa
86 C4 **Calabar** Nigeria
69 J3 **Calabogie** Can.
81 D2 **Calabozo** Venez.
19 K3 **Calafat** Romania
80 B8 **Calafate** Arg.
43 B3 **Calagua Islands** *is* Phil.
15 F1 **Calahorra** Spain
89 B5 **Calai** Angola
14 E1 **Calais** France
71 K2 **Calais** U.S.A.
71 F5 **Calama** Brazil
80 C2 **Calama** Chile
81 B2 **Calamar** *Bolívar* Col.
81 B4 **Calamar** *Guaviare* Col.
43 A4 **Calamian Group** *is* Phil.
15 F2 **Calamocha** Spain
89 B4 **Calandula** Angola
87 E2 **Calanscio Sand Sea** *des.* Libya
43 B3 **Calapan** Phil.
19 M2 **Călărași** Romania
15 F2 **Calatayud** Spain
43 B3 **Calauag** Phil.
43 B2 **Calavite, Cape** *pt* Phil.
43 A3 **Calawit** *i.* Phil.
43 B2 **Calayan** *i.* Phil.
43 C3 **Calbayog** Phil.
13 K3 **Calbe (Saale)** Ger.
43 C4 **Calbiga** Phil.
83 B4 **Calbuco** Chile
79 L5 **Calcanhar, Ponta do** *pt* Brazil
65 E6 **Calcasieu L.** *l.* U.S.A.
79 H3 **Calçoene** Brazil
35 G5 **Calcutta** India
15 B3 **Caldas da Rainha** Port.
82 C2 **Caldas Novas** Brazil
13 H3 **Calden** Ger.
80 B3 **Caldera** Chile
29 J2 **Çaldıran** Turkey
62 C3 **Caldwell** U.S.A.
69 H4 **Caledon** Can.
90 C7 **Caledon** S. Africa
91 G5 **Caledon** *r.* Lesotho/S. Africa
69 H4 **Caledonia** Can.
68 B4 **Caledonia** U.S.A.
80 C7 **Caleta Olivia** Arg.
73 E5 **Calexico** U.S.A.
8 C3 **Calf of Man** *i.* U.K.
56 G4 **Calgary** Can.
67 C5 **Calhoun** U.S.A.
81 A4 **Cali** Col.
43 C4 **Calicoan** *i.* Phil.
33 A4 **Calicut** India
72 C4 **Caliente** *CA* U.S.A.
73 E3 **Caliente** *NV* U.S.A.
72 B3 **California** *div.* U.S.A.
72 B3 **California Aqueduct** *canal* U.S.A.
74 B2 **California, Golfo de** *g.* Mex.
72 C4 **California Hot Springs** U.S.A.
29 M2 **Cälilabad** Azer.
63 D5 **Calipatria** U.S.A.
72 A2 **Calistoga** U.S.A.
90 D6 **Calitzdorp** S. Africa
72 D2 **Callaghan, Mt** *mt* U.S.A.
67 D6 **Callahan** U.S.A.
11 D5 **Callan** Rep. of Ireland
69 H2 **Callander** Can.
10 D4 **Callander** U.K.
78 C6 **Callao** Peru
73 F2 **Callao** U.S.A.
71 F4 **Callicoon** U.S.A.
9 C7 **Callington** U.K.
69 G2 **Callum** Can.
56 G4 **Calmar** Can.
68 B4 **Calmar** U.S.A.
73 E4 **Cal-Nev-Ari** U.S.A.
67 D7 **Caloosahatchee** *r.* U.S.A.
72 B2 **Calpine** U.S.A.
18 F6 **Caltanissetta** *Sicily* Italy
68 C2 **Calumet** U.S.A.
89 B5 **Calunga** Angola
89 B5 **Caluquembe** Angola
43 B4 **Calusa** *i.* Phil.
88 F2 **Caluula** Somalia
73 G5 **Calva** U.S.A.
56 D4 **Calvert I.** *i.* Can.
18 C3 **Calvi** *Corsica* France
15 H3 **Calvià** Spain
90 C5 **Calvinia** S. Africa
18 F4 **Calvo, Monte** *mt* Italy
9 H5 **Cam** *r.* U.K.
82 E1 **Camaçari** Brazil
72 B2 **Camache Reservoir** U.S.A.
89 B5 **Camacuio** Angola
89 B5 **Camacupa** Angola
81 D2 **Camaguán** Venez.
75 J4 **Camagüey** Cuba
75 J4 **Camagüey, Arch. de** *is* Cuba
45 B1 **Camah, Gunung** *mt* Malaysia
**Çamalan** *see* **Gülek**
78 D7 **Camana** Peru
89 C5 **Camanongue** Angola
82 B2 **Camapuã** Brazil
83 G1 **Camaquã** Brazil
83 G1 **Camaquã** *r.* Brazil
28 E3 **Çamardı** Turkey
65 D7 **Camargo** Mex.
80 C6 **Camarones** Arg.
80 C6 **Camarones, Bahía** *b.* Arg.
62 B2 **Camas** U.S.A.
44 C3 **Ca Mau** Vietnam
**Cambay** *see* **Khambhat**
**Cambay, Gulf of** *g. see* **Khambhat, Gulf of**
9 G6 **Camberley** U.K.
23 K8 **Cambodia** *country* Asia
9 B7 **Camborne** U.K.
14 F1 **Cambrai** France
72 B4 **Cambria** U.S.A.
9 D5 **Cambrian Mountains** *reg.* U.K.
69 G4 **Cambridge** Can.
51 E2 **Cambridge** N.Z.
9 H5 **Cambridge** U.K.
68 B5 **Cambridge** *IL* U.S.A.
71 H3 **Cambridge** *MA* U.S.A.
71 E5 **Cambridge** *MD* U.S.A.
64 E2 **Cambridge** *MN* U.S.A.
71 G3 **Cambridge** *NY* U.S.A.
70 C4 **Cambridge** *OH* U.S.A.
59 G2 **Cambrien, Lac** *l.* Can.
50 H3 **Camden** Austr.
67 C5 **Camden** *AL* U.S.A.
65 E5 **Camden** *AR* U.S.A.
71 J2 **Camden** *ME* U.S.A.
71 F5 **Camden** *NJ* U.S.A.
71 F3 **Camden** *NY* U.S.A.
67 D5 **Camden** *SC* U.S.A.
80 B8 **Camden, Isla** *i.* Chile
89 C5 **Cameia, Parque Nacional da** *nat. park* Angola
73 G4 **Cameron** *AZ* U.S.A.
65 E6 **Cameron** *LA* U.S.A.
64 E4 **Cameron** *MO* U.S.A.
65 D6 **Cameron** *TX* U.S.A.
68 B3 **Cameron** *WV* U.S.A.
44 B4 **Cameron Highlands** Malaysia
56 F3 **Cameron Hills** *h.* Can.
72 B2 **Cameron Park** U.S.A.
85 E5 **Cameroon** *country* Africa
86 C4 **Cameroun, Mt** *mt* Cameroon
79 J4 **Cametá** Brazil
43 B2 **Camiguin** *i.* Phil.
43 C4 **Camiguin** *i.* Phil.
43 B3 **Camiling** Phil.
67 C6 **Camilla** U.S.A.
78 F8 **Camiri** Bol.
79 K4 **Camocim** Brazil
48 D3 **Camooweal** Austr.
43 C4 **Camotes Sea** *g.* Phil.
83 E2 **Campana** Arg.
81 B4 **Campana, Co** *h.* Col.
80 A7 **Campana, I.** *i.* Chile
83 B2 **Campanario** *mt* Arg./Chile
56 D4 **Campania I.** *i.* Can.
90 E4 **Campbell** S. Africa
51 E4 **Campbell, Cape** *c.* N.Z.
46 H9 **Campbell Island** *i.* N.Z.
56 D4 **Campbell River** Can.
69 J3 **Campbells Bay** Can.
66 C4 **Campbellsville** U.S.A.
59 G4 **Campbellton** Can.
10 C5 **Campbeltown** U.K.
74 F5 **Campeche** Mex.
74 F5 **Campeche, Bahía de** *g.* Mex.
50 D5 **Camperdown** Austr.
19 L2 **Câmpina** Romania
79 L5 **Campina Grande** Brazil
82 C3 **Campinas** Brazil
82 C2 **Campina Verde** Brazil
86 C4 **Campo** Cameroon
81 B4 **Campoalegre** Col.
18 F4 **Campobasso** Italy
82 D3 **Campo Belo** Brazil
79 H6 **Campo de Diauarum** Brazil
82 C2 **Campo Florido** Brazil
80 D3 **Campo Gallo** Arg.
82 A3 **Campo Grande** Brazil
79 K4 **Campo Maior** Brazil
15 C3 **Campo Maior** Port.
82 B4 **Campo Mourão** Brazil
82 E3 **Campos** Brazil
82 C2 **Campos Altos** Brazil
82 D3 **Campos do Jordão** Brazil
82 B4 **Campos Erê** *reg.* Brazil
10 D4 **Campsie Fells** *h.* U.K.
70 B6 **Campton** *KY* U.S.A.
71 H3 **Campton** *NH* U.S.A.
19 L2 **Câmpulung** Romania
17 M7 **Câmpulung Moldovenesc** Romania
73 G4 **Camp Verde** U.S.A.
44 D3 **Cam Ranh** Vietnam
56 G4 **Camrose** Can.
9 B6 **Camrose** U.K.
57 G2 **Camsell Lake** *l.* Can.
57 H3 **Camsell Portage** Can.
21 C7 **Çan** Turkey
71 G3 **Canaan** U.S.A.
53 E4 **Canada** N. America
83 E2 **Cañada de Gómez** Arg.
71 H2 **Canada Falls Lake** *l.* U.S.A.
65 C5 **Canadian** *r.* U.S.A.
81 E3 **Canaima, Parque Nacional** *nat. park* Venez.
71 F3 **Canajoharie** U.S.A.
21 C7 **Çanakkale** Turkey
**Çanakkale Boğazı** *str. see* **Dardanelles**
83 C2 **Canalejas** Arg.
70 E3 **Canandaigua** U.S.A.
70 E3 **Canandaigua Lake** *l.* U.S.A.
74 B2 **Cananea** Mex.
59 H2 **Cananée, Lac** *l.* Can.
82 C4 **Cananéia** Brazil
81 C4 **Canapiare, Co** *h.* Col.
78 C4 **Cañar** Ecuador
**Canarias, Islas** *is see* **Canary Islands**
96 G4 **Canary Basin** *sea feature* Atl. Ocean
84 A3 **Canary Islands** *is* Atlantic Ocean
71 F3 **Canastota** U.S.A.
82 C2 **Canastra, Serra da** *mts* Brazil
67 D6 **Canaveral, Cape** *c.* U.S.A.
15 E2 **Cañaveras** Spain
82 E1 **Canavieiras** Brazil
50 F1 **Canbelego** Austr.
50 G3 **Canberra** Austr.
62 B3 **Canby** *CA* U.S.A.
64 D2 **Canby** *MN* U.S.A.
74 G4 **Cancún** Mex.
63 F6 **Candelaria** *Chihuahua* Mex.
15 D2 **Candeleda** Spain
50 G4 **Candelo** Austr.
79 J4 **Cândido Mendes** Brazil
28 D1 **Çandır** Turkey
57 H4 **Candle Lake** Can.
57 H4 **Candle Lake** *l.* Can.
92 C1 **Candlemas I.** *i.* Atl. Ocean
71 G4 **Candlewood, Lake** *l.* U.S.A.
64 D1 **Cando** U.S.A.
43 B2 **Candon** Phil.
83 B1 **Canela Baja** Chile
83 F2 **Canelones** Uru.
83 B3 **Cañete** Chile
15 F2 **Cañete** Spain
78 D6 **Cangallo** Peru
89 B5 **Cangamba** Angola
15 C1 **Cangas del Narcea** Spain
90 E6 **Cango Caves** *caves* S. Africa
79 L5 **Canguaretama** Brazil
83 G1 **Canguçu** Brazil
83 G1 **Canguçu, Sa do** *h.* Brazil
39 D6 **Cangwu** China
38 E2 **Cangzhou** China
59 G3 **Caniapiscau** Can.
59 G2 **Caniapiscau** *r.* Can.
59 G3 **Caniapiscau, Lac** *l.* Can.
18 E6 **Canicattì** *Sicily* Italy
56 E4 **Canim Lake** Can.
56 E4 **Canim Lake** *l.* Can.
79 L4 **Canindé** Brazil
79 K5 **Canindé** *r.* Brazil
10 C2 **Canisp** *h.* U.K.
70 E3 **Canisteo** U.S.A.
70 E3 **Canisteo** *r.* U.S.A.
28 D1 **Çankırı** Turkey
43 B4 **Canlaon** Phil.
56 F4 **Canmore** Can.
10 B3 **Canna** *i.* U.K.
33 A4 **Cannanore** India
33 A4 **Cannanore Islands** *is* India
14 H5 **Cannes** France
9 E5 **Cannock** U.K.
50 G4 **Cann River** Austr.
81 E2 **Caño Araguao** *r.* Venez.
80 F3 **Canoas** Brazil
57 H3 **Canoe L.** *l.* Can.
82 B4 **Canoinhas** Brazil
81 E2 **Caño Macareo** *r.* Venez.
81 E2 **Caño Manamo** *r.* Venez.
81 E2 **Caño Mariusa** *r.* Venez.
63 F4 **Canon City** U.S.A.
50 C2 **Canopus** Austr.
57 J4 **Canora** Can.
50 G2 **Canowindra** Austr.
59 H4 **Canso, C.** *hd* Can.
15 D1 **Cantábrica, Cordillera** *mts* Spain
**Cantábrico, Mar** *sea see* **Biscay, Bay of**
83 C2 **Cantantal** Arg.
81 D2 **Cantaura** Venez.
71 K2 **Canterbury** Can.
9 J6 **Canterbury** U.K.
51 C6 **Canterbury Bight** *b.* N.Z.
51 C5 **Canterbury Plains** *plain* N.Z.
44 C3 **Cần Thơ** Vietnam
43 C4 **Cantilan** Phil.
79 K5 **Canto do Buriti** Brazil
**Canton** *see* **Guangzhou**
68 B5 **Canton** *IL* U.S.A.
71 H2 **Canton** *ME* U.S.A.
68 B5 **Canton** *MO* U.S.A.
65 F5 **Canton** *MS* U.S.A.
71 F2 **Canton** *NY* U.S.A.
70 C4 **Canton** *OH* U.S.A.
70 E4 **Canton** *PA* U.S.A.
82 B4 **Cantu** *r.* Brazil
82 B4 **Cantu, Serra do** *h.* Brazil
83 E2 **Cañuelas** Arg.
79 G4 **Canumã** Brazil
78 F5 **Canutama** Brazil
51 D4 **Canvastown** N.Z.
9 H6 **Canvey Island** U.K.
65 C5 **Canyon** U.S.A.
62 C2 **Canyon City** U.S.A.
73 H3 **Canyon de Chelly National Monument** *res.* U.S.A.
62 D2 **Canyon Ferry L.** *l.* U.S.A.
73 H2 **Canyonlands National Park** U.S.A.
56 D2 **Canyon Ranges** *mts* Can.
62 B3 **Canyonville** U.S.A.
42 C3 **Cao** *r.* China
39 C6 **Cao Băng** Vietnam
44 D2 **Cao Nguyên Đắc Lắc** *plat.* Vietnam
42 C2 **Caoshi** China
38 E3 **Cao Xian** China
43 B5 **Cap** *i.* Phil.
81 D3 **Capanaparo** *r.* Venez.
79 J4 **Capanema** Brazil
82 B4 **Capanema** *r.* Brazil
82 C4 **Capão Bonito** Brazil
81 C3 **Caparo** *r.* Venez.
81 C4 **Caparro, Co** *h.* Brazil
43 B3 **Capas** Phil.
59 H4 **Cap-aux-Meules** Can.
59 F4 **Cap-de-la-Madeleine** Can.
48 E6 **Cape Barren Island** *i.* Austr.
96 K8 **Cape Basin** *sea feature* Atl. Ocean
59 H4 **Cape Breton Highlands Nat. Park** *nat. park* Can.
59 H4 **Cape Breton Island** *i.* Can.

42 B4 Changhai China
42 D6 Changhang S. Korea
42 D5 Changhowan S. Korea
39 F5 Chang-hua Taiwan
44 D1 Changhua Jiang r. China
42 D6 Changhung S. Korea
44 □ Changi Sing.
39 C7 Changjiang China
Chang Jiang r. see Yangtze
Changjiang Kou est. see Yangtze, Mouth of the
42 D3 Changjin N. Korea
42 D3 Changjin Reservoir N. Korea
39 F5 Changle China
38 F2 Changli China
42 B1 Changling China
39 D5 Changning China
42 C4 Changnyŏn N. Korea
38 E1 Changping China
42 E5 Changp'yŏng S. Korea
42 C4 Changsan-got pt N. Korea
39 D4 Changsha China
39 F4 Changshan China
42 B4 Changshan Qundao is China
39 C4 Changshou China
39 D4 Changshoujie China
38 F4 Changshu China
39 C5 Changshun China
42 D6 Changsŏng S. Korea
39 E5 Changtai China
39 E5 Changting Fujian China
42 E1 Changting Heilongjiang China
42 C2 Changtu China
42 E6 Ch'angwŏn S. Korea
38 C3 Changwu China
42 A4 Changxing Dao i. China
39 D4 Changyang China
38 F2 Changyi China
42 C4 Changyŏn N. Korea
38 E3 Changyuan China
38 D2 Changzhi China
38 F4 Changzhou China
19 L7 Chania Greece
42 D3 Chanjin r. N. Korea
38 B3 Chankou China
33 B3 Channapatna India
72 C5 Channel Islands is U.S.A.
4 C4 Channel Islands terr. English Channel
72 B5 Channel Is Nat. Park U.S.A.
59 J4 Channel-Port-aux-Basques Can.
9 J6 Channel Tunnel tunnel France/U.K.
68 C2 Channing U.S.A.
15 C1 Chantada Spain
44 B2 Chanthaburi Thai.
14 F2 Chantilly France
65 E4 Chanute U.S.A.
24 J4 Chany, Ozero salt l. Rus. Fed.
38 E2 Chaobai Xinhe r. China
38 E4 Chao Hu l. China
44 B2 Chao Phraya r. Thai.
86 B1 Chaouèn Morocco
35 H2 Chaowula Shan mts China
38 E4 Chao Xian China
39 E6 Chaoyang Guangdong China
38 F1 Chaoyang Liaoning China
39 E6 Chaozhou China
82 E1 Chapada Diamantina, Parque Nacional nat. park Brazil
82 A1 Chapada dos Guimarães Brazil
82 C1 Chapada dos Veadeiros, Parque Nacional da nat. park Brazil
74 D4 Chapala, L. de l. Mex.
81 B4 Chaparral Col.
26 D1 Chapayev Kazak.
20 J4 Chapayevsk Rus. Fed.
80 F3 Chapecó Brazil
80 F3 Chapecó r. Brazil
9 F4 Chapel-en-le-Frith U.K.
67 E5 Chapel Hill U.S.A.
12 C4 Chapelle-lez-Herlaimont Belgium
9 F4 Chapeltown U.K.
68 D5 Chapin, Lake l. U.S.A.
69 F2 Chapleau Can.
20 F4 Chaplygin Rus. Fed.
21 E6 Chaplynka Ukr.
70 B6 Chapmanville U.S.A.
31 G3 Chapri Pass Afgh.
78 E7 Chaqui Bol.
34 D2 Char Jammu and Kashmir
35 H3 Char Chu r. China
92 A2 Charcot I. i. Ant.
57 G3 Chard Can.
9 E7 Chard U.K.
29 L3 Chārdagh Iran
29 L5 Chardāvol Iran
70 C4 Chardon U.S.A.
31 F2 Chardzhev Turkm.
14 E3 Charente r. France
31 H3 Chārīkār Afgh.
64 E3 Chariton r. U.S.A.
69 F3 Charity Is i. U.S.A.
24 G3 Charkayuvom Rus. Fed.
34 D4 Charkhari India
12 C4 Charleroi Belgium
61 L4 Charles, Cape pt VA U.S.A.
68 A4 Charles City U.S.A.
12 A5 Charles de Gaulle airport France
65 E6 Charles, Lake U.S.A.
51 C4 Charleston N.Z.
66 B4 Charleston IL U.S.A.
71 J2 Charleston ME U.S.A.
65 F4 Charleston MO U.S.A.
67 E5 Charleston SC U.S.A.
70 C5 Charleston WV U.S.A.
73 E3 Charleston Peak summit U.S.A.
11 C4 Charlestown Rep. of Ireland
71 G3 Charlestown NH U.S.A.
71 H4 Charlestown RI U.S.A.
70 E5 Charles Town U.S.A.
48 E4 Charleville Austr.
14 G2 Charleville-Mézières France
68 E3 Charlevoix U.S.A.
56 E3 Charlie Lake Can.
68 E4 Charlotte MI U.S.A.
67 D5 Charlotte NC U.S.A.
67 D7 Charlotte Harbor b. U.S.A.
70 D5 Charlottesville U.S.A.
59 H4 Charlottetown Can.
81 E2 Charlotteville Trinidad and Tobago
50 D4 Charlton Austr.
58 E3 Charlton I. i. Can.
20 F2 Charozero Rus. Fed.
34 B2 Charsadda Pak.
48 E4 Charters Towers Austr.
14 E2 Chartres France
83 E2 Chascomús Arg.
56 F4 Chase Can.
31 F2 Chashkent Turkm.
29 L4 Chashmeh Iran
30 E3 Chashmeh Nūrī Iran
30 D3 Chashmeh ye Palasi Iran
30 D3 Chashmeh ye Shotoran well Iran
20 D4 Chashniki Belarus
51 B7 Chaslands Mistake c. N.Z.
42 D3 Chasŏng N. Korea
30 D3 Chastab, Kūh-e mts Iran
14 D3 Châteaubriant France
14 E3 Château-du-Loir France
14 E2 Châteaudun France
71 F2 Chateaugay U.S.A.
71 G2 Châteauguay Can.
14 B2 Châteaulin France
14 F3 Châteauneuf-sur-Loire France
14 E3 Châteauroux France
12 E6 Château-Salins France
14 F2 Château-Thierry France
12 C4 Châtelet Belgium
14 E3 Châtellerault France
68 A4 Chatfield U.S.A.
59 G4 Chatham N.B. Can.
69 F4 Chatham Ont. Can.
9 H6 Chatham U.K.
71 H4 Chatham MA U.S.A.
71 G3 Chatham NY U.S.A.
70 D6 Chatham VA U.S.A.
49 J6 Chatham Islands is N.Z.
94 G8 Chatham Rise sea feature Pac. Oc.
56 C4 Chatham Sd chan. Can.
56 C3 Chatham Strait chan. U.S.A.
35 F4 Chatra India
69 G3 Chatsworth Can.
68 C5 Chatsworth U.S.A.
67 C5 Chattanooga U.S.A.
9 H5 Chatteris U.K.
44 B2 Chatturat Thai.
44 C3 Châu Đốc Vietnam
34 B4 Chauhtan India
35 H5 Chauk Myanmar
34 E4 Chauka r. India
14 G2 Chaumont France
44 A2 Chaungwabyin Myanmar
25 S3 Chaunskaya Guba b. Rus. Fed.
14 F2 Chauny France
35 F4 Chauparan India
70 D3 Chautauqua, Lake l. U.S.A.
33 C4 Chavakachcheri Sri Lanka
30 B3 Chavār Iran
79 J4 Chaves Brazil
15 C2 Chaves Port.
58 E2 Chavigny, Lac l. Can.
20 D4 Chavusy Belarus
34 A3 Chawal r. Pak.
39 B6 Chây r. Vietnam
Chāyul see Qayü
83 D2 Chazón Arg.
71 G2 Chazy U.S.A.
9 F5 Cheadle U.K.
70 D5 Cheat r. U.S.A.
16 F5 Cheb Czech Rep.
18 D7 Chebba Tunisia
20 H3 Cheboksary Rus. Fed.
68 E3 Cheboygan U.S.A.
21 H7 Chechen', Ostrov i. Rus. Fed.
21 H7 Chechenskaya Respublika div. Rus. Fed.
42 E5 Chech'ŏn S. Korea
65 E5 Checotah U.S.A.
42 A5 Chedao China
9 E6 Cheddar U.K.
57 G3 Cheecham Can.
92 B5 Cheetham, C. c. Ant.
54 B3 Chefornak AK U.S.A.
91 K1 Chefu Moz.
86 B2 Chegga Maur.
89 D5 Chegutu Zimbabwe
62 B2 Chehalis U.S.A.
31 H3 Chehardar Pass Afgh.
29 L5 Cheharīz Iraq
30 E4 Chehell'āyeh Iran
42 D7 Cheju S. Korea
42 D7 Cheju-do i. S. Korea
42 D7 Cheju-haehyŏp chan. S. Korea
20 F4 Chekhov Rus. Fed.
62 B1 Chelan, L. l. U.S.A.
30 D2 Cheleken Turkm.
83 C3 Chelforó Arg.
15 G4 Chélif r. Alg.
26 D2 Chelkar Kazak.
17 L5 Chełm Pol.
9 H6 Chelmer r. U.K.
17 J4 Chełmno Pol.
9 H6 Chelmsford U.K.
71 H3 Chelmsford U.S.A.
9 E6 Cheltenham U.K.
15 F3 Chelva Spain
24 H4 Chelyabinsk Rus. Fed.
89 D5 Chemba Moz.
34 D2 Chem Co l. China
13 L4 Chemnitz Ger.
70 E3 Chemung r. U.S.A.
34 B3 Chenab r. Pak.
86 B2 Chenachane Alg.
71 F3 Chenango r. U.S.A.
62 C2 Cheney U.S.A.
65 D4 Cheney Res. resr U.S.A.
33 C3 Chengalpattu India
38 E2 Cheng'an China
39 D5 Chengbu China
38 E1 Chengde China
39 B4 Chengdu China
38 C3 Chenggu China
39 E6 Chenghai China
38 C4 Chengkou China
37 D5 Chengmai China
42 B4 Chengzitan China
38 F3 Cheniu Shan i. China
68 C5 Chenoa U.S.A.
39 D5 Chenxi China
39 D5 Chenzhou China
44 D2 Cheo Reo Vietnam
78 C5 Chepén Peru
83 C1 Chepes Arg.
9 E6 Chepstow U.K.
20 J3 Cheptsa r. Rus. Fed.
29 L5 Cheqad Kabūd Iran
68 B2 Chequamegon Bay b. U.S.A.
14 F3 Cher r. France
67 E5 Cheraw U.S.A.
14 D2 Cherbourg France
15 H4 Cherchell Alg.
20 J4 Cherdakly Rus. Fed.
36 C1 Cheremkhovo Rus. Fed.
20 D2 Cheremshany Rus. Fed.
20 F3 Cherepovets Rus. Fed.
20 H2 Cherevkovo Rus. Fed.
18 B7 Chéria Alg.
21 E5 Cherkasy Ukr.
21 G6 Cherkessk Rus. Fed.
33 C2 Cherla India
89 C5 Chermenze Angola
24 K2 Chernaya Rus. Fed.
20 J3 Chernaya Kholunitsa Rus. Fed.
40 C2 Chernigovka Rus. Fed.
21 D5 Chernihiv Ukr.
21 F6 Cherninivka Ukr.
21 C5 Chernivtsi Ukr.
36 B1 Chernogorsk Rus. Fed.
20 H3 Chernovskoye Rus. Fed.
21 D5 Chernyakhiv Ukr.
17 K3 Chernyakhovsk Rus. Fed.
21 F5 Chernyanka Rus. Fed.
25 N3 Chernyshevskiy Rus. Fed.
21 H6 Chernyye Zemli reg. Rus. Fed.
21 H5 Chernyy Yar Rus. Fed.
64 E3 Cherokee IA U.S.A.
65 D4 Cherokee OK U.S.A.
65 E4 Cherokees, Lake o' the l. U.S.A.
67 E7 Cherokee Sound Bahamas
83 B3 Cherquenco Chile
35 G4 Cherrapunji India
72 E2 Cherry Creek U.S.A.
73 E1 Cherry Creek Mts mts U.S.A.
71 K2 Cherryfield U.S.A.
49 G3 Cherry Island i. Solomon Is
69 J4 Cherry Valley Can.
71 F3 Cherry Valley U.S.A.
25 Q3 Cherskogo, Khrebet mts Rus. Fed.
21 G5 Chertkovo Rus. Fed.
20 J2 Cherva Rus. Fed.
19 L3 Cherven Bryag Bulg.
21 C5 Chervonohrad Ukr.
21 E5 Chervonozavods'ke Ukr.
20 D4 Chervyen' Belarus
9 F6 Cherwell r. U.K.
20 D4 Cherykaw Belarus
69 E4 Chesaning U.S.A.
71 E6 Chesapeake U.S.A.
71 E5 Chesapeake Bay b. U.S.A.
9 G6 Chesham U.K.
71 G3 Cheshire U.S.A.
9 E4 Cheshire Plain lowland U.K.
31 F2 Cheshme 2-y Turkm.
24 F3 Cheshskaya Guba b. Rus. Fed.
31 F3 Chesht-e Sharīf Afgh.
9 G6 Cheshunt U.K.
9 E4 Chester U.K.
72 B1 Chester CA U.S.A.
66 B4 Chester IL U.S.A.
62 E1 Chester MT U.S.A.
71 F5 Chester PA U.S.A.
67 D5 Chester SC U.S.A.
71 E5 Chester r. U.S.A.
9 F4 Chesterfield U.K.
49 F3 Chesterfield, Îles is New Caledonia
55 J3 Chesterfield Inlet N.W.T. Can.
57 L2 Chesterfield Inlet Can.
57 L2 Chesterfield Inlet in. Can.
8 F3 Chester-le-Street U.K.
71 E5 Chestertown MD U.S.A.
71 G3 Chestertown NY U.S.A.
71 F2 Chesterville Can.
70 D4 Chestnut Ridge ridge U.S.A.
71 J1 Chesuncook U.S.A.
71 J1 Chesuncook Lake l. U.S.A.
18 B6 Chetaïbi Alg.
59 H4 Chéticamp Can.
33 A4 Chetlat i. India
74 G5 Chetumal Mex.
56 E3 Chetwynd Can.
39 □ Cheung Chau H.K. China
39 □ Cheung Chau i. H.K. China
51 D5 Cheviot N.Z.
8 E2 Cheviot Hills h. U.K.
8 E2 Cheviot, The h. U.K.
62 C1 Chewelah U.S.A.
65 D5 Cheyenne OK U.S.A.
62 F3 Cheyenne WY U.S.A.
64 C3 Cheyenne r. U.S.A.
64 C4 Cheyenne Wells U.S.A.
56 E4 Chezacut Can.
34 C4 Chhapar India
35 F4 Chhapra India
34 D4 Chhatarpur India
34 B3 Chhatr Pak.
34 D5 Chhindwara India
34 C5 Chhota Udepur India
34 C4 Chhoti Sadri India
35 G4 Chhukha Bhutan
39 F6 Chia-i Taiwan
44 B1 Chiang Kham Thai.
44 B1 Chiang Khan Thai.
44 A1 Chiang Mai Thai.
18 C2 Chiari Italy
41 G7 Chiba Japan
89 B5 Chibia Angola
89 D6 Chiboma Moz.
58 F4 Chibougamau Can.
58 F4 Chibougamau L. l. Can.
58 F4 Chibougamau, Parc de res. Can.
41 E6 Chibu-Sangaku Nat. Park Japan
91 K2 Chibuto Moz.
35 G2 Chibuzhang Hu l. China
Chicacole see Srikakulam
68 D5 Chicago U.S.A.
68 D5 Chicago airport IL U.S.A.
68 D5 Chicago Heights U.S.A.
68 C5 Chicago Ship Canal canal U.S.A.
81 B3 Chicamocha r. Col.
81 E3 Chicanán r. Venez.
56 B3 Chichagof U.S.A.
56 B3 Chichagof Island i. U.S.A.
38 E1 Chicheng China
9 G7 Chichester U.K.
48 B4 Chichester Range mts Austr.
41 F7 Chichibu Japan
41 F7 Chichibu-Tama National Park Japan
70 E6 Chickahominy r. U.S.A.
67 C5 Chickamauga L. l. U.S.A.
65 D5 Chickasha U.S.A.
15 C4 Chiclana de la Frontera Spain
78 C5 Chiclayo Peru
72 B2 Chico U.S.A.
80 C6 Chico r. Chubut Arg.
83 B4 Chico r. Chubut/Río Negro Arg.
80 C7 Chico r. Santa Cruz Arg.
91 L2 Chicomo Moz.
71 G3 Chicopee U.S.A.
43 B2 Chico Sapocoy, Mt mt Phil.
59 F4 Chicoutimi Can.
91 J1 Chicualacuala Moz.
33 B4 Chidambaram India
91 L2 Chidenguele Moz.
59 H1 Chidley, C. c. Can.
42 D6 Chido S. Korea
91 L2 Chiducuane Moz.
67 D6 Chiefland U.S.A.
16 F7 Chiemsee l. Ger.
12 D5 Chiers r. France
18 F3 Chieti Italy
38 F1 Chifeng China
82 E2 Chifre, Serra do mts Brazil
24 J5 Chiganak Kazak.
59 G4 Chignecto B. b. Can.
81 A3 Chigorodó Col.
89 D6 Chigubo Moz.
35 G3 Chigu Co l. China
74 C3 Chihuahua Mex.
65 B6 Chihuahua div. Mex.
39 D6 Chikan China
33 B3 Chik Ballapur India
20 D3 Chikhachevo Rus. Fed.
34 D5 Chikhali Kalan Parasia India
34 D5 Chikhli India
33 A3 Chikmagalur India
41 F6 Chikuma-gawa r. Japan
56 E4 Chilanko Forks Can.
27 F3 Chilas Jammu and Kashmir
33 B5 Chilaw Sri Lanka
72 B2 Chilcoot U.S.A.
56 E4 Chilcotin r. Can.
65 C5 Childress U.S.A.
77 C7 Chile country S. America
95 O8 Chile Basin sea feature Pac. Oc.
80 C3 Chilecito Arg.
21 H6 Chilgir Rus. Fed.
68 C5 Chilicothe IL U.S.A.
35 F6 Chilika Lake l. India
89 C5 Chililabombwe Zambia
56 E4 Chilko r. Can.
56 E4 Chilko L. l. Can.
56 B2 Chilkoot Trail National Historic Site U.S.A.
83 B3 Chillán Chile
83 B3 Chillán, Nevado mts Chile
83 E3 Chillar Arg.
64 E4 Chillicothe MO U.S.A.
70 B5 Chillicothe OH U.S.A.
34 C1 Chillinji Pak.
56 E5 Chilliwack Can.
30 D1 Chil'mamedkum, Peski des. Turkm.
80 B6 Chiloé, Isla de i. Chile
62 B3 Chiloquin U.S.A.
74 E5 Chilpancingo Mex.
50 F4 Chiltern Austr.
9 G6 Chiltern Hills h. U.K.
68 C3 Chilton U.S.A.
39 F5 Chi-lung Taiwan
34 D2 Chilung Pass India
89 D4 Chimala Tanz.
12 C4 Chimay Belgium
83 C1 Chimbas Arg.
78 C4 Chimborazo mt Ecuador
78 C5 Chimbote Peru
81 B2 Chimichaguá Col.
89 D5 Chimoio Moz.
65 D7 China Mex.
23 H6 China country Asia
81 B3 Chinácota Col.
72 D4 China Lake l. CA U.S.A.
71 J2 China Lake l. ME U.S.A.
74 G6 Chinandega Nic.
72 C5 China Pt pt U.S.A.
78 C6 Chincha Alta Peru
56 F3 Chinchaga r. Can.
71 F6 Chincoteague B. b. U.S.A.
89 D5 Chinde Moz.
42 D6 Chindo S. Korea
42 D6 Chin-do i. S. Korea
36 B3 Chindu China
35 H5 Chindwin r. Myanmar
34 C2 Chineni Jammu and Kashmir
81 B3 Chingaza, Parque Nacional nat. park Col.
42 C4 Chinghwa N. Korea
89 C5 Chingola Zambia
89 B5 Chinguar Angola
42 E6 Chinhae S. Korea
89 D5 Chinhoyi Zimbabwe
34 C3 Chiniot Pak.
42 E6 Chinju S. Korea
88 C3 Chinko r. C.A.R.
73 H3 Chinle U.S.A.
73 H3 Chinle Valley v. U.S.A.
73 H3 Chinle Wash r. U.S.A.
39 F5 Chinmen Taiwan
39 F5 Chinmen Tao i. Taiwan
33 B2 Chinnur India
41 F7 Chino Japan
14 E3 Chinon France
73 F4 Chino Valley U.S.A.
89 D5 Chinsali Zambia
33 B3 Chintamani India
18 E2 Chioggia Italy
19 M5 Chios Greece
19 L5 Chios i. Greece
89 D5 Chipata Zambia
83 C4 Chipchihua, Sa de mts Arg.
89 B5 Chipindo Angola
89 D6 Chipinge Zimbabwe
33 A2 Chiplun India
9 E6 Chippenham U.K.
68 B3 Chippewa r. U.S.A.
68 B3 Chippewa Falls U.S.A.
68 B3 Chippewa, Lake l. U.S.A.
9 F6 Chipping Norton U.K.
9 E6 Chipping Sodbury U.K.
71 K2 Chiputneticook Lakes l. U.S.A.
74 G6 Chiquimula Guatemala
81 B3 Chiquinquira Col.
21 G5 Chir r. Rus. Fed.
33 C3 Chirada India
33 A4 Chirakkal India
33 C3 Chirala India
31 G3 Chiras Afgh.
34 C3 Chirāwa India
89 D6 Chiredzi Zimbabwe
73 H5 Chiricahua National Monument res. U.S.A.
73 H6 Chiricahua Peak summit U.S.A.
81 B2 Chiriguaná Col.
54 C4 Chirikof I. i. U.S.A.
75 H7 Chiriquí, Golfo de b. Panama
9 D5 Chirk U.K.
10 F5 Chirnside U.K.
19 L3 Chirpan Bulg.
75 H7 Chirripo mt Costa Rica
89 C5 Chirundu Zambia
58 E3 Chisasibi Can.
68 A2 Chisholm U.S.A.
34 C3 Chishtian Mandi Pak.
39 B4 Chishur China
21 D6 Chişinău Moldova
17 K7 Chişineu-Criş Romania
20 J4 Chistopol' Rus. Fed.
36 D1 Chita Rus. Fed.
89 B5 Chitado Angola
89 D5 Chitambo Zambia
88 C4 Chitato Angola
57 H4 Chitek Lake Can.
89 B5 Chitembo Angola
89 D4 Chitipa Malawi
89 C5 Chitokoloki Zambia
40 G3 Chitose Japan
33 B3 Chitradurga India
34 B2 Chitral Pak.
34 B2 Chitral r. Pak.
75 H7 Chitré Panama
35 G5 Chittagong Bangl.
35 F5 Chittaranjan India
34 C4 Chittaurgarh India
33 B3 Chittoor India
33 B4 Chittur India
89 D5 Chitungulu Zambia
89 D5 Chitungwiza Zimbabwe
89 C5 Chiume Angola
89 D5 Chivhu Zimbabwe
83 E2 Chivilcoy Arg.
39 D6 Chixi China
29 J3 Chiya-e Linik h. Iraq
41 D7 Chizu Japan
20 G3 Chkalovsk Rus. Fed.
40 C2 Chkalovskoye Rus. Fed.
42 D6 Ch'o i. S. Korea
44 □ Choa Chu Kang Sing.
44 □ Choa Chu Kang h. Sing.
44 C2 Choâm Khsant Cambodia
83 B1 Choapa r. Chile
89 C5 Chobe National Park Botswana
42 D5 Choch'iwŏn S. Korea
73 E5 Chocolate Mts mts U.S.A.
81 B3 Chocontá Col.
42 C4 Cho Do i. N. Korea
13 L4 Chodov Czech Rep.
83 D3 Choele Choel Arg.
34 C2 Chogo Lungma Gl. gl. Pak.
21 H6 Chograyskoye Vdkhr. resr Rus. Fed.
57 J4 Choiceland Can.
49 F2 Choiseul i. Solomon Is
80 E8 Choiseul Sound chan. Falkland Is
16 H4 Chojnice Pol.
40 G5 Chōkai-san volc. Japan
65 D6 Choke Canyon L. l. U.S.A.
88 D2 Ch'ok'ē Mts mts Eth.
35 F3 Choksum China
25 Q2 Chokurdakh Rus. Fed.
89 D6 Chókwé Moz.
14 D3 Cholet France
83 B4 Cholila Arg.
74 G6 Choluteca Honduras
89 C5 Choma Zambia
42 E5 Chŏmch'ŏn S. Korea
35 G4 Chomo Lhari mt Bhutan
44 A1 Chom Thong Thai.
16 F5 Chomutov Czech Rep.
25 M3 Chona r. Rus. Fed.
42 D5 Ch'ŏnan S. Korea
44 B2 Chon Buri Thai.
42 D3 Ch'ŏnch'ŏn N. Korea
78 B4 Chone Ecuador
39 F5 Chong'an China
42 C4 Chongchon r. N. Korea
42 E6 Chongdo S. Korea
42 E3 Ch'ŏngjin N. Korea
42 C4 Chŏngju N. Korea
42 D6 Chŏngju S. Korea
42 D5 Ch'ŏngju S. Korea
44 B2 Chŏng Kal Cambodia
42 D4 Chŏngp'yŏng N. Korea
39 C4 Chongqing China
39 E5 Chongren China
91 K2 Chonguene Moz.
89 C5 Chongwe Zambia
39 D4 Chongyang China
39 F5 Chongyang Xi r. China
39 E5 Chongyi China
39 C6 Chongzuo China
42 D6 Ch'ŏnju S. Korea
35 F3 Cho Oyu mt China
44 C3 Chơ Phươc Hai Vietnam
82 B4 Chopim r. Brazil
82 B4 Chopimzinho Brazil
71 F5 Choptank r. U.S.A.
34 B4 Chor Pak.
8 E4 Chorley U.K.
21 D5 Chornobyl' Ukr.
21 E6 Chornomors'ke Ukr.
21 C5 Chortkiv Ukr.
42 D4 Ch'ŏrwŏn S. Korea
42 C3 Ch'osan N. Korea
41 G7 Chōshi Japan
83 B3 Chos Malal Arg.
16 G4 Choszczno Pol.
78 C5 Chota Peru
62 D2 Choteau U.S.A.
34 B3 Choti Pak.
86 A2 Choûm Maur.
72 B3 Chowchilla U.S.A.
56 F4 Chown, Mt mt Can.
36 D2 Choybalsan Mongolia
36 C2 Choyr Mongolia
16 H6 Chřiby h. Czech Rep.
68 D6 Chrisman U.S.A.
91 J3 Chrissiesmeer S. Africa
51 D5 Christchurch N.Z.
9 F7 Christchurch U.K.
91 F3 Christiana S. Africa
55 M2 Christian, C. pt Can.
69 G3 Christian I. i. Can.
Christiansåb see Qasigiannguit
70 C6 Christiansburg U.S.A.
56 C3 Christian Sound chan. U.S.A.
57 G3 Christina r. Can.
49 G6 Christina, Mt mt N.Z.
Christmas Island i. see Kiritimati
37 C8 Christmas Island terr. Ind. Ocean
16 G6 Chrudim Czech Rep.
19 L7 Chrysi i. Greece
27 F2 Chu Kazak.
24 H5 Chu r. Kazak.
35 G5 Chuadanga Bangl.
91 K2 Chuali, L. l. Moz.
38 F4 Chuansha China
62 D3 Chubbuck U.S.A.
83 C4 Chubut div. Arg.
80 C6 Chubut r. Arg.
73 E5 Chuckwalla Mts mts U.S.A.
21 D5 Chudniv Ukr.
20 D3 Chudovo Rus. Fed.
Chudskoye Ozero l. see Peipus, Lake
54 C4 Chugach Mountains U.S.A.
41 C7 Chūgoku-sanchi mts Japan
40 C2 Chuguyevka Rus. Fed.
62 F3 Chugwater U.S.A.
21 F5 Chuhuyiv Ukr.
73 G5 Chuichu U.S.A.
36 F1 Chukchagirskoye, Ozero l. Rus. Fed.
25 V3 Chukchi Sea sea Rus. Fed./U.S.A.
20 G3 Chukhloma Rus. Fed.
25 U3 Chukotskiy Poluostrov pen. Rus. Fed.
20 H1 Chulasa Rus. Fed.
72 D5 Chula Vista U.S.A.
24 K4 Chulym Rus. Fed.
35 G4 Chumbi China
80 C3 Chumbicha Arg.
36 F1 Chumikan Rus. Fed.
44 B1 Chum Phae Thai.
44 A3 Chumphon Thai.
44 B2 Chum Saeng Thai.
25 L4 Chuna r. Rus. Fed.
39 F4 Chun'an China
42 D5 Ch'unch'ŏn S. Korea
42 D5 Ch'ungju S. Korea
Chungking see Chongqing
42 E6 Ch'ungmu S. Korea
42 C4 Chŭngsan N. Korea
31 H3 Chungur, Koh-i- h. Afgh.
42 F2 Chunhua China
35 F3 Chunit Tso salt l. China
25 M3 Chunya r. Rus. Fed.
44 C3 Chuŏr Phnum Dâmrei mts Cambodia
44 C2 Chuŏr Phnum Dângrêk mts Cambodia/Thai.
44 B2 Chuŏr Phnum Krâvanh mts Cambodia
38 A4 Chuosijia China
29 L3 Chūplū Iran
78 D7 Chuquibamba Peru
80 C2 Chuquicamata Chile
16 D7 Chur Switz.
25 P3 Churapcha Rus. Fed.
57 L3 Churchill Can.
57 K3 Churchill r. Man./Sask. Can.
59 H3 Churchill r. Nfld Can.
57 J4 Churchill r. Sask. Can.
57 L3 Churchill, Cape c. Can.
59 H3 Churchill Falls Can.
57 H3 Churchill Lake l. Can.

# D

13 G2 Damme Ger.
34 D5 Damoh India
86 B4 Damongo Ghana
48 E2 Dampier Strait chan. P.N.G.
37 F7 Dampir, Selat chan. Indon.
Damqoq Kanbab r. see Maquan He
35 H2 Dam Qu r. China
35 H3 Damroh India
12 E1 Damwoude Neth.
86 B4 Danané Côte d'Ivoire
44 D1 Đa Năng Vietnam
43 C4 Danao Phil.
38 A4 Danba China
71 G4 Danbury CT U.S.A.
71 H3 Danbury NH U.S.A.
71 G3 Danby U.S.A.
73 E4 Danby Lake l. U.S.A.
38 E3 Dancheng China
88 D3 Dande Eth.
33 A3 Dandeli India
50 E4 Dandenong Austr.
42 C3 Dandong China
9 E4 Dane r. U.K.
55 Q2 Daneborg Greenland
71 K2 Danforth U.S.A.
39 E6 Dangan Liedao is China
35 G3 Dangbe La pass China
32 B2 Dangbizhen Rus. Fed.
38 B3 Dangchang China
46 L5 Danger Islands is Cook Islands Pac. Oc.
90 C7 Danger Pt pt S. Africa
88 D2 Dangila Eth.
Dangla mts see Tanggula Shan
35 G3 Dangqên China
74 G5 Dangriga Belize
38 E3 Dangshan China
38 F4 Dangtu China
39 D4 Dangyang China
62 E3 Daniel U.S.A.
90 E4 Daniëlskuil S. Africa
20 G3 Danilov Rus. Fed.
21 H5 Danilovka Rus. Fed.
20 G3 Danilovskaya Vozvyshennost' reg. Rus. Fed.
38 D2 Daning China
29 M1 Dänizkänarı Azer.
38 D3 Danjiangkou Sk. resr China
30 E6 Ḑank Oman
34 D2 Dankhar India
20 F4 Dankov Rus. Fed.
39 B4 Danleng China
74 G6 Danlí Honduras
Dannebrogsø i. see Qillak
71 G2 Dannemora U.S.A.
13 K1 Dannenberg (Elbe) Ger.
13 M1 Dannenwalde Ger.
51 F4 Dannevirke N.Z.
91 J4 Dannhauser S. Africa
44 B1 Dan Sai Thai.
70 E3 Dansville U.S.A.
34 C4 Danta India
33 C2 Dantewara India
19 M3 Danube r. Europe
68 D5 Danville IL U.S.A.
68 D6 Danville IN U.S.A.
66 C4 Danville KY U.S.A.
69 J5 Danville PA U.S.A.
70 D6 Danville VA U.S.A.
39 C7 Dan Xian China
38 F4 Danyang China
39 C5 Danzhai China
43 B4 Dao Phil.
39 C6 Đao Bach Long Vi i. Vietnam
39 C6 Đao Cai Bâu i. Vietnam
39 C6 Đao Cat Ba i. Vietnam
44 B3 Đao Phu Quôc i. Vietnam
44 B3 Đao Thô Chu' i. Vietnam
86 B4 Daoukro Côte d'Ivoire
44 B3 Đao Vây i. Vietnam
39 D5 Dao Xian China
39 C4 Daozhen China
43 C4 Dapa Phil.
86 C3 Dapaong Togo
35 J4 Daphabum mt India
43 B4 Dapiak, Mt mt Phil.
43 B4 Dapitan Phil.
27 H3 Da Qaidam China
36 E2 Daqing China
38 D1 Daqing Shan mts China
30 D3 Daqq-e Dombūn Iran
31 F3 Daqq-e-Tundi, Dasht-e l. Afgh.
29 K4 Dāqūq Iraq
39 G4 Daqu Shan i. China
28 F5 Dar'ā Syria
30 D4 Dārāb Iran
43 B3 Daraga Phil.
17 O4 Darahanava Belarus
86 D1 Daraj Libya
30 D4 Dārākūyeh Iran
43 C4 Daram i. Phil.
30 D3 Darang, Kūh-e h. Iran
25 N4 Darasun Rus. Fed.
30 E4 Darband Iran
35 F4 Darbhanga India
72 C2 Dardanelle U.S.A.
65 E5 Dardanelle, Lake l. U.S.A.
19 M4 Dardanelles str. Turkey
13 J3 Dardesheim Ger.
28 F2 Darende Turkey
88 D4 Dar es Salaam Tanz.
12 D2 Darfo Boario Terme Italy
34 B2 Dargai Pak.
31 F1 Dargan-Ata Turkm.
51 D1 Dargaville N.Z.
50 F4 Dargo Austr.
36 C2 Darhan Mongolia
38 D1 Darhan Muminggan Lianheqi China
67 D6 Darien U.S.A.
81 A2 Darién, Golfo del g. Col.
75 J7 Darién, Parque Nacional de nat. park Panama
81 A2 Darién, Serranía del mts Panama
35 G4 Dārjiling India
30 C4 Darkhazīneh Iran
36 B3 Darlag China
50 D2 Darling r. Austr.
48 E4 Darling Downs reg. Austr.
48 B5 Darling Range h. Austr.
8 F3 Darlington U.K.
68 B4 Darlington U.S.A.
50 F3 Darlington Point Austr.
16 H3 Darłowo Pol.
30 B5 Darmā S. Arabia
34 E3 Darma Pass China/India
33 B2 Darmaraopet India
30 E4 Dar Mazār Iran
13 G5 Darmstadt Ger.
34 C5 Darna r. India
87 E1 Darnah Libya
91 J4 Darnall S. Africa
50 D2 Darnick Austr.
54 F3 Darnley Bay b. Can.
92 D5 Darnley, C. c. Ant.
15 F2 Daroca Spain
20 G3 Darovka Rus. Fed.
20 H3 Darovskoy Rus. Fed.
83 D3 Darregueira Arg.
30 E3 Darreh Bīd Iran
31 E2 Darreh Gaz Iran
29 L4 Darreh Gozaru r. Iran
31 H3 Darreh-ye Shekārī r. Afgh.
33 B3 Darsi India
29 M6 Darsīyeh Iran
9 D7 Dart r. U.K.
9 H6 Dartford U.K.
50 C4 Dartmoor Austr.
9 C7 Dartmoor reg. U.K.
9 D7 Dartmoor National Park U.K.
59 H5 Dartmouth Can.
9 D7 Dartmouth U.K.
8 F4 Darton U.K.
11 C3 Darty Mts h. Rep. of Ireland
48 E2 Daru P.N.G.
86 A4 Daru Sierra Leone
35 G3 Darum Tso l. China
18 G2 Daruvar Croatia
31 E1 Darvaza Turkm.
30 C4 Darvīsla Iran
31 G4 Darwazgai Afgh.
8 E4 Darwen U.K.
31 G4 Darweshan Afgh.
48 D3 Darwin Austr.
80 C8 Darwin, Mte mt Chile
34 B3 Darya Khan Pak.
31 E4 Dārzīn Iran
30 D5 Dās i. U.A.E.
38 D4 Dashennongjia mt China
32 E1 Dashkhovuz Turkm.
30 E2 Dasht Iran
31 F5 Dasht r. Pak.
30 E4 Dasht Āb Iran
30 C4 Dasht-e Palang r. Iran
31 F5 Dashtiari Iran
31 H2 Dashtiobburdon Tajik.
38 C2 Dashuikeng China
38 B2 Dashuitou China
34 C2 Daska Pak.
29 L1 Daşkäsän Azer.
34 C1 Daspar mt Pak.
13 H3 Dassel Ger.
90 C6 Dassen Island i. S. Africa
29 L2 Dastakert Armenia
30 E3 Dastgardān Iran
42 F2 Da Suifen r. China
19 M6 Datça Turkey
40 G3 Date Japan
73 F5 Dateland U.S.A.
34 D4 Datia India
39 E5 Datian China
38 A2 Datong Qinghai China
38 D1 Datong Shanxi China
38 B2 Datong He r. China
38 A2 Datong Shan mts China
43 B5 Datu Piang Phil.
45 C2 Datu, Tanjung c. Indon./Malaysia
20 C3 Daugava r. Belarus/Latvia
7 U9 Daugavpils Latvia
31 G2 Daulatabad Afgh.
34 C6 Daulatabad India
Daulatabad see Malāyer
12 E4 Daun Ger.
33 A2 Daund India
44 A2 Daung Kyun i. Myanmar
57 J4 Dauphin Can.
14 G4 Dauphiné reg. France
65 F6 Dauphin I. i. U.S.A.
57 K4 Dauphin L. l. Can.
34 D4 Dausa India
10 E3 Dava U.K.
29 M1 Däväçi Azer.
33 A3 Davangere India
43 C5 Davao Phil.
43 C5 Davao Gulf b. Phil.
31 F5 Dāvar Panāh Iran
91 H3 Davel S. Africa
72 A3 Davenport CA U.S.A.
68 B5 Davenport IA U.S.A.
9 F5 Daventry U.K.
91 H3 Daveyton S. Africa
75 H7 David Panama
57 H4 Davidson Can.
57 J3 Davin Lake l. Can.
72 B2 Davis U.S.A.
92 D5 Davis Austr. Base Ant.
73 E4 Davis Dam U.S.A.
59 H2 Davis Inlet Can.
92 D5 Davis Sea sea Ant.
55 N3 Davis Strait str. Can./Greenland
16 D7 Davos Switz.
42 B3 Dawa China
38 A1 Dawan China
35 F3 Dawaxung China
38 B4 Dawe China
Dawei see Tavoy
38 E3 Dawen r. China
30 C5 Dawḩat Salwah b. Qatar/S. Arabia
44 A1 Dawna Range mts Myanmar/Thai.
32 D6 Dawqah Oman
54 E3 Dawson Y.T. Can.
67 C6 Dawson GA U.S.A.
64 D2 Dawson ND U.S.A.
57 J4 Dawson Bay b. Can.
56 E3 Dawson Creek Can.
57 L2 Dawson Inlet in. Can.
56 B2 Dawson Range mts Can.
38 E4 Dawu Hubei China
36 C3 Dawu Sichuan China
14 D5 Dax France
38 C4 Daxian China
39 C6 Daxin China
38 E2 Daxing China
39 A4 Daxue Shan mts China
42 B4 Dayang r. China
35 H4 Dayang r. India
39 D6 Dayao Shan mts China
39 E4 Daye China
39 B4 Dayi China
50 E4 Daylesford Austr.
72 D3 Daylight Pass U.S.A.
83 F1 Daymán r. Uru.
83 F1 Daymán, Cuchilla del h. Uru.
39 D4 Dayong China
29 H4 Dayr az Zawr Syria
70 A5 Dayton OH U.S.A.
67 C5 Dayton TN U.S.A.
62 C2 Dayton WA U.S.A.
67 D6 Daytona Beach U.S.A.
39 E5 Dayu China
39 D5 Dayu Ling mts China
38 F3 Da Yunhe r. China
62 C2 Dayville U.S.A.
39 D7 Dazhou Dao i. China
39 C4 Dazhu China
39 B4 Dazu China
90 F5 De Aar S. Africa
68 D2 Dead r. U.S.A.
67 F7 Deadman's Cay Bahamas
73 E4 Dead Mts mts U.S.A.
71 H2 Dead River r. U.S.A.
28 E6 Dead Sea salt l. Asia
9 J6 Deal U.K.
91 F4 Dealesville S. Africa
39 E4 De'an China
56 D4 Dean r. Can.
9 E6 Dean, Forest of forest U.K.
83 D1 Deán Funes Arg.
69 F4 Dearborn U.S.A.
56 D3 Dease r. Can.
56 C3 Dease Lake Can.
54 H3 Dease Strait chan. Can.
72 D3 Death Valley v. U.S.A.
72 D3 Death Valley Junction U.S.A.
72 D3 Death Valley National Monument res. U.S.A.
14 E2 Deauville France
45 D2 Debak Malaysia
39 C6 Debao China
19 J4 Debar Macedonia
57 H4 Debden Can.
9 J5 Debenham U.K.
73 H2 De Beque U.S.A.
71 J2 Deblois U.S.A.
88 D3 Debre Birhan Eth.
17 K7 Debrecen Hungary
88 D2 Debre Markos Eth.
88 D2 Debre Tabor Eth.
88 D3 Debre Zeyit Eth.
67 C5 Decatur AL U.S.A.
67 C5 Decatur GA U.S.A.
68 C6 Decatur IL U.S.A.
68 E5 Decatur IN U.S.A.
68 E4 Decatur MI U.S.A.
33 B2 Deccan plat. India
69 H2 Decelles, Réservoir resr Can.
16 G5 Děčín Czech Rep.
68 B4 Decorah U.S.A.
9 F6 Deddington U.K.
13 J2 Dedeleben Ger.
13 J2 Dedelstorf Ger.
12 E2 Dedemsvaart Neth.
82 C4 Dedo de Deus mt Brazil
90 C6 De Doorns S. Africa
29 L1 Dedoplis Tsqaro Georgia
86 B3 Dédougou Burkina
20 D3 Dedovichi Rus. Fed.
89 D5 Dedza Malawi
9 D4 Dee est. Wales U.K.
9 E4 Dee r. Eng./Wales U.K.
10 F3 Dee r. Scot. U.K.
11 C5 Deel r. Rep. of Ireland
11 D3 Deele r. Rep. of Ireland
39 D6 Deep Bay b. H.K. China
70 D5 Deep Creek Lake l. U.S.A.
73 F2 Deep Creek Range mts U.S.A.
69 J2 Deep River Can.
71 G4 Deep River U.S.A.
57 K1 Deep Rose Lake l. Can.
72 D3 Deep Springs U.S.A.
70 B5 Deer Creek Lake l. U.S.A.
71 K2 Deer I. i. Can.
71 J2 Deer I. i. U.S.A.
71 J2 Deer Isle U.S.A.
58 B3 Deer L. l. Can.
59 J4 Deer Lake Nfld Can.
58 B3 Deer Lake Ont. Can.
62 D2 Deer Lodge U.S.A.
80 D2 Defensores del Chaco, Parque Nacional nat. park Para.
70 A4 Defiance U.S.A.
67 C6 De Funiak Springs U.S.A.
36 B3 Dêgê China
88 E3 Degeh Bur Eth.
35 G3 Dêgên China
13 L6 Deggendorf Ger.
34 C3 Degh r. Pak.
12 B3 De Haan Belgium
30 D4 Dehaj Iran
31 F4 Dehak Iran
31 F5 Dehak Iran
30 D4 Deh Bīd Iran
30 C4 Deh-Dasht Iran
30 C4 Deh-e Khalīfeh Iran
30 C3 Deheq Iran
30 C2 Dehgāh Iran
30 B3 Dehgolān Iran
33 B5 Dehiwala-Mount Lavinia Sri Lanka
30 D5 Dehkūyeh Iran
30 B3 Dehlonān Iran
34 D3 Dehra Dun India
35 F4 Dehri India
31 E4 Deh Salm Iran
30 E4 Deh Sard Iran
29 K4 Deh Sheykh Iran
31 F4 Deh Shū Afgh.
39 F5 Dehua China
42 C1 Dehui China
12 B4 Deinze Belgium
28 E5 Deir el Qamer Lebanon
Deir-ez-Zor see Dayr az Zawr
17 L7 Dej Romania
39 C4 Dejiang China
68 C5 De Kalb IL U.S.A.
65 E5 De Kalb TX U.S.A.
71 F2 De Kalb Junction U.S.A.
32 A6 Dekemhare Eritrea
88 C4 Dekese Congo(Zaire)
31 G2 Dekhkanabad Uzbek.
12 C1 De Koog Neth.
12 C2 De Kooy Neth.
72 C4 Delano U.S.A.
73 F2 Delano Peak summit U.S.A.
31 F3 Delārām Afgh.
91 F3 Delareyville S. Africa
57 H4 Delaronde Lake l. Can.
68 C5 Delavan IL U.S.A.
68 C4 Delavan WV U.S.A.
70 B4 Delaware U.S.A.
71 F5 Delaware div. U.S.A.
71 F4 Delaware r. U.S.A.
71 F5 Delaware Bay b. U.S.A.
70 B4 Delaware Lake l. U.S.A.
71 F4 Delaware Water Gap National Recreational Area res. U.S.A.
13 G3 Delbrück Ger.
50 G4 Delegate Austr.
16 C7 Delémont Switz.
12 C2 Delft Neth.
33 B4 Delft I. i. Sri Lanka
12 E1 Delfzijl Neth.
89 E5 Delgado, Cabo pt Moz.
69 G4 Delhi Can.
34 D3 Delhi India
63 F4 Delhi CO U.S.A.
71 F3 Delhi NY U.S.A.
29 J2 Deli r. Turkey
28 E2 Delice Turkey
28 E1 Delice r. Turkey
30 C3 Delījān Iran
56 E1 Déline Can.
36 B3 Delingha China
57 H4 Delisle Can.
13 L3 Delitzsch Ger.
13 H3 Delligsen Ger.
64 D3 Dell Rapids U.S.A.
15 H4 Dellys Alg.
72 D5 Del Mar U.S.A.
73 E3 Delmar L. l. U.S.A.
13 G1 Delmenhorst Ger.
25 R2 De-Longa, O-va is Rus. Fed.
54 B3 De Long Mts mts U.S.A.
57 J5 Deloraine Can.
68 D5 Delphi U.S.A.
70 A4 Delphos U.S.A.
90 F4 Delportshoop S. Africa
67 D7 Delray Beach U.S.A.
63 E6 Del Río Mex.
65 C6 Del Rio U.S.A.
7 P6 Delsbo Sweden
63 F4 Delta CO U.S.A.
68 A5 Delta IA U.S.A.
73 F2 Delta UT U.S.A.
54 D3 Delta Junction U.S.A.
73 F3 Delta Reservoir U.S.A.
67 D6 Deltona U.S.A.
11 D4 Delvin Rep. of Ireland
19 J5 Delvinë Albania
15 E1 Demanda, Sierra de la mts Spain
88 C4 Demba Congo(Zaire)
88 D3 Dembī Dolo Eth.
20 D4 Demidov Rus. Fed.
63 F5 Deming U.S.A.
81 E4 Demini r. Brazil
28 B2 Demirci Turkey
19 M4 Demirköy Turkey
16 F4 Demmin Ger.
67 C5 Demopolis U.S.A.
68 D5 Demotte U.S.A.
83 B4 Dempo, G. volc. Indon.
34 D2 Dêmqog China/India
20 H2 Dem'yanovo Rus. Fed.
17 Q2 Demyansk Rus. Fed.
90 D5 De Naawte S. Africa
82 E2 Denakil reg. Eritrea
88 E3 Denan Eth.
57 J4 Denare Beach Can.
31 G2 Denau Uzbek.
69 J3 Denbigh Can.
9 D4 Denbigh U.K.
12 C1 Den Burg Neth.
44 B1 Den Chai Thai.
45 C3 Dendang Indon.
12 C3 Dendermonde Belgium
91 H1 Dendron S. Africa
39 C1 Dengkou China
35 H3 Dêngqên China
38 D3 Deng Xian China
Den Haag see The Hague
48 B4 Denham Austr.
12 D2 Den Ham Neth.
12 C2 Den Helder Neth.
15 G3 Denia Spain
50 E3 Deniliquin Austr.
62 C3 Denio U.S.A.
64 E3 Denison IA U.S.A.
65 D5 Denison TX U.S.A.
28 B3 Denizli Turkey
50 H2 Denman Austr.
92 C5 Denman Glacier gl. Ant.
48 B5 Denmark Austr.
5 D3 Denmark country Europe
55 Q3 Denmark Strait Greenland/Iceland
73 H3 Dennehotso U.S.A.
71 H4 Dennis Port U.S.A.
10 E4 Denny U.K.
71 K2 Dennysville U.S.A.
45 E4 Denpasar Indon.
71 F5 Denton MD U.S.A.
65 D5 Denton TX U.S.A.
48 F2 D'Entrecasteaux Islands is P.N.G.
48 B5 d'Entrecasteaux, Pt pt Austr.
49 G3 d'Entrecasteaux, Récifs rf New Caledonia
62 F4 Denver U.S.A.
35 F4 Deo India
34 D3 Deoband India
35 F5 Deogarh India
35 E5 Deogarh mt India
35 F4 Deoghar India
34 D5 Deori India
35 E4 Deoria India
34 C2 Deosai, Plains of plain Pak.
35 E5 Deosil India
12 A3 De Panne Belgium
12 D3 De Peel reg. Neth.
68 C3 De Pere U.S.A.
71 F3 Deposit U.S.A.
69 J2 Depot-Forbes Can.
69 J2 Depot-Rowanton Can.
68 C5 Depue U.S.A.
25 P3 Deputatskiy Rus. Fed.
36 B4 Dêqên China
39 D6 Deqing Guangdong China
39 F4 Deqing Zhejiang China
39 F5 Deqiu China
65 E5 De Queen U.S.A.
34 B3 Dera Bugti Pak.
34 B3 Dera Ghazi Khan Pak.
34 B3 Dera Ismail Khan Pak.
34 B3 Derawar Fort Pak.
21 J7 Derbent Rus. Fed.
31 G2 Derbent Uzbek.
48 C3 Derby Austr.
9 F5 Derby U.K.
71 G4 Derby CT U.S.A.
65 D4 Derby KS U.S.A.
11 D3 Derg r. Rep. of Ireland/U.K.
21 J5 Dergachi Rus. Fed.
11 C5 Derg, Lough l. Rep. of Ireland
21 F5 Derhachi Ukr.
65 E6 De Ridder U.S.A.
29 H3 Derik Turkey
28 E2 Derinkuyu Turkey
21 F5 Derkul r. Rus. Fed./Ukr.
90 C1 Derm Namibia
11 D4 Derravaragh, Lough l. Rep. of Ireland
71 H3 Derry U.S.A.
11 E5 Derry r. Rep. of Ireland
11 C3 Derryveagh Mts h. Rep. of Ireland
38 A1 Derstei China
87 F3 Derudeb Sudan
90 E6 De Rust S. Africa
18 G2 Derventa Bos.-Herz.
48 E6 Derwent r. Austr.
8 G4 Derwent r. U.K.
10 G6 Derwent Reservoir U.K.
8 D3 Derwent Water l. U.K.
26 E1 Derzhavinsk Kazak.
83 C2 Desaguadero r. Arg.
78 E7 Desaguadero r. Bol.
46 N5 Désappointement, Îles de is Pac. Oc.
72 D2 Desatoya Mts mts U.S.A.
69 F2 Desbarats Can.
54 F3 Des Bois, Lac l. Can.
57 J3 Deschambault L. l. Can.
57 J4 Deschambault Lake Can.
62 B2 Deschutes r. U.S.A.
88 D2 Desē Eth.
80 C7 Deseado Arg.
80 C7 Deseado r. Arg.
69 J3 Deseronto Can.
84 B3 Desert Canal canal Pak.
73 E5 Desert Center U.S.A.
73 F1 Desert Peak summit U.S.A.
56 G3 Desmarais Can.
64 E3 Des Moines IA U.S.A.
63 G4 Des Moines NM U.S.A.
68 A5 Des Moines r. IA U.S.A.
21 D5 Desna Ukr.
20 E5 Desna r. Rus. Fed.
20 E4 Desnogorsk Rus. Fed.
43 C4 Desolation Point pt Phil.
68 D4 Des Plaines U.S.A.
13 L3 Dessau Ger.
12 B3 Destelbergen Belgium
69 H1 Destor Can.
56 B2 Destruction Bay Can.
76 C5 Desventurados, Islas de los is Chile
19 J2 Deta Romania
56 G2 Detah Can.
89 C5 Dete Zimbabwe
13 G3 Detmold Ger.
68 D3 Detour, Pt pt U.S.A.
69 F3 De Tour Village U.S.A.
69 F4 Detroit U.S.A.
69 F4 Detroit airport MI U.S.A.
64 E2 Detroit Lakes U.S.A.
50 G3 Deua Nat. Park Austr.
13 L3 Deuben Ger.
12 D3 Deurne Neth.
18 F1 Deutschlandsberg Austria
13 L3 Deutzen Ger.
69 H2 Deux-Rivières Can.
19 K2 Deva Romania
33 B2 Devarkonda India
28 E2 Develi Turkey
12 E2 Deventer Neth.
16 H6 Devét Skal h. Czech Rep.
34 B4 Devikot India
11 D5 Devils Bit Mountain h. Rep. of Ireland
9 D5 Devil's Bridge U.K.
72 C4 Devils Den U.S.A.
72 C2 Devils Gate pass U.S.A.
68 B2 Devils I. i. U.S.A.
64 D1 Devils Lake U.S.A.
72 C3 Devils Peak summit U.S.A.
72 C3 Devils Postpile National Monument res. U.S.A.
67 F7 Devil's Pt Bahamas
9 F6 Devizes U.K.
34 C4 Devli India
19 M3 Devnya Bulg.
56 G4 Devon Can.
9 G5 Devon r. U.K.
55 J2 Devon Island i. Can.
48 E6 Devonport Austr.
28 C1 Devrek Turkey
28 D1 Devrekâni Turkey
28 E1 Devrez r. Turkey
33 A2 Devrukh India
34 D5 Dewas India
45 A2 Dewa, Tanjung pt Indon.
91 G4 Dewetsdorp S. Africa
70 B6 Dewey Lake l. U.S.A.
65 F5 De Witt AR U.S.A.
68 B5 De Witt IA U.S.A.
8 F4 Dewsbury U.K.
39 E4 Dexing China
71 J2 Dexter ME U.S.A.
65 F4 Dexter MO U.S.A.
71 E2 Dexter NY U.S.A.
38 B4 Deyang China
30 E3 Deyhuk Iran
29 M3 Deylaman Iran
31 F2 Deynau Turkm.
48 D2 Deyong, Tg pt Indon.
30 C5 Deyyer Iran
29 M6 Dez r. Iran
30 C3 Dezfūl Iran
30 C4 Dez Gerd Iran
38 E2 Dezhou China
30 B5 Dhahlān, J. h. S. Arabia
32 D4 Dhahran S. Arabia
35 G5 Dhaka Bangl.
35 G5 Dhaleswari r. Bangl.
35 H4 Dhaleswari r. India
32 B7 Dhamār Yemen
35 F5 Dhāmara India
34 C5 Dhamnod India
35 E5 Dhamtari India
34 B3 Dhana Sar Pak.
35 F5 Dhanbad India
34 C5 Dhandhuka India
35 E3 Dhang Ra. mts Nepal
34 C5 Dhar India
35 F4 Dharan Bazar Nepal
33 B4 Dharapuram India
34 B5 Dhari India
33 B3 Dharmapuri India
33 B3 Dharmavaram India
34 D2 Dharmshala India
33 A3 Dhārwād India
34 D4 Dhasan r. India
35 E3 Dhaulagiri mt Nepal
34 D4 Dhaulpur India
34 C4 Dhebar L. l. India
35 H4 Dhekiajuli India
28 E6 Dhībān Jordan
35 H4 Dhing India
33 B3 Dhone India
34 B5 Dhoraji India
34 B5 Dhrangadhra India
34 C5 Dhule India
35 F4 Dhulian India
35 F4 Dhunche Nepal
34 D4 Dhund r. India
88 E3 Dhuusa Marreeb Somalia
19 L7 Dia i. Greece
72 B3 Diablo, Mt mt U.S.A.
72 B3 Diablo Range mts U.S.A.
83 E2 Diamante Arg.
83 C2 Diamante r. Arg.
82 D2 Diamantina Brazil
48 D4 Diamantina watercourse Austr.
79 K6 Diamantina, Chapada plat. Brazil
82 A1 Diamantino Brazil
72 □1 Diamond Head hd U.S.A.
73 E2 Diamond Peak summit U.S.A.
39 D6 Dianbai China
39 B5 Dian Chi l. China
39 C4 Dianjiang China
79 J6 Dianópolis Brazil
86 B4 Dianra Côte d'Ivoire
40 B2 Diaoling China
86 C3 Diapaga Burkina
31 E6 Ḑibab Oman
35 H4 Dibang r. India
88 C4 Dibaya Congo(Zaire)
90 E3 Dibeng S. Africa
58 F2 D'Iberville, Lac l. Can.
91 G1 Dibete Botswana
35 H4 Dibrugarh India
65 C5 Dickens U.S.A.
71 J1 Dickey U.S.A.
64 C2 Dickinson U.S.A.
67 C4 Dickson U.S.A.
71 F4 Dickson City U.S.A.
Dicle r. see Tigris
43 B2 Didicas i. Phil.
34 C4 Didwana India
19 M4 Didymoteicho Greece
14 G4 Die France
12 F4 Dieblich Ger.
86 B3 Diébougou Burkina
13 G5 Dieburg Ger.
57 H4 Diefenbaker, L. l. Can.
93 J4 Diego Garcia i. British Indian Ocean Terr.
12 E5 Diekirch Lux.
86 B3 Diéma Mali
13 H3 Diemel r. Ger.
39 B6 Điên Biên Vietnam
44 C1 Diên Châu Vietnam
44 D2 Diên Khanh Vietnam
13 G2 Diepholz Ger.
14 E2 Dieppe France
38 C2 Di'er Nonchang Qu r. China
42 C1 Di'er Songhua Jiang r. China
12 D3 Diessen Neth.
12 D4 Diest Belgium
16 D7 Dietikon Switz.
13 G4 Diez Ger.
87 D3 Diffa Niger
33 D2 Digapahandi India
59 G5 Digby Can.

35 F5 Digha India
14 H4 Digne-les-Bains France
14 F3 Digoin France
43 C5 Digos Phil.
34 D5 Digras India
34 B4 Digri Pak.
37 F7 Digul *r.* Indon.
86 B4 Digya National Park Ghana
14 G3 Dijon France
88 E2 Dikhil Djibouti
19 M5 Dikili Turkey
12 A3 Diksmuide Belgium
24 K2 Dikson Rus. Fed.
87 D3 Dikwa Nigeria
88 D3 Dīla Eth.
31 E4 Dilaram Iran
48 C2 Dili Indon.
29 K1 Dilijan Armenia
44 D3 Di Linh Vietnam
13 G4 Dillenburg Ger.
65 D6 Dilley U.S.A.
16 E6 Dillingen an der Donau Ger.
12 E5 Dillingen (Saar) Ger.
54 C4 Dillingham U.S.A.
57 H3 Dillon Can.
62 D2 Dillon *MT* U.S.A.
67 E5 Dillon *SC* U.S.A.
89 C5 Dilolo Congo(Zaire)
12 D3 Dilsen Belgium
29 K5 Diltāwa Iraq
35 H4 Dimapur India
28 F5 Dimashq Syria
88 C4 Dimbelenge Congo(Zaire)
86 B4 Dimbokro Côte d'Ivoire
50 D4 Dimboola Austr.
19 L3 Dimitrovgrad Bulg.
20 J4 Dimitrovgrad Rus. Fed.
28 E6 Dīmona Israel
90 D2 Dimpho Pan *salt pan* Botswana
43 C4 Dinagat *i.* Phil.
35 G4 Dinajpur Bangl.
14 C2 Dinan France
34 C2 Dinanagar India
12 C4 Dinant Belgium
35 F4 Dinapur India
28 C2 Dinar Turkey
18 G2 Dinara *mts* Croatia
30 C4 Dīnār, Kūh-e *mt* Iran
87 F3 Dinder National Park Sudan
33 B4 Dindigul India
91 K1 Dindiza Moz.
34 E5 Dindori India
28 D3 Dinek Turkey
38 C2 Dingbian China
88 B4 Dinge Angola
13 J3 Dingelstädt Ger.
39 G4 Dinghai China
35 F4 Dingla Nepal
11 A5 Dingle Rep. of Ireland
11 A5 Dingle Bay *b.* Rep. of Ireland
39 E5 Dingnan China
43 B2 Dingras Phil.
38 E3 Dingtao China
86 A3 Dinguiraye Guinea
10 D3 Dingwall U.K.
38 B3 Dingxi China
38 E2 Ding Xian China
38 E2 Dingxing China
38 E3 Dingyuan China
38 F2 Dingzi Gang *harbour* China
39 C6 Dinh Lâp Vietnam
13 J5 Dinkelsbühl Ger.
73 G3 Dinnebito Wash *r.* U.S.A.
35 F3 Dinngyê China
91 G1 Dinokwe Botswana
57 L5 Dinorwic Lake U.S.A.
73 H1 Dinosaur U.S.A.
62 E3 Dinosaur Nat. Mon. *res.* U.S.A.
12 E3 Dinslaken Ger.
86 B3 Dioïla Mali
82 B4 Dionísio Cerqueira Brazil
86 A3 Diourbel Senegal
35 H4 Diphu India
34 B4 Diplo Pak.
43 B4 Dipolog Phil.
51 B6 Dipton N.Z.
28 F2 Dirckli Turkey
86 B3 Diré Mali
48 E3 Direction, C. *c.* Austr.
88 E3 Dirē Dawa Eth.
89 C5 Dirico Angola
48 B4 Dirk Hartog I. *i.* Austr.
48 E4 Dirranbandi Austr.
73 G2 Dirty Devil *r.* U.S.A.
34 C4 Dīsa India
80 Disappointment, C. *c.* Atl. Ocean
62 A2 Disappointment, C. *c.* U.S.A.
48 C4 Disappointment, L. *salt flat* Austr.
50 G4 Disaster B. *b.* Austr.
50 C5 Discovery Bay *b.* Austr.
39 Discovery Bay *b.* *H.K.* China
Disko *i.* *see* Qeqertarsuatsiaq
Disko Bugt *b.* *see* Qeqertarsuup Tunua
71 E6 Dismal Swamp *swamp* U.S.A.
12 A6 Disneyland Paris France
35 G4 Dispur India
9 J5 Diss U.K.
82 C1 Distrito Federal *div.* Brazil
28 C6 Disūq Egypt
43 B4 Dit *i.* Phil.
90 E4 Ditloung S. Africa
18 F6 Dittaino *r.* *Sicily* Italy
43 C4 Diuata Mountains Phil.
43 C4 Diuata Pt *pt* Phil.
30 B3 Dīvāndarreh Iran
20 G4 Diveyevo Rus. Fed.
43 B2 Divilacan Bay *b.* Phil.
82 D3 Divinópolis Brazil
21 G6 Divnoye Rus. Fed.
86 B4 Divo Côte d'Ivoire
28 G2 Divriği Turkey
31 G5 Diwana Pak.
71 H2 Dixfield U.S.A.
71 J2 Dixmont U.S.A.
72 B2 Dixon *CA* U.S.A.
68 C5 Dixon *IL* U.S.A.
56 C4 Dixon Entrance *chan.* Can./U.S.A.
56 F3 Dixonville Can.
71 H2 Dixville Can.
29 J2 Diyadin Turkey
29 K5 Diyālā *r.* Iraq
29 H3 Diyarbakır Turkey
34 B4 Diyodar India
Dizak *see* Dāvar Panāh
30 D3 Diz Chah Iran
87 D2 Djado Niger
87 D2 Djado, Plateau du *plat.* Niger
88 B4 Djambala Congo
86 C2 Djanet Alg.
86 C1 Djelfa Alg.
88 C3 Djéma C.A.R.
86 B3 Djenné Mali
86 B3 Djibo Burkina
88 E2 Djibouti Djibouti
85 H4 Djibouti *country* Africa
11 E4 Djouce Mountain *h.* Rep. of Ireland
86 C4 Djougou Benin
6 F4 Djúpivogur Iceland
7 O6 Djurås Sweden
29 K1 Dmanisi Georgia
25 Q2 Dmitriya Lapteva, Proliv *chan.* Rus. Fed.
40 C2 Dmitriyevka *Primorskiy Kray* Rus. Fed.
20 G4 Dmitriyevka *Tambov.* Rus. Fed.
21 E4 Dmitriyev-L'govskiy Rus. Fed.
20 F3 Dmitrov Rus. Fed.
17 P5 Dnieper *r.* Europe
17 N6 Dniester *r.* Ukr.
17 Q7 Dnipro *r.* Ukr.
21 E5 Dniprodzerzhyns'k Ukr.
21 E5 Dnipropetrovs'k Ukr.
21 E6 Dniprorudne Ukr.
20 D3 Dno Rus. Fed.
Dnyapro *r.* *see* Dnieper
87 D4 Doba Chad
35 G3 Doba China
69 G3 Dobbinton Can.
7 S8 Dobele Latvia
13 M3 Döbeln Ger.
37 F7 Doberai, Jazirah *pen.* Indon.
83 D3 Doblas Arg.
37 F7 Dobo Indon.
19 H2 Doboj Bos.-Herz.
13 K4 Döbra-berg *h.* Ger.
19 M3 Dobrich Bulg.
21 G4 Dobrinka Rus. Fed.
21 D4 Dobrush Belarus
43 A5 Doc Can *rf* Phil.
82 E2 Doce *r.* Brazil
9 H5 Docking U.K.
63 F6 Doctor B. Domínguez Mex.
33 B3 Dod Ballapur India
19 M6 Dodecanese *is* Greece
Dodekanisos *is* *see* Dodecanese
62 C2 Dodge U.S.A.
68 A3 Dodge Center U.S.A.
65 C4 Dodge City U.S.A.
68 B4 Dodgeville U.S.A.
9 C7 Dodman Point *pt* U.K.
88 D4 Dodoma Tanz.
12 E3 Doetinchem Neth.
37 E6 Dofa Indon.
35 G2 Dogai Coring *salt l.* China
28 F2 Doğanşehir Turkey
56 E4 Dog Creek Can.
35 G3 Dogên Co *l.* China
59 H2 Dog Island *i.* Can.
57 K4 Dog L. *l.* Can.
69 E1 Dog Lake *l.* Can.
41 C6 Dōgo *i.* Japan
86 C3 Dogondoutchi Niger
41 C7 Dōgo-yama *mt* Japan
29 K2 Doğubeyazıt Turkey
35 G3 Do'gyaling China
30 C5 Doha Qatar
Dohad *see* Dāhod
35 H5 Dohazar Bangl.
35 G3 Doilungdêqên China
44 A1 Doi Saket Thai.
79 K5 Dois Irmãos, Serra dos *h.* Brazil
19 K4 Dojran, Lake *l.* Greece/Macedonia
7 M6 Dokka Norway
12 E1 Dokkum Neth.
34 B4 Dokri Pak.
17 N3 Dokshytsy Belarus
21 F6 Dokuchayevs'k Ukr.
37 F7 Dolak, Pulau *i.* Indon.
59 F4 Dolbeau Can.
9 C5 Dolbenmaen U.K.
14 D2 Dol-de-Bretagne France
14 G3 Dole France
9 D5 Dolgellau U.K.
13 M1 Dolgen Ger.
71 F3 Dolgeville U.S.A.
21 F4 Dolgorukovo Rus. Fed.
21 F4 Dolgoye Rus. Fed.
18 C5 Dolianova *Sardinia* Italy
36 G2 Dolinsk Rus. Fed.
92 B2 Dolleman I. *i.* Ant.
13 K6 Dollnstein Ger.
88 E3 Dolo Odo Eth.
83 F3 Dolores Arg.
83 E2 Dolores Uru.
73 H2 Dolores *r.* U.S.A.
54 G3 Dolphin and Union Str. Can.
39 B7 Đô Lương Vietnam
21 B5 Dolyna Ukr.
28 B2 Domaniç Turkey
34 E2 Domar China
16 F6 Domažlice Czech Rep.
35 H2 Domba China
7 L5 Dombås Norway
16 J7 Dombóvár Hungary
92 C4 Dome Argus *ice feature* Ant.
92 C5 Dome Circe *ice feature* Ant.
56 E4 Dome Creek Can.
56 D2 Dome Pk *summit* Can.
73 E5 Dome Rock Mts *mts* U.S.A.
14 D2 Domfront France
53 K8 Dominica *country* Caribbean Sea
53 J8 Dominican Republic *country* Caribbean Sea
13 K1 Dömitz Ger.
44 C2 Dom Noi, L. *r.* Thai.
18 C1 Domodossola Italy
19 K5 Domokos Greece
83 F1 Dom Pedrito Brazil
45 E4 Dompu Indon.
83 B3 Domuyo, Volcán *volc.* Arg.
33 B2 Don *r.* India
21 G5 Don *r.* Rus. Fed.
10 F3 Don *r.* U.K.
11 E3 Donaghadee U.K.
11 E3 Donaghmore U.K.
50 D4 Donald Austr.
Donau *r.* *see* Danube
16 D7 Donaueschingen Ger.
16 E6 Donauwörth Ger.
15 D3 Don Benito Spain
8 F4 Doncaster U.K.
89 B4 Dondo Angola
89 D5 Dondo Moz.
43 B4 Dondonay *i.* Phil.
33 C5 Dondra Head *c.* Sri Lanka
11 C3 Donegal Rep. of Ireland
11 C3 Donegal Bay *g.* Rep. of Ireland
21 F6 Donets'k Ukr.
21 F5 Donets'kyy Kryazh *h.* Rus. Fed./Ukr.
39 D5 Dong'an China
48 B4 Dongara Austr.
34 E5 Dongargarh India
39 B5 Dongchuan China
35 F2 Dongco China
39 C7 Dongfang China
40 C1 Dongfanghong China
42 C2 Dongfeng China
45 E3 Donggala Indon.
42 C4 Donggou China
39 E5 Donggu China
39 D6 Dongguan China
44 C1 Đông Ha Vietnam
38 F3 Donghai China
39 D6 Donghai Dao *i.* China
38 C3 Dong He *r.* *Sichuan* China
38 A1 Dong He *watercourse* *Nei Monggol* China
44 C1 Đông Hơi Vietnam
42 E1 Dongjingcheng China
35 H3 Dongjug *Xizang* China
35 H3 Dongjug *Xizang* China
39 D5 Dongkou China
35 G4 Dongkya La *pass* India
39 C5 Donglan China
38 A2 Dongle China
42 C2 Dongliao *r.* China
42 B1 Dongminzhutun China
42 F2 Dongning China
89 B5 Dongo Angola
88 B3 Dongou Congo
44 B1 Dong Phraya Fai *mts* Thai.
44 B2 Dong Phraya Yen *esc.* Thai.
39 D6 Dongping *Guangdong* China
38 E3 Dongping *Shandong* China
35 G3 Dongqiao China
39 E6 Dongshan China
39 E6 Dongshan Dao *i.* China
38 D2 Dongsheng China
38 F3 Dongtai *Jiangsu* China
38 F3 Dongtai *r.* China
39 D4 Dongting Hu *l.* China
39 F5 Dongtou China
38 D2 Dong Ujimqin Qi China
39 E4 Dongxiang China
38 B3 Dongxiangzu China
39 F4 Dongyang China
39 F4 Dongying China
38 B2 Dongzhen China
39 E4 Dongzhi China
56 B2 Donjek *r.* Can.
12 E1 Donkerbroek Neth.
35 G5 Donmanick Islands *is* Bangl.
65 C7 Don Martin Mex.
59 F4 Donnacona Can.
56 F3 Donnelly Can.
51 D1 Donnellys Crossing N.Z.
72 B2 Donner Pass U.S.A.
Donostia-San Sebastián *see* San Sebastián
19 L6 Donoussa *i.* Greece
20 F4 Donskoy Rus. Fed.
21 G6 Donskoye Rus. Fed.
43 B3 Donsol Phil.
44 C2 Don, Xé *r.* Laos
11 A4 Dooagh Rep. of Ireland
11 B5 Doonbeg *r.* Rep. of Ireland
10 D5 Doon, Loch *l.* U.K.
12 D2 Doorn Neth.
68 D3 Door Peninsula U.S.A.
12 D3 Doorwerth Neth.
88 E3 Dooxo Nugaaleed *v.* Somalia
31 F4 Dor *watercourse* Afgh.
65 C5 Dora U.S.A.
18 C2 Dora Baltea *r.* Italy
9 E7 Dorchester U.K.
89 B6 Dordabis Namibia
14 E4 Dordogne *r.* France
12 C3 Dordrecht Neth.
91 G5 Dordrecht S. Africa
90 C1 Doreenville Namibia
57 H4 Doré L. *l.* Can.
57 H4 Doré Lake Can.
18 C4 Dorgali *Sardinia* Italy
86 B3 Dori Burkina
31 G4 Dori *r.* Afgh.
90 C5 Doring *r.* S. Africa
9 G6 Dorking U.K.
12 E3 Dormagen Ger.
12 B5 Dormans France
38 C1 Dorngovĭ *div.* Mongolia
10 D3 Dornoch Firth *est.* U.K.
12 F1 Dornum Ger.
20 E4 Dorogobuzh Rus. Fed.
17 N7 Dorohoi Romania
36 B2 Döröö Nuur *l.* Mongolia
6 P4 Dorotea Sweden
48 B4 Dorre I. *i.* Austr.
62 B3 Dorris U.S.A.
86 D4 Dorsale Camerounaise *slope* Cameroon/Nigeria
69 H3 Dorset Can.
12 F3 Dortmund Ger.
70 B6 Dorton U.S.A.
28 F3 Dörtyol Turkey
13 G1 Dorum Ger.
88 C3 Doruma Congo(Zaire)
30 E3 Dorūneh Iran
71 G2 Dorval Can.
13 H2 Dörverden Ger.
80 C6 Dos Bahías, C. *pt* Arg.
73 H5 Dos Cabezas U.S.A.
78 C5 Dos de Mayo Peru
39 C6 Đo Son Vietnam
72 B3 Dos Palos U.S.A.
13 L2 Dosse *r.* Ger.
86 C3 Dosso Niger
67 C6 Dothan U.S.A.
14 F1 Douai France
86 C4 Douala Cameroon
14 B2 Douarnenez France
39 Double I. *i.* *H.K.* China
72 C4 Double Peak *summit* U.S.A.
14 H3 Doubs *r.* France
51 A6 Doubtful Sound *in.* N.Z.
51 D1 Doubtless Bay *b.* N.Z.
86 B3 Douentza Mali
8 C3 Douglas Isle of Man
90 E4 Douglas S. Africa
10 E5 Douglas *Scot.* U.K.
56 C3 Douglas *AK* U.S.A.
73 H6 Douglas *AZ* U.S.A.
67 D6 Douglas *GA* U.S.A.
62 F3 Douglas *WY* U.S.A.
73 H6 Douglas *airport* *AZ* U.S.A.
56 D4 Douglas Chan. *chan.* Can.
73 H2 Douglas Creek *r.* U.S.A.
14 F1 Doullens France
10 D4 Doune U.K.
82 C2 Dourada, Cach. *waterfall* Brazil
82 B2 Dourada, Serra *h.* Brazil
82 C1 Dourada, Serra *mts* Brazil
82 A3 Dourados Brazil
82 A3 Dourados *r.* Brazil
82 B3 Dourados, Serra dos *h.* Brazil
15 C2 Douro *r.* Port.
12 D5 Douzy France
9 F4 Dove *r.* *Eng.* U.K.
9 J5 Dove *r.* *Eng.* U.K.
59 J3 Dove Brook Can.
73 H3 Dove Creek U.S.A.
9 J6 Dover U.K.
71 F5 Dover *DE* U.S.A.
71 H3 Dover *NH* U.S.A.
71 F4 Dover *NJ* U.S.A.
70 C4 Dover *OH* U.S.A.
71 J2 Dover-Foxcroft U.S.A.
9 J7 Dover, Strait of *str.* France/U.K.
29 L5 Doveyrīch *r.* Iran/Iraq
75 D5 Dowagiac U.S.A.
30 D4 Dow Chāh Iran
31 E2 Dowgha'ī Iran
44 A5 Dowi, Tg *pt* Indon.
31 F3 Dowlatābād Afgh.
31 G2 Dowlatābād Afgh.
30 D4 Dowlatābād Iran
30 E4 Dowlatābād Iran
30 D4 Dowlatābād Iran
31 F2 Dowlatābād Iran
31 G3 Dowl at Yār Afgh.
72 B2 Downieville U.S.A.
11 F3 Downpatrick U.K.
71 F3 Downsville U.S.A.
30 C3 Dow Rūd Iran
29 L4 Dow Sar Iran
31 E4 Dowsārī Iran
31 H3 Dowshī Afgh.
72 B1 Doyle U.S.A.
71 F4 Doylestown U.S.A.
41 C6 Dōzen *is* Japan
69 J2 Dozois, Réservoir *resr* Can.
82 B3 Dracena Brazil
12 E1 Drachten Neth.
19 L2 Drăgănești-Olt Romania
19 L2 Drăgășani Romania
81 E2 Dragon's Mouths *str.* Trinidad/Venez.
7 S6 Dragsfjärd Fin.
14 H5 Draguignan France
21 C4 Drahichyn Belarus
73 F4 Drake *AZ* U.S.A.
57 J5 Drake *ND* U.S.A.
91 H5 Drakensberg *mts* Lesotho/ S. Africa
91 J2 Drakensberg *mts* S. Africa
96 E9 Drake Passage *str.* Ant.
19 L4 Drama Greece
7 M7 Drammen Norway
7 L7 Drangedal Norway
31 G5 Dran juk *h.* Pak.
13 H3 Dransfeld Ger.
11 E3 Draperstown U.K.
34 C2 Dras Jammu and Kashmir
16 F7 Drau *r.* Austria
56 G4 Drayton Valley Can.
18 B6 Dréan Alg.
13 H4 Dreistelz-berge *h.* Ger.
16 F5 Dresden Ger.
20 D4 Dretun' Belarus
14 E2 Dreux France
7 N6 Drevsjø Norway
70 D4 Driftwood U.S.A.
11 B6 Drimoleague Rep. of Ireland
18 G3 Drniš Croatia
19 K2 Drobeta-Turnu Severin Romania
13 H1 Drochtersen Ger.
11 E4 Drogheda Rep. of Ireland
21 B5 Drohobych Ukr.
Droichead Átha *see* Drogheda
9 E5 Droitwich U.K.
35 G4 Drokung India
13 J2 Drömling *reg.* Ger.
11 D4 Dromod Rep. of Ireland
11 E3 Dromore *Co. Down* U.K.
11 D3 Dromore *Co. Tyrone* U.K.
9 F4 Dronfield U.K.
55 Q2 Dronning Louise Land *reg.* Greenland
92 C3 Dronning Maud Land *reg.* Ant.
12 D2 Dronten Neth.
34 B2 Drosh Pak.
21 F4 Droskovo Rus. Fed.
50 E5 Drouin Austr.
80 D2 Dr Pedro P. Peña Para.
56 G4 Drumheller Can.
62 D2 Drummond *MT* U.S.A.
68 B2 Drummond *WV* U.S.A.
69 F3 Drummond Island *i.* U.S.A.
59 F4 Drummondville Can.
10 D6 Drummore U.K.
10 D4 Drumochter Pass U.K.
7 T10 Druskininkai Lith.
25 Q3 Druzhina Rus. Fed.
19 L3 Dryanovo Bulg.
56 B3 Dry Bay *b.* U.S.A.
57 L5 Dryberry L. *l.* Can.
68 E2 Dryburg U.S.A.
58 B4 Dryden Can.
92 D5 Drygalski I. *i.* Ant.
92 B5 Drygalski Ice Tongue *ice feature* Ant.
72 D2 Dry Lake *l.* U.S.A.
10 D4 Drymen U.K.
48 C3 Drysdale *r.* Austr.
30 C3 Dūāb *r.* Iran
39 C6 Du'an China
71 F2 Duane U.S.A.
35 G4 Duars *reg.* India
26 B4 Ḍubā S. Arabia
32 E4 Dubai U.A.E.
57 J2 Dubawnt *r.* Can.
54 H3 Dubawnt Lake *l.* *N.W.T.* Can.
57 J2 Dubawnt Lake *l.* Can.
Dubayy *see* Dubai
26 B4 Dubbagh, J. ad *mt* S. Arabia
50 G2 Dubbo Austr.
68 D1 Dublin Can.
11 E4 Dublin Rep. of Ireland
67 D5 Dublin U.S.A.
20 F3 Dubna Rus. Fed.
21 C5 Dubno Ukr.
62 D2 Dubois *ID* U.S.A.
62 E3 Dubois *WY* U.S.A.
70 D4 Du Bois U.S.A.
21 H5 Dubovka Rus. Fed.
21 G6 Dubovskoye Rus. Fed.
29 M1 Dübrar P. *pass* Azer.
86 A4 Dubréka Guinea
19 H3 Dubrovnik Croatia
21 C5 Dubrovytsya Ukr.
20 D4 Dubrowna Belarus
68 B4 Dubuque U.S.A.
7 S9 Dubysa *r.* Lith.
39 E4 Duchang China
73 G1 Duchesne U.S.A.
46 P6 Ducie Island *i.* *Pitcairn Is* Pac. Oc.
67 C5 Duck *r.* U.S.A.
57 J4 Duck Bay Can.
57 H4 Duck Lake Can.
68 E4 Duck Lake U.S.A.
73 E2 Duckwater U.S.A.
73 E2 Duckwater Peak *summit* U.S.A.
44 D2 Đưc Pho Vietnam
44 D3 Đưc Trong Vietnam
81 B4 Duda *r.* Col.
12 E5 Dudelange Lux.
13 J3 Duderstadt Ger.
35 E4 Dudhi India
35 G4 Dudhnai India
24 K3 Dudinka Rus. Fed.
9 E5 Dudley U.K.
34 D6 Dudna *r.* India
10 F3 Dudwick, Hill of *h.* U.K.
86 B4 Duékoué Côte d'Ivoire
15 C2 Duero *r.* Spain
69 H1 Dufault, Lac *l.* Can.
92 B4 Dufek Coast *coastal area* Ant.
12 C3 Duffel Belgium
58 E2 Dufferin, Cape *hd* Can.
70 B6 Duffield U.S.A.
49 G2 Duff Is *is* Solomon Is
10 E3 Dufftown U.K.
58 F1 Dufrost, Pte *pt* Can.
31 G2 Dugab Uzbek.
18 F3 Dugi Otok *i.* Croatia
38 C2 Dugui Qarag China
39 C5 Du He *r.* China
81 D4 Duida, Co *mt* Venez.
78 E3 Duida-Marahuaca, Parque Nacional *nat. park* Venez.
12 E3 Duisburg Ger.
81 B3 Duitama Col.
91 J1 Duiwelskloof S. Africa
29 K4 Dukān Dam *dam* Iraq
91 G5 Dukathole S. Africa
56 C4 Duke I. *i.* U.S.A.
30 C5 Dukhān Qatar
17 Q3 Dukhovshchina Rus. Fed.
34 B3 Duki Pak.
39 A5 Dukou China
7 U9 Dūkštas Lith.
36 B3 Dulan China
80 D3 Dulce *r.* Arg.
35 E2 Dulishi Hu *salt l.* China
91 J2 Dullstroom S. Africa
12 F3 Dülmen Ger.
19 M3 Dulovo Bulg.
68 A2 Duluth U.S.A.
68 A2 Duluth/Superior *airport* U.S.A.
9 D6 Dulverton U.K.
28 F5 Dūmā Syria
43 B4 Dumaguete Phil.
45 B2 Dumai Indon.
43 B4 Dumaran *i.* Phil.
65 F5 Dumas *AR* U.S.A.
65 C5 Dumas *TX* U.S.A.
28 F5 Ḍumayr Syria
30 B3 Dumbakh Iran
10 D5 Dumbarton U.K.
91 J3 Dumbe S. Africa
17 J6 Ďumbier *mt* Slovakia
34 D2 Dumchele Jammu and Kashmir
35 H4 Dum Duma India
10 E5 Dumfries U.K.
35 F4 Dumka India
13 G2 Dümmer *l.* Ger.
58 E4 Dumoine, L. *l.* Can.
92 B6 Dumont d'Urville *France base* Ant.
92 B6 Dumont d'Urville Sea *sea* Ant.
12 E4 Dümpelfeld Ger.
87 F1 Dumyât Egypt
13 J3 Dün *ridge* Ger.
Duna *r.* *see* Danube
16 H7 Dunajská Streda Slovakia
17 J7 Dunakeszi Hungary
11 E4 Dunany Point *pt* Rep. of Ireland
19 N2 Dunării, Delta *delta* Romania
17 J7 Dunaújváros Hungary
Dunav *r.* *see* Danube
21 C5 Dunayivtsi Ukr.
51 C6 Dunback N.Z.
10 F4 Dunbar U.K.
10 E4 Dunblane U.K.
11 E4 Dunboyne Rep. of Ireland
56 E5 Duncan Can.
73 H5 Duncan *AZ* U.S.A.
65 D5 Duncan *OK* U.S.A.
58 D3 Duncan, Cape *c.* Can.
58 E3 Duncan, L. *l.* Can.
70 E4 Duncannon U.S.A.
10 E2 Duncansby Head *hd* U.K.
68 B5 Duncans Mills U.S.A.
11 E5 Duncormick Rep. of Ireland
7 S8 Dundaga Latvia
69 G3 Dundalk Can.
11 E3 Dundalk Rep. of Ireland
70 E5 Dundalk U.S.A.
11 E4 Dundalk Bay *b.* Rep. of Ireland
Dundas *see* Uummannaq
56 C4 Dundas I. *i.* Can.
Dun Dealgan *see* Dundalk
91 J4 Dundee S. Africa
10 F4 Dundee U.K.
69 F5 Dundee *MI* U.S.A.
70 E3 Dundee *NY* U.S.A.
11 F3 Dundonald U.K.
10 E6 Dundrennan U.K.
11 F3 Dundrum U.K.
11 F3 Dundrum Bay *b.* U.K.
35 E4 Dundwa Range *mts* India/Nepal
51 C6 Dunedin N.Z.
67 D6 Dunedin U.S.A.
50 G2 Dunedoo Austr.
58 F2 Dune, Lac *l.* Can.
10 E4 Dunfermline U.K.
11 E3 Dungannon U.K.
34 C5 Dungarpur India
11 D5 Dungarvan Rep. of Ireland
9 H7 Dungeness *hd* U.K.
80 C8 Dungeness, Pta *pt* Arg.
12 F4 Düngenheim Ger.
11 E3 Dungiven U.K.
11 C3 Dungloe Rep. of Ireland
50 H2 Dungog Austr.
88 C3 Dungu Congo(Zaire)
45 B2 Dungun Malaysia
87 F2 Dungunab Sudan
42 E2 Dunhua China
36 B2 Dunhuang China
50 D4 Dunkeld Austr.
10 E4 Dunkeld U.K.
Dunkerque *see* Dunkirk
9 D6 Dunkery Beacon *h.* U.K.
14 F1 Dunkirk France
70 D3 Dunkirk U.S.A.
86 B4 Dunkwa Ghana
11 E4 Dún Laoghaire Rep. of Ireland
11 E4 Dunlavin Rep. of Ireland
11 E4 Dunleer Rep. of Ireland
11 F2 Dunloy U.K.
11 B6 Dunmanus Bay *b.* Rep. of Ireland
11 B6 Dunmanway Rep. of Ireland
11 C4 Dunmore Rep. of Ireland
67 E7 Dunmore Town Bahamas
72 D3 Dunmovin U.S.A.
11 F3 Dunmurry U.K.
67 E5 Dunn U.S.A.
10 E2 Dunnet Bay *b.* U.K.
10 E2 Dunnet Head *hd* U.K.
72 B2 Dunnigan U.S.A.
64 C3 Dunning U.S.A.
69 H4 Dunnville Can.
50 D4 Dunolly Austr.
10 D5 Dunoon U.K.
10 F5 Duns U.K.
64 C1 Dunseith U.S.A.
62 B3 Dunsmuir U.S.A.
9 G6 Dunstable U.K.
51 B6 Dunstan Mts *mts* N.Z.
12 D5 Dun-sur-Meuse France
51 C6 Duntroon N.Z.
10 B3 Dunvegan, Loch *in.* U.K.
34 B3 Dunyapur Pak.
38 E1 Duolon China
39 D5 Dupang Ling *mts* China
69 H1 Duparquet, Lac *l.* Can.
64 C2 Dupree U.S.A.
66 B4 Du Quoin U.S.A.
48 C3 Durack *r.* Austr.
Dura Europos *see* Qal'at as Ṣāliḥīyah
28 E1 Durağan Turkey
14 G5 Durance *r.* France
69 F4 Durand *MI* U.S.A.

68 B3 Durand WV U.S.A.
74 D4 Durango Mex.
15 E1 Durango Spain
63 F4 Durango U.S.A.
65 B7 Durango div. Mex.
65 D5 Durant U.S.A.
83 F2 Durazno Uru.
83 F1 Durazno, Cuchilla Grande del h. Uru.
91 J4 Durban S. Africa
14 F5 Durban-Corbières France
90 C6 Durbanville S. Africa
70 D5 Durbin U.S.A.
12 D4 Durbuy Belgium
12 E4 Düren Ger.
34 E5 Durg India
35 F5 Durgapur India
69 G3 Durham Can.
8 F3 Durham U.K.
72 B2 Durham CA U.S.A.
67 E4 Durham NC U.S.A.
71 H3 Durham NH U.S.A.
21 D6 Durleşti Moldova
13 G6 Durmersheim Ger.
19 H3 Durmitor mt Yugo.
10 D2 Durness U.K.
19 H4 Durrës Albania
9 F6 Durrington U.K.
11 A6 Dursey Island i. Rep. of Ireland
28 B2 Dursunbey Turkey
31 F3 Dūruḩ Iran
28 F5 Durūz, Jabal ad mt Syria
51 D4 D'Urville Island i. N.Z.
48 D2 d'Urville, Tanjung pt Indon.
31 G3 Durzab Afgh.
31 G4 Dushai Pak.
31 E2 Dushak Turkm.
39 C5 Dushan China
31 H2 Dushanbe Tajik.
21 H7 Dushet'i Georgia
51 A6 Dusky Sound in. N.Z.
12 E3 Düsseldorf Ger.
73 F1 Dutch Mt mt U.S.A.
90 E1 Dutlwe Botswana
86 C3 Dutse Nigeria
72 F2 Dutton, Mt mt U.S.A.
20 H3 Duvannoye Rus. Fed.
59 F2 Duvert, Lac l. Can.
39 C5 Duyun China
31 F5 Duzab Pak.
28 C1 Düzce Turkey
Duzdab see Zāhedān
20 D4 Dvina, Western r. Rus. Fed.
21 F5 Dvorichna Ukr.
40 B2 Dvoryanka Rus. Fed.
34 B5 Dwarka India
91 G2 Dwarsberg S. Africa
68 C5 Dwight U.S.A.
12 E2 Dwingelderveld, Nationaal Park nat. park Neth.
62 C2 Dworshak Res. resr U.S.A.
90 D6 Dwyka S. Africa
20 E4 Dyat'kovo Rus. Fed.
10 F3 Dyce U.K.
68 D5 Dyer IN U.S.A.
72 C3 Dyer NV U.S.A.
69 G3 Dyer Bay Can.
55 M3 Dyer, C. c. Can.
67 B4 Dyersburg U.S.A.
68 B4 Dyersville U.S.A.
9 D5 Dyfi r. U.K.
10 E3 Dyke U.K.
21 G7 Dykh Tau mt Georgia/Rus. Fed.
13 L5 Dyleň h. Czech Rep.
17 J4 Dylewska Góra h. Pol.
91 H5 Dyoki S. Africa
68 A4 Dysart U.S.A.
90 E6 Dysselsdorp S. Africa
36 D2 Dzamïn Üüd Mongolia
89 E5 Dzaoudzi Mayotte Africa
20 G3 Dzerzhinsk Rus. Fed.
17 N5 Dzerzhyns'k Ukr.
30 D1 Dzhanga Turkm.
21 E6 Dzhankoy Ukr.
21 H5 Dzhanybek Rus. Fed.
31 G2 Dzharkurgan Uzbek.
31 D2 Dzhebel Turkm.
26 E1 Dzhetygara Kazak.
26 E2 Dzhezkazgan Kazak.
25 R3 Dzhigudzhak Rus. Fed.
31 G1 Dzhizak Uzbek.
31 F1 Dzhugdzhur, Khrebet mts Rus. Fed.
Dzhul'fa see Culfa
31 G2 Dzhuma Uzbek.
27 F2 Dzhungarskiy Alatau, Khr. mts China/Kazak.
24 H5 Dzhusaly Kazak.
17 K4 Działdowo Pol.
36 C2 Dzuunmod Mongolia
20 C4 Dzyaniskavichy Belarus
20 C4 Dzyarzhynsk Belarus
17 N4 Dzyatlavichy Belarus

# E

58 C3 Eabamet L. l. Can.
73 H4 Eagar U.S.A.
63 F4 Eagle U.S.A.
59 J3 Eagle r. Can.
71 F3 Eagle Bay U.S.A.
57 H4 Eagle Cr. r. Can.
72 D4 Eagle Crags summit U.S.A.
57 L5 Eagle L. l. Can.
62 B3 Eagle L. l. CA U.S.A.
71 J1 Eagle Lake ME U.S.A.
71 J1 Eagle Lake l. ME U.S.A.
68 B2 Eagle Mtn h. U.S.A.
65 C6 Eagle Pass U.S.A.
54 D3 Eagle Plain plain Can.
68 C2 Eagle River MI U.S.A.
68 C3 Eagle River WI U.S.A.
56 F3 Eaglesham Can.
73 F5 Eagle Tail Mts mts U.S.A.
58 B3 Ear Falls Can.
72 C4 Earlimart U.S.A.
10 F5 Earlston U.K.
69 H2 Earlton Can.
10 E4 Earn r. U.K.
10 D4 Earn, L. l. U.K.
65 C5 Earth U.S.A.
8 H4 Easington U.K.
67 D5 Easley U.S.A.
92 C5 East Antarctica reg. Ant.
71 F4 East Ararat U.S.A.
70 D3 East Aurora U.S.A.
65 F6 East Bay b. U.S.A.
71 G2 East Berkshire U.S.A.
9 H7 Eastbourne U.K.
70 D4 East Branch Clarion River Reservoir U.S.A.
71 H4 East Brooklyn U.S.A.
51 G2 East Cape c. N.Z.
73 G2 East Carbon U.S.A.
94 E5 East Caroline Basin sea feature Pac. Oc.
68 D5 East Chicago U.S.A.
36 E3 East China Sea Asia
51 E2 East Coast Bays N.Z.
71 G2 East Corinth U.S.A.
9 H5 East Dereham U.K.
95 M7 Easter Island i. Pac. Oc.
95 M7 Easter Island Fracture Zone sea feature Pac. Oc.
91 G5 Eastern Cape div. S. Africa
87 F2 Eastern Desert Egypt
35 E6 Eastern Ghats mts India
34 B4 Eastern Nara canal Pak.
Eastern Transvaal div. see Mpumalanga
57 K4 Easterville Can.
80 E8 East Falkland i. Falkland Is
71 H4 East Falmouth U.S.A.
12 E1 East Frisian Islands is Ger.
72 D2 Eastgate U.S.A.
64 D2 East Grand Forks U.S.A.
9 G6 East Grinstead U.K.
71 G4 East Hampton U.S.A.
71 G3 Easthampton U.S.A.
70 D4 East Hickory U.S.A.
71 G3 East Jamaica U.S.A.
96 K1 East Jan Mayen Ridge sea feature Atl. Ocean
68 E3 East Jordan U.S.A.
10 D5 East Kilbride U.K.
68 D3 Eastlake U.S.A.
39 □ East Lamma Channel H.K. China
9 F7 Eastleigh U.K.
70 C4 East Liverpool U.S.A.
10 B3 East Loch Tarbert b. U.K.
91 G6 East London S. Africa
70 B5 East Lynn Lake l. U.S.A.
58 E3 Eastmain Que. Can.
58 F3 Eastmain r. Que. Can.
71 G2 Eastman Can.
67 D5 Eastman U.S.A.
71 J2 East Millinocket U.S.A.
68 B5 East Moline U.S.A.
68 C5 Easton IL U.S.A.
71 E5 Easton MD U.S.A.
71 F4 Easton PA U.S.A.
95 M8 East Pacific Ridge sea feature Pac. Oc.
95 N5 East Pacific Rise sea feature Pac. Oc.
72 A2 East Park Res. resr U.S.A.
67 C5 East Point U.S.A.
59 H4 East Point pt P.E.I. Can.
71 K2 Eastport ME U.S.A.
68 E3 Eastport MI U.S.A.
72 D1 East Range mts U.S.A.
East Retford see Retford
66 B4 East St Louis U.S.A.
25 R2 East Siberian Sea sea Rus. Fed.
23 M10 East Timor reg Asia
35 F4 East Tons r. India
68 C4 East Troy U.S.A.
71 F6 Eastville U.S.A.
72 C2 East Walker r. U.S.A.
71 G3 East Wallingford U.S.A.
67 D5 Eatonton U.S.A.
68 B3 Eau Claire U.S.A.
68 B3 Eau Claire r. U.S.A.
58 F2 Eau Claire, Lac à l' l. Can.
37 G6 Eauripik Atoll Micronesia
94 E5 Eauripik - New Guinea Rise sea feature Pac. Oc.
74 E4 Ebano Mex.
9 D6 Ebbw Vale U.K.
86 D4 Ebebiyin Equatorial Guinea
90 B2 Ebenerde Namibia
70 D4 Ebensburg U.S.A.
28 C2 Eber Gölü l. Turkey
13 J3 Ebergötzen Ger.
16 F4 Eberswalde-Finow Ger.
69 F4 Eberts Can.
40 G3 Ebetsu Japan
39 B4 Ebian China
18 F4 Eboli Italy
86 D4 Ebolowa Cameroon
94 G5 Ebon i. Pac. Oc.
29 K3 Ebrāhim Ḩeşār Iran
15 G2 Ebro r. Spain
13 J1 Ebstorf Ger.
19 M4 Eceabat Turkey
43 B2 Echague Phil.
15 E1 Echarri-Aranaz Spain
86 C1 Ech Chélif Alg.
15 E1 Echegárate, Puerto pass Spain
39 E4 Echeng China
56 F1 Echo Bay N.W.T. Can.
69 E2 Echo Bay Ont. Can.
73 G3 Echo Cliffs cliff U.S.A.
58 B3 Echoing r. Can.
69 K2 Échouani, Lac l. Can.
12 D3 Echt Neth.
12 E5 Echternach Lux.
50 E4 Echuca Austr.
13 G4 Echzell Ger.
15 D4 Écija Spain
13 K5 Eckental Ger.
68 E2 Eckerman U.S.A.
16 D3 Eckernförde Ger.
55 L2 Eclipse Sound chan. Can.
77 C3 Ecuador country S. America
58 E2 Écueils, Pte aux pt Can.
88 E2 Ed Eritrea
7 M7 Ed Sweden
57 H4 Edam Can.
12 D2 Edam Neth.
10 F1 Eday i. U.K.
87 E3 Ed Da'ein Sudan
87 F3 Ed Damazin Sudan
87 F3 Ed Damer Sudan
87 F3 Ed Debba Sudan
87 F3 Ed Dueim Sudan
48 E6 Eddystone Pt pt Austr.
12 D2 Ede Neth.
86 D4 Edéa Cameroon
57 K2 Edehon Lake l. Can.
82 C2 Edéia Brazil
50 G4 Eden Austr.
65 D6 Eden TX U.S.A.
8 E3 Eden r. U.K.
91 F4 Edenburg S. Africa
51 B7 Edendale N.Z.
11 D4 Edenderry Rep. of Ireland
50 C4 Edenhope Austr.
67 E4 Edenton U.S.A.
91 G3 Edenville S. Africa
19 K4 Edessa Greece
13 F1 Edewecht Ger.
71 H4 Edgartown U.S.A.
64 D2 Edgeley U.S.A.
64 C3 Edgemont U.S.A.
68 C4 Edgerton U.S.A.
11 D4 Edgeworthstown Rep. of Ireland
68 A5 Edina U.S.A.
65 D7 Edinburg U.S.A.
10 E5 Edinburgh U.K.
21 C7 Edirne Turkey
56 F4 Edith Cavell, Mt mt Can.
62 B2 Edmonds U.S.A.
56 G4 Edmonton Can.
57 K5 Edmore U.S.A.
68 B4 Edmund U.S.A.
57 L4 Edmund L. l. Can.
59 G4 Edmundston Can.
65 D6 Edna U.S.A.
56 C3 Edna Bay U.S.A.
19 M5 Edremit Turkey
7 O6 Edsbyn Sweden
56 F4 Edson Can.
83 D2 Eduardo Castex Arg.
50 E3 Edward r. Austr.
68 C1 Edward I. i. Can.
88 C4 Edward, Lake l. Congo(Zaire)/Uganda
71 F2 Edwards U.S.A.
65 C6 Edwards Plateau plat. U.S.A.
68 C6 Edwardsville U.S.A.
92 D4 Edward VIII Ice Shelf ice feature Ant.
92 A4 Edward VII Pen. pen. Ant.
56 C3 Edziza Pk mt Can.
12 B3 Eeklo Belgium
72 A1 Eel r. U.S.A.
12 E1 Eemshaven pt Neth.
12 E1 Eenrum Neth.
90 D3 Eenzamheid Pan salt pan S. Africa
49 G3 Éfaté i. Vanuatu
66 B4 Effingham U.S.A.
28 D1 Eflâni Turkey
73 E2 Egan Range mts U.S.A.
69 J3 Eganville Can.
17 K7 Eger Hungary
7 K7 Egersund Norway
13 G3 Eggegebirge h. Ger.
13 K5 Eggolsheim Ger.
12 C4 Eghezée Belgium
6 F4 Egilsstaðir Iceland
28 C3 Eğirdir Turkey
28 C3 Eğirdir Gölü l. Turkey
14 F4 Égletons France
11 D2 Eglinton U.K.
54 F2 Eglinton I. i. Can.
12 C2 Egmond aan Zee Neth.
51 D3 Egmont, Cape c. N.Z.
51 E3 Egmont, Mt volc. N.Z.
51 E3 Egmont National Park N.Z.
28 B2 Eğrigöz Dağı mts Turkey
8 G3 Egton U.K.
82 D1 Éguas r. Brazil
25 V3 Egvekinot Rus. Fed.
85 F3 Egypt country Africa
16 D6 Ehingen (Donau) Ger.
13 J2 Ehra-Lessien Ger.
73 E5 Ehrenberg U.S.A.
13 J5 Eibelstadt Ger.
12 E2 Eibergen Neth.
13 H4 Eichenzell Ger.
13 K6 Eichstätt Ger.
7 K6 Eidfjord Norway
7 M6 Eidsvoll Norway
12 E4 Eifel reg. Ger.
10 B4 Eigg i. U.K.
33 A4 Eight Degree Chan. India/Maldives
92 A3 Eights Coast coastal area Ant.
48 C3 Eighty Mile Beach beach Austr.
50 E4 Eildon Austr.
50 F4 Eildon, Lake l. Austr.
10 C4 Eilean Shona i. U.K.
57 H2 Eileen Lake l. Can.
13 L3 Eilenburg Ger.
13 J2 Eimke Ger.
13 H3 Einbeck Ger.
12 D3 Eindhoven Neth.
16 D7 Einsiedeln Switz.
78 E5 Eirunepé Brazil
13 H3 Eisberg h. Ger.
89 C5 Eiseb watercourse Namibia
13 J4 Eisenach Ger.
13 K4 Eisenberg Ger.
16 G4 Eisenhüttenstadt Ger.
16 H7 Eisenstadt Austria
13 J4 Eisfeld Ger.
10 C3 Eishort, Loch in. U.K.
13 K3 Eisleben Lutherstadt Ger.
13 H4 Eiterfeld Ger.
Eivissa see Ibiza
Eivissa i. see Ibiza
15 F1 Ejea de los Caballeros Spain
89 E6 Ejeda Madag.
74 B3 Ejido Insurgentes Mex.
38 C2 Ejin Horo Qi China
38 A1 Ejin Qi China
29 K1 Ejmiatsin Armenia
7 S7 Ekenäs Fin.
12 C3 Ekeren Belgium
51 E4 Eketahuna N.Z.
27 F1 Ekibastuz Kazak.
25 M3 Ekonda Rus. Fed.
7 N6 Ekshärad Sweden
7 O8 Eksjö Sweden
90 B4 Eksteenfontein S. Africa
88 C4 Ekuku Congo(Zaire)
58 D3 Ekwan r. Can.
58 D3 Ekwan Point pt Can.
19 K6 Elafonisou, Steno chan. Greece
28 B6 El 'Alamein Egypt
28 B6 El 'Âmirîya Egypt
91 H2 Elands r. S. Africa
91 H2 Elandsdoorn S. Africa
18 B7 El Aouinet Alg.
28 B6 El 'Arab, Khalîg b. Egypt
28 D6 El 'Arîsh Egypt
19 K5 Elassona Greece
28 E7 Elat Israel
29 G2 Elazığ Turkey
18 D3 Elba, Isola d' i. Italy
36 F1 El'ban Rus. Fed.
81 B2 El Banco Col.
28 D6 El Bardawîl, Sabkhet lag. Egypt
19 J4 Elbasan Albania
28 G2 Elbaşı Turkey
81 C2 El Baúl Venez.
86 C1 El Bayadh Alg.
13 J1 Elbe r. Ger.
68 D3 Elberta MI U.S.A.
73 G2 Elberta UT U.S.A.
63 F4 Elbert, Mount mt U.S.A.
67 D5 Elberton U.S.A.
14 E2 Elbeuf France
28 F2 Elbistan Turkey
17 J3 Elbląg Pol.
83 B4 El Bolsón Arg.
67 E7 Elbow Cay i. Bahamas
21 G7 Elbrus mt Rus. Fed.
12 D2 Elburg Neth.
15 E2 El Burgo de Osma Spain
83 C4 El Cain Arg.
72 D5 El Cajon U.S.A.
81 E3 El Callao Venez.
65 D6 El Campo U.S.A.
73 E5 El Centro U.S.A.
78 F7 El Cerro Bol.
81 D2 El Chaparro Venez.
15 F3 Elche Spain
48 D3 Elcho I. i. Austr.
81 B3 El Cocuy Col.
15 F3 Elda Spain
13 K1 Elde r. Ger.
69 H2 Eldee Can.
72 D5 El Descanso Mex.
81 B2 El Difícil Col.
25 P3 El'dikan Rus. Fed.
81 A4 El Diviso Col.
73 E6 El Doctor Mex.
68 A5 Eldon IA U.S.A.
64 E4 Eldon MO U.S.A.
80 F3 Eldorado Arg.
74 C4 El Dorado Mex.
65 E5 El Dorado AR U.S.A.
65 D4 El Dorado KS U.S.A.
65 C6 Eldorado U.S.A.
81 E3 El Dorado Venez.
88 D3 Eldoret Kenya
62 E2 Electric Peak summit U.S.A.
86 B2 El Eglab plat. Alg.
15 E4 El Ejido Spain
20 F4 Elektrostal' Rus. Fed.
78 D4 El Encanto Col.
13 J3 Elend Ger.
63 F5 Elephant Butte Res. resr U.S.A.
92 B1 Elephant I. i. Ant.
35 H5 Elephant Point pt Bangl.
29 J2 Eleşkirt Turkey
86 C1 El Eulma Alg.
67 E7 Eleuthera i. Bahamas
18 C6 El Fahs Tunisia
87 F2 El Faiyûm Egypt
87 E3 El Fasher Sudan
13 H4 Elfershausen Ger.
60 E6 El Fuerte Mex.
87 E3 El Geneina Sudan
87 F3 El Geteina Sudan
10 E3 Elgin U.K.
68 C4 Elgin IL U.S.A.
64 C2 Elgin ND U.S.A.
73 E3 Elgin NV U.S.A.
73 G2 Elgin UT U.S.A.
25 Q3 El'ginskiy Rus. Fed.
87 F2 El Gîza Egypt
86 C1 El Goléa Alg.
87 F4 Elgon, Mount mt Uganda
18 B6 El Hadjar Alg.
28 B6 El Hammâm Egypt
28 F6 El Hazim Jordan
86 A2 El Hierro i. Canary Is
86 C2 El Homr Alg.
10 F4 Elie U.K.
51 C5 Elie de Beaumont mt N.Z.
54 B3 Elim AK U.S.A.
59 H2 Eliot, Mount mt Can.
15 F1 Elizondo Spain
El Iskandarîya see Alexandria
21 H6 Elista Rus. Fed.
68 B4 Elizabeth IL U.S.A.
71 F4 Elizabeth NJ U.S.A.
70 C5 Elizabeth WV U.S.A.
67 E4 Elizabeth City U.S.A.
71 H4 Elizabeth Is is U.S.A.
67 D4 Elizabethton U.S.A.
66 C4 Elizabethtown KY U.S.A.
67 E5 Elizabethtown NC U.S.A.
71 G2 Elizabethtown NY U.S.A.
70 E4 Elizabethtown PA U.S.A.
86 B1 El Jadida Morocco
28 F6 El Jafr Jordan
65 B7 El Jaralito Mex.
18 D7 El Jem Tunisia
17 L4 Ełk Pol.
72 A2 Elk U.S.A.
56 G4 Elk r. Can.
70 C5 Elk r. U.S.A.
28 F4 El Kaa Lebanon
18 C6 El Kala Alg.
87 F3 El Kamlin Sudan
65 D5 Elk City U.S.A.
72 A2 Elk Creek U.S.A.
72 B2 Elk Grove U.S.A.
87 F2 El Khârga Egypt
68 E5 Elkhart U.S.A.
El Khartum see Khartoum
86 B2 El Khnâchîch esc. Mali
68 C4 Elkhorn U.S.A.
64 D3 Elkhorn r. U.S.A.
32 B1 El'khotovo Rus. Fed.
19 M3 Elkhovo Bulg.
70 D5 Elkins U.S.A.
56 G4 Elk Island Nat. Park Can.
69 G2 Elk Lake Can.
68 E3 Elk Lake l. U.S.A.
70 E4 Elkland U.S.A.
56 F5 Elko Can.
62 D3 Elko U.S.A.
57 G4 Elk Point Can.
64 E2 Elk River U.S.A.
71 F5 Elkton MD U.S.A.
70 D5 Elkton VA U.S.A.
29 G4 El Kubar Syria
57 M2 Ell Bay b. Can.
55 H2 Ellef Ringnes I. i. Can.
34 C3 Ellenabad India
64 D2 Ellendale U.S.A.
73 G2 Ellen, Mt mt U.S.A.
62 B2 Ellensburg U.S.A.
71 F4 Ellenville U.S.A.
50 G4 Ellery, Mt mt Austr.
55 K2 Ellesmere Island i. Can.
51 D5 Ellesmere, Lake l. N.Z.
9 E4 Ellesmere Port U.K.
54 H3 Ellice r. Can.
70 D3 Ellicottville U.S.A.
13 J5 Ellingen Ger.
91 G5 Elliot S. Africa
91 H5 Elliotdale S. Africa
69 F2 Elliot Lake Can.
62 D2 Ellis U.S.A.
91 G1 Ellisras S. Africa
10 F3 Ellon U.K.
71 J2 Ellsworth ME U.S.A.
68 A3 Ellsworth WI U.S.A.
92 A3 Ellsworth Land reg. Ant.
92 B3 Ellsworth Mountains Ant.
13 J6 Ellwangen (Jagst) Ger.
28 B3 Elmalı Turkey
87 F1 El Manşûra Egypt
81 E3 El Manteco Venez.
86 C1 El Meghaïer Alg.
81 E3 El Miamo Venez.
28 E4 El Mîna Lebanon
87 F2 El Minya Egypt
68 E3 Elmira MI U.S.A.
70 E3 Elmira NY U.S.A.
73 F5 El Mirage U.S.A.
15 E4 El Moral Spain
50 E4 Elmore Austr.
83 D2 El Morro mt Arg.
86 B2 El Mreyyé reg. Maur.
13 H1 Elmshorn Ger.
87 E3 El Muglad Sudan
69 G3 Elmwood Can.
68 C5 Elmwood IL U.S.A.
68 A3 Elmwood WI U.S.A.
6 K5 Elnesvågen Norway
81 B3 El Nevado, Cerro mt Col.
43 A4 El Nido Phil.
87 F3 El Obeid Sudan
81 C3 Elorza Venez.
86 C1 El Oued Alg.
73 G5 Eloy U.S.A.
65 B7 El Palmito Mex.
81 E2 El Pao Bolívar Venez.
81 C2 El Pao Cojedes Venez.
68 C5 El Paso IL U.S.A.
63 F6 El Paso TX U.S.A.
10 C2 Elphin U.K.
72 C3 El Portal U.S.A.
15 H2 El Prat de Llobregat Spain
15 C4 El Puerto de Santa María Spain
El Qâhira see Cairo
28 D6 El Qantara Egypt
28 E7 El Quweira Jordan
65 D5 El Reno U.S.A.
68 B4 Elroy U.S.A.
56 B2 Elsa Can.
28 C7 El Saff Egypt
28 D6 El Sâlhîya Egypt
74 C4 El Salto Mex.
43 C4 El Salvador Phil.
53 H8 El Salvador country Central America
81 C3 El Samán de Apure Venez.
69 F1 Elsas Can.
13 G2 Else r. Ger.
35 H2 Elsen Nur l. China
28 D7 El Shatt Egypt
81 D2 El Sombrero Venez.
83 C2 El Sosneado Arg.
El Suweis see Suez
95 L9 Eltanin Fracture Zone sea feature Pac. Oc.
18 C6 El Tarf Alg.
15 C1 El Teleno mt Spain
28 E7 El Thamad Egypt
81 D2 El Tigre Venez.
13 J5 Eltmann Ger.
81 C2 El Tocuyo Venez.
21 H5 El'ton Rus. Fed.
21 H5 El'ton, Ozero l. Rus. Fed.
62 C2 Eltopia U.S.A.
81 E2 El Toro Venez.
83 E2 El Trébol Arg.
81 C3 El Tuparro, Parque Nacional nat. park Col.
87 F2 El Tur Egypt
80 B8 El Turbio Chile
33 C2 Eluru India
7 U7 Elva Estonia
81 A3 El Valle Col.
10 E5 Elvanfoot U.K.
15 C3 Elvas Port.
7 M6 Elverum Norway
81 B3 El Viejo mt Col.
81 C2 El Vigía Venez.
78 D5 Elvira Brazil
88 E3 El Wak Kenya
68 E5 Elwood U.S.A.
13 J3 Elxleben Ger.
9 H5 Ely U.K.
68 B2 Ely MN U.S.A.
73 E2 Ely NV U.S.A.
70 B4 Elyria U.S.A.
13 G4 Elz Ger.
13 H2 Elze Ger.
49 G3 Émaé i. Vanuatu
30 D2 Emāmrūd Iran
31 H2 Emām Şaḩēb Afgh.
29 L5 Emāmzadeh Naşrod Dīn Iran
7 O8 Emån r. Sweden
82 B2 Emas, Parque Nacional das nat. park Brazil
26 D2 Emba Kazak.
91 H3 Embalenhle S. Africa
57 G3 Embarras Portage Can.
82 C2 Emborcação, Represa de resr Brazil
71 F2 Embrun Can.
88 D4 Embu Kenya
12 F1 Emden Ger.
39 B4 Emei China
39 B4 Emei Shan mt China
50 E4 Emerald Vic. Austr.
48 E4 Emerald Austr.
59 G3 Emeril Can.
57 K5 Emerson Can.
28 B2 Emet Turkey
91 J2 eMgwenya S. Africa
73 E3 Emigrant Valley v. U.S.A.
91 J2 eMijindini S. Africa
87 D3 Emi Koussi mt Chad
19 M3 Eminska Planina h. Bulg.
28 C2 Emir D. mt Turkey
28 C2 Emirdağ Turkey
7 O8 Emmaboda Sweden
7 S7 Emmaste Estonia
12 D2 Emmeloord Neth.
12 F4 Emmelshausen Ger.
12 E2 Emmen Neth.
16 D7 Emmen Switz.
12 E3 Emmerich Ger.
33 B3 Emmiganuru India
65 C6 Emory Pk summit U.S.A.
74 B3 Empalme Mex.
91 J4 Empangeni S. Africa
80 E3 Empedrado Arg.
94 G3 Emperor Seamount Chain sea feature Pac. Oc.
18 D3 Empoli Italy
64 D4 Emporia KS U.S.A.
70 E6 Emporia VA U.S.A.
70 D4 Emporium U.S.A.
57 G4 Empress Can.
31 E3 'Emrānī Iran
12 F2 Ems r. Ger.
69 H3 Emsdale Can.
12 F2 Emsdetten Ger.
12 F1 Ems-Jade-Kanal canal Ger.
12 F2 Emsland reg. Ger.
91 H3 Emzinoni S. Africa
6 N5 Enafors Sweden
37 F7 Enarotali Indon.
41 E7 Ena-san mt Japan
74 A2 Encantada, Co de la mt Mex.
83 G1 Encantadas, Serra das h. Brazil
43 B3 Encanto, Cape pt Phil.
80 E3 Encarnación Para.
65 D6 Encinal U.S.A.
72 D5 Encinitas U.S.A.
63 F5 Encino U.S.A.
50 B3 Encounter Bay b. Austr.
82 E1 Encruzilhada Brazil
83 G1 Encruzilhada do Sul Brazil
56 D4 Endako Can.
44 B5 Endau Malaysia
48 E3 Endeavour Strait chan. Austr.
37 E7 Endeh Indon.
92 D4 Enderby Land reg. Ant.
71 E3 Endicott U.S.A.
56 C3 Endicott Arm in. U.S.A.
54 C3 Endicott Mts mts U.S.A.
83 E3 Energía Arg.
21 E6 Enerhodar Ukr.
94 F5 Enewetak i. Pac. Oc.
18 D6 Enfidaville Tunisia
71 G3 Enfield U.S.A.
68 E2 Engadine U.S.A.
6 L5 Engan Norway
43 B2 Engaño, Cape c. Phil.
Engaños, Río de los r. see Yari
40 H2 Engaru Japan
91 G5 Engcobo S. Africa
21 H5 Engel's Rus. Fed.
12 C1 Engelschmangat chan. Neth.
45 B4 Enggano i. Indon.
12 C4 Enghien Belgium
9 E5 England div. U.K.
59 J3 Englee Can.
67 F5 Englehard U.S.A.
69 H2 Englehart Can.
9 D7 English Channel str. France/U.K.
21 G7 Enguri r. Georgia
91 J4 Enhlalakahle S. Africa
65 D4 Enid U.S.A.
40 G3 Eniwa Japan
12 D2 Enkhuizen Neth.
7 P7 Enköping Sweden
18 F6 Enna Sicily Italy
57 J2 Ennadai Lake l. Can.
87 E3 En Nahud Sudan
87 E3 Ennedi, Massif mts Chad
11 D4 Ennell, Lough l. Rep. of Ireland
64 C2 Enning U.S.A.

# F

# G

35 G4 Goalpara India
10 C5 Goat Fell *h.* U.K.
88 E3 Goba Eth.
89 B6 Gobabis Namibia
90 C3 Gobas Namibia
83 E1 Gobernador Crespo Arg.
83 C3 Gobernador Duval Arg.
80 B7 Gobernador Gregores Arg.
22 H5 Gobi *des.* Mongolia
41 D8 Gobō Japan
12 E3 Goch Ger.
89 B6 Gochas Namibia
44 C3 Go Công Vietnam
9 G6 Godalming U.K.
33 C2 Godavari *r.* India
33 C2 Godavari, Mouths of the *river mouth* India
59 G4 Godbout Can.
72 C3 Goddard, Mt *mt* U.S.A.
88 E3 Godere Eth.
69 G4 Goderich Can.
34 C5 Godhra India
83 C2 Godoy Cruz Arg.
57 L3 Gods *r.* Can.
57 L4 Gods Lake *l.* Can.
57 M2 Gods Mercy, Bay of *b.* Can.
Godwin Austen *mt see* K2
12 B3 Goedereede Neth.
58 E4 Goéland, Lac au *l.* Can.
59 H2 Goélands, Lac aux *l.* Can.
12 B3 Goes Neth.
69 E2 Goetzville U.S.A.
73 E4 Goffs U.S.A.
62 G2 Gogama Can.
68 C2 Gogebic, Lake *l.* U.S.A.
68 C2 Gogebic Range *h.* U.S.A.
Gogra *r. see* Ghaghara
34 D4 Gohad India
79 M5 Goiana Brazil
82 C2 Goiandira Brazil
82 C2 Goiânia Brazil
82 B1 Goiás Brazil
82 B2 Goiás *div.* Brazil
82 B4 Goio-Erê Brazil
34 C3 Gojra Pak.
33 A2 Gokak India
21 C7 Gökçeada *i.* Turkey
28 B2 Gökçedağ Turkey
35 G3 Gokhar La *pass* China
28 E1 Gökirmak *r.* Turkey
31 F5 Gokprosh Hills *mts* Pak.
28 F2 Göksun Turkey
28 E3 Göksu Nehri *r.* Turkey
89 C5 Gokwe Zimbabwe
7 L6 Gol Norway
34 E3 Gola India
35 H4 Golaghat India
28 F3 Gölbaşı Turkey
24 K2 Gol'chikha Rus. Fed.
28 B1 Gölcük Turkey
17 J3 Gołdap Pol.
13 L1 Goldberg Ger.
49 F4 Gold Coast Austr.
86 B4 Gold Coast *coastal area* Ghana
56 F4 Golden Can.
51 D4 Golden Bay *b.* N.Z.
13 J3 Goldene Aue *reg.* Ger.
72 A3 Golden Gate National Recreation Area *res.* U.S.A.
56 D5 Golden Hinde *mt* Can.
13 G2 Goldenstedt Ger.
11 C5 Golden Vale *lowland* Rep. of Ireland
72 D3 Goldfield U.S.A.
72 D3 Gold Point U.S.A.
67 E5 Goldsboro U.S.A.
65 D6 Goldthwaite U.S.A.
29 J1 Göle Turkey
31 F3 Golestān Afgh.
30 D4 Golestānak Iran
72 C4 Goleta U.S.A.
65 D6 Goliad U.S.A.
42 A1 Golin Baixing China
25 F1 Gölköy Turkey
13 L2 Golm Ger.
29 K3 Golmānkhānen Iran
36 B3 Golmud China
35 H1 Golmud He *r.* China
43 B3 Golo *i.* Phil.
40 J3 Golovnino Rus. Fed.
30 C3 Golpāyegān Iran
28 C1 Gölpazarı Turkey
12 E3 Golspie U.K.
31 F3 Gol Vardeh Iran
19 L4 Golyama Syutkya *mt* Bulg.
19 L4 Golyam Persenk *mt* Bulg.
13 L2 Golzow Ger.
88 C4 Goma Congo(Zaire)
35 G3 Gomang Co *salt l.* China
34 E4 Gomati *r.* India
44 □ Gombak, Bukit *h.* Sing.
86 D3 Gombe Nigeria
88 D4 Gombe *r.* Tanz.
87 D3 Gombi Nigeria
86 A2 Gomera, La *i.* Canary Is
65 C7 Gómez Palacio Mex.
65 D7 Gómez, Presa M. R. *resr* Mex.
30 D2 Gomīshān Iran
13 K2 Gommern Ger.
35 F2 Gomo Co *salt l.* China
31 E2 Gonābād Iran
Gonabad *see* Jūymand
75 K5 Gonaïves Haiti
91 J1 Gonarezhou National Park Zimbabwe
75 K5 Gonâve, Île de la *i.* Haiti
30 D2 Gonbad-e Kavus Iran
35 E4 Gonda India
34 B5 Gondal India
88 D2 Gonder Eth.
34 E5 Gondia India
28 A1 Gönen Turkey
39 D4 Gong'an China
39 D5 Gongcheng China
39 A4 Gongga Shan *mt* China
38 A2 Gonghe China
38 E1 Gonghui China
82 E1 Gongogi *r.* Brazil
86 D3 Gongola *r.* Nigeria
39 B5 Gongwang Shan *mts* China
38 D3 Gong Xian *Henan* China
39 B4 Gong Xian *Sichuan* China
91 H6 Gonubie S. Africa
72 B3 Gonzales *CA* U.S.A.
65 D6 Gonzales *TX* U.S.A.
83 D2 González Moreno Arg.
70 E6 Goochland U.S.A.
92 C6 Goodenough, C. *c.* Ant.
48 F2 Goodenough I. *i.* P.N.G.
69 H3 Gooderham Can.
68 E3 Good Harbor Bay *b.* U.S.A.
90 C7 Good Hope, Cape of *c.* S. Africa
62 D3 Gooding U.S.A.
64 C4 Goodland U.S.A.
8 G4 Goole U.K.
50 E3 Goolgowi Austr.
50 G2 Goolma Austr.
50 G2 Gooloogong Austr.
50 B3 Goolwa Austr.
48 F4 Goondiwindi Austr.
59 H3 Goose *r.* Can.
62 B3 Goose L. *l.* U.S.A.
33 B3 Gooty India
16 D6 Göppingen Ger.
35 E4 Gorakhpur India
19 H3 Goražde Bos.-Herz.
20 G3 Gorchukha Rus. Fed.
67 E7 Gorda Cay *i.* Bahamas
28 B2 Gördes Turkey
17 P4 Gordeyevka Rus. Fed.
10 F5 Gordon U.K.
48 E6 Gordon, L. *l.* Austr.
56 G2 Gordon Lake *l.* Can.
70 D5 Gordon Lake *l.* U.S.A.
70 D5 Gordonsville U.S.A.
87 D4 Goré Chad
88 D3 Gorē Eth.
51 B7 Gore N.Z.
69 F3 Gore Bay Can.
10 E5 Gorebridge U.K.
11 E5 Gorey Rep. of Ireland
31 E4 Gorg Iran
30 D2 Gorgān Iran
81 A4 Gorgona, I. *i.* Col.
71 H2 Gorham U.S.A.
21 H7 Gori Georgia
12 C3 Gorinchem Neth.
29 L2 Goris Armenia
18 E2 Gorizia Italy
Gor'kiy *see* Nizhniy Novgorod
21 H5 Gor'ko-Solenoye, Ozero *l.* Rus. Fed.
20 G3 Gor'kovskoye Vdkhr. *resr* Rus. Fed.
17 K6 Gorlice Pol.
16 G5 Görlitz Ger.
34 D4 Gormi India
19 L3 Gorna Oryakhovitsa Bulg.
19 J2 Gornji Milanovac Yugo.
18 G3 Gornji Vakuf Bos.-Herz.
36 A1 Gorno-Altaysk Rus. Fed.
40 G1 Gornozavodsk Rus. Fed.
24 K4 Gornyak Rus. Fed.
40 C2 Gornye Klyuchi Rus. Fed.
40 C2 Gornyy *Primorskiy Kray* Rus. Fed.
21 J5 Gornyy *Saratov. Obl.* Rus. Fed.
21 H5 Gornyy Balykley Rus. Fed.
21 G5 Gorodets Rus. Fed.
21 H5 Gorodishche Rus. Fed.
21 G6 Gorodovikovsk Rus. Fed.
48 E2 Goroka P.N.G.
50 C4 Goroke Austr.
20 G3 Gorokhovets Rus. Fed.
86 B3 Gorom Gorom Burkina
89 D5 Gorongosa Moz.
37 E6 Gorontalo Indon.
21 F5 Gorshechnoye Rus. Fed.
11 C4 Gort Rep. of Ireland
11 C2 Gortahork Rep. of Ireland
82 D1 Gorutuba *r.* Brazil
21 F6 Goryachiy Klyuch Rus. Fed.
13 L2 Görzke Ger.
16 G4 Gorzów Wielkopolski Pol.
50 H2 Gosford Austr.
8 F2 Gosforth U.K.
68 E5 Goshen *IN* U.S.A.
71 F4 Goshen *NY* U.S.A.
40 G4 Goshogawara Japan
13 J3 Goslar Ger.
18 F2 Gospić Croatia
9 F7 Gosport U.K.
19 J4 Gostivar Macedonia
Göteborg *see* Gothenburg
7 N7 Götene Sweden
13 J4 Gotha Ger.
7 M8 Gothenburg Sweden
64 C3 Gothenburg U.S.A.
7 Q8 Gotland *i.* Sweden
19 K4 Gotse Delchev Bulg.
7 Q7 Gotska Sandön *i.* Sweden
41 C7 Götsu Japan
13 H3 Göttingen Ger.
56 E4 Gott Peak *summit* Can.
Gottwaldow *see* Zlín
42 A3 Goubangzi China
12 C2 Gouda Neth.
86 A3 Goudiri Senegal
86 D3 Goudoumaria Niger
68 E1 Goudreau Can.
96 J8 Gough Island *i.* Atl. Ocean
58 F4 Gouin, Réservoir *resr* Can.
68 E2 Goulais River Can.
50 G3 Goulburn Austr.
50 H2 Goulburn *r.* *N.S.W.* Austr.
50 E4 Goulburn *r.* *Vic.* Austr.
48 D3 Goulburn Is *is* Austr.
68 E2 Gould City U.S.A.
92 B4 Gould Coast *coastal area* Ant.
86 B3 Goundam Mali
15 G4 Gouraya Alg.
86 D3 Gouré Niger
90 D7 Gourits *r.* S. Africa
86 B3 Gourma-Rharous Mali
14 E2 Gournay-en-Bray France
50 G4 Gourock Range *mts* Austr.
12 A5 Goussainville France
71 F2 Gouverneur U.S.A.
57 H5 Govenlock Can.
82 E2 Governador Valadares Brazil
43 C5 Governor Generoso Phil.
67 E7 Governor's Harbour Bahamas
36 B2 Govĭ Altayn Nuruu *mts* Mongolia
35 E4 Govind Ballash Pant Sāgar *resr* India
34 D3 Govind Sagar *resr* India
31 G2 Govurdak Turkm.
70 D3 Gowanda U.S.A.
31 G4 Gowārān Afgh.
30 D4 Gowd-e Aḩmad Iran
30 E3 Gowd-e Hasht Tekkeh *waterhole* Iran
30 D4 Gowd-e Mokh *l.* Iran
9 C6 Gower *pen.* U.K.
69 G2 Gowganda Can.
31 E4 Gowk Iran
11 D4 Gowna, Lough *l.* Rep. of Ireland
80 E3 Goya Arg.
29 L1 Göyçay Azer.
29 H2 Göynük Turkey
40 G5 Goyō-zan *mt* Japan
29 M2 Göytäpä Azer.
31 F3 Gōzareh Afgh.
28 G2 Gözene Turkey
34 E2 Gozha Co *salt l.* China
18 F6 Gozo *i.* Malta
90 F6 Graaff-Reinet S. Africa
90 C6 Graafwater S. Africa
13 J4 Grabfeld *plain* Ger.
86 B4 Grabo Côte d'Ivoire
90 C7 Grabouw S. Africa
13 K1 Grabow Ger.
18 F2 Gračac Croatia
69 J2 Gracefield Can.
13 L3 Gräfenhainichen Ger.
13 K5 Grafenwöhr Ger.
49 F4 Grafton Austr.
64 D1 Grafton *ND* U.S.A.
68 D4 Grafton *WV* U.S.A.
70 C5 Grafton *WV* U.S.A.
73 E2 Grafton, Mt *mt* U.S.A.
65 D5 Graham U.S.A.
Graham Bell Island *i. see* Greem-Bell, Ostrov
55 J2 Graham I. *i.* Can.
56 C4 Graham Island *i.* Can.
71 J2 Graham Lake *l.* U.S.A.
92 B2 Graham Land *reg.* Ant.
73 H5 Graham, Mt *mt* U.S.A.
91 G6 Grahamstown S. Africa
11 E5 Graigue Rep. of Ireland
86 A4 Grain Coast *coastal area* Liberia
79 J5 Grajaú Brazil
10 B1 Gralisgeir *i.* U.K.
19 J4 Grámmos *mt* Greece
10 D4 Grampian Mountains U.K.
50 D4 Grampians *mts* Austr.
90 C5 Granaatboskolk S. Africa
81 B4 Granada Col.
75 G6 Granada Nic.
15 E4 Granada Spain
64 C4 Granada U.S.A.
11 D4 Granard Rep. of Ireland
83 C3 Gran Bajo Salitroso *salt flat* Arg.
58 F4 Granby Can.
86 A2 Gran Canaria *i.* Canary Is
80 D3 Gran Chaco *reg.* Arg./Para.
66 C3 Grand *r.* *MI* U.S.A.
64 E3 Grand *r.* *MO* U.S.A.
67 E7 Grand Bahama *i.* Bahamas
59 J4 Grand Bank Can.
96 F2 Grand Banks *sea feature* Atl. Ocean
86 B4 Grand-Bassam Côte d'Ivoire
59 G4 Grand Bay Can.
69 G4 Grand Bend Can.
11 D4 Grand Canal *canal* Rep. of Ireland
73 F3 Grand Canyon U.S.A.
73 F3 Grand Canyon *gorge* U.S.A.
73 F3 Grand Canyon Nat. Park U.S.A.
75 H5 Grand Cayman *i.* Cayman Is
57 G4 Grand Centre Can.
62 C2 Grand Coulee U.S.A.
83 C3 Grande *r.* Arg.
79 J6 Grande *r.* *Bahia* Brazil
82 B2 Grande *r.* *São Paulo* Brazil
80 C8 Grande, Bahía *b.* Arg.
56 F4 Grande Cache Can.
14 H4 Grande Casse, Pointe de la *mt* France
89 E5 Grande Comore *i.* Comoros
83 F1 Grande, Cuchilla *h.* Uru.
82 D3 Grande, Ilha *i.* Brazil
56 F3 Grande Prairie Can.
87 D3 Grand Erg de Bilma *sand dunes* Niger
86 B1 Grand Erg Occidental *des.* Alg.
86 C2 Grand Erg Oriental *des.* Alg.
59 H4 Grande-Rivière Can.
58 F3 Grande Rivière de la Baleine *r.* Can.
62 C2 Grande Ronde *r.* U.S.A.
81 E4 Grande, Serra *mt* Brazil
59 G4 Grand Falls *N.B.* Can.
59 J4 Grand Falls *Nfld* Can.
56 F5 Grand Forks Can.
64 D2 Grand Forks U.S.A.
71 F3 Grand Gorge U.S.A.
71 K2 Grand Harbour Can.
68 D4 Grand Haven U.S.A.
56 F2 Grandin, Lac *l.* Can.
64 D3 Grand Island U.S.A.
68 D2 Grand Island *i.* U.S.A.
65 F6 Grand Isle *LA* U.S.A.
71 J1 Grand Isle *ME* U.S.A.
73 H2 Grand Junction U.S.A.
86 B4 Grand-Lahou Côte d'Ivoire
59 G4 Grand Lake *l.* *N.B.* Can.
59 J4 Grand Lake *l.* *Nfld* Can.
59 H3 Grand Lake *l.* *Nfld* Can.
65 E6 Grand Lake *l.* *LA* U.S.A.
71 K2 Grand Lake *l.* *ME* U.S.A.
69 F3 Grand Lake *l.* *MI* U.S.A.
71 J1 Grand Lake Matagamon *l.* U.S.A.
70 A4 Grand Lake St Marys *l.* U.S.A.
71 J1 Grand Lake Seboeis *l.* U.S.A.
71 K2 Grand Lake Stream U.S.A.
68 E4 Grand Ledge U.S.A.
59 G5 Grand Manan I. *i.* Can.
68 E2 Grand Marais *MI* U.S.A.
68 B2 Grand Marais *MN* U.S.A.
59 F4 Grand-Mère Can.
15 B3 Grândola Port.
49 G3 Grand Passage *chan.* New Caledonia
68 C2 Grand Portage U.S.A.
57 K4 Grand Rapids Can.
68 E4 Grand Rapids *MI* U.S.A.
64 E2 Grand Rapids *MN* U.S.A.
49 G3 Grand Récif de Cook *rf* New Caledonia
49 G4 Grand Récif du Sud *rf* New Caledonia
62 E3 Grand Teton *mt* U.S.A.
62 E3 Grand Teton Nat. Park U.S.A.
68 E3 Grand Traverse Bay *b.* U.S.A.
59 G4 Grand Vallée Can.
62 C2 Grandview U.S.A.
73 F3 Grand Wash *r.* U.S.A.
73 E4 Grand Wash Cliffs *cliff* U.S.A.
83 B2 Graneros Chile
11 D6 Grange Rep. of Ireland
62 E3 Granger U.S.A.
7 O6 Grängesberg Sweden
62 C2 Grangeville U.S.A.
56 D3 Granisle Can.
64 E2 Granite Falls U.S.A.
59 J4 Granite Lake *l.* Can.
73 E4 Granite Mts *mts* U.S.A.
62 E2 Granite Peak *summit MT* U.S.A.
73 F1 Granite Peak *summit UT* U.S.A.
18 E6 Granitola, Capo *c.* *Sicily* Italy
80 C6 Gran Laguna Salada *l.* Arg.
7 O7 Gränna Sweden
18 B2 Gran Paradiso *mt* Italy
16 E7 Gran Pilastro *mt* Austria/Italy
13 L3 Granschütz Ger.
13 M1 Gransee Ger.
9 G5 Grantham U.K.
92 A4 Grant I. *i.* Ant.
72 D2 Grant, Mt *mt* *NV* U.S.A.
72 C2 Grant, Mt *mt* *NV* U.S.A.
10 E3 Grantown-on-Spey U.K.
73 E2 Grant Range *mts* U.S.A.
63 F5 Grants U.S.A.
62 B3 Grants Pass U.S.A.
14 D2 Granville France
68 C5 Granville *IL* U.S.A.
71 G3 Granville *NY* U.S.A.
57 J3 Granville Lake *l.* Can.
82 D2 Grão Mogol Brazil
72 C4 Grapevine U.S.A.
72 D3 Grapevine Mts *mts* U.S.A.
71 G3 Graphite U.S.A.
91 J2 Graskop S. Africa
57 G2 Gras, Lac de *l.* Can.
71 F2 Grass *r.* U.S.A.
14 H5 Grasse France
8 F3 Grassington U.K.
57 H5 Grasslands Nat. Park Can.
62 E2 Grassrange U.S.A.
57 J4 Grass River Prov. Park *res.* Can.
72 B2 Grass Valley U.S.A.
67 E7 Grassy Cr. *r.* Bahamas
7 N7 Grästorp Sweden
68 B4 Gratiot U.S.A.
15 G1 Graus Spain
57 J2 Gravel Hill Lake *l.* Can.
12 A4 Gravelines France
91 J1 Gravelotte S. Africa
69 H3 Gravenhurst Can.
9 H6 Gravesend U.K.
18 G4 Gravina in Puglia Italy
68 E3 Grawn U.S.A.
14 G3 Gray France
71 H3 Gray U.S.A.
68 E3 Grayling U.S.A.
9 H6 Grays U.K.
62 A2 Grays Harbor *in.* U.S.A.
62 E3 Grays L. *l.* U.S.A.
70 B5 Grayson U.S.A.
59 H1 Gray Strait *chan.* Can.
66 B4 Grayville U.S.A.
16 G7 Graz Austria
67 E7 Great Abaco *i.* Bahamas
48 C5 Great Australian Bight *g.* Austr.
9 H6 Great Baddow U.K.
75 J3 Great Bahama Bank *sea feature* Bahamas
51 E2 Great Barrier Island *i.* N.Z.
48 E3 Great Barrier Reef *rf* Austr.
71 G3 Great Barrington U.S.A.
63 C4 Great Basin *basin* U.S.A.
73 E2 Great Basin Nat. Park U.S.A.
71 F5 Great Bay *b.* U.S.A.
56 E1 Great Bear *r.* Can.
56 E1 Great Bear Lake *l.* Can.
64 D4 Great Bend U.S.A.
90 C6 Great Berg *r.* S. Africa
10 B2 Great Bernera *i.* U.K.
11 A5 Great Blasket I. *i.* Rep. of Ireland
8 D3 Great Clifton U.K.
10 D5 Great Cumbrae *i.* U.K.
50 F4 Great Dividing Range *mts* Austr.
8 G3 Great Driffield U.K.
69 F3 Great Duck I. *i.* Can.
71 F5 Great Egg Harbor *in.* U.S.A.
75 H4 Greater Antilles *is* Caribbean Sea
75 J4 Great Exuma *i.* Bahamas
62 E2 Great Falls U.S.A.
91 G6 Great Fish *r.* S. Africa
91 G6 Great Fish Point *pt* S. Africa
35 F4 Great Gandak *r.* India
67 E7 Great Guana Cay *i.* Bahamas
67 E7 Great Harbour Cay *i.* Bahamas
75 K4 Great Inagua *i.* Bahamas
90 D5 Great Karoo *plat.* S. Africa
91 H6 Great Kei *r.* S. Africa
48 E6 Great Lake *l.* Austr.
9 E5 Great Malvern U.K.
70 A5 Great Miami *r.* U.S.A.
87 F2 Great Oasis, The *oasis* Egypt
9 D4 Great Ormes Head *hd* U.K.
9 H5 Great Ouse *r.* U.K.
71 G4 Great Peconic Bay *b.* U.S.A.
71 H4 Great Pt *pt* U.S.A.
9 D5 Great Rhos *h.* U.K.
88 D4 Great Ruaha *r.* Tanz.
71 F3 Great Sacandaga L. *l.* U.S.A.
18 B2 Great St Bernard Pass Italy/Switz.
67 E7 Great Sale Cay *i.* Bahamas
62 D3 Great Salt Lake *l.* U.S.A.
62 D3 Great Salt Lake Desert U.S.A.
87 E2 Great Sand Sea *des.* Egypt/Libya
48 C4 Great Sandy Desert Austr.
49 H3 Great Sea Reef *rf* Fiji
54 G3 Great Slave Lake *N.W.T.* Can.
56 G2 Great Slave Lake *l.* Can.
67 D5 Great Smoky Mts *mts* U.S.A.
67 D5 Great Smoky Mts Nat. Park U.S.A.
56 E3 Great Snow Mtn *mt* Can.
71 G4 Great South Bay *b.* U.S.A.
9 H7 Greatstone-on-Sea U.K.
9 J6 Great Stour *r.* U.K.
9 C7 Great Torrington U.K.
48 C4 Great Victoria Desert Austr.
38 F1 Great Wall China
9 H6 Great Waltham U.K.
71 K2 Great Wass I. *i.* U.S.A.
8 F3 Great Whernside *h.* U.K.
9 J5 Great Yarmouth U.K.
29 J3 Great Zab *r.* Iraq
18 E4 Greco, Monte *mt* Italy
15 D2 Gredos, Sa de *mts* Spain
5 F5 Greece *country* Europe
62 F3 Greeley U.S.A.
55 K1 Greely Fiord *in.* Can.
24 H1 Greem-Bell, Ostrov *i.* Rus. Fed.
66 C4 Green *r.* *KY* U.S.A.
73 H2 Green *r.* *UT/WY* U.S.A.
69 H3 Greenbank Can.
68 C3 Green Bay U.S.A.
68 D3 Green Bay *b.* U.S.A.
50 H4 Green C. *hd* Austr.
68 E3 Greencastle U.K.
66 C4 Greencastle U.S.A.
67 E7 Green Cay *i.* Bahamas
67 D6 Green Cove Springs U.S.A.
68 A4 Greene *IA* U.S.A.
71 F3 Greene *NY* U.S.A.
67 D4 Greeneville U.S.A.
72 B3 Greenfield *CA* U.S.A.
68 E6 Greenfield *IN* U.S.A.
71 G3 Greenfield *MA* U.S.A.
70 B5 Greenfield *OH* U.S.A.
68 C4 Greenfield *WV* U.S.A.
43 A4 Green Island Bay *b.* Phil.
57 H4 Green Lake Can.
68 C4 Green Lake *l.* U.S.A.
53 M2 Greenland *terr.* Arctic Ocean
96 J1 Greenland Basin *sea feature* Arctic Ocean
10 F5 Greenlaw U.K.
71 G2 Green Mountains U.S.A.
10 D5 Greenock U.K.
11 E3 Greenore Rep. of Ireland
71 G4 Greenport U.S.A.
63 E4 Green River *UT* U.S.A.
62 E3 Green River *WY* U.S.A.
67 E4 Greensboro U.S.A.
66 C4 Greensburg *IN* U.S.A.
65 D4 Greensburg *KS* U.S.A.
70 D4 Greensburg *PA* U.S.A.
10 C3 Greenstone Point *pt* U.K.
61 L5 Green Swamp *swamp NC* U.S.A.
70 B5 Greenup U.S.A.
71 F2 Green Valley Can.
73 G6 Green Valley U.S.A.
68 C5 Greenview U.S.A.
86 B4 Greenville Liberia
67 C6 Greenville *AL* U.S.A.
72 B1 Greenville *CA* U.S.A.
67 D6 Greenville *FL* U.S.A.
71 J2 Greenville *ME* U.S.A.
68 E4 Greenville *MI* U.S.A.
65 F5 Greenville *MS* U.S.A.
67 E5 Greenville *NC* U.S.A.
71 H3 Greenville *NH* U.S.A.
70 A4 Greenville *OH* U.S.A.
70 C4 Greenville *PA* U.S.A.
67 D5 Greenville *SC* U.S.A.
65 D5 Greenville *TX* U.S.A.
57 J4 Greenwater Provincial Park *res.* Can.
50 H3 Greenwell Point Austr.
71 G4 Greenwich *CT* U.S.A.
71 G3 Greenwich *NY* U.S.A.
73 G2 Greenwich *UT* U.S.A.
65 F5 Greenwood *MS* U.S.A.
67 D5 Greenwood *SC* U.S.A.
65 E5 Greers Ferry Lake *l.* U.S.A.
64 D3 Gregory U.S.A.
48 C4 Gregory Lake *salt flat* Austr.
48 E3 Gregory Range *h.* Austr.
16 F3 Greifswald Ger.
13 L4 Greiz Ger.
28 E4 Greko, Cape *c.* Cyprus
7 M8 Grenå Denmark
65 F5 Grenada U.S.A.
53 K8 Grenada *country* Caribbean Sea
14 E5 Grenade France
7 M8 Grenen *spit* Denmark
50 G2 Grenfell Austr.
57 J4 Grenfell Can.
14 G4 Grenoble France
81 E1 Grenville Grenada
48 E3 Grenville, C. *hd* Austr.
62 B2 Gresham U.S.A.
8 F3 Greta *r.* U.K.
10 E6 Gretna U.K.
65 F6 Gretna U.S.A.
13 J3 Greußen Ger.
12 B3 Grevelingen *chan.* Neth.
12 F2 Greven Ger.
19 J4 Grevena Greece
12 D3 Grevenbicht Neth.
12 E3 Grevenbroich Ger.
12 E5 Grevenmacher Lux.
16 E4 Grevesmühlen Ger.
51 C5 Grey *r.* N.Z.
62 E2 Greybull U.S.A.
56 B2 Grey Hunter Pk *summit* Can.
59 J3 Grey Is *is* Can.
51 C5 Greymouth N.Z.
48 E4 Grey Range *h.* Austr.
91 J4 Greytown S. Africa
12 C4 Grez-Doiceau Belgium
21 G5 Gribanovskiy Rus. Fed.
72 B2 Gridley *CA* U.S.A.
68 C5 Gridley *IL* U.S.A.
67 C5 Griffin U.S.A.
50 F3 Griffith Austr.
69 J3 Griffith Can.
54 F2 Griffiths Point *pt* Can.
13 L3 Grimma Ger.
16 F3 Grimmen Ger.
69 H4 Grimsby Can.
8 G4 Grimsby U.K.
6 E3 Grímsey *i.* Iceland
56 F3 Grimshaw Can.
6 E4 Grímsstaðir Iceland
7 L7 Grimstad Norway
6 B5 Grindavík Iceland
7 L9 Grindsted Denmark
19 N2 Grindul Chituc *spit* Romania
64 E3 Grinnell U.S.A.
91 H5 Griqualand East *reg.* S. Africa
90 E4 Griqualand West *reg.* S. Africa
90 E4 Griquatown S. Africa
55 K2 Grise Fiord Can.
45 B3 Grisik Indon.
9 J7 Gris Nez, Cap *pt* France
10 F2 Gritley U.K.
18 G2 Grmeč *mts* Bos.-Herz.
12 C3 Grobbendonk Belgium
91 H2 Groblersdal S. Africa
90 E4 Groblershoop S. Africa
40 B2 Grodekovo Rus. Fed.
Grodno *see* Hrodna
90 B5 Groen *watercourse* Northern Cape S. Africa
90 E5 Groen *watercourse* Northern Cape S. Africa
14 C3 Groix, Île de *i.* France
18 D6 Grombalia Tunisia
12 F2 Gronau (Westfalen) Ger.
6 N4 Grong Norway
12 E1 Groningen Neth.
12 E1 Groninger Wad *tidal flats* Neth.
73 E3 Groom L. *l.* U.S.A.
90 D3 Groot-Aar Pan *salt pan* S. Africa
90 E7 Groot Brakrivier S. Africa
91 H3 Grootdraaidam *dam* S. Africa
90 D4 Grootdrink S. Africa
48 D3 Groote Eylandt *i.* Austr.
89 B5 Grootfontein Namibia
90 C3 Groot Karas Berg *plat.* Namibia
91 J1 Groot Letaba *r.* S. Africa
91 G2 Groot Marico S. Africa
90 D6 Groot Swartberg *mts* S. Africa
90 D5 Grootvloer *salt pan* S. Africa
91 G6 Groot Winterberg *mt* S. Africa
68 E3 Gros Cap U.S.A.
59 J4 Gros Morne Nat. Pk *nat. park* Can.
13 J3 Großengottern Ger.
13 G2 Großenkneten Ger.
13 H4 Großenlüder Ger.
13 J4 Großer Beerberg *h.* Ger.
13 J4 Großer Gleichberg *h.* Ger.
16 G7 Grosser Speikkogel *mt* Austria
18 D3 Grosseto Italy
13 G5 Groß-Gerau Ger.
18 E1 Großglockner *mt* Austria
13 J2 Groß Oesingen Ger.
13 K3 Großrudestedt Ger.
13 M2 Groß Schönebeck Ger.
90 C1 Gross Ums Namibia
62 E3 Gros Ventre Range *mts* U.S.A.
59 J3 Groswater Bay *b.* Can.
71 E3 Groton U.S.A.
70 D5 Grottoes U.S.A.
56 F3 Grouard Can.
58 D4 Groundhog *r.* Can.
12 D1 Grouw Neth.
70 C4 Grove City U.S.A.
67 C6 Grove Hill U.S.A.
72 B3 Groveland U.S.A.
92 D5 Grove Mts *mts* Ant.
72 B4 Grover Beach U.S.A.
71 H2 Groveton U.S.A.

73 F5 Harcuvar Mts *mts* U.S.A.
34 D5 Harda Khās India
7 K6 Hardangervidda *plat.* Norway
7 K6 Hardangervidda Nasjonalpark *nat. park* Norway
90 B2 Hardap *div.* Namibia
90 B2 Hardap Dam *dam* Namibia
12 E2 Hardenberg Neth.
45 E2 Harden, Bukit *mt* Indon.
12 D2 Harderwijk Neth.
90 C5 Hardeveld *mts* S. Africa
13 H5 Hardheim Ger.
62 F2 Hardin U.S.A.
91 H5 Harding S. Africa
57 G4 Hardisty Can.
56 F2 Hardisty Lake *l.* Can.
34 E4 Hardoi India
71 G2 Hardwick U.S.A.
65 F4 Hardy U.S.A.
68 E4 Hardy Reservoir U.S.A.
28 D6 Hareidîn, W. *watercourse* Egypt
12 B4 Harelbeke Belgium
12 E1 Haren Neth.
12 F2 Haren (Ems) Ger.
88 E3 Hārer Eth.
71 F4 Harford U.S.A.
88 E3 Hargeysa Somalia
17 M7 Harghita-Mădăraş, Vârful *mt* Romania
29 H2 Harhal D. *mts* Turkey
38 C2 Harhatan China
36 B3 Har Hu *l.* China
34 D3 Haridwar India
33 A3 Harihar India
51 C5 Harihari N.Z.
41 D7 Harima-nada *b.* Japan
35 G5 Haringhat *r.* Bangl.
12 C3 Haringvliet *est.* Neth.
31 G3 Hari Rūd *r.* Afgh./Iran
7 S6 Harjavalta Fin.
64 E3 Harlan *IA* U.S.A.
70 B6 Harlan *KY* U.S.A.
9 C5 Harlech U.K.
62 E1 Harlem U.S.A.
9 J5 Harleston U.K.
12 D1 Harlingen Neth.
65 D7 Harlingen U.S.A.
9 H6 Harlow U.K.
62 E2 Harlowtown U.S.A.
12 B5 Harly France
71 J2 Harmony *ME* U.S.A.
68 A4 Harmony *MN* U.S.A.
13 J1 Harmsdorf Ger.
34 A3 Harnai Pak.
12 A4 Harnes France
62 B3 Harney Basin *basin* U.S.A.
62 C3 Harney L. *l.* U.S.A.
7 P5 Härnösand Sweden
36 E2 Har Nur China
36 B2 Har Nuur *l.* Mongolia
10 □ Haroldswick U.K.
86 B4 Harper Liberia
72 D4 Harper Lake *l.* U.S.A.
70 E5 Harpers Ferry U.S.A.
59 H2 Harp Lake *l.* Can.
13 G2 Harpstedt Ger.
29 G2 Harput Turkey
38 F1 Harqin China
38 F1 Harqin Qi China
73 F5 Harquahala Mts *mts* U.S.A.
29 G3 Harran Turkey
28 F5 Harrat er Rujeila *lava* Jordan
58 E3 Harricana *r.* Can.
67 C5 Harriman U.S.A.
71 G3 Harriman Reservoir U.S.A.
71 F5 Harrington U.S.A.
59 J3 Harrington Harbour Can.
10 B3 Harris U.K.
66 B4 Harrisburg *IL* U.S.A.
70 E4 Harrisburg *PA* U.S.A.
91 H4 Harrismith S. Africa
65 E4 Harrison *AR* U.S.A.
68 E3 Harrison *MI* U.S.A.
54 C2 Harrison Bay *b.* U.S.A.
70 D5 Harrisonburg U.S.A.
59 J3 Harrison, Cape *c.* Can.
56 E5 Harrison L. *l.* Can.
64 E4 Harrisonville U.S.A.
10 A3 Harris, Sound of *chan.* U.K.
69 F3 Harrisville *MI* U.S.A.
71 F2 Harrisville *NY* U.S.A.
70 C5 Harrisville *WV* U.S.A.
8 F4 Harrogate U.K.
13 H1 Harsefeld Ger.
30 B3 Harsin Iran
28 G1 Harşit *r.* Turkey
19 M2 Hârşova Romania
6 P2 Harstad Norway
13 H2 Harsum Ger.
68 D4 Hart U.S.A.
42 B2 Hartao China
90 D4 Hartbees *watercourse* S. Africa
16 G7 Hartberg Austria
7 K6 Harteigan *mt* Norway
10 E5 Hart Fell *h.* U.K.
71 G4 Hartford *CT* U.S.A.
68 D4 Hartford *MI* U.S.A.
64 D3 Hartford *SD* U.S.A.
68 C4 Hartford *WI* U.S.A.
56 E3 Hart Highway Can.
59 G4 Hartland Can.
9 C7 Hartland U.K.
71 J2 Hartland U.S.A.
9 C6 Hartland Point *pt* U.K.
8 F3 Hartlepool U.K.
65 C5 Hartley U.S.A.
56 D4 Hartley Bay Can.
7 U6 Hartola Fin.
56 E4 Hart Ranges *mts* Can.
16 E6 Härtsfeld *h.* Ger.
90 F3 Hartswater S. Africa
67 D5 Hartwell Res. *resr* U.S.A.
36 B2 Har Us Nuur *l.* Mongolia
31 F3 Harut *watercourse* Afgh.
68 C4 Harvard U.S.A.
63 F4 Harvard, Mt *mt* U.S.A.
71 K2 Harvey Can.
68 D2 Harvey *MI* U.S.A.
64 C2 Harvey *ND* U.S.A.
9 J6 Harwich U.K.
34 C3 Haryana *div.* India
28 F6 Ḩaşāh, Wādī al *watercourse* Jordan
30 B2 Hasan Iran
34 C2 Hasan Abdal Pak.
28 E2 Hasan Dağı *mts* Turkey
29 H3 Hasankeyf Turkey
30 E5 Ḩasan Langī Iran
33 B2 Hasanparti India
28 E5 Hasbani *r.* Lebanon
28 E2 Hasbek Turkey
29 K6 Ḩasb, Sha'īb *watercourse* Iraq
35 E5 Hasdo *r.* India
13 F2 Hase *r.* Ger.
12 F2 Haselünne Ger.
13 J4 Hasenkopf *h.* Ger.
30 C3 Hashtgerd Iran
30 C2 Hashtpar Iran
65 D5 Haskell U.S.A.
9 G6 Haslemere U.K.
17 M7 Hăşmaşul Mare *mt* Romania
33 B3 Hassan India
29 K4 Hassan Iraq
73 F5 Hassayampa *r.* U.S.A.
13 J4 Haßberge *reg.* Ger.
12 D4 Hasselt Belgium
12 E2 Hasselt Neth.
86 C1 Hassi Messaoud Alg.
7 N8 Hässleholm Sweden
50 E5 Hastings Austr.
51 F3 Hastings N.Z.
9 H7 Hastings U.K.
68 E4 Hastings *MI* U.S.A.
68 A3 Hastings *MN* U.S.A.
64 D3 Hastings *NE* U.S.A.
Hatay *see* Antakya
73 F3 Hatch U.S.A.
67 E7 Hatchet Bay Bahamas
57 J3 Hatchet Lake *l.* Can.
65 F5 Hatchie *r.* U.S.A.
50 D2 Hatfield Austr.
8 G4 Hatfield U.K.
36 C1 Hatgal Mongolia
34 D4 Hathras India
35 F4 Hatia Nepal
44 C3 Ha Tiên Vietnam
44 C1 Ha Tĩnh Vietnam
50 D3 Hattah Austr.
67 F5 Hatteras, Cape *c.* U.S.A.
6 N4 Hattfjelldal Norway
35 E6 Hatti *r.* India
65 F6 Hattiesburg U.S.A.
13 F3 Hattingen Ger.
88 E3 Haud *reg.* Eth.
7 K7 Hauge Norway
7 J7 Haugesund Norway
51 E3 Hauhungaroa *mt* N.Z.
7 K7 Haukeligrend Norway
6 T4 Haukipudas Fin.
7 V5 Haukivesi *l.* Fin.
57 H3 Haultain *r.* Can.
51 E2 Hauraki Gulf *g.* N.Z.
51 A7 Hauroko, L. *l.* N.Z.
86 B1 Haut Atlas *mts* Morocco
59 G4 Hauterive Can.
73 G2 Haut, Isle au *i.* U.S.A.
86 B1 Hauts Plateaux *plat.* Alg.
72 □1 Hauula U.S.A.
75 H4 Havana Cuba
68 B5 Havana U.S.A.
9 G7 Havant U.K.
73 E4 Havasu Lake *l.* U.S.A.
13 L2 Havel *r.* Ger.
12 D4 Havelange Belgium
13 L2 Havelberg Ger.
13 L2 Havelländisches Luch *marsh* Ger.
69 J3 Havelock Can.
67 E5 Havelock U.S.A.
51 F3 Havelock North N.Z.
9 C6 Haverfordwest U.K.
71 H3 Haverhill U.S.A.
33 A3 Haveri India
12 D4 Haversin Belgium
12 F3 Havixbeck Ger.
16 G6 Havlíčkův Brod Czech Rep.
6 T1 Havøysund Norway
19 M5 Havran Turkey
62 E1 Havre U.S.A.
59 H4 Havre Aubert, Île du *i.* Can.
71 E5 Havre de Grace U.S.A.
59 H3 Havre-St-Pierre Can.
19 M4 Havsa Turkey
28 E1 Havza Turkey
72 □2 Hawaii *i.* U.S.A.
46 M2 Hawaii *is* Pac. Oc.
94 H4 Hawaiian Ridge *sea feature* Pac. Oc.
72 □2 Hawaii Volcanoes National Park U.S.A.
29 L7 Ḩawallī Kuwait
9 D4 Hawarden U.K.
51 B6 Hawea, L. *l.* N.Z.
51 E3 Hawera N.Z.
8 E3 Hawes U.K.
72 □2 Hawi U.S.A.
10 F5 Hawick U.K.
29 L6 Ḩawīzah, Hawr al *l.* Iraq
51 B6 Hawkdun Range *mts* N.Z.
51 F3 Hawke Bay *b.* N.Z.
59 J3 Hawke Island *i.* Can.
50 B1 Hawker Austr.
50 F2 Hawkesbury Can.
73 F3 Hawkins Peak *summit* U.S.A.
69 F3 Hawks U.S.A.
57 K2 Hawkshaw Can.
71 F4 Hawley U.S.A.
29 J5 Ḩawrān, Wādī *watercourse* Iraq
90 C7 Hawston S. Africa
72 C2 Hawthorne U.S.A.
42 C1 Haxat China
8 F3 Haxby U.K.
50 E3 Hay Austr.
56 F2 Hay *r.* Can.
68 B3 Hay *r.* U.S.A.
38 B1 Haya China
40 G5 Hayachine-san *mt* Japan
30 B2 Haydarābad Iran
73 G5 Hayden *AZ* U.S.A.
62 C2 Hayden *ID* U.S.A.
57 L3 Hayes *r.* Can.
55 M2 Hayes Halvø *pen.* Greenland
9 B7 Hayle U.K.
28 D2 Haymana Turkey
70 E5 Haymarket U.S.A.
55 J3 Haynes *r.* Can.
71 J2 Haynesville U.S.A.
9 D5 Hay-on-Wye U.K.
21 C7 Hayrabolu Turkey
56 F2 Hay River Can.
64 D4 Hays U.S.A.
21 D5 Haysyn Ukr.
72 A3 Hayward *CA* U.S.A.
68 B2 Hayward *WI* U.S.A.
9 G7 Haywards Heath U.K.
31 G3 Hazarajat *reg.* Afgh.
70 B6 Hazard U.S.A.
35 F5 Hazāribāg India
35 E5 Hazaribagh Range *mts* India
12 A4 Hazebrouck France
56 D3 Hazelton Can.
71 F4 Hazelton U.S.A.
54 G2 Hazen Strait *chan.* Can.
12 C2 Hazerswoude-Rijndijk Neth.
29 G6 Ḩazm al Jalāmid *ridge* S. Arabia
31 G2 Hazrat Sultan Afgh.
29 H2 Hazro Turkey
11 B4 Headford Rep. of Ireland
72 A2 Healdsburg U.S.A.
50 E4 Healesville Austr.
9 F4 Heanor U.K.
93 J7 Heard Island *i.* Ind. Ocean
65 D6 Hearne U.S.A.
58 D4 Hearst Can.
92 B2 Hearst I. *i.* Ant.
9 H7 Heathfield U.K.
71 E6 Heathsville U.S.A.
65 D7 Hebbronville U.S.A.
38 E2 Hebei *div.* China
65 E5 Heber Springs U.S.A.
38 E3 Hebi China
59 H2 Hebron Can.
68 D5 Hebron *IN* U.S.A.
64 D3 Hebron *NE* U.S.A.
71 G3 Hebron *NY* U.S.A.
28 E6 Hebron West Bank
59 H2 Hebron Fiord *in.* Can.
54 E4 Hecate Strait *B.C.* Can.
56 C4 Hecate Strait *chan.* Can.
56 C3 Heceta I. *i.* U.S.A.
39 C5 Hechi China
39 C4 Hechuan China
7 N5 Hede Sweden
7 O6 Hedemora Sweden
39 D6 Hede Sk. *resr* China
62 C2 He Devil Mt. *mt* U.S.A.
68 A5 Hedrick U.S.A.
12 D2 Heeg Neth.
12 F2 Heek Ger.
12 C4 Heer Belgium
12 E2 Heerde Neth.
12 D2 Heerenveen Neth.
12 C2 Heerhugowaard Neth.
12 D4 Heerlen Neth.
Ḩefa *see* Haifa
38 E4 Hefei China
39 D4 Hefeng China
40 B1 Hegang China
41 E6 Hegura-jima *i.* Japan
13 K3 Heidberg *h.* Ger.
16 D3 Heide Ger.
89 B6 Heide Namibia
13 G5 Heidelberg Ger.
91 H3 Heidelberg *Gauteng* S. Africa
90 D7 Heidelberg *Western Cape* S. Africa
91 G3 Heilbron S. Africa
13 H5 Heilbronn Ger.
16 E3 Heiligenhafen Ger.
39 □ Hei Ling Chau *i.* *H.K.* China
42 E1 Heilongjiang *div.* China
36 E2 Heilong Jiang *r.* China/Rus. Fed.
13 J5 Heilsbronn Ger.
6 M5 Heimdal Norway
7 U6 Heinola Fin.
44 A2 Heinze Is *is* Myanmar
42 B3 Heishan China
12 C3 Heist-op-den-Berg Belgium
42 E2 Hejian China
38 B4 Hejiang China
39 D6 He Jiang *r.* China
38 D3 Hejin China
28 F2 Hekimhan Turkey
6 D5 Hekla *volc.* Iceland
38 B2 Hekou *Gansu* China
39 B6 Hekou *Yunnan* China
6 N5 Helagsfjället *mt* Sweden
38 B2 Helan Shan *mts* China
13 K3 Helbra Ger.
35 H4 Helem India
65 F5 Helena *AR* U.S.A.
62 E2 Helena *MT* U.S.A.
73 D3 Helen, Mt *mt* U.S.A.
10 D4 Helensburgh U.K.
28 E6 Ḩelez Israel
16 C3 Helgoland *i.* Ger.
16 D3 Helgoländer Bucht *b.* Ger.
6 C5 Hella Iceland
6 P2 Helland Norway
30 C4 Helleh *r.* Iran
12 C3 Hellevoetsluis Neth.
6 R2 Helligskogen Norway
15 F3 Hellín Spain
62 C2 Hells Canyon *gorge* U.S.A.
31 F4 Helmand *r.* Afgh.
13 K4 Helmbrechts Ger.
13 J3 Helme *r.* Ger.
89 B6 Helmeringhausen Namibia
90 E6 Helmeringhausen S. Africa
12 D3 Helmond Neth.
10 E2 Helmsdale U.K.
10 E2 Helmsdale *r.* U.K.
13 K2 Helmstedt Ger.
42 E2 Helong China
73 G2 Helper U.S.A.
7 N8 Helsingborg Sweden
7 N8 Helsingør Denmark
7 T6 Helsinki Fin.
9 B7 Helston U.K.
8 D3 Helvellyn *mt* U.K.
11 D5 Helvick Head *hd* Rep. of Ireland
87 F2 Helwân Egypt
9 G6 Hemel Hempstead U.K.
72 D5 Hemet U.S.A.
70 E3 Hemlock Lake *l.* U.S.A.
13 H2 Hemmingen Ger.
71 G2 Hemmingford Can.
13 H1 Hemmoor Ger.
65 D6 Hempstead U.S.A.
9 J5 Hemsby U.K.
7 Q8 Hemse Sweden
38 A3 Henan *Qinghai* China
38 D3 Henan *div.* China
15 E2 Henares *r.* Spain
40 F4 Henashi-zaki *pt* Japan
28 C1 Hendek Turkey
83 E3 Henderson Arg.
66 C4 Henderson *KY* U.S.A.
67 E4 Henderson *NC* U.S.A.
73 E3 Henderson *NV* U.S.A.
71 E3 Henderson *NY* U.S.A.
65 E5 Henderson *TX* U.S.A.
46 P6 Henderson Island *i.* *Pitcairn Is* Pac. Oc.
67 D5 Hendersonville *NC* U.S.A.
67 C4 Hendersonville *TN* U.S.A.
30 C4 Hendījān Iran
9 G6 Hendon U.K.
30 D5 Hendorābī *i.* Iran
36 B4 Hengduan Shan *mts* China
12 E2 Hengelo Neth.
39 D5 Hengshan *Hunan* China
38 C2 Hengshan *Shaanxi* China
42 F1 Hengshan China
39 D5 Heng Shan *mt* *Hunan* China
38 D2 Heng Shan *mt* China
38 E2 Hengshui China
39 C6 Heng Xian China
39 D5 Hengyang *Hunan* China
39 D5 Hengyang *Hunan* China
21 E6 Heniches'k Ukr.
51 C6 Henley N.Z.
9 G6 Henley-on-Thames U.K.
71 F5 Henlopen, Cape *pt* U.S.A.
12 F4 Hennef (Sieg) Ger.
91 G3 Hennenman S. Africa
13 M2 Hennigsdorf Berlin Ger.
71 H3 Henniker U.S.A.
65 D5 Henrietta U.S.A.
58 D2 Henrietta Maria, Cape *c.* Can.
73 G3 Henrieville U.S.A.
68 C5 Henry U.S.A.
92 B3 Henry Ice Rise *ice feature* Ant.
55 M3 Henry Kater, C. *hd* Can.
73 G2 Henry Mts *mts* U.S.A.
69 G4 Hensall Can.
13 H1 Henstedt-Ulzburg Ger.
89 B6 Hentiesbaai Namibia
50 F3 Henty Austr.
37 B5 Henzada Myanmar
57 H4 Hepburn Can.
39 E5 Heping China
39 C6 Hepu China
38 D2 Hequ China
31 F3 Herāt Afgh.
14 F5 Hérault *r.* France
57 H4 Herbert Can.
13 G4 Herborn Ger.
13 H4 Herbstein Ger.
92 B4 Hercules Dome *ice feature* Ant.
12 F3 Herdecke Ger.
13 F4 Herdorf Ger.
9 E5 Hereford U.K.
65 C5 Hereford U.S.A.
46 N5 Héréhérétué *i.* Pac. Oc.
12 C4 Herent Belgium
13 G2 Herford Ger.
13 J4 Heringen (Werra) Ger.
64 D4 Herington U.S.A.
30 B2 Herīs Iran
16 D7 Herisau Switz.
92 B3 Heritage Ra. *mts* Ant.
71 F3 Herkimer U.S.A.
13 J3 Herleshausen Ger.
10 □ Herma Ness *hd* U.K.
13 J2 Hermannsburg Ger.
90 C7 Hermanus S. Africa
91 H5 Hermes, Cape *pt* S. Africa
50 F1 Hermidale Austr.
62 C2 Hermiston U.S.A.
80 C9 Hermite, Is *i.* Chile
48 E2 Hermit Is *is* P.N.G.
Hermon, Mount *mt* *see* Sheikh, Jebel esh
83 B2 Hermosa, P. de V. *pass* Chile
81 B4 Hermosas, Parque Nacional las *nat. park* Col.
74 B3 Hermosillo Mex.
80 F3 Hernandarias Para.
12 F3 Herne Ger.
9 J6 Herne Bay U.K.
7 L8 Herning Denmark
68 D1 Heron Bay Can.
15 D3 Herrera del Duque Spain
65 B7 Herreras Mex.
13 J5 Herrieden Ger.
70 E4 Hershey U.S.A.
9 G6 Hertford U.K.
91 F4 Hertzogville S. Africa
12 D4 Herve Belgium
49 F4 Hervey Bay *b.* Austr.
46 M5 Hervey Is *is* Pac. Oc.
13 L2 Herzberg *Brandenburg* Ger.
13 M3 Herzberg *Brandenburg* Ger.
12 F2 Herzlake Ger.
13 J5 Herzogenaurach Ger.
13 L1 Herzsprung Ger.
29 M4 Ḩeşār Iran
12 C4 Hesbaye *reg.* Belgium
12 F1 Hesel Ger.
39 C6 Heshan China
38 C3 Heshui China
38 D2 Heshun China
72 D4 Hesperia U.S.A.
56 C2 Hess *r.* Can.
13 J5 Heßdorf Ger.
13 J5 Hesselberg *h.* Ger.
13 H4 Hessen *div.* Ger.
13 H3 Hessisch Lichtenau Ger.
39 B6 Het *r.* Laos
72 B3 Hetch Hetchy Aqueduct *canal* U.S.A.
12 D3 Heteren Neth.
64 C2 Hettinger U.S.A.
8 E3 Hetton U.K.
13 K3 Hettstedt Ger.
8 E3 Hexham U.K.
38 F4 He Xian *Anhui* China
39 D5 He Xian *Guangxi* China
38 B2 Hexibao China
38 E1 Hexigten Qi China
90 C6 Hex River Pass S. Africa
38 D3 Heyang China
30 D4 Ḩeydarābād Iran
31 F4 Ḩeydarābād Iran
8 E3 Heysham U.K.
39 E6 Heyuan China
50 C5 Heywood Austr.
8 E4 Heywood U.K.
68 C5 Heyworth U.S.A.
38 E3 Heze China
39 B5 Hezhang China
38 B3 Hezheng China
38 B3 Hezuozhen China
67 D7 Hialeah U.S.A.
64 E4 Hiawatha U.S.A.
68 A2 Hibbing U.S.A.
67 D5 Hickory U.S.A.
51 G2 Hicks Bay N.Z.
57 K2 Hicks L. *l.* Can.
44 A4 Hicksville U.S.A.
65 D5 Hico U.S.A.
40 H3 Hidaka-sanmyaku *mts* Japan
74 C3 Hidalgo del Parral Mex.
74 C3 Hidalgo, Psa M. *resr* Mex.
82 C2 Hidrolândia Brazil
41 C7 Higashi-Hiroshima Japan
40 G5 Higashine Japan
41 D7 Higashi-ōsaka Japan
41 A8 Higashi-suidō *chan.* Japan
71 F3 Higgins Bay U.S.A.
68 E3 Higgins Lake *l.* U.S.A.
High Atlas *mts* *see* Haut Atlas
62 B3 High Desert U.S.A.
68 C3 High Falls Reservoir U.S.A.
68 E3 High I. *i.* U.S.A.
39 □ High Island Res. *resr* *H.K.* China
68 D4 Highland Park U.S.A.
72 C2 Highland Peak *summit* *CA* U.S.A.
73 E3 Highland Peak *summit* *NV* U.S.A.
56 F3 High Level Can.
35 F5 High Level Canal *canal* India
67 E5 High Point U.S.A.
56 F3 High Prairie Can.
56 G4 High River Can.
67 E7 High Rock Bahamas
57 J3 Highrock Lake *l.* Can.
8 E3 High Seat *h.* U.K.
71 F4 Hightstown U.S.A.
9 G6 High Wycombe U.K.
81 D2 Higuerote Venez.
7 S7 Hiiumaa *i.* Estonia
32 A4 Hijaz *reg.* S. Arabia
73 E3 Hiko U.S.A.
41 E7 Hikone Japan
51 G2 Hikurangi *mt* N.Z.
73 F3 Hildale U.S.A.
13 J4 Hildburghausen Ger.
13 J4 Hilders Ger.
13 H2 Hildesheim Ger.
35 G4 Hili Bangl.
92 B5 Hillary Coast *coastal area* Ant.
64 D4 Hill City U.S.A.
73 H2 Hill Creek *r.* U.S.A.
12 C2 Hillegom Neth.
7 N9 Hillerød Denmark
64 D2 Hillsboro *ND* U.S.A.
71 H3 Hillsboro *NH* U.S.A.
70 B5 Hillsboro *OH* U.S.A.
65 D5 Hillsboro *TX* U.S.A.
70 C5 Hillsboro *WV* U.S.A.
68 B4 Hillsboro *WI* U.S.A.
68 E5 Hillsdale *MI* U.S.A.
71 G3 Hillsdale *NY* U.S.A.
70 E4 Hillsgrove U.S.A.
10 F4 Hillside U.K.
73 F4 Hillside U.S.A.
50 E2 Hillston Austr.
70 C6 Hillsville U.S.A.
50 H3 Hilltop Austr.
72 □2 Hilo U.S.A.
91 J4 Hilton S. Africa
70 E3 Hilton U.S.A.
69 F2 Hilton Beach Can.
67 D5 Hilton Head Island U.S.A.
29 G3 Hilvan Turkey
12 D2 Hilversum Neth.
34 D3 Himachal Pradesh *div.* India
22 F6 Himalaya *mts* Asia
35 F3 Himalchul *mt* Nepal
6 S4 Himanka Fin.
19 H4 Himarë Albania
34 C5 Himatnagar India
41 D7 Himeji Japan
40 G5 Himekami-dake *mt* Japan
91 H4 Himeville S. Africa
41 E6 Himi Japan
28 F4 Ḩimş Syria
28 F4 Ḩimş, Baḩrat *resr* Syria
43 C4 Hinatuan Phil.
48 E3 Hinchinbrook I. *i.* Austr.
9 F5 Hinckley U.K.
68 A2 Hinckley *MN* U.S.A.
73 F2 Hinckley *UT* U.S.A.
71 F3 Hinckley Reservoir U.S.A.
34 D3 Hindan *r.* India
34 D4 Hindaun India
8 G3 Hinderwell U.K.
29 K5 Hindīyah Barrage Iraq
8 E4 Hindley U.K.
70 B6 Hindman U.S.A.
50 C4 Hindmarsh, L. *l.* Austr.
35 F5 Hindola India
31 G3 Hindu Kush *mts* Afgh./Pak.
33 B3 Hindupur India
56 F3 Hines Creek Can.
67 D6 Hinesville U.S.A.
34 D5 Hinganghat India
31 G5 Hinglaj Pak.
31 G5 Hingol *r.* Pak.
34 D6 Hingoli India
29 H2 Hınıs Turkey
72 D4 Hinkley U.S.A.
6 O2 Hinnøya *i.* Norway
43 B4 Hinobaan Phil.
15 D3 Hinojosa del Duque Spain
41 C7 Hino-misaki *pt* Japan
71 G3 Hinsdale U.S.A.
12 F1 Hinte Ger.
56 F4 Hinton Can.
70 C6 Hinton U.S.A.
12 C2 Hippolytushoef Neth.
29 K2 Hirabit Dağ *mt* Turkey
41 A8 Hirado Japan
41 A8 Hirado-shima *i.* Japan
35 E5 Hirakud Reservoir India
40 H3 Hiroo Japan
40 G4 Hirosaki Japan
41 C7 Hiroshima Japan
13 K5 Hirschaid Ger.
13 K4 Hirschberg Ger.
16 E7 Hirschberg *mt* Ger.
14 G2 Hirson France
7 L8 Hirtshals Denmark
29 M3 Hisar Iran
31 G3 Hisar, Koh-i- *mts* Afgh.
28 D1 Hisarönü Turkey
28 E6 Hisban Jordan
31 H2 Hisor Tajik.
75 K4 Hispaniola *i.* Caribbean Sea
34 C3 Hissar India
35 F4 Hisua India
29 J5 Hīt Iraq
41 G6 Hitachi Japan
41 G6 Hitachi-ōta Japan
41 B8 Hitoyoshi Japan
6 L5 Hitra *i.* Norway
13 K1 Hitzacker Ger.
41 C7 Hiuchi-nada *b.* Japan
46 O4 Hiva Oa *i.* *Fr. Polynesia* Pac. Oc.
56 E4 Hixon Can.
29 J2 Hizan Turkey
7 O7 Hjälmaren *l.* Sweden
57 H2 Hjalmar Lake *l.* Can.
7 L5 Hjerkinn Norway
7 O7 Hjo Sweden
7 M8 Hjørring Denmark
91 J4 Hlabisa S. Africa
35 F3 Hlako Kangri *mt* China
91 J3 Hlatikulu Swaziland
21 E5 Hlobyne Ukr.
91 G4 Hlohlowane S. Africa
91 H4 Hlotse Lesotho
91 K4 Hluhluwe S. Africa
21 E5 Hlukhiv Ukr.
17 O4 Hlusha Belarus
20 C4 Hlybokaye Belarus
86 C4 Ho Ghana
89 B6 Hoachanas Namibia
48 E6 Hobart Austr.
65 D5 Hobart U.S.A.
65 C5 Hobbs U.S.A.
92 A4 Hobbs Coast *coastal area* Ant.
67 D7 Hobe Sound U.S.A.
7 L8 Hobro Denmark
88 E3 Hobyo Somalia
13 H5 Höchberg Ger.
44 C3 Hô Chi Minh Vietnam
16 G7 Hochschwab *mt* Austria
13 G5 Hockenheim Ger.
70 B5 Hocking *r.* U.S.A.
34 D4 Hodal India
8 E4 Hodder *r.* U.K.
9 G6 Hoddesdon U.K.
Hodeida *see* Al Hudaydah
71 K1 Hodgdon U.S.A.
17 K7 Hódmezővásárhely Hungary
15 J5 Hodna, Chott el *salt l.* Alg.
42 D4 Hodo dan *pt* N. Korea
12 C3 Hoek van Holland Neth.
12 D4 Hoensbroek Neth.
42 E2 Hoeryŏng N. Korea
42 D4 Hoeyang N. Korea
13 K4 Hof Ger.
13 J4 Hofheim in Unterfranken Ger.
91 F5 Hofmeyr S. Africa
6 F4 Höfn Iceland
7 P6 Hofors Sweden
6 D4 Hofsjökull *ice cap* Iceland
41 B7 Hōfu Japan
7 N8 Höganäs Sweden
86 C2 Hoggar *plat.* Alg.
71 F6 Hog I. *i.* U.S.A.
7 P8 Högsby Sweden
13 H5 Hohenloher Ebene *plain* Ger.
13 L2 Hohenmölsen Ger.
13 L2 Hohennauen Ger.
13 K4 Hohenwarte-talsperre *resr* Ger.
13 H4 Hohe Rhön *mts* Ger.
16 F7 Hohe Tauern *mts* Austria
12 E4 Hohe Venn *moorland* Belgium
38 D1 Hohhot China
35 G2 Hoh Xil Hu *salt l.* China
35 G2 Hoh Xil Shan *mts* China
44 D2 Hôi An Vietnam
88 D3 Hoima Uganda

89 E6 Ikongo Madag.
21 H6 Ikryanoye Rus. Fed.
88 D4 Ikungu Tanz.
43 B2 Ilagan Phil.
88 D3 Ilaisamis Kenya
30 B3 Īlām Iran
35 F4 Ilam Nepal
86 C4 Ilaro Nigeria
17 J4 Iława Pol.
57 H3 Île-à-la-Crosse Can.
57 H3 Île-à-la-Crosse, Lac *l.* Can.
88 C4 Ilebo Congo(Zaire)
88 D3 Ileret Kenya
20 G2 Ileza Rus. Fed.
57 K3 Ilford Can.
9 H6 Ilford U.K.
9 C6 Ilfracombe U.K.
28 D1 Ilgaz Turkey
28 D1 Ilgaz D. *mts* Turkey
28 C2 Ilgın Turkey
81 D5 Ilha Grande Brazil
82 D3 Ilha Grande, Baía da *b.* Brazil
82 B3 Ilha Grande, Represa *resr* Brazil
82 B3 Ilha Solteíra, Represa *resr* Brazil
15 B2 Ílhavo Port.
82 E1 Ilhéus Brazil
86 □ Ilhéus Secos ou do Rombo *i.* Cape Verde
54 C4 Iliamna Lake *l.* U.S.A.
28 G2 İliç Turkey
43 C4 Iligan Phil.
43 C4 Iligan Bay *b.* Phil.
20 H2 Il'insko-Podomskoye Rus. Fed.
71 F3 Ilion U.S.A.
33 B3 Ilkal India
9 F5 Ilkeston U.K.
8 F4 Ilkley U.K.
43 B5 Illana Bay *b.* Phil.
83 B1 Illapel Chile
83 B1 Illapel *r.* Chile
16 E7 Iller *r.* Ger.
21 D6 Illichivs'k Ukr.
78 E7 Illimani, Nevado de *mt* Bol.
68 C5 Illinois *div.* U.S.A.
68 C5 Illinois *r.* U.S.A.
68 B5 Illinois and Mississippi Canal *canal* U.S.A.
21 D5 Illintsi Ukr.
86 C2 Illizi Alg.
13 K4 Ilm *r.* Ger.
6 S5 Ilmajoki Fin.
13 J4 Ilmenau Ger.
13 J1 Ilmenau *r.* Ger.
20 D3 Il'men', Ozero *l.* Rus. Fed.
9 E7 Ilminster U.K.
78 D7 Ilo Peru
43 A4 Iloc *i.* Phil.
43 B4 Iloilo Phil.
6 W5 Ilomantsi Fin.
86 C4 Ilorin Nigeria
21 F6 Ilovays'k Ukr.
21 G5 Ilovlya Rus. Fed.
21 H5 Ilovlya *r.* Rus. Fed.
13 J2 Ilsede Ger.
55 N3 Ilulissat Greenland
41 C7 Imabari Japan
41 F6 Imaichi Japan
29 K6 Imām al Ḥamzah Iraq
28 E3 İmamOğlu Turkey
29 K5 Imām Ḥamīd Iraq
40 D2 Iman *r.* Rus. Fed.
41 A8 Imari Japan
81 E3 Imataca, Serranía de *mts* Venez.
7 V6 Imatra Fin.
41 E7 Imazu Japan
80 G3 Imbituba Brazil
82 B4 Imbituva Brazil
20 G3 imeni Babushkina Rus. Fed.
31 F2 imeni Chapayeva Turkm.
88 E3 Īmī Eth.
29 M2 İmişli Azer.
42 D6 Imja-do *i.* S. Korea
42 D4 Imjin *r.* N. Korea
18 D2 Imola Italy
91 H4 Impendle S. Africa
79 J5 Imperatriz Brazil
18 C3 Imperia Italy
64 C3 Imperial U.S.A.
72 D5 Imperial Beach U.S.A.
73 E5 Imperial Valley *v.* U.S.A.
88 B3 Impfondo Congo
35 H4 Imphal India
19 L4 İmroz Turkey
28 F5 Imtān Syria
43 A4 Imuruan Bay *b.* Phil.
41 E7 Ina Japan
78 E6 Inambari *r.* Peru
86 C2 In Aménas Alg.
51 C4 Inangahua Junction N.Z.
37 F7 Inanwatan Indon.
6 U2 Inari Fin.
6 U2 Inarijärvi *l.* Fin.
6 T2 Inarijoki *r.* Fin./Norway
15 H3 Inca Spain
21 C7 İnce Burnu *pt* Turkey
21 E7 İnce Burnu *pt* Turkey
28 D3 İncekum Burnu *pt* Turkey
28 E2 İncesu Turkey
11 E5 Inch Rep. of Ireland
10 C2 Inchard, Loch *b.* U.K.
10 E4 Inchkeith *i.* U.K.
42 D5 Inch'ŏn S. Korea
91 K2 Incomati *r.* Moz.
10 B5 Indaal, Loch *in.* U.K.
82 D2 Indaiá *r.* Brazil
82 B3 Indaiá Grande *r.* Brazil
6 P5 Indalsälven *r.* Sweden
7 J6 Indalstø Norway
65 B7 Indé Mex.
72 C3 Independence *CA* U.S.A.
68 B4 Independence *IA* U.S.A.
65 E4 Independence *KS* U.S.A.
68 A2 Independence *MN* U.S.A.
64 E4 Independence *MO* U.S.A.
70 C6 Independence *VA* U.S.A.
68 B3 Independence *WV* U.S.A.
62 C3 Independence Mts *mts* U.S.A.
26 D2 Inderborskiy Kazak.
33 B2 Indi India
23 G7 India *country* Asia
68 D2 Indian *r.* U.S.A.
70 D4 Indiana U.S.A.
68 D5 Indiana *div.* U.S.A.
68 D5 Indiana Dunes National Lakeshore *res.* U.S.A.
93 M7 Indian-Antarctic Basin *sea feature* Ind. Ocean
93 O7 Indian-Antarctic Ridge *sea feature* Pac. Oc.
68 D6 Indianapolis U.S.A.
Indian Desert *see* Thar Desert
59 J3 Indian Harbour Can.
71 F3 Indian Lake *NY* U.S.A.
68 D3 Indian Lake *l. MI* U.S.A.
70 B4 Indian Lake *l. OH* U.S.A.
70 D4 Indian Lake *l. PA* U.S.A.
64 E3 Indianola *IA* U.S.A.
65 F5 Indianola *MS* U.S.A.
73 F2 Indian Peak *summit* U.S.A.
68 E3 Indian River U.S.A.
73 E3 Indian Springs U.S.A.
73 G4 Indian Wells U.S.A.
25 Q2 Indigirka *r.* Rus. Fed.
19 J2 Inđija Yugo.
56 F2 Indin Lake *l.* Can.
72 D5 Indio U.S.A.
49 G3 Indispensable Reefs *rf* Solomon Is
23 K10 Indonesia *country* Asia
34 C5 Indore India
45 C4 Indramayu, Tanjung *pt* Indon.
45 B3 Indrapura Indon.
33 C2 Indravati *r.* India
14 E3 Indre *r.* France
Indur *see* Nizamabad
34 B4 Indus *r.* Pak.
34 A5 Indus, Mouths of the *est.* Pak.
91 G5 Indwe S. Africa
28 E1 İnebolu Turkey
28 B1 İnegöl Turkey
70 B6 Inez U.S.A.
90 D7 Infanta, Cape *hd* S. Africa
74 D5 Infiernillo, L. *l.* Mex.
68 D3 Ingalls U.S.A.
57 J2 Ingalls Lake *l.* Can.
72 B2 Ingalls, Mt *mt* U.S.A.
12 B4 Ingelmunster Belgium
83 C4 Ingeniero Jacobacci Arg.
69 G4 Ingersoll Can.
30 G2 Ingichka Uzbek.
8 E3 Ingleborough *h.* U.K.
55 L2 Inglefield Land *reg.* Greenland
8 E3 Ingleton U.K.
50 D4 Inglewood Austr.
9 H4 Ingoldmells U.K.
16 E6 Ingolstadt Ger.
59 H4 Ingonish Can.
35 G5 Ingrāj Bāzār India
56 F2 Ingray Lake *l.* Can.
92 D5 Ingrid Christensen Coast *coastal area* Ant.
21 H7 Ingushskaya Respublika *div.* Rus. Fed.
91 K3 Ingwavuma S. Africa
91 K3 Inhaca Moz.
91 K2 Inhaca e dos Portugueses, Ilhas da S. Africa
91 K3 Inhaca, Peninsula *pen.* Moz.
89 D6 Inhambane Moz.
91 K1 Inhambane *div.* Moz.
89 D5 Inhaminga Moz.
82 A3 Inhanduízinho *r.* Brazil
82 D1 Inhaúmas Brazil
81 C4 Inírida *r.* Col.
11 A4 Inishark *i.* Rep. of Ireland
11 A4 Inishbofin *i.* Rep. of Ireland
11 A3 Inishkea North *i.* Rep. of Ireland
11 A3 Inishkea South *i.* Rep. of Ireland
11 B4 Inishmaan *i.* Rep. of Ireland
11 B4 Inishmore *i.* Rep. of Ireland
11 C3 Inishmurray *i.* Rep. of Ireland
11 D2 Inishowen *pen.* Rep. of Ireland
11 E2 Inishowen Head *hd* Rep. of Ireland
11 D2 Inishtrahull *i.* Rep. of Ireland
11 D2 Inishtrahull Sound *chan.* Rep. of Ireland
11 A4 Inishturk *i.* Rep. of Ireland
31 F2 Inkylap Turkm.
51 D5 Inland Kaikoura Range *mts* N.Z.
6 O3 Inndyr Norway
Inner Mongolian Aut. Region *div. see* Nei Monggol Zizhiqu
10 C3 Inner Sound *chan.* U.K.
48 E3 Innisfail Austr.
16 E7 Innsbruck Austria
11 D4 Inny *r.* Rep. of Ireland
88 B4 Inongo Congo(Zaire)
16 J4 Inowrocław Pol.
86 C2 In Salah Alg.
20 H4 Insar Rus. Fed.
10 F3 Insch U.K.
42 D6 Insil S. Korea
24 H3 Inta Rus. Fed.
83 D2 Intendente Alvear Arg.
16 C7 Interlaken Switz.
64 E1 International Falls U.S.A.
41 G7 Inubō-zaki *pt* Japan
58 E2 Inukjuak Can.
54 E3 Inuvik Can.
10 C4 Inveraray U.K.
10 F4 Inverbervie U.K.
51 B7 Invercargill N.Z.
48 F4 Inverell Austr.
10 D3 Invergordon U.K.
10 E4 Inverkeithing U.K.
59 H4 Inverness Can.
10 D3 Inverness U.K.
67 D6 Inverness U.S.A.
10 F3 Inverurie U.K.
48 D5 Investigator Strait *chan.* Austr.
27 G1 Inya Rus. Fed.
63 C5 Inyokern U.S.A.
72 C3 Inyo Mts *mts* U.S.A.
88 D4 Inyonga Tanz.
20 H4 Inza Rus. Fed.
21 G4 Inzhavino Rus. Fed.
19 J5 Ioannina Greece
36 G4 Iō-Jima Japan
65 E4 Iola U.S.A.
10 B4 Iona *i.* U.K.
62 C1 Ione U.S.A.
68 E4 Ionia U.S.A.
19 H5 Ionian Islands *is* Greece
18 G6 Ionian Sea *sea* Greece/Italy
Ionoi Nisoi *is see* Ionian Islands
36 G1 Iony, Ostrov *i.* Rus. Fed.
29 L1 Iori *r.* Georgia
19 L6 Ios *i.* Greece
41 B9 Iō-shima *i.* Japan
68 A4 Iowa *div.* U.S.A.
68 B5 Iowa *r.* U.S.A.
68 B5 Iowa City U.S.A.
64 E3 Iowa Falls U.S.A.
82 C2 Ipameri Brazil
78 D5 Iparía Peru
82 D2 Ipatinga Brazil
21 G6 Ipatovo Rus. Fed.
91 F3 Ipelegeng S. Africa
81 A4 Ipiales Col.
82 E1 Ipiaú Brazil
82 B4 Ipiranga Brazil
45 B2 Ipoh Malaysia
79 L5 Ipojuca *r.* Brazil
82 B2 Iporá Brazil
88 C3 Ippy C.A.R.
19 M4 İpsala Turkey
9 J5 Ipswich U.K.
55 M3 Iqaluit Can.
80 B2 Iquique Chile
78 D4 Iquitos Peru
31 F5 Īrafshān *reg.* Iran
41 E7 Irago-misaki *pt* Japan
19 L6 Irakleia *i.* Greece
Irakleio *see* Iraklion
19 L7 Iraklion Greece
82 E1 Iramaia Brazil
23 E6 Iran *country* Asia
45 D2 Iran, Pegunungan *mts* Indon.
30 B2 Irānshāh Iran
31 F5 Īrānshahr Iran
Iranshahr *see* Fahraj
74 D4 Irapuato Mex.
23 D6 Iraq *country* Asia
71 G2 Irasville U.S.A.
82 B4 Irati Brazil
28 E5 Irbid Jordan
24 H4 Irbit Rus. Fed.
79 K6 Irecê Brazil
5 C3 Ireland, Republic of *country* Europe
88 C4 Irema Congo(Zaire)
26 E2 Irgiz Kazak.
42 D6 Iri S. Korea
37 F7 Irian Jaya *reg.* Indon.
29 L2 Īrī Dagh *mt* Iran
43 B3 Iriga Phil.
86 B3 Irîgui *reg.* Mali/Maur.
89 D4 Iringa Tanz.
33 B4 Irinjalakuda India
79 H4 Iriri *r.* Brazil
8 B4 Irish Sea *sea* Rep. of Ireland
79 J4 Irituia Brazil
30 C5 'Irj *well* S. Arabia
36 C1 Irkutsk Rus. Fed.
28 D2 Irmak Turkey
69 F2 Iron Bridge Can.
70 E3 Irondequoit U.S.A.
68 C3 Iron Mountain *MI* U.S.A.
73 F3 Iron Mountain *mt UT* U.S.A.
68 C2 Iron River U.S.A.
65 F4 Ironton *MO* U.S.A.
70 B5 Ironton *OH* U.S.A.
68 B2 Ironwood U.S.A.
71 F2 Iroquois Can.
68 D5 Iroquois *r.* U.S.A.
43 C3 Irosin Phil.
41 F7 Irō-zaki *pt* Japan
21 D5 Irpin' Ukr.
30 A5 Irq al Mazḥūr *sand dunes* S. Arabia
30 B5 'Irq ath Thāmām *sand dunes* S. Arabia
30 B5 Irq Jahām *sand dunes* S. Arabia
35 H Irrawaddy *r.* China/Myanmar
37 B5 Irrawaddy, Mouths of the *est.* Myanmar
34 C1 Irshad Pass Afgh./Pak.
20 J2 Irta Rus. Fed.
8 E3 Irthing *r.* U.K.
27 F1 Irtysh *r.* Kazak./Rus. Fed.
88 C3 Irumu Congo(Zaire)
15 F1 Irún Spain
10 D5 Irvine U.K.
72 D5 Irvine *CA* U.S.A.
70 B6 Irvine *KY* U.S.A.
65 D5 Irving U.S.A.
43 B5 Isabela Phil.
78 □ Isabela, Isla *i. Galapagos Is* Ecuador
75 G6 Isabelia, Cordillera *mts* Nic.
68 B2 Isabella U.S.A.
72 C4 Isabella Lake *l.* U.S.A.
68 D2 Isabelle, Pt *pt* U.S.A.
6 B3 Ísafjarðardjúp *est.* Iceland
6 B3 Ísafjörður Iceland
41 B8 Isahaya Japan
34 B2 Isà Khel Pak.
20 G1 Isakogorka Rus. Fed.
89 E6 Isalo, Massif de l' *mts* Madag.
89 E6 Isalo, Parc National de l' *nat. park* Madag.
81 C4 Isana *r.* Col.
10 □ Isbister U.K.
18 E4 Ischia, Isola d' *i.* Italy
81 A4 Iscuande *r.* Col.
41 E7 Ise Japan
88 C3 Isengi Congo(Zaire)
14 H4 Isère *r.* France
13 F3 Iserlohn Ger.
13 H2 Isernhagen Ger.
18 F4 Isernia Italy
41 F6 Isesaki Japan
41 E7 Ise-shima National Park Japan
41 E7 Ise-wan *b.* Japan
86 C4 Iseyin Nigeria
Isfahan *see* Eşfahan
31 H2 Isfana Kyrg.
29 K5 Isḥāq Iraq
20 J4 Isheyevka Rus. Fed.
40 G3 Ishikari-gawa *r.* Japan
40 G3 Ishikari-wan *b.* Japan
40 G5 Ishinomaki Japan
40 G5 Ishinomaki-wan *b.* Japan
41 G6 Ishioka Japan
41 C8 Ishizuchi-san *mt* Japan
34 C1 Ishkuman Pak.
68 D2 Ishpeming U.S.A.
31 G2 Ishtykhan Uzbek.
35 G4 Ishurdi Bangl.
78 E7 Isiboro Sécure, Parque Nacional *nat. park* Bol.
28 B2 Işıklı Turkey
28 B2 Işıklı Barajı *resr* Turkey
24 J4 Isil'kul' Rus. Fed.
91 J4 Isipingo S. Africa
88 C3 Isiro Congo(Zaire)
31 G2 Iskabad Canal *canal* Afgh.
28 F3 İskenderun Turkey
28 E1 İskilip Turkey
36 A1 Iskitim Rus. Fed.
19 L3 Iskŭr *r.* Bulg.
56 C3 Iskut Can.
56 C3 Iskut *r.* Can.
28 F3 Islahiye Turkey
34 C2 Islamabad Pak.
34 C3 Islam Barrage *barrage* Pak.
34 B4 Islamgarh Pak.
34 B4 Islamkot Pak.
67 D7 Islamorada U.S.A.
31 F3 Islam Qala Afgh.
43 A4 Island Bay *b.* Phil.
71 J1 Island Falls U.S.A.
57 L4 Island L. *l.* Can.
48 D5 Island Lagoon *salt flat* Austr.
57 L4 Island Lake Can.
68 A2 Island Lake *l.* U.S.A.
11 F3 Island Magee *pen.* U.K.
72 A1 Island Mountain U.S.A.
62 E2 Island Park U.S.A.
71 H2 Island Pond U.S.A.
51 E1 Islands, Bay of *b.* N.Z.
10 B5 Islay *i.* U.K.
70 E6 Isle of Wight U.S.A.
68 C2 Isle Royale National Park U.S.A.
87 F1 Ismâ'ilîya Egypt
29 M1 İsmayıllı Azer.
7 R5 Isojoki Fin.
89 D5 Isoka Zambia
6 U3 Isokylä Fin.
18 G5 Isola di Capo Rizzuto Italy
28 C3 Isparta Turkey
19 M3 Isperikh Bulg.
31 F5 Ispikan Pak.
29 H1 İspir Turkey
23 C6 Israel *country* Asia
20 H4 Issa Rus. Fed.
12 E3 Isselburg Ger.
86 B4 Issia Côte d'Ivoire
29 K6 Issin Iraq
14 F4 Issoire France
29 J4 Iştablāt Iraq
28 B1 İstanbul Turkey
İstanbul Boğazı *str. see* Bosporus
30 C3 Īstgāh-e Eznā Iran
19 K5 Istiaia Greece
81 A3 Istmina Col.
67 D7 Istokpoga, L. *l.* U.S.A.
18 E2 Istra *pen.* Croatia
14 G5 Istres France
Istria *pen. see* Istra
35 G5 Iswaripur Bangl.
79 L6 Itabaianinha Brazil
79 K6 Itaberaba Brazil
82 D2 Itabira Brazil
82 D3 Itabirito Brazil
82 E1 Itabuna Brazil
79 G4 Itacoatiara Brazil
82 B3 Itaguajé Brazil
82 C3 Itaí Brazil
82 A4 Itaimbey *r.* Para.
79 G4 Itaituba Brazil
80 G3 Itajaí Brazil
82 D3 Itajubá Brazil
35 F5 Itaki India
5 E4 Italy *country* Europe
79 L7 Itamaraju Brazil
82 D2 Itamarandiba Brazil
82 E2 Itambacuri Brazil
82 E2 Itambacuri *r.* Brazil
82 D2 Itambé, Pico de *mt* Brazil
89 E6 Itampolo Madag.
35 H4 Itanagar India
82 D1 Itanguari *r.* Brazil
82 C4 Itanhaém Brazil
82 E2 Itanhém Brazil
82 E2 Itanhém *r.* Brazil
82 E2 Itaobim Brazil
82 C2 Itapajipe Brazil
82 E1 Itaparica, Ilha *i.* Brazil
82 E1 Itapebi Brazil
82 E3 Itapemirim Brazil
82 E3 Itaperuna Brazil
82 E1 Itapetinga Brazil
82 C3 Itapetininga Brazil
82 C3 Itapeva Brazil
79 L6 Itapicuru *r. Bahia* Brazil
79 K5 Itapicuru *r. Maranhão* Brazil
79 K4 Itapicuru Mirim Brazil
79 L4 Itapipoca Brazil
82 C4 Itararé Brazil
82 C3 Itararé *r.* Brazil
34 D5 Itarsi India
82 B2 Itarumã Brazil
43 B1 Itbayat *i.* Phil.
56 G1 Itchen Lake *l.* Can.
19 K5 Itea Greece
68 E4 Ithaca *MI* U.S.A.
70 E3 Ithaca *NY* U.S.A.
13 H2 Ith Hils *ridge* Ger.
28 F6 Ithrah S. Arabia
88 C3 Itimbiri *r.* Congo(Zaire)
82 E2 Itinga Brazil
82 A2 Itiquira Brazil
82 A2 Itiquira *r.* Brazil
41 F7 Itō Japan
41 E6 Itoigawa Japan
18 C4 Ittiri *Sardinia* Italy
82 C3 Itu Brazil
81 B3 Ituango Col.
78 D5 Ituí *r.* Brazil
82 C2 Ituiutaba Brazil
88 C4 Itula Congo(Zaire)
82 C2 Itumbiara Brazil
79 G2 Ituni Guyana
79 J5 Itupiranga Brazil
82 B3 Iturama Brazil
82 A4 Iturbe Para.
36 G2 Iturup, Ostrov *i.* Rus. Fed.
78 E5 Ituxi *r.* Brazil
16 D4 Itzehoe Ger.
81 C4 Iuaretê Brazil
25 V3 Iultin Rus. Fed.
81 C4 Iutica Brazil
82 B3 Ivaí *r.* Brazil
6 U2 Ivalo Fin.
6 U2 Ivalojoki *r.* Fin.
21 C4 Ivanava Belarus
19 H3 Ivangrad Yugo.
50 E2 Ivanhoe Austr.
69 F1 Ivanhoe *r.* Can.
57 H2 Ivanhoe Lake *l. N.W.T.* Can.
69 F1 Ivanhoe Lake *l. Ont.* Can.
17 O5 Ivankiv Ukr.
21 C5 Ivano-Frankivs'k Ukr.
20 G3 Ivanovo Rus. Fed.
20 G3 Ivanovskaya Oblast' *div.* Rus. Fed.
73 E4 Ivanpah Lake *l.* U.S.A.
20 J4 Ivanteyevka Rus. Fed.
20 C4 Ivatsevichy Belarus
19 M4 Ivaylovgrad Bulg.
24 H3 Ivdel' Rus. Fed.
82 B3 Ivinheima Brazil
82 B3 Ivinheima *r.* Brazil
55 O3 Ivittuut Greenland
89 E6 Ivohibe Madag.
Ivory Coast *country see* Côte d'Ivoire
18 B2 Ivrea Italy
19 M5 İvrindi Turkey
21 H7 Ivris Ugheltekhili *pass* Georgia
55 L3 Ivujivik Can.
17 N4 Ivyanyets Belarus
40 G5 Iwaizumi Japan
41 G6 Iwaki Japan
40 G4 Iwaki-san *volc.* Japan
41 C7 Iwakuni Japan
40 G3 Iwamizawa Japan
40 G5 Iwate-san *volc.* Japan
86 C4 Iwo Nigeria
Iwo Jima *see* Iō-Jima
20 C4 Iwye Belarus
12 C4 Ixelles Belgium
74 E4 Ixmiquilpán Mex.
91 J5 Ixopo S. Africa
9 H5 Ixworth U.K.
41 C8 Iyo Japan
41 C8 Iyo-nada *b.* Japan
74 G5 Izabal, L. de *l.* Guatemala
40 G3 Izari-dake *mt* Japan
88 D4 Izazi Tanz.
21 H7 Izberbash Rus. Fed.
17 Q3 Izdeshkovo Rus. Fed.
12 B4 Izegem Belgium
30 C4 Īzeh Iran
24 G4 Izhevsk Rus. Fed.
24 G3 Izhma Rus. Fed.
20 K1 Izhma *r.* Rus. Fed.
21 F4 Izmalkovo Rus. Fed.
21 D6 Izmayil Ukr.
19 M5 İzmir Turkey
19 M5 İzmir Körfezi *g.* Turkey
28 B1 İznik Gölü *l.* Turkey
21 G6 Izobil'nyy Rus. Fed.
41 F7 Izu-hantō *pen.* Japan
41 A7 Izuhara Japan
41 D7 Izumisano Japan
41 C7 Izumo Japan
41 F7 Izu-shotō *is* Japan
21 C5 Izyaslav Ukr.
21 F5 Izyum Ukr.


## J


30 E3 Jaba *watercourse* Iran
Jabal, Bahr el *r. see* White Nile
15 E3 Jabalón *r.* Spain
34 D5 Jabalpur India
28 F3 Jabbūl Syria
48 D3 Jabiru Austr.
28 E4 Jablah Syria
18 G3 Jablanica Bos.-Herz.
79 M5 Jaboatão Brazil
82 C3 Jaboticabal Brazil
15 F1 Jaca Spain
79 K6 Jacaré *r.* Brazil
79 G5 Jacareacanga Brazil
82 C3 Jacareí Brazil
83 C1 Jáchal *r.* Arg.
13 L4 Jáchymov Czech Rep.
82 E2 Jacinto Brazil
78 F5 Jaciparaná *r.* Brazil
68 D1 Jackfish Can.
69 H3 Jack Lake *l.* Can.
71 H2 Jackman U.S.A.
65 D5 Jacksboro U.S.A.
65 G6 Jackson *AL* U.S.A.
72 B2 Jackson *CA* U.S.A.
70 B6 Jackson *KY* U.S.A.
68 E4 Jackson *MI* U.S.A.
64 E3 Jackson *MN* U.S.A.
65 F4 Jackson *MO* U.S.A.
65 F5 Jackson *MS* U.S.A.
70 B5 Jackson *OH* U.S.A.
67 B5 Jackson *TN* U.S.A.
62 E3 Jackson *WY* U.S.A.
51 B5 Jackson Head *hd* N.Z.
62 E2 Jackson L. *l.* U.S.A.
65 E6 Jackson, Lake U.S.A.
68 D3 Jacksonport U.S.A.
65 E5 Jacksonville *AR* U.S.A.
67 D6 Jacksonville *FL* U.S.A.
68 B6 Jacksonville *IL* U.S.A.
67 E5 Jacksonville *NC* U.S.A.
65 E6 Jacksonville *TX* U.S.A.
67 D6 Jacksonville Beach U.S.A.
75 K5 Jacmel Haiti
34 B3 Jacobabad Pak.
79 K6 Jacobina Brazil
73 F3 Jacob Lake U.S.A.
90 F4 Jacobsdal S. Africa
Jacobshavn *see* Ilulissat
59 H4 Jacques-Cartier, Détroit de *chan.* Can.
59 G4 Jacques Cartier, Mt *mt* Can.
59 G4 Jacquet River Can.
83 G1 Jacuí *r.* Brazil
79 L6 Jacuípe *r.* Brazil
79 J4 Jacunda Brazil
82 C4 Jacupiranga Brazil
81 C2 Jacura Venez.
33 B2 Jadcherla India
31 F5 Jaddi, Ras *pt* Pak.
13 G1 Jadebusen *b.* Ger.
87 D1 Jādū Libya
78 C5 Jaén Peru
43 B3 Jaen Phil.
15 E4 Jaén Spain
30 C3 Ja'farābād Iran
Jaffa *see* Tel Aviv-Yafo
50 B4 Jaffa, C. *pt* Austr.
33 B4 Jaffna Sri Lanka
71 G3 Jaffrey U.S.A.
34 D3 Jagadhri India
33 B3 Jagalur India
33 C2 Jagdalpur India
91 F4 Jagersfontein S. Africa
34 D2 Jaggang China
31 E5 Jagīn *watercourse* Iran
Jagok Tso *salt l. see* Urru Co
34 C3 Jagraon India
13 H5 Jagst *r.* Ger.
33 B2 Jagtial India
83 G2 Jaguarão Brazil
83 G2 Jaguarão *r.* Brazil/Uru.
82 C4 Jaguariaíva Brazil
35 F4 Jahanabad India
29 M3 Jahan Dagh *mt* Iran
34 C4 Jahazpur India
29 K7 Jahmah *well* Iraq
30 D4 Jahrom Iran
38 B3 Jainca China
34 C4 Jaipur India
34 B4 Jaisalmer India
34 E5 Jaisinghnagar India
34 D5 Jaitgarh *mt* India
35 E3 Jajarkot Nepal
30 E2 Jajarm Iran
18 G2 Jajce Bos.-Herz.
45 C4 Jakarta Indon.
56 C2 Jakes Corner Can.
34 B5 Jakhan India
31 G4 Jakin *mt* Afgh.
6 P3 Jäkkvik Sweden
6 S5 Jakobstad Fin.
65 C5 Jal U.S.A.
31 H3 Jalālābād Afgh.
27 F2 Jalal-Abad Kyrg.
34 C3 Jalandhar India
74 E5 Jalapa Enríquez Mex.
7 S5 Jalasjärvi Fin.
35 G4 Jaldhaka *r.* Bangl.
33 B2 Jaldrug India
82 B3 Jales Brazil
35 F5 Jaleshwar India
34 D5 Jalgaon *Maharashtra* India
34 C5 Jalgaon *Maharashtra* India
29 L6 Jalībah Iraq
86 D4 Jalingo Nigeria
34 C6 Jalna India
31 F5 Jālo Iran
15 F2 Jalón *r.* Spain
35 G4 Jalpaiguri India
87 E2 Jālū Libya
29 K4 Jalūlā Iraq
31 F3 Jām *r.* Iran
31 F3 Jām *reg.* Iran
34 D5 Jamai India
53 J8 Jamaica *country* Caribbean Sea
75 J5 Jamaica Channel Haiti/Jamaica
30 C3 Jamālābād Iran
29 L3 Jamalabad Iran
35 G4 Jamalpur Bangl.
35 F4 Jamalpur India
79 G5 Jamanxim *r.* Brazil
45 B3 Jambi Indon.
34 C4 Jambo India
45 A2 Jamboaye *r.* Indon.
45 A5 Jambongan *i.* Malaysia
44 A4 Jambuair, Tg *pt* Indon.
29 K4 Jambur Iraq
33 A1 Jambusar India
64 D2 James *r. ND* U.S.A.
70 D6 James *r. VA* U.S.A.
34 B4 Jamesabad Pak.
58 D3 James Bay *b.* Can.
83 D2 James Craik Arg.
55 Q2 Jameson Land *reg.* Greenland

51 B6 James Pk *mt* N.Z.
92 B2 James Ross I. *i.* Ant.
55 J3 James Ross Strait *chan.* Can.
50 B2 Jamestown Austr.
91 G5 Jamestown S. Africa
64 D2 Jamestown *ND* U.S.A.
70 D3 Jamestown *NY* U.S.A.
29 M4 Jamīlābād Iran
33 A2 Jamkhandi India
33 A2 Jamkhed India
33 B3 Jammalamadugu India
34 C2 Jammu Jammu and Kashmir
34 C2 Jammu and Kashmir *terr.* Asia
34 B5 Jamnagar India
34 D4 Jamni *r.* India
45 C4 Jampang Kulon Indon.
34 B3 Jampur Pak.
7 T6 Jämsä Fin.
7 T6 Jämsänkoski Fin.
35 F5 Jamshedpur India
35 G5 Jamuna *r.* Bangl.
82 D1 Janaúba Brazil
82 B2 Jandaia Brazil
30 D3 Jandaq Iran
34 B2 Jandola Pak.
72 B1 Janesville *CA* U.S.A.
68 C4 Janesville *WV* U.S.A.
31 E3 Jangal Iran
35 G4 Jangipur India
29 L2 Jānī Beyglū Iran
13 M2 Jänickendorf Ger.
96 J1 Jan Mayen *i.* Arctic Ocean
29 L5 Jannah Iraq
31 F3 Jannatabad Iran
90 F6 Jansenville S. Africa
82 D1 Januária Brazil
34 C5 Jaora India
23 O6 Japan *country* Asia
Japan Alps Nat. Park *see* Chibu-Sangaku Nat. Park
40 C5 Japan, Sea of *sea* Pac. Oc.
94 E4 Japan Tr. *sea feature* Pac. Oc.
78 E4 Japurá *r.* Brazil
35 H4 Jāpvo Mount *mt* India
81 A3 Jaqué Panama
28 G3 Jarābulus Syria
82 A3 Jaraguari Brazil
28 E5 Jarash Jordan
82 A3 Jardim Brazil
75 J4 Jardines de la Reina, Archipiélago de los *is* Cuba
42 B2 Jargalang China
36 D2 Jargalant Mongolia
29 K4 Jarmo Iraq
7 P7 Järna Sweden
16 H5 Jarocin Pol.
17 L5 Jarosław Pol.
6 N5 Järpen Sweden
30 C4 Jarrāhi *watercourse* Iran
38 B2 Jartai China
78 F6 Jarú Brazil
42 A1 Jarud Qi China
7 T7 Järvakandi Estonia
7 T6 Järvenpää Fin.
46 L4 Jarvis Island *i.* Pac. Oc.
34 B5 Jasdan India
31 E5 Jāsk Iran
17 K6 Jasło Pol.
80 D8 Jason Is *is* Falkland Is
92 B2 Jason Pen. *pen.* Ant.
56 F4 Jasper Can.
67 C5 Jasper *AL* U.S.A.
65 E4 Jasper *AR* U.S.A.
67 D6 Jasper *FL* U.S.A.
66 C4 Jasper *IN* U.S.A.
70 E3 Jasper *NY* U.S.A.
70 B5 Jasper *OH* U.S.A.
65 E6 Jasper *TX* U.S.A.
56 F4 Jasper Nat. Park Can.
29 K5 Jaşşān Iraq
17 J6 Jastrzębie-Zdrój Pol.
34 C4 Jaswantpura India
17 J7 Jászberény Hungary
82 B2 Jataí Brazil
79 G4 Jatapu *r.* Brazil
33 A2 Jath India
34 B4 Jati Pak.
34 B3 Jatoi Pak.
82 C3 Jaú Brazil
78 F4 Jaú *r.* Brazil
81 E5 Jauaperi *r.* Brazil
81 D3 Jaua Sarisariñama, Parque Nacional *nat. park* Venez.
7 S8 Jaunlutriņi Latvia
7 U8 Jaunpiebalga Latvia
35 E4 Jaunpur India
78 F4 Jaú, Parque Nacional do *nat. park* Brazil
31 F4 Jauri Iran
82 A2 Jauru Brazil
82 B2 Jauru *r.* Brazil
21 G7 Java Georgia
45 C4 Java *i.* Indon.
33 B3 Javadi Hills *mts* India
31 G3 Javand Afgh.
93 M4 Java Ridge *sea feature* Ind. Ocean
36 D2 Javarthushuu Mongolia
45 D3 Java Sea *sea* Indon.
Java Trench *sea feature* *see* Sunda Trench
13 K2 Jävenitz Ger.
Jawa *i.* *see* Java
34 C4 Jawad India
34 B4 Jawai *r.* India
28 F3 Jawbān Bayk Syria
34 C6 Jawhar India
88 E3 Jawhar Somalia
16 H5 Jawor Pol.
37 F7 Jaya, Pk *mt* Indon.
37 G7 Jayapura Indon.
35 F4 Jaynagar India
28 F5 Jayrūd Syria
32 B6 Jazā'ir Farasān *is* S. Arabia
29 M3 Jazvān Iran
29 G4 Jdaide Syria
73 E4 Jean U.S.A.
56 E2 Jean Marie River Can.
59 G2 Jeannin, Lac *l.* Can.
31 E4 Jebāl Bārez, Kūh-e *mts* Iran
86 C4 Jebba Nigeria
87 E3 Jebel Abyad Plateau *plat.* Sudan
34 C3 Jech Doab *lowland* Pak.
10 F5 Jedburgh U.K.
32 A5 Jedda S. Arabia
18 C6 Jedeida Tunisia
13 K1 Jeetze *r.* Ger.
71 F3 Jefferson *NY* U.S.A.
68 C4 Jefferson *WV* U.S.A.
62 D2 Jefferson *r.* U.S.A.
64 E4 Jefferson City U.S.A.
72 D2 Jefferson, Mt *mt* *NV* U.S.A.
62 B2 Jefferson, Mt *volc.* *OR* U.S.A.
66 C4 Jeffersonville U.S.A.
90 F7 Jeffrey's Bay S. Africa
80 E2 Jejuí Guazú *r.* Para.
7 T8 Jēkabpils Latvia
16 G5 Jelenia Góra Pol.
35 G4 Jelep La *pass* China
7 S8 Jelgava Latvia
70 A6 Jellico U.S.A.
44 C5 Jemaja *i.* Indon.
45 D4 Jember Indon.
45 E3 Jempang, Danau *l.* Indon.
13 K4 Jena Ger.
86 C1 Jendouba Tunisia
28 E5 Jenin West Bank
70 B6 Jenkins U.S.A.
72 A2 Jenner U.S.A.
65 E6 Jennings U.S.A.
57 K4 Jenpeg Can.
50 D4 Jeparit Austr.
82 E1 Jequié Brazil
82 D2 Jequitaí Brazil
82 D2 Jequitaí *r.* Brazil
82 E2 Jequitinhonha Brazil
82 E2 Jequitinhonha *r.* Brazil
44 B5 Jerantut Malaysia
87 F4 Jerbar Sudan
75 K5 Jérémie Haiti
15 C4 Jerez de la Frontera Spain
15 C3 Jerez de los Caballeros Spain
19 J5 Jergucat Albania
28 E6 Jericho West Bank
13 L2 Jerichow Ger.
50 E3 Jerilderie Austr.
29 K2 Jermuk Armenia
62 D3 Jerome U.S.A.
14 C2 Jersey *i.* *Channel Is* U.K.
71 F4 Jersey City U.S.A.
70 E4 Jersey Shore U.S.A.
66 B4 Jerseyville U.S.A.
79 K5 Jerumenha Brazil
28 E6 Jerusalem Israel/West Bank
50 H3 Jervis B. *b.* Austr.
50 H3 Jervis Bay Austr.
50 H3 Jervis Bay Terr. Austr.
18 F1 Jesenice Slovenia
18 E3 Jesi Italy
13 L3 Jessen Ger.
7 M6 Jessheim Norway
35 G5 Jessore Bangl.
13 H1 Jesteburg Ger.
67 D6 Jesup U.S.A.
74 F5 Jesús Carranza Mex.
83 D1 Jesús María Arg.
34 B5 Jetalsar India
64 D4 Jetmore U.S.A.
13 F1 Jever Ger.
35 F4 Jha Jha India
34 D3 Jhajjar India
34 C4 Jhajju India
34 A3 Jhal Pak.
35 G5 Jhalakati Bangl.
31 G5 Jhal Jhao Pak.
34 C3 Jhang Pak.
34 D4 Jhansi India
35 F5 Jharia India
35 F5 Jharsuguda India
34 B3 Jhatpat Pak.
34 C2 Jhelum Pak.
34 C2 Jhelum *r.* Pak.
35 G5 Jhenida Bangl.
34 B4 Jhudo Pak.
35 F4 Jhumritilaiya India
34 C3 Jhunjhunūn India
38 C3 Jiachuan China
38 F4 Jiading China
38 D5 Jiahe China
39 B4 Jiajiang China
38 B3 Jialing Jiang *r.* China
40 B1 Jiamusi China
39 E5 Ji'an *Jiangxi* China
39 E5 Ji'an *Jiangxi* China
42 D3 Ji'an China
38 F1 Jianchang China
39 F4 Jiande China
39 B4 Jiang'an China
39 C4 Jiangbei China
39 A6 Jiangcheng China
39 B5 Jiangchuan China
38 B4 Jiange China
39 D5 Jianghua China
39 C4 Jiangjin China
39 C5 Jiangkou China
39 E5 Jiangle China
39 D4 Jiangling China
38 B3 Jiangluozhen China
39 D6 Jiangmen China
39 F4 Jiangshan China
38 F3 Jiangsu *div.* China
39 E5 Jiangxi *div.* China
38 D3 Jiang Xian China
38 F4 Jiangyin China
39 D5 Jiangyong China
38 B4 Jiangyou China
38 F3 Jianhu China
39 D6 Jian Jiang *r.* China
39 D4 Jianli China
39 E5 Jianning China
39 F5 Jian'ou China
38 F1 Jianping *Liaoning* China
38 F1 Jianping *Liaoning* China
39 C4 Jianshi China
39 B6 Jianshui China
39 F5 Jianyang *Fujian* China
39 B4 Jianyang *Sichuan* China
38 D2 Jiaocheng China
38 E2 Jiaohe *Hebei* China
42 D2 Jiaohe China
39 F4 Jiaojiang China
42 A2 Jiaolai *r.* *Nei Monggol* China
38 F2 Jiaolai *r.* *Shandong* China
39 E5 Jiaoling China
38 F3 Jiaonan China
38 F2 Jiao Xian China
38 F2 Jiaozhou Wan *b.* China
38 D3 Jiaozuo China
42 D2 Jiapigou China
38 F3 Jiashan China
38 D2 Jia Xian China
38 F4 Jiaxing China
39 D4 Jiayu China
38 B3 Jiayuguan China
39 E6 Jiazi China
30 B6 Jibāl al Ḩawshah *mts* S. Arabia
Jiddah *see* Jedda
32 E6 Jiddat al Ḩarāsīs *gravel area* Oman
42 F1 Jidong China
38 B2 Jiehebe China
6 Q2 Jiehkkevarri *mt* Norway
39 E6 Jieshi China
39 E6 Jieshi Wan *b.* China
38 E3 Jieshou China
6 T2 Iešjávri *l.* Norway
39 E6 Jiexi China
38 D2 Jiexiu China
39 E6 Jieyang China
7 T9 Jieznas Lith.
38 A3 Jigzhi China
16 G6 Jihlava Czech Rep.
31 F3 Jija Sarai Afgh.
88 E3 Jijiga Eth.
39 A4 Jiju China
41 H3 Jilga *r.* Afgh.
34 D2 Jilganang Kol, S. *salt l.* China/Jammu and Kashmir
88 E3 Jilib Somalia
42 D2 Jilin China
42 C2 Jilin *div.* China
42 A2 Jiling China
42 C2 Jilin Handa Ling *mts* China
88 D3 Jīma Eth.
74 D3 Jiménez *Chihuahua* Mex.
74 E4 Jiménez *Tamaulipas* Mex.
38 F2 Jimo China
71 F4 Jim Thorpe U.S.A.
38 E2 Jinan China
38 B2 Jinchang China
38 D3 Jincheng China
38 B4 Jinchuan China
34 D3 Jind India
50 G4 Jindabyne Austr.
50 F3 Jindera Austr.
16 G6 Jindřichův Hradec Czech Rep.
38 C3 Jing *r.* China
39 E4 Jing'an China
39 E4 Jingbian China
38 C3 Jingchuan China
39 F4 Jingde China
39 E4 Jingdezhen China
39 E5 Jinggangshan China
39 E4 Jinggongqiao China
38 E2 Jinghai China
37 C4 Jinghong China
38 E3 Jingjiang China
38 D2 Jingle China
38 D4 Jingmen China
38 B3 Jingning China
42 E2 Jingpo China
42 E2 Jingpo Hu *resr* China
38 B2 Jingtai China
39 C6 Jingxi China
39 F4 Jing Xian *Anhui* China
39 C5 Jing Xian *Hunan* China
42 D2 Jingyu China
38 B2 Jingyuan China
39 F3 Jinhu China
39 F4 Jinhua China
38 D1 Jining *Nei Monggol* China
38 E3 Jining *Shandong* China
88 D3 Jinja Uganda
39 F5 Jinjiang China
39 E4 Jin Jiang *r.* China
88 D3 Jinka Eth.
43 A3 Jinlingsi China
39 C7 Jinmu Jiao *pt* China
74 G6 Jinotepe Nic.
39 C5 Jinping *Guizhou* China
39 B6 Jinping *Yunnan* China
39 A5 Jinping Shan *mts* China
39 C5 Jinsha China
Jinsha Jiang *r.* *see* Yangtze
38 F4 Jinshan China
39 D4 Jinshi China
38 B4 Jintang China
43 B4 Jintotolo *i.* Phil.
43 B4 Jintotolo Channel Phil.
34 D6 Jintur India
39 E5 Jinxi *Jiangxi* China
42 A3 Jinxi China
42 A3 Jin Xian *Liaoning* China
42 A4 Jin Xian *Liaoning* China
39 E4 Jinxian China
38 E3 Jinxiang *Shandong* China
39 F5 Jinxiang *Zhejiang* China
39 B5 Jinyang China
39 F4 Jinyun China
38 E4 Jinzhai China
42 A3 Jinzhou China
42 A4 Jinzhou Wan *b.* China
78 F5 Jiparaná *r.* Brazil
78 B4 Jipijapa Ecuador
31 H2 Jirgatol Tajik.
31 E4 Jīroft Iran
30 C6 Jirwan *well* S. Arabia
39 C4 Jishou China
39 E5 Jishui China
28 F4 Jisr ash Shughūr Syria
44 B4 Jitra Malaysia
38 C2 Jiudengkou China
38 B4 Jiuding Shan *mt* China
38 C3 Jiufoping China
39 E4 Jiujiang *Jiangxi* China
39 E4 Jiujiang *Jiangxi* China
39 E4 Jiuling Shan *mts* China
39 A4 Jiulong China
42 A2 Jiumiao China
42 B5 Jiurongcheng China
42 C1 Jiutai China
39 C5 Jiuxu China
31 F5 Jiwani Pak.
39 F4 Jixi *Anhui* China
42 F1 Jixi China
38 E2 Ji Xian *Hebei* China
38 E3 Ji Xian *Henan* China
40 B1 Jixian China
38 D3 Jiyuan China
32 B6 Jīzān S. Arabia
41 C7 Jizō-zaki *pt* Japan
79 M5 João Pessoa Brazil
82 C2 João Pinheiro Brazil
72 C2 Job Peak *summit* U.S.A.
13 L4 Jocketa Ger.
35 F5 Joda India
34 C4 Jodhpur India
6 V5 Joensuu Fin.
41 F6 Jōetsu Japan
89 D6 Jofane Moz.
56 F4 Joffre, Mt *mt* Can.
7 U7 Jõgeva Estonia
7 U7 Jõgua Estonia
91 G3 Johannesburg S. Africa
72 D4 Johannesburg U.S.A.
34 E5 Johilla *r.* India
62 C2 John Day U.S.A.
62 B2 John Day *r.* U.S.A.
56 F3 John d'Or Prairie Can.
70 D6 John H. Kerr Res. *resr* U.S.A.
10 E2 John o'Groats U.K.
67 D4 Johnson City U.S.A.
56 C2 Johnson's Crossing Can.
67 D5 Johnston U.S.A.
10 D5 Johnstone U.K.
46 L2 Johnston I. *i.* Pac. Oc.
11 D5 Johnstown Rep. of Ireland
71 F3 Johnstown *NY* U.S.A.
70 D4 Johnstown *PA* U.S.A.
69 F3 Johnswood U.S.A.
45 B2 Johor Bahru Malaysia
7 U7 Jõhvi Estonia
80 G3 Joinville Brazil
14 G2 Joinville France
92 B2 Joinville I. *i.* Ant.
6 Q3 Jokkmokk Sweden
6 F4 Jökulsá á Brú *r.* Iceland
6 E3 Jökulsá á Fjöllum *r.* Iceland
6 F4 Jökulsá í Fljótsdal *r.* Iceland
30 B2 Jolfa Iran
68 C5 Joliet U.S.A.
58 F4 Joliette Can.
43 B5 Jolo Phil.
43 B5 Jolo *i.* Phil.
43 B3 Jomalig *i.* Phil.
45 D4 Jombang Indon.
7 T9 Jonava Lith.
38 B3 Jonê China
65 F5 Jonesboro *AR* U.S.A.
71 K2 Jonesboro *ME* U.S.A.
92 A3 Jones Mts *mts* Ant.
71 K2 Jonesport U.S.A.
55 K2 Jones Sound *chan.* Can.
70 B6 Jonesville U.S.A.
87 F4 Jonglei Canal *canal* Sudan
35 E5 Jonk *r.* India
7 O8 Jönköping Sweden
59 F4 Jonquière Can.
65 E4 Joplin U.S.A.
71 E5 Joppatowne U.S.A.
34 D4 Jora India
62 F2 Jordan U.S.A.
23 C6 Jordan *country* Asia
28 E6 Jordan *r.* Asia
62 E3 Jordan *r.* U.S.A.
62 C3 Jordan Valley U.S.A.
82 B4 Jordão *r.* Brazil
7 N6 Jordet Norway
35 H4 Jorhat India
13 H1 Jork Ger.
6 R4 Jörn Sweden
7 U5 Joroinen Fin.
7 K7 Jørpeland Norway
86 C4 Jos Nigeria
43 C5 Jose Abad Santos Phil.
80 B6 José de San Martin Arg.
82 A2 Joselândia Brazil
83 F2 José Pedro Varela Uru.
48 C3 Joseph Bonaparte Gulf *g.* Austr.
73 G4 Joseph City U.S.A.
59 G3 Joseph, Lac *l.* Can.
55 M4 Joseph, Lake *l.* Can.
41 F6 Jōshinetsu-kōgen National Park Japan
73 E5 Joshua Tree National Monument *res.* U.S.A.
86 C4 Jos Plateau *plat.* Nigeria
7 K6 Jostedalsbreen Nasjonalpark *nat. park* Norway
7 L6 Jotunheimen Nasjonalpark *nat. park* Norway
90 E6 Joubertina S. Africa
91 G3 Jouberton S. Africa
12 D2 Joure Neth.
7 U6 Joutsa Fin.
7 V6 Joutseno Fin.
12 E5 Jouy-aux-Arches France
35 H4 Jowai India
11 B4 Joyce's Country *reg.* Rep. of Ireland
62 A1 Juan de Fuca, Str. of *chan.* U.S.A.
89 E5 Juan de Nova *i.* Ind. Ocean
76 B6 Juan Fernández, Islas *is* Chile
6 V5 Juankoski Fin.
79 K5 Juàzeiro Brazil
79 L5 Juàzeiro do Norte Brazil
87 F4 Juba Sudan
88 E3 Jubba *r.* Somalia
72 D4 Jubilee Pass U.S.A.
15 F3 Júcar *r.* Spain
74 E5 Juchitán Mex.
82 E2 Jucuruçu *r.* Brazil
7 J7 Judaberg Norway
29 H6 Judaidat al Hamir Iraq
29 H6 Judayyidat 'Ar'ar *well* Iraq
16 G7 Judenburg Austria
7 M9 Juelsminde Denmark
38 C2 Juh China
38 F1 Juhua Dao *i.* China
75 G6 Juigalpa Nic.
12 F1 Juist *i.* Ger.
82 D3 Juiz de Fora Brazil
78 E8 Julaca Bol.
64 C3 Julesburg U.S.A.
78 D7 Juliaca Peru
12 C2 Julianadorp Neth.
79 G3 Juliana Top *summit* Suriname
12 E4 Jülich Ger.
18 E1 Julijske Alpe *mts* Slovenia
83 E2 Julio, 9 de Arg.
78 C5 Jumbilla Peru
15 F3 Jumilla Spain
35 E3 Jumla Nepal
34 B5 Junagadh India
35 E6 Junagarh India
38 F3 Junan China
83 B2 Juncal *mt* Chile
83 D4 Juncal, L. *l.* Arg.
65 D6 Junction *TX* U.S.A.
63 D4 Junction *UT* U.S.A.
64 D4 Junction City U.S.A.
82 C3 Jundiaí Brazil
56 C3 Juneau U.S.A.
50 F3 Junee Austr.
16 C7 Jungfrau *mt* Switz.
36 A2 Junggar Pendi *basin* China
34 A4 Jungshahi Pak.
70 E4 Juniata *r.* U.S.A.
83 E2 Junín Arg.
83 B3 Junín de los Andes Arg.
71 K1 Juniper Can.
72 B3 Junipero Serro Peak *summit* U.S.A.
39 B4 Junlian China
33 A2 Junnar India
6 P5 Junsele Sweden
62 C3 Juntura U.S.A.
38 D3 Jun Xian China
7 T8 Juodupė Lith.
82 C4 Juquiá Brazil
87 E4 Jur *r.* Sudan
10 C4 Jura *i.* U.K.
14 H3 Jura *mts* France/Switz.
82 E1 Jurací Brazil
81 A3 Juradó Col.
10 C5 Jura, Sound of *chan.* U.K.
7 S9 Jurbarkas Lith.
28 E6 Jurf ed Darāwīsh Jordan
13 L1 Jürgenstorf Ger.
42 A1 Jurh China
42 A1 Jurhe China
35 G2 Jurhen Ul Shan *mts* China
7 S8 Jūrmala Latvia
6 U4 Jurmu Fin.
38 F4 Jurong China
44 □ Jurong Sing.
78 E4 Juruá *r.* Brazil
79 G6 Juruena *r.* Brazil
6 R5 Jurva Fin.
30 E2 Jūshqān Iran
83 D2 Justo Daract Arg.
78 E4 Jutaí *r.* Brazil
13 M3 Jüterbog Ger.
82 A3 Juti Brazil
74 G6 Jutiapa Guatemala
74 G6 Juticalpa Honduras
6 P3 Jutis Sweden
6 V5 Juuka Fin.
7 U6 Juva Fin.
75 H4 Juventud, Isla de la *i.* Cuba
31 F4 Juwain Afgh.
38 F3 Ju Xian China
38 A1 Juyan China
38 E3 Juye China
31 E3 Jūymand Iran
30 D4 Jūyom Iran
89 C6 Jwaneng Botswana
7 T5 Jyväskylä Fin.


# K


34 D2 K2 *mt* China/Jammu and Kashmir
42 C4 Ka *i.* N. Korea
31 E2 Kaakhka Turkm.
72 □1 Kaala *mt* U.S.A.
88 E4 Kaamboni Kenya
7 S6 Kaarina Fin.
13 K1 Kaarßen Ger.
12 E3 Kaarst Ger.
6 V5 Kaavi Fin.
31 F2 Kabakly Turkm.
86 A4 Kabala Sierra Leone
88 C4 Kabale Uganda
88 C4 Kabalo Congo(Zaire)
88 C4 Kabambare Congo(Zaire)
89 C5 Kabangu Congo(Zaire)
44 A5 Kabanjahe Indon.
21 G7 Kabardino-Balkarskaya Respublika *div.* Rus. Fed.
88 C4 Kabare Congo(Zaire)
6 R3 Kåbdalis Sweden
68 E1 Kabenung Lake *l.* Can.
58 D4 Kabinakagami Lake *l.* Can.
88 C4 Kabinda Congo(Zaire)
30 B3 Kabīrkūh *mts* Iran
34 B3 Kabirwala Pak.
88 B3 Kabo C.A.R.
89 C5 Kabompo Zambia
88 C4 Kabongo Congo(Zaire)
31 F3 Kabūdeh Iran
31 E2 Kabūd Gonbad Iran
30 C3 Kabūd Rāhang Iran
43 B2 Kabugao Phil.
31 H3 Kābul Afgh.
31 H3 Kabul *r.* Afgh.
43 C6 Kaburuang *i.* Indon.
89 C5 Kabwe Zambia
31 F4 Kacha Kuh *mts* Iran/Pak.
21 H5 Kachalinskaya Rus. Fed.
34 B5 Kachchh, Gulf of *g.* India
34 C1 Kach Pass Afgh.
36 C1 Kachug Rus. Fed.
29 H1 Kaçkar Dağı *mt* Turkey
33 B4 Kadaiyanallur India
34 A3 Kadanai *r.* Afgh./Pak.
44 A2 Kadan Kyun *i.* Myanmar
49 H3 Kadavu *i.* Fiji
49 H3 Kadavu Passage *chan.* Fiji
86 B4 Kade Ghana
29 K5 Kādhimain Iraq
34 C5 Kadi India
28 B1 Kadıköy Turkey
50 A2 Kadina Austr.
28 D2 Kadınhanı Turkey
86 B3 Kadiolo Mali
33 B3 Kadiri India
28 F3 Kadirli Turkey
33 A4 Kadmat *i.* India
64 C3 Kadoka U.S.A.
89 C5 Kadoma Zimbabwe
87 E3 Kadugli Sudan
86 C3 Kaduna Nigeria
86 C3 Kaduna *r.* Nigeria
35 J3 Kadusam *mt* China
20 F3 Kaduy Rus. Fed.
33 A2 Kadwa *r.* India
20 G3 Kadyy Rus. Fed.
24 G3 Kadzherom Rus. Fed.
42 C4 Kaechon N. Korea
86 A3 Kaédi Maur.
87 D3 Kaélé Cameroon
72 □1 Kaena Pt *pt* U.S.A.
51 D1 Kaeo N.Z.
42 D5 Kaesŏng N. Korea
28 F6 Kāf S. Arabia
89 C4 Kafakumba Congo(Zaire)
86 A3 Kaffrine Senegal
19 L5 Kafireas, Akra *pt* Greece
28 C6 Kafr el Sheik Egypt
89 C5 Kafue Zambia
89 C5 Kafue *r.* Zambia
89 C5 Kafue National Park Zambia
41 E6 Kaga Japan
88 B3 Kaga Bandoro C.A.R.
21 G6 Kagal'nitskaya Rus. Fed.
31 G2 Kagan Uzbek.
69 F3 Kagawong Can.
6 R4 Kåge Sweden
29 J1 Kağızman Turkey
45 A3 Kagologolo Indon.
41 B9 Kagoshima Japan
30 C2 Kahak Iran
72 □1 Kahaluu U.S.A.
88 D4 Kahama Tanz.
72 □1 Kahana U.S.A.
21 D5 Kaharlyk Ukr.
45 D3 Kahayan *r.* Indon.
88 B4 Kahemba Congo(Zaire)
51 A6 Kaherekoau Mts *mts* N.Z.
13 K4 Kahla Ger.
Kahnu *see* Kahnūj
31 E5 Kahnūj Iran
68 B5 Kahoka U.S.A.
72 □2 Kahoolawe *i.* U.S.A.
28 F3 Kahraman Maraş Turkey
34 B3 Kahror Pak.
28 G3 Kahta Turkey
72 □1 Kahuku U.S.A.
72 □1 Kahuku Pt *pt* U.S.A.
72 □2 Kahului U.S.A.
51 D4 Kahurangi Point *pt* N.Z.
34 C2 Kahuta Pak.
88 C4 Kahuzi-Biega, Parc National du *nat. park* Congo(Zaire)
86 C4 Kaiama Nigeria
51 D5 Kaiapoi N.Z.
73 F3 Kaibab U.S.A.
63 D4 Kaibab Plat. *plat.* U.S.A.
37 F7 Kai Besar *i.* Indon.
73 G3 Kaibito U.S.A.
73 G3 Kaibito Plateau *plat.* U.S.A.
38 E3 Kaifeng *Henan* China
38 E3 Kaifeng *Henan* China
39 F4 Kaihua China
90 D4 Kaiingveld *reg.* S. Africa
38 C4 Kaijiang China
37 F7 Kai Kecil *i.* Indon.
37 F7 Kai, Kepulauan *is* Indon.
51 D5 Kaikoura N.Z.
51 D5 Kaikoura Peninsula N.Z.
39 □ Kai Kung Leng *h.* *H.K.* China
86 A4 Kailahun Sierra Leone
Kailas *mt* *see* Kangrinboqê Feng
35 G4 Kailāshahar India
Kailas Range *mts* *see* Gangdisê Shan
39 C5 Kaili China
42 A2 Kailu China
72 □1 Kailua U.S.A.
72 □2 Kailua Kona U.S.A.
51 E2 Kaimai Range *h.* N.Z.
48 D2 Kaimana Indon.
51 E3 Kaimanawa Mountains N.Z.
35 H2 Kaimar China
34 E4 Kaimur Range *h.* India
7 S7 Käina Estonia
41 D8 Kainan Japan
41 D7 Kainan Japan
86 C3 Kainji Lake National Park Nigeria
86 C3 Kainji Reservoir Nigeria
51 E2 Kaipara Harbour *in.* N.Z.
73 G3 Kaiparowits Plateau *plat.* U.S.A.
39 D6 Kaiping China
59 J3 Kaipokok Bay *in.* Can.
34 D3 Kairana India
86 D1 Kairouan Tunisia
13 F5 Kaiserslautern Ger.
42 E2 Kaishantun China
51 D1 Kaitaia N.Z.
51 B7 Kaitangata N.Z.
51 F3 Kaitawa N.Z.
34 D3 Kaithal India
6 R3 Kaitum Sweden
48 C2 Kaiwatu Indon.
72 □1 Kaiwi Channel U.S.A.
38 C4 Kai Xian China

39 C5 Kaiyang China
39 B6 Kaiyuan *Yunnan* China
42 C2 Kaiyuan China
6 U4 Kajaani Fin.
48 E4 Kajabbi Austr.
31 G3 Kajaki Afgh.
44 B5 Kajang Malaysia
34 B3 Kajanpur Pak.
29 L2 K'ajaran Armenia
31 G3 Kajrān Afgh.
29 L3 Kaju Iran
58 C4 Kakabeka Falls Can.
90 D4 Kakamas S. Africa
88 D3 Kakamega Kenya
51 C6 Kakanui Mts *mts* N.Z.
Kakar Range *mts see* Toba & Kakar Ranges
86 A4 Kakata Liberia
51 E3 Kakatahi N.Z.
35 H4 Kakching India
41 C7 Kake Japan
56 C3 Kake U.S.A.
88 C4 Kakenge Congo(Zaire)
13 K2 Kakerbeck Ger.
21 E6 Kakhovka Ukr.
21 E6 Kakhovs'ke Vodoskhovyshche *resr* Ukr.
30 C4 Kākī Iran
33 C2 Kākināda India
56 F2 Kakisa Can.
56 F2 Kakisa *r.* Can.
56 F2 Kakisa Lake *l.* Can.
41 D7 Kakogawa Japan
88 C4 Kakoswa Congo(Zaire)
34 D4 Kakrala India
54 D2 Kaktovik U.S.A.
41 G6 Kakuda Japan
56 F4 Kakwa *r.* Can.
34 B3 Kala Pak.
18 D7 Kalaâ Kebira Tunisia
34 B2 Kalabagh Pak.
37 E7 Kalabahi Indon.
43 A5 Kalabakan Malaysia
50 C1 Kalabity Austr.
89 C5 Kalabo Zambia
21 G5 Kalach Rus. Fed.
88 D3 Kalacha Dida Kenya
21 G5 Kalach-na-Donu Rus. Fed.
35 H5 Kaladan *r.* India/Myanmar
69 J3 Kaladar Can.
72 □2 Ka Lae *c.* U.S.A.
84 D8 Kalahari Desert *des.* Africa
89 B6 Kalahari Gemsbok National Park S. Africa
31 F3 Kala-I-Mor Turkm.
6 S4 Kalajoki Fin.
6 T4 Kalajoki *r.* Fin.
34 C2 Kalam Pak.
91 G1 Kalamare Botswana
19 K4 Kalamaria Greece
19 K6 Kalamata Greece
68 E4 Kalamazoo U.S.A.
68 D4 Kalamazoo *r.* U.S.A.
19 J5 Kalampaka Greece
34 C3 Kalanaur India
21 E6 Kalanchak Ukr.
31 F4 Kalandi Pak.
50 C4 Kalangadoo Austr.
34 C3 Kalanwali India
43 C5 Kalaong Phil.
33 C4 Kala Oya *r.* Sri Lanka
29 K4 Kalār Iraq
31 F5 Kalar *watercourse* Iran
Kalāt *see* Kabūd Gonbad
31 G4 Kalat Pak.
72 □2 Kalaupapa U.S.A.
21 G6 Kalaus *r.* Rus. Fed.
29 L1 Kälbäcär Azer.
48 B4 Kalbarri Austr.
13 K2 Kalbe (Milde) Ger.
31 E3 Kalbū Iran
28 B3 Kale *Denizli* Turkey
29 G1 Kale Turkey
28 D1 Kalecik Turkey
13 J3 Kalefeld Ger.
29 M3 Kaleh Sarai Iran
88 C4 Kalema Congo(Zaire)
88 C4 Kalémié Congo(Zaire)
68 D3 Kaleva U.S.A.
6 W4 Kalevala Rus. Fed.
35 H5 Kalewa Myanmar
48 C5 Kalgoorlie Austr.
18 F2 Kali Croatia
34 E3 Kali *r.* India/Nepal
43 B4 Kalibo Phil.
35 F4 Kali Gadaki *r.* Nepal
88 C4 Kalima Congo(Zaire)
45 D3 Kalimantan *reg.* Indon.
33 A3 Kalinadi *r.* India
34 E4 Kali Nadi *r.* India
20 B4 Kaliningrad Rus. Fed.
20 B4 Kaliningradskaya Oblast' *div.* Rus. Fed.
20 G3 Kalinino Rus. Fed.
21 H5 Kalininsk Rus. Fed.
21 F6 Kalininskaya Rus. Fed.
21 D4 Kalinkavichy Belarus
34 D4 Kali Sindh *r.* India
62 D1 Kalispell U.S.A.
16 J5 Kalisz Pol.
21 G5 Kalitva *r.* Rus. Fed.
88 D4 Kaliua Tanz.
6 S4 Kalix Sweden
6 S3 Kalixälven *r.* Sweden
35 H4 Kalkalighat India
28 B3 Kalkan Turkey
68 E3 Kalkaska U.S.A.
89 B6 Kalkfeld Namibia
91 F4 Kalkfonteindam *dam* S. Africa
12 E4 Kall Ger.
44 □ Kallang Sing.
7 U7 Kallaste Estonia
6 U5 Kallavesi *l.* Fin.
6 N5 Kallsedet Sweden
6 N5 Kallsjön *l.* Sweden
7 P8 Kalmar Sweden
7 P8 Kalmarsund *chan.* Sweden
13 G5 Kalmit *h.* Ger.
21 F6 Kal'mius *r.* Ukr.
33 C5 Kalmunai Sri Lanka
21 H6 Kalmykiya, Respublika *div.* Rus. Fed.
35 G4 Kalni *r.* Bangl.
17 N5 Kalodnaye Belarus
34 C5 Kalol India
43 C6 Kaloma *i.* Indon.
89 C5 Kalomo Zambia
56 D4 Kalone Pk *summit* Can.
30 B2 Kalow *r.* Iran
34 D3 Kalpa India
33 A4 Kalpeni *i.* India
34 D4 Kalpi India
29 L4 Kal Safīd Iran
54 C3 Kaltag U.S.A.
13 H1 Kaltenkirchen Ger.
13 J4 Kaltensundheim Ger.
34 C3 Kalu India
20 F4 Kaluga Rus. Fed.
7 M9 Kalundborg Denmark
34 B2 Kalur Kot Pak.
21 C5 Kalush Ukr.
33 B5 Kalutara Sri Lanka
20 E4 Kaluzhskaya Oblast' *div.* Rus. Fed.
6 S5 Kälviä Fin.
33 A2 Kalyan India
20 F3 Kalyazin Rus. Fed.
19 M6 Kalymnos *i.* Greece
17 M6 Kalynivka Ukr.
88 C4 Kama Congo(Zaire)
40 G5 Kamaishi Japan
34 C3 Kamalia Pak.
28 D2 Kaman Turkey
89 B5 Kamanjab Namibia
33 B2 Kamareddi India
31 F5 Kamarod Pak.
31 G2 Kamashi Uzbek.
48 C5 Kambalda Austr.
33 B4 Kambam India
42 E3 Kambo Ho *mt* N. Korea
89 C5 Kambove Congo(Zaire)
25 S4 Kamchatka *r.* Rus. Fed.
25 R4 Kamchatka Peninsula Rus. Fed.
19 M3 Kamchiya *r.* Bulg.
13 F3 Kamen Ger.
19 K4 Kamenitsa *mt* Bulg.
20 H4 Kamenka *Penzen.* Rus. Fed.
22 E2 Kamenka *Primorskiy Kray* Rus. Fed.
24 K4 Kamen'-na-Obi Rus. Fed.
20 F3 Kamenniki Rus. Fed.
20 D2 Kamennogorsk Rus. Fed.
21 G6 Kamennomostskiy Rus. Fed.
21 G6 Kamenolomni Rus. Fed.
40 C2 Kamen'-Rybolov Rus. Fed.
25 S3 Kamenskoye Rus. Fed.
21 G5 Kamensk-Shakhtinskiy Rus. Fed.
24 H4 Kamensk-Ural'skiy Rus. Fed.
20 G3 Kameshkovo Rus. Fed.
34 D3 Kamet *mt* China
90 C5 Kamiesberge *mts* S. Africa
90 B5 Kamieskroon S. Africa
57 J2 Kamilukuak Lake *l.* Can.
89 C4 Kamina Congo(Zaire)
57 L2 Kaminak Lake *l.* Can.
17 M5 Kamin'-Kashyrs'kyy Ukr.
40 H3 Kamishihoro Japan
35 H4 Kamjong India
35 F4 Kamla *r.* India
56 E4 Kamloops Can.
29 K1 Kamo Armenia
41 G7 Kamogawa Japan
33 C3 Kamoke Pak.
88 C4 Kamonia Congo(Zaire)
44 C2 Kamon, Xé *r.* Laos
88 D3 Kampala Uganda
44 B4 Kampar Malaysia
45 B2 Kampar *r.* Indon.
12 D2 Kampen Neth.
88 C4 Kampene Congo(Zaire)
44 A1 Kamphaeng Phet Thai.
33 B3 Kampli India
44 C3 Kâmpóng Cham Cambodia
44 C2 Kâmpóng Chhnăng Cambodia
44 C2 Kâmpóng Khleăng Cambodia
44 C3 Kâmpóng Spoe Cambodia
44 C2 Kâmpóng Thum Cambodia
44 C3 Kâmpôt Cambodia
Kampuchea *country see* Cambodia
37 F7 Kamrau, Teluk *b.* Indon.
57 J4 Kamsack Can.
24 G4 Kamskoye Vdkhr. *resr* Rus. Fed.
88 E3 Kamsuuma Somalia
57 J3 Kamuchawie Lake *l.* Can.
88 D3 Kamuli Uganda
21 C5 Kam"yane Ukr.
21 C5 Kam"yanets'-Podil's'kyy Ukr.
21 C5 Kam"yanka-Buz'ka Ukr.
17 L4 Kamyanyets Belarus
30 B3 Kāmyārān Iran
21 F6 Kamyshevatskaya Rus. Fed.
21 H5 Kamyshin Rus. Fed.
21 J6 Kamyzyak Rus. Fed.
30 E5 Kamzar Oman
58 F3 Kanaaupscow *r.* Can.
63 F3 Kanab U.S.A.
73 F3 Kanab Creek *r.* U.S.A.
31 G4 Kanak Pak.
29 K5 Kan'ān Iraq
88 C4 Kananga Congo(Zaire)
50 H2 Kanangra Nat. Park Austr.
73 F3 Kanarraville U.S.A.
20 H4 Kanash Rus. Fed.
70 C5 Kanawha *r.* U.S.A.
41 E7 Kanayama Japan
41 E6 Kanazawa Japan
44 A2 Kanchanaburi Thai.
33 B3 Kanchipuram India
34 A3 Kand *mt* Pak.
31 G4 Kandahār Afgh.
6 X3 Kandalaksha Rus. Fed.
44 A5 Kandang Indon.
34 B2 Kandhura Pak.
86 C3 Kandi Benin
31 G4 Kandi Pak.
34 B4 Kandiaro Pak.
28 C1 Kandıra Turkey
50 G2 Kandos Austr.
89 E5 Kandreho Madag.
33 B3 Kandukur India
33 C5 Kandy Sri Lanka
70 D4 Kane U.S.A.
55 M2 Kane Basin *b.* Can./Greenland
30 D5 Kaneh *watercourse* Iran
72 □1 Kaneohe U.S.A.
72 □1 Kaneohe Bay *b.* U.S.A.
21 F6 Kanevskaya Rus. Fed.
89 C6 Kang Botswana
35 G5 Kanga *r.* Bangl.
55 N3 Kangaatsiaq Greenland
86 B3 Kangaba Mali
28 F2 Kangal Turkey
30 D5 Kangan Iran
31 E5 Kangān Iran
45 B1 Kangar Malaysia
50 A3 Kangaroo I. *i.* Austr.
6 V5 Kangaslampi Fin.
7 U6 Kangasniemi Fin.
30 B3 Kangāvar Iran
38 E1 Kangbao China
35 G4 Kangchenjunga *mt* Nepal
39 A4 Kangding China
42 D4 Kangdong N. Korea
55 M3 Kangeak Pt *pt* Can.
45 E4 Kangean, Kepulauan *is* Indon.
55 O3 Kangeq *hd* Greenland
55 O4 Kangerlussuaq *in.* Greenland
55 N2 Kangersuatsiaq Greenland
55 P3 Kangertittivatsiaq *in.* Greenland
42 D3 Kanggye N. Korea
42 D5 Kanghwa S. Korea
42 D5 Kanghwa Do *i.* S. Korea
59 G2 Kangiqsualujjuaq Can.
55 L3 Kangiqsujuaq Can.
59 G1 Kangirsuk Can.
38 B3 Kangle China
35 F3 Kangmar *Xizang* China
35 G3 Kangmar *Xizang* China
42 E5 Kangnŭng S. Korea
88 B3 Kango Gabon
42 B2 Kangping China
35 J3 Kangri Karpo Pass India
34 E3 Kangrinboqê Feng *mt* China
35 H4 Kangto *mt* China
35 F2 Kangtog China
38 B3 Kang Xian China
34 D5 Kanhan *r.* India
35 E4 Kanhar *r.* India
88 C4 Kaniama Congo(Zaire)
51 C5 Kaniere, L. *l.* N.Z.
33 B3 Kanigiri India
24 F3 Kanin, Poluostrov *pen.* Rus. Fed.
29 K3 Kānī Ṛash Iraq
21 D5 Kaniv Ukr.
50 C4 Kaniva Austr.
7 S6 Kankaanpää Fin.
68 D5 Kankakee U.S.A.
68 C5 Kankakee *r.* U.S.A.
86 B3 Kankan Guinea
35 E5 Kanker India
33 C4 Kankesanturai Sri Lanka
44 A3 Kanmaw Kyun *i.* Myanmar
34 D4 Kannanj India
67 D5 Kannapolis U.S.A.
33 B4 Kanniyakumari India
Kanniya Kumari *c. see* Comorin, Cape
34 D5 Kannod India
6 T5 Kannonkoski Fin.
Kannur *see* Cannanore
6 S5 Kannus Fin.
86 C3 Kano Nigeria
90 D7 Kanonpunt *pt* S. Africa
34 C4 Kanor India
41 B9 Kanoya Japan
34 E4 Kanpur India
34 B3 Kanpur Pak.
31 G5 Kanrach *reg.* Pak.
64 D4 Kansas *div.* U.S.A.
64 D4 Kansas *r.* U.S.A.
64 E4 Kansas City *KS* U.S.A.
64 E4 Kansas City *MO* U.S.A.
36 B1 Kansk Rus. Fed.
42 E4 Kansŏng S. Korea
35 G4 Kantanagar Bangl.
44 C2 Kantaralak Thai.
86 C3 Kantchari Burkina
21 F5 Kantemirovka Rus. Fed.
35 F5 Kānthi India
35 F4 Kanti India
34 C3 Kantli *r.* India
49 J2 Kanton Island *i.* Kiribati
11 C5 Kanturk Rep. of Ireland
90 C3 Kanus Namibia
91 J2 KaNyamazane S. Africa
89 C6 Kanye Botswana
44 B3 Kaôh Kŏng *i.* Cambodia
44 B3 Kaôh Rŭng *i.* Cambodia
44 B3 Kaôh Rŭng Sânlŏem *i.* Cambodia
39 F6 Kao-hsiung Taiwan
44 B3 Kaôh Smăch *i.* Cambodia
89 B5 Kaokoveld *plat.* Namibia
86 A3 Kaolack Senegal
89 C5 Kaoma Zambia
72 □2 Kapaa U.S.A.
72 □2 Kapaau U.S.A.
29 L2 Kapan Armenia
89 C4 Kapanga Congo(Zaire)
27 F2 Kapchagay Kazak.
12 C3 Kapellen Belgium
19 K6 Kapello, Akra *pt* Greece
7 Q7 Kapellskär Sweden
28 A1 Kapıdağı Yarımadası *pen.* Turkey
35 G4 Kapili *r.* India
94 F5 Kapingamarangi Rise *sea feature* Pac. Oc.
94 F5 Kapingamarangi *i.* Pac. Oc.
34 B3 Kapip Pak.
89 C5 Kapiri Mposhi Zambia
55 N3 Kapisigdlit Greenland
58 D3 Kapiskau Can.
58 D3 Kapiskau *r.* Can.
69 G2 Kapiskong Lake *l.* Can.
51 E4 Kapiti I. *i.* N.Z.
44 A3 Kapoe Thai.
87 F4 Kapoeta Sudan
16 H7 Kaposvár Hungary
31 F5 Kappar Pak.
12 F5 Kappel Ger.
13 D3 Kappeln Ger.
34 D4 Kapran India
88 D3 Kapsabet Kenya
42 E3 Kapsan N. Korea
45 D3 Kapuas *r.* Indon.
45 D2 Kapuas *r.* Indon.
50 B3 Kapunda Austr.
34 C4 Kapūriya India
34 C3 Kapurthala India
58 D4 Kapuskasing Can.
58 D4 Kapuskasing *r.* Can.
21 H5 Kapustin Yar Rus. Fed.
88 D3 Kaputir Kenya
16 H7 Kapuvár Hungary
20 C4 Kapyl' Belarus
42 D5 Kap'yŏng S. Korea
86 C4 Kara Togo
29 H2 Kara *r.* Turkey
19 M5 Kara Ada *i.* Turkey
28 D2 Karaali Turkey
31 F2 Karabil', Vozvyshennost' *reg.* Turkm.
32 D1 Kara-Bogaz Gol, Zaliv *b.* Turkm.
28 D1 Karabük Turkey
26 E2 Karabutak Kazak.
28 B1 Karacabey Turkey
29 G3 Karacadağ Turkey
28 D3 Karacadağ *mts* Turkey
28 B1 Karacaköy Turkey
29 G3 Karacalı Dağ *mt* Turkey
28 B3 Karacasu Turkey
28 C3 Karaca Yarımadası *pen.* Turkey
21 G7 Karachayevo-Cherkesskaya Respublika *div.* Rus. Fed.
21 G7 Karachayevsk Rus. Fed.
20 E4 Karachev Rus. Fed.
31 G5 Karachi Pak.
29 J2 Karaçoban Turkey
33 A2 Karad India
29 J3 Kara Dağ *mt* Turkey
28 D3 Kara Dağ *mt* Turkey
Kara Deniz *sea see* Black Sea
27 F2 Karaganda Kazak.
27 F2 Karagayly Kazak.
25 S4 Karaginskiy Zaliv *b.* Rus. Fed.
28 B2 Karahallı Turkey
28 E2 Karahasanlı Turkey
33 B4 Kāraikāl India
33 B4 Karaikkudi India
28 E3 Karaisalı Turkey
30 C3 Karaj Iran
30 C3 Karaj *r.* Iran
28 E6 Karak Jordan
30 E2 Kara Kala Turkm.
34 E1 Karakax He *r.* China
29 G3 Karakeçi Turkey
28 D2 Karakeçili Turkey
37 E6 Karakelong *i.* Indon.
29 H2 Karakoçan Turkey
24 J5 Kara-Köl Kyrg.
27 F2 Karakol Kyrg.
34 D2 Karakoram Pass China/Jammu and Kashmir
27 F3 Karakoram Range *mts* Asia
88 D2 Kara K'orē Eth.
31 F2 Karakul' Uzbek.
31 F2 Karakul' Uzbek.
31 F2 Karakum Desert Turkm.
26 D2 Karakum, Peski *des.* Kazak.
31 F2 Karakumskiy Kanal *canal* Turkm.
31 E2 Kara Kumy *reg.* Turkm.
Karakumy, Peski *des. see* Karakum Desert
29 J1 Karakurt Turkey
7 R7 Karala Estonia
28 D3 Karaman Turkey
28 B3 Karamanlı Turkey
27 G2 Karamay China
34 C1 Karambar Pass Afgh./Pak.
51 D4 Karamea N.Z.
51 C4 Karamea Bight *b.* N.Z.
31 G2 Karamet-Niyaz Turkm.
35 F1 Karamiran China
35 F1 Karamiran Shankou *pass* China
28 B1 Karamürsel Turkey
20 D3 Karamyshevo Rus. Fed.
30 C5 Karān *i.* S. Arabia
30 B3 Karand Iran
34 D5 Karanja India
33 B2 Karanja *r.* India
35 F5 Karanjia India
34 C3 Karanpura India
28 D3 Karapınar Turkey
90 B3 Karas *div.* Namibia
90 B3 Karas *watercourse* Namibia
89 B6 Karasburg Namibia
24 J2 Kara Sea *sea* Rus. Fed.
6 T2 Karasjok Norway
28 C1 Karasu Turkey
29 J2 Karasu *r.* Turkey
24 J4 Karasuk Rus. Fed.
28 E3 Karataş Turkey
28 E3 Karataş Burun *pt* Turkey
26 F2 Karatau Kazak.
26 E2 Karatau, Khr. *mts* Kazak.
34 E2 Karatau Shan *mts* China
44 A3 Karathuri Myanmar
33 B4 Karativu *i.* Sri Lanka
35 G4 Karatoya *r.* Bangl.
41 A8 Karatsu Japan
43 C5 Karatung *i.* Indon.
31 G2 Karaulbazar Uzbek.
34 D4 Karauli India
29 J1 Karaurgan Turkey
45 C4 Karawang Indon.
29 K5 Karbalā' Iraq
13 G4 Karben Ger.
17 K7 Karcag Hungary
12 F4 Karden Ger.
19 J5 Karditsa Greece
7 S7 Kärdla Estonia
91 G4 Karee S. Africa
90 D5 Kareeberge *mts* S. Africa
87 F3 Kareima Sudan
21 G7 K'areli Georgia
34 D5 Kareli India
20 E2 Kareliya, Respublika *div.* Rus. Fed.
36 D1 Karenga *r.* Rus. Fed.
34 D4 Karera India
6 S2 Karesuando Sweden
31 F5 Kārevāndar Iran
21 H7 Kargalinskaya Rus. Fed.
29 H2 Kargapazarı Dağları *mts* Turkey
28 E1 Kargı Turkey
34 D2 Kargil Jammu and Kashmir
20 F2 Kargopol' Rus. Fed.
7 P6 Karholmsbruk Sweden
89 C5 Kariba Zimbabwe
89 C5 Kariba, Lake *resr* Zambia/Zimbabwe
40 F3 Kariba-yama *volc.* Japan
90 E6 Kariega *r.* S. Africa
6 T2 Karigasniemi Fin.
7 R5 Karijoki Fin.
51 D1 Karikari, Cape *c.* N.Z.
30 D3 Karīmābād Iran
45 C3 Karimata, Pulau Pulau *is* Indon.
45 C3 Karimata, Selat *str.* Indon.
33 B2 Karimnagar India
45 D4 Karimunjawa, Pulau Pulau *is* Indon.
88 E2 Karin Somalia
30 E3 Karit Iran
33 A2 Karjat India
35 F5 Karkai *r.* India
33 A3 Karkal India
43 C5 Karkaralong, Kepulauan *is* Indon.
48 E2 Karkar I. *i.* P.N.G.
30 C4 Karkheh *r.* Iran
31 E5 Kārkīn Dar Iran
21 E6 Karkinits'ka Zatoka *g.* Ukr.
7 T6 Kärkölä Fin.
7 T7 Karksi-Nuia Estonia
29 H2 Karlıova Turkey
21 E5 Karlivka Ukr.
Karl-Marx-Stadt *see* Chemnitz
18 F2 Karlovac Croatia
19 L3 Karlovo Bulg.
16 F5 Karlovy Vary Czech Rep.
13 G6 Karlsbad Ger.
7 O7 Karlsborg Sweden
7 O8 Karlshamn Sweden
7 O7 Karlskoga Sweden
7 O8 Karlskrona Sweden
13 G5 Karlsruhe Ger.
7 N7 Karlstad Sweden
64 D1 Karlstad U.S.A.
13 H5 Karlstadt Ger.
20 D4 Karma Belarus
33 A2 Karmala India
7 J7 Karmøy *i.* Norway
35 H5 Karnafuli Reservoir Bangl.
34 D3 Karnal India
35 E3 Karnali *r.* Nepal
33 A3 Karnataka *div.* India
19 M3 Karnobat Bulg.
31 G5 Karodi Pak.
89 C5 Karoi Zimbabwe
35 G3 Karo La *pass* China
35 H4 Karong India
89 D4 Karonga Malawi
90 E6 Karoo National Park S. Africa
50 B3 Karoonda Austr.
34 B3 Karor Pak.
88 D2 Karora Eritrea
13 L1 Karow Ger.
19 M7 Karpathos *i.* Greece
19 M6 Karpathou, Steno *chan.* Greece
Karpaty *see* Carpathian Mountains
19 J5 Karpenisi Greece
20 H1 Karpogory Rus. Fed.
48 B4 Karratha Austr.
31 F3 Karrukh Afgh.
29 J1 Kars Turkey
6 T5 Kärsämäki Fin.
7 U8 Kārsava Latvia
31 G2 Karshi Uzbek.
35 G4 Kārsiyāng India
24 G3 Karskiye Vorota, Proliv *str.* Rus. Fed.
Karskoye More *sea see* Kara Sea
13 K1 Karstädt Ger.
6 T5 Karstula Fin.
28 B1 Kartal Turkey
24 H4 Kartaly Rus. Fed.
6 U5 Karttula Fin.
30 C4 Kārūn *r.* Iran
30 C4 Karun, Kūh-e *h.* Iran
33 B4 Karur India
7 S5 Karvia Fin.
7 S6 Karvianjoki *r.* Fin.
33 A3 Karwar India
36 D1 Karymskoye Rus. Fed.
19 L5 Karystos Greece
28 B3 Kaş Turkey
58 C3 Kasabonika Can.
58 C3 Kasabonika Lake *l.* Can.
88 B4 Kasai *r.* Congo(Zaire)
89 C5 Kasaji Congo(Zaire)
89 D5 Kasama Zambia
31 G2 Kasan Uzbek.
89 C5 Kasane Botswana
88 B4 Kasangulu Congo(Zaire)
33 A3 Kasaragod India
57 J2 Kasba Lake *l.* Can.
86 B1 Kasba Tadla Morocco
41 B9 Kaseda Japan
29 L4 Kaseh Garan Iran
89 C5 Kasempa Zambia
89 C5 Kasenga Congo(Zaire)
88 C4 Kasese Congo(Zaire)
88 D3 Kasese Uganda
34 D4 Kasganj India
30 C3 Kāshān Iran
58 D3 Kashechewan Can.
Kashgar *see* Kashi
27 F3 Kashi China
41 D7 Kashihara Japan
41 B8 Kashima Japan
41 G6 Kashima-nada *b.* Japan
20 F3 Kashin Rus. Fed.
34 D3 Kashipur India
41 F6 Kashiwazaki Japan
29 L5 Kashkan *r.* Iran
31 E3 Kāshmar Iran
34 C2 Kashmir, Vale of *v.* India
34 B3 Kashmor Pak.
31 H3 Kashmund *reg.* Afgh.
88 C4 Kashyukulu Congo(Zaire)
20 G4 Kasimov Rus. Fed.
66 B4 Kaskaskia *r.* U.S.A.
57 L3 Kaskattama *r.* Can.
7 R5 Kaskinen Fin.
88 C4 Kasongo Congo(Zaire)
88 B4 Kasongo-Lunda Congo(Zaire)
19 M7 Kasos *i.* Greece
19 M7 Kasou, Steno *chan.* Greece
21 H7 Kaspi Georgia
21 H7 Kaspiysk Rus. Fed.
Kaspiyskoye More *sea see* Caspian Sea
17 P3 Kasplya Rus. Fed.
87 F3 Kassala Sudan
19 K4 Kassandra *pen.* Greece
19 K4 Kassandras, Kolpos *b.* Greece
13 H3 Kassel Ger.
86 C1 Kasserine Tunisia
68 A3 Kasson U.S.A.
28 D1 Kastamonu Turkey
12 F4 Kastellaun Ger.
19 K7 Kastelli Greece
12 C3 Kasterlee Belgium
19 J4 Kastoria Greece
20 E4 Kastsyukovichy Belarus
41 E7 Kasugai Japan
88 D4 Kasulu Tanz.
41 D7 Kasumi Japan
41 G6 Kasumiga-ura *l.* Japan
21 J7 Kasumkent Rus. Fed.
89 D5 Kasungu Malawi
34 C3 Kasur Pak.
71 J2 Katahdin, Mt *mt* U.S.A.
34 D2 Kataklik Jammu and Kashmir
88 C4 Katako-Kombe Congo(Zaire)
34 D5 Katangi India
48 B5 Katanning Austr.
31 H3 Katawaz Afgh.
88 C4 Katea Congo(Zaire)
19 K4 Katerini Greece
56 C3 Kate's Needle *mt* Can./U.S.A.
89 D5 Katete Zambia
35 E5 Katghora India
36 B4 Katha Myanmar
48 D3 Katherine *r.* Austr.
34 B5 Kathiawar *pen.* India
28 D6 Kathīb el Henu *sand dunes* Egypt
33 C4 Kathiraveli Sri Lanka
91 H3 Kathlehong S. Africa
35 F4 Kathmandu Nepal
90 E3 Kathu S. Africa
34 C2 Kathua Jammu and Kashmir
86 B3 Kati Mali
35 F4 Katihar India
51 E2 Katikati N.Z.
91 G6 Kati-Kati S. Africa
89 C5 Katima Mulilo Namibia
86 B4 Katiola Côte d'Ivoire
90 D4 Katkop Hills *reg.* S. Africa
Katmandu *see* Kathmandu
19 J5 Kato Achaïa Greece
34 D5 Katol India
44 □ Katong Sing.
50 H2 Katoomba Austr.
17 J5 Katowice Pol.
35 G5 Katoya India
7 P7 Katrineholm Sweden
10 D4 Katrine, Loch *l.* U.K.
86 C3 Katsina Nigeria
86 C4 Katsina-Ala Nigeria
41 G6 Katsuta Japan
41 G7 Katsuura Japan
41 E6 Katsuyama Japan
59 G2 Kattaktoc, Cap *hd* Can.
31 G2 Kattakurgan Uzbek.
31 G3 Kattasang Hills *mts* Afgh.
7 M8 Kattegat *str.* Denmark/Sweden
34 B3 Katuri Pak.
12 C2 Katwijk aan Zee Neth.
13 H5 Katzenbuckel *h.* Ger.
72 □2 Kauai *i.* U.S.A.
72 □2 Kauai Channel U.S.A.
13 F4 Kaub Ger.
13 H3 Kaufungen Ger.
7 S5 Kauhajoki Fin.
6 S5 Kauhava Fin.
6 T3 Kaukonen Fin.
72 □2 Kaula *i.* U.S.A.
72 □2 Kaulakahi Channel U.S.A.
59 H2 Kaumajet Mts *mts* Can.
72 □2 Kaunakakai U.S.A.
7 S9 Kaunas Lith.
7 U8 Kaunata Latvia
86 C3 Kaura-Namoda Nigeria
39 □ Kau Sai Chau *i.* *H.K.* China
6 S5 Kaustinen Fin.
6 S2 Kautokeino Norway
44 A3 Kau-ye Kyun *i.* Myanmar
19 K4 Kavadarci Macedonia
28 F1 Kavak Turkey
19 L4 Kavala Greece
40 D2 Kavalerovo Rus. Fed.
33 C3 Kavali India

30 D4 Kavār Iran
33 A4 Kavaratti i. India
19 N3 Kavarna Bulg.
33 A3 Kāveri r. India
33 B4 Kāveri r. India
30 D4 Kavīr des. Iran
30 D3 Kavir salt flat Iran
30 D3 Kavir salt flat Iran
30 D3 Kavir, Dasht-e des. Iran
30 D3 Kavīr-e Hāj Ali Qoli salt l. Iran
31 E3 Kavir-i-Namak salt flat Iran
41 F7 Kawagoe Japan
41 F7 Kawaguchi Japan
72 □2 Kawaihae U.S.A.
51 E1 Kawakawa N.Z.
89 C4 Kawambwa Zambia
58 E5 Kawartha Lakes l. Can.
41 F7 Kawasaki Japan
51 E2 Kawau I. i. N.Z.
59 G2 Kawawachikamach Can.
51 F3 Kawerau N.Z.
51 E3 Kawhia N.Z.
51 E3 Kawhia Harbour in. N.Z.
72 D3 Kawich Range mts U.S.A.
44 A1 Kawkareik Myanmar
44 A1 Kawludo Myanmar
30 E6 Kawr, J. mt Oman
44 A3 Kawthaung Myanmar
86 B3 Kaya Burkina
28 F2 Kayadibi Turkey
25 M2 Kayak Rus. Fed.
45 E2 Kayan r. Indon.
88 C4 Kayanaza Burundi
33 B4 Kayankulam India
62 F3 Kaycee U.S.A.
89 C4 Kayembe-Mukulu Congo(Zaire)
73 G3 Kayenta U.S.A.
86 A3 Kayes Mali
86 A4 Kayima Sierra Leone
27 F2 Kaynar Kazak.
28 F2 Kaynar Turkey
28 F3 Kaypak Turkey
21 H5 Kaysatskoye Rus. Fed.
28 E2 Kayseri Turkey
45 B3 Kayuagung Indon.
24 K3 Kayyerkan Rus. Fed.
25 P2 Kazach'ye Rus. Fed.
Kazakh see Qazax
26 F1 Kazakskiy Melkosopochnik reg. Kazak.
23 E5 Kazakstan country Asia
20 J4 Kazan' Rus. Fed.
57 K2 Kazan r. Can.
28 D3 Kazancı Turkey
20 J4 Kazanka r. Rus. Fed.
19 L3 Kazanlŭk Bulg.
36 G4 Kazan-rettō is Japan
21 G5 Kazanskaya Rus. Fed.
21 H7 Kazbek mt Georgia/Rus. Fed.
19 M5 Kaz Dağı mts Turkey
30 C4 Kāzerūn Iran
20 J2 Kazhim Rus. Fed.
31 F5 Kazhmak r. Pak.
17 K6 Kazincbarcika Hungary
31 F5 Kazmīr Iran
21 H7 Kazret'i Georgia
21 J5 Kaztalovka Kazak.
40 G4 Kazuno Japan
24 H3 Kazymskiy Mys Rus. Fed.
19 L6 Kea i. Greece
11 E3 Keady U.K.
72 □2 Kealakekua Bay b. U.S.A.
29 M4 K-e-Alvand mt Iran
73 G4 Keams Canyon U.S.A.
64 D3 Kearney U.S.A.
73 G5 Kearny U.S.A.
28 G2 Keban Turkey
28 G2 Keban Barajı resr Turkey
86 A3 Kébémèr Senegal
28 F4 Kebīr r. Lebanon/Syria
87 E3 Kebkabiya Sudan
6 Q3 Kebnekaise mt Sweden
10 B2 Kebock Head hd U.K.
88 E3 K'ebrī Dehar Eth.
45 C4 Kebumen Indon.
56 D3 Kechika r. Can.
28 C3 Keçiborlu Turkey
17 J7 Kecskemét Hungary
29 H1 K'eda Georgia
7 S9 Kėdainiai Lith.
29 L4 K-e Dalakhāni h. Iraq
34 D3 Kedar Kanta mt India
34 D3 Kedarnath Peak mt India
59 G4 Kedgwick Can.
45 D4 Kediri Indon.
86 A3 Kédougou Senegal
56 D2 Keele r. Can.
56 C2 Keele Pk summit Can.
63 C4 Keeler U.S.A.
Keeling Is terr. see Cocos Is
43 A5 Keenapusan i. Phil.
71 G3 Keene U.S.A.
10 F4 Keen, Mount mt U.K.
50 H1 Keepit Reservoir Austr.
12 C3 Keerbergen Belgium
89 B6 Keetmanshoop Namibia
57 L5 Keewatin Can.
57 L5 Keewatin U.S.A.
19 J5 Kefallonia i. Greece
37 E7 Kefamenanu Indon.
6 B4 Keflavík Iceland
33 C5 Kegalla Sri Lanka
27 F2 Kegen Kazak.
59 G2 Keglo, Baie de b. Can.
21 H6 Kegul'ta Rus. Fed.
7 T7 Kehra Estonia
8 F4 Keighley U.K.
7 T7 Keila Estonia
90 D4 Keimoes S. Africa
6 U5 Keitele Fin.
6 T5 Keitele l. Fin.
50 C4 Keith Austr.
10 F3 Keith U.K.
56 E1 Keith Arm b. Can.
59 G5 Kejimkujik National Park Can.
72 □2 Kekaha U.S.A.
17 K7 Kékes mt Hungary
34 C4 Kekri India
27 F6 Kelai i. Maldives
38 D2 Kelan China
45 B2 Kelang Malaysia
44 B4 Kelantan r. Malaysia
12 E4 Kelberg Ger.
13 K6 Kelheim Ger.
18 D6 Kelibia Tunisia
31 G2 Kelif Turkm.
31 F2 Kelifskiy Uzboy marsh Turkm.
13 G4 Kelkheim (Taunus) Ger.
29 G1 Kelkit Turkey
28 F1 Kelkit r. Turkey
56 E2 Keller Lake l. Can.
70 B4 Kelleys I. i. U.S.A.
62 C2 Kellogg U.S.A.
6 V3 Kelloselkä Fin.
11 E4 Kells Rep. of Ireland
7 S9 Kelmė Lith.
12 E4 Kelmis Belgium
87 D4 Kelo Chad
56 F5 Kelowna Can.
56 D4 Kelsey Bay Can.
72 A2 Kelseyville U.S.A.
10 F5 Kelso U.K.
73 E4 Kelso CA U.S.A.
62 B2 Kelso WA U.S.A.
45 B2 Keluang Malaysia
57 J4 Kelvington Can.
20 E1 Kem' Rus. Fed.
20 E1 Kem' r. Rus. Fed.
29 G2 Kemah Turkey
28 G2 Kemaliye Turkey
19 M5 Kemalpaşa Turkey
56 D4 Kemano Can.
28 C3 Kemer Antalya Turkey
28 B3 Kemer Muğla Turkey
28 B3 Kemer Barajı resr Turkey
36 A1 Kemerovo Rus. Fed.
6 T4 Kemi Fin.
6 U3 Kemijärvi Fin.
6 U3 Kemijärvi l. Fin.
6 T3 Kemijoki r. Fin.
62 E3 Kemmerer U.S.A.
13 K5 Kemnath Ger.
10 F3 Kemnay U.K.
6 T4 Kempele Fin.
12 E3 Kempen Ger.
12 C3 Kempen reg. Belgium
65 D5 Kemp, L. l. U.S.A.
92 D4 Kemp Land reg. Ant.
92 B2 Kemp Pen. pen. Ant.
67 E7 Kemp's Bay Bahamas
16 E7 Kempten (Allgäu) Ger.
58 F4 Kempt, L. l. Can.
91 H3 Kempton Park S. Africa
69 K3 Kemptville Can.
45 D4 Kemujan i. Indon.
34 E4 Ken r. India
54 C3 Kenai U.S.A.
54 C4 Kenai Mts mts U.S.A.
31 F3 Kenar-e-Kapeh Afgh.
8 E3 Kendal U.K.
57 M2 Kendall, Cape hd Can.
68 E5 Kendallville U.S.A.
45 C4 Kendang, Gunung volc. Indon.
37 E7 Kendari Indon.
45 D3 Kendawangan Indon.
87 D3 Kendégué Chad
35 F5 Kendrāparha India
62 C2 Kendrick U.S.A.
73 G4 Kendrick Peak summit U.S.A.
50 G1 Kenebri Austr.
65 D6 Kenedy U.S.A.
86 A4 Kenema Sierra Leone
88 B4 Kenge Congo(Zaire)
37 B4 Kengtung Myanmar
90 D4 Kenhardt S. Africa
86 A3 Kéniéba Mali
86 B1 Kénitra Morocco
38 F2 Kenli China
11 B6 Kenmare Rep. of Ireland
64 C1 Kenmare U.S.A.
11 A6 Kenmare River in. Rep. of Ireland
12 E5 Kenn Ger.
63 G5 Kenna U.S.A.
71 J2 Kennebec r. U.S.A.
71 H3 Kennebunk U.S.A.
71 H3 Kennebunkport U.S.A.
65 F6 Kenner U.S.A.
9 F6 Kennet r. U.K.
65 F4 Kennett U.S.A.
62 C2 Kennewick U.S.A.
56 B2 Keno Can.
69 G1 Kenogami Lake Can.
69 G1 Kenogamissi Lake l. Can.
57 L5 Kenora Can.
68 D4 Kenosha U.S.A.
20 F2 Kenozero, Ozero l. Rus. Fed.
71 G4 Kent CT U.S.A.
65 B6 Kent TX U.S.A.
62 B2 Kent WA U.S.A.
8 E3 Kent r. U.K.
91 H6 Kentani S. Africa
68 D5 Kentland U.S.A.
70 B4 Kenton U.S.A.
70 A6 Kentucky div. U.S.A.
61 K4 Kentucky r. KY U.S.A.
67 B4 Kentucky Lake l. U.S.A.
59 H4 Kentville Can.
65 F6 Kentwood LA U.S.A.
68 E4 Kentwood MI U.S.A.
85 G5 Kenya country Africa
Kenya, Mount mt see Kirinyaga
68 A3 Kenyon U.S.A.
92 B2 Kenyon Pen. pen. Ant.
72 □2 Keokea U.S.A.
68 B5 Keokuk U.S.A.
44 C1 Keo Neua, Col de pass Laos/Vietnam
68 B5 Keosauqua U.S.A.
48 F4 Keppel Bay b. Austr.
44 □ Keppel Harbour chan. Sing.
28 B2 Kepsut Turkey
31 E4 Kerāh Iran
33 A4 Kerala div. India
50 D3 Kerang Austr.
86 C4 Kéran, Parc National de la nat. park Togo
7 T6 Kerava Fin.
15 G4 Kerba Alg.
21 F6 Kerch Ukr.
48 E2 Kerema P.N.G.
56 F5 Keremeos Can.
21 E7 Kerempe Burun pt Turkey
88 D2 Keren Eritrea
30 E2 Kergeli Turkm.
93 J7 Kerguélen i. Ind. Ocean
93 J7 Kerguelen Ridge sea feature Ind. Ocean
88 D4 Kericho Kenya
51 D1 Kerikeri N.Z.
7 V6 Kerimäki Fin.
45 B3 Kerinci, G. volc. Indon.
35 E2 Keriya Shankou pass China
12 E3 Kerken Ger.
31 G2 Kerki Turkm.
31 G2 Kerkichi Turkm.
19 K4 Kerkinitis, Limni l. Greece
19 H5 Kerkyra Greece
Kerkyra i. see Corfu
87 F3 Kerma Sudan
46 K7 Kermadec Is. is N.Z.
94 H8 Kermadec Tr. sea feature Pac. Oc.
30 E4 Kermān Iran
72 B3 Kerman U.S.A.
31 E4 Kermān Desert Iran
30 B3 Kermānshāh Iran
30 D4 Kermānshāhān Iran
65 C6 Kermit U.S.A.
63 C5 Kern r. U.S.A.
59 G2 Kernertut, Cap pt Can.
72 C4 Kernville U.S.A.
20 K2 Keros Rus. Fed.
19 L6 Keros i. Greece
86 B4 Kérouané Guinea
12 E4 Kerpen Ger.
92 B5 Kerr, C. c. Ant.
57 H4 Kerrobert Can.
65 D6 Kerrville U.S.A.
11 B5 Kerry Head hd Rep. of Ireland
44 B4 Kerteh Malaysia
7 M9 Kerteminde Denmark
28 D4 Keryneia Cyprus
20 H3 Kerzhenets r. Rus. Fed.
58 D3 Kesagami Lake l. Can.
7 V6 Kesälahti Fin.
28 A1 Keşan Turkey
28 G1 Keşap Turkey
40 G5 Kesennuma Japan
31 H2 Keshem Afgh.
31 G2 Keshendeh-ye Bala Afgh.
34 B4 Keshod India
29 M5 Keshvar Iran
28 D2 Keskin Turkey
20 E2 Keskozero Rus. Fed.
12 E3 Kessel Neth.
91 H4 Kestell S. Africa
6 W4 Kesten'ga Rus. Fed.
6 U4 Kestilä Fin.
69 H3 Keswick Can.
8 D3 Keswick U.K.
16 H7 Keszthely Hungary
24 K4 Ket' r. Rus. Fed.
86 C4 Keta Ghana
44 □ Ketam, P. i. Sing.
45 D3 Ketapang Indon.
56 C3 Ketchikan U.S.A.
12 D2 Ketelmeer l. Neth.
31 G5 Keti Bandar Pak.
9 G5 Kettering U.K.
70 A5 Kettering U.S.A.
56 F5 Kettle r. Can.
68 A2 Kettle r. U.S.A.
70 E4 Kettle Creek r. U.S.A.
72 C3 Kettleman City U.S.A.
62 C1 Kettle River Ra. mts U.S.A.
70 E3 Keuka Lake l. U.S.A.
7 T5 Keuruu Fin.
68 C5 Kewanee U.S.A.
68 D3 Kewaunee U.S.A.
68 C2 Keweenaw Bay b. U.S.A.
68 C2 Keweenaw Peninsula U.S.A.
68 D2 Keweenaw Pt pt U.S.A.
81 E3 Keweigek Guyana
58 E3 Keyano Can.
69 G3 Key Harbour Can.
67 D7 Key Largo U.S.A.
11 C3 Key, Lough l. Rep. of Ireland
9 E6 Keynsham U.K.
70 D5 Keyser U.S.A.
70 D5 Keysers Ridge U.S.A.
73 G6 Keystone Peak summit U.S.A.
70 D6 Keysville U.S.A.
51 A6 Key, The N.Z.
29 M4 Keytū Iran
67 D7 Key West FL U.S.A.
68 B4 Key West IA U.S.A.
71 H3 Kezar Falls U.S.A.
89 C6 Kezi Zimbabwe
17 K6 Kežmarok Slovakia
90 D1 Kgalagadi div. Botswana
91 G2 Kgatleng div. Botswana
90 D1 Kgomofatshe Pan salt pan Botswana
90 F2 Kgoro Pan salt pan Botswana
91 G3 Kgotsong S. Africa
36 F2 Khabarovsk Rus. Fed.
Khabis see Shahdāb
29 H4 Khabur r. Syria
29 J7 Khadd, W. al watercourse S. Arabia
30 B6 Khafs Daghrah S. Arabia
34 E4 Khaga India
35 G5 Khagrachari Bangl.
34 B3 Khairgarh Pak.
34 B4 Khairpur Pak.
31 G2 Khaja du Koh h. Afgh.
34 D4 Khajurāho India
89 C6 Khakhea Botswana
31 G3 Khakīr Afgh.
31 G4 Khak-rēz Afgh.
31 G4 Khakriz reg. Afgh.
31 G2 Khalach Turkm.
30 C4 Khalafabād Iran
30 C3 Khalajestan reg. Iran
34 D2 Khalatse Jammu and Kashmir
34 A3 Khalifat mt Pak.
31 E3 Khalilabad Iran
30 C3 Khalkhāl Iran
35 F6 Khallikot India
20 D4 Khalopyenichy Belarus
36 C1 Khamar-Daban, Khrebet mts Rus. Fed.
34 C5 Khambhat India
34 B5 Khambhat, Gulf of g. India
34 D5 Khamgaon India
44 C1 Khamkkeut Laos
30 B5 Khamma well S. Arabia
33 C2 Khammam India
25 N3 Khamra Rus. Fed.
30 C3 Khamseh reg. Iran
31 H2 Khānābād Afgh.
29 J5 Khān al Baghdādī Iraq
29 K5 Khān al Maḩāwīl Iraq
29 K5 Khān al Mashāhidah Iraq
29 K5 Khān al Muşalla Iraq
33 A3 Khanapur India
30 B2 Khānaqāh Iran
29 K4 Khānaqīn Iraq
29 K2 Khanasur Pass Iran/Turkey
28 F6 Khān az Zabīb Jordan
34 C2 Khanbari Pass Jammu and Kashmir
50 G4 Khancoban Austr.
34 B2 Khand Pass Afgh./Pak.
34 D5 Khandwa India
25 P3 Khandyga Rus. Fed.
34 B3 Khanewal Pak.
44 D2 Khanh Dương Vietnam
34 D4 Khaniadhana India
30 D4 Khanīyak Iran
29 K5 Khān Jadwal Iraq
40 C2 Khanka, Lake l. China/Rus. Fed.
Khanka, Ozero l. see Khanka, Lake
34 C2 Khanki Weir barrage Pak.
34 D3 Khanna India
34 B3 Khanpur Pak.
28 F4 Khān Ruḩābah Iraq
28 F4 Khān Shaykhūn Syria
27 F2 Khantau Kazak.
24 L3 Khantayskoye, Ozero l. Rus. Fed.
24 H3 Khanty-Mansiysk Rus. Fed.
28 E6 Khān Yūnis Gaza
44 A3 Khao Chum Thong Thai.
34 D5 Khapa India
30 C3 Khar r. Iran
21 H6 Kharabali Rus. Fed.
35 F5 Kharagpur India
31 E5 Kharakī Iran
31 G4 Kharan Pak.
30 E5 Khārān r. Iran
30 D3 Kharānáq Iran
34 B2 Kharbin Pass Afgh.
34 C6 Khardi India
34 D2 Khardung La pass India
31 F3 Kharez Ilias Afgh.
29 L6 Kharfiyah Iraq
30 C4 Khārg Islands is Iran
34 C5 Khargon India
34 C4 Khari r. Rajasthan India
34 C4 Khari r. Rajasthan India
34 C2 Kharian Pak.
35 E5 Khariar India
30 C6 Kharit S. Arabia
21 F5 Kharkiv Ukr.
Khar'kov see Kharkiv
19 L4 Kharmanli Bulg.
20 G3 Kharovsk Rus. Fed.
35 E5 Kharsia India
87 F3 Khartoum Sudan
30 E2 Khasardag, Gora mt Turkm.
21 H7 Khasav'yurt Rus. Fed.
31 F4 Khash Afgh.
31 F4 Khāsh Iran
31 F4 Khash Desert Afgh.
30 C5 Khashm Bijrān h. S. Arabia
31 F4 Khash Rūd r. Afgh.
21 G7 Khashuri Georgia
35 G4 Khāsi Hills h. India
19 L4 Khaskovo Bulg.
25 M2 Khatanga Rus. Fed.
25 M2 Khatanga, Gulf of b. Rus. Fed.
28 D6 Khatmia Pass Egypt
25 T3 Khatyrka Rus. Fed.
30 C4 Khāvar Iran
34 B5 Khavda India
31 H3 Khawak Pass Afgh.
30 E5 Khawr Fakkan U.A.E.
44 A2 Khawsa Myanmar
91 F5 Khayamnandi S. Africa
90 C7 Khayelitsha S. Africa
29 J3 Khāzir r. Iraq
44 C1 Khê Bo Vietnam
33 A2 Khed India
34 C4 Khedbrahma India
31 E3 Khedrī Iran
34 E3 Khela India
15 H4 Khemis Miliana Alg.
86 C1 Khenchela Alg.
86 B1 Khenifra Morocco
30 D4 Kherāmeh Iran
34 D4 Kherli India
30 C4 Khersan r. Iran
21 E6 Kherson Ukr.
30 C4 Khesht Iran
25 L2 Kheta r. Rus. Fed.
30 D4 Kheyrābād Iran
30 D2 Khezerābād Iran
34 D4 Khilchipur India
28 F4 Khirbat Isrīyah Syria
29 J6 Khirr, Wādī al watercourse S. Arabia
34 D2 Khitai P. pass China/Jammu and Kashmir
30 B2 Khīyāv Iran
7 V6 Khiytola Rus. Fed.
21 C5 Khmel'nyts'kyy Ukr.
21 C5 Khmil'nyk Ukr.
30 B2 Khodā Āfarīn Iran
31 G2 Khodzhambass Turkm.
26 D2 Khodzheyli Uzbek.
90 D2 Khokhowe Pan salt pan Botswana
34 B4 Khokhropar Pak.
20 G1 Kholmogory Rus. Fed.
36 G2 Kholmsk Rus. Fed.
17 Q3 Kholm-Zhirkovskiy Rus. Fed.
29 M3 Khoman Iran
90 B1 Khomas div. Namibia
90 A1 Khomas Highland reg. Namibia
30 C3 Khomeyn Iran
29 M4 Khondāb Iran
21 G7 Khoni Georgia
30 D5 Khonj Iran
25 Q3 Khonuu Rus. Fed.
21 G5 Khoper r. Rus. Fed.
36 F2 Khor Rus. Fed.
36 F2 Khor r. Rus. Fed.
34 B4 Khora Pak.
35 F5 Khordha India
30 C5 Khor Duweihin b. S. Arabia/U.A.E.
36 C1 Khorinsk Rus. Fed.
89 B6 Khorixas Namibia
40 C2 Khorol Rus. Fed.
21 E5 Khorol Ukr.
29 L2 Khoroslū Dāgh h. Iran
30 C3 Khorramābād Iran
29 M3 Khorram Darreh Iran
30 C4 Khorramshahr Iran
31 H2 Khorugh Tajik.
31 E3 Khosf Iran
21 H6 Khosheutovo Rus. Fed.
30 C4 Khosravī Iran
30 C4 Khosrowabad Iran
29 K4 Khosrowvī Iran
30 D4 Khowrjān Iran
30 D3 Khowrnag, Kūh-e mt Iran
31 H3 Khowst Afgh.
36 E1 Khrebet Dzhagdy mts Rus. Fed.
35 H5 Khreum Myanmar
35 G4 Khri r. India
20 H2 Khristoforovo Rus. Fed.
25 Q2 Khroma r. Rus. Fed.
26 D1 Khromtau Kazak.
40 D2 Khrustalnyy Rus. Fed.
17 O6 Khrystynivka Ukr.
31 G5 Khude Hills mts Pak.
90 F1 Khudumelapye Botswana
30 B5 Khuff S. Arabia
31 F5 Khūh Lab, Ra's pt Iran
90 D3 Khuis Botswana
26 E2 Khŭjand Tajik.
44 C2 Khu Khan Thai.
31 G3 Khulm r. Afgh.
35 G5 Khulna Bangl.
29 J1 Khulo Georgia
91 G3 Khuma S. Africa
34 C2 Khunjerab Pass China/Jammu and Kashmir
30 C3 Khunsar Iran
35 F5 Khunti India
31 E3 Khūr Iran
34 D4 Khurai India
30 D5 Khūran chan. Iran
31 G3 Khurd, Koh-i- mt Afgh.
34 D3 Khurja India
31 F3 Khurmalik Afgh.
34 C2 Khushab Pak.
29 M3 Khūshāvar Iran
31 E4 Khushk Rud Iran
31 F3 Khuspas Afgh.
21 B5 Khust Ukr.
91 G3 Khutsong S. Africa
31 G5 Khuzdar Pak.
31 F3 Khvāf Iran
20 J4 Khvalynsk Rus. Fed.
30 D3 Khvor Iran
30 E3 Khvord Nārvan Iran
30 C4 Khvormūj Iran
29 L3 Khvosh Maqām Iran
30 B2 Khvoy Iran
20 E3 Khvoynaya Rus. Fed.
44 A2 Khwae Noi r. Thai.
31 F4 Khwaja Ali Afgh.
31 H2 Khwaja Muhammad Range mts Afgh.
34 B2 Khyber Pass Afgh./Pak.
50 H3 Kiama Austr.
43 C5 Kiamba Phil.
88 C4 Kiambi Congo(Zaire)
65 E5 Kiamichi r. U.S.A.
6 V4 Kiantajärvi l. Fin.
30 D2 Kīāseh Iran
34 D2 Kibar India
43 C5 Kibawe Phil.
88 D4 Kibaya Tanz.
89 D4 Kibiti Tanz.
88 C4 Kibombo Congo(Zaire)
88 D4 Kibondo Tanz.
19 J4 Kičevo Macedonia
20 H3 Kichmengskiy Gorodok Rus. Fed.
86 C3 Kidal Mali
9 E5 Kidderminster U.K.
88 D3 Kidepo Valley National Park Uganda
86 A3 Kidira Senegal
34 D2 Kidmang Jammu and Kashmir
51 F3 Kidnappers, Cape c. N.Z.
9 E4 Kidsgrove U.K.
16 E3 Kiel Ger.
68 C4 Kiel U.S.A.
17 K5 Kielce Pol.
8 E2 Kielder Water resr U.K.
16 E3 Kieler Bucht b. Ger.
89 C5 Kienge Congo(Zaire)
12 F3 Kierspe Ger.
21 D5 Kiev Ukr.
86 A3 Kiffa Maur.
19 K5 Kifisia Greece
29 K4 Kifrī Iraq
88 D4 Kigali Rwanda
29 H2 Kiğı Turkey
59 H2 Kiglapait Mts mts Can.
88 C4 Kigoma Tanz.
6 S3 Kihlanki Fin.
7 S5 Kihniö Fin.
6 T4 Kiiminki Fin.
41 D8 Kii-sanchi mts Japan
41 D8 Kii-suidō chan. Japan
19 J2 Kikinda Yugo.
31 F5 Kikki Pak.
20 H3 Kiknur Rus. Fed.
40 G4 Kikonai Japan
89 C4 Kikondja Congo(Zaire)
48 E2 Kikori P.N.G.
48 E2 Kikori r. P.N.G.
88 B4 Kikwit Congo(Zaire)
7 P6 Kilafors Sweden
33 B4 Kilakkarai India
34 D2 Kilar India
72 □2 Kilauea U.S.A.
72 □2 Kilauea Crater crater U.S.A.
10 C5 Kilbrannan Sound chan. U.K.
42 E3 Kilchu N. Korea
11 E4 Kilcoole Rep. of Ireland
11 D4 Kilcormac Rep. of Ireland
11 E4 Kildare Rep. of Ireland
6 X2 Kil'dinstroy Rus. Fed.
88 B4 Kilembe Congo(Zaire)
10 C5 Kilfinan U.K.
65 E5 Kilgore U.S.A.
8 E2 Kilham U.K.
88 D4 Kilifi Kenya
88 D4 Kilimanjaro mt Tanz.
49 F2 Kilinailau Is is P.N.G.
89 D4 Kilindoni Tanz.
7 T7 Kilingi-Nõmme Estonia
28 F3 Kilis Turkey
21 D6 Kiliya Ukr.
11 B5 Kilkee Rep. of Ireland
11 F3 Kilkeel U.K.
11 D5 Kilkenny Rep. of Ireland
9 C7 Kilkhampton U.K.
19 K4 Kilkis Greece
11 B3 Killala Rep. of Ireland
11 B3 Killala Bay b. Rep. of Ireland
11 C5 Killaloe Rep. of Ireland
69 J3 Killaloe Station Can.
57 G4 Killam Can.
69 G3 Killarney Can.
11 B5 Killarney Rep. of Ireland
69 G2 Killarney National Park Can.
11 B6 Killarney National Park Rep. of Ireland
11 B4 Killary Harbour b. Rep. of Ireland
65 D6 Killeen U.S.A.
11 D5 Killenaule Rep. of Ireland
11 C4 Killimor Rep. of Ireland
10 D4 Killin U.K.
11 F3 Killinchy U.K.
11 E5 Killinick Rep. of Ireland
59 H1 Killiniq Can.
59 H1 Killiniq Island i. Can.
11 B5 Killorglin Rep. of Ireland
11 E5 Killurin Rep. of Ireland
11 C3 Killybegs Rep. of Ireland
11 D2 Kilmacrenan Rep. of Ireland
11 B4 Kilmaine Rep. of Ireland
11 C5 Kilmallock Rep. of Ireland
10 B3 Kilmaluag U.K.
10 D5 Kilmarnock U.K.
10 C4 Kilmelford U.K.
20 J3 Kil'mez' Rus. Fed.
20 J3 Kil'mez' r. Rus. Fed.
11 C6 Kilmona Rep. of Ireland
50 E4 Kilmore Austr.
11 E5 Kilmore Quay Rep. of Ireland
88 D4 Kilosa Tanz.
6 R2 Kilpisjärvi Fin.
6 X2 Kilp"yavr Rus. Fed.
11 E3 Kilrea U.K.
11 B5 Kilrush Rep. of Ireland
10 D5 Kilsyth U.K.
33 A4 Kiltān i. India
11 C4 Kiltullagh Rep. of Ireland
89 C4 Kilwa Congo(Zaire)
89 D4 Kilwa Masoko Tanz.
10 D5 Kilwinning U.K.
89 D4 Kimambi Tanz.
88 B4 Kimba Congo
64 C3 Kimball U.S.A.
48 F2 Kimbe P.N.G.
56 F5 Kimberley Can.
90 F4 Kimberley S. Africa
48 C3 Kimberley Plateau plat. Austr.
51 E4 Kimbolton N.Z.
42 E3 Kimch'aek N. Korea
42 E5 Kimch'ŏn S. Korea
7 S6 Kimito Fin.
42 D6 Kimje S. Korea
19 L6 Kimolos i. Greece
20 F4 Kimovsk Rus. Fed.
88 B4 Kimpese Congo(Zaire)
41 F5 Kimpoku-san mt Japan
20 F3 Kimry Rus. Fed.
88 B4 Kimvula Congo(Zaire)
45 E1 Kinabalu, Gunung mt Malaysia
43 A5 Kinabatangan r. Malaysia
19 M6 Kinaros i. Greece
60 C1 Kinbasket Lake l. B.C. Can.
10 E2 Kinbrace U.K.
69 G3 Kincardine Can.
10 E4 Kincardine U.K.
50 D2 Kinchega National Park Austr.
56 D3 Kincolith Can.
89 C4 Kinda Congo(Zaire)
35 H5 Kindat Myanmar
65 E6 Kinder U.S.A.
9 F4 Kinder Scout h. U.K.
57 H4 Kindersley Can.
86 A3 Kindia Guinea
88 C4 Kindu Congo(Zaire)
20 G3 Kineshma Rus. Fed.
49 F4 Kingaroy Austr.
72 B3 King City U.S.A.
92 C1 King Edward Point U.K. Base Ant.
70 E3 King Ferry U.S.A.
71 H2 Kingfield U.S.A.

# L

39 F4 Longquan Xi r. China
55 N5 Long Range Mountains Can.
59 J4 Long Range Mts h. Can.
48 E4 Longreach Austr.
38 B3 Longriba China
39 C4 Longshan China
39 D5 Longsheng China
62 F3 Longs Peak summit U.S.A.
9 J5 Long Stratton U.K.
39 D4 Longtian China
8 E2 Longtown U.K.
58 F4 Longueuil Can.
12 D5 Longuyon France
72 A2 Longvale U.S.A.
73 F3 Long Valley Junction U.S.A.
65 E5 Longview TX U.S.A.
62 B2 Longview WA U.S.A.
40 C2 Longwangmiao Rus. Fed.
38 B3 Longxi China
38 C3 Long Xian China
39 E5 Longxi Shan mt China
44 C3 Long Xuyên Vietnam
39 E5 Longyan China
38 E2 Longyao China
39 C6 Longzhou China
13 F2 Löningen Ger.
7 O8 Lönsboda Sweden
50 D4 Lonsdale, Lake l. Austr.
14 G3 Lons-le-Saunier France
58 B2 Lontra r. Brazil
43 B3 Looc Phil.
68 E4 Looking Glass r. U.S.A.
71 F4 Lookout U.S.A.
58 D2 Lookout, Cape c. Can.
67 E5 Lookout, Cape c. U.S.A.
72 C3 Lookout Mt mt U.S.A.
69 F3 Lookout, Pt pt U.S.A.
68 C1 Loon Can.
56 F3 Loon r. Can.
57 H4 Loon Lake Can.
71 J1 Loon Lake l. U.S.A.
11 B5 Loop Head hd Rep. of Ireland
34 E1 Lop China
36 G1 Lopatina, Gora mt Rus. Fed.
20 H4 Lopatino Rus. Fed.
44 B2 Lop Buri Thai.
43 B3 Lopez Phil.
71 E4 Lopez U.S.A.
36 B2 Lop Nur l. China
88 C3 Lopori r. Congo(Zaire)
6 R1 Lopphavet b. Norway
20 J2 Loptyuga Rus. Fed.
31 G4 Lora r. Afgh.
81 B2 Lora r. Venez.
15 D4 Lora del Río Spain
70 B4 Lorain U.S.A.
34 B3 Loralai Pak.
34 B3 Loralai r. Pak.
70 A4 Loramie, Lake l. U.S.A.
15 F4 Lorca Spain
13 F4 Lorch Ger.
43 A4 Lord Auckland sand bank Phil.
30 C4 Lordegān Iran
49 F5 Lord Howe Island i. Pac. Oc.
94 F8 Lord Howe Rise sea feature Pac. Oc.
73 H5 Lordsburg U.S.A.
13 F4 Loreley Ger.
82 D3 Lorena Brazil
37 F7 Lorentz r. Indon.
78 F7 Loreto Bol.
79 J5 Loreto Brazil
74 B3 Loreto Mex.
43 C4 Loreto Phil.
81 B2 Lorica Col.
13 C3 Lorient France
57 L1 Lorillard r. Can.
50 D5 Lorne Austr.
10 C4 Lorn, Firth of est. U.K.
35 H3 Loro r. China
14 G2 Lorraine reg. France
13 G5 Lorsch Ger.
12 F2 Lorup Ger.
34 C4 Losal India
63 F5 Los Alamos U.S.A.
83 B2 Los Andes Chile
83 B3 Los Angeles Chile
72 C5 Los Angeles CA U.S.A.
72 C4 Los Angeles Aqueduct canal U.S.A.
72 B3 Los Banos U.S.A.
80 D2 Los Blancos Arg.
80 B7 Los Chonos, Archipiélago de is Chile
72 D5 Los Coronados is Mex.
72 B3 Los Gatos U.S.A.
80 B8 Los Glacieres, Parque Nacional nat. park Arg.
12 E5 Losheim Ger.
18 F2 Lošinj i. Croatia
91 H2 Loskop Dam dam S. Africa
83 B4 Los Lagos div. Chile
63 F5 Los Lunas U.S.A.
83 C4 Los Menucos Arg.
74 C3 Los Mochis Mex.
72 A1 Los Molinos U.S.A.
88 B3 Losombo Congo(Zaire)
81 D2 Los Roques, Islas is Venez.
12 E2 Losser Neth.
10 E3 Lossie r. U.K.
10 E3 Lossiemouth U.K.
13 L4 Lößnitz Ger.
81 C2 Los Taques Venez.
81 D2 Los Teques Venez.
81 E2 Los Testigos is Venez.
72 C4 Lost Hills U.S.A.
62 D2 Lost Trail Pass U.S.A.
9 C7 Lostwithiel U.K.
80 C2 Los Vientos Chile
83 B1 Los Vilos Chile
83 B3 Lota Chile
31 E2 Lotfābād Iran
91 J3 Lothair S. Africa
88 D3 Lotikipi Plain plain Kenya
88 C4 Loto Congo(Zaire)
20 E3 Lotoshino Rus. Fed.
91 G1 Lotsane r. Botswana
6 V2 Lotta r. Fin./Rus. Fed.
13 F2 Lotte Ger.
37 C4 Louang Namtha Laos
37 C5 Louangphrabang Laos
88 B4 Loubomo Congo
14 C2 Loudéac France
39 D5 Loudi China
88 B4 Loudima Congo
70 B4 Loudonville U.S.A.
86 A3 Louga Senegal
9 F5 Loughborough U.K.
9 C6 Loughor r. U.K.
11 C4 Loughrea Rep. of Ireland
9 H6 Loughton U.K.
70 B5 Louisa KY U.S.A.
70 E5 Louisa VA U.S.A.
11 B4 Louisburgh Rep. of Ireland
56 C4 Louise I. i. Can.
49 F3 Louisiade Archipelago is P.N.G.
65 E6 Louisiana div. U.S.A.
91 H1 Louis Trichardt S. Africa
67 D5 Louisville GA U.S.A.
66 C4 Louisville KY U.S.A.
65 F5 Louisville MS U.S.A.
58 E3 Louis-XIV, Pointe c. Can.
24 E3 Loukhi Rus. Fed.
15 B4 Loulé Port.
57 L4 Lount L. l. Can.
16 F5 Louny Czech Rep.
64 D3 Loup r. U.S.A.
58 F2 Loups Marins, Lacs des l. Can.
59 J4 Lourdes Can.
14 D5 Lourdes France
15 B2 Lousã Port.
42 E1 Loushan China
9 G4 Louth U.K.
19 K5 Loutra Aidipsou Greece
Louvain see Leuven
90 B1 Louwater-Suid Namibia
91 J3 Louwsburg S. Africa
6 R4 Lövånger Sweden
20 D3 Lovat' r. Rus. Fed.
19 L3 Lovech Bulg.
62 F3 Loveland U.S.A.
62 E2 Lovell U.S.A.
72 C1 Lovelock U.S.A.
12 B3 Lovendegem Belgium
7 U6 Loviisa Fin.
70 D6 Lovingston U.S.A.
68 C6 Lovington IL U.S.A.
65 C5 Lovington NM U.S.A.
69 K3 Low Can.
88 C4 Lowa Congo(Zaire)
34 B2 Lowarai Pass Pak.
57 M2 Low, Cape c. Can.
71 H3 Lowell MA U.S.A.
68 E4 Lowell MI U.S.A.
71 G2 Lowell VT U.S.A.
56 F5 Lower Arrow L. l. Can.
73 F4 Lower Granite Gorge gorge U.S.A.
51 E4 Lower Hutt N.Z.
72 A2 Lower Lake U.S.A.
11 D3 Lower Lough Erne l. U.K.
44 Lower Peirce Res. resr Sing.
56 D3 Lower Post Can.
59 H5 Lower Sackville Can.
9 J5 Lowestoft U.K.
17 J4 Łowicz Pol.
58 E3 Low, Lac l. Can.
10 E5 Lowther Hills h. U.K.
71 F3 Lowville U.S.A.
13 G1 Loxstedt Ger.
50 C3 Loxton Austr.
90 E5 Loxton S. Africa
70 E4 Loyalsock Creek r. U.S.A.
72 B2 Loyalton U.S.A.
Loyalty Is is see Loyauté, Îs
49 G4 Loyauté, Îs is New Caledonia
21 D5 Loyew Belarus
19 H2 Loznica Yugo.
21 F5 Lozova Ukr.
89 C5 Luacano Angola
38 E4 Lu'an China
38 D3 Luanchuan China
89 B4 Luanda Angola
44 A3 Luang, Khao mt Thai.
89 D5 Luangwa r. Zambia
35 H2 Luanhaizi China
38 F1 Luan He r. China
38 F2 Luannan China
38 E1 Luanping China
89 C5 Luanshya Zambia
38 F2 Luan Xian China
89 C4 Luanza Congo(Zaire)
15 C1 Luarca Spain
45 D2 Luar, Danau l. Indon.
89 C5 Luau Angola
17 L5 Lubaczów Pol.
7 U8 Lubānas l. Latvia
43 B3 Lubang Phil.
43 B3 Lubang i. Phil.
43 A3 Lubang Islands is Phil.
89 B5 Lubango Angola
88 C4 Lubao Congo(Zaire)
17 L5 Lubartów Pol.
13 G2 Lübbecke Ger.
90 C4 Lubbeskolk salt pan S. Africa
65 C5 Lubbock U.S.A.
13 K2 Lübbow Ger.
13 J1 Lübeck Ger.
17 L5 Lubelska, Wyżyna reg. Pol.
88 C4 Lubero Congo(Zaire)
16 H5 Lubin Pol.
17 L5 Lublin Pol.
21 E5 Lubny Ukr.
45 D2 Lubok Antu Malaysia
13 K1 Lübstorf Ger.
13 K1 Lübtheen Ger.
43 B2 Lubuagan Phil.
89 C4 Lubudi Congo(Zaire)
45 B3 Lubuklinggau Indon.
44 A5 Lubukpakam Indon.
89 C5 Lubumbashi Congo(Zaire)
89 C5 Lubungu Zambia
88 C4 Lubutu Congo(Zaire)
13 L1 Lübz Ger.
89 B4 Lucala Angola
11 E4 Lucan Rep. of Ireland
56 A2 Lucania, Mt mt Can.
89 C4 Lucapa Angola
67 E7 Lucaya Bahamas
18 D3 Lucca Italy
10 D6 Luce Bay b. U.K.
82 B3 Lucélia Brazil
43 B3 Lucena Phil.
15 D4 Lucena Spain
17 J6 Lučenec Slovakia
18 F4 Lucera Italy
Lucerne see Luzern
40 D1 Luchegorsk Rus. Fed.
39 D6 Luchuan China
39 B6 Lüchun China
50 C4 Lucindale Austr.
89 B5 Lucira Angola
35 F4 Luckeesarai India
13 M2 Luckenwalde Ger.
90 F4 Luckhoff S. Africa
69 G4 Lucknow Can.
34 E4 Lucknow India
89 C5 Lucusse Angola
20 F1 Luda Rus. Fed.
12 F3 Lüdenscheid Ger.
89 B6 Lüderitz Namibia
13 J1 Lüdersdorf Ger.
34 C3 Ludhiana India
39 B5 Ludian China
68 D4 Ludington U.S.A.
9 E5 Ludlow U.K.
72 D4 Ludlow CA U.S.A.
71 J1 Ludlow ME U.S.A.
71 G3 Ludlow VT U.S.A.
19 M3 Ludogorie reg. Bulg.
7 O6 Ludvika Sweden
13 H6 Ludwigsburg Ger.
13 M2 Ludwigsfelde Ger.
13 G5 Ludwigshafen am Rhein Ger.
13 K1 Ludwigslust Ger.
7 U8 Ludza Latvia
88 C4 Luebo Congo(Zaire)
89 B5 Luena Angola
81 E3 Luepa Venez.
38 C3 Lüeyang China
39 E6 Lufeng China
65 E6 Lufkin U.S.A.
20 D3 Luga Rus. Fed.
20 D3 Luga r. Rus. Fed.
18 C1 Lugano Switz.
13 L4 Lugau Ger.
13 H3 Lügde Ger.
89 D5 Lugenda r. Moz.
9 D5 Lugg r. U.K.
18 D2 Lugo Italy
15 C1 Lugo Spain
19 J2 Lugoj Romania
43 B5 Lugus i. Phil.
21 F5 Luhans'k Ukr.
38 F3 Luhe China
13 J1 Luhe r. Ger.
35 H4 Luhit r. India
89 D4 Luhombero Tanz.
21 D5 Luhyny Ukr.
89 C5 Luiana Angola
Luik see Liège
88 C4 Luilaka r. Congo(Zaire)
10 C4 Luing i. U.K.
18 C2 Luino Italy
6 U3 Luiro r. Fin.
88 C4 Luiza Congo(Zaire)
83 E2 Luján r. Arg.
83 C2 Luján de Cuyo Arg.
38 E4 Lujiang China
19 H2 Lukavac Bos.-Herz.
88 C4 Lukenie r. Congo(Zaire)
73 F6 Lukeville U.S.A.
20 G3 Lukh r. Rus. Fed.
20 F4 Lukhovitsy Rus. Fed.
19 L3 Lukovit Bulg.
17 L5 Łuków Pol.
20 H4 Lukoyanov Rus. Fed.
89 C5 Lukulu Zambia
89 D4 Lukumburu Tanz.
6 S4 Luleå Sweden
6 S4 Luleälven r. Sweden
28 A1 Lüleburgaz Turkey
39 B5 Luliang China
38 D2 Lüliang Shan mts China
65 D6 Luling U.S.A.
38 F2 Lulong China
35 F3 Lülung China
35 F3 Lumachomo China
45 D4 Lumajang Indon.
35 E2 Lumajangdong Co salt l. China
89 C5 Lumbala Kaquengue Angola
89 C5 Lumbala N'guimbo Angola
67 E5 Lumberton U.S.A.
15 C2 Lumbrales Spain
35 H4 Lumding India
6 T4 Lumijoki Fin.
44 C2 Lumphăt Cambodia
51 B6 Lumsden N.Z.
45 C3 Lumut, Tanjung pt Indon.
43 B2 Luna Phil.
73 H5 Luna U.S.A.
10 F4 Lunan Bay b. U.K.
57 L2 Lunan Lake l. Can.
69 F5 Luna Pier U.S.A.
34 C5 Lunavada India
34 B4 Lund Pak.
7 N9 Lund Sweden
73 F2 Lund U.S.A.
57 K4 Lundar Can.
89 D5 Lundazi Zambia
9 C6 Lundy Island i. U.K.
8 E3 Lune r. U.K.
13 J1 Lüneburg Ger.
13 J1 Lüneburger Heide reg. Ger.
12 F3 Lünen Ger.
14 H2 Lunéville France
89 C5 Lunga r. Zambia
35 E2 Lungdo China
35 E3 Lunggar China
86 A4 Lungi Sierra Leone
39 Lung Kwu Chau h. H.K. China
35 H5 Lunglei India
11 E5 Lungnaquilla Mountain mt Rep. of Ireland
89 C5 Lungwebungu r. Zambia
34 C4 Luni India
34 C4 Luni r. India
34 B3 Luni r. Pak.
72 C2 Luning U.S.A.
20 H4 Lunino Rus. Fed.
21 C4 Luninyets Belarus
34 C1 Lunkho mt Afgh./Pak.
12 F2 Lünne Ger.
86 A4 Lunsar Sierra Leone
91 H2 Lunsklip S. Africa
27 G2 Luntai China
38 D3 Luo r. Henan China
38 C3 Luo r. Shaanxi China
39 C5 Luocheng China
38 C3 Luochuan China
39 C5 Luodian China
39 D6 Luoding China
39 D6 Luodou Sha i. China
38 E3 Luohe China
38 D3 Luoning China
39 B5 Luoping China
38 E3 Luoshan China
39 E4 Luotian China
38 D3 Luoyang China
39 F5 Luoyuan China
42 F2 Luozigou China
89 C5 Lupane Zimbabwe
45 D2 Lupar r. Malaysia
19 K2 Lupeni Romania
89 D5 Lupilichi Moz.
43 C5 Lupon Phil.
73 H4 Lupton U.S.A.
38 B3 Luqu China
39 B5 Luquan China
29 K3 Lūrā Shīrīn Iran
89 B4 Luremo Angola
10 C2 Lurgainn, Loch l. U.K.
11 E3 Lurgan U.K.
89 E5 Lúrio Moz.
89 D5 Lurio r. Moz.
89 C5 Lusaka Zambia
88 C4 Lusambo Congo(Zaire)
48 F2 Lusancay Islands and Reefs is P.N.G.
56 F4 Luscar Can.
57 H4 Luseland Can.
38 D3 Lushi China
19 H4 Lushnjë Albania
42 D2 Lushuihe China
42 A4 Lüshun China
91 H5 Lusikisiki S. Africa
62 F3 Lusk U.S.A.
31 E4 Lut, Dasht-e des. Iran
69 G4 Luther Lake l. Can.
13 L3 Lutherstadt Wittenberg Ger.
9 G6 Luton U.K.
45 D2 Lutong Malaysia
57 G2 Łutselk'e Can.
21 C5 Luts'k Ukr.
12 D2 Luttelgeest Neth.
12 E2 Luttenberg Neth.
13 H5 Lützelbach Ger.
92 D4 Lützow-Holmbukta b. Ant.
90 D4 Lutzputs S. Africa
90 C5 Lutzville S. Africa
43 B5 Luuk Phil.
7 U6 Luumäki Fin.
88 E3 Luuq Somalia
64 D3 Luverne U.S.A.
88 C4 Luvua r. Congo(Zaire)
91 J1 Luvuvhu r. S. Africa
88 D3 Luwero Uganda
48 C2 Luwuk Indon.
12 E5 Luxembourg Lux.
5 D4 Luxembourg country Europe
14 H3 Luxeuil-les-Bains France
39 D4 Luxi Hunan China
39 B5 Luxi Yunnan China
91 F5 Luxolweni S. Africa
87 F2 Luxor Egypt
38 E3 Luyi China
12 D3 Luyksgestel Neth.
20 H2 Luza Rus. Fed.
20 J2 Luza r. Rus. Fed.
16 D7 Luzern Switz.
39 C5 Luzhai China
39 E5 Luzhi China
39 B4 Luzhou China
82 C2 Luziânia Brazil
79 K4 Luzilândia Brazil
43 B3 Luzon i. Phil.
43 B1 Luzon Strait str. Phil.
14 F3 Luzy France
21 C5 L'viv Ukr.
L'vov see L'viv
20 D3 Lyady Rus. Fed.
20 C4 Lyakhavichy Belarus
56 G5 Lyall, Mt mt Can.
Lyallpur see Faisalabad
6 Q4 Lycksele Sweden
9 H7 Lydd U.K.
92 C3 Lyddan I. i. Ant.
91 J2 Lydenburg S. Africa
9 E6 Lydney U.K.
21 D5 Lyel'chytsy Belarus
56 C4 Lyell I. i. Can.
72 C3 Lyell, Mt mt U.S.A.
20 D4 Lyepyel' Belarus
70 E4 Lykens U.S.A.
62 E3 Lyman U.S.A.
9 E7 Lyme Bay b. U.K.
9 E7 Lyme Regis U.K.
9 F7 Lymington U.K.
70 D6 Lynchburg U.S.A.
71 H2 Lynchville U.S.A.
50 G2 Lyndhurst Austr.
71 G2 Lyndonville U.S.A.
10 E2 Lyness U.K.
7 K7 Lyngdal Norway
71 H3 Lynn U.S.A.
56 B3 Lynn Canal chan. U.S.A.
73 F2 Lynndyl U.S.A.
57 J3 Lynn Lake Can.
9 D6 Lynton U.K.
57 H2 Lynx Lake l. Can.
14 G4 Lyon France
71 G2 Lyon Mountain U.S.A.
67 D5 Lyons GA U.S.A.
70 E3 Lyons NY U.S.A.
71 F3 Lyons Falls U.S.A.
20 D4 Lyozna Belarus
49 F2 Lyra Reef rf P.N.G.
7 M7 Lysekil Sweden
20 H3 Lyskovo Rus. Fed.
24 G4 Lys'va Rus. Fed.
21 F5 Lysychans'k Ukr.
8 D4 Lytham St Anne's U.K.
56 E4 Lytton Can.
20 D4 Lyuban' Belarus
21 C5 Lyubeshiv Ukr.
20 E4 Lyudinovo Rus. Fed.
20 H3 Lyunda r. Rus. Fed.


# M


89 C5 Maamba Zambia
28 E6 Ma'an Jordan
6 U5 Maaninka Fin.
6 V3 Maaninkavaara Fin.
38 F4 Ma'anshan China
7 T7 Maardu Estonia
28 F4 Ma'arrat an Nu'mān Syria
12 D2 Maarssen Neth.
12 E3 Maas r. Neth.
12 D3 Maaseik Belgium
43 C4 Maasin Phil.
12 D4 Maasmechelen Belgium
12 D4 Maastricht Neth.
91 H1 Maastroom S. Africa
43 B3 Mabalacat Phil.
89 D6 Mabalane Moz.
78 G2 Mabaruma Guyana
69 J3 Maberly Can.
39 B4 Mabian China
9 H4 Mablethorpe U.K.
91 H2 Mabopane S. Africa
89 D6 Mabote Moz.
43 B1 Mabudis i. Phil.
90 F2 Mabule Botswana
90 E2 Mabutsane Botswana
83 D3 Macachín Arg.
71 K2 McAdam Can.
82 E3 Macaé Brazil
43 C4 Macajalar Bay b. Phil.
65 E5 McAlester U.S.A.
70 E4 McAlevys Fort U.S.A.
50 G3 McAlister mt Austr.
50 F4 Macalister r. Austr.
65 D7 McAllen U.S.A.
89 D5 Macaloge Moz.
54 H3 MacAlpine Lake l. Can.
80 B7 Macá, Mt mt Chile
91 K1 Macandze Moz.
79 H3 Macapá Brazil
78 C4 Macará Ecuador
82 E1 Macarani Brazil
81 B4 Macarena, Cordillera mts Col.
81 B4 Macarena, Parque Nacional La nat. park Col.
50 D5 Macarthur Austr.
70 B5 McArthur U.S.A.
69 J3 McArthur Mills Can.
56 B2 McArthur Wildlife Sanctuary res. Can.
78 C4 Macas Ecuador
45 E3 Macassar Strait str. Indon.
79 L5 Macau Brazil
39 D6 Macau Macau
79 H6 Macaúba Brazil
82 D1 Macaúbas Brazil
81 B4 Macaya r. Col.
81 B4 Macayari Col.
56 E4 McBride Can.
62 C2 McCall U.S.A.
65 C6 McCamey U.S.A.
62 D3 McCammon U.S.A.
91 K2 Maccaretane Moz.
56 C4 McCauley I. i. Can.
9 E4 Macclesfield U.K.
54 H2 McClintock Chan. Can.
72 B3 McClure, L. l. U.S.A.
54 F2 McClure Strait Can.
65 F6 McComb U.S.A.
64 C3 McConaughy, L. l. U.S.A.
70 E5 McConnellsburg U.S.A.
70 C5 McConnelsville U.S.A.
64 C3 McCook U.S.A.
57 K4 McCreary Can.
73 E4 McCullough Range mts U.S.A.
56 D3 McDame Can.
62 C3 McDermitt U.S.A.
48 C4 Macdonald, L. salt flat Austr.
62 D2 McDonald Peak summit U.S.A.
48 D4 Macdonnell Ranges mts Austr.
90 B4 McDougall's Bay b. S. Africa
58 B3 MacDowell L. l. Can.
73 G5 McDowell Peak summit U.S.A.
10 F3 Macduff U.K.
15 C2 Macedo de Cavaleiros Port.
50 E4 Macedon mt Austr.
5 F4 Macedonia country Europe
79 L5 Maceió Brazil
86 B4 Macenta Guinea
18 E3 Macerata Italy
72 C4 McFarland U.S.A.
57 H3 McFarlane r. Can.
48 D5 Macfarlane, L. salt flat Austr.
73 E2 McGill U.S.A.
11 B6 Macgillycuddy's Reeks mts Rep. of Ireland
54 C3 McGrath U.S.A.
90 C6 McGregor S. Africa
68 A2 McGregor U.S.A.
56 E4 McGregor r. Can.
69 G2 McGregor Bay Can.
62 D2 McGuire, Mt mt U.S.A.
34 A3 Mach Pak.
78 C4 Machachi Ecuador
82 D3 Machado Brazil
89 D6 Machaila Moz.
88 D4 Machakos Kenya
78 C4 Machala Ecuador
89 D6 Machanga Moz.
91 K2 Machatuine Moz.
12 C5 Machault France
38 E4 Macheng China
33 B2 Macherla India
33 C2 Māchhakund Dam dam India
71 K2 Machias ME U.S.A.
70 D3 Machias NY U.S.A.
71 J1 Machias r. U.S.A.
33 C2 Machilipatnam India
81 B2 Machiques Venez.
10 C5 Machrihanish U.K.
9 D5 Machynlleth U.K.
91 K2 Macia Moz.
19 N2 Măcin Romania
71 G2 McIndoe Falls U.S.A.
64 C2 McIntosh U.S.A.
73 H2 Mack U.S.A.
29 G1 Maçka Turkey
48 E4 Mackay Austr.
62 D2 Mackay U.S.A.
57 G2 Mackay Lake l. Can.
48 C4 Mackay, Lake salt flat Austr.
49 J2 McKean Island i. Kiribati
70 A6 McKee U.S.A.
70 D4 McKeesport U.S.A.
71 F3 McKeever U.S.A.
56 E3 Mackenzie B.C. Can.
68 C1 Mackenzie Ont. Can.
67 B4 McKenzie U.S.A.
54 E3 Mackenzie r. Can.
92 D5 Mackenzie Bay b. Ant.
54 E3 Mackenzie Bay b. Y.T. Can.
56 F2 Mackenzie Bison Sanctuary res. Can.
54 G2 Mackenzie King I. Can.
56 C2 Mackenzie Mountains Can.
54 E3 Mackenzie Mts Can.
68 E3 Mackinac I. i. U.S.A.
68 E3 Mackinac, Straits of chan. U.S.A.
68 C5 Mackinaw r. U.S.A.
68 E3 Mackinaw City U.S.A.
54 C3 McKinley, Mt U.S.A.
65 D5 McKinney U.S.A.
92 B5 Mackintosh, C. c. Ant.
72 C4 McKittrick U.S.A.
57 H4 Macklin Can.
49 F5 Macksville Austr.
64 C2 McLaughlin U.S.A.
91 H5 Maclear S. Africa
56 F3 McLennan Can.
56 F4 McLeod r. Can.
56 E3 McLeod Lake Can.
48 B4 Macleod, Lake l. Austr.
62 B3 McLoughlin, Mt mt U.S.A.
68 E2 McMillan U.S.A.
56 C2 Macmillan r. Can.
62 B2 McMinnville OR U.S.A.
67 C5 McMinnville TN U.S.A.
92 B5 McMurdo U.S.A. Base Ant.
73 H4 McNary U.S.A.
56 F4 McNaughton Lake l. Can.
73 H6 McNeal U.S.A.
68 B5 Macomb U.S.A.
18 C4 Macomer Sardinia Italy
14 G3 Mâcon France
67 D5 Macon GA U.S.A.
64 E4 Macon MO U.S.A.
89 C5 Macondo Angola
64 D4 McPherson U.S.A.
50 F1 Macquarie r. Austr.
48 E6 Macquarie Harbour in. Austr.
46 G9 Macquarie Island i. Austr.
50 H2 Macquarie, L. b. Austr.
50 F1 Macquarie Marshes marsh Austr.
50 G2 Macquarie Mt mt Austr.
94 F9 Macquarie Ridge sea feature Pac. Oc.
56 B2 McQuesten r. Can.
67 D5 McRae U.S.A.
44 MacRitchie Res. resr Sing.
92 D4 Mac. Robertson Land reg. Ant.
11 C6 Macroom Rep. of Ireland
81 C1 Macuira, Parque Nacional nat. park Col.
81 B4 Macuje Col.
48 D4 Macumba watercourse Austr.
78 D6 Macusani Peru
60 E6 Macuzari, Presa resr Mex.
56 E1 McVicar Arm b. Can.
71 J2 Macwahoc U.S.A.
28 E6 Mādabā Jordan
91 J3 Madadeni S. Africa
85 H8 Madagascar country Africa
93 H5 Madagascar Basin sea feature Ind. Ocean
93 G6 Madagascar Ridge sea feature Ind. Ocean
33 B3 Madakasira India
87 D2 Madama Niger
19 L4 Madan Bulg.
33 B3 Madanapalle India
48 E2 Madang P.N.G.
86 C3 Madaoua Niger
35 G5 Madaripur Bangl.
69 J3 Madawaska Can.
71 J1 Madawaska U.S.A.
69 J3 Madawaska r. Can.
84 A2 Madeira is Atlantic Ocean
78 F5 Madeira r. Brazil
59 H4 Madeleine, Îles de la is Can.
68 B2 Madeline I. i. U.S.A.
29 G2 Maden Turkey
74 C3 Madera Mex.
72 B3 Madera U.S.A.
33 A3 Madgaon India
35 F4 Madhepura India
33 C2 Madhira India
35 F4 Madhubani India
34 D5 Madhya Pradesh div. India
91 F3 Madibogo S. Africa
33 A3 Madikeri India

88 B4 Madingou Congo
78 E6 Madini r. Bol.
89 E5 Madirovalo Madag.
66 C4 Madison IN U.S.A.
71 J2 Madison ME U.S.A.
64 D2 Madison MN U.S.A.
64 D3 Madison NE U.S.A.
64 D2 Madison SD U.S.A.
70 C5 Madison WV U.S.A.
68 C4 Madison WV U.S.A.
60 D2 Madison r. MT U.S.A.
66 C4 Madisonville KY U.S.A.
65 E6 Madisonville TX U.S.A.
45 D4 Madiun Indon.
69 J3 Madoc Can.
88 D3 Mado Gashi Kenya
36 B3 Madoi China
7 U8 Madona Latvia
34 B4 Madpura India
19 M5 Madra Dağı mts Turkey
33 C3 Madras India
62 B2 Madras U.S.A.
78 D6 Madre de Dios r. Peru
80 A8 Madre de Dios, I. i. Chile
74 D5 Madre del Sur, Sierra mts Mex.
74 E4 Madre, Laguna lag. Mex.
65 D7 Madre, Laguna lag. U.S.A.
74 C3 Madre Occidental, Sierra mts Mex.
74 D3 Madre Oriental, Sierra mts Mex.
43 B2 Madre, Sierra mt Phil.
43 C4 Madrid Phil.
15 E2 Madrid Spain
43 B4 Madridejos Phil.
15 E3 Madridejos Spain
33 C2 Madugula India
45 D4 Madura i. Indon.
33 B4 Madurai India
45 D4 Madura, Selat chan. Indon.
35 E4 Madwas India
34 C2 Madyan Pak.
21 H7 Madzhalis Rus. Fed.
41 F6 Maebashi Japan
44 A1 Mae Hong Son Thai.
44 B2 Mae Khlong r. Thai.
44 A1 Mae Lao r. Thai.
44 A1 Mae Li r. Thai.
44 B1 Mae Nam Ing r. Thai.
44 C2 Mae Nam Mun r. Thai.
44 B2 Mae Nam Nan r. Thai.
44 B2 Mae Nam Pa Sak r. Thai.
44 B2 Mae Nam Ping r. Thai.
44 A1 Mae Nam Wang r. Thai.
44 B2 Mae Nam Yom r. Thai.
75 J5 Maestra, Sierra mts Cuba
89 E5 Maevatanana Madag.
49 G3 Maéwo i. Vanuatu
44 A1 Mae Yuam r. Myanmar/Thai.
57 J4 Mafeking Can.
91 G4 Mafeteng Lesotho
50 F4 Maffra Austr.
89 D4 Mafia I. i. Tanz.
91 F2 Mafikeng S. Africa
89 D4 Mafinga Tanz.
82 C4 Mafra Brazil
28 F5 Mafraq Jordan
91 J5 Magabeni S. Africa
25 R4 Magadan Rus. Fed.
88 D4 Magadi Kenya
91 K1 Magaiza Moz.
43 B3 Magallanes Phil.
80 B8 Magallanes, Estrecho de chan. Chile
81 B2 Magangue Col.
28 D3 Mağara Turkey
Magas see Zābolī
43 B2 Magat r. Phil.
83 F2 Magdalena Arg.
78 F6 Magdalena Bol.
74 B2 Magdalena Mex.
63 F5 Magdalena U.S.A.
81 B3 Magdalena r. Col.
60 D7 Magdalena, Bahía b. Mex.
80 B6 Magdalena, Isla i. Chile
43 A5 Magdaleno, Mt mt Malaysia
13 K2 Magdeburg Ger.
94 F4 Magellan Seamounts sea feature Pac. Oc.
6 T1 Magerøya i. Norway
41 B9 Mage-shima i. Japan
18 C2 Maggiorasca, Monte mt Italy
18 C2 Maggiore, Lago l. Italy
86 A3 Maghama Maur.
11 E3 Maghera U.K.
11 E3 Magherafelt U.K.
8 E4 Maghull U.K.
62 D3 Magna U.S.A.
18 F6 Magna Grande mt Sicily Italy
92 D4 Magnet Bay b. Ant.
48 E3 Magnetic I. i. Austr.
6 X2 Magnetity Rus. Fed.
24 G4 Magnitogorsk Rus. Fed.
65 E5 Magnolia U.S.A.
59 F4 Magog Can.
59 H3 Magpie Can.
68 E1 Magpie r. Can.
59 H3 Magpie L. l. Can.
68 E1 Magpie Lake l. Can.
56 G5 Magrath Can.
72 D3 Magruder Mt mt U.S.A.
86 A3 Magṭa' Laḥjar Maur.
88 D4 Magu Tanz.
39 B6 Maguan China
79 J4 Maguarinho, Cabo pt Brazil
91 K2 Magude Moz.
71 K2 Magundy Can.
57 K2 Maguse Lake l. Can.
35 H5 Magwe Myanmar
35 H5 Magyichaung Myanmar
30 B2 Mahābād Iran
33 A2 Mahabaleshwar India
Mahabalipuram see Māmallapuram
35 F4 Mahabharat Range mts Nepal
89 E6 Mahabo Madag.
33 A2 Mahad India
34 D5 Mahadeo Hills h. India
88 D3 Mahagi Congo(Zaire)
34 C3 Mahajan India
89 E5 Mahajanga Madag.
45 D2 Mahakam r. Indon.
89 C6 Mahalapye Botswana
89 E5 Mahalevona Madag.
30 C3 Mahallāt Iran
34 D3 Maham India
45 D4 Mahameru, Gunung volc. Indon.
30 E4 Mahān Iran
35 F5 Mahanadi r. India
89 E5 Mahanoro Madag.
34 C6 Maharashtra div. India
35 E5 Mahasamund India
44 B1 Maha Sarakham Thai.
89 E6 Mahatalaky Madag.
89 E5 Mahavanona Madag.
89 E5 Mahavavy r. Madag.
33 C5 Mahaweli Ganga r. Sri Lanka
44 C1 Mahaxai Laos
33 C2 Mahbubabad India
33 B2 Mahbubnagar India
30 D5 Mahḍah Oman
79 G2 Mahdia Guyana
18 D7 Mahdia Tunisia
93 H4 Mahé i. Seychelles
33 D2 Mahendragiri mt India
34 C5 Mahesāna India
34 C5 Maheshwar India
34 C5 Mahi r. India
31 E4 Māhī watercourse Iran
51 F3 Mahia Peninsula N.Z.
20 D4 Mahilyow Belarus
33 C5 Mahiyangana Sri Lanka
91 J4 Mahlabatini S. Africa
13 K2 Mahlsdorf Ger.
31 H3 Maḥmūd-e 'Erāqī Afgh.
29 M4 Mahnīān Iran
64 D2 Mahnomen U.S.A.
34 D4 Mahoba India
15 J3 Mahón Spain
70 D4 Mahoning Creek Lake l. U.S.A.
35 H5 Mahudaung Hgts mts Myanmar
34 B5 Mahuva India
19 M4 Mahya Dağı mt Turkey
30 C3 Mahyār Iran
35 H4 Maibang India
81 B2 Maicao Col.
58 E4 Maicasagi, Lac l. Can.
39 C6 Maichen China
9 G6 Maidenhead U.K.
57 H4 Maidstone Can.
9 H6 Maidstone U.K.
87 D3 Maiduguri Nigeria
81 D3 Maigualida, Sierra mts Venez.
11 C5 Maigue r. Rep. of Ireland
34 E4 Maihar India
38 C3 Maiji Shan mt China
35 E4 Maikala Range h. India
88 C4 Maiko, Parc National de la nat. park Congo(Zaire)
34 E3 Mailani India
13 H5 Main r. Ger.
11 E3 Main r. U.K.
59 J3 Main Brook Can.
69 F3 Main Channel Can.
88 B4 Mai-Ndombe, Lac l. Congo(Zaire)
13 K5 Main-Donau-Kanal canal Ger.
69 J4 Main Duck I. i. Can.
71 J2 Maine div. U.S.A.
86 D3 Maïné-Soroa Niger
44 A2 Maingy I. i. Myanmar
13 H5 Mainhardt Ger.
43 C4 Mainit Phil.
43 C4 Mainit, Lake l. Phil.
10 E1 Mainland i. Orkney U.K.
10 □ Mainland i. Shetland U.K.
13 K4 Mainleus Ger.
35 E5 Mainpat reg. India
34 D4 Mainpuri India
89 E5 Maintirano Madag.
13 G4 Mainz Ger.
86 □ Maio i. Cape Verde
83 C2 Maipó, Vol. volc. Chile
83 F3 Maipú Buenos Aires Arg.
83 C2 Maipú Mendoza Arg.
81 D2 Maiquetía Venez.
35 G5 Maiskhal I. i. Bangl.
89 C6 Maitengwe Botswana
50 H2 Maitland N.S.W. Austr.
50 A3 Maitland S.A. Austr.
92 D3 Maitri India Base Ant.
35 G3 Maizhokunggar China
75 H6 Maíz, Islas del is Nic.
41 D7 Maizuru Japan
19 H3 Maja Jezercë mt Albania
33 B2 Mājalgaon India
81 E4 Majari r. Brazil
45 E3 Majene Indon.
30 C6 Majhūd well S. Arabia
88 D3 Majī Eth.
38 E2 Majia r. China
39 D6 Majiang China
Majorca i. see Mallorca
35 H4 Majuli I. i. India
94 G5 Majuro i. Pac. Oc.
91 G4 Majwemasweu S. Africa
88 B4 Makabana Congo
72 □1 Makaha U.S.A.
37 D7 Makale Indon.
35 F4 Makalu, Mt mt China
88 C4 Makamba Burundi
27 G2 Makanchi Kazak.
72 □1 Makapuu Hd hd U.S.A.
20 J2 Makar-Ib Rus. Fed.
18 G3 Makarska Croatia
26 D2 Makat Kazak.
91 K3 Makatini Flats lowland S. Africa
86 A4 Makeni Sierra Leone
89 C6 Makgadikgadi salt pan Botswana
21 H7 Makhachkala Rus. Fed.
28 G4 Makhfar al Ḥammām Syria
29 J4 Makhmūr Iraq
88 D4 Makindu Kenya
24 F1 Makinsk Kazak.
21 F5 Makiyivka Ukr.
Makkah see Mecca
59 J2 Makkovik Can.
59 J2 Makkovik, Cape c. Can.
12 D1 Makkum Neth.
19 J1 Makó Hungary
88 B3 Makokou Gabon
89 D4 Makongolosi Tanz.
89 C6 Makopong Botswana
88 B4 Makotipoko Congo
31 F5 Makran reg. Iran/Pak.
34 C4 Makrana India
Makran Coast Range mts see Talar-i-Band
35 E6 Makri India
19 L6 Makronisi i. Greece
20 E3 Maksatikha Rus. Fed.
41 E1 Maksimovka Rus. Fed.
31 F4 Maksotag Iran
30 B2 Mākū Iran
35 H4 Makum India
89 D4 Makumbako Tanz.
89 D5 Makunguwiro Tanz.
41 B9 Makurazaki Japan
86 C4 Makurdi Nigeria
30 D4 Makūyeh Iran
91 F3 Makwassie S. Africa
6 Q4 Malå Sweden
43 C5 Malabang Phil.
33 A3 Malabar Coast coastal area India
86 C4 Malabo Equatorial Guinea
43 A4 Malabuñgan Phil.
42 A5 Malacca, Strait of str. Indon./Malaysia
62 D3 Malad City U.S.A.
20 C4 Maladzyechna Belarus
15 D4 Málaga Spain
71 F5 Malaga NJ U.S.A.
63 F5 Malaga NM U.S.A.
49 G2 Malaita i. Solomon Is
87 F4 Malakal Sudan
33 C2 Malakanagiri India
49 G3 Malakula i. Vanuatu
34 C2 Malakwal Pak.
37 E7 Malamala Indon.
45 D4 Malang Indon.
89 B4 Malanje Angola
31 G5 Malan, Ras pt Pak.
83 C1 Malanzán, Sa de mts Arg.
33 B4 Malappuram India
75 H7 Mala, Pta pt Panama
7 P7 Mälaren l. Sweden
83 C2 Malargüe Arg.
69 H1 Malartic Can.
69 H1 Malartic, Lac l. Can.
56 A3 Malaspina Glacier gl. U.S.A.
28 G2 Malatya Turkey
34 C3 Malaut India
29 L5 Malāvi Iran
45 E3 Malawali i. Malaysia
85 G7 Malawi country Africa
Malawi, Lake l. see Nyasa, Lake
44 B5 Malaya reg. Malaysia
33 E3 Malaya Vishera Rus. Fed.
43 C4 Malaybalay Phil.
30 C3 Malāyer Iran
23 K9 Malaysia country Asia
29 J2 Malazgirt Turkey
17 J3 Malbork Pol.
12 E5 Malborn Ger.
13 L1 Malchin Ger.
13 L1 Malchiner See l. Ger.
35 G4 Māldah India
12 B3 Maldegem Belgium
65 F4 Malden U.S.A.
46 M4 Malden Island i. Kiribati
93 J4 Maldive Ridge sea feature Ind. Ocean
23 G9 Maldives country Ind. Ocean
9 H6 Maldon U.K.
83 F2 Maldonado Uru.
19 K6 Maleas, Akra i. Greece
27 F6 Male Atoll Maldives
91 F4 Malebogo S. Africa
34 C5 Malegaon India
34 B2 Malegaon India
16 H6 Malé Karpaty h. Slovakia
30 C3 Malek Kandī Iran
88 B4 Malele Congo(Zaire)
89 D5 Malema Moz.
34 C3 Maler Kōtla India
31 G3 Mālestān Afgh.
21 H7 Malgobek Rus. Fed.
6 P4 Malgomaj l. Sweden
30 B5 Malham S. Arabia
62 C3 Malheur L. l. U.S.A.
88 C4 Mali Congo(Zaire)
86 A3 Mali Guinea
85 C4 Mali country Africa
38 C3 Malian r. China
34 C4 Malihabad India
34 F4 Malik Naro mt Pak.
44 A2 Mali Kyun i. Myanmar
37 E7 Malili Indon.
45 C4 Malimping Indon.
88 E4 Malindi Kenya
11 D2 Malin Head hd Rep. of Ireland
11 C3 Malin More Rep. of Ireland
40 D2 Malinovka r. Rus. Fed.
39 B6 Malipo China
18 F2 Mali Raginac mt Croatia
43 C5 Malita Phil.
44 A3 Maliwun Myanmar
34 B5 Maliya India
29 L5 Malkaili Iran
34 D5 Malkapur India
21 C7 Malkara Turkey
17 N4 Mal'kavichy Belarus
19 M3 Malko Tŭrnovo Bulg.
50 G4 Mallacoota Austr.
50 G4 Mallacoota Inlet Austr.
10 C4 Mallaig U.K.
50 B3 Mallala Austr.
50 D3 Mallee Cliffs Nat. Park Austr.
57 K2 Mallery Lake l. Can.
15 H3 Mallorca i. Spain
11 C5 Mallow Rep. of Ireland
9 D5 Mallwyd U.K.
6 M4 Malm Norway
6 R3 Malmberget Sweden
12 E4 Malmédy Belgium
90 C6 Malmesbury S. Africa
9 E6 Malmesbury U.K.
7 N9 Malmö Sweden
20 J3 Malmyzh Rus. Fed.
49 G3 Malo i. Vanuatu
43 B3 Malolos Phil.
71 F2 Malone U.S.A.
39 B5 Malong China
89 C5 Malonga Congo(Zaire)
20 F2 Maloshuyka Rus. Fed.
7 J6 Måløy Norway
20 F4 Maloyaroslavets Rus. Fed.
78 B3 Malpelo, Isla de i. Col.
33 A3 Malprabha r. India
7 U8 Malta Latvia
62 F1 Malta U.S.A.
5 E5 Malta country Europe
18 F6 Malta Channel Italy/Malta
89 B6 Maltahöhe Namibia
9 F4 Maltby U.K.
9 H4 Maltby le Marsh U.K.
8 G3 Malton U.K.
37 E7 Maluku is Indon.
7 N6 Malung Sweden
91 H4 Maluti Mountains Lesotho
49 G2 Malu'u Solomon Is
33 A2 Malvan India
65 E5 Malvern U.S.A.
Malvinas, Islas terr. see Falkland Islands
21 D5 Malyn Ukr.
25 S3 Malyy Anyuy r. Rus. Fed.
30 D2 Malyy Balkhan, Khrebet h. Turkm.
21 H6 Malyye Derbety Rus. Fed.
21 G7 Malyy Kavkaz mts Asia
25 Q2 Malyy Lyakhovskiy, Ostrov i. Rus. Fed.
21 J5 Malyy Uzen' r. Kazak./Rus. Fed.
25 Q3 Mama r. Rus. Fed.
91 H3 Mamafubedu S. Africa
33 C3 Māmallapuram India
43 A5 Mambahenauhan i. Phil.
43 C4 Mambajao Phil.
88 C3 Mambasa Congo(Zaire)
88 B3 Mambéré r. C.A.R.
43 B3 Mamburao Phil.
91 H2 Mamelodi S. Africa
86 C4 Mamfé Cameroon
73 G5 Mammoth U.S.A.
66 C4 Mammoth Cave Nat. Park U.S.A.
72 C3 Mammoth Lakes U.S.A.
78 E6 Mamoré r. Bol./Brazil
86 A3 Mamou Guinea
89 E5 Mampikony Madag.
86 B4 Mampong Ghana
83 B3 Mamuil Malal, P. pass Arg./Chile
45 E3 Mamuju Indon.
90 D1 Mamuno Botswana
86 B4 Man Côte d'Ivoire
81 B3 Manacacias r. Col.
78 F4 Manacapuru Brazil
15 H3 Manacor Spain
37 E6 Manadao Indon.
74 G6 Managua Nic.
74 G6 Managua, L. de l. Nic.
89 E6 Manakara Madag.
51 D5 Manakau mt N.Z.
48 E2 Manam I. i. P.N.G.
72 □1 Manana i. U.S.A.
89 E6 Mananara r. Madag.
89 E5 Mananara Avaratra Madag.
89 E5 Mananara, Parc National de nat. park Madag.
50 D3 Manangatang Austr.
89 E6 Mananjary Madag.
33 B4 Mānantavādi India
81 D2 Manapire r. Venez.
51 A6 Manapouri, L. l. N.Z.
89 E5 Manarantsandry Madag.
35 G4 Manas r. Bhutan
34 D3 Mana Shankou pass India
35 G2 Manas Hu l. China
35 F3 Manaslu mt Nepal
70 E5 Manassas U.S.A.
37 E7 Manatuto Indon.
78 F4 Manaus Brazil
28 C3 Manavgat Turkey
51 E4 Manawatu r. N.Z.
43 C5 Manay Phil.
28 F3 Manbij Syria
9 H4 Manby U.K.
68 E3 Mancelona U.S.A.
9 E4 Manchester U.K.
72 A2 Manchester CA U.S.A.
71 G4 Manchester CT U.S.A.
68 B4 Manchester IA U.S.A.
70 B6 Manchester KY U.S.A.
69 E4 Manchester MI U.S.A.
71 H3 Manchester NH U.S.A.
70 B5 Manchester OH U.S.A.
67 C5 Manchester TN U.S.A.
71 G3 Manchester VT U.S.A.
34 A4 Manchhar L. l. Pak.
28 F2 Mancılık Turkey
73 H3 Mancos U.S.A.
73 H3 Mancos r. U.S.A.
31 F5 Mand Pak.
30 D4 Mand r. Iran
89 E6 Mandabe Madag.
45 B2 Mandah Indon.
44 □ Mandai Sing.
31 F3 Mandal Afgh.
34 C4 Mandal India
7 K7 Mandal Norway
37 G7 Mandala, Pk mt Indon.
37 B4 Mandalay Myanmar
36 C2 Mandalgovĭ Mongolia
29 K5 Mandalī Iraq
38 D1 Mandalt Sum China
64 C2 Mandan U.S.A.
43 B3 Mandaon Phil.
87 D4 Manda, Parc National de nat. park Chad
87 D3 Mandara Mountains Cameroon/Nigeria
18 C5 Mandas Sardinia Italy
88 E3 Mandera Kenya
73 F2 Manderfield U.S.A.
12 E4 Manderscheid Ger.
75 J5 Mandeville Jamaica
51 B6 Mandeville N.Z.
34 B4 Mandha India
86 B3 Mandiana Guinea
34 C3 Mandi Burewala Pak.
89 D5 Mandié Moz.
89 D5 Mandimba Moz.
91 J4 Mandini S. Africa
35 F5 Mandira Dam dam India
34 E5 Mandla India
89 E5 Mandritsara Madag.
34 C4 Mandsaur India
43 A6 Mandul i. Indon.
48 B5 Mandurah Austr.
18 G4 Manduria Italy
34 B5 Mandvi Gujarat India
34 C5 Mandvi Gujarat India
33 B3 Mandya India
33 B2 Maner r. India
18 D2 Manerbio Italy
17 M5 Manevychi Ukr.
18 F4 Manfredonia Italy
18 G4 Manfredonia, Golfo di g. Italy
82 D1 Manga Brazil
86 B3 Manga Burkina
88 B4 Mangai Congo(Zaire)
46 M6 Mangaia i. Cook Is Pac. Oc.
51 E3 Mangakino N.Z.
33 C2 Mangalagiri India
35 H4 Mangaldai India
19 N3 Mangalia Romania
33 A3 Mangalore India
33 A2 Mangalvedha India
35 G4 Mangan India
33 C2 Mangapet India
43 C6 Mangarang Indon.
91 G4 Mangaung S. Africa
51 E3 Mangaweka N.Z.
35 G4 Mangde r. Bhutan
11 B6 Mangerton Mt h. Rep. of Ireland
45 C3 Manggar Indon.
36 B3 Mangnai China
89 D5 Mangochi Malawi
37 E7 Mangole i. Indon.
9 E6 Mangotsfield U.K.
34 B5 Māngral India
67 E7 Mangrove Cay Bahamas
15 C2 Mangualde Port.
31 G4 Manguchar Pak.
83 G2 Mangueira, L. l. Brazil
82 B4 Mangueirinha Brazil
87 D2 Manguéni, Plateau de plat. Niger
36 E1 Mangui China
43 C5 Mangupung i. Indon.
26 D2 Mangyshlak Kazak.
64 D4 Manhattan KS U.S.A.
72 D2 Manhattan NV U.S.A.
89 D6 Manhica Moz.
91 K3 Manhoca Moz.
82 D3 Manhuaçu Brazil
82 E2 Manhuaçu r. Brazil
81 B3 Mani Col.
89 E5 Mania r. Madag.
18 E1 Maniago Italy
78 F5 Manicoré Brazil
59 G3 Manicouagan Can.
59 G3 Manicouagan r. Can.
59 G3 Manicouagan, Réservoir resr Can.
30 C5 Manīfah S. Arabia
46 L5 Manihiki i. Cook Is Pac. Oc.
Manikgarh see Rajura
34 E4 Manikpur India
43 B3 Manila Phil.
62 E3 Manila U.S.A.
50 G2 Manildra Austr.
50 H1 Manilla Austr.
Manipur see Imphal
35 H4 Manipur div. India
19 M5 Manisa Turkey
29 L5 Manisht Kūh mt Iran
8 C3 Man, Isle of terr. Europe
68 D3 Manistee U.S.A.
68 E3 Manistee r. U.S.A.
68 D3 Manistique U.S.A.
68 E2 Manistique Lake l. U.S.A.
58 B2 Manitoba div. Can.
57 K4 Manitoba, Lake l. Can.
57 H4 Manito L. l. Can.
57 K5 Manitou Can.
70 E3 Manitou Beach U.S.A.
58 B3 Manitou Falls Can.
68 D2 Manitou Island i. U.S.A.
66 C2 Manitou Islands is U.S.A.
69 G3 Manitou, Lake l. Can.
69 F3 Manitoulin I. i. Can.
69 G3 Manitouwaning Can.
58 D4 Manitowik Lake l. Can.
68 D3 Manitowoc U.S.A.
69 K2 Maniwaki Can.
81 B3 Manizales Col.
89 E6 Manja Madag.
91 K2 Manjacaze Moz.
33 B4 Manjeri India
42 D3 Man Jiang r. China
29 M3 Manjil Iran
33 B2 Manjra r. India
64 E2 Mankato U.S.A.
91 J3 Mankayane Swaziland
86 B4 Mankono Côte d'Ivoire
33 C4 Mankulam Sri Lanka
50 H2 Manly Austr.
34 C5 Manmad India
45 B3 Manna Indon.
50 B2 Mannahill Austr.
33 B4 Mannar Sri Lanka
27 F6 Mannar, Gulf of India/Sri Lanka
33 B4 Mannar, Gulf of g. India/Sri Lanka
33 B3 Manneru r. India
13 G5 Mannheim Ger.
11 A4 Mannin Bay b. Rep. of Ireland
56 F3 Manning Can.
67 D5 Manning U.S.A.
9 J6 Manningtree U.K.
18 C4 Mannu, Capo pt Sardinia Italy
50 B3 Mannum Austr.
37 F7 Manokwari Indon.
88 C4 Manono Congo(Zaire)
44 A3 Manoron Myanmar
14 G5 Manosque France
55 L4 Manouane Lake l. Can.
42 D3 Manp'o N. Korea
49 J2 Manra i. Kiribati
15 G2 Manresa Spain
34 C3 Mānsa India
89 C5 Mansa Zambia
86 A3 Mansa Konko The Gambia
34 C2 Mansehra Pak.
55 L3 Mansel Island i. Can.
50 F4 Mansfield Austr.
9 F4 Mansfield U.K.
65 E5 Mansfield LA U.S.A.
70 B4 Mansfield OH U.S.A.
70 E4 Mansfield PA U.S.A.
79 H6 Manso r. Brazil
56 E3 Manson Creek Can.
29 M6 Manṣūrī Iran
28 E3 Mansurlu Turkey
78 B4 Manta Ecuador
78 B4 Manta, B. de b. Ecuador
43 A4 Mantalingajan, Mount mt Phil.
42 E3 Mantapsan mt N. Korea
72 B3 Manteca U.S.A.
81 C3 Mantecal Venez.
13 L5 Mantel Ger.
67 F5 Manteo U.S.A.
14 E2 Mantes-la-Jolie France
33 B2 Manthani India
73 G2 Manti U.S.A.
82 D3 Mantiqueira, Serra da mts Brazil
68 E3 Manton U.S.A.
18 D2 Mantova Italy
7 T6 Mäntsälä Fin.
7 T5 Mänttä Fin.
Mantua see Mantova
20 H3 Manturovo Rus. Fed.
7 U6 Mäntyharju Fin.
6 U3 Mäntyjärvi Fin.
46 L5 Manua Islands is Pac. Oc.
73 H4 Manuelito U.S.A.
83 F2 Manuel J. Cobo Arg.
82 E1 Manuel Vitorino Brazil
79 H5 Manuelzinho Brazil
37 E7 Manui i. Indon.
31 E5 Manūjān Iran
43 B4 Manukan Phil.
51 E2 Manukau N.Z.
51 E2 Manukau Harbour in. N.Z.
43 A5 Manuk Manka i. Phil.
50 B2 Manunda r. Austr.
78 D6 Manu, Parque Nacional nat. park Peru
48 E2 Manus I. i. P.N.G.
33 B3 Manvi India
91 F2 Manyana Botswana
21 G6 Manych-Gudilo, Ozero l. Rus. Fed.
73 H3 Many Farms U.S.A.
88 D4 Manyoni Tanz.
28 D6 Manzala, Bahra el l. Egypt
15 E3 Manzanares Spain
75 J4 Manzanillo Cuba
74 D5 Manzanillo Mex.
30 C3 Manzariyeh Iran
36 D2 Manzhouli China
91 J3 Manzini Swaziland
87 D3 Mao Chad
Maó see Mahón
38 D4 Maocifan China
38 C2 Maojiachuan China
91 G3 Maokeng S. Africa
37 F7 Maoke, Pegunungan mts Indon.
42 B3 Maokui Shan h. China
42 B2 Maolin China
38 B2 Maomao Shan mt China
39 D6 Maoming China
39 □ Ma On Shan h. H.K. China
89 D6 Mapai Moz.
35 E3 Mapam Yumco l. China
91 F5 Maphodi S. Africa
65 C7 Mapimí Mex.
43 A5 Mapin i. Phil.
89 D6 Mapinhane Moz.
81 D3 Mapire Venez.
68 E4 Maple r. U.S.A.
57 H5 Maple Creek Can.
91 G4 Mapoteng Lesotho
79 G4 Mapuera r. Brazil
91 K2 Mapulanguene Moz.
89 D6 Maputo Moz.
91 K2 Maputo div. Moz.
91 K3 Maputo r. Moz.
91 G4 Maputsoe Lesotho
29 H6 Maqar an Na'am well Iraq
35 H3 Maqu China
35 E3 Maquan He r. China
88 B4 Maquela do Zombo Angola
83 C4 Maquinchao Arg.
83 C4 Maquinchao r. Arg.
68 B4 Maquoketa U.S.A.
68 B4 Maquoketa r. U.S.A.
31 G5 Mar r. Pak.
35 E5 Māra India
91 H1 Mara S. Africa
81 C2 Mara Venez.
57 H1 Mara r. Can.
78 E4 Maraã Brazil
79 J5 Maraba Brazil
81 C2 Maracaibo Venez.
81 C2 Maracaibo, Lago de l. Venez.
79 H3 Maracá, Ilha de i. Brazil
82 A3 Maracaju Brazil

13 L5 **Mitterteich** Ger.
13 L4 **Mittweida** Ger.
81 C4 **Mitú** Col.
81 C4 **Mituas** Col.
89 C5 **Mitumba, Chaîne des** *mts* Congo(Zaire)
88 C4 **Mitumba, Monts** *mts* Congo(Zaire)
88 B3 **Mitzic** Gabon
41 F7 **Miura** Japan
29 G4 **Miyah, Wādī el** *watercourse* Syria
41 F7 **Miyake-jima** *i.* Japan
40 G5 **Miyako** Japan
41 B9 **Miyakonojō** Japan
38 B4 **Miyaluo** China
34 B5 **Miyāni** India
41 B9 **Miyazaki** Japan
41 D7 **Miyazu** Japan
39 B5 **Miyi** China
41 C7 **Miyoshi** Japan
38 E1 **Miyun** China
38 E1 **Miyun Sk.** *resr* China
31 G3 **Mīzāni** Afgh.
88 D3 **Mīzan Teferī** Eth.
87 D1 **Mizdah** Libya
11 B6 **Mizen Head** *hd* Rep. of Ireland
21 B5 **Mizhhir''ya** Ukr.
38 D2 **Mizhi** China
35 H5 **Mizoram** *div.* India
40 G5 **Mizusawa** Japan
7 O7 **Mjölby** Sweden
88 D4 **Mkata** Tanz.
88 D4 **Mkomazi** Tanz.
89 C5 **Mkushi** Zambia
16 G5 **Mladá Boleslav** Czech Rep.
19 J2 **Mladenovac** Yugo.
17 K4 **Mława** Pol.
18 G3 **Mljet** *i.* Croatia
91 G5 **Mlungisi** S. Africa
17 M5 **Mlyniv** Ukr.
91 F2 **Mmabatho** S. Africa
91 G1 **Mmamabula** Botswana
91 F2 **Mmathethe** Botswana
7 J6 **Mo** Norway
73 H2 **Moab** U.S.A.
48 E3 **Moa I.** *i.* Austr.
49 H3 **Moala** *i.* Fiji
30 D3 **Mo'alla** Iran
91 K2 **Moamba** Moz.
73 E3 **Moapa** U.S.A.
11 D4 **Moate** Rep. of Ireland
88 C4 **Moba** Congo(Zaire)
41 G7 **Mobara** Japan
30 C3 **Mobārakeh** Iran
88 C3 **Mobayi-Mbongo** Congo(Zaire)
64 E4 **Moberly** U.S.A.
67 B6 **Mobile** *AL* U.S.A.
73 F5 **Mobile** *AZ* U.S.A.
67 B6 **Mobile Bay** *b.* U.S.A.
64 C2 **Mobridge** U.S.A.
**Mobutu, Lake** *l. see* **Albert, Lake**
79 J4 **Mocajuba** Brazil
89 E5 **Moçambique** Moz.
81 D2 **Mocapra** *r.* Venez.
39 B6 **Môc Châu** Vietnam
81 D2 **Mochirma, Parque Nacional** *nat. park* Venez.
89 C6 **Mochudi** Botswana
89 E5 **Mocimboa da Praia** Moz.
13 K2 **Möckern** Ger.
13 H5 **Möckmühl** Ger.
6 R4 **Mockträsk** Sweden
81 A4 **Mocoa** Col.
82 C3 **Mococa** Brazil
89 D5 **Mocuba** Moz.
14 H4 **Modane** France
34 C5 **Modasa** India
90 F4 **Modder** *r.* S. Africa
18 D2 **Modena** Italy
73 F3 **Modena** U.S.A.
72 B3 **Modesto** U.S.A.
50 F5 **Moe** Austr.
9 D5 **Moel Sych** *h.* U.K.
7 M6 **Moely** Norway
6 Q2 **Moen** Norway
73 G3 **Moenkopi** U.S.A.
51 C6 **Moeraki Pt** *pt* N.Z.
13 E3 **Moers** Ger.
10 E5 **Moffat** U.K.
34 C3 **Moga** India
**Mogadishu** *see* **Muqdisho**
70 C4 **Mogadore Reservoir** U.S.A.
91 H1 **Mogalakwena** *r.* S. Africa
91 H2 **Moganyaka** S. Africa
13 L2 **Mögelin** Ger.
31 G2 **Moghiyon** Tajik.
82 C3 **Mogi-Mirim** Brazil
36 D1 **Mogocha** Rus. Fed.
18 C6 **Mogod** *mts* Tunisia
91 F2 **Mogoditshane** Botswana
36 B4 **Mogok** Myanmar
73 H5 **Mogollon Baldy** *mt* U.S.A.
73 H5 **Mogollon Mts** *mts* U.S.A.
73 G4 **Mogollon Rim** *plat.* U.S.A.
91 G2 **Mogwase** S. Africa
19 H2 **Mohács** Hungary
51 F3 **Mohaka** *r.* N.Z.
91 G5 **Mohale's Hoek** Lesotho
57 J5 **Mohall** U.S.A.
31 E3 **Mohammad** Iran
**Moḩammadābād** *see* **Darreh Gaz**
15 G5 **Mohammadia** Alg.
34 E3 **Mohan** *r.* India/Nepal
73 E4 **Mohave, L.** *l.* U.S.A.
73 F5 **Mohawk** U.S.A.
71 F3 **Mohawk** *r.* U.S.A.
73 F5 **Mohawk Mts** *mts* U.S.A.
89 E5 **Moheli** *i.* Comoros
11 D4 **Mohill** Rep. of Ireland
13 G3 **Möhne** *r.* Ger.
73 F4 **Mohon Peak** *summit* U.S.A.
89 D4 **Mohoro** Tanz.
65 C7 **Mohovano Ranch** Mex.
29 M5 **Moh Reza Shah Pahlavi** *resr* Iran
21 C5 **Mohyliv Podil's'kyy** Ukr.
7 K7 **Moi** Norway
91 G1 **Moijabana** Botswana
91 K2 **Moine** Moz.
17 N7 **Moinești** Romania
71 F2 **Moira** U.S.A.
6 O3 **Mo i Rana** Norway
35 H4 **Moirang** India
7 T7 **Mõisaküla** Estonia
83 E1 **Moisés Ville** Arg.
59 G3 **Moisie** Can.
59 G3 **Moisie** *r.* Can.
14 E4 **Moissac** France
72 C4 **Mojave** U.S.A.
72 D4 **Mojave** *r.* U.S.A.
72 D4 **Mojave Desert** U.S.A.
82 C3 **Moji das Cruzes** Brazil
82 C3 **Moji-Guaçu** *r.* Brazil
41 B8 **Mojikō** Japan
35 F4 **Mokāma** India
72 □1 **Mokapu Pen.** *pen.* U.S.A.
51 E3 **Mokau** N.Z.
51 E3 **Mokau** *r.* N.Z.
72 B2 **Mokelumne** *r.* U.S.A.
91 H4 **Mokhoabong Pass** Lesotho
91 H4 **Mokhotlong** Lesotho
18 D7 **Moknine** Tunisia
51 E1 **Mokohinau Is** *is* N.Z.
87 D3 **Mokolo** Cameroon
91 G2 **Mokolo** *r.* S. Africa
42 D6 **Mokp'o** S. Korea
20 G4 **Moksha** *r.* Rus. Fed.
20 H4 **Mokshan** Rus. Fed.
72 □1 **Mokuauia I.** *i.* U.S.A.
72 □1 **Mokulua Is** *is* U.S.A.
15 F3 **Molatón** *mt* Spain
**Moldavia** *country see* **Moldova**
6 K5 **Molde** Norway
6 O3 **Moldjord** Norway
5 F4 **Moldova** *country* Europe
19 L2 **Moldoveanu, Vârful** *mt* Romania
9 D7 **Mole** *r.* U.K.
86 B4 **Mole National Park** Ghana
89 C6 **Molepolole** Botswana
7 T9 **Molėtai** Lith.
18 G4 **Molfetta** Italy
42 C2 **Molihong Shan** *h.* China
15 F2 **Molina de Aragón** Spain
68 B5 **Moline** U.S.A.
7 N7 **Molkom** Sweden
29 M4 **Mollā Bodāgh** Iran
35 H4 **Mol Len** *mt* India
13 M1 **Möllenbeck** Ger.
78 D7 **Mollendo** Peru
13 J1 **Mölln** Ger.
7 N8 **Mölnlycke** Sweden
20 F3 **Molochnoye** Rus. Fed.
6 X2 **Molochnyy** Rus. Fed.
92 D4 **Molodezhnaya** *Rus. Fed. Base* Ant.
20 E3 **Molodoy Tud** Rus. Fed.
72 □2 **Molokai** *i.* U.S.A.
95 K4 **Molokai Fracture Zone** *sea feature* Pac. Oc.
20 J3 **Moloma** *r.* Rus. Fed.
50 G2 **Molong** Austr.
90 F2 **Molopo** *watercourse* Botswana/S. Africa
87 D4 **Moloundou** Cameroon
57 K4 **Molson L.** *l.* Can.
**Moluccas** *is see* **Maluku**
37 E7 **Molucca Sea** *g.* Indon.
89 D5 **Moma** Moz.
50 D1 **Momba** Austr.
88 D4 **Mombasa** Kenya
35 H4 **Mombi New** India
82 B2 **Mombuca, Serra da** *h.* Brazil
21 C7 **Momchilgrad** Bulg.
68 D5 **Momence** U.S.A.
81 B2 **Mompós** Col.
7 N9 **Møn** *i.* Denmark
73 G2 **Mona** U.S.A.
10 A3 **Monach Islands** *is* U.K.
10 A3 **Monach, Sound of** *chan.* U.K.
5 D4 **Monaco** *country* Europe
10 D3 **Monadhliath Mountains** U.K.
11 E3 **Monaghan** Rep. of Ireland
65 C6 **Monahans** U.S.A.
75 L5 **Mona, I.** *i.* Puerto Rico
75 L5 **Mona Passage** *chan.* Dom. Rep./Puerto Rico
89 E5 **Monapo** Moz.
56 D4 **Monarch Mt.** *mt* Can.
63 F4 **Monarch Pass** U.S.A.
10 C3 **Monar, Loch** *l.* U.K.
56 F4 **Monashee Mts** *mts* Can.
18 D7 **Monastir** Tunisia
17 P3 **Monastyrshchina** Rus. Fed.
21 D5 **Monastyryshche** Ukr.
40 H2 **Monbetsu** Japan
40 H3 **Monbetsu** Japan
18 B2 **Moncalieri** Italy
15 F2 **Moncayo** *mt* Spain
6 X3 **Monchegorsk** Rus. Fed.
12 E3 **Mönchengladbach** Ger.
15 B4 **Monchique** Port.
67 E5 **Moncks Corner** U.S.A.
74 D3 **Monclova** Mex.
59 H4 **Moncton** Can.
15 C2 **Mondego** *r.* Port.
91 J3 **Mondlo** S. Africa
18 B2 **Mondovì** Italy
68 B3 **Mondovi** U.S.A.
18 E4 **Mondragone** Italy
19 K6 **Monemvasia** Greece
40 G1 **Moneron, Ostrov** *i.* Rus. Fed.
70 D4 **Monessen** U.S.A.
69 K1 **Monet** Can.
11 D5 **Moneygall** Rep. of Ireland
11 E3 **Moneymore** U.K.
18 E2 **Monfalcone** Italy
15 C1 **Monforte** Spain
88 C3 **Monga** Congo(Zaire)
39 C6 **Mông Cai** Vietnam
42 C4 **Monggŭmp'o-ri** N. Korea
44 A1 **Mong Mau** Myanmar
23 J5 **Mongolia** *country* Asia
34 C2 **Mongora** Pak.
89 C5 **Mongu** Zambia
71 J3 **Monhegan I.** *i.* U.S.A.
10 E5 **Moniaive** U.K.
72 D2 **Monitor Mt** *mt* U.S.A.
72 D2 **Monitor Range** *mts* U.S.A.
11 C4 **Monivea** Rep. of Ireland
69 G4 **Monkton** Can.
35 F3 **Mon La** *pass* China
9 E6 **Monmouth** U.K.
68 B5 **Monmouth** *IL* U.S.A.
71 H2 **Monmouth** *ME* U.S.A.
56 E4 **Monmouth Mt.** *mt* Can.
9 E6 **Monnow** *r.* U.K.
86 C3 **Mono** *r.* Togo
72 C3 **Mono Lake** *l.* U.S.A.
71 H4 **Monomoy Pt** *pt* U.S.A.
68 D5 **Monon** U.S.A.
68 B4 **Monona** U.S.A.
18 G4 **Monopoli** Italy
70 C5 **Monongahela** *r.* U.S.A.
15 F2 **Monreal del Campo** Spain
18 E5 **Monreale** *Sicily* Italy
65 E5 **Monroe** *LA* U.S.A.
69 F5 **Monroe** *MI* U.S.A.
67 D5 **Monroe** *NC* U.S.A.
71 F4 **Monroe** *NY* U.S.A.
73 F2 **Monroe** *UT* U.S.A.
68 C4 **Monroe** *WV* U.S.A.
68 B6 **Monroe City** U.S.A.
67 C6 **Monroeville** U.S.A.
86 A4 **Monrovia** Liberia
12 B4 **Mons** Belgium
12 E4 **Monschau** Ger.
18 D2 **Monselice** Italy
13 F4 **Montabaur** Ger.
89 E5 **Montagne d'Ambre, Parc National de la** *nat. park* Madag.
90 D6 **Montagu** S. Africa
68 D4 **Montague** U.S.A.
92 C1 **Montagu I.** *i.* Atl. Ocean
18 F5 **Montalto** *mt* Italy
18 G5 **Montalto Uffugo** Italy
19 K3 **Montana** Bulg.
62 E2 **Montana** *div.* U.S.A.
14 F3 **Montargis** France
14 E4 **Montauban** France
71 G4 **Montauk** U.S.A.
71 H4 **Montauk Pt** *pt* U.S.A.
14 G3 **Montbard** France
15 G2 **Montblanc** Spain
14 G4 **Montbrison** France
14 G3 **Montceau-les-Mines** France
12 C5 **Montcornet** France
14 D5 **Mont-de-Marsan** France
14 F2 **Montdidier** France
79 H4 **Monte Alegre** Brazil
82 C1 **Monte Alegre de Goiás** Brazil
82 D1 **Monte Azul** Brazil
58 E4 **Montebello** Can.
18 F6 **Montebello Ionico** Italy
18 E2 **Montebelluna** Italy
83 D2 **Monte Buey** Arg.
14 H5 **Monte Carlo** Monaco
83 F1 **Monte Caseros** Arg.
91 G1 **Monte Christo** S. Africa
83 C2 **Monte Comán** Arg.
75 K5 **Monte Cristi** Dom. Rep.
18 D3 **Montecristo, Isola di** *i.* Italy
75 J5 **Montego Bay** Jamaica
14 G4 **Montélimar** France
80 E2 **Monte Lindo** *r.* Para.
18 F4 **Montella** Italy
68 C4 **Montello** U.S.A.
74 E3 **Montemorelos** Mex.
15 B3 **Montemor-o-Novo** Port.
19 H3 **Montenegro** *div.* Yugo.
89 D5 **Montepuez** Moz.
18 D3 **Montepulciano** Italy
14 F2 **Montereau-faut-Yonne** France
72 B3 **Monterey** *CA* U.S.A.
70 D5 **Monterey** *VA* U.S.A.
72 B3 **Monterey Bay** *b.* U.S.A.
81 B2 **Montería** Col.
78 F7 **Montero** Bol.
65 C7 **Monterrey** Mex.
18 F4 **Montesano sulla Marcellana** Italy
79 L6 **Monte Santo** Brazil
82 D2 **Montes Claros** Brazil
18 F3 **Montesilvano** Italy
18 D3 **Montevarchi** Italy
83 F2 **Montevideo** Uru.
64 E2 **Montevideo** U.S.A.
63 F4 **Monte Vista** U.S.A.
68 A5 **Montezuma** U.S.A.
73 G4 **Montezuma Castle National Monument** *res.* U.S.A.
73 H3 **Montezuma Creek** U.S.A.
72 D3 **Montezuma Peak** *summit* U.S.A.
12 D3 **Montfort** Neth.
9 D5 **Montgomery** U.K.
67 C5 **Montgomery** U.S.A.
16 C7 **Monthey** Switz.
65 F5 **Monticello** *AR* U.S.A.
67 D6 **Monticello** *FL* U.S.A.
68 B4 **Monticello** *IA* U.S.A.
68 D5 **Monticello** *IN* U.S.A.
71 K1 **Monticello** *ME* U.S.A.
68 B5 **Monticello** *MO* U.S.A.
71 F4 **Monticello** *NY* U.S.A.
73 H3 **Monticello** *UT* U.S.A.
68 C4 **Monticello** *WV* U.S.A.
83 E1 **Montiel, Cuchilla de** *h.* Arg.
14 E4 **Montignac** France
12 C4 **Montignies-le-Tilleul** Belgium
12 E5 **Montigny-lès-Metz** France
15 D4 **Montilla** Spain
59 G4 **Mont Joli** Can.
69 K2 **Mont-Laurier** Can.
59 G4 **Mont Louis** Can.
14 F3 **Montluçon** France
59 F4 **Montmagny** Can.
12 D5 **Montmédy** France
12 B6 **Montmirail** France
68 D5 **Montmorenci** U.S.A.
59 F4 **Montmorency** Can.
14 E3 **Montmorillon** France
12 B6 **Montmort-Lucy** France
48 F4 **Monto** Austr.
62 E3 **Montpelier** *ID* U.S.A.
68 E5 **Montpelier** *IN* U.S.A.
70 A4 **Montpelier** *OH* U.S.A.
71 G2 **Montpelier** *VT* U.S.A.
14 F5 **Montpellier** France
58 F4 **Montréal** Can.
69 G2 **Montreal** *r.* Can.
69 F2 **Montreal** *r.* Can.
68 E2 **Montreal I.** *i.* Can.
57 H4 **Montreal L.** *l.* Can.
57 H4 **Montreal Lake** Can.
71 F2 **Montréal-Mirabel** Can.
68 E2 **Montreal River** Can.
16 C7 **Montreux** Switz.
10 F4 **Montrose** U.K.
63 F4 **Montrose** *CO* U.S.A.
69 F4 **Montrose** *MI* U.S.A.
71 F4 **Montrose** *PA* U.S.A.
90 D3 **Montrose** *well* S. Africa
53 K8 **Montserrat** *terr.* Caribbean Sea
59 G4 **Monts, Pte des** *pt* Can.
73 G3 **Monument Valley** *reg.* U.S.A.
36 B4 **Monywa** Myanmar
18 C2 **Monza** Italy
89 C5 **Monze** Zambia
15 G2 **Monzón** Spain
91 J4 **Mooi** *r.* S. Africa
90 B3 **Mooifontein** Namibia
91 J4 **Mooirivier** S. Africa
91 G1 **Mookane** Botswana
50 H1 **Moonbi Ra.** *mts* Austr.
50 A3 **Moonta** Austr.
62 F2 **Moorcroft** U.S.A.
70 D5 **Moorefield** U.S.A.
48 B4 **Moore, Lake** *salt flat* Austr.
67 E7 **Moores I.** *i.* Bahamas
71 K2 **Moores Mills** Can.
10 E5 **Moorfoot Hills** *h.* U.K.
64 D2 **Moorhead** U.S.A.
50 D2 **Moornanyah Lake** Austr.
50 C3 **Moorook** Austr.
50 E4 **Mooroopna** Austr.
90 C6 **Moorreesburg** S. Africa
58 D3 **Moose** *r.* Can.
58 D3 **Moose Factory** Can.
71 J2 **Moosehead Lake** *l.* U.S.A.
57 H4 **Moose Jaw** Can.
68 A2 **Moose Lake** U.S.A.
57 J4 **Moose Lake** *l.* Can.
71 H2 **Mooselookmeguntic Lake** *l.* U.S.A.
58 D3 **Moose River** Can.
57 J4 **Moosomin** Can.
58 D3 **Moosonee** Can.
50 D1 **Mootwingee** Austr.
91 H1 **Mopane** S. Africa
86 B3 **Mopti** Mali
31 G3 **Moqor** Afgh.
78 D7 **Moquegua** Peru
87 D3 **Mora** Cameroon
15 E3 **Mora** Spain
7 O6 **Mora** Sweden
83 B2 **Mora, Cerro** *mt* Arg./Chile
34 A3 **Morad** *r.* Pak.
34 D3 **Moradabad** India
89 E5 **Morafenobe** Madag.
33 B2 **Moram** India
89 E5 **Moramanga** Madag.
68 E3 **Moran** *MI* U.S.A.
62 E3 **Moran** *WY* U.S.A.
10 C4 **Morar, Loch** *l.* U.K.
33 B5 **Moratuwa** Sri Lanka
16 H6 **Morava** *r.* Austria/Slovakia
30 D2 **Moraveh Tappeh** Iran
71 E3 **Moravia** U.S.A.
10 E3 **Moray Firth** *est.* U.K.
12 F5 **Morbach** Ger.
18 C1 **Morbegno** Italy
34 B5 **Morbi** India
14 D4 **Morcenx** France
36 E1 **Mordaga** China
29 K3 **Mor Dağı** *mt* Turkey
57 K5 **Morden** Can.
50 E5 **Mordialloc** Austr.
20 H4 **Mordoviya, Respublika** *div.* Rus. Fed.
21 G4 **Mordovo** Rus. Fed.
64 C2 **Moreau** *r.* U.S.A.
8 E3 **Morecambe** U.K.
8 D3 **Morecambe Bay** *b.* U.K.
48 E4 **Moree** Austr.
48 E2 **Morehead** P.N.G.
70 B5 **Morehead** U.S.A.
67 E5 **Morehead City** U.S.A.
34 D4 **Morel** *r.* India
**More Laptevykh** *sea see* **Laptev Sea**
74 D5 **Morelia** Mex.
15 F2 **Morella** Spain
10 D2 **More, Loch** *l.* U.K.
34 D4 **Morena** India
15 D3 **Morena, Sierra** *mts* Spain
73 H5 **Morenci** *AZ* U.S.A.
69 E5 **Morenci** *MI* U.S.A.
19 L2 **Moreni** Romania
83 E2 **Moreno** Arg.
63 E6 **Moreno** Mex.
72 D5 **Moreno Valley** U.S.A.
56 C4 **Moresby Island** *i.* Can.
90 F1 **Moreswe Pan** *salt pan* Botswana
9 F6 **Moreton-in-Marsh** U.K.
12 A5 **Moreuil** France
28 D4 **Morfou** Cyprus
28 D4 **Morfou Bay** *b.* Cyprus
50 B3 **Morgan** Austr.
65 F6 **Morgan City** U.S.A.
72 B3 **Morgan Hill** U.S.A.
72 C3 **Morgan, Mt** *mt* U.S.A.
71 F4 **Morgantown** *PA* U.S.A.
70 D5 **Morgantown** *WV* U.S.A.
91 H3 **Morgenzon** S. Africa
16 C7 **Morges** Switz.
35 F4 **Morhar** *r.* India
40 G3 **Mori** Japan
73 E2 **Moriah, Mt** *mt* U.S.A.
63 F5 **Moriarty** U.S.A.
81 C4 **Morichal** Col.
81 E2 **Morichal Largo** *r.* Venez.
91 G4 **Morija** Lesotho
13 H3 **Moringen** Ger.
20 D3 **Morino** Rus. Fed.
40 G5 **Morioka** Japan
50 H2 **Morisset** Austr.
40 G5 **Moriyoshi-zan** *volc.* Japan
6 S3 **Morjärv** Sweden
31 F4 **Morjen** *r.* Pak.
20 J3 **Morki** Rus. Fed.
14 C2 **Morlaix** France
8 F4 **Morley** U.K.
73 G4 **Mormon Lake** *l.* U.S.A.
48 D3 **Mornington I.** *i.* Austr.
80 A7 **Mornington, I.** *i.* Chile
34 A4 **Moro** Pak.
48 E2 **Morobe** P.N.G.
68 D5 **Morocco** U.S.A.
85 C2 **Morocco** *country* Africa
88 D4 **Morogoro** Tanz.
43 B5 **Moro Gulf** *g.* Phil.
91 G4 **Morojaneng** S. Africa
90 E3 **Morokweng** S. Africa
89 E6 **Morombe** Madag.
75 J4 **Morón** Cuba
36 C2 **Mörön** Mongolia
89 E6 **Morondava** Madag.
15 D4 **Morón de la Frontera** Spain
89 E5 **Moroni** Comoros
37 E6 **Morotai** *i.* Indon.
88 D3 **Moroto** Uganda
21 G5 **Morozovsk** Rus. Fed.
69 G4 **Morpeth** Can.
8 F2 **Morpeth** U.K.
82 C2 **Morrinhos** Brazil
57 K5 **Morris** Can.
68 C5 **Morris** *IL* U.S.A.
64 E2 **Morris** *MN* U.S.A.
71 F2 **Morrisburg** Can.
68 C5 **Morrison** U.S.A.
73 F5 **Morristown** *AZ* U.S.A.
71 F4 **Morristown** *NJ* U.S.A.
71 F2 **Morristown** *NY* U.S.A.
67 D4 **Morristown** *TN* U.S.A.
71 F4 **Morrisville** *PA* U.S.A.
71 G2 **Morrisville** *VT* U.S.A.
72 B4 **Morro Bay** U.S.A.
81 C2 **Morrocoy, Parque Nacional** *nat. park* Venez.
79 H4 **Morro Grande** *h.* Brazil
80 B3 **Morro, Pta** *pt* Chile
81 B2 **Morrosquillo, Golfo de** *b.* Col.
13 H3 **Morschen** Ger.
68 D5 **Morse Reservoir** U.S.A.
20 G4 **Morshansk** Rus. Fed.
20 E2 **Morskaya Masel'ga** Rus. Fed.
18 C7 **Morsott** Alg.
14 E2 **Mortagne-au-Perche** France
14 D3 **Mortagne-sur-Sèvre** France
9 C6 **Mortehoe** U.K.
83 E1 **Morteros** Arg.
**Mortes** *r. see* **Manso**
50 D5 **Mortlake** Austr.
**Mortlock Is** *is see* **Tauu**
9 G5 **Morton** U.K.
68 C5 **Morton** *IL* U.S.A.
62 B2 **Morton** *WA* U.S.A.
50 H3 **Morton Nat. Park** Austr.
50 F3 **Morundah** Austr.
91 G1 **Morupule** Botswana
50 H3 **Moruya** Austr.
10 C4 **Morvern** *reg.* U.K.
**Morvi** *see* **Morbi**
50 F5 **Morwell** Austr.
13 H5 **Mosbach** Ger.
9 F4 **Mosborough** U.K.
20 F4 **Moscow** Rus. Fed.
62 C2 **Moscow** U.S.A.
92 C6 **Moscow Univ. Ice Shelf** *ice feature* Ant.
92 B6 **Mose, C.** *c.* Ant.
12 F4 **Mosel** *r.* Ger.
90 E2 **Moselebe** *watercourse* Botswana
14 H2 **Moselle** *r.* France
13 K2 **Möser** Ger.
62 C2 **Moses Lake** U.S.A.
72 D1 **Moses, Mt** *mt* U.S.A.
51 C6 **Mosgiel** N.Z.
90 E3 **Moshaweng** *watercourse* S. Africa
88 D4 **Moshi** Tanz.
68 C3 **Mosinee** U.S.A.
6 N4 **Mosjøen** Norway
6 N3 **Moskenesøy** *i.* Norway
20 F4 **Moskovskaya Oblast'** *div.* Rus. Fed.
**Moskva** *see* **Moscow**
16 H7 **Mosonmagyaróvár** Hungary
81 A4 **Mosquera** Col.
63 F5 **Mosquero** U.S.A.
75 H5 **Mosquitia** *reg.* Honduras
82 E1 **Mosquito** *r.* Brazil
70 C4 **Mosquito Creek Lake** *l.* U.S.A.
75 H7 **Mosquitos, Golfo de los** *b.* Panama
57 J2 **Mosquitto Lake** *l.* Can.
7 M7 **Moss** Norway
10 F3 **Mossat** U.K.
51 B6 **Mossburn** N.Z.
90 E7 **Mossel Bay** S. Africa
90 E7 **Mossel Bay** *b.* S. Africa
88 B4 **Mossendjo** Congo
50 E2 **Mossgiel** Austr.
48 E3 **Mossman** Austr.
79 L5 **Mossoró** Brazil
50 H3 **Moss Vale** Austr.
16 F5 **Most** Czech Rep.
30 D3 **Moşţafaabad** Iran
86 C1 **Mostaganem** Alg.
18 G3 **Mostar** Bos.-Herz.
80 F4 **Mostardas** Brazil
57 G3 **Mostoos Hills** *h.* Can.
21 G6 **Mostovskoy** Rus. Fed.
45 E2 **Mostyn** Malaysia
29 J3 **Mosul** Iraq
7 L7 **Møsvatnet** *l.* Norway
7 O7 **Motala** Sweden
81 C2 **Motatán** *r.* Venez.
91 K2 **Motaze** Moz.
91 H2 **Motetema** S. Africa
34 D4 **Moth** India
10 E5 **Motherwell** U.K.
35 F4 **Motihari** India
15 F3 **Motilla del Palancar** Spain
51 F2 **Motiti I.** *i.* N.Z.
42 B3 **Motlan Ling** *h.* China
90 E2 **Motokwe** Botswana
15 E4 **Motril** Spain
19 K2 **Motru** Romania
74 G4 **Motul** Mex.
46 M5 **Motu One** *i.* Pac. Oc.
39 A5 **Mouding** China
86 A3 **Moudjéria** Maur.
19 L5 **Moudros** Greece
7 S6 **Mouhijärvi** Fin.
88 B4 **Mouila** Gabon
50 E3 **Moulamein** Austr.
50 E3 **Moulamein** *r.* Austr.
88 B4 **Moulèngui Binza** Gabon
14 F3 **Moulins** France
44 A1 **Moulmein** Myanmar
67 D6 **Moultrie** U.S.A.
61 L5 **Moultrie, Lake** *l. SC* U.S.A.
66 B4 **Mound City** *IL* U.S.A.
64 E3 **Mound City** *MO* U.S.A.
87 D4 **Moundou** Chad
70 C5 **Moundsville** U.S.A.
34 C4 **Mount Abu** India
67 C5 **Mountain Brook** U.S.A.
70 C6 **Mountain City** U.S.A.
65 E4 **Mountain Grove** U.S.A.
65 E4 **Mountain Home** *AR* U.S.A.
62 D3 **Mountain Home** *ID* U.S.A.
91 F6 **Mountain Zebra National Park** S. Africa
70 C6 **Mount Airy** U.S.A.
51 B6 **Mount Aspiring National Park** N.Z.
91 H5 **Mount Ayliff** S. Africa
64 E3 **Mount Ayr** U.S.A.
50 B3 **Mount Barker** Austr.
50 F4 **Mount Beauty** Austr.
11 C4 **Mount Bellew** Rep. of Ireland
50 F4 **Mt Bogong Nat.Park** Austr.
50 F4 **Mount Buffalo National Park** Austr.
71 K1 **Mount Carleton Provincial Park** *res.* Can.
73 F3 **Mount Carmel Junction** U.S.A.
68 C4 **Mount Carroll** U.S.A.
51 C5 **Mount Cook** N.Z.
51 C5 **Mount Cook National Park** N.Z.
89 D5 **Mount Darwin** Zimbabwe
71 J2 **Mount Desert Island** *i.* U.S.A.
91 H5 **Mount Fletcher** S. Africa
69 G4 **Mount Forest** Can.
91 H5 **Mount Frere** S. Africa
50 C4 **Mount Gambier** Austr.
70 B4 **Mount Gilead** U.S.A.
48 E2 **Mount Hagen** P.N.G.
50 E2 **Mount Hope** *N.S.W.* Austr.
70 C6 **Mount Hope** U.S.A.
48 D4 **Mount Isa** Austr.
71 G4 **Mount Kisco** U.S.A.
50 B3 **Mount Lofty Range** *mts* Austr.
69 G2 **Mount MacDonald** Can.
48 B4 **Mount Magnet** Austr.
50 D2 **Mount Manara** Austr.
72 B1 **Mount Meadows Reservoir** U.S.A.
11 D4 **Mountmellick** Rep. of Ireland
91 G5 **Mount Moorosi** Lesotho
50 D1 **Mount Murchison** Austr.
68 B5 **Mount Pleasant** *IA* U.S.A.
68 E4 **Mount Pleasant** *MI* U.S.A.
66 C3 **Mount Pleasant** *MI* U.S.A.
70 D4 **Mount Pleasant** *PA* U.S.A.
67 E5 **Mount Pleasant** *SC* U.S.A.
65 E5 **Mount Pleasant** *TX* U.S.A.
73 G2 **Mount Pleasant** *UT* U.S.A.
68 C5 **Mount Pulaski** U.S.A.
62 B2 **Mount Rainier Nat. Park** U.S.A.
56 F4 **Mount Robson Prov. Park** *res.* Can.
70 C6 **Mount Rogers National Recreation Area** *res.* U.S.A.
9 B7 **Mount's Bay** *b.* U.K.
9 F5 **Mountsorrel** U.K.
68 B6 **Mount Sterling** *IL* U.S.A.
70 B5 **Mount Sterling** *KY* U.S.A.
70 D5 **Mount Storm** U.S.A.
70 E4 **Mount Union** U.S.A.
67 B6 **Mount Vernon** *AL* U.S.A.
68 B5 **Mount Vernon** *IA* U.S.A.
66 B4 **Mount Vernon** *IL* U.S.A.
70 A6 **Mount Vernon** *KY* U.S.A.
70 B4 **Mount Vernon** *OH* U.S.A.
62 B1 **Mount Vernon** *WA* U.S.A.
92 C3 **Mt. Victor** *mt* Ant.
48 E4 **Moura** Austr.
78 F4 **Moura** Brazil
87 E3 **Mourdi, Dépression du** *depression* Chad
11 D3 **Mourne** *r.* U.K.
11 E3 **Mourne Mountains** *h.* U.K.
12 B4 **Mouscron** Belgium
87 D3 **Moussoro** Chad
37 E6 **Moutong** Indon.
12 A5 **Mouy** France
86 C2 **Mouydir, Mts de** *plat.* Alg.
12 D5 **Mouzon** France
11 C4 **Moy** *r.* Rep. of Ireland
88 D3 **Moyale** Eth.
86 A4 **Moyamba** Sierra Leone
33 B4 **Moyar** *r.* India
86 B1 **Moyen Atlas** *mts* Morocco

# N

71 H4 Nantucket U.S.A.
71 H4 Nantucket I. i. U.S.A.
71 H4 Nantucket Sound g. U.S.A.
9 E4 Nantwich U.K.
49 H2 Nanumanga i. Tuvalu
49 H2 Nanumea i. Tuvalu
82 E2 Nanuque Brazil
43 C5 Nanusa, Kepulauan is Indon.
39 B4 Nanxi China
39 D4 Nan Xian China
39 E5 Nanxiong China
38 D3 Nanyang China
42 C3 Nanzamu China
38 D4 Nanzhang China
38 D3 Nanzhao China
15 G3 Nao, Cabo de la hd Spain
59 F3 Naococane, Lac l. Can.
35 G4 Naogaon Bangl.
34 B4 Naokot Pak.
40 C1 Naoli r. China
31 F3 Naomid, Dasht-e des. Afgh./Iran
34 C2 Naoshera Jammu and Kashmir
39 D6 Naozhou Dao i. China
72 A2 Napa U.S.A.
71 K1 Napadogan Can.
69 J3 Napanee Can.
34 C4 Napasar India
55 N3 Napasoq Greenland
68 C5 Naperville U.S.A.
51 F3 Napier N.Z.
92 D4 Napier Mts mts Ant.
71 G2 Napierville Can.
18 F4 Naples Italy
67 D7 Naples FL U.S.A.
71 H3 Naples ME U.S.A.
39 B6 Napo China
78 D4 Napo r. Ecuador/Peru
70 A4 Napoleon U.S.A.
Napoli see Naples
83 D3 Naposta Arg.
83 D3 Naposta r. Arg.
68 E5 Nappanee U.S.A.
29 K3 Naqadeh Iran
28 E6 Naqb Ashtar Jordan
29 M4 Naqqash Iran
41 D7 Nara Japan
86 B3 Nara Mali
17 N3 Narach Belarus
50 C4 Naracoorte Austr.
50 F2 Naradhan Austr.
34 C4 Naraina India
34 E6 Narainpur India
33 D2 Narasannapeta India
33 C2 Narasapatnam, Pt pt India
33 C2 Narasapur India
33 C2 Narasaraopet India
35 F5 Narasinghapur India
44 B4 Narathiwat Thai.
33 A2 Narayangaon India
Narbada r. see Narmada
9 C6 Narberth U.K.
14 F5 Narbonne France
15 C1 Narcea r. Spain
30 D2 Nardin Iran
19 H4 Nardò Italy
83 E1 Nare Arg.
34 B3 Narechi r. Pak.
55 M1 Nares Strait str. Can./Greenland
17 K4 Narew r. Pol.
32 D2 Narhong China
34 A3 Nari r. Pak.
89 B6 Narib Namibia
90 B5 Nariep S. Africa
21 H6 Narimanov Rus. Fed.
31 H2 Narin Afgh.
31 H3 Narin reg. Afgh.
28 G3 Narince Turkey
35 H1 Narin Gol watercourse China
41 G7 Narita Japan
34 C5 Narmada r. India
29 H1 Narman Turkey
34 D3 Narnaul India
18 E3 Narni Italy
17 O5 Narodychi Ukr.
20 F4 Naro-Fominsk Rus. Fed.
50 H4 Narooma Austr.
20 G4 Narovchat Rus. Fed.
21 D5 Narowlya Belarus
7 R5 Närpes Fin.
48 E5 Narrabri Austr.
71 H4 Narragansett Bay b. U.S.A.
50 F3 Narrandera Austr.
50 G2 Narromine Austr.
57 J4 Narrow Hills Provincial Park res. Can.
70 C6 Narrows U.S.A.
71 F4 Narrowsburg U.S.A.
34 D5 Narsimhapur India
35 G5 Narsingdi Bangl.
34 D5 Narsinghgarh India
33 C2 Narsipatnam India
38 E1 Nart China
41 D7 Naruto Japan
7 V7 Narva Estonia
7 U7 Narva Bay b. Estonia/Rus. Fed.
43 B2 Narvacan Phil.
6 P2 Narvik Norway
7 V7 Narvskoye Vdkhr. resr Estonia/Rus. Fed.
34 D3 Narwana India
34 D4 Narwar India
24 G3 Nar'yan-Mar Rus. Fed.
27 F2 Naryn Kyrg.
6 P5 Nasåker Sweden
73 H3 Naschitti U.S.A.
51 C6 Naseby N.Z.
68 A4 Nashua IA U.S.A.
71 H3 Nashua NH U.S.A.
67 C4 Nashville U.S.A.
28 F5 Nasib Syria
7 S6 Näsijärvi l. Fin.
34 C5 Nasik India
87 F4 Nasir Sudan
Nasirabad see Mymensingh
34 B3 Nasirabad Pak.
89 C5 Nasondoye Congo(Zaire)
28 C6 Nasr Egypt
30 C3 Naşrābād Iran
31 E3 Naşrābād Iran
Nasratabad see Zābol
29 L5 Nasrīān-e-Pā'īn Iran
56 D3 Nass r. Can.
67 E7 Nassau Bahamas
46 L5 Nassau i. Cook Is Pac. Oc.
87 F2 Nasser, Lake resr Egypt
7 O8 Nässjö Sweden
58 E2 Nastapoca r. Can.
58 E2 Nastapoka Islands is Can.
41 F6 Nasu-dake volc. Japan
43 B3 Nasugbu Phil.
17 P2 Nasva Rus. Fed.
89 C6 Nata Botswana
88 D4 Nata Tanz.
81 B4 Natagaima Col.
79 L5 Natal Brazil
Natal div. see Kwazulu-Natal
93 G6 Natal Basin sea feature Ind. Ocean
30 C3 Naţanz Iran
59 H3 Natashquan Can.
59 H3 Natashquan r. Can.
65 F6 Natchez U.S.A.
65 E6 Natchitoches U.S.A.
50 E4 Nathalia Austr.
34 C4 Nathdwara India
50 C4 Natimuk Austr.
72 D5 National City U.S.A.
15 H2 Nati, Pta pt Spain
86 C3 Natitingou Benin
79 J6 Natividade Brazil
40 G5 Natori Japan
88 D4 Natron, Lake salt l. Tanz.
44 A1 Nattaung mt Myanmar
45 C2 Natuna Besar i. Indon.
45 C2 Natuna, Kepulauan is Indon.
71 F2 Natural Bridge U.S.A.
73 G3 Natural Bridges National Monument res. U.S.A.
93 M6 Naturaliste Plateau sea feature Ind. Ocean
73 H2 Naturita U.S.A.
68 E2 Naubinway U.S.A.
89 B6 Nauchas Namibia
13 L2 Nauen Ger.
71 G4 Naugatuck U.S.A.
43 B3 Naujan Phil.
43 B3 Naujan, L. l. Phil.
7 S8 Naujoji Akmenė Lith.
34 C4 Naukh India
13 H3 Naumburg (Hessen) Ger.
13 K3 Naumburg (Saale) Ger.
44 A1 Naungpale Myanmar
28 E6 Na'ūr Jordan
31 G4 Nauroz Kalat Pak.
47 H4 Nauru country Pac. Oc.
34 B4 Naushara Pak.
7 J6 Naustdal Norway
78 D4 Nauta Peru
30 C3 Naute Dam dam Namibia
74 E4 Nautla Mex.
31 G3 Nauzad Afgh.
35 G5 Navadwīp India
20 C4 Navahrudak Belarus
73 H4 Navajo U.S.A.
63 F4 Navajo Lake l. U.S.A.
73 G3 Navajo Mt mt U.S.A.
43 C4 Naval Phil.
15 D3 Navalmoral de la Mata Spain
15 D3 Navalvillar de Pela Spain
11 E4 Navan Rep. of Ireland
20 D4 Navapolatsk Belarus
25 T3 Navarin, Mys c. Rus. Fed.
80 C9 Navarino, I. i. Chile
15 F1 Navarra div. Spain
50 D4 Navarre Austr.
72 A2 Navarro U.S.A.
20 G4 Navashino Rus. Fed.
65 D6 Navasota U.S.A.
6 O5 Näverede Sweden
10 D2 Naver, Loch l. U.K.
83 B2 Navidad Chile
79 H3 Navio, Serra do Brazil
20 E4 Navlya Rus. Fed.
19 N2 Năvodari Romania
31 G1 Navoi Uzbek.
74 C3 Navojoa Mex.
20 G3 Navoloki Rus. Fed.
34 C5 Navsari India
34 C4 Nawa India
28 F5 Nawá Syria
35 G4 Nawabganj Bangl.
34 B4 Nawabshah Pak.
35 F4 Nawada India
31 G3 Nāwah Afgh.
34 C4 Nawalgarh India
29 K2 Naxçıvan Azer.
39 B4 Naxi China
19 L6 Naxos Greece
19 L6 Naxos i. Greece
81 A4 Naya Col.
75 F5 Nayagarh India
30 D5 Nāy Band Iran
40 H2 Nayoro Japan
33 B3 Nāyudupeta India
82 E1 Nazaré Brazil
33 B4 Nazareth India
28 E5 Nazareth Israel
65 B7 Nazas Mex.
74 D3 Nazas r. Mex.
78 D6 Nazca Peru
Nazca Ridge sea feature see South-West Peru Ridge
29 M5 Nazian Iran
29 K2 Nāzīk Iran
29 J2 Nazik Gölü l. Turkey
29 F4 Nāzīl Iran
28 B3 Nazilli Turkey
31 G5 Nazimabad Pak.
29 G2 Nazımiye Turkey
35 H4 Nazira India
54 E4 Nazko Can.
56 E4 Nazko r. Can.
29 K3 Nāzlū r. Iran
21 H7 Nazran' Rus. Fed.
88 D3 Nazrēt Eth.
32 E5 Nazwá Oman
89 C4 Nchelenge Zambia
89 C6 Ncojane Botswana
89 B4 N'dalatando Angola
88 C3 Ndélé C.A.R.
88 B4 Ndendé Gabon
49 G3 Ndeni i. Solomon Is
87 D3 Ndjamena Chad
89 C5 Ndola Zambia
91 H4 Ndwedwe S. Africa
11 E3 Neagh, Lough l. U.K.
62 A1 Neah Bay U.S.A.
48 D4 Neale, L. salt flat Austr.
19 K5 Nea Liosia Greece
19 K6 Neapoli Greece
9 D6 Neath U.K.
9 D6 Neath r. U.K.
30 D2 Nebitdag Turkm.
20 E3 Nebolchi Rus. Fed.
73 G2 Nebo, Mount mt U.S.A.
64 C3 Nebraska div. U.S.A.
64 E3 Nebraska City U.S.A.
18 F6 Nebrodi, Monti mts Sicily Italy
65 E6 Neches r. U.S.A.
81 B3 Nechí r. Col.
88 D3 Nechisar National Park Eth.
13 G5 Neckar r. Ger.
13 H5 Neckarsulm Ger.
94 H4 Necker I. HI U.S.A.
83 E3 Necochea Arg.
13 M1 Neddemin Ger.
58 F2 Neddouc, Lac l. Can.
6 R2 Nedre Soppero Sweden
73 E4 Needles U.S.A.
9 F7 Needles, The stack U.K.
68 C3 Neenah U.S.A.
57 K4 Neepawa Can.
55 K2 Neergaard Lake l. Can.
12 D3 Neerijnen Neth.
12 D3 Neerpelt Belgium
29 M2 Neftçala Azer.
24 G4 Neftekamsk Rus. Fed.
21 H6 Neftekumsk Rus. Fed.
24 J3 Nefteyugansk Rus. Fed.
9 C5 Nefyn U.K.
18 C6 Nefza Tunisia
88 B4 Negage Angola
88 D3 Negēlē Eth.
82 A3 Negla r. Para.
89 D5 Negomane Moz.
33 B5 Negombo Sri Lanka
19 K4 Negotino Macedonia
78 C5 Negra, Cordillera mts Peru
78 B5 Negra, Pta pt Peru
18 B7 Négrine Alg.
78 B4 Negritos Peru
83 D4 Negro r. Arg.
82 A2 Negro r. Mato Grosso do Sul Brazil
78 F4 Negro r. S. America
83 F2 Negro r. Uru.
43 B4 Negros i. Phil.
19 N3 Negru Vodă Romania
29 M4 Nehavand Iran
31 F4 Nehbandān Iran
36 E2 Nehe China
39 B4 Neijiang China
57 H4 Neilburg Can.
42 A2 Nei Monggol Zizhiqu div. China
13 K3 Neinstedt Ger.
16 G5 Neiß r. Ger./Pol.
81 B4 Neiva Col.
38 D3 Neixiang China
57 K3 Nejanilini Lake l. Can.
30 D2 Neka Iran
88 D3 Nek'emtē Eth.
40 E2 Nekrasovka Rus. Fed.
7 O9 Neksø Denmark
20 E3 Nelidovo Rus. Fed.
64 D3 Neligh U.S.A.
36 F1 Nel'kan Rus. Fed.
25 Q3 Nel'kan Rus. Fed.
33 B3 Nellore India
56 F5 Nelson Can.
51 D4 Nelson N.Z.
8 E4 Nelson U.K.
73 E4 Nelson U.S.A.
55 J4 Nelson r. Man. Can.
57 L3 Nelson r. Can.
50 J2 Nelson Bay Austr.
50 C5 Nelson, C. c. Austr.
80 B8 Nelson, Estrecho chan. Chile
56 E3 Nelson Forks Can.
57 K3 Nelson House Can.
91 J2 Nelspruit S. Africa
86 B3 Néma Maur.
20 J3 Nema Rus. Fed.
68 A2 Nemadji r. U.S.A.
20 B4 Neman Rus. Fed.
28 F5 Nemara Syria
20 G3 Nemda r. Rus. Fed.
20 K2 Nemed Rus. Fed.
69 F2 Nemegos Can.
6 W2 Nemetskiy, Mys c. Rus. Fed.
14 F2 Nemours France
29 J2 Nemrut Dağı h. Turkey
40 J3 Nemuro Japan
40 J3 Nemuro-kaikyō chan. Japan
21 D5 Nemyriv Ukr.
11 C5 Nenagh Rep. of Ireland
9 H5 Nene r. U.K.
36 E2 Nenjiang China
12 E5 Nennig Ger.
20 F1 Nenoksa Rus. Fed.
65 E4 Neosho U.S.A.
64 E4 Neosho r. U.S.A.
23 H7 Nepal country Asia
69 K3 Nepean Can.
73 G2 Nephi U.S.A.
11 B3 Nephin h. Rep. of Ireland
11 B3 Nephin Beg Range h. Rep. of Ireland
88 C3 Nepoko r. Congo(Zaire)
71 F4 Neptune U.S.A.
14 E4 Nérac France
36 D1 Nerchinsk Rus. Fed.
20 G3 Nerekhta Rus. Fed.
18 G3 Neretva r. Bos.-Herz./Croatia
89 C5 Neriquinha Angola
7 T9 Neris r. Lith.
20 F3 Nerl' r. Rus. Fed.
82 C2 Nerópolis Brazil
25 O4 Neryungri Rus. Fed.
12 D1 Nes Neth.
7 L6 Nes Norway
7 L6 Nesbyen Norway
6 G4 Neskaupstaður Iceland
12 A5 Nesle France
6 N3 Nesna Norway
64 D4 Ness City U.S.A.
13 J4 Nesse r. Ger.
56 C3 Nesselrode, Mt mt Can./U.S.A.
10 D3 Ness, Loch l. U.K.
19 L4 Nestos r. Greece
28 E5 Netanya Israel
5 D3 Netherlands country Europe
53 K8 Netherlands Antilles terr. Caribbean Sea
13 G4 Netphen Ger.
35 G4 Netrakona Bangl.
34 C5 Netrang India
55 L3 Nettilling Lake l. Can.
68 A1 Nett Lake U.S.A.
68 A1 Nett Lake l. U.S.A.
74 F5 Netzahualcóyotl, Presa resr Mex.
13 M1 Neubrandenburg Ger.
16 C7 Neuchâtel Switz.
16 C7 Neuchâtel, Lac de l. Switz.
13 J5 Neuendettelsau Ger.
12 E2 Neuenhaus Ger.
13 H1 Neuenkirchen Ger.
13 G2 Neuenkirchen (Oldenburg) Ger.
12 D5 Neufchâteau Belgium
14 G2 Neufchâteau France
14 E2 Neufchâtel-en-Bray France
13 F1 Neuharlingersiel Ger.
13 H1 Neuhaus (Oste) Ger.
13 H4 Neuhof Ger.
13 K1 Neu Kaliß Ger.
13 H4 Neukirchen Hessen Ger.
13 L4 Neukirchen Sachsen Ger.
57 K2 Neultin Lake l. Can.
13 K5 Neumarkt in der Oberpfalz Ger.
92 C2 Neumayer Ger. Base Ant.
16 D3 Neumünster Ger.
13 L5 Neunburg vorm Wald Ger.
16 H7 Neunkirchen Austria
12 F5 Neunkirchen Ger.
83 C3 Neuquén Arg.
83 C3 Neuquén div. Arg.
83 C3 Neuquén r. Arg.
13 L2 Neuruppin Ger.
67 E5 Neuse r. U.S.A.
16 H7 Neusiedler See l. Austria/Hungary
12 E3 Neuss Ger.
13 H2 Neustadt am Rübenberge Ger.
13 J5 Neustadt an der Aisch Ger.
13 L5 Neustadt an der Waldnaab Ger.
13 G5 Neustadt an der Weinstraße Ger.
13 K4 Neustadt bei Coburg Ger.
13 K1 Neustadt-Glewe Ger.
12 F4 Neustadt (Wied) Ger.
13 M1 Neustrelitz Ger.
13 L6 Neutraubling Ger.
12 F4 Neuwied Ger.
13 H1 Neu Wulmstorf Ger.
65 E4 Nevada MO U.S.A.
72 D2 Nevada div. U.S.A.
15 E4 Nevada, Sierra mts Spain
83 C2 Nevado, Cerro mt Arg.
74 D5 Nevado de Colima volc. Mex.
83 C3 Nevado, Sierra del mts Arg.
20 D3 Nevel' Rus. Fed.
14 F3 Nevers France
50 F1 Nevertire Austr.
19 H3 Nevesinje Bos.-Herz.
21 G6 Nevinnomyssk Rus. Fed.
10 C3 Nevis, Loch in. U.K.
28 E2 Nevşehir Turkey
40 C2 Nevskoye Rus. Fed.
73 E5 New r. CA U.S.A.
70 C6 New r. WV U.S.A.
66 C4 New Albany IN U.S.A.
65 F5 New Albany MS U.S.A.
71 E4 New Albany PA U.S.A.
79 G2 New Amsterdam Guyana
71 F5 Newark DE U.S.A.
71 F5 Newark MD U.S.A.
71 F4 Newark NJ U.S.A.
70 E3 Newark NY U.S.A.
70 B4 Newark OH U.S.A.
73 E2 Newark Lake l. U.S.A.
9 G4 Newark-on-Trent U.K.
71 E3 Newark Valley U.S.A.
71 H4 New Bedford U.S.A.
62 B2 Newberg U.S.A.
71 F3 New Berlin U.S.A.
67 E5 New Bern U.S.A.
68 E2 Newberry MI U.S.A.
67 D5 Newberry SC U.S.A.
72 D4 Newberry Springs U.S.A.
8 F2 Newbiggin-by-the-Sea U.K.
69 J3 Newboro Can.
71 G3 New Boston MA U.S.A.
70 B5 New Boston OH U.S.A.
65 D6 New Braunfels U.S.A.
11 E4 Newbridge Rep. of Ireland
64 G2 New Britain U.S.A.
48 E2 New Britain i. P.N.G.
71 F4 New Brunswick U.S.A.
59 G4 New Brunswick div. Can.
68 D5 New Buffalo U.S.A.
10 F3 Newburgh U.K.
71 F4 Newburgh U.S.A.
9 F6 Newbury U.K.
71 H3 Newburyport U.S.A.
8 E3 Newby Bridge U.K.
47 G6 New Caledonia is Pac. Oc.
59 G4 New Carlisle Can.
50 H2 Newcastle Austr.
59 G4 Newcastle N.B. Can.
69 H4 Newcastle Ont. Can.
11 E4 Newcastle Rep. of Ireland
91 H3 Newcastle S. Africa
11 F3 Newcastle N. Ireland U.K.
72 B2 Newcastle CA U.S.A.
68 E6 New Castle IN U.S.A.
70 B4 Newcastle OH U.S.A.
70 C4 New Castle PA U.S.A.
73 F3 Newcastle UT U.S.A.
70 C6 New Castle VA U.S.A.
62 F3 Newcastle WY U.S.A.
9 C5 Newcastle Emlyn U.K.
9 E4 Newcastle-under-Lyme U.K.
8 F3 Newcastle upon Tyne U.K.
11 B5 Newcastle West Rep. of Ireland
71 F6 New Church U.S.A.
73 H3 Newcomb U.S.A.
10 D5 New Cumnock U.K.
10 F3 New Deer U.K.
34 D3 New Delhi India
71 K1 New Denmark Can.
72 B3 New Don Pedro Reservoir U.S.A.
50 H1 New England Range mts Austr.
9 E6 Newent U.K.
59 J4 Newfoundland div. Can.
55 N5 Newfoundland i. Can.
96 G2 Newfoundland Basin sea feature Atl. Ocean
10 D5 New Galloway U.K.
49 F2 New Georgia i. Solomon Is
49 F2 New Georgia Islands is Solomon Is
59 H4 New Glasgow Can.
37 G7 New Guinea i. Asia
70 B4 New Hampshire OH U.S.A.
71 G3 New Hampshire div. U.S.A.
68 A4 New Hampton U.S.A.
91 J4 New Hanover S. Africa
48 F2 New Hanover i. P.N.G.
71 G4 New Haven U.S.A.
56 D3 New Hazelton Can.
72 B2 New Hogan Reservoir U.S.A.
68 C4 New Holstein U.S.A.
65 F6 New Iberia U.S.A.
91 J2 Newington S. Africa
11 D5 Newinn Rep. of Ireland
48 F2 New Ireland i. P.N.G.
71 F5 New Jersey div. U.S.A.
70 E6 New Kent U.S.A.
70 B5 New Lexington U.S.A.
68 B3 New Lisbon U.S.A.
69 H2 New Liskeard Can.
71 G4 New London CT U.S.A.
68 B5 New London IA U.S.A.
68 B6 New London MO U.S.A.
68 C3 New London WV U.S.A.
48 B4 Newman Austr.
68 D6 Newman U.S.A.
69 H3 Newmarket Can.
11 B5 Newmarket Rep. of Ireland
9 H5 Newmarket U.K.
70 D5 New Market U.S.A.
11 C5 Newmarket on-Fergus Rep. of Ireland
70 C5 New Martinsville U.S.A.
62 C2 New Meadows U.S.A.
72 B3 New Melanes L. l. U.S.A.
63 F5 New Mexico div. U.S.A.
67 C5 Newnan U.S.A.
65 F6 New Orleans U.S.A.
71 F4 New Paltz U.S.A.
70 C4 New Philadelphia U.S.A.
10 F3 New Pitsligo U.K.
51 E3 New Plymouth N.Z.
11 B4 Newport Mayo Rep. of Ireland
11 C5 Newport Tipperary Rep. of Ireland
9 F7 Newport Eng. U.K.
9 E5 Newport Eng. U.K.
9 D6 Newport Wales U.K.
65 F5 Newport AR U.S.A.
70 A5 Newport KY U.S.A.
71 J2 Newport ME U.S.A.
69 F5 Newport MI U.S.A.
71 G3 Newport NH U.S.A.
62 A2 Newport OR U.S.A.
71 H4 Newport RI U.S.A.
71 G2 Newport VT U.S.A.
62 C1 Newport WA U.S.A.
72 D5 Newport Beach U.S.A.
70 E6 Newport News U.S.A.
9 G5 Newport Pagnell U.K.
67 E7 New Providence i. Bahamas
9 B7 Newquay U.K.
59 G4 New Richmond Can.
68 A3 New Richmond U.S.A.
73 F5 New River U.S.A.
65 F6 New Roads U.S.A.
9 H7 New Romney U.K.
11 E5 New Ross Rep. of Ireland
11 E3 Newry U.K.
10 E4 New Scone U.K.
68 A5 New Sharon U.S.A.
New Siberian Islands is see Novosibirskiye Ostrova
67 D6 New Smyrna Beach U.S.A.
50 D2 New South Wales div. Austr.
39 □ New Territories reg. H.K. China
8 E4 Newton U.K.
64 D4 Newton IA U.S.A.
64 D4 Newton KS U.S.A.
71 H3 Newton MA U.S.A.
65 F5 Newton MS U.S.A.
71 F4 Newton NJ U.S.A.
9 D7 Newton Abbot U.K.
10 F3 Newtonhill U.K.
10 D5 Newton Mearns U.K.
10 D6 Newton Stewart U.K.
11 C5 Newtown Rep. of Ireland
9 E5 Newtown Eng. U.K.
9 D5 Newtown Wales U.K.
64 C1 New Town U.S.A.
11 F3 Newtownabbey U.K.
11 F3 Newtownards U.K.
11 D3 Newtownbutler U.K.
11 E4 Newtownmountkennedy Rep. of Ireland
10 F5 Newtown St Boswells U.K.
11 D3 Newtownstewart U.K.
64 E2 New Ulm U.S.A.
72 A2 Newville U.S.A.
56 E5 New Westminster Can.
71 G4 New York U.S.A.
71 E3 New York div. U.S.A.
71 G4 New York-John F. Kennedy airport U.S.A.
71 F4 New York-Newark airport U.S.A.
47 J8 New Zealand country Oceania
94 G9 New Zealand Plateau sea feature Pac. Oc.
20 G3 Neya Rus. Fed.
30 D4 Neyrīz Iran
31 E2 Neyshābūr Iran
33 B4 Neyyattinkara India
45 D2 Ngabang Indon.
88 B4 Ngabé Congo
44 A2 Nga Chong, Khao mt Myanmar/Thai.
43 C6 Ngalipaëng Indon.
89 C6 Ngami, Lake l. Botswana
35 F3 Ngamring China
35 E3 Ngangla Ringco salt l. China
34 E2 Nganglong Kangri mt China
34 E2 Nganglong Kangri mts Xizang China
35 F3 Ngangzê Co salt l. China
44 A1 Ngao Thai.
87 D4 Ngaoundéré Cameroon
51 E2 Ngaruawahia N.Z.
51 F3 Ngaruroro r. N.Z.
51 E3 Ngauruhoe, Mt volc. N.Z.
44 B1 Ngiap r. Laos
88 B4 Ngo Congo
44 C2 Ngoc Linh mt Vietnam
35 F3 Ngoin, Co salt l. China
86 D4 Ngol Bembo Nigeria
35 H2 Ngom Qu r. China
35 F2 Ngoqumaima China
36 B3 Ngoring Hu l. China
87 D3 Ngourti Niger
87 D3 Nguigmi Niger
37 F6 Ngulu i. Micronesia
86 D3 Nguru Nigeria
39 B6 Nguyên Binh Vietnam
90 E2 Ngwaketse div. Botswana
91 G3 Ngwathe S. Africa
91 J3 Ngwavuma r. Swaziland
91 J4 Ngwelezana S. Africa
89 D5 Nhamalabué Moz.
44 D2 Nha Trang Vietnam
50 C4 Nhill Austr.
91 J3 Nhlangano Swaziland
39 B6 Nho Quan Vietnam
48 D3 Nhulunbuy Austr.
57 J4 Niacam Can.
86 B3 Niafounké Mali
68 D3 Niagara U.S.A.
69 H4 Niagara Falls Can.
70 D3 Niagara Falls U.S.A.
69 H4 Niagara River r. Can./U.S.A.
86 C3 Niamey Niger
43 C5 Niampak Indon.
89 D4 Niangandu Tanz.
88 C3 Niangara Congo(Zaire)
45 A2 Nias i. Indon.
Niassa, Lago l. see Nyasa, Lake
7 R8 Nīca Latvia
53 H8 Nicaragua country Central America
75 G6 Nicaragua, Lago de l. Nic.
18 G5 Nicastro Italy
14 H5 Nice France
59 F3 Nichicun, Lac l. Can.
35 E4 Nichlaul India
67 E7 Nicholl's Town Bahamas
69 F2 Nicholson Can.
27 H6 Nicobar Islands is Andaman and Nicobar Is
28 D4 Nicosia Cyprus
75 H7 Nicoya, G. de b. Costa Rica
75 G7 Nicoya, Pen. de pen. Costa Rica
71 K1 Nictau Can.
7 R9 Nida Lith.
8 F4 Nidd r. U.K.
13 H4 Nidda Ger.
13 H4 Nidder r. Ger.
17 K4 Nidzica Pol.
16 D3 Niebüll Ger.
12 E5 Niederanven Lux.
13 H4 Niederaula Ger.
16 F7 Niedere Tauern mts Austria
13 G2 Niedersachsen div. Ger.
12 E1 Niedersächsisches Wattenmeer, Nationalpark nat. park Ger.
86 D4 Niefang Equatorial Guinea
86 B3 Niellé Côte d'Ivoire
13 H2 Nienburg (Weser) Ger.
12 E3 Niers r. Ger.
13 G5 Nierstein Ger.
79 G2 Nieuw Amsterdam Suriname
12 C2 Nieuwe-Niedorp Neth.
12 E1 Nieuwe Pekela Neth.
12 C3 Nieuwerkerk aan de IJssel Neth.
79 G2 Nieuw Nickerie Suriname
12 E1 Nieuwolda Neth.
90 C5 Nieuwoudtville S. Africa
12 A3 Nieuwpoort Belgium
12 C3 Nieuw-Vossemeer Neth.
28 E3 Niğde Turkey
85 D4 Niger country Africa
86 C4 Niger r. Africa
85 D5 Nigeria country Africa

35 F3 Nyonni Ri *mt* China
14 G4 Nyons France
24 G3 Nyrob Rus. Fed.
16 H5 Nysa Pol.
Nysa Łużycka *r. see* Neiß
20 J2 Nyuchpas Rus. Fed.
40 F5 Nyūdō-zaki *pt* Japan
88 C4 Nyunzu Congo(Zaire)
25 N3 Nyurba Rus. Fed.
20 J2 Nyuvchim Rus. Fed.
21 E6 Nyzhn'ohirs'kyy Ukr.
88 D4 Nzega Tanz.
86 B4 Nzérékoré Guinea
88 B4 N'zeto Angola
91 J1 Nzhelele Dam *dam* S. Africa
Nzwani *i. see* Anjouan

## O

64 C2 Oahe, Lake *l.* U.S.A.
72 □1 Oahu *i.* U.S.A.
50 C2 Oakbank Austr.
73 F2 Oak City U.S.A.
65 E6 Oakdale U.S.A.
64 D2 Oakes U.S.A.
9 G5 Oakham U.K.
62 B1 Oak Harbor U.S.A.
70 C6 Oak Hill U.S.A.
72 C3 Oakhurst U.S.A.
68 B2 Oak I. *i.* U.S.A.
72 A3 Oakland *CA* U.S.A.
70 D5 Oakland *MD* U.S.A.
64 D3 Oakland *NE* U.S.A.
62 B3 Oakland *OR* U.S.A.
72 A3 Oakland *airport CA* U.S.A.
50 F3 Oaklands Austr.
68 D5 Oak Lawn U.S.A.
64 C4 Oakley U.S.A.
48 C4 Oakover *r.* Austr.
62 B3 Oakridge U.S.A.
67 C4 Oak Ridge U.S.A.
50 C2 Oakvale Austr.
69 H4 Oakville Can.
51 C6 Oamaru N.Z.
10 B5 Oa, Mull of *hd* U.K.
51 D5 Oaro N.Z.
43 B3 Oas Phil.
73 D2 Oasis U.S.A.
92 B5 Oates Land *reg.* Ant.
73 E4 Oatman U.S.A.
74 E5 Oaxaca Mex.
24 H3 Ob' *r.* Rus. Fed.
86 D4 Obala Cameroon
41 D7 Obama Japan
10 C4 Oban U.K.
40 G5 Obanazawa Japan
15 C1 O Barco Spain
58 F4 Obatogama L. *l.* Can.
56 F4 Obed Can.
51 B6 Obelisk *mt* N.Z.
13 H4 Oberaula Ger.
13 J3 Oberdorla Ger.
13 J3 Oberharz *nat. park* Ger.
12 E3 Oberhausen Ger.
64 C4 Oberlin *KS* U.S.A.
70 B4 Oberlin *OH* U.S.A.
13 F5 Obermoschel Ger.
50 G2 Oberon Austr.
13 L5 Oberpfälzer Wald *mts* Ger.
13 H4 Obersinn Ger.
13 H4 Oberthulba Ger.
13 G4 Obertshausen Ger.
13 H3 Oberwälder Land *reg.* Ger.
37 E7 Obi *i.* Indon.
79 G4 Óbidos Brazil
31 H2 Obigarm Tajik.
40 H3 Obihiro Japan
21 H6 Obil'noye Rus. Fed.
81 C2 Obispos Venez.
36 F2 Obluch'ye Rus. Fed.
20 F4 Obninsk Rus. Fed.
88 C3 Obo C.A.R.
38 A2 Obo China
88 E2 Obock Djibouti
88 C4 Obokote Congo(Zaire)
42 E3 Obŏk-tong N. Korea
88 B4 Obouya Congo
21 F5 Oboyan' Rus. Fed.
20 G2 Obozerskiy Rus. Fed.
35 E4 Obra India
35 E4 Obra Dam *dam* India
60 E6 Obregón, Presa *resr* Mex.
19 J2 Obrenovac Yugo.
28 D2 Obruk Turkey
24 J2 Obskaya Guba *chan.* Rus. Fed.
86 B4 Obuasi Ghana
21 D5 Obukhiv Ukr.
20 J2 Ob''yachevo Rus. Fed.
67 D6 Ocala U.S.A.
81 D4 Ocamo *r.* Venez.
81 B2 Ocaña Col.
15 E3 Ocaña Spain
78 E7 Occidental, Cordillera *mts* Chile
81 A4 Occidental, Cordillera *mts* Col.
78 C6 Occidental, Cordillera *mts* Peru
56 B3 Ocean Cape *pt* U.S.A.
71 F5 Ocean City *MD* U.S.A.
71 F5 Ocean City *NJ* U.S.A.
56 D4 Ocean Falls Can.
96 G3 Oceanographer Fracture *sea feature* Atl. Ocean
72 D5 Oceanside U.S.A.
65 F6 Ocean Springs U.S.A.
21 D6 Ochakiv Ukr.
21 G7 Och'amch'ire Georgia
10 E4 Ochil Hills *h.* U.K.
34 C1 Ochili Pass Afgh.
13 J5 Ochsenfurt Ger.
12 F2 Ochtrup Ger.
7 P6 Ockelbo Sweden
17 M7 Ocolaşul Mare, Vârful *mt* Romania
61 K5 Oconee *r. GA* U.S.A.
68 C4 Oconomowoc U.S.A.
68 D3 Oconto U.S.A.
72 D5 Ocotillo Wells U.S.A.
86 B4 Oda Ghana
41 C7 Ōda Japan
6 E4 Ódáðahraun *lava* Iceland
42 E3 Odaejin N. Korea
40 G4 Ōdate Japan
41 F7 Odawara Japan
7 K6 Odda Norway
57 K3 Odei *r.* Can.
68 C5 Odell U.S.A.
15 B4 Odemira Port.
28 A2 Ödemiş Turkey
91 G3 Odendaalsrus S. Africa
7 M9 Odense Denmark
13 G5 Odenwald *reg.* Ger.
13 J3 Oder *r.* Ger./Pol.
16 G3 Oderbucht *b.* Ger.
21 D6 Odesa Ukr.
7 O7 Ödeshog Sweden
65 C6 Odessa U.S.A.
15 C4 Odiel *r.* Spain
86 B4 Odienné Côte d'Ivoire
20 F4 Odintsovo Rus. Fed.
44 C2 Ŏdŏngk Cambodia
16 J6 Odra *r.* Ger./Pol.
79 K5 Oeiras Brazil
64 C3 Oelrichs U.S.A.
13 L4 Oelsnitz Ger.
68 B4 Oelwein U.S.A.
12 D1 Oenkerk Neth.
46 O6 Oeno *i. Pitcairn Is* Pac. Oc.
29 H1 Of Turkey
64 B4 Ofanto *r.* Italy
13 G4 Offenbach am Main Ger.
12 F6 Offenburg Ger.
19 M6 Ofidoussa *i.* Greece
65 G5 Ōfunato Japan
40 F5 Oga Japan
88 E3 Ogadēn *reg.* Eth.
40 F5 Oga-hantō *pen.* Japan
41 E7 Ōgaki Japan
64 C3 Ogallala U.S.A.
36 G4 Ogasawara-shotō *is* Japan
69 H2 Ogascanane, Lac *l.* Can.
86 C4 Ogbomoso Nigeria
64 E3 Ogden *IA* U.S.A.
62 E3 Ogden *UT* U.S.A.
56 C3 Ogden, Mt *mt* Can.
71 F2 Ogdensburg U.S.A.
54 E3 Ogilvie *r.* Can.
54 E3 Ogilvie Mts *mts* Can.
30 D2 Oglanly Turkm.
67 C5 Oglethorpe, Mt *mt* U.S.A.
18 D1 Oglio *r.* Italy
86 C4 Ogoja Nigeria
58 C3 Ogoki *r.* Can.
58 C3 Ogoki Res. *resr* Can.
19 K3 Ogosta *r.* Bulg.
7 T8 Ogre Latvia
18 F2 Ogulin Croatia
30 D2 Ogurchinskiy, Ostrov *i.* Turkm.
29 L1 Oğuz Azer.
51 A6 Ohai N.Z.
51 E3 Ohakune N.Z.
41 G4 Ōhata Japan
51 B6 Ohau, L. *l.* N.Z.
83 B7 O'Higgins *div.* Chile
80 B7 O'Higgins, L. *l.* Chile
70 B4 Ohio *div.* U.S.A.
66 C4 Ohio *r.* U.S.A.
13 G4 Ohm *r.* Ger.
13 J4 Ohrdruf Ger.
13 L4 Ohře *r.* Czech Rep.
13 K2 Ohre *r.* Ger.
19 J4 Ohrid Macedonia
19 J4 Ohrid, Lake *l.* Albania/Macedonia
91 J2 Ohrigstad S. Africa
13 H5 Öhringen Ger.
51 E3 Ohura N.Z.
79 H3 Oiapoque Brazil
10 D3 Oich, Loch *l.* U.K.
35 H3 Oiga China
12 A4 Oignies France
70 D4 Oil City U.S.A.
72 C4 Oildale U.S.A.
14 F2 Oise *r.* France
12 B5 Oise à l'Aisne, Canal de l' *canal* France
41 B8 Ōita Japan
19 K5 Oiti *mt* Greece
72 C4 Ojai U.S.A.
83 D2 Ojeda Arg.
68 B3 Ojibwa U.S.A.
74 D3 Ojinaga Mex.
41 F6 Ojiya Japan
80 C3 Ojos del Salado *mt* Arg.
20 G4 Oka *r.* Rus. Fed.
86 B6 Okahandja Namibia
51 E3 Okahukura N.Z.
89 B6 Okakarara Namibia
59 H2 Okak Islands *is* Can.
56 F5 Okanagan Falls Can.
56 F4 Okanagan Lake *l.* Can.
56 F5 Okanogan U.S.A.
62 C1 Okanogan *r.* Can./U.S.A.
62 B1 Okanogan Range *mts* U.S.A.
88 C3 Okapi, Parc National de la *nat. park* Congo(Zaire)
34 C3 Okara Pak.
30 D2 Okarem Turkm.
89 B5 Okaukuejo Namibia
89 C5 Okavango *r.* Botswana/Namibia
89 C5 Okavango Delta *swamp* Botswana
41 F6 Okaya Japan
41 C7 Okayama Japan
41 E7 Okazaki Japan
67 D7 Okeechobee U.S.A.
67 D7 Okeechobee, L. *l.* U.S.A.
67 D6 Okefenokee Swamp *swamp* U.S.A.
9 C7 Okehampton U.K.
86 C4 Okene Nigeria
13 J2 Oker *r.* Ger.
35 F4 Okha India
36 G1 Okha Rus. Fed.
35 F4 Okhaldhunga Nepal
34 B5 Okha Rann *marsh* India
25 Q3 Okhotka *r.* Rus. Fed.
25 Q4 Okhotsk Rus. Fed.
36 G2 Okhotsk, Sea of *g.* Rus. Fed.
21 E5 Okhtyrka Ukr.
36 E4 Okinawa *i.* Japan
41 B7 Okino-shima *i.* Japan
41 C6 Oki-shotō *is* Japan
65 D5 Oklahoma *div.* U.S.A.
65 D5 Oklahoma City U.S.A.
65 D5 Okmulgee U.S.A.
88 B4 Okondja Gabon
56 G4 Okotoks Can.
20 E4 Okovskiy Les *forest* Rus. Fed.
88 B4 Okoyo Congo
6 S1 Øksfjord Norway
20 F2 Oksovskiy Rus. Fed.
31 H2 Oktyabr' Tajik.
26 D2 Oktyabr'sk Kazak.
20 J4 Oktyabr'sk Rus. Fed.
20 G2 Oktyabr'skiy *Archangel.* Rus. Fed.
21 G6 Oktyabr'skiy *Volgograd.* Rus. Fed.
36 H1 Oktyabr'skiy Rus. Fed.
24 G4 Oktyabr'skiy Rus. Fed.
31 G2 Oktyabr'skiy Uzbek.
24 H3 Oktyabr'skoye Rus. Fed.
25 L2 Oktyabr'skoy Revolyutsii, Ostrov *i.* Rus. Fed.
20 E3 Okulovka Rus. Fed.
40 F3 Okushiri-tō *i.* Japan
90 E1 Okwa *watercourse* Botswana
6 B4 Ólafsvík Iceland
72 C3 Olancha U.S.A.
72 C3 Olancha Peak *summit* U.S.A.
7 P8 Öland *i.* Sweden
6 W3 Olanga Rus. Fed.
50 C2 Olary Austr.
50 C2 Olary *r.* Austr.
64 E4 Olathe U.S.A.
83 E3 Olavarría Arg.
16 H5 Oława Pol.
73 G5 Olberg U.S.A.
18 C4 Olbia *Sardinia* Italy
70 D3 Olcott U.S.A.
33 C2 Old Bastar India
11 D4 Oldcastle Rep. of Ireland
54 E3 Old Crow Can.
12 D1 Oldeboorn Neth.
13 G1 Oldenburg Ger.
16 E3 Oldenburg in Holstein Ger.
12 E2 Oldenzaal Neth.
6 R2 Olderdalen Norway
71 F3 Old Forge *NY* U.S.A.
71 F4 Old Forge *PA* U.S.A.
8 E4 Oldham U.K.
11 C6 Old Head of Kinsale *hd* Rep. of Ireland
56 G4 Oldman *r.* Can.
10 F3 Oldmeldrum U.K.
71 H3 Old Orchard Beach U.S.A.
59 K4 Old Perlican Can.
56 G4 Olds Can.
71 J2 Old Town U.S.A.
57 H4 Old Wives L. *l.* Can.
73 E4 Old Woman Mts *mts* U.S.A.
70 D3 Olean U.S.A.
17 L3 Olecko Pol.
25 O4 Olekma *r.* Rus. Fed.
25 O3 Olekminsk Rus. Fed.
21 E5 Oleksandriya Ukr.
20 H1 Olema Rus. Fed.
7 J7 Ølen Norway
6 X2 Olenegorsk Rus. Fed.
25 N3 Olenek Rus. Fed.
25 O2 Olenek *r.* Rus. Fed.
25 O2 Olenek B. *b.* Rus. Fed.
20 E3 Olenino Rus. Fed.
21 C5 Olevs'k Ukr.
40 D3 Ol'ga Rus. Fed.
15 C4 Olhão Port.
91 J2 Olifants S. Africa
90 C5 Olifants *r.* S. Africa
90 C2 Olifants *watercourse* Namibia
90 E3 Olifantshoek S. Africa
90 C6 Olifantsrivierberg *mts* S. Africa
83 F2 Olimar Grande *r.* Uru.
82 C3 Olímpia Brazil
79 M5 Olinda Brazil
89 D5 Olinga Moz.
91 G2 Oliphants Drift Botswana
82 D4 Oliva Arg.
15 F3 Oliva Spain
80 C3 Oliva, Cordillera de *mts* Arg./Chile
83 C1 Olivares, Co del *mt* Chile
70 B5 Olive Hill U.S.A.
82 D3 Oliveira Brazil
15 C3 Olivenza Spain
64 E2 Olivia U.S.A.
40 G4 Ol'khi Rus. Fed.
80 C2 Ollagüe Chile
83 B1 Ollita, Cordillera de *mts* Arg./Chile
83 B1 Ollitas *mt* Arg.
78 C5 Olmos Peru
71 G3 Olmstedville U.S.A.
9 G5 Olney U.K.
66 C4 Olney U.S.A.
7 O8 Olofström Sweden
16 H6 Olomouc Czech Rep.
20 E2 Olonets Rus. Fed.
43 B3 Olongapo Phil.
14 D5 Oloron-Ste-Marie France
15 H1 Olot Spain
36 D1 Olovyannaya Rus. Fed.
34 C5 Olpad India
13 F3 Olpe Ger.
17 K4 Olsztyn Pol.
16 C7 Olten Switz.
19 M2 Olteniţa Romania
29 H1 Oltu Turkey
43 B5 Olutanga *i.* Phil.
62 B2 Olympia U.S.A.
62 B2 Olympic Nat. Park *WA* U.S.A.
62 A2 Olympic Nat. Park *WA* U.S.A.
Olympus *mt see* Troödos, Mount
19 K4 Olympus *mt* Greece
62 B2 Olympus, Mt *mt* U.S.A.
25 S3 Olyutorskiy Rus. Fed.
25 T4 Olyutorskiy, Mys *c.* Rus. Fed.
25 S4 Olyutorskiy Zaliv *b.* Rus. Fed.
35 E2 Oma China
40 G4 Ōma Japan
41 E6 Ōmachi Japan
41 F7 Omae-zaki *pt* Japan
11 D3 Omagh U.K.
64 E3 Omaha U.S.A.
90 C1 Omaheke *div.* Namibia
62 C1 Omak U.S.A.
23 E8 Oman *country* Asia
31 E5 Oman, Gulf of *g.* Asia
51 B6 Omarama N.Z.
89 B6 Omaruru Namibia
89 B5 Omatako *watercourse* Namibia
78 D7 Omate Peru
90 E2 Omaweneno Botswana
40 G4 Ōma-zaki *c.* Japan
88 A4 Omboué Gabon
18 D3 Ombrone *r.* Italy
35 F3 Ombu China
90 E5 Omdraaisvlei S. Africa
87 F3 Omdurman Sudan
18 C2 Omegna Italy
50 F4 Omeo Austr.
88 D2 Om Hājer Eritrea
30 C4 Omīdīyeh Iran
56 D3 Omineca Mountains Can.
90 C1 Omitara Namibia
41 F7 Ōmiya Japan
56 C3 Ommaney, Cape *hd* U.S.A.
12 E2 Ommen Neth.
38 B1 Ömnögovĭ *div.* Mongolia
25 R3 Omolon *r.* Rus. Fed.
88 D3 Omo National Park Eth.
40 G5 Omono-gawa *r.* Japan
24 J4 Omsk Rus. Fed.
25 R3 Omsukchan Rus. Fed.
40 H2 Ōmu Japan
41 A8 Ōmura Japan
19 L2 Omu, Vârful *mt* Romania
68 B4 Onalaska U.S.A.
71 F6 Onancock U.S.A.
58 D4 Onaping Lake *l.* Can.
69 E3 Onaway U.S.A.
44 A2 Onbingwin Myanmar
83 D1 Oncativo Arg.
8 C3 Onchan U.K.
89 B5 Oncócua Angola
89 B5 Ondangwa Namibia
90 B1 Ondekaremba Namibia
90 D5 Onderstedorings S. Africa
89 B5 Ondjiva Angola
86 C4 Ondo Nigeria
36 D2 Öndörhaan Mongolia
42 A1 Ondor Had China
38 B1 Ondor Mod China
38 D1 Ondor Sum China
20 E2 Ondozero Rus. Fed.
90 D1 One Botswana
20 F2 Onega Rus. Fed.
20 F2 Onega *r.* Rus. Fed.
20 E2 Onega, Lake *l.* Rus. Fed.
56 E4 100 Mile House Can.
71 F3 Oneida U.S.A.
71 F3 Oneida Lake *l.* U.S.A.
64 D3 O'Neill U.S.A.
36 H2 Onekotan, O. *i.* Rus. Fed.
71 F3 Oneonta U.S.A.
51 E2 Oneroa N.Z.
17 N7 Oneşti Romania
20 E1 Onezhskaya Guba *g.* Rus. Fed.
Onezhskoye Ozero *l. see* Onega, Lake
35 E5 Ong *r.* India
88 B4 Onga Gabon
51 F3 Ongaonga N.Z.
90 E4 Ongers *watercourse* S. Africa
42 C5 Ongjin N. Korea
38 F1 Ongniud Qi China
33 C3 Ongole India
21 G7 Oni Georgia
89 E6 Onilahy *r.* Madag.
86 C4 Onitsha Nigeria
90 B1 Onjati Mountain *mt* Namibia
41 E7 Ōno Japan
49 J4 Ono-i-Lau *i.* Fiji
41 C7 Onomichi Japan
49 H2 Onotoa *i.* Kiribati
56 G4 Onoway Can.
90 C4 Onseepkans S. Africa
48 B4 Onslow Austr.
67 E5 Onslow Bay *b.* U.S.A.
42 F2 Onsong N. Korea
12 F1 Onstwedde Neth.
41 E7 Ontake-san *volc.* Japan
62 C2 Ontario U.S.A.
58 B3 Ontario *div.* Can.
69 H4 Ontario, Lake *l.* Can./U.S.A.
68 C2 Ontonagon U.S.A.
49 F2 Ontong Java Atoll *atoll* Solomon Is
48 D4 Oodnadatta Austr.
65 E4 Oologah L. *resr* U.S.A.
12 B3 Oostburg Neth.
Oostende *see* Ostend
12 D2 Oostendorp Neth.
12 C3 Oosterhout Neth.
12 B3 Oosterschelde *est.* Neth.
12 E2 Oosterwolde Neth.
12 A4 Oostvleteren Belgium
12 D1 Oost-Vlieland Neth.
56 D4 Ootsa Lake Can.
56 D4 Ootsa Lake *l.* Can.
70 E5 Opal U.S.A.
88 C4 Opala Congo(Zaire)
20 J3 Oparino Rus. Fed.
58 B3 Opasquia Can.
58 B3 Opasquia Provincial Park *res.* Can.
58 F3 Opataca L. *l.* Can.
16 H6 Opava Czech Rep.
67 C5 Opelika U.S.A.
65 E6 Opelousas U.S.A.
62 F1 Opheim U.S.A.
69 F2 Ophir Can.
45 B2 Ophir, Gunung *volc.* Indon.
51 C6 Opihi *r.* N.Z.
58 E3 Opinaca *r.* Can.
58 E3 Opinaca, Réservoir *resr* Can.
58 D3 Opinnagau *r.* Can.
29 K5 Opis Iraq
59 G3 Opiscotéo L. *l.* Can.
12 C2 Opmeer Neth.
20 D3 Opochka Rus. Fed.
16 H5 Opole Pol.
15 B2 Oporto Port.
51 F3 Opotiki N.Z.
67 C6 Opp U.S.A.
6 L5 Oppdal Norway
51 D3 Opunake N.Z.
89 B5 Opuwo Namibia
68 B5 Oquawka U.S.A.
71 H2 Oquossoc U.S.A.
73 G5 Oracle U.S.A.
73 G5 Oracle Junction U.S.A.
17 K7 Oradea Romania
6 E4 Öræfajökull *gl.* Iceland
19 J3 Orahovac Yugo.
34 D4 Orai India
86 B1 Oran Alg.
80 D2 Orán Arg.
44 C2 O Rang Cambodia
42 E3 Orang N. Korea
50 G2 Orange Austr.
14 G4 Orange France
71 G3 Orange *MA* U.S.A.
65 E6 Orange *TX* U.S.A.
70 D5 Orange *VA* U.S.A.
89 B6 Orange *r.* Namibia/S. Africa
67 D5 Orangeburg U.S.A.
79 H3 Orange, Cabo *c.* Brazil
Orange Free State *div. see* Free State
69 G3 Orangeville Can.
73 G2 Orangeville U.S.A.
74 G5 Orange Walk Belize
43 B3 Orani Phil.
13 M2 Oranienburg Ger.
89 B6 Oranjemund Namibia
81 C1 Oranjestad Aruba
11 C4 Oranmore Rep. of Ireland
89 C6 Orapa Botswana
43 C3 Oras Phil.
19 K2 Orăştie Romania
6 S5 Oravais Fin.
19 J2 Oravita Romania
34 E2 Orba Co *l.* China
18 D3 Orbetello Italy
15 D1 Orbigo *r.* Spain
50 G4 Orbost Austr.
92 B1 Orcadas *Arg. Base* Ant.
73 H3 Orchard Mesa U.S.A.
81 D2 Orchila, Isla *i.* Venez.
72 B4 Orcutt U.S.A.
48 C3 Ord *r.* Austr.
63 D4 Orderville U.S.A.
15 B1 Ordes Spain
48 C3 Ord, Mt *h.* Austr.
72 D4 Ord Mt *mt* U.S.A.
28 F1 Ordu Turkey
29 L2 Ordubad Azer.
63 G4 Ordway U.S.A.
Ordzhonikidze *see* Vladikavkaz
21 E6 Ordzhonikidze Ukr.
72 C1 Oreana U.S.A.
7 O7 Örebro Sweden
68 C4 Oregon *IL* U.S.A.
70 B4 Oregon *OH* U.S.A.
68 C4 Oregon *WV* U.S.A.
62 B3 Oregon *div.* U.S.A.
62 B2 Oregon City U.S.A.
20 F4 Orekhovo-Zuyevo Rus. Fed.
20 F4 Orel Rus. Fed.
36 F1 Orel', Ozero *l.* Rus. Fed.
73 G1 Orem U.S.A.
19 M6 Ören Turkey
28 A2 Ören Turkey
24 G4 Orenburg Rus. Fed.
83 E3 Orense Arg.
51 A7 Orepuki N.Z.
7 N9 Øresund *str.* Denmark
51 B7 Oreti *r.* N.Z.
51 E2 Orewa N.Z.
12 D4 Oreye Belgium
19 K4 Orfanou, Kolpos *b.* Greece
9 J5 Orford U.K.
9 J5 Orford Ness *spit* U.K.
73 F5 Organ Pipe Cactus National Monument *res.* U.S.A.
31 H3 Orgūn Afgh.
28 B2 Orhaneli Turkey
21 D7 Orhangazi Turkey
20 J3 Orichi Rus. Fed.
71 K2 Orient U.S.A.
78 E7 Oriental, Cordillera *mts* Bol.
81 B3 Oriental, Cordillera *mts* Col.
78 D6 Oriental, Cordillera *mts* Peru
83 E3 Oriente Arg.
15 F3 Orihuela Spain
21 E6 Orikhiv Ukr.
69 H3 Orillia Can.
7 T6 Orimattila Fin.
81 E2 Orinoco *r.* Col./Venez.
81 E2 Orinoco Delta *delta* Venez.
35 F5 Orissa *div.* India
7 S7 Orissaare Estonia
18 C5 Oristano *Sardinia* Italy
7 T6 Orivesi Fin.
6 V5 Orivesi *l.* Fin.
79 G4 Oriximiná Brazil
74 E5 Orizaba Mex.
6 L5 Orkanger Norway
7 N8 Örkelljunga Sweden
6 L5 Orkla *r.* Norway
91 G3 Orkney S. Africa
10 E1 Orkney Islands *is* U.K.
65 C6 Orla U.S.A.
72 A2 Orland U.S.A.
82 C3 Orlândia Brazil
67 D6 Orlando U.S.A.
14 E3 Orléans France
71 J4 Orleans *MA* U.S.A.
71 G2 Orleans *VT* U.S.A.
20 J3 Orlov Rus. Fed.
20 F4 Orlovskaya Oblast' *div.* Rus. Fed.
21 G6 Orlovskiy Rus. Fed.
31 G5 Ormara Pak.
31 G5 Ormara, Ras *hd* Pak.
43 C4 Ormoc Phil.
67 D6 Ormond Beach U.S.A.
8 E4 Ormskirk U.K.
71 G2 Ormstown Can.
14 D2 Orne *r.* France
6 N3 Ørnes Norway
6 Q5 Örnsköldsvik Sweden
42 D4 Oro N. Korea
81 C3 Orocué Col.
86 B3 Orodara Burkina
62 C2 Orofino U.S.A.
63 F5 Orogrande U.S.A.
59 G4 Oromocto Can.
28 E6 Oron Israel
49 J2 Orona *i.* Kiribati
71 J2 Orono U.S.A.
10 B4 Oronsay *i.* U.K.
Orontes *r. see* 'Āṣī, Nahr al
36 E1 Oroqen Zizhiqi China
43 B4 Oroquieta Phil.
79 L5 Orós, Açude *resr* Brazil
18 C4 Orosei *Sardinia* Italy
18 C4 Orosei, Golfo di *b. Sardinia* Italy
17 K7 Orosháza Hungary
73 G5 Oro Valley U.S.A.
72 B2 Oroville *CA* U.S.A.
62 C1 Oroville *WA* U.S.A.
72 B2 Oroville, Lake *l.* U.S.A.
50 B2 Orroroo Austr.
7 O6 Orsa Sweden
20 D4 Orsha Belarus
24 G4 Orsk Rus. Fed.
7 K5 Ørsta Norway
15 C1 Ortegal, Cabo *c.* Spain
14 D5 Orthez France
15 C1 Ortigueira Spain
81 D2 Ortíz Venez.
18 D1 Ortles *mt* Italy
8 E3 Orton U.K.
18 F3 Ortona Italy
64 D2 Ortonville U.S.A.
25 O3 Orulgan, Khrebet *mts* Rus. Fed.
90 B1 Orumbo Namibia
30 B2 Orūmīyeh Iran
30 B2 Orūmīyeh, Daryācheh-ye *salt l.* Iran
78 E7 Oruro Bol.
12 D5 Orval, Abbaye d' Belgium
18 E3 Orvieto Italy
92 B3 Orville Coast *coastal area* Ant.
70 C4 Orwell *OH* U.S.A.
71 G3 Orwell *VT* U.S.A.
7 M5 Os Norway
68 A4 Osage U.S.A.
64 E4 Osage *r.* U.S.A.
41 D7 Ōsaka Japan
75 H7 Osa, Pen. de *pen.* Costa Rica
7 N8 Osby Sweden
65 F5 Osceola *AR* U.S.A.
64 E3 Osceola *IA* U.S.A.
13 M3 Oschatz Ger.
13 K2 Oschersleben (Bode) Ger.
18 C4 Oschiri *Sardinia* Italy
69 F3 Oscoda U.S.A.
20 F4 Osetr *r.* Rus. Fed.
41 A8 Ōse-zaki *pt* Japan
69 K3 Osgoode Can.
27 F2 Osh Kyrg.
89 B5 Oshakati Namibia
40 G3 Oshamanbe Japan
69 H4 Oshawa Can.
40 G5 Oshika-hantō *pen.* Japan
40 F4 Ō-shima *i.* Japan
41 F7 Ō-shima *i.* Japan
64 C3 Oshkosh *NE* U.S.A.
68 C3 Oshkosh *WV* U.S.A.
30 B2 Oshnovīyeh Iran
86 C4 Oshogbo Nigeria
29 M5 Oshtorān Kūh *mt* Iran
29 M5 Oshtorīnān Iran
88 B4 Oshwe Congo(Zaire)
19 H2 Osijek Croatia
18 E3 Osimo Italy
34 C4 Osiyān India
91 J3 Osizweni S. Africa
18 G2 Osječenica *mt* Bos.-Herz.
6 O5 Osjön *l.* Sweden
64 E3 Oskaloosa U.S.A.
7 P8 Oskarshamn Sweden
69 K1 Oskélanéo Can.
21 F5 Oskol *r.* Rus. Fed.
7 M7 Oslo Norway
43 B4 Oslob Phil.
7 M7 Oslofjorden *chan.* Norway
33 B2 Osmanabad India
28 E1 Osmancık Turkey
28 B1 Osmaneli Turkey
28 F3 Osmaniye Turkey
7 V7 Os'mino Rus. Fed.
13 G2 Osnabrück Ger.
19 K3 Osogovske Planine *mts* Bulg./Macedonia
83 B4 Osorno Chile
15 D1 Osorno Spain
83 B4 Osorno, Vol. *volc.* Chile
56 F5 Osoyoos Can.
7 J6 Osøyri Norway
48 E3 Osprey Reef *rf* Coral Sea Is Terr.
12 D3 Oss Neth.
48 E6 Ossa, Mt *mt* Austr.

40 H3 **Rubeshibe** Japan
10 C2 **Rubha Coigeach** *pt* U.K.
10 B3 **Rubha Hunish** *pt* U.K.
10 C3 **Rubha Reidh** *pt* U.K.
72 B2 **Rubicon** *r.* U.S.A.
21 F5 **Rubizhne** Ukr.
24 K4 **Rubtsovsk** Rus. Fed.
54 C3 **Ruby** U.S.A.
73 E1 **Ruby Lake** *l.* U.S.A.
73 E1 **Ruby Mountains** U.S.A.
39 D5 **Rucheng** China
70 D5 **Ruckersville** U.S.A.
30 E5 **Rudan** Iran
35 E4 **Rudauli** India
31 F4 **Rudbar** Afgh.
29 M3 **Rūdbār** Iran
30 E2 **Rūd-e Kāl-Shūr** *r.* Iran
31 E4 **Rūd-i-Shur** *watercourse* Iran
7 M9 **Rudkøbing** Denmark
36 F2 **Rudnaya Pristan'** Rus. Fed.
20 K3 **Rudnichnyy** Rus. Fed.
20 D4 **Rudnya** Rus. Fed.
26 E1 **Rudnyy** Kazak.
40 D2 **Rudnyy** Rus. Fed.
24 G1 **Rudolfa, O.** *i.* Rus. Fed.
13 K4 **Rudolstadt** Ger.
38 F3 **Rudong** China
30 C2 **Rūdsar** Iran
68 E2 **Rudyard** U.S.A.
89 D4 **Rufiji** *r.* Tanz.
83 D2 **Rufino** Arg.
86 A3 **Rufisque** Senegal
89 C5 **Rufunsa** Zambia
38 F3 **Rugao** China
9 F5 **Rugby** U.K.
64 C1 **Rugby** U.S.A.
9 F5 **Rugeley** U.K.
16 F3 **Rügen** *i.* Ger.
70 B4 **Ruggles** U.S.A.
13 J5 **Rügland** Ger.
30 B5 **Ruḩayyat al Ḩamr'ā'** *waterhole* S. Arabia
88 C4 **Ruhengeri** Rwanda
7 S8 **Ruhnu** *i.* Estonia
12 E4 **Ruhr** *r.* Ger.
39 F5 **Rui'an** China
63 F5 **Ruidoso** U.S.A.
39 E5 **Ruijin** China
57 N2 **Ruin Point** *pt* Can.
89 D4 **Ruipa** Tanz.
81 B3 **Ruiz, Nevado del** *volc.* Col.
7 T8 **Rūjiena** Latvia
30 C5 **Rukbah** *well* S. Arabia
35 E3 **Rukumkot** Nepal
88 D4 **Rukwa, Lake** *l.* Tanz.
30 E5 **Rūl Dadnah** U.A.E.
31 E3 **Rūm** Iran
10 B4 **Rum** *i. Scot.* U.K.
19 H2 **Ruma** Yugo.
30 B5 **Rumāh** S. Arabia
87 E4 **Rumbek** Sudan
67 F7 **Rum Cay** *i.* Bahamas
71 H2 **Rumford** U.S.A.
14 G4 **Rumilly** France
48 D3 **Rum Jungle** Austr.
40 G3 **Rumoi** Japan
38 E3 **Runan** China
51 C5 **Runanga** N.Z.
51 F2 **Runaway, Cape** *c.* N.Z.
9 E4 **Runcorn** U.K.
89 B5 **Rundu** Namibia
6 Q5 **Rundvik** Sweden
38 E3 **Runheji** China
38 A3 **Ru'nying** China
7 V6 **Ruokolahti** Fin.
36 A3 **Ruoqiang** China
35 H4 **Rupa** India
83 B4 **Rupanco, L.** *l.* Chile
54 D4 **Rupanyup** Austr.
45 B2 **Rupat** *i.* Indon.
62 D3 **Rupert** U.S.A.
58 E3 **Rupert** *r.* Can.
58 E3 **Rupert Bay** *b.* Can.
92 A4 **Ruppert Coast** *coastal area* Ant.
46 M6 **Rurutu** *i. Fr. Polynesia* Pac. Oc.
89 D5 **Rusape** Zimbabwe
19 L3 **Ruse** Bulg.
42 A5 **Rushan** China
9 G5 **Rushden** U.K.
68 B4 **Rushford** U.S.A.
68 C4 **Rush Lake** *l.* U.S.A.
35 E3 **Rushon** India
31 H2 **Rushon** Tajik.
68 B5 **Rushville** *IL* U.S.A.
64 C3 **Rushville** *NE* U.S.A.
50 E4 **Rushworth** Austr.
65 E6 **Rusk** U.S.A.
67 D7 **Ruskin** U.S.A.
57 J4 **Russell** *Man.* Can.
71 F2 **Russell** *Ont.* Can.
51 E1 **Russell** N.Z.
64 D4 **Russell** U.S.A.
56 F2 **Russell Lake** *l.* Can.
55 J2 **Russell I.** *i.* Can.
49 F2 **Russell Is** *is* Solomon Is
67 C4 **Russellville** *AL* U.S.A.
65 E5 **Russellville** *AR* U.S.A.
66 C4 **Russellville** *KY* U.S.A.
13 G4 **Rüsselsheim** Ger.
23 E3 **Russian Federation** *country* Asia/Europe
40 C3 **Russkiy, Ostrov** *i.* Rus. Fed.
29 K1 **Rust'avi** Georgia
91 G2 **Rustenburg** S. Africa
65 E5 **Ruston** U.S.A.
37 E7 **Ruteng** Indon.
73 E2 **Ruth** U.S.A.
13 G3 **Rüthen** Ger.
69 H2 **Rutherglen** Can.
9 D4 **Ruthin** U.K.
20 H3 **Rutka** *r.* Rus. Fed.
71 G3 **Rutland** U.S.A.
9 G5 **Rutland Water** *resr* U.K.
57 G2 **Rutledge Lake** *l.* Can.
34 D2 **Rutog** China
69 G2 **Rutter** Can.
6 T4 **Ruukki** Fin.
30 E5 **Rū'us al Jibāl** *pen.* Oman
89 D5 **Ruvuma** *r.* Moz./Tanz.
28 F5 **Ruwayshid, Wādī** *watercourse* Jordan
30 D5 **Ruweis** U.A.E.
39 D5 **Ruyuan** China
26 E1 **Ruzayevka** Kazak.
20 H4 **Ruzayevka** Rus. Fed.
17 J6 **Ružomberok** Slovakia
85 F6 **Rwanda** *country* Africa
30 D2 **Ryābād** Iran
20 H2 **Ryadovo** Rus. Fed.
10 C5 **Ryan, Loch** *b.* U.K.
20 F4 **Ryazan'** Rus. Fed.
20 G4 **Ryazanskaya Oblast'** *div.* Rus. Fed.
20 G4 **Ryazhsk** Rus. Fed.
24 E2 **Rybachiy, Poluostrov** *pen.* Rus. Fed.
20 F3 **Rybinsk** Rus. Fed.
20 F3 **Rybinskoye Vdkhr.** *resr* Rus. Fed.
20 J4 **Rybnaya Sloboda** Rus. Fed.
17 J5 **Rybnik** Pol.
20 F4 **Rybnoye** Rus. Fed.
56 F3 **Rycroft** Can.
7 O8 **Ryd** Sweden
92 B3 **Rydberg Pen.** *pen.* Ant.
9 F7 **Ryde** U.K.
9 H7 **Rye** U.K.
8 G3 **Rye** *r.* U.K.
21 E5 **Ryl'sk** Rus. Fed.
50 G2 **Rylstone** Austr.
42 D5 **Ryoju** S. Korea
41 F5 **Ryōtsu** Japan
17 L5 **Rzeszów** Pol.
21 G4 **Rzhaksa** Rus. Fed.
20 E3 **Rzhev** Rus. Fed.


# S


30 E3 **Sa'ābād** Iran
30 D4 **Sa'ādatābād** Iran
30 D4 **Sa'ādatābād** Iran
13 K6 **Saal an der Donau** Ger.
13 K3 **Saale** *r.* Ger.
13 K4 **Saalfeld** Ger.
12 E5 **Saar** *r.* Ger.
12 E5 **Saarbrücken** Ger.
7 S7 **Saaremaa** *i.* Estonia
6 T3 **Saarenkylä** Fin.
12 E5 **Saargau** *reg.* Ger.
6 T5 **Saarijärvi** Fin.
6 U3 **Saari-Kämä** Fin.
6 R2 **Saarikoski** Fin.
12 E5 **Saarland** *div.* Ger.
12 E5 **Saarlouis** Ger.
29 M2 **Saatlı** Azer.
83 D3 **Saavedra** Arg.
28 F5 **Şab' Ābār** Syria
19 H2 **Šabac** Yugo.
15 H2 **Sabadell** Spain
41 E7 **Sabae** Japan
45 E1 **Sabah** *div.* Malaysia
44 B5 **Sabak** Malaysia
45 E4 **Sabalana, Kep.** *is* Indon.
34 D4 **Sabalgarh** India
75 H4 **Sabana, Arch. de** *is* Cuba
81 B2 **Sabanalarga** Col.
28 D1 **Şabanözü** Turkey
82 D2 **Sabará** Brazil
33 C2 **Sabari** *r.* India
34 C5 **Sabarmati** *r.* India
18 E4 **Sabaudia** Italy
31 E3 **Sabeh** Iran
90 E5 **Sabelo** S. Africa
87 D2 **Sabhā** Libya
30 B6 **Şabḩā'** S. Arabia
34 D3 **Sabi** *r.* India
91 K2 **Sabie** Moz.
91 J2 **Sabie** S. Africa
91 K2 **Sabie** *r.* Moz./S. Africa
74 D3 **Sabinas** Mex.
74 D3 **Sabinas Hidalgo** Mex.
65 E6 **Sabine L.** *l.* U.S.A.
29 M1 **Sabirabad** Azer.
43 B3 **Sablayan** Phil.
67 D7 **Sable, Cape** *c.* U.S.A.
49 F3 **Sable, Île de** *i.* New Caledonia
55 N5 **Sable Island** *i. N.S.* Can.
69 F2 **Sables, River aux** *r.* Can.
92 C6 **Sabrina Coast** *coastal area* Ant.
43 B1 **Sabtang** *i.* Phil.
15 C2 **Sabugal** Port.
68 B4 **Sabula** U.S.A.
32 B6 **Şabyā** S. Arabia
**Sabzawar** *see* **Shīndand**
31 E2 **Sabzevār** Iran
19 N2 **Sacalinul Mare, Insula** *i.* Romania
19 L2 **Săcele** Romania
89 B5 **Sachanga** Angola
58 B3 **Sachigo** *r.* Can.
58 B3 **Sachigo L.** *l.* Can.
34 C5 **Sachin** India
42 E6 **Sach'ŏn** S. Korea
34 D2 **Sach Pass** India
13 L3 **Sachsen** *div.* Ger.
13 K3 **Sachsen-Anhalt** *div.* Ger.
13 H6 **Sachsenheim** Ger.
54 F2 **Sachs Harbour** Can.
71 E3 **Sackets Harbor** U.S.A.
13 G4 **Sackpfeife** *h.* Ger.
59 H4 **Sackville** Can.
71 H3 **Saco** *ME* U.S.A.
62 F1 **Saco** *MT* U.S.A.
43 B5 **Sacol** *i.* Phil.
72 B2 **Sacramento** U.S.A.
72 B2 **Sacramento** *airport CA* U.S.A.
72 B2 **Sacramento** *r.* U.S.A.
63 F5 **Sacramento Mts** *mts* U.S.A.
62 B3 **Sacramento Valley** *v.* U.S.A.
91 G6 **Sada** S. Africa
15 F1 **Sádaba** Spain
30 C4 **Sa'dabad** Iran
28 F4 **Şadad** Syria
44 B4 **Sadao** Thai.
91 J2 **Saddleback** *pass* S. Africa
44 C3 **Sa Đec** Vietnam
35 H3 **Sadêng** China
31 E5 **Sadīj** *watercourse* Iran
34 B3 **Sadiqabad** Pak.
34 C1 **Sad Istragh** *mt* Afgh./Pak.
29 L5 **Sa'dīyah, Hawr as** *l.* Iraq
30 D5 **Sa'diyyat** *i.* U.A.E.
30 E2 **Sad-Kharv** Iran
15 B3 **Sado** *r.* Port.
41 F6 **Sadoga-shima** *i.* Japan
36 F3 **Sado-Shima** *i.* Japan
15 H3 **Sa Dragonera** *i.* Spain
7 M8 **Sæby** Denmark
**Safad** *see* **Zefat**
29 L6 **Safayal Maqūf** *well* Iraq
31 H2 **Safed Khirs** *mts* Afgh.
31 G3 **Safed Koh** *mts* Afgh.
7 N7 **Säffle** Sweden
73 H5 **Safford** U.S.A.
9 H5 **Saffron Walden** U.K.
28 E6 **Safi** Jordan
86 B1 **Safi** Morocco
30 C2 **Safīd** *r.* Iran
30 D3 **Safīd Ab** Iran
31 F4 **Safidabeh** Iran
29 M5 **Safid Dasht** Iran
28 F4 **Şāfītā** Syria
6 X2 **Safonovo** *Murmansk.* Rus. Fed.
20 E4 **Safonovo** *Smolensk.* Rus. Fed.
24 F3 **Safonovo** Rus. Fed.
30 A5 **Safrā' al Asyāḩ** *esc.* S. Arabia
28 D1 **Safranbolu** Turkey
29 L6 **Safwān** Iraq
35 F3 **Saga** China
41 B8 **Saga** Japan
41 F7 **Sagamihara** Japan
41 F7 **Sagami-nada** *g.* Japan
41 F7 **Sagami-wan** *b.* Japan
81 B3 **Sagamoso** *r.* Col.
44 A2 **Saganthit Kyun** *i.* Myanmar
33 B2 **Sagar** *Karnataka* India
33 A3 **Sagar** *Karnataka* India
34 D5 **Sagar** *Madhya Pradesh* India
21 H7 **Sagarejo** Georgia
35 G5 **Sagar I.** *i.* India
25 O2 **Sagastyr** Rus. Fed.
30 D3 **Saghand** Iran
31 F3 **Saghar** Afgh.
33 B3 **Sagileru** *r.* India
69 F4 **Saginaw** U.S.A.
69 F4 **Saginaw Bay** *b.* U.S.A.
59 H2 **Saglek Bay** *b.* Can.
18 C3 **Sagone, Golfe de** *b. Corsica* France
15 B4 **Sagres** Port.
35 H5 **Sagu** Myanmar
63 F4 **Saguache** U.S.A.
75 H4 **Sagua la Grande** Cuba
73 G5 **Saguaro National Monument** *res.* U.S.A.
59 F4 **Saguenay** *r.* Can.
15 F3 **Sagunto-Sagunt** Spain
34 C5 **Sagwara** India
81 B2 **Sahagún** Col.
15 D1 **Sahagún** Spain
29 L3 **Sahand, Kūh-e** *mt* Iran
84 B3 **Sahara** *des.* Africa
**Saharan Atlas** *mts see* **Atlas Saharien**
34 D3 **Saharanpur** India
35 F4 **Saharsa** India
34 D3 **Sahaswan** India
30 C6 **Sahba', W. as** *watercourse* S. Arabia
34 C3 **Sahiwal** Pak.
30 E3 **Sahlābād** Iran
29 L4 **Şahneh** Iran
29 K6 **Şahrā al Ḩijārah** *reg.* Iraq
73 G6 **Sahuarita** U.S.A.
44 D2 **Sa Huynh** Vietnam
**Sahyadri** *mts see* **Western Ghats**
34 C5 **Sahyadriparvat Range** *h.* India
34 E4 **Sai** *r.* India
44 B4 **Sai Buri** Thai.
44 B4 **Sai Buri** *r.* Thai.
**Saïda** *see* **Sidon**
30 D4 **Sa'īdābād** Iran
44 B2 **Sai Dao Tai, Khao** *mt* Thai.
31 F5 **Sa'īdī** Iran
35 G4 **Saidpur** Bangl.
34 C2 **Saidu** Pak.
41 C6 **Saigō** Japan
**Saigon** *see* **Hô Chi Minh**
35 H5 **Saiha** India
38 A1 **Saihan Toroi** China
41 C8 **Saijō** Japan
41 B8 **Saiki** Japan
39 □ **Sai Kung** *H.K.* China
7 V6 **Saimaa** *l.* Fin.
28 F2 **Saimbeyli** Turkey
30 D4 **Sā'īn** Iran
31 F4 **Saindak** Pak.
30 B2 **Sa'īndezh** Iran
10 F5 **St Abb's Head** *hd* U.K.
9 B7 **St Agnes** U.K.
9 A8 **St Agnes** *i.* U.K.
59 J4 **St Alban's** Can.
9 G6 **St Albans** U.K.
71 G2 **St Albans** *VT* U.S.A.
70 C5 **St Albans** *WV* U.S.A.
9 E7 **St Alban's Head** *hd* U.K.
56 G4 **St Albert** Can.
12 B4 **St-Amand-les-Eaux** France
14 F3 **St-Amand-Montrond** France
14 G3 **St-Amour** France
71 K2 **St Andrews** Can.
10 F4 **St Andrews** U.K.
75 J5 **St Ann's Bay** Jamaica
11 F6 **St Ann's Head** *hd* U.K.
59 J3 **St Anthony** Can.
62 E3 **St Anthony** U.S.A.
50 D4 **St Arnaud** Austr.
51 D5 **St Arnaud Range** *mts* N.Z.
59 J3 **St-Augustin** Can.
12 F4 **St Augustin** Ger.
67 D6 **St Augustine** U.S.A.
9 C7 **St Austell** U.K.
14 E3 **St-Avertin** France
12 E5 **St-Avold** France
75 M5 **St Barthélémy** *i.* Guadeloupe
8 D3 **St Bees** U.K.
8 D3 **St Bees Head** *hd* U.K.
9 B6 **St Bride's Bay** *b.* U.K.
14 C2 **St-Brieuc** France
73 G5 **St Carlos Lake** *l.* U.S.A.
69 H4 **St Catharines** Can.
67 D6 **St Catherines I.** *i.* U.S.A.
9 F7 **St Catherine's Point** *pt* U.K.
14 E4 **St-Céré** France
71 G2 **St-Césaire** Can.
14 G4 **St-Chamond** France
62 E3 **St Charles** *ID* U.S.A.
70 E5 **St Charles** *MD* U.S.A.
68 A4 **St Charles** *MN* U.S.A.
64 F4 **St Charles** *MO* U.S.A.
69 F4 **St Clair** U.S.A.
69 F4 **St Clair Shores** U.S.A.
14 G3 **St-Claude** France
9 C6 **St Clears** U.K.
64 E2 **St Cloud** U.S.A.
75 M5 **St Croix** *i.* Virgin Is
59 G4 **St Croix** *r.* Can.
68 A2 **St Croix** *r.* U.S.A.
68 A3 **St Croix Falls** U.S.A.
73 G6 **St David** U.S.A.
11 F6 **St David's** U.K.
9 B6 **St David's Head** *hd* U.K.
12 A6 **St-Denis** France
14 H2 **St-Dié** France
14 G2 **St-Dizier** France
57 K5 **Ste Anne** Can.
59 F4 **Ste-Anne-de-Beaupré** Can.
71 J1 **Sainte-Anne-de-Madawaska** Can.
69 K2 **Sainte-Anne-du-Lac** Can.
59 G3 **Ste Anne, L.** *l.* Can.
71 H1 **Ste-Camille-de-Lellis** Can.
14 G4 **St-Égrève** France
71 H1 **Sainte-Justine** Can.
71 J1 **St-Éleuthère** Can.
56 B2 **St Elias Mountains** Can.
59 G3 **Ste Marguerite** *r.* Can.
14 H5 **Ste-Maxime** France
14 D4 **Saintes** France
71 G2 **Ste-Thérèse** Can.
14 G4 **St-Étienne** France
71 F2 **St Eugene** Can.
71 G2 **St-Eustache** Can.
75 M5 **St Eustatius** *i.* Neth. Ant.
59 F4 **St-Félicien** Can.
11 F3 **Saintfield** U.K.
18 C3 **St-Florent** *Corsica* France
14 F3 **St-Florent-sur-Cher** France
88 C3 **St. Floris, Parc National** *nat. park* C.A.R.
64 C4 **St Francis** *KS* U.S.A.
71 J1 **St Francis** *ME* U.S.A.
71 J1 **St-Francis** *r.* Can./U.S.A.
65 F4 **St Francis** *r.* U.S.A.
59 K4 **St Francis, C.** *c.* Can.
71 J1 **St Froid Lake** *l.* U.S.A.
16 D7 **St Gallen** Switz.
14 E5 **St-Gaudens** France
71 H2 **St-Gédéon** Can.
48 F4 **St George** Austr.
71 K2 **St George** Can.
67 D5 **St George** *SC* U.S.A.
73 F3 **St George** *UT* U.S.A.
49 F2 **St George, C.** *pt* P.N.G.
67 C6 **St George I.** *i.* U.S.A.
62 A3 **St George, Pt** *pt* U.S.A.
59 J4 **St Georges** Can.
75 M6 **St George's** Grenada
59 J4 **St George's B.** *b.* Can.
48 F2 **St George's Channel** P.N.G.
9 A6 **St George's Channel** Rep. of Ireland/U.K.
9 C6 **St Govan's Head** *hd* U.K.
68 E3 **St Helen** U.S.A.
72 A2 **St Helena** U.S.A.
85 C7 **St Helena** *terr.* Atl. Ocean
90 C6 **St Helena Bay** S. Africa
90 C6 **St Helena Bay** *b.* S. Africa
96 J7 **St Helena Fracture** *sea feature* Atl. Ocean
9 E4 **St Helens** U.K.
62 B2 **St Helens** U.S.A.
62 B2 **St Helens, Mt** *volc.* U.S.A.
14 C2 **St Helier** *Channel Is* U.K.
12 D4 **St-Hubert** Belgium
58 F4 **St-Hyacinthe** Can.
68 E3 **St Ignace** U.S.A.
68 C1 **St Ignace I.** *i.* Can.
9 C6 **St Ishmael** U.K.
9 B7 **St Ives** *Eng.* U.K.
9 G5 **St Ives** *Eng.* U.K.
71 J1 **St-Jacques** Can.
68 E3 **St James** U.S.A.
56 C4 **St James, Cape** *pt* Can.
14 D4 **St-Jean-d'Angély** France
14 C3 **St-Jean-de-Monts** France
59 F4 **St-Jean, Lac** *l.* Can.
58 F4 **St-Jean-sur-Richelieu** Can.
58 F4 **St-Jérôme** Can.
62 C2 **St Joe** *r.* U.S.A.
59 G4 **St John** Can.
73 F1 **St John** U.S.A.
75 M5 **St John** *i.* Virgin Is
71 K2 **St John** *r.* Can./U.S.A.
75 M5 **St John's** Antigua
59 K4 **St John's** Can.
73 H4 **St Johns** *AZ* U.S.A.
68 E4 **St Johns** *MI* U.S.A.
67 D6 **St Johns** *r.* U.S.A.
71 H2 **St Johnsbury** U.S.A.
8 E3 **St John's Chapel** U.K.
59 F4 **St Joseph** Can.
68 D4 **St Joseph** *MI* U.S.A.
64 E4 **St Joseph** *MO* U.S.A.
68 E5 **St Joseph** *r.* U.S.A.
69 F2 **St Joseph I.** *i.* Can.
65 D7 **St Joseph I.** *i.* U.S.A.
58 B3 **St Joseph, Lac** *l.* Can.
58 F4 **St Jovité** Can.
14 E4 **St-Junien** France
9 B7 **St Just** U.K.
12 A5 **St-Just-en-Chaussée** France
9 B7 **St Keverne** U.K.
53 K8 **St Kitts-Nevis** *country* Caribbean Sea
12 B3 **St-Laureins** Belgium
79 H2 **St Laurent** Fr. Guiana
**St-Laurent, Golfe du** *g. see* **St Lawrence, Gulf of**
59 K4 **St Lawrence** *Nfld* Can.
59 G4 **St Lawrence** *in. Que.* Can.
59 H4 **St Lawrence, Gulf of** *g.* Can./U.S.A.
54 B3 **St Lawrence I.** *i. AK* U.S.A.
69 K3 **St Lawrence Islands National Park** Can.
71 F2 **St Lawrence Seaway** *chan.* Can./U.S.A.
59 G4 **St-Léonard** Can.
59 J3 **St Lewis** Can.
59 J3 **Saint Lewis** *r.* Can.
14 D2 **St-Lô** France
86 A3 **St Louis** Senegal
68 E4 **St Louis** *MI* U.S.A.
64 F4 **St Louis** *MO* U.S.A.
68 A2 **St Louis** *r.* U.S.A.
53 K8 **St Lucia** *country* Caribbean Sea
91 K4 **St Lucia Estuary** S. Africa
91 K3 **St Lucia, Lake** *l.* S. Africa
75 M5 **St Maarten** *i.* Neth. Ant.
10 □ **St Magnus Bay** *b.* U.K.
14 D3 **St-Maixent-l'École** France
14 C2 **St-Malo** France
14 C2 **St-Malo, Golfe de** *g.* France
91 G6 **St Marks** S. Africa
75 M5 **Saint Martin** *i.* Guadeloupe
90 B6 **St Martin, Cape** *hd* S. Africa
68 D3 **St Martin I.** *i.* U.S.A.
57 K4 **St Martin, L.** *l.* Can.
9 A8 **St Martin's** *i.* U.K.
35 H5 **St Martin's I.** *i.* Bangl.
50 B1 **St Mary Pk** *mt* Austr.
69 G4 **St Mary's** Can.
10 F2 **St Mary's** U.K.
70 A4 **St Marys** *OH* U.S.A.
70 D4 **St Marys** *PA* U.S.A.
70 C5 **Saint Marys** U.S.A.
9 A8 **St Mary's** *i.* U.K.
70 A4 **St Marys** *r.* U.S.A.
59 K4 **St Mary's, C.** *hd* Can.
54 A3 **St Matthew I.** *i. AK* U.S.A.
48 E2 **St Matthias Group** *is* P.N.G.
58 F4 **St Maurice** *r.* Can.
9 B7 **St Mawes** U.K.
14 D4 **St-Médard-en-Jalles** France
59 J3 **St Michaels Bay** *b.* Can.
16 D7 **St Moritz** Switz.
14 C3 **St-Nazaire** France
9 G5 **St Neots** U.K.
14 H2 **St-Nicolas-de-Port** France
12 C3 **St-Niklaas** Belgium
14 F1 **St-Omer** France
71 J1 **St-Pamphile** Can.
59 G4 **St Pascal** Can.
57 G4 **St Paul** Can.
68 A3 **St Paul** *MN* U.S.A.
64 D3 **St Paul** *NE* U.S.A.
70 B6 **St Paul** *VA* U.S.A.
93 K6 **St Paul, Île** *i.* Ind. Ocean
61 H3 **St Peter** *MN* U.S.A.
14 C2 **St Peter Port** *Channel Is* U.K.
20 D3 **St Petersburg** Rus. Fed.
67 D7 **St Petersburg** U.S.A.
59 J4 **St-Pierre** *St Pierre and Miquelon* N. America
14 G5 **St-Pierre** *mt* France
55 N5 **St Pierre and Miquelon** *terr.* N. America
14 D4 **St-Pierre-d'Oléron** France
58 F4 **St Pierre, Lac** *l.* Can.
14 F3 **St-Pierre-le-Moûtier** France
12 A4 **St-Pol-sur-Ternoise** France
16 G6 **St Pölten** Austria
14 F3 **St-Pourçain-sur-Sioule** France
71 H1 **Saint-Prosper** Can.
14 F2 **St-Quentin** France
14 H5 **St-Raphaël** France
71 F2 **St Regis** *r.* U.S.A.
71 F2 **St Regis Falls** U.S.A.
71 G2 **St-Rémi** Can.
71 H2 **St-Sébastien** Can.
59 G4 **St Siméon** Can.
67 D6 **St Simons I.** *i.* U.S.A.
71 K2 **St Stephen** Can.
67 E5 **St Stephen** U.S.A.
71 H2 **St-Théophile** Can.
57 L4 **St Theresa Point** Can.
69 G4 **St Thomas** Can.
14 H5 **St-Tropez** France
12 D4 **St-Truiden** Belgium
57 K5 **St Vincent** U.S.A.
53 K8 **St Vincent and the Grenadines** *country* Caribbean Sea
**St Vincent, Cape** *c. see* **São Vicente, Cabo de**
50 A3 **St. Vincent, Gulf** Austr.
12 E4 **St-Vith** Belgium
57 H4 **St Walburg** Can.
12 F5 **St Wendel** Ger.
69 G4 **St Williams** Can.
14 E4 **St-Yrieix-la-Perche** France
34 E3 **Saipal** *mt* Nepal
37 G5 **Saipan** *i.* N. Mariana Is
35 H5 **Saitlai** Myanmar
6 T3 **Saittanulkki** *h.* Fin.
39 □ **Sai Wan** *H.K.* China
78 E7 **Sajama, Nevado** *mt* Bol.
30 B5 **Sājir** S. Arabia
90 D5 **Sak** *watercourse* S. Africa
41 D7 **Sakai** Japan
41 C7 **Sakaide** Japan
41 C7 **Sakaiminato** Japan
32 B3 **Sakākah** S. Arabia
31 G5 **Saka Kalat** Pak.
64 C2 **Sakakawea, Lake** *l.* U.S.A.
58 E3 **Sakami** Can.
58 F3 **Sakami** *r.* Can.
58 E3 **Sakami, Lac** *l.* Can.
19 M4 **Sakar** *mts* Bulg.
28 C1 **Sakarya** Turkey
28 C1 **Sakarya** *r.* Turkey
40 F5 **Sakata** Japan
42 C3 **Sakchu** N. Korea
44 B2 **Sa Keo** *r.* Thai.
86 C4 **Sakété** Benin
36 G2 **Sakhalin** *i.* Rus. Fed.
36 G1 **Sakhalinskiy Zaliv** *b.* Rus. Fed.
34 C3 **Sakhi** India
91 H3 **Sakhile** S. Africa
30 C2 **Sakht-Sar** Iran
29 L1 **Şäki** Azer.
7 S9 **Šakiai** Lith.
34 A3 **Sakir** *mt* Pak.
36 E4 **Sakishima-guntō** *is* Japan
34 B4 **Sakrand** Pak.
44 □ **Sakra, P.** *i.* Sing.
90 D5 **Sakrivier** S. Africa
41 B9 **Sakura-jima** *volc.* Japan
21 E6 **Saky** Ukr.
7 S6 **Säkylä** Fin.
86 □ **Sal** *i.* Cape Verde
21 G6 **Sal** *r.* Rus. Fed.
7 S8 **Sala** Latvia
7 P7 **Sala** Sweden
58 F4 **Salaberry-de-Valleyfield** Can.
7 T8 **Salacgrīva** Latvia
18 F4 **Sala Consilina** Italy
73 E5 **Salada, Laguna** *salt l.* Mex.
83 E2 **Saladillo** *Buenos Aires* Arg.
83 D2 **Saladillo** *r. Córdoba* Arg.
83 E2 **Salado** *r. Buenos Aires* Arg.
83 C2 **Salado** *r. Mendoza/San Luis* Arg.
83 D4 **Salado** *r. Río Negro* Arg.
83 E1 **Salado** *r. Santa Fé* Arg.
74 E3 **Salado** *r.* Mex.
80 B3 **Salado, Quebrada de** *r.* Chile
86 B4 **Salaga** Ghana
90 F1 **Salajwe** Botswana
87 D3 **Salal** Chad
32 D6 **Şalālah** Oman
83 B1 **Salamanca** Chile
74 D4 **Salamanca** Mex.
15 D2 **Salamanca** Spain
70 D3 **Salamanca** U.S.A.
91 K3 **Salamanga** Moz.
30 B3 **Salamatabad** Iran
81 B3 **Salamina** Col.
28 F4 **Salamīyah** Syria
68 E5 **Salamonie** *r.* U.S.A.
68 E5 **Salamonie Lake** *l.* U.S.A.
35 F5 **Salandi** *r.* India
7 R8 **Salantai** Lith.
80 C2 **Salar de Arizaro** *salt flat* Arg.
80 C2 **Salar de Atacama** *salt flat* Chile
15 C1 **Salas** Spain
7 T8 **Salaspils** Latvia
37 F7 **Salawati** *i.* Indon.
34 B5 **Salaya** India
37 E7 **Salayar** *i.* Indon.
95 N7 **Sala y Gómez, Isla** *i.* Chile
83 D3 **Salazar** Arg.
7 T9 **Šalčininkai** Lith.
9 D7 **Salcombe** U.K.
15 D1 **Saldaña** Spain
81 B4 **Saldaña** *r.* Col.
90 B6 **Saldanha** S. Africa
90 B6 **Saldanha Bay** *b.* S. Africa
83 E3 **Saldungaray** Arg.
7 S8 **Saldus** Latvia
50 F5 **Sale** Austr.
29 L5 **Şālehābād** Iran
30 C3 **Şālehābād** Iran
24 H3 **Salekhard** Rus. Fed.
33 B4 **Salem** India
71 H3 **Salem** *MA* U.S.A.
65 F4 **Salem** *MO* U.S.A.
66 F4 **Salem** *NJ* U.S.A.
71 G3 **Salem** *NY* U.S.A.
70 C4 **Salem** *OH* U.S.A.
62 B2 **Salem** *OR* U.S.A.
66 D4 **Salem** *VA* U.S.A.
10 C4 **Salen** U.K.
10 C4 **Salen** U.K.
18 F4 **Salerno** Italy
18 F4 **Salerno, Golfo di** *g.* Italy
9 E4 **Salford** U.K.
79 L5 **Salgado** *r.* Brazil
17 J6 **Salgótarján** Hungary
79 L5 **Salgueiro** Brazil
31 F4 **Salian** Afgh.
43 C6 **Salibabu** *i.* Indon.
60 E4 **Salida** *CO* U.S.A.
14 D5 **Salies-de-Béarn** France
28 B2 **Salihli** Turkey
20 C4 **Salihorsk** Belarus
89 D5 **Salima** Malawi
89 D5 **Salimo** Moz.
64 D4 **Salina** *KS* U.S.A.
73 G2 **Salina** *UT* U.S.A.
74 E5 **Salina Cruz** Mex.
83 D4 **Salina Gualicho** *salt flat* Arg.
18 F5 **Salina, Isola** *i.* Italy
83 C2 **Salina Llancanelo** *salt flat* Arg.
82 D2 **Salinas** Brazil
78 B4 **Salinas** Ecuador
72 B3 **Salinas** *CA* U.S.A.
72 B3 **Salinas** *r. CA* U.S.A.
80 C4 **Salinas Grandes** *salt flat* Arg.
63 F5 **Salinas Peak** *summit* U.S.A.
65 E4 **Saline** *r. AR* U.S.A.
64 C4 **Saline** *r. KS* U.S.A.
15 H3 **Salines, Cap de ses** *pt* Spain
72 D3 **Saline Valley** *v.* U.S.A.
79 J4 **Salinópolis** Brazil

18 E5 San Vito, Capo c. Sicily Italy
39 C7 Sanya China
38 C3 Sanyuan China
42 C2 Sanyuanpu China
88 B4 Sanza Pombo Angola
82 C3 São Bernardo do Campo Brazil
80 E3 São Borja Brazil
82 C3 São Carlos Brazil
82 C1 São Domingos Brazil
82 B2 São Domingos r. Brazil
79 H6 São Félix Mato Grosso Brazil
79 H5 São Félix Pará Brazil
82 E3 São Fidélis Brazil
86 □ São Filipe Cape Verde
82 D1 São Francisco Brazil
79 L5 São Francisco r. Brazil
80 G3 São Francisco do Sul Brazil
83 F1 São Gabriel Brazil
82 D3 São Gonçalo Brazil
82 D2 São Gotardo Brazil
82 C1 São João da Aliança Brazil
82 E3 São João da Barra Brazil
82 C3 São João da Boa Vista Brazil
15 B2 São João da Madeira Port.
82 D1 São João do Paraíso Brazil
82 D3 São João Nepomuceno Brazil
82 C3 São Joaquim da Barra Brazil
81 D5 São José Brazil
82 E3 São José do Calçado Brazil
83 G2 São José do Norte Brazil
82 C3 São José do Rio Preto Brazil
82 D3 São José dos Campos Brazil
82 C4 São José dos Pinhais Brazil
82 D3 São Lourenço Brazil
82 A2 São Lourenço r. Brazil
83 G1 São Lourenço do Sul Brazil
79 K4 São Luís Brazil
82 C3 São Manuel Brazil
82 C2 São Marcos r. Brazil
79 K4 São Marcos, Baía de b. Brazil
82 E2 São Mateus Brazil
82 E2 São Mateus r. Brazil
82 C2 São Miguel r. Brazil
14 G3 Saône r. France
86 □ São Nicolau i. Cape Verde
82 C3 São Paulo Brazil
82 C3 São Paulo div. Brazil
96 H5 São Pedro e São Paulo is Atl. Ocean
79 K5 São Raimundo Nonato Brazil
82 D2 São Romão Brazil
79 L5 São Roque, Cabo de pt Brazil
82 C3 São Sebastião do Paraíso Brazil
82 D3 São Sebastião, Ilha de i. Brazil
83 G1 São Sepé Brazil
82 B2 São Simão Brazil
82 B2 São Simão, Barragem de resr Brazil
37 E6 Sao-Siu Indon.
86 □ São Tiago i. Cape Verde
86 C4 São Tomé i. Sao Tome and Principe
85 D5 São Tomé and Príncipe country Africa
82 E3 São Tomé, Cabo de c. Brazil
82 C3 São Vicente Brazil
86 □ São Vicente i. Cape Verde
15 B4 São Vicente, Cabo de c. Port.
28 C1 Sapanca Turkey
48 C2 Saparua Indon.
28 C2 Şaphane Dağı mt Turkey
86 B4 Sapo National Park Liberia
40 G3 Sapporo Japan
18 F4 Sapri Italy
45 D4 Sapudi i. Indon.
65 D4 Sapulpa U.S.A.
31 E3 Sāqī Iran
30 B2 Saqqez Iran
30 B2 Sarāb Iran
29 L5 Sarābe Meymeh Iran
44 B2 Sara Buri Thai.
Saragossa see Zaragoza
78 C4 Saraguro Ecuador
19 H3 Sarajevo Bos.-Herz.
31 F2 Sarakhs Iran
26 D1 Saraktash Rus. Fed.
35 H4 Saramati mt India
71 G2 Saranac r. U.S.A.
71 F2 Saranac Lake U.S.A.
58 E5 Saranac Lakes l. U.S.A.
19 J5 Sarandë Albania
83 F2 Sarandí del Yí Uru.
83 F2 Sarandí Grande Uru.
43 C5 Sarangani i. Phil.
43 C5 Sarangani Bay b. Phil.
43 C5 Sarangani Islands is Phil.
43 C5 Sarangani Str. chan. Phil.
45 D3 Saran, Gunung mt Indon.
20 H4 Saransk Rus. Fed.
24 G4 Sarapul Rus. Fed.
81 C3 Sarare r. Venez.
67 D7 Sarasota U.S.A.
34 B5 Saraswati r. India
21 D6 Sarata Ukr.
62 F3 Saratoga U.S.A.
71 G3 Saratoga Springs U.S.A.
45 D2 Saratok Malaysia
21 H5 Saratov Rus. Fed.
21 H5 Saratovskaya Oblast' div. Rus. Fed.
20 J4 Saratovskoye Vdkhr. resr Rus. Fed.
31 F5 Saravan Iran
44 C2 Saravan Laos
44 A2 Sarawa r. Myanmar
45 D2 Sarawak div. Malaysia
28 A1 Saray Turkey
28 B3 Sarayköy Turkey
28 D2 Sarayönü Turkey
31 F5 Sarbāz Iran
31 F5 Sarbāz r. Iran
31 E3 Sarbīsheh Iran
18 D2 Sarca r. Italy
29 M3 Sarcham Iran
34 E3 Sarda r. India/Nepal
35 E3 Sarda r. Nepal
34 C3 Sardarshahr India
29 M5 Sardasht Iran
30 B2 Sar Dasht Iran
Sardegna i. see Sardinia
81 B2 Sardinata Col.
18 C4 Sardinia i. Sardinia Italy
29 L3 Sardrūd Iran
30 C5 Sareb, Rās-as pt U.A.E.
6 P3 Sareks Nationalpark nat. park Sweden
6 P3 Sarektjåkkå mt Sweden
31 G2 Sar-e Pol Afgh.
30 B3 Sar-e-Pol-e-Zahāb Iran
30 D4 Sare Yazd Iran
96 E4 Sargasso Sea sea Atl. Ocean
34 C2 Sargodha Pak.
87 D4 Sarh Chad
30 D2 Sārī Iran
19 M7 Saria i. Greece
28 B2 Sarıgöl Turkey
29 J1 Sarıkamış Turkey
28 D3 Sarıkavak Turkey
34 D4 Sarila India
44 □ Sarimbun Res. resr Sing.
48 E4 Sarina Austr.
28 E2 Sarıoğlan Turkey
31 G3 Sar-i-Pul Afgh.
87 D2 Sarīr Tibesti des. Libya
29 J2 Sarısu Turkey
42 C4 Sariwŏn N. Korea
28 C2 Sarıyar Barajı resr Turkey
28 B1 Sarıyer Turkey
28 F2 Sarız Turkey
34 E4 Sarju r. India
27 F2 Sarkand Kazak.
34 B4 Sarkāri Tala India
28 C2 Şarkikaraağaç Turkey
28 F2 Şarkışla Turkey
21 C7 Şarköy Turkey
31 G4 Sarlath Range mts Afgh./Pak.
14 E4 Sarlat-la-Canéda France
37 F7 Sarmi Indon.
7 N6 Särna Sweden
29 L5 Sarneh Iran
18 C1 Sarnen Switz.
69 F4 Sarnia Can.
21 C5 Sarny Ukr.
45 B3 Sarolangun Indon.
40 H2 Saroma-ko l. Japan
19 K6 Saronikos Kolpos g. Greece
21 C7 Saros Körfezi b. Turkey
34 C4 Sarotra India
20 G4 Sarova Rus. Fed.
31 H3 Sarowbī Afgh.
21 H6 Sarpa, Ozero l. Kalmykiya Rus. Fed.
21 H5 Sarpa, Ozero l. Volgograd. Rus. Fed.
7 M7 Sarpsborg Norway
14 H2 Sarrebourg France
12 F5 Sarreguemines France
15 C1 Sarria Spain
15 F2 Sarrión Spain
12 C6 Sarry France
18 C4 Sartène Corsica France
30 C3 Sarud r. Iran
31 G5 Saruna Pak.
29 M4 Saruq Iran
29 K2 Şärur Azer.
31 F4 Ṡaru Tara Afgh.
29 L4 Sarvabad Iran
16 H7 Sárvár Hungary
30 D4 Sarvestān Iran
32 E1 Sarykamyshkoye Ozero salt l. Turkm.
27 F2 Saryozek Kazak.
27 F2 Saryshagan Kazak.
27 F3 Sary-Tash Kyrg.
31 F2 Sary Yazikskoye Vdkhr. resr Turkm.
73 G6 Sasabe U.S.A.
35 F4 Sasaram India
41 A8 Sasebo Japan
57 H4 Saskatchewan div. Can.
57 J4 Saskatchewan r. Can.
57 H4 Saskatoon Can.
25 N2 Saskylakh Rus. Fed.
91 G3 Sasolburg S. Africa
20 G4 Sasovo Rus. Fed.
71 F5 Sassafras U.S.A.
86 B4 Sassandra Côte d'Ivoire
18 C4 Sassari Sardinia Italy
13 G3 Sassenberg Ger.
16 F3 Sassnitz Ger.
21 H6 Sasykoli Rus. Fed.
86 A3 Satadougou Mali
41 B9 Sata-misaki c. Japan
34 C5 Satana India
33 A2 Satara India
91 J2 Satara S. Africa
21 G4 Satinka Rus. Fed.
35 G5 Satkhira Bangl.
33 B2 Satmala Range h. India
34 E4 Satna India
34 C5 Satpura Range mts India
41 B9 Satsuma-hantō pen. Japan
13 J5 Satteldorf Ger.
34 D2 Satti Jammu and Kashmir
17 L7 Satu Mare Romania
44 B4 Satun Thai.
83 E1 Sauce Arg.
65 C7 Sauceda Mex.
73 F5 Sauceda Mts mts U.S.A.
7 K7 Sauda Norway
6 D4 Sauðárkrókur Iceland
23 D7 Saudi Arabia country Asia
13 F3 Sauerland reg. Ger.
68 D4 Saugatuck U.S.A.
71 G3 Saugerties U.S.A.
64 E2 Sauk Center U.S.A.
68 C4 Sauk City U.S.A.
14 G3 Saulieu France
69 E2 Sault Ste Marie Can.
68 E2 Sault Ste Marie U.S.A.
37 F7 Saumlakki Indon.
14 D3 Saumur France
92 A4 Saunders Coast coastal area Ant.
92 C1 Saunders I. i. Atl. Ocean
35 F4 Saura r. India
89 C4 Saurimo Angola
19 J2 Sava r. Europe
49 J3 Savaii i. Western Samoa
21 G5 Savala r. Rus. Fed.
86 C4 Savalou Benin
Savanat see Eşţahbānāt
68 B4 Savanna U.S.A.
67 D6 Savannah GA U.S.A.
67 B5 Savannah TN U.S.A.
67 D5 Savannah r. U.S.A.
67 E7 Savannah Sound Bahamas
44 C1 Savannakhét Laos
75 J5 Savanna la Mar Jamaica
58 B3 Savant Lake Can.
33 A3 Savanur India
6 R5 Sävar Sweden
19 M5 Savaştepe Turkey
86 C4 Savè Benin
89 D6 Save r. Moz.
30 C3 Sāveh Iran
6 V5 Saviaho Fin.
24 F3 Savinskiy Rus. Fed.
14 H4 Savoie reg. France
18 C2 Savona Italy
7 V6 Savonlinna Fin.
6 V5 Savonranta Fin.
29 J1 Şavşat Turkey
7 O8 Sävsjö Sweden
6 V3 Savukoski Fin.
29 H3 Savur Turkey
34 D4 Sawai Madhopur India
44 A1 Sawankhalok Thai.
63 F4 Sawatch Mts mts U.S.A.
10 A6 Sawel Mt h. U.K.
68 B2 Sawtooth Mountains h. U.S.A.
37 E7 Sawu Sea g. Indon.
9 G4 Saxilby U.K.
9 J5 Saxmundham U.K.
6 O4 Saxnäs Sweden
36 B1 Sayano-Shushenskoye Vdkhr. resr Rus. Fed.
31 F2 Sayat Turkm.
32 D6 Sayḥūt Yemen
21 H5 Saykhin Kazak.
88 E3 Saylac Somalia
36 D2 Saynshand Mongolia
15 F1 Sayoa mt Spain
42 E2 Sayon Rus. Fed.
65 D5 Sayre OK U.S.A.
70 E4 Sayre PA U.S.A.
34 C2 Sazin Pak.
23 E3 Sazonovo Rus. Fed.
86 B2 Sbaa Alg.
86 C1 Sbeitla Tunisia
8 D3 Scafell Pike mt U.K.
10 B4 Scalasaig U.K.
18 F5 Scalea Italy
10 □ Scalloway U.K.
11 C5 Scalp h. Rep. of Ireland
10 C3 Scalpay i. Scot. U.K.
10 B3 Scalpay i. Scot. U.K.
10 A5 Scalp Mountain h. Rep. of Ireland
10 E2 Scapa Flow in. U.K.
10 C4 Scarba i. U.K.
69 H4 Scarborough Can.
81 E2 Scarborough Trinidad and Tobago
8 G3 Scarborough U.K.
43 A3 Scarborough Shoal sand bank Phil.
10 A2 Scarp i. U.K.
Scarpanto i. see Karpathos
13 J1 Schaale r. Ger.
13 J1 Schaalsee l. Ger.
12 C4 Schaerbeek Belgium
16 D7 Schaffhausen Switz.
13 K3 Schafstädt Ger.
12 C2 Schagen Neth.
12 C2 Schagerbrug Neth.
90 B3 Schakalskuppe Namibia
31 F4 Schao watercourse Afgh./Iran
16 F6 Schärding Austria
12 B3 Scharendijke Neth.
13 J5 Schebheim Ger.
13 H1 Scheeßel Ger.
59 G3 Schefferville Can.
12 C3 Schelde r. Belgium
73 E2 Schell Creek Range mts U.S.A.
13 J2 Schellerten Ger.
71 G3 Schenectady U.S.A.
13 H1 Schenefeld Ger.
12 C2 Schermerhorn Neth.
10 D4 Schiehallion mt U.K.
13 L6 Schierling Ger.
12 E1 Schiermonnikoog Neth.
12 E1 Schiermonnikoog i. Neth.
12 E1 Schiermonnikoog Nationaal Park nat. park Neth.
13 G1 Schiffdorf Ger.
13 K1 Schilde r. Ger.
12 D4 Schinnen Neth.
18 D2 Schio Italy
13 L3 Schkeuditz Ger.
13 L4 Schleiden Ger.
13 K4 Schleiz Ger.
16 D3 Schleswig Ger.
13 H1 Schleswig-Holstein div. Ger.
13 J4 Schleusingen Ger.
13 H4 Schlitz Ger.
13 G3 Schloß Holte-Stukenbrock Ger.
13 H4 Schlüchtern Ger.
13 J5 Schlüsselfeld Ger.
13 G3 Schmallenberg Ger.
13 L4 Schneeberg Ger.
13 K3 Schneidlingen Ger.
13 H1 Schneverdingen Ger.
71 G3 Schodack Center U.S.A.
68 C3 Schofield U.S.A.
72 □1 Schofield Barracks U.S.A.
13 L1 Schönebeck Ger.
13 K2 Schönebeck (Elbe) Ger.
13 J2 Schöningen Ger.
13 H5 Schöntal Ger.
71 J2 Schoodic Lake l. U.S.A.
68 E4 Schoolcraft U.S.A.
12 C3 Schoonhoven Neth.
13 J5 Schopfloch Ger.
13 J2 Schöppenstedt Ger.
13 F1 Schortens Ger.
48 E2 Schouten Islands is P.N.G.
68 D1 Schreiber Can.
71 G3 Schroon Lake l. U.S.A.
73 F5 Schuchuli U.S.A.
11 B6 Schull Rep. of Ireland
57 K2 Schultz Lake l. Can.
72 C2 Schurz U.S.A.
12 F2 Schüttorf Ger.
71 G3 Schuylerville U.S.A.
13 K5 Schwabach Ger.
13 H5 Schwäbisch Hall Ger.
16 E6 Schwabmünchen Ger.
13 G2 Schwaförden Ger.
13 H4 Schwalmstadt-Ziegenhain Ger.
13 L5 Schwandorf Ger.
45 D3 Schwaner, Pegunungan mts Indon.
13 G1 Schwanewede Ger.
13 G1 Schwarmstedt Ger.
13 M3 Schwarze Elster r. Ger.
13 J1 Schwarzenbek Ger.
13 L4 Schwarzenberg Ger.
12 E4 Schwarzer Mann h. Ger.
90 B2 Schwarzrand mts Namibia
16 F7 Schwaz Austria
16 G4 Schwedt Ger.
13 G5 Schwegenheim Ger.
12 E5 Schweich Ger.
13 J4 Schweinfurt Ger.
13 M3 Schweinitz Ger.
13 L1 Schweinrich Ger.
91 F3 Schweizer-Reneke S. Africa
12 F3 Schwelm Ger.
16 D6 Schwenningen Ger.
13 K1 Schwerin Ger.
13 K1 Schweriner See l. Ger.
13 G5 Schwetzingen Ger.
16 D7 Schwyz Switz.
18 E6 Sciacca Sicily Italy
9 A8 Scilly, Isles of is U.K.
70 B5 Scioto r. U.S.A.
73 F2 Scipio U.S.A.
62 F1 Scobey U.S.A.
9 J5 Scole U.K.
50 H2 Scone Austr.
55 Q2 Scoresby Land reg. Greenland
55 Q2 Scoresby Sund chan. Greenland
96 F9 Scotia Ridge sea feature Atl. Ocean
96 F9 Scotia Sea sea Atl. Ocean
69 G4 Scotland Can.
10 D4 Scotland div. U.K.
92 B5 Scott Base N.Z. Base Ant.
91 J5 Scottburgh S. Africa
56 D4 Scott, C. c. Can.
64 C4 Scott City U.S.A.
92 B5 Scott Coast coastal area Ant.
70 D4 Scottdale U.S.A.
92 B4 Scott Gl. gl. Ant.
55 L2 Scott Inlet in. Can.
92 A5 Scott Island i. Ant.
57 H3 Scott Lake l. Can.
92 B4 Scott Mts mts Ant.
64 C3 Scottsbluff U.S.A.
67 C5 Scottsboro U.S.A.
66 C4 Scottsburg U.S.A.
63 E5 Scottsdale U.S.A.
72 A3 Scotts Valley U.S.A.
68 D4 Scottville U.S.A.
72 D3 Scotty's Junction U.S.A.
10 C2 Scourie U.K.
10 □ Scousburgh U.K.
10 E2 Scrabster U.K.
71 F4 Scranton U.S.A.
10 B4 Scridain, Loch in. U.K.
8 G4 Scunthorpe U.K.
9 H7 Seaford U.K.
71 F5 Seaford U.S.A.
69 G4 Seaforth Can.
43 A4 Seahorse Bank sand bank Phil.
57 K3 Seal r. Can.
50 D3 Sea Lake Austr.
90 E7 Seal, Cape pt S. Africa
71 J3 Seal I. i. U.S.A.
59 H3 Seal Lake l. Can.
90 F7 Seal Point pt S. Africa
73 E3 Seaman Range mts U.S.A.
8 G3 Seamer U.K.
73 E4 Searchlight U.S.A.
65 F5 Searcy U.S.A.
72 D4 Searles Lake l. U.S.A.
68 E4 Sears U.S.A.
71 J2 Searsport U.S.A.
72 B3 Seaside CA U.S.A.
62 B2 Seaside OR U.S.A.
10 D3 Seaton Eng. U.K.
8 D3 Seaton U.K.
62 B2 Seattle U.S.A.
71 F5 Seaville U.S.A.
71 H3 Sebago Lake l. U.S.A.
74 B3 Sebastián Vizcaíno, Bahía b. Mex.
71 J2 Sebasticook r. U.S.A.
45 E2 Sebatik i. Indon.
28 C1 Seben Turkey
19 K2 Sebeş Romania
45 C4 Sebesi i. Indon.
69 F4 Sebewaing U.S.A.
20 D3 Sebezh Rus. Fed.
28 E3 Sebil Turkey
28 G1 Şebinkarahisar Turkey
71 J2 Seboeis Lake l. U.S.A.
71 J2 Seboomook U.S.A.
71 J2 Seboomook Lake l. U.S.A.
67 D7 Sebring U.S.A.
21 G5 Sebrovo Rus. Fed.
78 B5 Sechura Peru
78 B5 Sechura, Bahía de b. Peru
13 H5 Seckach Ger.
71 H2 Second Lake l. U.S.A.
51 A6 Secretary Island i. N.Z.
91 H3 Secunda S. Africa
33 B2 Secunderabad India
64 E4 Sedalia U.S.A.
33 B2 Sedam India
50 B3 Sedan Austr.
14 G2 Sedan France
51 E4 Seddon N.Z.
51 C4 Seddonville N.Z.
31 E3 Sedeh Iran
71 J2 Sedgwick U.S.A.
86 A3 Sédhiou Senegal
16 G6 Sedlčany Czech Rep.
28 E6 Sedom Israel
73 G4 Sedona U.S.A.
18 B6 Sédrata Alg.
7 S9 Šeduva Lith.
13 J1 Seedorf Ger.
11 D5 Seefin h. Rep. of Ireland
13 K2 Seehausen Ger.
13 K2 Seehausen (Altmark) Ger.
89 B6 Seeheim Namibia
13 G5 Seeheim-Jugenheim Ger.
90 E6 Seekoegat S. Africa
73 E5 Seeley U.S.A.
92 B3 Seelig, Mt mt Ant.
13 H2 Seelze Ger.
14 E2 Sées France
13 J3 Seesen Ger.
13 J1 Seevetal Ger.
86 A4 Sefadu Sierra Leone
91 G1 Sefare Botswana
19 M5 Seferihisar Turkey
91 G1 Sefophe Botswana
7 M6 Segalstad Norway
43 A5 Segama r. Malaysia
45 B2 Segamat Malaysia
13 L2 Segeletz Ger.
20 E2 Segezha Rus. Fed.
15 F3 Segorbe Spain
86 B3 Ségou Mali
81 B3 Segovia Col.
15 D2 Segovia Spain
Segovia r. see Coco
20 E2 Segozerskoye, Oz. resr Rus. Fed.
15 G1 Segre r. Spain
87 D2 Séguédine Niger
86 B4 Séguéla Côte d'Ivoire
65 D6 Seguin U.S.A.
83 D1 Segundo r. Arg.
15 F3 Segura r. Spain
89 C6 Sehithwa Botswana
91 H4 Sehlabathebe National Park Lesotho
34 D5 Sehore India
6 S1 Seiland i. Norway
65 D4 Seiling U.S.A.
6 S5 Seinäjoki Fin.
58 B4 Seine r. Can.
14 E2 Seine r. France
14 D2 Seine, Baie de b. France
14 F2 Seine, Val de v. France
17 L3 Sejny Pol.
45 B3 Sekayu Indon.
90 F2 Sekhutlane watercourse Botswana
90 E2 Sekoma Botswana
86 B4 Sekondi Ghana
31 F4 Sekūheh Iran
44 D5 Sekura Indon.
62 B2 Selah U.S.A.
37 F7 Selaru i. Indon.
45 D3 Selatan, Tanjung pt Indon.
44 □ Selat Johor chan. Malaysia/Sing.
44 □ Selat Jurong chan. Sing.
44 □ Selat Pandan chan. Sing.
54 B3 Selawik U.S.A.
13 L4 Selb Ger.
6 L5 Selbekken Norway
6 M5 Selbu Norway
8 F4 Selby U.K.
64 C2 Selby U.S.A.
89 C6 Selebi-Phikwe Botswana
36 F1 Selemdzhinsky Khr. mts Rus. Fed.
28 B2 Selendi Turkey
14 H2 Sélestat France
44 □ Seletar Sing.
44 □ Seletar, P. i. Sing.
44 □ Seletar Res. resr Sing.
27 F1 Seletyteniz, Ozero l. Kazak.
Seleucia Pieria see Samandağı
64 C2 Selfridge U.S.A.
20 J2 Selib Rus. Fed.
86 A3 Sélibabi Maur.
13 G4 Seligenstadt Ger.
20 E3 Seliger, Oz. l. Rus. Fed.
73 F4 Seligman U.S.A.
87 E2 Selima Oasis oasis Sudan
69 J5 Selinsgrove U.S.A.
17 Q2 Selishche Rus. Fed.
21 H6 Selitrennoye Rus. Fed.
17 Q2 Selizharovo Rus. Fed.
7 L7 Seljord Norway
13 K3 Selke r. Ger.
57 K4 Selkirk Can.
10 F5 Selkirk U.K.
56 F4 Selkirk Mountains Can.
8 D3 Sellafield U.K.
73 G6 Sells U.S.A.
12 F3 Selm Ger.
67 C5 Selma AL U.S.A.
72 C3 Selma CA U.S.A.
67 B5 Selmer U.S.A.
31 F4 Selseleh-ye Pīr Shūrān mts Iran
9 G7 Selsey Bill hd U.K.
44 C4 Seluan i. Indon.
78 D5 Selvas reg. Brazil
57 J3 Selwyn Lake l. Can.
56 C2 Selwyn Mountains Can.
54 E3 Selwyn Mts Can.
48 D4 Selwyn Range h. Austr.
45 D4 Semarang Indon.
45 C2 Sematan Malaysia
45 E3 Semayang, Danau l. Indon.
43 A6 Sembakung r. Indon.
44 □ Sembawang Sing.
88 B3 Sembé Congo
29 K3 Şemdinli Turkey
45 D4 Semenanjung Blambangan pen. Indon.
21 E4 Semenivka Ukr.
20 H3 Semenov Rus. Fed.
21 G6 Semikarakorsk Rus. Fed.
21 F5 Semiluki Rus. Fed.
62 F3 Seminoe Res. resr U.S.A.
65 C5 Seminole U.S.A.
67 C6 Seminole, L. l. U.S.A.
27 G1 Semipalatinsk Kazak.
43 B3 Semirara i. Phil.
43 B4 Semirara Islands is Phil.
30 C4 Semīrom Iran
30 D3 Semnān Iran
12 D5 Semois r. Belgium
12 D5 Semois, Vallée de la v. Belgium/France
45 E2 Semporna Malaysia
45 D4 Sempu i. Indon.
43 A5 Senaja Malaysia
21 G7 Senaki Georgia
78 E5 Sena Madureira Brazil
33 C5 Senanayake Samudra l. Sri Lanka
89 C5 Senanga Zambia
40 G5 Sendai Japan
41 B9 Sendai Japan
35 H3 Sêndo China
44 B5 Senebui, Tanjung pt Indon.
73 G5 Seneca AZ U.S.A.
68 C5 Seneca IL U.S.A.
62 C2 Seneca OR U.S.A.
70 E3 Seneca Falls U.S.A.
70 E3 Seneca Lake l. U.S.A.
70 D5 Seneca Rocks U.S.A.
70 C5 Senecaville Lake l. U.S.A.
85 B4 Senegal country Africa
86 A3 Sénégal r. Maur./Senegal
91 G4 Senekal S. Africa
68 E2 Seney U.S.A.
16 G5 Senftenberg Ger.
34 D4 Sengar r. India
88 D4 Sengerema Tanz.
20 J4 Sengiley Rus. Fed.
79 K6 Senhor do Bonfim Brazil
18 E3 Senigallia Italy
18 F2 Senj Croatia
6 P2 Senja i. Norway
29 J1 Şenkaya Turkey
34 D2 Senku Jammu and Kashmir
90 E2 Senlac S. Africa
42 F2 Senlin Shan mt China
14 F2 Senlis France
44 C2 Senmonorom Cambodia
9 B7 Sennen U.K.
69 J1 Senneterre Can.
91 H5 Senqu r. Lesotho
14 F2 Sens France
12 B4 Sensée r. France
74 G6 Sensuntepeque El Salvador
19 J2 Senta Yugo.
34 D3 Senthal India
73 F5 Sentinel U.S.A.
56 E3 Sentinel Pk summit Can.
92 B3 Sentinel Ra. mts Ant.
44 □ Sentosa i. Sing.
29 H3 Şenyurt Turkey
34 D5 Seoni India
35 E5 Seorinarayan India
42 D5 Seoul S. Korea
51 D4 Separation Pt pt N.Z.
29 L4 Separ Shāhābād Iran
83 D3 Sepetiba, Baía de b. Brazil
30 C4 Sepīdān Iran
48 E2 Sepik r. P.N.G.
42 D4 Sep'o N. Korea
59 G3 Sept-Îles Can.
72 C3 Sequoia National Park U.S.A.
29 L3 Serā Iran
21 G5 Serafimovich Rus. Fed.
31 F2 Serakhs Turkm.
37 E7 Seram i. Indon.
37 F7 Seram Sea g. Indon.
45 C4 Serang Indon.
44 □ Serangoon Harbour chan. Sing.
44 D5 Serasan i. Indon.
44 D5 Serasan, Selat chan. Indon.
44 D5 Seraya i. Indon.
44 □ Seraya, P. i. Sing.
19 J3 Serbia div. Yugo.
Serdar see Kaypak
88 E2 Serdo Eth.
21 H4 Serdoba r. Rus. Fed.
21 H4 Serdobsk Rus. Fed.
20 D3 Seredka Rus. Fed.
28 D2 Şereflikoçhisar Turkey
45 B2 Seremban Malaysia
88 D4 Serengeti National Park Tanz.
89 D5 Serenje Zambia
20 H4 Sergach Rus. Fed.
40 C3 Sergeyevka Rus. Fed.
20 F3 Sergiyev Posad Rus. Fed.
45 D2 Seria Brunei
45 D2 Serian Malaysia
19 L6 Serifos i. Greece
59 G2 Sérigny, Lac l. Can.
28 C3 Serik Turkey
37 E7 Sermata, Kepulauan is Indon.
20 J3 Sernur Rus. Fed.
31 E2 Sernyy Zavod Turkm.
21 H6 Seroglazka Rus. Fed.
24 H4 Serov Rus. Fed.
89 C6 Serowe Botswana
15 C4 Serpa Port.
81 E2 Serpent's Mouth chan. Trinidad/Venez.
20 F4 Serpukhov Rus. Fed.
82 C3 Serra da Canastra, Parque Nacional da nat. park Brazil
81 D4 Serranía de la Neblina, Parque Nacional nat. park Venez.

73 G6 Sonoita U.S.A.
73 F6 Sonoita r. Mex.
72 B3 Sonora CA U.S.A.
65 C6 Sonora TX U.S.A.
60 D6 Sonora div. Mex.
74 B3 Sonora r. Mex.
73 F6 Sonoyta Mex.
30 B3 Sonqor Iran
81 B3 Sonsón Col.
74 G6 Sonsonate El Salvador
39 B6 Sơn Tây Vietnam
91 H5 Sonwabile S. Africa
83 F1 Sopas r. Uru.
25 S4 Sopka Shiveluch mt Rus. Fed.
87 E4 Sopo watercourse Sudan
19 L3 Sopot Bulg.
17 J3 Sopot Pol.
16 H7 Sopron Hungary
18 E4 Sora Italy
35 F6 Sorada India
7 P5 Soråker Sweden
42 E4 Sŏraksan mt S. Korea
58 F4 Sorel Can.
46 E6 Sorell Austr.
28 E2 Sorgun Turkey
15 E2 Soria Spain
24 C2 Sørkappøya i. Svalbard
30 D3 Sorkheh Iran
30 D3 Sorkh, Kūh-e mts Iran
6 N4 Sørli Norway
35 F5 Soro India
21 D5 Soroca Moldova
82 C3 Sorocaba Brazil
24 G4 Sorochinsk Rus. Fed.
36 G6 Sorol i. Micronesia
37 F7 Sorong Indon.
88 D3 Soroti Uganda
6 S1 Sørøya i. Norway
15 B3 Sorraia r. Port.
6 O2 Sorreisa Norway
50 E5 Sorrento Austr.
89 B6 Sorris Sorris Namibia
92 D3 Sør-Rondane mts Ant.
6 P4 Sorsele Sweden
43 C3 Sorsogon Phil.
20 D2 Sortavala Rus. Fed.
6 O2 Sortland Norway
20 J2 Sortopolovskaya Rus. Fed.
20 J3 Sorvizhi Rus. Fed.
42 D5 Sŏsan S. Korea
91 H2 Soshanguve S. Africa
21 F4 Sosna r. Rus. Fed.
83 C2 Sosneado mt Arg.
20 K2 Sosnogorsk Rus. Fed.
20 H2 Sosnovka Archangel. Rus. Fed.
20 G4 Sosnovka Tambov. Rus. Fed.
24 F3 Sosnovka Rus. Fed.
6 X4 Sosnovyy Rus. Fed.
7 V7 Sosnovyy Bor Rus. Fed.
17 J5 Sosnowiec Pol.
21 F6 Sosyka r. Rus. Fed.
81 A4 Sotara, Volcán volc. Col.
6 V4 Sotkamo Fin.
83 D1 Soto Arg.
74 E4 Soto la Marina Mex.
88 B3 Souanké Congo
86 B4 Soubré Côte d'Ivoire
71 F4 Souderton U.S.A.
19 M4 Soufli Greece
14 E4 Souillac France
12 D5 Souilly France
86 C1 Souk Ahras Alg.
Sŏul see Seoul
14 D5 Soulom France
Soûr see Tyre
15 H4 Sour el Ghozlane Alg.
57 J5 Souris Man. Can.
59 H4 Souris P.E.I. Can.
57 J5 Souris r. Can./U.S.A.
79 L5 Sousa Brazil
86 D1 Sousse Tunisia
14 D5 Soustons France
32 C7 South div. Yemen
85 F9 South Africa, Republic of country Africa
69 G3 Southampton Can.
9 F7 Southampton U.K.
71 G4 Southampton U.S.A.
55 K3 Southampton I. Can.
57 M2 Southampton Island i. Can.
70 E6 South Anna r. U.S.A.
9 F4 South Anston U.K.
59 H2 South Aulatsivik Island i. Can.
48 D5 South Australia div. Austr.
93 N6 South Australian Basin sea feature Ind. Ocean
65 F5 Southaven U.S.A.
63 F5 South Baldy mt U.S.A.
8 F3 South Bank U.K.
70 B4 South Bass I. i. U.S.A.
57 N2 South Bay b. Can.
69 F3 South Baymouth Can.
68 D5 South Bend IN U.S.A.
62 B2 South Bend WA U.S.A.
67 E7 South Bight chan. Bahamas
70 D6 South Boston U.S.A.
51 D5 Southbridge N.Z.
71 G3 Southbridge U.S.A.
South Cape c. see Ka Lae
67 D5 South Carolina div. U.S.A.
71 J2 South China U.S.A.
45 C1 South China Sea sea Pac. Oc.
64 C2 South Dakota div. U.S.A.
71 G3 South Deerfield U.S.A.
9 G7 South Downs h. U.K.
91 F2 South East div. Botswana
50 F5 South East Cape Vic. Austr.
48 E6 South East Cape c. Austr.
95 N10 South-East Pacific Basin sea feature Pac. Oc.
57 J3 Southend Can.
10 C5 Southend U.K.
9 H6 Southend-on-Sea U.K.
68 A5 South English U.S.A.
51 C5 Southern Alps mts N.Z.
48 B5 Southern Cross Austr.
57 K3 Southern Indian Lake l. Can.
87 E4 Southern National Park Sudan
47 C7 Southern Ocean ocean
67 E5 Southern Pines U.S.A.
92 C1 Southern Thule I. i. Atl. Ocean
10 D5 Southern Uplands reg. U.K.
10 F4 South Esk r. U.K.
68 B6 South Fabius r. U.S.A.
94 G7 South Fiji Basin sea feature Pac. Oc.
63 F4 South Fork U.S.A.
72 A2 South Fork Eel r. U.S.A.
72 C4 South Fork Kern r. U.S.A.
70 D5 South Fork South Branch r. U.S.A.
68 E3 South Fox I. i. U.S.A.
92 C5 South Geomagnetic Pole Ant.
10 A3 South Harris i. U.K.
35 G5 South Hatia I. i. Bangl.
68 D4 South Haven U.S.A.
57 K2 South Henik Lake l. Can.
71 G2 South Hero U.S.A.
70 D6 South Hill U.S.A.
94 E4 South Honshu Ridge sea feature Pac. Oc.
57 K3 South Indian Lake Can.
71 G4 Southington U.S.A.
51 C6 South Island i. N.Z.
43 A4 South Islet rf Phil.
35 F5 South Koel r. India
72 B2 South Lake Tahoe U.S.A.
89 D5 South Luangwa National Park Zambia
92 B6 South Magnetic Pole Ant.
68 D3 South Manitou I. i. U.S.A.
67 D7 South Miami U.S.A.
9 H6 Southminster U.K.
57 J4 South Moose L. l. Can.
70 E5 South Mts h. U.S.A.
56 D2 South Nahanni r. Can.
10 □ South Nesting Bay b. U.K.
96 G10 South Orkney Is is Atl. Ocean
71 H2 South Paris U.S.A.
62 G3 South Platte r. U.S.A.
92 B4 South Pole Ant.
69 G1 South Porcupine Can.
8 D4 Southport U.K.
71 H3 South Portland U.S.A.
69 H3 South River Can.
10 F2 South Ronaldsay i. U.K.
71 G3 South Royalton U.S.A.
91 J5 South Sand Bluff pt S. Africa
96 H9 South Sandwich Islands is Atl. Ocean
96 H9 South Sandwich Trench sea feature Atl. Ocean
57 H4 South Saskatchewan r. Can.
57 K3 South Seal r. Can.
96 F9 South Shetland Is is Ant.
8 F3 South Shields U.K.
8 G4 South Skirlaugh U.K.
68 A5 South Skunk r. U.S.A.
51 E3 South Taranaki Bight b. N.Z.
73 G2 South Tent summit U.S.A.
35 E4 South Tons r. India
58 E3 South Twin I. i. Can.
8 E3 South Tyne r. U.K.
10 A3 South Uist i. U.K.
51 A7 South West Cape c. N.Z.
93 H6 South-West Indian Ridge sea feature Ind. Ocean
95 J8 South-West Pacific Basin sea feature Pa. Oc.
95 O7 South-West Peru Ridge sea feature Pac. Oc.
68 E5 South Whitley U.S.A.
71 H3 South Windham U.S.A.
9 J5 Southwold U.K.
91 H1 Soutpansberg mts S. Africa
18 G5 Soverato Italy
20 B4 Sovetsk Kaliningrad. Rus. Fed.
20 J3 Sovetsk Kirovsk. Rus. Fed.
36 G2 Sovetskaya Gavan' Rus. Fed.
20 D2 Sovetskiy Leningrad. Rus. Fed.
20 J3 Sovetskiy Mariy El. Rus. Fed.
24 H3 Sovetskiy Rus. Fed.
91 G3 Soweto S. Africa
30 E4 Sowghān Iran
40 G2 Sōya-misaki c. Japan
42 D4 Soyang-ho l. S. Korea
17 P4 Sozh r. Belarus
19 M3 Sozopol Bulg.
12 D4 Spa Belgium
92 B3 Spaatz I. i. Ant.
5 C4 Spain country Europe
9 G5 Spalding U.K.
9 D6 Span Head h. U.K.
69 F2 Spanish Can.
69 G2 Spanish r. Can.
73 G1 Spanish Fork U.S.A.
75 J5 Spanish Town Jamaica
72 C2 Sparks U.S.A.
70 C6 Sparta NC U.S.A.
68 B4 Sparta WV U.S.A.
67 D5 Spartanburg U.S.A.
19 K6 Sparti Greece
18 G6 Spartivento, Capo c. Italy
56 G5 Sparwood Can.
20 E4 Spas-Demensk Rus. Fed.
20 E2 Spasskaya Guba Rus. Fed.
36 F2 Spassk-Dal'niy Rus. Fed.
19 K7 Spatha, Akra pt Greece
56 D3 Spatsizi Plateau Wilderness Provincial Park res. Can.
64 C2 Spearfish U.S.A.
65 C4 Spearman U.S.A.
71 F3 Speculator U.S.A.
64 E3 Spencer IA U.S.A.
62 D2 Spencer ID U.S.A.
70 C5 Spencer WV U.S.A.
56 B3 Spencer, Cape c. U.S.A.
48 D5 Spencer Gulf est. Austr.
56 E4 Spences Bridge Can.
8 F3 Spennymoor U.K.
11 D3 Sperrin Mountains h. U.K.
70 D5 Sperryville U.S.A.
13 H5 Spessart reg. Ger.
19 K6 Spetses i. Greece
10 E3 Spey r. U.K.
13 G5 Speyer Ger.
31 G4 Spezand Pak.
13 F1 Spiekeroog i. Ger.
16 C7 Spiez Switz.
12 E1 Spijk Neth.
12 C3 Spijkenisse Neth.
18 E1 Spilimbergo Italy
9 H4 Spilsby U.K.
31 G4 Spīn Būldak Afgh.
34 B3 Spintangi Pak.
56 F3 Spirit River Can.
68 C3 Spirit River Flowage resr U.S.A.
57 H4 Spiritwood Can.
31 G3 Spirsang Pass Afgh.
17 K6 Spišská Nová Ves Slovakia
29 K1 Spitak Armenia
34 D3 Spiti r. India
24 C2 Spitsbergen i. Svalbard
16 F7 Spittal an der Drau Austria
18 G3 Split Croatia
57 K3 Split Lake Can.
57 K3 Split Lake l. Can.
62 C2 Spokane U.S.A.
18 E3 Spoleto Italy
44 C2 Spong Cambodia
68 B3 Spooner U.S.A.
13 K1 Spornitz Ger.
62 F2 Spotted Horse U.S.A.
59 J3 Spotted Island Can.
69 F2 Spragge Can.
56 E4 Spranger, Mt mt Can.
62 C2 Spray U.S.A.
16 G5 Spree r. Ger.
12 D4 Sprimont Belgium
69 F3 Spring Bay Can.
90 B4 Springbok S. Africa
59 J4 Springdale Can.
65 E4 Springdale U.S.A.
13 H2 Springe Ger.
63 F4 Springer U.S.A.
73 H4 Springerville U.S.A.
65 C4 Springfield CO U.S.A.
68 C6 Springfield IL U.S.A.
71 G3 Springfield MA U.S.A.
71 J2 Springfield ME U.S.A.
64 E2 Springfield MN U.S.A.
65 E4 Springfield MO U.S.A.
70 B5 Springfield OH U.S.A.
62 B2 Springfield OR U.S.A.
71 G3 Springfield VT U.S.A.
70 D5 Springfield WV U.S.A.
68 C6 Springfield, Lake l. U.S.A.
91 F5 Springfontein S. Africa
68 B4 Spring Green U.S.A.
68 B4 Spring Grove U.S.A.
59 H4 Springhill Can.
67 D6 Spring Hill U.S.A.
68 D4 Spring Lake U.S.A.
73 E3 Spring Mountains U.S.A.
51 D5 Springs Junction N.Z.
68 A4 Spring Valley U.S.A.
70 D3 Springville NY U.S.A.
73 G1 Springville UT U.S.A.
9 J5 Sprowston U.K.
56 G4 Spruce Grove Can.
70 D5 Spruce Knob-Seneca Rocks National Recreation Area res. U.S.A.
62 D3 Spruce Mt. mt U.S.A.
8 H4 Spurn Head c. U.K.
56 E5 Spuzzum Can.
56 E5 Squamish Can.
71 H3 Squam Lake l. U.S.A.
71 J1 Squapan Lake l. U.S.A.
71 J1 Square Lake l. U.S.A.
18 G5 Squillace, Golfo di g. Italy
74 A2 S. Quintín, C. pt Mex.
Srbija div. see Serbia
44 B3 Srê Âmběl Cambodia
25 R4 Sredinnyy Khrebet mts Rus. Fed.
19 K3 Sredna Gora mts Bulg.
25 R3 Srednekolymsk Rus. Fed.
24 E4 Sredne-Russkaya Vozvyshennost' reg. Rus. Fed.
25 M3 Sredne-Sibirskoye Ploskogor'ye plat. Rus. Fed.
6 W4 Sredneye Kuyto, Oz. l. Rus. Fed.
19 L3 Srednogorie Bulg.
44 C2 Srêpok, T. r. Cambodia
36 D1 Sretensk Rus. Fed.
33 C3 Sriharikota I. i. India
33 D2 Srikakulam India
33 B3 Sri Kalahasti India
34 D3 Sri Kanta mt India
23 H9 Sri Lanka country Asia
34 D3 Srinagar India
34 C2 Srinagar Jammu and Kashmir
33 B4 Srirangam India
44 B1 Sri Thep Thai.
33 B4 Srivaikuntam India
33 A2 Srivardhan India
33 B4 Srivilliputtur India
33 C2 Srungavarapukota India
13 H1 Stade Ger.
12 B4 Staden Belgium
12 E2 Stadskanaal Neth.
13 H4 Stadtallendorf Ger.
13 H2 Stadthagen Ger.
13 K4 Stadtilm Ger.
12 E3 Stadtlohn Ger.
13 H3 Stadtoldendorf Ger.
13 K4 Stadtroda Ger.
10 B4 Staffa i. U.K.
13 K4 Staffelberg h. Ger.
13 J4 Staffelstein Ger.
9 E5 Stafford U.K.
70 E5 Stafford U.S.A.
7 T8 Staicele Latvia
9 G6 Staines U.K.
21 F5 Stakhanov Ukr.
9 E7 Stalbridge U.K.
9 J5 Stalham U.K.
Stalingrad see Volgograd
56 E3 Stalin, Mt mt Can.
17 L5 Stalowa Wola Pol.
19 L3 Stamboliyski Bulg.
9 G5 Stamford U.K.
71 G4 Stamford CT U.S.A.
71 F3 Stamford NY U.S.A.
Stampalia i. see Astypalaia
89 B6 Stampriet Namibia
6 N2 Stamsund Norway
64 E3 Stanberry U.S.A.
12 C3 Standdaarbuiten Neth.
91 H3 Standerton S. Africa
69 F4 Standish U.S.A.
66 C4 Stanford U.S.A.
91 J4 Stanger S. Africa
67 E7 Staniard Ck Bahamas
19 K3 Stanke Dimitrov Bulg.
13 M5 Staňkov Czech Rep.
71 K1 Stanley Can.
39 □ Stanley H.K. China
80 E8 Stanley Falkland Is
8 F3 Stanley U.K.
62 D2 Stanley ID U.S.A.
64 C1 Stanley ND U.S.A.
68 B3 Stanley WV U.S.A.
88 C3 Stanley, Mount mt Congo(Zaire)/Uganda
33 B4 Stanley Reservoir India
8 F2 Stannington U.K.
25 R3 Stanovaya Rus. Fed.
36 D1 Stanovoye Nagor'ye mts Rus. Fed.
36 E1 Stanovoy Khrebet mts Rus. Fed.
9 H5 Stanton U.K.
70 B6 Stanton KY U.S.A.
68 E4 Stanton MI U.S.A.
64 C3 Stapleton U.S.A.
17 K5 Starachowice Pol.
Stara Planina mts see Balkan Mountains
20 H4 Staraya Kulatka Rus. Fed.
21 H5 Staraya Poltavka Rus. Fed.
20 D3 Staraya Russa Rus. Fed.
17 P2 Staraya Toropa Rus. Fed.
20 J4 Staraya Tumba Rus. Fed.
19 L3 Stara Zagora Bulg.
46 M4 Starbuck Island i. Kiribati
16 G4 Stargard Szczeciński Pol.
20 E3 Staritsa Rus. Fed.
67 D6 Starke U.S.A.
65 F5 Starkville U.S.A.
16 E7 Starnberger See l. Ger.
21 F5 Starobil's'k Ukr.
17 Q4 Starodub Rus. Fed.
17 J4 Starogard Gdański Pol.
21 C5 Starokostyantyniv Ukr.
21 F6 Starominskaya Rus. Fed.
21 F6 Staroshcherbinovskaya Rus. Fed.
72 C1 Star Peak mt U.S.A.
9 D7 Start Point pt U.K.
17 O4 Staryya Darohi Belarus
21 F5 Staryy Oskol Rus. Fed.
13 K3 Staßfurt Ger.
70 E4 State College U.S.A.
67 D5 Statesboro U.S.A.
67 D5 Statesville U.S.A.
13 M3 Stauchitz Ger.
13 G4 Staufenberg Ger.
70 D5 Staunton U.S.A.
7 J7 Stavanger Norway
9 F4 Staveley U.K.
21 G6 Stavropol' Rus. Fed.
21 G6 Stavropol'skaya Vozvyshennost' reg. Rus. Fed.
21 G6 Stavropol'skiy Kray div. Rus. Fed.
50 D4 Stawell Austr.
91 H4 Steadville S. Africa
72 C2 Steamboat U.S.A.
62 F3 Steamboat Springs U.S.A.
92 B2 Steele I. i. Ant.
70 E4 Steelton U.S.A.
12 E2 Steenderen Neth.
91 J2 Steenkampsberge mts S. Africa
56 F3 Steen River Can.
62 C3 Steens Mt. mt U.S.A.
55 N2 Steenstrup Gletscher gl. Greenland
12 A4 Steenvoorde France
12 E2 Steenwijk Neth.
92 D4 Stefansson Bay b. Ant.
54 H2 Stefansson I. i. Can.
13 J5 Steigerwald forest Ger.
13 K5 Stein Ger.
13 K4 Steinach Ger.
57 K5 Steinbach Can.
13 G2 Steinfeld (Oldenburg) Ger.
12 F2 Steinfurt Ger.
89 B6 Steinhausen Namibia
13 H3 Steinheim Ger.
13 H2 Steinhuder Meer l. Ger.
6 M4 Steinkjer Norway
90 B4 Steinkopf S. Africa
73 H5 Steins U.S.A.
6 M4 Steinsdalen Norway
90 F3 Stella S. Africa
90 C6 Stellenbosch S. Africa
18 C3 Stello, Monte mt Corsica France
12 D5 Stenay France
13 K2 Stendal Ger.
39 □ Stenhouse, Mt h. H.K. China
10 E4 Stenhousemuir U.K.
7 M7 Stenungsund Sweden
Stepanakert see Xankändi
21 H7 Step'anavan Armenia
57 K5 Stephen U.S.A.
50 C2 Stephens r. Austr.
51 D4 Stephens, Cape c. N.Z.
50 C1 Stephens Creek Austr.
68 D3 Stephenson U.S.A.
56 C3 Stephens Passage chan. U.S.A.
59 J4 Stephenville Can.
65 D5 Stephenville U.S.A.
21 H5 Stepnoye Rus. Fed.
91 H4 Sterkfontein Dam resr S. Africa
91 G5 Sterkstroom S. Africa
90 D5 Sterling S. Africa
62 G3 Sterling CO U.S.A.
68 C5 Sterling IL U.S.A.
64 C2 Sterling ND U.S.A.
73 G2 Sterling UT U.S.A.
65 C6 Sterling City U.S.A.
69 F4 Sterling Hgts U.S.A.
26 D1 Sterlitamak Rus. Fed.
13 K1 Sternberg Ger.
56 G4 Stettler Can.
68 D2 Steuben U.S.A.
70 C4 Steubenville U.S.A.
9 G6 Stevenage U.K.
57 K4 Stevenson L. l. Can.
68 C3 Stevens Point U.S.A.
54 D3 Stevens Village U.S.A.
56 D3 Stewart Can.
56 B2 Stewart r. Can.
56 B2 Stewart Crossing Can.
51 A7 Stewart Island i. N.Z.
49 G2 Stewart Islands is Solomon Is
55 K3 Stewart Lake l. Can.
10 D5 Stewarton U.K.
68 A4 Stewartville U.S.A.
91 F5 Steynsburg S. Africa
16 G6 Steyr Austria
90 F6 Steytlerville S. Africa
12 D1 Stiens Neth.
56 C3 Stikine r. Can./U.S.A.
56 C3 Stikine Ranges mts Can.
90 D7 Stilbaai S. Africa
68 A3 Stillwater MN U.S.A.
72 C2 Stillwater NV U.S.A.
65 D4 Stillwater OK U.S.A.
63 C4 Stillwater Ra. mts U.S.A.
9 G5 Stilton U.K.
19 K4 Štip Macedonia
50 B3 Stirling Austr.
10 E4 Stirling U.K.
72 B2 Stirling City U.S.A.
50 A2 Stirling North Austr.
6 M5 Stjørdalshalsen Norway
16 H6 Stockerau Austria
13 K4 Stockheim Ger.
7 Q7 Stockholm Sweden
71 J1 Stockholm U.S.A.
9 E4 Stockport U.K.
72 B3 Stockton CA U.S.A.
64 D4 Stockton KS U.S.A.
73 F1 Stockton UT U.S.A.
68 B2 Stockton I. i. U.S.A.
65 E4 Stockton L. l. U.S.A.
8 F3 Stockton-on-Tees U.K.
71 J2 Stockton Springs U.S.A.
7 P5 Stöde Sweden
44 B2 Stœng Sângke r. Cambodia
44 C2 Stœng Sên r. Cambodia
44 C2 Stœng Trêng Cambodia
10 C2 Stoer, Point of pt U.K.
9 E4 Stoke-on-Trent U.K.
8 F3 Stokesley U.K.
6 C5 Stokkseyri Iceland
6 N3 Stokkvågen Norway
6 O2 Stokmarknes Norway
18 G3 Stolac Bos.-Herz.
12 E4 Stolberg (Rheinland) Ger.
21 C5 Stolin Belarus
13 L4 Stollberg Ger.
13 H2 Stolzenau Ger.
9 E5 Stone U.K.
69 J2 Stonecliffe Can.
71 F5 Stone Harbor U.S.A.
10 F4 Stonehaven U.K.
56 E3 Stone Mountain Prov. Park res. Can.
73 H3 Stoner U.S.A.
71 F4 Stone Ridge U.S.A.
57 K4 Stonewall Can.
70 C5 Stonewall Jackson Lake l. U.S.A.
69 F4 Stoney Point Can.
71 J2 Stonington U.S.A.
72 A2 Stonyford U.S.A.
71 E3 Stony Pt pt U.S.A.
57 H3 Stony Rapids Can.
6 Q3 Stora Inlevatten l. Sweden
6 P3 Stora Sjöfallets Nationalpark nat. park Sweden
6 Q4 Storavan l. Sweden
7 M9 Store Bælt chan. Denmark
6 M5 Støren Norway
6 O3 Storforshei Norway
6 O3 Storjord Norway
54 H2 Storkerson Peninsula Can.
91 G5 Stormberg S. Africa
91 G5 Stormberg mts S. Africa
64 E3 Storm Lake U.S.A.
7 K6 Stornosa mt Norway
10 B2 Stornoway U.K.
20 K2 Storozhevsk Rus. Fed.
21 C5 Storozhynets' Ukr.
71 G4 Storrs U.S.A.
10 B3 Storr, The h. U.K.
6 P4 Storseleby Sweden
6 O5 Storsjön l. Sweden
7 L5 Storskrymten mt Norway
6 R2 Storslett Norway
12 D1 Stortemelk chan. Neth.
6 P4 Storuman Sweden
6 P4 Storuman l. Sweden
7 P6 Storvik Sweden
7 M8 Storvorde Denmark
7 P7 Storvreta Sweden
9 G5 Stotfold U.K.
68 C4 Stoughton U.S.A.
9 E7 Stour r. Eng. U.K.
9 J6 Stour r. Eng. U.K.
9 H6 Stour r. Eng. U.K.
9 F5 Stour r. Eng. U.K.
9 E5 Stourbridge U.K.
9 E5 Stourport-on-Severn U.K.
57 L4 Stout L. l. Can.
20 C4 Stowbtsy Belarus
71 F4 Stowe U.S.A.
9 H5 Stowmarket U.K.
11 D3 Strabane U.K.
11 D4 Stradbally Rep. of Ireland
9 J5 Stradbroke U.K.
18 C2 Stradella Italy
73 G3 Straight Cliffs cliff U.S.A.
16 F6 Strakonice Czech Rep.
16 F3 Stralsund Ger.
90 C7 Strand S. Africa
6 K5 Stranda Norway
67 E7 Strangers Cay i. Bahamas
11 F3 Strangford U.K.
11 F3 Strangford Lough l. U.K.
10 C6 Stranraer U.K.
14 H2 Strasbourg France
70 D5 Strasburg U.S.A.
50 F4 Stratford Austr.
69 G4 Stratford Can.
51 E3 Stratford N.Z.
65 C4 Stratford TX U.S.A.
68 B3 Stratford WV U.S.A.
9 F5 Stratford-upon-Avon U.K.
50 B3 Strathalbyn Austr.
10 D5 Strathaven U.K.
10 G3 Strathbeg, Loch of l. U.K.
10 D3 Strathcarron v. U.K.
56 D5 Strathcona Prov. Park res. Can.
10 D3 Strathconon v. U.K.
10 D3 Strath Dearn v. U.K.
10 D2 Strath Fleet v. U.K.
56 G4 Strathmore Can.
56 E4 Strathnaver Can.
10 D2 Strathnaver v. U.K.
10 E2 Strath of Kildonan v. U.K.
69 G4 Strathroy Can.
10 E3 Strathspey v. U.K.
10 E2 Strathy U.K.
10 D2 Strathy Point pt U.K.
9 C7 Stratton U.K.
71 H2 Stratton U.S.A.
13 L6 Straubing Ger.
6 B3 Straumnes pt Iceland
68 B4 Strawberry Point U.S.A.
73 G1 Strawberry Reservoir U.S.A.
48 D5 Streaky Bay Austr.
48 D5 Streaky Bay b. Austr.
68 C5 Streator U.S.A.
9 E6 Street U.K.
19 K2 Strehaia Romania
13 M3 Strehla Ger.
25 R3 Strelka Rus. Fed.
7 T8 Strenči Latvia
13 L5 Stříbro Czech Rep.
10 F3 Strichen U.K.
19 K4 Strimonas r. Greece
83 D4 Stroeder Arg.
11 C4 Strokestown Rep. of Ireland
10 E2 Stroma, Island of i. U.K.
18 F5 Stromboli, Isola i. Italy
10 E2 Stromness U.K.
64 D3 Stromsburg U.S.A.
7 M7 Strömstad Sweden
6 O5 Strömsund Sweden
70 C4 Strongsville U.S.A.
10 F1 Stronsay i. U.K.
50 H2 Stroud Austr.
9 E6 Stroud U.K.
50 H2 Stroud Road Austr.
71 F4 Stroudsburg U.S.A.
7 L8 Struer Denmark
19 J4 Struga Macedonia
20 D3 Strugi-Krasnyye Rus. Fed.
90 D7 Struis Bay S. Africa
13 J5 Strullendorf Ger.
19 K4 Struma r. Bulg.
9 B5 Strumble Head hd U.K.
19 K4 Strumica Macedonia
19 L3 Stryama r. Bulg.
90 E4 Strydenburg S. Africa
7 K6 Stryn Norway
21 B5 Stryy Ukr.
67 D7 Stuart FL U.S.A.
70 C6 Stuart VA U.S.A.
56 E4 Stuart Lake l. Can.
70 D5 Stuarts Draft U.S.A.
50 G2 Stuart Town Austr.
51 C6 Studholme Junction N.Z.
6 Q5 Studsviken Sweden
65 C6 Study Butte U.S.A.
57 L4 Stull L. l. Can.
44 C2 Stung Chinit r. Cambodia
20 F4 Stupino Rus. Fed.
92 A6 Sturge I. i. Ant.
68 D2 Sturgeon r. U.S.A.
68 D3 Sturgeon Bay WV U.S.A.
57 K4 Sturgeon Bay b. Can.
68 E3 Sturgeon Bay b. U.S.A.
68 D3 Sturgeon Bay Canal chan. U.S.A.
69 H2 Sturgeon Falls Can.
58 B3 Sturgeon L. l. Can.
66 C4 Sturgis KY U.S.A.
68 E5 Sturgis MI U.S.A.
64 C2 Sturgis SD U.S.A.
48 C3 Sturt Creek r. Austr.
48 E4 Sturt Desert Austr.
91 G6 Stutterheim S. Africa
16 D6 Stuttgart Ger.
65 F5 Stuttgart U.S.A.
6 B4 Stykkishólmur Iceland
17 M5 Styr r. Ukr.
82 D2 Suaçuí Grande r. Brazil
87 F3 Suakin Sudan
39 F5 Su'ao Taiwan
63 E6 Suaqui Gde Mex.
81 B3 Suárez r. Col.
17 M3 Subačius Lith.
35 H4 Subansiri r. India
35 F5 Subarnarekha r. India
29 G6 Şubayḩah S. Arabia
45 C2 Subi Besar i. Indon.
19 H1 Subotica Yugo.
17 N7 Suceava Romania
40 C3 Suchan r. Rus. Fed.
11 C4 Suck r. Rep. of Ireland
13 K1 Suckow Ger.
78 E7 Sucre Bol.
81 B2 Sucre Col.
81 C3 Sucuaro Col.
82 B2 Sucuriú r. Brazil
21 E6 Sudak Ukr.

85 F4 Sudan *country* Africa
20 G3 Suday Rus. Fed.
29 K6 Sudayr *watercourse* Iraq
69 G2 Sudbury Can.
9 H5 Sudbury U.K.
87 E4 Sudd *swamp* Sudan
13 K1 Sude *r.* Ger.
16 H5 Sudety *mts* Czech Rep./Pol.
71 F5 Sudlersville U.S.A.
20 G4 Sudogda Rus. Fed.
28 D7 Sudr Egypt
6 □ Suðuroy *i.* Faroe Is
87 E4 Sue *watercourse* Sudan
15 F3 Sueca Spain
87 F2 Suez Egypt
87 F1 Suez Canal *canal* Egypt
87 F2 Suez, Gulf of *g.* Egypt
70 E6 Suffolk U.S.A.
30 B2 Sūfiān Iran
68 C4 Sugar *r.* U.S.A.
71 H2 Sugarloaf Mt. *mt* U.S.A.
43 C4 Sugbuhan Point *pt* Phil.
45 E1 Sugut *r.* Malaysia
43 A5 Sugut, Tg *pt* Malaysia
38 D2 Suhait China
32 E5 Şuḩār Oman
36 C1 Sühbaatar Mongolia
13 J4 Suhl Ger.
13 J2 Suhlendorf Ger.
28 C2 Şuhut Turkey
34 B3 Sui Pak.
40 B1 Suibin China
39 F4 Suichang China
39 E5 Suichuan China
38 D2 Suide China
42 F1 Suifenhe China
34 B4 Suigam India
36 E2 Suihua China
39 B4 Suijiang China
39 D5 Suining *Hunan* China
38 E3 Suining *Jiangsu* China
39 B4 Suining *Sichuan* China
38 E3 Suiping China
12 C5 Suippes France
11 D5 Suir *r.* Rep. of Ireland
38 E3 Suixi China
38 E3 Sui Xian China
39 C5 Suiyang China
38 F1 Suizhong China
38 D4 Suizhou China
38 C1 Suj China
34 C4 Sujangarh India
34 D3 Sujanpur India
34 B4 Sujawal Pak.
45 C4 Sukabumi Indon.
45 C3 Sukadana Indon.
41 G6 Sukagawa Japan
43 A5 Sukau Malaysia
42 C4 Sukchŏn N. Korea
40 C1 Sukhanovka Rus. Fed.
20 E4 Sukhinichi Rus. Fed.
20 H2 Sukhona *r.* Rus. Fed.
44 A1 Sukhothai Thai.
20 E2 Sukkozero Rus. Fed.
34 B4 Sukkur Pak.
33 C2 Sukma India
34 C4 Sukri *r.* India
20 F3 Sukromny Rus. Fed.
41 C8 Sukumo Japan
7 J6 Sula *i.* Norway
34 B3 Sulaiman Ranges *mts* Pak.
21 H7 Sulak *r.* Rus. Fed.
37 E7 Sula, Kepulauan *is* Indon.
30 C4 Sūlār Iran
10 B1 Sula Sgeir *i.* U.K.
45 E3 Sulawesi *i.* Indon.
29 K4 Sulaymān Beg Iraq
30 C2 Suledeh Iran
10 D1 Sule Skerry *i.* U.K.
10 D1 Sule Stack *i.* U.K.
28 F3 Süleymanlı Turkey
86 A4 Sulima Sierra Leone
13 G2 Sulingen Ger.
6 P3 Sulitjelma Norway
7 V6 Sulkava Fin.
78 B4 Sullana Peru
64 F4 Sullivan U.S.A.
57 G4 Sullivan L. *l.* Can.
71 J1 Sully Can.
18 E3 Sulmona Italy
65 E6 Sulphur U.S.A.
65 E5 Sulphur Springs U.S.A.
69 F2 Sultan Can.
Sultanabad *see* Arāk
28 C2 Sultan Dağları *mts* Turkey
28 D2 Sultanhanı Turkey
31 F4 Sultan, Koh-i- *mts* Pak.
35 E4 Sultanpur India
43 B5 Sulu Archipelago *is* Phil.
31 H2 Sülüktü Kyrg.
28 F2 Sulusaray Turkey
43 A4 Sulu Sea *sea* Phil.
13 K5 Sulzbach-Rosenberg Ger.
92 A4 Sulzberger Bay *b.* Ant.
31 E6 Sumāil Oman
80 D3 Sumampa Arg.
81 B4 Sumapaz, Parque Nacional *nat. park* Col.
29 K5 Sūmar Iran
45 B3 Sumatera *i.* Indon.
Sumatra *i.* *see* Sumatera
16 F6 Šumava *mts* Czech Rep.
37 E7 Sumba *i.* Indon.
30 D2 Sumbar *r.* Turkm.
37 D7 Sumba, Selat *chan.* Indon.
45 E4 Sumbawa *i.* Indon.
45 E4 Sumbawabesar Indon.
89 D4 Sumbawanga Tanz.
89 B5 Sumbe Angola
10 □ Sumburgh U.K.
10 □ Sumburgh Head *hd* U.K.
34 D2 Sumdo China/Jammu and Kashmir
29 M3 Sume'eh Sarā Iran
45 D4 Sumenep Indon.
Sumgait *see* Sumqayıt
41 F9 Sumisu-jima *i.* Japan
29 J3 Summēl Iraq
58 C3 Summer Beaver Can.
59 K4 Summerford Can.
68 D3 Summer I. *i.* U.S.A.
10 C2 Summer Isles *is* U.K.
59 H4 Summerside Can.
70 C5 Summersville U.S.A.
70 C5 Summersville Lake *l.* U.S.A.
56 E4 Summit Lake Can.
68 E5 Summit Lake *l.* U.S.A.
72 D2 Summit Mt *mt* U.S.A.
34 D2 Sumnal China/India
51 D5 Sumner N.Z.
68 A4 Sumner U.S.A.
51 D5 Sumner, L. *l.* N.Z.
56 C3 Sumner Strait *chan.* U.S.A.
41 F6 Sumon-dake *mt* Japan
41 D7 Sumoto Japan
16 H6 Šumperk Czech Rep.
29 M1 Sumqayıt Azer.
29 M1 Sumqayıt *r.* Azer.
34 B4 Sumrahu Pak.
67 D5 Sumter U.S.A.
21 E5 Sumy Ukr.
62 D2 Sun *r.* U.S.A.
20 J3 Suna Rus. Fed.
40 G3 Sunagawa Japan
35 G4 Sunamganj Bangl.
42 C4 Sunan N. Korea
10 C4 Sunart, Loch *in.* U.K.
30 D6 Şunaynah Oman
29 K4 Sunbula Kuh *mts* Iran
62 E1 Sunburst U.S.A.
50 E4 Sunbury Austr.
70 B4 Sunbury *OH* U.S.A.
70 E4 Sunbury *PA* U.S.A.
83 E1 Sunchales Arg.
42 C4 Sunch'ŏn N. Korea
42 D6 Sunch'ŏn S. Korea
91 G2 Sun City S. Africa
71 H3 Suncook U.S.A.
62 F2 Sundance U.S.A.
35 F5 Sundargarh India
34 D3 Sundarnagar India
45 C4 Sunda, Selat *chan.* Indon.
93 M4 Sunda Trench *sea feature* Ind. Ocean
8 F3 Sunderland U.K.
13 G3 Sundern (Sauerland) Ger.
28 C2 Sündiken Dağları *mts* Turkey
69 H3 Sundridge Can.
7 P5 Sundsvall Sweden
31 F2 Sundukli, Peski *des.* Turkm.
91 J4 Sundumbili S. Africa
34 D4 Sunel India
44 B5 Sungaikabung Indon.
45 C3 Sungailiat Indon.
45 B2 Sungai Pahang *r.* Malaysia
45 B3 Sungaipenuh Indon.
45 B1 Sungei Petani Malaysia
44 □ Sungei Seletar Res. *resr* Sing.
28 E1 Sungurlu Turkey
35 F4 Sun Kosi *r.* Nepal
7 K6 Sunndal Norway
6 L5 Sunndalsøra Norway
7 N7 Sunne Sweden
62 C2 Sunnyside U.S.A.
72 A3 Sunnyvale U.S.A.
68 C4 Sun Prairie U.S.A.
72 □1 Sunset Beach U.S.A.
73 G4 Sunset Crater National Monument *res.* U.S.A.
25 N3 Suntar Rus. Fed.
31 F5 Suntsar Pak.
62 D3 Sun Valley U.S.A.
42 C5 Sunwi Do *i.* N. Korea
86 B4 Sunyani Ghana
6 U3 Suolijärvet *l.* Fin.
68 C1 Suomi Can.
6 V4 Suomussalmi Fin.
41 B8 Suō-nada *b.* Japan
6 U5 Suonenjoki Fin.
44 C2 Suŏng Cambodia
39 B7 Suong *r.* Laos
20 E2 Suoyarvi Rus. Fed.
33 A3 Supa India
73 F3 Supai U.S.A.
81 E3 Supamo *r.* Venez.
35 F4 Supaul India
73 G5 Superior *AZ* U.S.A.
64 D3 Superior *NE* U.S.A.
68 A2 Superior *WV* U.S.A.
68 C2 Superior, Lake *l.* Can./U.S.A.
44 B2 Suphan Buri Thai.
29 J2 Süphan Dağı *mt* Turkey
20 E4 Suponevo Rus. Fed.
92 B3 Support Force Glacier *gl.* Ant.
42 C3 Supung N. Korea
29 L6 Sūq ash Shuyūkh Iraq
38 F3 Suqian China
Suqutrā *i.* *see* Socotra
32 E5 Şūr Oman
20 H4 Sura Rus. Fed.
20 H4 Sura *r.* Rus. Fed.
29 M1 Şuraabad Azer.
31 G4 Surab Pak.
45 D4 Surabaya Indon.
31 E5 Sūrak Iran
45 D4 Surakarta Indon.
34 C5 Surat India
34 C3 Suratgarh India
44 A3 Surat Thani Thai.
20 E4 Surazh Rus. Fed.
29 K4 Sūrdāsh Iraq
19 K3 Surdulica Yugo.
12 E5 Sûre *r.* Lux.
34 B5 Surendranagar India
72 B4 Surf U.S.A.
24 J3 Surgut Rus. Fed.
33 B2 Suriapet India
43 C4 Surigao Phil.
43 C4 Surigao Str. *chan.* Phil.
44 B2 Surin Thai.
77 E2 Suriname *country* S. America
31 H3 Surkhab *r.* Afgh.
31 G2 Surkhandar'ya *r.* Uzbek.
35 E3 Surkhet Nepal
31 H2 Surkhob *r.* Tajik.
30 D4 Surmāq Iran
29 H1 Sürmene Turkey
21 G5 Surovikino Rus. Fed.
72 B3 Sur, Pt *pt* U.S.A.
83 F3 Sur, Pta *pt* Arg.
70 E6 Surry U.S.A.
20 H4 Sursk Rus. Fed.
Surt *see* Sirte
Surt, Khalīj *g.* *see* Sirte, Gulf of
6 C5 Surtsey *i.* Iceland
28 G3 Sürüç Turkey
41 F7 Suruga-wan *b.* Japan
45 B3 Surulangun Indon.
43 C5 Surup Phil.
12 F2 Surwold Ger.
30 B2 Şuşa Azer.
41 B7 Susa Japan
41 C8 Susaki Japan
30 C4 Süsangerd Iran
20 G3 Susanino Rus. Fed.
72 B1 Susanville U.S.A.
28 G1 Suşehri Turkey
44 A4 Suso Thai.
39 E4 Susong China
71 E4 Susquehanna *r.* U.S.A.
59 G4 Sussex Can.
71 F4 Sussex U.S.A.
43 A5 Susul Malaysia
25 Q3 Susuman Rus. Fed.
28 B2 Susurluk Turkey
34 D2 Sutak Jammu and Kashmir
72 C2 Sutcliffe U.S.A.
90 D6 Sutherland S. Africa
64 C3 Sutherland U.S.A.
34 C3 Sutlej *r.* Pak.
72 B2 Sutter Creek U.S.A.
9 G5 Sutterton U.K.
69 G2 Sutton Can.
9 H5 Sutton U.K.
70 C5 Sutton U.S.A.
58 D3 Sutton *r.* Can.
9 F5 Sutton Coldfield U.K.
9 F4 Sutton in Ashfield U.K.
58 D3 Sutton L. *l.* Can.
70 C5 Sutton Lake *l.* U.S.A.
40 G3 Suttsu Japan
40 D1 Sutungu Rus. Fed.
49 H3 Suva Fiji
20 F4 Suvorov Rus. Fed.
46 L5 Suvorov I. *i.* *Cook Is* Pac. Oc.
41 F6 Suwa Japan
17 L3 Suwałki Pol.
44 B2 Suwannaphum Thai.
67 D6 Suwannee *r.* U.S.A.
29 K5 Suwayqīyah, Hawr as *l.* Iraq
29 H6 Suwayr *well* S. Arabia
45 D5 Suwŏn S. Korea
41 E6 Suzaka Japan
20 G3 Suzdal' Rus. Fed.
38 E3 Suzhou *Anhui* China
38 F4 Suzhou *Jiangsu* China
42 C3 Suzi *r.* China
41 E6 Suzu Japan
41 E7 Suzuka Japan
41 E6 Suzu-misaki *pt* Japan
6 U1 Sværholthalvøya *pen.* Norway
96 K1 Svalbard *terr.* Arctic Ocean
55 N2 Svartenhuk Halvø *pen.* Greenland
21 F5 Svatove Ukr.
44 C3 Svay Riĕng Cambodia
7 O5 Sveg Sweden
7 U8 Sveķi Latvia
7 J6 Svelgen Norway
6 L5 Svellingen Norway
7 T9 Švenčionėliai Lith.
7 U9 Švenčionys Lith.
7 M9 Svendborg Denmark
6 Q2 Svensby Norway
6 O5 Svenstavik Sweden
Sverdlovsk *see* Yekaterinburg
21 F5 Sverdlovs'k Ukr.
55 J1 Sverdrup Channel Can.
19 J4 Sveti Nikole Macedonia
36 F2 Svetlaya Rus. Fed.
24 K3 Svetlogorsk Rus. Fed.
20 B4 Svetlogorsk Rus. Fed.
21 G6 Svetlograd Rus. Fed.
20 B4 Svetlyy Rus. Fed.
21 H5 Svetlyy Yar Rus. Fed.
20 D2 Svetogorsk Rus. Fed.
6 E4 Svíahnúkar *volc.* Iceland
19 M4 Svilengrad Bulg.
19 K2 Svinecea Mare, Vârful *mt* Romania
20 C4 Svir Belarus
20 E2 Svir' *r.* Rus. Fed.
19 L3 Svishtov Bulg.
16 H6 Svitava *r.* Czech Rep.
16 H6 Svitavy Czech Rep.
21 E5 Svitlovods'k Ukr.
20 J4 Sviyaga *r.* Rus. Fed.
36 E1 Svobodnyy Rus. Fed.
6 O2 Svolvær Norway
19 H3 Svrljiške Planine *mts* Yugo.
20 D4 Svyetlahorsk Belarus
9 F5 Swadlincote U.K.
9 H5 Swaffham U.K.
48 F4 Swain Reefs *rf* Austr.
67 D5 Swainsboro U.S.A.
46 K5 Swains Island *i.* Pac. Oc.
89 B6 Swakopmund Namibia
8 F3 Swale *r.* U.K.
49 G3 Swallow Is *is* Solomon Is
57 J4 Swan *r.* Can.
9 F7 Swanage U.K.
50 D3 Swan Hill Austr.
56 F4 Swan Hills Can.
75 H5 Swan Islands *is* Honduras
57 J4 Swan L. *l.* Can.
9 H6 Swanley U.K.
50 B3 Swan Reach Austr.
57 J4 Swan River Can.
50 H2 Swansea *N.S.W.* Austr.
9 D6 Swansea U.K.
9 D6 Swansea Bay *b.* U.K.
71 J2 Swans I. *i.* U.S.A.
71 G2 Swanton U.S.A.
91 G2 Swartruggens S. Africa
73 F2 Swasey Peak *summit* U.S.A.
69 G1 Swastika Can.
34 B2 Swat *r.* Pak.
Swatow *see* Shantou
85 G8 Swaziland *country* Africa
5 E3 Sweden *country* Europe
62 B2 Sweet Home U.S.A.
67 C5 Sweetwater *TN* U.S.A.
65 C5 Sweetwater *TX* U.S.A.
62 E3 Sweetwater *r.* U.S.A.
90 D7 Swellendam S. Africa
16 H5 Świdnica Pol.
16 G4 Świdwin Pol.
16 G4 Świebodzin Pol.
17 J4 Świecie Pol.
71 H2 Swift *r.* U.S.A.
57 H4 Swift Current Can.
57 H5 Swiftcurrent Cr. *r.* Can.
56 C2 Swift River Can.
11 D2 Swilly, Lough *in.* Rep. of Ireland
9 F6 Swindon U.K.
11 C4 Swinford Rep. of Ireland
16 G4 Świnoujście Pol.
10 F5 Swinton U.K.
5 D4 Switzerland *country* Europe
11 E4 Swords Rep. of Ireland
40 D1 Syain Rus. Fed.
21 F6 Syamozero, Oz. *l.* Rus. Fed.
20 G2 Syamzha Rus. Fed.
17 O3 Syanno Belarus
20 E2 Syas'troy Rus. Fed.
20 H3 Syava Rus. Fed.
68 C5 Sycamore U.S.A.
50 H2 Sydney Austr.
59 H4 Sydney Can.
57 L4 Sydney L. *l.* Can.
59 H4 Sydney Mines Can.
21 F5 Syeverodonets'k Ukr.
13 G2 Syke Ger.
20 J2 Syktyvkar Rus. Fed.
67 C5 Sylacauga U.S.A.
6 N5 Sylarna *mt* Norway/Sweden
35 G4 Sylhet Bangl.
20 G2 Syloga Rus. Fed.
16 G3 Sylt *i.* Ger.
67 D5 Sylvania *GA* U.S.A.
70 B4 Sylvania *OH* U.S.A.
56 G4 Sylvan Lake Can.
67 D6 Sylvester U.S.A.
56 E3 Sylvia, Mt *mt* Can.
19 M6 Symi *i.* Greece
21 E5 Synel'nykove Ukr.
92 D4 Syowa *Japan Base* Ant.
18 F6 Syracuse *Sicily* Italy
64 C4 Syracuse *KS* U.S.A.
71 E3 Syracuse *NY* U.S.A.
71 E3 Syracuse *airport* *NY* U.S.A.
26 E2 Syrdar'ya *r.* Kazak.
23 C6 Syria *country* Asia
32 A3 Syrian Desert Asia
19 M6 Syrna *i.* Greece
19 L6 Syros *i.* Greece
7 T6 Sysmä Fin.
20 J2 Sysola *r.* Rus. Fed.
20 J4 Syzran' Rus. Fed.
16 G4 Szczecin Pol.
16 H4 Szczecinek Pol.
17 K4 Szczytno Pol.
17 K7 Szeged Hungary
17 J7 Székesfehérvár Hungary
17 J7 Szekszárd Hungary
17 K7 Szentes Hungary
16 H7 Szentgotthárd Hungary
18 G1 Szigetvár Hungary
17 K7 Szolnok Hungary
16 H7 Szombathely Hungary


# T


43 B3 Taal, L. *l.* Phil.
43 B3 Tabaco Phil.
91 H5 Tabankulu S. Africa
28 G4 Ţabaqah Syria
48 F2 Tabar Is *is* P.N.G.
28 E4 Tabarja Lebanon
18 C6 Tabarka Tunisia
30 E3 Ţabas Iran
31 E4 Tabāsin Iran
30 C4 Tābask, Kūh-e *mt* Iran
59 J3 Tabatière Can.
78 E4 Tabatinga Col.
43 B2 Tabayoo, Mt *mt* Phil.
53 E3 Tabbita Austr.
86 B2 Tabelbala Alg.
57 G5 Taber Can.
35 F3 Tabia Tsaka *salt l.* China
49 H2 Tabiteuea *i.* Kiribati
7 U7 Tabivere Estonia
43 B3 Tablas *i.* Phil.
43 B3 Tablas Strait *chan.* Phil.
51 F3 Table Cape *c.* N.Z.
90 C6 Table Mountain *mt* S. Africa
65 E4 Table Rock Res. *resr* U.S.A.
82 A2 Tabocó *r.* Brazil
16 G6 Tábor Czech Rep.
88 D4 Tabora Tanz.
86 B4 Tabou Côte d'Ivoire
30 B2 Tabrīz Iran
46 M3 Tabueran *i.* Kiribati
32 A4 Tabūk S. Arabia
49 G3 Tabwémasana *mt* Vanuatu
7 Q7 Täby Sweden
81 A2 Tacarcuna, Cerro *mt* Panama
27 G2 Tacheng China
16 F6 Tachov Czech Rep.
43 C4 Tacloban Phil.
78 D7 Tacna Peru
62 B2 Tacoma U.S.A.
83 F1 Tacuarembó Uru.
83 G2 Tacuari *r.* Uru.
81 E4 Tacutu *r.* Brazil
8 F4 Tadcaster U.K.
86 C2 Tademaït, Plateau du *plat.* Alg.
49 G4 Tadine New Caledonia
88 E2 Tadjoura Djibouti
28 G4 Tadmur Syria
57 K3 Tadoule Lake *l.* Can.
59 G4 Tadoussac Can.
42 D4 T'aebaek Sanmaek *mts* N. Korea/S. Korea
42 D5 Taech'ŏn S. Korea
42 C5 Taech'ŏngdo *i.* N. Korea
42 C4 Taedasa-do N. Korea
42 D4 Taedong *r.* N. Korea
42 C5 Taedong man *b.* N. Korea
42 E6 Taegu S. Korea
42 C6 Taehŭksan-kundo *i.* S. Korea
42 D5 Taejŏn S. Korea
42 D7 Taejŏng S. Korea
42 E5 T'aepaek S. Korea
9 C6 Taf *r.* U.K.
49 J3 Tafahi *i.* Tonga
15 F1 Tafalla Spain
30 D4 Tafihān Iran
28 E6 Tafila Jordan
86 B4 Tafiré Côte d'Ivoire
80 C3 Tafí Viejo Arg.
30 C3 Tafresh Iran
30 D4 Taft Iran
72 C4 Taft U.S.A.
31 F4 Taftān, Kūh-e *mt* Iran
21 F6 Taganrog Rus. Fed.
21 F6 Taganrog, Gulf of *b.* Rus. Fed./Ukr.
43 C3 Tagapula *i.* Phil.
43 B3 Tagaytay City Phil.
43 B4 Tagbilaran Phil.
35 E2 Tagchagpu Ri *mt* China
11 E5 Taghmon Rep. of Ireland
56 C2 Tagish Can.
18 E1 Tagliamento *r.* Italy
15 J4 Tagma, Col de *pass* Alg.
43 C4 Tagoloan *r.* Phil.
43 B4 Tagolo Point *pt* Phil.
49 F3 Tagula I. *i.* P.N.G.
43 C5 Tagum Phil.
15 B3 Tagus *r.* Port./Spain
56 F4 Tahaetkun Mt. *mt* Can.
44 B4 Tahan, Gunung *mt* Malaysia
86 C2 Tahat, Mt *mt* Alg.
36 E1 Tahe China
51 D1 Taheke N.Z.
46 N5 Tahiti *i.* Pac. Oc.
31 F4 Tahlab *r.* Iran/Pak.
31 F4 Tahlab, Dasht-i *plain* Pak.
65 E5 Tahlequah U.S.A.
72 B2 Tahoe City U.S.A.
54 H3 Tahoe Lake *l.* Can.
72 B2 Tahoe, Lake *l.* U.S.A.
65 C5 Tahoka U.S.A.
86 C3 Tahoua Niger
56 D4 Tahtsa Pk *summit* Can.
43 C6 Tahuna Indon.
39 □ Tai a Chau *i.* *H.K.* China
42 B3 Tai'an *Liaoning* China
38 E2 Tai'an *Shandong* China
38 C3 Taibai Shan *mt* China
38 E1 Taibus Qi China
39 F5 T'ai-chung Taiwan
51 C6 Taieri *r.* N.Z.
38 D2 Taigu China
38 D2 Taihang Shan *mts* China
51 E3 Taihape N.Z.
38 E3 Taihe *Anhui* China
39 E5 Taihe *Jiangxi* China
39 E4 Taihu China
36 E3 Tai Hu *l.* China
39 C5 Taijiang China
38 E3 Taikang China
39 □ Tai Lam Chung Res. *resr* *H.K.* China
50 B3 Tailem Bend Austr.
39 □ Tai Long Bay *b.* *H.K.* China
39 F5 T'ai-lu-ko Taiwan
31 F3 Taimani *reg.* Afgh.
39 □ Tai Mo Shan *h.* *H.K.* China
39 F6 T'ai-nan Taiwan
39 F6 T'ainan Taiwan
19 K6 Tainaro, Akra *pt* Greece
39 E5 Taining China
39 □ Tai O *H.K.* China
82 D1 Taiobeiras Brazil
86 B4 Taï, Parc National de *nat. park* Côte d'Ivoire
39 F5 T'ai-pei Taiwan
39 F4 Taiping *Anhui* China
39 D6 Taiping *Guangxi* China
45 B2 Taiping Malaysia
38 A2 Taipingbao China
42 B1 Taipingchuan China
39 □ Tai Po *H.K.* China
40 H3 Taisetsu-zan National Park Japan
41 C7 Taisha Japan
39 D6 Taishan China
39 F5 Taishun China
12 C5 Taissy France
51 D5 Taitanu N.Z.
80 B7 Taitao, Peninsula de *pen.* Chile
39 F6 T'ai-tung Taiwan
6 V4 Taivalkoski Fin.
6 T2 Taivaskero *h.* Fin.
23 M7 Taiwan *country* Asia
39 F6 Taiwan Shan *mts* Taiwan
39 F5 Taiwan Strait *str.* China/Taiwan
38 F3 Tai Xian China
38 F3 Taixing China
38 D2 Taiyuan China
38 D2 Taiyue Shan *mts* China
38 F3 Taizhou China
39 F4 Taizhou Wan *b.* China
42 C3 Taizi *r.* China
32 B7 Ta'izz Yemen
34 B4 Tajal Pak.
74 F5 Tajamulco, Volcano de *volc.* Guatemala
18 C7 Tajerouine Tunisia
23 G6 Tajikistan *country* Asia
Tajo *r.* *see* Tagus
44 A1 Tak Thai.
30 B2 Takāb Iran
41 C7 Takahashi Japan
51 D4 Takaka N.Z.
34 D5 Takal India
41 D7 Takamatsu Japan
34 D4 Takanpur India
41 E6 Takaoka Japan
51 F4 Takapau N.Z.
51 E2 Takapuna N.Z.
41 F6 Takasaki Japan
90 F2 Takatokwane Botswana
90 D1 Takatshwaane Botswana
41 C8 Takatsuki-yama *mt* Japan
41 E6 Takayama Japan
44 B4 Tak Bai Thai.
41 E7 Takefu Japan
41 B8 Takeo Japan
Take-shima *i.* *see* Tok-tō
41 B9 Take-shima *i.* Japan
30 C2 Takestān Iran
41 B8 Taketa Japan
44 C3 Takêv Cambodia
29 K7 Takhādīd *well* Iraq
32 E1 Takhiatash Uzbek.
44 C3 Ta Khmau Cambodia
31 F3 Takhta-Bazar Turkm.
29 M5 Takht Apān, Kūh-e *mt* Iran
31 G4 Takhta Pul Post Afgh.
34 B3 Takht-i-Sulaiman *mt* Pak.
30 C2 Takht-i-Suleiman *mt* Iran
57 G1 Takijuq Lake *l.* Can.
40 G3 Takikawa Japan
40 H2 Takinoue Japan
51 A6 Takitimu Mts *mts* N.Z.
56 D3 Takla Lake *l.* Can.
56 D3 Takla Landing Can.
Taklimakan Desert *see* Taklimakan Shamo
22 F6 Taklimakan Shamo *des.* China
31 H2 Takob Tajik.
35 H3 Takpa Shiri *mt* China
56 C3 Taku *r.* Can.
86 C4 Takum Nigeria
83 F2 Tala Uru.
20 D4 Talachyn Belarus
33 B4 Talaimannar Sri Lanka
34 C5 Talaja India
35 H4 Talap India
78 B4 Talara Peru
31 F5 Talar-i-Band *mts* Pak.
37 E6 Talaud, Kepulauan *is* Indon.
15 D3 Talavera de la Reina Spain
25 R3 Talaya Rus. Fed.
43 C5 Talayan Phil.
55 L2 Talbot Inlet *b.* Can.
53 G2 Talbragar *r.* Austr.
83 B2 Talca Chile
83 B3 Talcahuano Chile
35 F5 Talcher India
27 F2 Taldykorgan Kazak.
29 M5 Taleh Zang Iran
30 C2 Tālesh Iran
9 D6 Talgarth U.K.
37 E7 Taliabu *i.* Indon.
43 C4 Talibon Phil.
33 B2 Talikota India
31 G2 Talimardzhan Uzbek.
29 J1 T'alin Armenia
33 A3 Taliparamba India
43 B4 Talisay Phil.
43 C4 Talisayan Phil.
29 M2 Talış Dağları *mts* Azer./Iran
20 H3 Talitsa Rus. Fed.
45 E4 Taliwang Indon.
67 C5 Talladega U.S.A.
29 J3 Tall 'Afar Iraq
67 C6 Tallahassee U.S.A.
50 F4 Tallangatta Austr.
67 C5 Tallassee U.S.A.
28 F6 Tall as Suwaysh *h.* Jordan
29 H3 Tall Baydar Syria
29 H4 Tall Fadghāmī Syria
7 T7 Tallinn Estonia
28 F4 Tall Kalakh Syria
29 J3 Tall Kayf Iraq
11 C5 Tallow Rep. of Ireland
65 F5 Tallulah U.S.A.
29 J3 Tall 'Uwaynāt Iraq
14 D3 Talmont-St-Hilaire France
21 D5 Tal'ne Ukr.
87 F3 Talodi Sudan
59 G2 Talon, Lac *l.* Can.
31 H2 Tāloqān Afgh.
21 G5 Talovaya Rus. Fed.
55 J3 Taloyoak Can.
34 C2 Tal Pass Pak.
7 S8 Talsi Latvia
80 B3 Taltal Chile
57 G2 Taltson *r.* Can.
30 B3 Talvar *r.* Iran
6 S1 Talvik Norway
21 G5 Taly Rus. Fed.
50 D2 Talyawalka *r.* Austr.
68 A4 Tama U.S.A.
81 B2 Tamalameque Col.
86 B4 Tamale Ghana
49 H2 Tamana *i.* Kiribati
81 A3 Tamana *mt* Col.
41 C7 Tamano Japan
86 C2 Tamanrasset Alg.
35 H4 Tamanthi Myanmar
81 B3 Tama, Parque Nacional el *nat. park* Venez.
71 F4 Tamaqua U.S.A.
9 C7 Tamar *r.* U.K.
91 G1 Tamasane Botswana
65 D7 Tamaulipas *div.* Mex.
74 E4 Tamazunchale Mex.
88 D3 Tambach Kenya
86 A3 Tambacounda Senegal
35 F4 Tamba Kosi *r.* Nepal
43 A5 Tambisan Malaysia
50 F4 Tambo *r.* Austr.
45 E4 Tambora, Gunung *volc.* Indon.
50 F4 Tamboritha *mt* Austr.
20 G4 Tambov Rus. Fed.
20 G4 Tambovskaya Oblast' *div.* Rus. Fed.
15 B1 Tambre *r.* Spain
43 A5 Tambunan, Bukit *h.* Malaysia
87 E4 Tambura Sudan
43 A5 Tambuyukon, Gunung *mt* Malaysia
86 A3 Tâmchekkeţ Maur.

34 C5 Thandla India
34 B5 Thangadh India
44 D2 Thăng Binh Vietnam
44 C1 Thanh Hoa Vietnam
33 B4 Thanjavur India
44 B1 Tha Pla Thai.
44 A3 Thap Put Thai.
44 A3 Thap Sakae Thai.
34 B4 Tharad India
34 B4 Thar Desert India/Pak.
19 L4 Thasos *i.* Greece
73 H5 Thatcher U.S.A.
39 C6 Thât Khê Vietnam
37 B5 Thaton Myanmar
35 H4 Thaungdut Myanmar
44 A1 Thaungyin *r.* Myanmar/Thai.
37 B5 Thayetmyo Myanmar
73 F5 Theba U.S.A.
64 C3 Thedford U.S.A.
12 C2 The Hague Neth.
44 A3 Theinkun Myanmar
57 H2 Thekulthili Lake *l.* Can.
57 J2 Thelon *r.* Can.
57 J2 Thelon Game Sanctuary *res.* Can.
13 J4 Themar Ger.
90 F6 Thembalesizwe S. Africa
91 H3 Thembalihle S. Africa
15 H4 Thenia Alg.
15 H5 Theniet El Had Alg.
78 F5 Theodore Roosevelt *r.* Brazil
73 G5 Theodore Roosevelt Lake *l.* U.S.A.
64 C2 Theodore Roosevelt Nat. Park U.S.A.
12 A5 Thérain *r.* France
71 F2 Theresa U.S.A.
19 K4 Thermaïkos Kolpos *g.* Greece
72 B2 Thermalito U.S.A.
62 E3 Thermopolis U.S.A.
12 A4 Thérouanne France
54 F2 Thesiger Bay *b.* Can.
69 F2 Thessalon Can.
19 K4 Thessaloniki Greece
9 H5 Thet *r.* U.K.
9 H5 Thetford U.K.
59 F4 Thetford Mines Can.
44 C1 Theun *r.* Laos
91 G4 Theunissen S. Africa
65 F6 Thibodaux U.S.A.
57 K3 Thicket Portage Can.
64 D1 Thief River Falls U.S.A.
92 B4 Thiel Mts *mts* Ant.
14 F4 Thiers France
86 A3 Thiès Senegal
88 D4 Thika Kenya
33 A5 Thiladhunmathee Atoll *atoll* Maldives
35 G4 Thimphu Bhutan
14 H2 Thionville France
Thira *i. see* Santorini
19 L6 Thirasia *i.* Greece
8 F3 Thirsk U.K.
Thiruvananthapuram *see* Trivandrum
7 L8 Thisted Denmark
19 K5 Thiva Greece
57 K2 Thlewiaza *r.* Can.
57 H2 Thoa *r.* Can.
91 J1 Thohoyandou S. Africa
12 C3 Tholen Neth.
12 F5 Tholey Ger.
70 D5 Thomas U.S.A.
67 C5 Thomaston *GA* U.S.A.
71 J2 Thomaston *ME* U.S.A.
71 K2 Thomaston Corner Can.
11 D5 Thomastown Rep. of Ireland
67 D6 Thomasville U.S.A.
12 E4 Thommen Belgium
57 K3 Thompson *Man.* Can.
68 D3 Thompson *MI* U.S.A.
71 F4 Thompson *PA* U.S.A.
56 E4 Thompson *r.* Can.
64 E3 Thompson *r.* U.S.A.
62 D2 Thompson Falls U.S.A.
67 D5 Thomson U.S.A.
44 C1 Thôn Cư Lai Vietnam
16 C7 Thonon-les-Bains France
44 D3 Thôn Sơn Hai Vietnam
63 E5 Thoreau U.S.A.
12 D3 Thorn Neth.
8 F3 Thornaby-on-Tees U.K.
68 E4 Thornapple *r.* U.S.A.
9 E6 Thornbury U.K.
69 H2 Thorne Can.
8 G4 Thorne U.K.
72 C2 Thorne U.S.A.
56 C3 Thorne Bay U.S.A.
68 D5 Thorntown U.S.A.
68 B3 Thorp U.S.A.
92 D3 Thorshavnheiane *mts* Ant.
91 G4 Thota-ea-Moli Lesotho
14 D3 Thouars France
71 E2 Thousand Islands *is* Can.
73 G2 Thousand Lake Mt *mt* U.S.A.
72 C4 Thousand Oaks U.S.A.
19 L4 Thrakiko Pelagos *sea* Greece
62 E2 Three Forks U.S.A.
56 G4 Three Hills Can.
51 D1 Three Kings Is *is* N.Z.
68 C3 Three Lakes U.S.A.
68 D5 Three Oaks U.S.A.
44 A2 Three Pagodas Pass Myanmar/Thai.
86 B4 Three Points, Cape *c.* Ghana
68 E5 Three Rivers *MI* U.S.A.
65 D6 Three Rivers *TX* U.S.A.
62 B2 Three Sisters *mt* U.S.A.
Thrissur *see* Trichur
65 D5 Throckmorton U.S.A.
57 G2 Thubun Lakes *l.* Can.
44 C3 Thu Dâu Một Vietnam
12 C4 Thuin Belgium
Thule *see* Qaanaaq
89 C6 Thuli Zimbabwe
16 C7 Thun Switz.
68 C1 Thunder Bay Can.
68 C1 Thunder Bay *b.* Can.
69 F3 Thunder Bay *b.* U.S.A.
13 H5 Thüngen Ger.
44 A3 Thung Song Thai.
44 A4 Thung Wa Thai.
13 J4 Thüringen *div.* Ger.
13 K3 Thüringer Becken *reg.* Ger.
13 J4 Thüringer Wald *mts* Ger.
11 D5 Thurles Rep. of Ireland
70 E5 Thurmont U.S.A.
16 F7 Thurn, Paß *pass* Austria
71 F2 Thurso Can.
10 E2 Thurso U.K.
10 E2 Thurso *r. Scot.* U.K.
92 A3 Thurston I. *i.* Ant.
13 H2 Thüster Berg *h.* Ger.
8 E3 Thwaite U.K.
92 A3 Thwaites Gl. *gl.* Ant.
7 L8 Thyborøn Denmark
38 A1 Tiancang China
38 F3 Tianchang China
39 C6 Tiandeng China
39 C6 Tiandong China
39 C5 Tian'e China
79 K4 Tianguá Brazil
38 E2 Tianjin China
38 E2 Tianjin *div.* China
36 B3 Tianjun China
39 C5 Tianlin China
39 D4 Tianmen China
39 F4 Tianmu Shan *mts* China
42 E2 Tianqiaoling China
39 B4 Tianquan China
42 C3 Tianshifu China
38 B3 Tianshui China
34 D2 Tianshuihai China/Jammu and Kashmir
39 F4 Tiantai China
38 E1 Tiantaiyong China
39 C6 Tianyang China
38 B2 Tianzhu *Gansu* China
39 C5 Tianzhu *Guizhou* China
86 C1 Tiaret Alg.
86 B4 Tiassalé Côte d'Ivoire
82 B4 Tibagi *r.* Brazil
29 J5 Tibal, Wādī *watercourse* Iraq
87 D4 Tibati Cameroon
18 E3 Tiber *r.* Italy
28 E5 Tiberias Israel
Tiberias, Lake *l. see* Galilee, Sea of
62 E1 Tiber Res. *resr* U.S.A.
87 D2 Tibesti *mts* Chad
Tibet Aut. Region *div. see* Xizang Zizhiqu
Tibet, Plateau of *plat. see* Xizang Gaoyuan
48 E4 Tibooburra Austr.
35 E3 Tibrikot Nepal
35 E3 Tibrikot Nepal
7 O7 Tibro Sweden
74 B3 Tiburón *i.* Mex.
43 B3 Ticao *i.* Phil.
9 H6 Ticehurst U.K.
69 J3 Tichborne Can.
86 B3 Tichît Maur.
86 A2 Tichla Western Sahara
16 D7 Ticino *r.* Switz.
71 G3 Ticonderoga U.S.A.
74 G4 Ticul Mex.
7 N7 Tidaholm Sweden
35 H5 Tiddim Myanmar
86 C2 Tidikelt, Plaine du *plain* Alg.
86 A3 Tidjikja Maur.
12 D3 Tiel Neth.
40 A1 Tieli China
42 B2 Tieling China
34 D2 Tielongtan China/Jammu and Kashmir
12 B4 Tielt Belgium
86 B4 Tiémé Côte d'Ivoire
12 C4 Tienen Belgium
22 E5 Tien Shan *mts* China/Kyrg.
Tientsin *see* Tianjin
7 P6 Tierp Sweden
63 F4 Tierra Amarilla U.S.A.
74 E5 Tierra Blanca Mex.
80 C8 Tierra del Fuego, Isla Grande de *i.* Arg./Chile
15 D2 Tiétar *r.* Spain
15 D2 Tiétar, Valle de *v.* Spain
82 C3 Tietê Brazil
82 B3 Tietê *r.* Brazil
70 B4 Tiffin U.S.A.
Tiflis *see* T'bilisi
67 D6 Tifton U.S.A.
19 L3 Tigheciului, Dealurile *h.* Moldova
21 D6 Tighina Moldova
35 F5 Tigiria India
87 D4 Tignère Cameroon
59 H4 Tignish Can.
78 C4 Tigre *r.* Ecuador/Peru
81 E2 Tigre *r.* Venez.
29 L5 Tigris *r.* Iraq/Turkey
32 B6 Tihāmah *reg.* S. Arabia
28 D7 Tīh, Gebel el *plat.* Egypt
74 A2 Tijuana Mex.
82 C2 Tijuco *r.* Brazil
34 D4 Tikamgarh India
21 G6 Tikhoretsk Rus. Fed.
20 E3 Tikhvin Rus. Fed.
20 E3 Tikhvinskaya Gryada *ridge* Rus. Fed.
51 F3 Tikokino N.Z.
49 G3 Tikopia *i.* Solomon Is
29 J4 Tikrīt Iraq
6 W3 Tiksheozero, Oz. *l.* Rus. Fed.
25 O2 Tiksi Rus. Fed.
35 E3 Tila *r.* Nepal
35 F4 Tilaiya Reservoir India
30 D2 Tilavar Iran
12 D3 Tilburg Neth.
9 H6 Tilbury U.K.
80 C2 Tilcara Arg.
35 H5 Tilin Myanmar
86 C3 Tillabéri Niger
62 B2 Tillamook U.S.A.
10 E4 Tillicoultry U.K.
69 G4 Tillsonburg Can.
10 F3 Tillyfourie U.K.
19 M6 Tilos *i.* Greece
50 E1 Tilpa Austr.
21 F5 Tim Rus. Fed.
20 K1 Timanskiy Kryazh *ridge* Rus. Fed.
29 J2 Timar Turkey
51 C6 Timaru N.Z.
21 F6 Timashevsk Rus. Fed.
86 B3 Timbedgha Maur.
48 D3 Timber Creek Austr.
72 D3 Timber Mt *mt* U.S.A.
70 D5 Timberville U.S.A.
50 D5 Timboon Austr.
86 B3 Timétrine *reg.* Mali
86 C2 Timimoun Alg.
19 J2 Timişoara Romania
69 G1 Timmins Can.
20 F3 Timokhino Rus. Fed.
79 K5 Timon Brazil
37 E7 Timor *i.* Indon.
48 C3 Timor Sea *sea* Austr./Indon.
20 H3 Timoshino Rus. Fed.
83 D2 Timote Arg.
7 P5 Timrå Sweden
67 C5 Tims Ford L. *l.* U.S.A.
34 D5 Timurni Muafi India
81 C2 Tinaco Venez.
33 B3 Tindivanam India
86 B2 Tindouf Alg.
44 C5 Tinggi *i.* Malaysia
39 E5 Ting Jiang *r.* China
35 F3 Tingri China
7 O8 Tingsryd Sweden
83 B2 Tinguiririca, Vol. *volc.* Chile
6 L5 Tingvoll Norway
10 E1 Tingwall U.K.
82 E1 Tinharé, Ilha de *i.* Brazil
44 C1 Tinh Gia Vietnam
43 G5 Tinian *i.* N. Mariana Is
80 C3 Tinogasta Arg.
19 L6 Tinos *i.* Greece
12 B5 Tinqueux France
86 C2 Tinrhert, Plateau du *plat.* Alg.
35 H4 Tinsukia India
9 C7 Tintagel U.K.
50 C3 Tintinara Austr.
15 E5 Tinto *h.* U.K.
70 E4 Tioga *r.* U.S.A.
45 B2 Tioman *i.* Malaysia
69 F1 Tionaga Can.
70 D4 Tionesta Lake *l.* U.S.A.
71 E3 Tioughnioga *r.* U.S.A.
15 H4 Tipasa Alg.
68 D5 Tippecanoe *r.* U.S.A.
68 E5 Tippecanoe Lake *l.* U.S.A.
11 C5 Tipperary Rep. of Ireland
35 F4 Tiptala Bhanjyang *pass* Nepal
68 B5 Tipton *IA* U.S.A.
68 D5 Tipton *IN* U.S.A.
73 E4 Tipton, Mt *mt* U.S.A.
68 E1 Tip Top Hill *h.* Can.
9 H6 Tiptree U.K.
81 C4 Tiquié *r.* Brazil
79 J4 Tiracambu, Serra do *h.* Brazil
19 H4 Tirana Albania
Tiranë *see* Tirana
18 D1 Tirano Italy
21 D6 Tiraspol Moldova
90 B3 Tiraz Mts *mts* Namibia
28 A2 Tire Turkey
10 B4 Tiree *i.* U.K.
34 B1 Tirich Mir *mt* Pak.
33 B2 Tirna *r.* India
33 A3 Tirthahalli India
35 F5 Tirtol India
33 B4 Tiruchchendur India
33 B4 Tiruchchirāppalli India
33 B4 Tiruchengodu India
33 B4 Tirunelveli India
33 B3 Tirupati India
33 B3 Tiruppattur India
33 B4 Tiruppur India
33 B4 Tirutturaippundi India
33 B3 Tiruvannamalai India
33 B3 Tisaiyanvilai India
57 J4 Tisdale Can.
33 C5 Tissamaharama Sri Lanka
15 G5 Tissemsilt Alg.
35 G4 Tista *r.* India
92 B4 Titan Dome *ice feature* Ant.
25 O2 Tit-Ary Rus. Fed.
78 E7 Titicaca, Lago *l.* Bol./Peru
35 E5 Titlagarh India
18 G2 Titov Drvar Bos.-Herz.
69 E4 Tittabawassee *r.* U.S.A.
19 L2 Titu Romania
67 D6 Titusville *FL* U.S.A.
70 D4 Titusville *PA* U.S.A.
69 G3 Tiverton Can.
9 D7 Tiverton U.K.
18 E4 Tivoli Italy
15 H4 Tizi El Arba *h.* Alg.
74 G4 Tizimín Mex.
15 J4 Tizi Ouzou Alg.
81 D2 Tiznados *r.* Venez.
86 B2 Tiznit Morocco
65 C7 Tizoc Mex.
91 J2 Tjaneni Swaziland
6 Q4 Tjappsåive Sweden
12 D2 Tjeukemeer *l.* Neth.
7 K7 Tjorhom Norway
65 C7 Tlahualilo Mex.
74 E5 Tlaxcala Mex.
86 B1 Tlemcen Alg.
90 E4 Tlhakalatlou S. Africa
91 H4 Tlholong S. Africa
91 F2 Tlokweng Botswana
56 D3 Toad River Can.
89 E5 Toamasina Madag.
83 D3 Toay Arg.
41 E7 Toba Japan
44 A5 Toba, Danau *l.* Indon.
78 F1 Tobago *i.* Trinidad and Tobago
34 A3 Toba & Kakar Ranges *mts* Pak.
37 E6 Tobelo Indon.
69 G3 Tobermory Can.
10 B4 Tobermory U.K.
57 J4 Tobin L. *l.* Can.
72 D1 Tobin, Mt *mt* U.S.A.
71 K1 Tobique *r.* Can.
40 F5 Tobi-shima *i.* Japan
45 C3 Toboali Indon.
24 H4 Tobol *r.* Kazak./Rus. Fed.
44 D2 Tô Bong Vietnam
79 J5 Tocantinópolis Brazil
79 J4 Tocantins *r.* Brazil
82 C1 Tocantinzinha *r.* Brazil
67 D5 Toccoa U.S.A.
34 B2 Tochi *r.* Pak.
7 M7 Töcksfors Sweden
80 B2 Tocopilla Chile
50 E3 Tocumwal Austr.
81 C2 Tocuyo *r.* Venez.
18 E3 Todi Italy
16 D7 Todi *mt* Switz.
40 H5 Todoga-saki *pt* Japan
40 G4 Todohokke Japan
78 E7 Todos Santos Bol.
72 D6 Todos Santos, Bahía de *b.* Mex.
56 G4 Tofield Can.
56 D5 Tofino Can.
10 □ Toft U.K.
68 B2 Tofte U.S.A.
49 J3 Tofua *i.* Tonga
37 E7 Togian, Kepulauan *is* Indon.
68 A2 Togo U.S.A.
85 D5 Togo *country* Africa
38 D1 Togtoh China
73 H4 Tohatchi U.S.A.
6 T5 Toholampi Fin.
38 B1 Tohom China
7 S6 Toijala Fin.
41 B9 Toi-misaki *pt* Japan
7 U5 Toivakka Fin.
72 D2 Toiyabe Range *mts* U.S.A.
31 H2 Tojikobod Tajik.
54 D3 Tok U.S.A.
41 F6 Tōkamachi Japan
51 B7 Tokanui N.Z.
87 F3 Tokar Sudan
36 E4 Tokara-rettō *is* Japan
28 F1 Tokat Turkey
42 D5 Tŏkchŏktŏ *i.* S. Korea
42 D4 Tŏkch'ŏn N. Korea
47 K4 Tokelau *terr.* Pac. Oc.
27 F2 Tokmak Kyrg.
21 E6 Tokmak Ukr.
51 G3 Tokomaru Bay N.Z.
51 E3 Tokoroa N.Z.
91 H3 Tokoza S. Africa
24 K5 Toksun China
41 B6 Tok-tō *i.* Japan
41 D7 Tokushima Japan
41 B7 Tokuyama Japan
41 F7 Tōkyō Japan
41 F7 Tōkyō-wan *b.* Japan
31 G3 Tokzār Afgh.
51 G3 Tolaga Bay N.Z.
89 E6 Tōlañaro Madag.
82 B4 Toledo Brazil
15 D3 Toledo Spain
68 A5 Toledo *IA* U.S.A.
70 B4 Toledo *OH* U.S.A.
65 E6 Toledo Bend Reservoir U.S.A.
15 D3 Toledo, Montes de *mts* Spain
83 B3 Tolhuaca, Parque Nacional *nat. park* Chile
89 E6 Toliara Madag.
81 B3 Tolima, Nev. del *volc.* Col.
37 E6 Tolitoli Indon.
24 K3 Tol'ka Rus. Fed.
13 M1 Tollensesee *l.* Ger.
20 D3 Tolmachevo Rus. Fed.
18 E1 Tolmezzo Italy
39 □ Tolo Channel *H.K.* China
39 □ Tolo Harbour *b. H.K.* China
15 E1 Tolosa Spain
42 D6 Tolsan-do *i.* S. Korea
69 F3 Tolsmaville Can.
10 B2 Tolsta Head *hd* U.K.
81 B2 Tolú Col.
74 E5 Toluca Mex.
60 B4 Tolumne *r. CA* U.S.A.
6 W3 Tolvand, Oz. *l.* Rus. Fed.
20 J4 Tol'yatti Rus. Fed.
68 B4 Tomah U.S.A.
68 C3 Tomahawk U.S.A.
40 G3 Tomakomai Japan
40 G2 Tomamae Japan
49 H3 Tomanivi *mt* Fiji
81 E5 Tomar Brazil
15 B3 Tomar Port.
28 E2 Tomarza Turkey
83 F1 Tomás Gomensoro Uru.
17 L5 Tomaszów Lubelski Pol.
17 K5 Tomaszów Mazowiecki Pol.
10 E3 Tomatin U.K.
67 B6 Tombigbee *r.* U.S.A.
88 B4 Tomboco Angola
82 D3 Tombos Brazil
86 B3 Tombouctou Mali
73 G6 Tombstone U.S.A.
89 B5 Tombua Angola
91 H1 Tom Burke S. Africa
83 B3 Tomé Chile
91 L1 Tome Moz.
7 N9 Tomelilla Sweden
15 E3 Tomelloso Spain
69 H2 Tomiko Can.
50 G2 Tomingley Austr.
86 B3 Tominian Mali
37 E7 Tomini, Teluk *g.* Indon.
10 E3 Tomintoul U.K.
18 G3 Tomislavgrad Bos.-Herz.
6 O3 Tømmerneset Norway
25 O4 Tommot Rus. Fed.
81 D4 Tomo Col.
81 C3 Tomo *r.* Col.
38 D1 Tomortei China
25 P3 Tompo Rus. Fed.
48 B4 Tom Price Austr.
36 A1 Tomsk Rus. Fed.
7 O8 Tomtabacken *h.* Sweden
25 Q3 Tomtor Rus. Fed.
40 H3 Tomuraushi-yama *mt* Japan
21 G6 Tomuzlovka *r.* Rus. Fed.
74 F5 Tonalá Mex.
73 G3 Tonalea U.S.A.
78 E4 Tonantins Brazil
62 C1 Tonasket U.S.A.
9 H6 Tonbridge U.K.
37 E6 Tondano Indon.
7 L9 Tønder Denmark
9 E6 Tone *r.* U.K.
47 K5 Tonga *country* Pac. Oc.
91 J4 Tongaat S. Africa
50 E4 Tongala Austr.
39 F5 Tong'an China
46 M4 Tongareva *i. Cook Is* Kiribati
51 E3 Tongariro National Park N.Z.
49 J4 Tongatapu Group *is* Tonga
94 H7 Tonga Tr. *sea feature* Pac. Oc.
38 D3 Tongbai China
38 D3 Tongbai Shan *mts* China
38 E4 Tongcheng *Anhui* China
39 D4 Tongcheng *Hubei* China
42 D4 T'ongch'ŏn N. Korea
38 C3 Tongchuan China
39 C5 Tongdao China
38 A3 Tongde China
42 D5 Tongduch'ŏn S. Korea
12 D4 Tongeren Belgium
39 E4 Tonggu China
39 D7 Tonggu Jiao *pt* China
42 E5 Tonghae S. Korea
39 B5 Tonghai China
40 A2 Tonghe China
42 C3 Tonghua *Jilin* China
42 C3 Tonghua *Jilin* China
38 C4 Tongjiang China
42 B2 Tongjiangkou China
42 D4 Tongjosŏn Man *b.* N. Korea
39 C6 Tongking, Gulf of *g.* China/Vietnam
39 C4 Tongliang China
42 B2 Tongliao China
38 E4 Tongling China
39 F4 Tonglu China
42 E6 Tongnae S. Korea
39 B4 Tongnan China
43 B5 Tongquil *i.* Phil.
39 C5 Tongren *Guizhou* China
38 A3 Tongren *Qinghai* China
35 G4 Tongsa *r.* Bhutan
39 E4 Tongshan China
35 H2 Tongtian He *r.* China
10 D2 Tongue U.K.
62 F2 Tongue *r.* U.S.A.
67 E7 Tongue of the Ocean *chan.* Bahamas
38 B3 Tongwei China
38 E2 Tong Xian China
38 B2 Tongxin China
38 E4 Tongyanghe China
42 B1 Tongyu China
42 B3 Tongyuanpu China
39 C4 Tongzi China
68 C5 Tonica U.S.A.
34 C4 Tonk India
30 C2 Tonkābon Iran
39 B6 Tonkin *reg.* Vietnam
20 H3 Tonkino Rus. Fed.
44 C3 Tônle Basăk *r.* Cambodia
44 C2 Tônle Repou *r.* Laos
44 B2 Tônlé Sab *l.* Cambodia
40 G5 Tōno Japan
72 D2 Tonopah U.S.A.
81 E2 Tonoro *r.* Venez.
7 M7 Tønsberg Norway
7 K7 Tonstad Norway
73 G5 Tonto National Monument *res.* U.S.A.
35 H5 Tonzang Myanmar
62 D3 Tooele U.S.A.
50 D3 Tooleybuc Austr.
50 G3 Tooma *r.* Austr.
50 F5 Toora Austr.
50 G1 Tooraweenah Austr.
90 F6 Toorberg *mt* S. Africa
48 F4 Toowoomba Austr.
73 G6 Topawa U.S.A.
72 C2 Topaz U.S.A.
64 E4 Topeka U.S.A.
56 D4 Topley Landing Can.
13 L2 Töplitz Ger.
83 B2 Topocalma, Pta *pt* Chile
73 E4 Topock U.S.A.
16 J6 Topoľčany Slovakia
74 C3 Topolobampo Mex.
19 M3 Topolovgrad Bulg.
6 W4 Topozero, Oz. *l.* Rus. Fed.
62 B2 Toppenish U.S.A.
71 K2 Topsfield U.S.A.
73 F3 Toquerville U.S.A.
88 D3 Tor Eth.
19 M5 Torbalı Turkey
31 E3 Torbat-e-Heydarīyeh Iran
31 F3 Torbat-e Jām Iran
20 G4 Torbeyevo Rus. Fed.
68 E3 Torch Lake *l.* U.S.A.
15 D2 Tordesillas Spain
6 S4 Töre Sweden
15 H1 Torelló Spain
12 D2 Torenberg *h.* Neth.
13 L3 Torgau Ger.
21 H5 Torgun *r.* Rus. Fed.
12 B3 Torhout Belgium
Torino *see* Turin
41 G9 Tori-shima *i.* Japan
87 F4 Torit Sudan
82 B2 Torixoreu Brazil
29 L3 Torkamān Iran
20 G3 Tor'kovskoye Vdkhr. *resr* Rus. Fed.
15 D2 Tormes *r.* Spain
6 S3 Torneälven *r.* Fin./Sweden
6 Q2 Torneträsk Sweden
6 Q2 Torneträsk *l.* Sweden
59 H2 Torngat Mountains Can.
6 T4 Tornio Fin.
83 D3 Tornquist Arg.
15 D2 Toro Spain
36 F1 Torom *r.* Rus. Fed.
50 H2 Toronto Austr.
69 H4 Toronto Can.
20 D3 Toropets Rus. Fed.
72 D5 Toro Pk *summit* U.S.A.
88 D3 Tororo Uganda
28 D3 Toros Dağları *mts* Turkey
10 F3 Torphins U.K.
9 D7 Torquay U.K.
72 C5 Torrance U.S.A.
15 B3 Torrão Port.
15 C2 Torre *mt* Port.
15 G2 Torreblanca Spain
18 F4 Torre del Greco Italy
15 D1 Torrelavega Spain
15 D4 Torremolinos Spain
50 A1 Torrens, Lake Austr.
15 F3 Torrent Spain
65 C7 Torreón Mex.
49 G3 Torres Islands *is* Vanuatu
15 B3 Torres Novas Port.
48 E2 Torres Strait *str.* Austr.
15 B3 Torres Vedras Port.
15 G3 Torreta, Sa *h.* Spain
15 F4 Torrevieja Spain
73 G2 Torrey U.S.A.
9 C7 Torridge *r.* U.K.
10 C3 Torridon, Loch *in.* U.K.
15 D3 Torrijos Spain
71 G4 Torrington *CT* U.S.A.
62 F3 Torrington *WY* U.S.A.
15 H1 Torroella de Montgrí Spain
7 N6 Torsby Sweden
6 □ Tórshavn Faroe Is
83 C1 Tórtolas, Cerro Las *mt* Chile
18 C5 Tortoli *Sardinia* Italy
18 C2 Tortona Italy
15 G2 Tortosa Spain
29 H1 Tortum Turkey
30 D3 Torūd Iran
29 G1 Torul Turkey
17 J4 Toruń Pol.
11 C2 Tory Island *i.* Rep. of Ireland
11 C2 Tory Sound *chan.* Rep. of Ireland
20 E3 Torzhok Rus. Fed.
41 C8 Tosa Japan
41 C8 Tosashimizu Japan
6 N4 Tosbotn Norway
90 E2 Tosca S. Africa
18 C3 Toscano, Arcipelago *is* Italy
40 G4 Tōshima-yama *mt* Japan
20 D3 Tosno Rus. Fed.
80 D3 Tostado Arg.
13 H1 Tostedt Ger.
41 B8 Tosu Japan
28 E1 Tosya Turkey
20 G3 Tot'ma Rus. Fed.
92 C6 Totten Glacier *gl.* Ant.
9 F7 Totton U.K.
41 D7 Tottori Japan
86 B4 Touba Côte d'Ivoire
86 A3 Touba Senegal
86 B1 Toubkal, Jbel *mt* Morocco
38 B2 Toudaohu China
86 B3 Tougan Burkina
86 C1 Touggourt Alg.
86 A3 Tougué Guinea
14 G2 Toul France
14 G5 Toulon France
14 E5 Toulouse France
86 B4 Toumodi Côte d'Ivoire
37 B5 Toungoo Myanmar
39 D5 Toupai China
44 B1 Tourakom Laos
12 B4 Tourcoing France
12 B4 Tournai Belgium
14 G4 Tournon-sur-Rhône France
14 G3 Tournus France
79 L5 Touros Brazil
14 E3 Tours France
90 D6 Touwsrivier S. Africa
13 L4 Toužim Czech Rep.
81 C2 Tovar Venez.
9 F5 Tove *r.* U.K.
29 K1 Tovuz Azer.
40 G4 Towada Japan
40 G5 Towada-Hachimantai National Park Japan
40 G4 Towada-ko *l.* Japan
51 E1 Towai N.Z.
71 E4 Towanda U.S.A.
73 H3 Towaoc U.S.A.
9 G5 Towcester U.K.
11 C6 Tower Rep. of Ireland
68 A2 Tower U.S.A.
57 J5 Towner U.S.A.
72 D3 Townes Pass U.S.A.
62 E2 Townsend U.S.A.
50 G4 Townsend, Mt *mt* Austr.
48 E3 Townsville Austr.
37 E7 Towori, Teluk *b.* Indon.
70 E5 Towson U.S.A.
40 G3 Tōya-ko *l.* Japan
41 E6 Toyama Japan
41 E6 Toyama-wan *b.* Japan
41 E7 Toyohashi Japan
41 E7 Toyokawa Japan
41 D7 Toyonaka Japan
41 D7 Toyooka Japan
41 E7 Toyota Japan
86 C1 Tozeur Tunisia
21 G7 Tqibuli Georgia
21 G7 Tqvarch'eli Georgia
12 F5 Traben Ger.
28 E4 Trâblous Lebanon
19 K4 Trabotivište Macedonia
29 G1 Trabzon Turkey
71 K2 Tracy Can.
72 B3 Tracy *CA* U.S.A.
64 E2 Tracy *MN* U.S.A.
68 A4 Traer U.S.A.
15 C4 Trafalgar, Cabo *pt* Spain
83 B3 Traiguén Chile
56 F5 Trail Can.
7 T9 Trakai Lith.
20 J2 Trakt Rus. Fed.
11 B5 Tralee Rep. of Ireland
11 B5 Tralee Bay *b.* Rep. of Ireland

81 E3 Tramán Tepui *mt* Venez.
11 D5 Tramore Rep. of Ireland
7 O7 Tranås Sweden
80 C3 Trancas Arg.
7 N8 Tranemo Sweden
10 F5 Tranent U.K.
44 A4 Trang Thai.
37 F7 Trangan *i.* Indon.
50 F2 Trangie Austr.
83 F1 Tranqueras Uru.
92 B5 Transantarctic Mountains Ant.
57 K5 Transcona Can.
19 K2 Transylvanian Alps *mts* Romania
18 E5 Trapani *Sicily* Italy
50 F5 Traralgon Austr.
18 E3 Trasimeno, Lago *l.* Italy
15 E3 Trasvase, Canal de *canal* Spain
44 B2 Trat Thai.
16 F7 Traunsee *l.* Austria
16 F7 Traunstein Ger.
50 D2 Travellers L. *l.* Austr.
92 C1 Traversay Is *is* Atl. Ocean
68 E3 Traverse City U.S.A.
51 D5 Travers, Mt *mt* N.Z.
44 C3 Tra Vinh Vietnam
65 D6 Travis, L. *l.* U.S.A.
18 G2 Travnik Bos.-Herz.
18 F1 Trbovlje Slovenia
49 F2 Treasury Is *is* Solomon Is
13 M2 Trebbin Ger.
16 G6 Třebíč Czech Rep.
19 H3 Trebinje Bos.-Herz.
17 K6 Trebišov Slovakia
18 F2 Trebnje Slovenia
13 G5 Trebur Ger.
13 J3 Treffurt Ger.
68 B3 Trego U.S.A.
10 D4 Treig, Loch *l.* U.K.
83 F2 Treinta-y-Tres Uru.
80 C6 Trelew Arg.
7 N9 Trelleborg Sweden
12 C4 Trélon France
9 C5 Tremadoc Bay *b.* U.K.
58 F4 Tremblant, Mt *h.* Can.
18 F3 Tremiti, Isole *is* Italy
62 D3 Tremonton U.S.A.
15 G1 Tremp Spain
68 B3 Trempealeau *r.* U.S.A.
9 B7 Trenance U.K.
16 J6 Trenčín Slovakia
13 H3 Trendelburg Ger.
83 D2 Trenque Lauquén Arg.
8 G4 Trent *r.* U.K.
18 D1 Trento Italy
69 J3 Trenton Can.
64 E3 Trenton *MO* U.S.A.
71 F4 Trenton *NJ* U.S.A.
59 K4 Trepassey Can.
83 E3 Tres Arroyos Arg.
9 A8 Tresco *i.* U.K.
82 D3 Três Corações Brazil
81 B4 Tres Esquinas Col.
10 B4 Treshnish Isles *is* U.K.
82 B3 Três Lagoas Brazil
80 B7 Tres Lagos Arg.
83 D3 Tres Lomas Arg.
82 D2 Três Marias, Represa *resr* Brazil
83 B4 Tres Picos *mt* Arg.
83 E3 Tres Picos, Cerro *mt* Arg.
63 F4 Tres Piedras U.S.A.
82 D3 Três Pontas Brazil
80 C7 Tres Puntas, C. *pt* Arg.
82 D3 Três Rios Brazil
7 M6 Tretten Norway
13 J6 Treuchtlingen Ger.
13 L2 Treuenbrietzen Ger.
7 L7 Treungen Norway
18 C2 Treviglio Italy
18 E2 Treviso Italy
9 B7 Trevose Head *hd* U.K.
19 M6 Tria Nisia *i.* Greece
19 N6 Trianta Greece
34 B2 Tribal Areas *div.* Pak.
19 H5 Tricase Italy
33 B4 Trichur India
12 A5 Tricot France
50 E2 Trida Austr.
12 E5 Trier Ger.
18 E2 Trieste Italy
18 E1 Triglav *mt* Slovenia
19 J5 Trikala Greece
28 D4 Trikomon Cyprus
37 F7 Trikora, Pk *mt* Indon.
11 E4 Trim Rep. of Ireland
33 C4 Trincomalee Sri Lanka
82 C2 Trindade Brazil
96 G7 Trindade, Ilha da *i.* Atl. Ocean
78 F6 Trinidad Bol.
81 C3 Trinidad Col.
75 J4 Trinidad Cuba
83 F2 Trinidad Uru.
63 F4 Trinidad U.S.A.
78 F1 Trinidad *i.* Trinidad and Tobago
53 K8 Trinidad and Tobago *country* Caribbean Sea
59 K4 Trinity Bay *b.* Can.
54 C4 Trinity Islands *is* U.S.A.
72 C1 Trinity Range *mts* U.S.A.
67 C5 Trion U.S.A.
13 K1 Tripkau Ger.
19 K6 Tripoli Greece
Tripoli *see* Trâblous
87 D1 Tripoli Libya
33 B4 Tripunittura India
35 G5 Tripura *div.* India
96 J8 Tristan da Cunha *i.* Atlantic Ocean
34 D3 Trisul *mt* India
35 F4 Trisul Dam *dam* Nepal
13 J1 Trittau Ger.
12 E5 Trittenheim Ger.
33 B4 Trivandrum India
18 F4 Trivento Italy
16 H6 Trnava Slovakia
48 F2 Trobriand Islands *is* P.N.G.
6 N4 Trofors Norway
18 G3 Trogir Croatia
18 F4 Troia Italy
12 F4 Troisdorf Ger.
12 D4 Trois-Ponts Belgium
59 F4 Trois-Rivières Can.
21 H6 Troitskoye Rus. Fed.
7 N7 Trollhättan Sweden
79 G3 Trombetas *r.* Brazil
93 H5 Tromelin, Île *i.* Ind. Ocean
83 B3 Tromen, Volcán *volc.* Arg.
91 F5 Trompsburg S. Africa
6 Q2 Tromsø Norway
72 D4 Trona U.S.A.
83 B4 Tronador, Monte *mt* Arg.
6 M5 Trondheim Norway
6 M5 Trondheimsfjorden *chan.* Norway
28 D4 Troodos Cyprus
28 D4 Troödos, Mount *mt* Cyprus
10 D5 Troon U.K.
82 D1 Tropeiros, Serra dos *h.* Brazil
73 F3 Tropic U.S.A.
10 D4 Trossachs, The *reg.* U.K.
11 E2 Trostan *h.* U.K.
10 F3 Troup Head *hd* U.K.
56 E2 Trout *r.* Can.
69 H3 Trout Creek Can.
62 E3 Trout Creek U.S.A.
58 B3 Trout L. *l.* Can.
56 G3 Trout Lake *Alta.* Can.
56 E2 Trout Lake *N.W.T.* Can.
68 E2 Trout Lake U.S.A.
56 E2 Trout Lake *l.* Can.
68 C2 Trout Lake *l.* U.S.A.
62 E2 Trout Peak *summit* U.S.A.
70 E4 Trout Run U.S.A.
9 E6 Trowbridge U.K.
67 C6 Troy *AL* U.S.A.
62 D1 Troy *MT* U.S.A.
71 G3 Troy *NH* U.S.A.
71 G3 Troy *NY* U.S.A.
70 A4 Troy *OH* U.S.A.
70 E4 Troy *PA* U.S.A.
19 L3 Troyan Bulg.
14 G2 Troyes France
10 F4 Troy Lake *l.* U.S.A.
73 E2 Troy Peak *summit* U.S.A.
19 J3 Trstenik Yugo.
21 E4 Trubchevsk Rus. Fed.
15 C1 Truchas Spain
20 E3 Trud Rus. Fed.
40 C3 Trudovoye Rus. Fed.
75 G5 Trujillo Honduras
78 C5 Trujillo Peru
15 D3 Trujillo Spain
81 C2 Trujillo Venez.
12 F5 Trulben Ger.
71 G4 Trumbull U.S.A.
73 F3 Trumbull, Mt *mt* U.S.A.
45 A2 Trumon Indon.
50 F2 Trundle Austr.
44 C2 Trung Hiệp Vietnam
39 C6 Trung Khanh China
59 H4 Truro Can.
9 B7 Truro U.K.
11 C3 Truskmore *h.* Rep. of Ireland
56 E3 Trutch Can.
63 F5 Truth or Consequences U.S.A.
16 G5 Trutnov Czech Rep.
19 L7 Trypiti, Akra *pt* Greece
7 N6 Trysil Norway
16 G3 Trzebiatów Pol.
36 A2 Tsagaannuur Mongolia
21 H6 Tsagan Aman Rus. Fed.
21 H6 Tsagan-Nur Rus. Fed.
21 G7 Ts'ageri Georgia
29 K1 Tsalka Georgia
89 E5 Tsaratanana, Massif du *mts* Madag.
90 B2 Tsaris Mts *mts* Namibia
21 H5 Tsatsa Rus. Fed.
90 A3 Tsaukaib Namibia
88 D4 Tsavo National Park Kenya
21 G6 Tselina Rus. Fed.
89 B6 Tses Namibia
89 C6 Tsetseng Botswana
36 C2 Tsetserleg Mongolia
89 C6 Tshabong Botswana
89 C6 Tshane Botswana
21 F6 Tshchikskoye Vdkhr. *resr* Rus. Fed.
88 B4 Tshela Congo(Zaire)
88 C4 Tshibala Congo(Zaire)
88 C4 Tshikapa Congo(Zaire)
88 C4 Tshikapa *r.* Congo(Zaire)
91 G3 Tshing S. Africa
91 J1 Tshipise S. Africa
89 C4 Tshitanzu Congo(Zaire)
88 C4 Tshofa Congo(Zaire)
91 J2 Tshokwane S. Africa
88 C4 Tshuapa *r.* Congo(Zaire)
21 G6 Tsimlyansk Rus. Fed.
21 G6 Tsimlyanskoye Vdkhr. *resr* Rus. Fed.
90 E3 Tsineng S. Africa
Tsingtao *see* Qingdao
39 □ Tsing Yi *i.* *H.K.* China
89 E6 Tsiombe Madag.
89 E5 Tsiroanomandidy Madag.
90 E6 Tsitsikamma Forest and Coastal National Park S. Africa
56 D4 Tsitsutl Pk *summit* Can.
20 H4 Tsivil'sk Rus. Fed.
21 G7 Ts'khinvali Georgia
20 G4 Tsna *r.* Rus. Fed.
34 D2 Tsokr Chumo *l.* India
91 H5 Tsolo S. Africa
91 G6 Tsomo S. Africa
34 D2 Tso Morari L. *l.* India
27 G7 Tsqaltubo Georgia
41 E7 Tsu Japan
41 G6 Tsuchiura Japan
39 □ Tsuen Wan *H.K.* China
40 G4 Tsugarū-Kaikyō *str.* Japan
89 B5 Tsumeb Namibia
89 B6 Tsumis Park Namibia
89 C5 Tsumkwe Namibia
35 G4 Tsunthang India
41 E7 Tsuruga Japan
41 D8 Tsurugi-san *mt* Japan
40 F5 Tsuruoka Japan
41 A7 Tsushima *i.* Japan
Tsushima-kaikyō *str. see* Korea Strait
41 D7 Tsuyama Japan
90 D1 Tswaane Botswana
91 F4 Tswaraganang S. Africa
91 F3 Tswelelang S. Africa
17 M4 Tsyelyakhany Belarus
6 X2 Tsyp-Navolok Rus. Fed.
21 E6 Tsyurupyns'k Ukr.
37 F7 Tual Indon.
11 C4 Tuam Rep. of Ireland
51 D4 Tuamarina N.Z.
46 N5 Tuamotu, Archipel des *arch.* Pac. Oc.
39 B6 Tuân Giao Vietnam
44 A5 Tuangku *i.* Indon.
21 F6 Tuapse Rus. Fed.
44 □ Tuas Sing.
51 A7 Tuatapere N.Z.
73 G3 Tuba City U.S.A.
45 D4 Tuban Indon.
80 G3 Tubarão Brazil
43 A4 Tubbataha Reefs *rf* Phil.
11 C3 Tubbercurry Rep. of Ireland
16 D6 Tübingen Ger.
86 A4 Tubmanburg Liberia
43 B4 Tubod Phil.
87 E1 Tubruq Libya
46 N6 Tubuai *i.* *Fr. Polynesia* Pac. Oc.
Tubuai Islands *is see* Australes, Îles
79 L6 Tucano Brazil
83 B3 Tucapel, Pta *pt* Chile
79 G7 Tucavaca Bol.
13 L1 Tüchen Ger.
13 L2 Tuchheim Ger.
56 D2 Tuchitua Can.
71 F5 Tuckerton U.S.A.
73 G5 Tucson U.S.A.
73 G5 Tucson Mts *mts* U.S.A.
81 B2 Tucuco *r.* Venez.
63 G5 Tucumcari U.S.A.
81 E2 Tucupita Venez.
79 J4 Tucuruí Brazil
79 J4 Tucuruí, Represa *resr* Brazil
29 M5 Tū Dār Iran
15 F1 Tudela Spain
15 C2 Tuela *r.* Port.
39 □ Tuen Mun *H.K.* China
35 H4 Tuensang India
30 C5 Ţufayḩ S. Arabia
91 J4 Tugela *r.* S. Africa
43 C4 Tugnug Point *pt* Phil.
43 B2 Tuguegarao Phil.
25 P4 Tugur Rus. Fed.
38 F2 Tuhai *r.* China
44 A5 Tuhemberua Indon.
15 B1 Tui Spain
81 A2 Tuira *r.* Panama
37 E7 Tukangbesi, Kepulauan *is* Indon.
58 E2 Tukarak Island *i.* Can.
51 F3 Tukituki *r.* N.Z.
54 E3 Tuktoyaktuk Can.
7 S8 Tukums Latvia
20 F4 Tula Rus. Fed.
35 H1 Tulagt Ar Gol *r.* China
74 E4 Tulancingo Mex.
72 C3 Tulare U.S.A.
72 C4 Tulare Lake Bed *l.* U.S.A.
63 F5 Tularosa U.S.A.
33 C2 Tulasi *mt* India
90 C6 Tulbagh S. Africa
78 C3 Tulcán Ecuador
19 N2 Tulcea Romania
21 D5 Tul'chyn Ukr.
72 C3 Tule *r.* U.S.A.
30 D3 Tuleh Iran
35 G4 Tule-la Pass Bhutan
57 J2 Tulemalu Lake *l.* Can.
65 C5 Tulia U.S.A.
28 E5 Tulkarm West Bank
11 C5 Tulla Rep. of Ireland
67 C5 Tullahoma U.S.A.
50 F2 Tullamore Austr.
11 D4 Tullamore Rep. of Ireland
14 E4 Tulle France
6 O5 Tulleråsen Sweden
50 F2 Tullibigeal Austr.
65 E6 Tullos U.S.A.
11 E5 Tullow Rep. of Ireland
48 E3 Tully Austr.
11 D3 Tully U.K.
71 E3 Tully U.S.A.
20 D2 Tulos Rus. Fed.
65 D4 Tulsa U.S.A.
20 F4 Tul'skaya Oblast' *div.* Rus. Fed.
81 A3 Tuluá Col.
54 B3 Tuluksak *AK* U.S.A.
83 C1 Tulum, Valle de *v.* Arg.
36 C1 Tulun Rus. Fed.
45 D4 Tulungagung Indon.
35 H4 Tulung La *pass* China
43 A4 Tuluran *i.* Phil.
81 A4 Tumaco Col.
91 G3 Tumahole S. Africa
21 J6 Tumak Rus. Fed.
7 P7 Tumba Sweden
88 B4 Tumba, Lac *l.* Congo(Zaire)
45 D3 Tumbangsamba Indon.
43 C5 Tumbao Phil.
78 B4 Tumbes Peru
56 E3 Tumbler Ridge Can.
38 D1 Tumd Youqi China
38 D1 Tumd Zuoqi China
42 E2 Tumen China
42 E2 Tumen Jiang *r.* China/N. Korea
38 B2 Tumenzi China
78 F2 Tumereng Guyana
43 A5 Tumindao *i.* Phil.
33 B3 Tumkur India
35 G3 Tum La *pass* China
10 E4 Tummel, Loch *l.* U.K.
36 G2 Tumnin *r.* Rus. Fed.
31 F5 Tump Pak.
44 B4 Tumpat Malaysia
86 B3 Tumu Ghana
79 G3 Tumucumaque, Serra *h.* Brazil
50 G3 Tumut Austr.
30 D5 Tunb al Kubrā *i.* Iran
9 H6 Tunbridge Wells, Royal U.K.
29 G2 Tunceli Turkey
39 D7 Tunchang China
34 D4 Tundla India
89 D5 Tunduru Tanz.
19 M3 Tundzha *r.* Bulg.
33 B3 Tungabhadra *r.* India
33 A3 Tungabhadra Reservoir India
35 H3 Tunga Pass China/India
43 B5 Tungawan Phil.
39 □ Tung Chung Wan *b.* *H.K.* China
6 D4 Tungnaá *r.* Iceland
56 D2 Tungsten Can.
20 E1 Tunguda Rus. Fed.
36 C1 Tunguska, Nizhnyaya *r.* Rus. Fed.
39 □ Tung Wan *b.* *H.K.* China
33 C2 Tuni India
86 D1 Tunis Tunisia
18 D6 Tunis, Golfe de *g.* Tunisia
85 D2 Tunisia *country* Africa
50 G3 Tuniut *r.* Austr.
81 B3 Tunja Col.
38 D2 Tunliu China
6 N4 Tunnsjøen *l.* Norway
9 J5 Tunstall U.K.
6 V3 Tuntsa Fin.
6 W3 Tuntsayoki *r.* Fin./Rus. Fed.
59 H2 Tunungayualok Island *i.* Can.
83 C2 Tunuyán Arg.
83 C2 Tunuyán *r.* Arg.
38 E3 Tuo He *r.* China
38 F2 Tuoji Dao *i.* China
44 C3 Tuŏl Khpos Cambodia
72 B3 Tuolumne U.S.A.
72 C3 Tuolumne Meadows U.S.A.
39 B5 Tuoniang Jiang *r.* China
35 H2 Tuotuo He *r.* China
35 H2 Tuotuoyan China
82 B3 Tupã Brazil
82 C2 Tupaciguara Brazil
29 L3 Tūp Āghāj Iran
80 F3 Tupanciretã Brazil
81 C3 Tuparro *r.* Col.
65 F5 Tupelo U.S.A.
78 E8 Tupiza Bol.
71 F2 Tupper Lake U.S.A.
71 F2 Tupper Lake *l.* U.S.A.
83 C2 Tupungato Arg.
83 C2 Tupungato, Cerro *mt* Arg./Chile
29 K7 Tuqayyid *well* Iraq
42 A1 Tuquan China
81 A4 Túquerres Col.
39 C7 Tuqu Wan *b.* China
35 G4 Tura India
25 M3 Tura Rus. Fed.
32 B5 Turabah S. Arabia
81 D3 Turagua, Serranía *mt* Venez.
51 E4 Turakina N.Z.
30 E3 Turan Iran
36 F1 Turana, Khrebet *mts* Rus. Fed.
51 E3 Turangi N.Z.
30 E2 Turan Lowland *lowland* Asia
28 G6 Turayf S. Arabia
30 C5 Turayf *well* S. Arabia
7 T7 Turba Estonia
81 B2 Turbaco Col.
31 F5 Turbat Pak.
81 A2 Turbo Col.
17 L7 Turda Romania
30 C3 Türeh Iran
Turfan *see* Turpan
26 E2 Turgay Kazak.
19 M3 Tŭrgovishte Bulg.
28 C2 Turgut Turkey
28 A2 Turgutlu Turkey
28 F1 Turhal Turkey
7 T7 Türi Estonia
15 F3 Turia *r.* Spain
81 D2 Turimo Venez.
18 B2 Turin Italy
40 B2 Turiy Rog Rus. Fed.
21 C5 Turiys'k Ukr.
88 D3 Turkana, Lake *salt l.* Eth./Kenya
19 M4 Türkeli Adası *i.* Turkey
26 E2 Turkestan Kazak.
31 G2 Turkestan Range *mts* Asia
23 C6 Turkey *country* Asia
68 B4 Turkey *r.* U.S.A.
21 G5 Turki Rus. Fed.
24 G6 Turkmenbashi Turkm.
28 C2 Türkmen Dağı *mt* Turkey
23 E5 Turkmenistan *country* Asia
31 F2 Turkmen-Kala Turkm.
30 D2 Turkmenskiy Zaliv *b.* Turkm.
28 F3 Türkoğlu Turkey
53 J7 Turks and Caicos Islands *terr.* Caribbean Sea
75 K4 Turks Islands *is* Turks and Caicos Is
7 S6 Turku Fin.
88 D3 Turkwel *watercourse* Kenya
72 B3 Turlock U.S.A.
72 B3 Turlock L. *l.* U.S.A.
51 F4 Turnagain, Cape *c.* N.Z.
10 D5 Turnberry U.K.
73 G5 Turnbull, Mt *mt* U.S.A.
74 G5 Turneffe Is *is* Belize
69 F3 Turner U.S.A.
12 C3 Turnhout Belgium
57 H3 Turnor Lake *l.* Can.
19 L3 Turnu Măgurele Romania
50 G2 Turon *r.* Austr.
20 G3 Turovets Rus. Fed.
36 A2 Turpan China
36 A2 Turpan Pendi China
75 J4 Turquino *mt* Cuba
10 F3 Turriff U.K.
29 K5 Tursāq Iraq
32 F1 Turtkul' Uzbek.
68 B2 Turtle Flambeau Flowage *resr* U.S.A.
57 H4 Turtleford Can.
68 A3 Turtle Lake U.S.A.
27 F2 Turugart Pass China/Kyrg.
82 B2 Turvo *r.* *Goiás* Brazil
82 C3 Turvo *r.* *São Paulo* Brazil
73 F4 Tusayan U.S.A.
67 C5 Tuscaloosa U.S.A.
70 C4 Tuscarawas *r.* U.S.A.
70 E4 Tuscarora Mts *h.* U.S.A.
68 C6 Tuscola *IL* U.S.A.
65 D5 Tuscola *TX* U.S.A.
30 E3 Tusharīk Iran
67 C5 Tuskegee U.S.A.
70 D4 Tussey Mts *h.* U.S.A.
31 E4 Tūtak Iran
29 J2 Tutak Turkey
20 F3 Tutayev Rus. Fed.
33 B4 Tuticorin India
64 D4 Tuttle Creek Res. *resr* U.S.A.
16 D7 Tuttlingen Ger.
55 Q2 Tuttut Nunaat *reg.* Greenland
49 J3 Tutuila *i.* Pac. Oc.
89 C6 Tutume Botswana
42 D3 Tuun, Mt *mt* N. Korea
6 W5 Tuupovaara Fin.
6 V5 Tuusniemi Fin.
47 J4 Tuvalu *country* Pac. Oc.
30 B5 Tuwayq, Jabal *h.* S. Arabia
74 E4 Tuxpan *Veracruz* Mex.
74 F5 Tuxtla Gutiérrez Mex.
81 D2 Tuy *r.* Venez.
44 C2 Tuy Đức Vietnam
39 B6 Tuyên Quang Vietnam
44 D2 Tuy Hoa Vietnam
30 C3 Tūysarkān Iran
28 D2 Tuz Gölü *salt l.* Turkey
73 F4 Tuzigoot National Monument *res.* U.S.A.
29 K4 Tuz Khurmātū Iraq
19 H2 Tuzla Bos.-Herz.
29 H2 Tuzla *r.* Turkey
Tuz, Lake *salt l. see* Tuz Gölü
21 F6 Tuzlov *r.* Rus. Fed.
7 L7 Tvedestrand Norway
20 E3 Tver' Rus. Fed.
20 E3 Tverskaya Oblast' *div.* Rus. Fed.
69 J3 Tweed Can.
10 F5 Tweed *r.* *Eng./Scot.* U.K.
56 D4 Tweedsmuir Prov. Park *res.* Can.
90 C6 Tweefontein S. Africa
90 C2 Twee Rivier Namibia
12 E2 Twente *reg.* Neth.
72 D4 Twentynine Palms U.S.A.
59 K4 Twillingate Can.
62 D2 Twin Bridges U.S.A.
65 C6 Twin Buttes Res. *resr* U.S.A.
59 H3 Twin Falls Can.
62 D3 Twin Falls U.S.A.
56 F3 Twin Lakes Can.
71 H2 Twin Mountain U.S.A.
70 C6 Twin Oaks U.S.A.
72 B2 Twin Peak *summit* U.S.A.
13 G2 Twistringen Ger.
50 G4 Twofold B. *b.* Austr.
73 G4 Two Guns U.S.A.
68 B2 Two Harbors U.S.A.
57 G4 Two Hills Can.
62 D1 Two Medicine *r.* U.S.A.
68 D3 Two Rivers U.S.A.
35 H5 Tyao *r.* India/Myanmar
6 M5 Tydal Norway
70 D5 Tygart Lake *l.* U.S.A.
70 D5 Tygart Valley *v.* U.S.A.
36 E1 Tygda Rus. Fed.
65 E5 Tyler U.S.A.
65 F6 Tylertown U.S.A.
36 E1 Tynda Rus. Fed.
56 A2 Tyndall Gl. *gl.* U.S.A.
10 F4 Tyne *r.* U.K.
8 F2 Tynemouth U.K.
7 M5 Tynset Norway
28 E5 Tyre Lebanon
57 H2 Tyrell Lake *l.* Can.
6 T4 Tyrnävä Fin.
19 K5 Tyrnavos Greece
70 D4 Tyrone U.S.A.
50 D3 Tyrrell *r.* Austr.
50 D3 Tyrrell, L. *l.* Austr.
18 D4 Tyrrhenian Sea *sea* France/Italy
25 Q3 Tyubelyakh Rus. Fed.
24 J4 Tyukalinsk Rus. Fed.
94 D4 Tyukyu Trench *sea feature* Pac. Oc.
24 H4 Tyumen' Rus. Fed.
25 N3 Tyung *r.* Rus. Fed.
9 C6 Tywi *r.* U.K.
9 C5 Tywyn U.K.
91 J1 Tzaneen S. Africa


# U


89 C5 Uamanda Angola
81 E4 Uatatás *r.* Brazil
79 L5 Uauá Brazil
81 D5 Uaupés Brazil
81 C4 Uaupés *r.* Brazil
30 B4 U'aywij *well* S. Arabia
29 J7 U'aywij, W. *watercourse* S. Arabia
82 D3 Ubá Brazil
82 D2 Ubaí Brazil
82 E1 Ubaitaba Brazil
88 B3 Ubangi *r.* C.A.R./Congo(Zaire)
81 B3 Ubate Col.
29 J5 Ubayyid, Wādī al *watercourse* Iraq/S. Arabia
41 B8 Ube Japan
15 E3 Úbeda Spain
82 C2 Uberaba Brazil
79 G7 Uberaba, Lagoa *l.* Bol./Brazil
82 C2 Uberlândia Brazil
44 □ Ubin, Pulau *i.* Sing.
44 B1 Ubolratna Res. *resr* Thai.
91 K3 Ubombo S. Africa
44 C2 Ubon Ratchathani Thai.
13 G5 Ubstadt-Weiher Ger.
88 C4 Ubundu Congo(Zaire)
29 L1 Ucar Azer.
78 D5 Ucayali *r.* Peru
34 B3 Uch Pak.
31 F2 Uch-Adzhi Turkm.
30 C2 Ūchān Iran
27 G2 Ucharal Kazak.
40 G3 Uchiura-wan *b.* Japan
13 G2 Uchte Ger.
13 K2 Uchte *r.* Ger.
36 F1 Uchur *r.* Rus. Fed.
9 H7 Uckfield U.K.
56 D5 Ucluelet Can.
73 H3 Ucolo U.S.A.
62 F2 Ucross U.S.A.
25 P4 Uda *r.* Rus. Fed.
21 H6 Udachnoye Rus. Fed.
25 N3 Udachnyy Rus. Fed.
33 B4 Udagamandalam India
34 C4 Udaipur *Rajasthan* India
35 G5 Udaipur *Tripura* India
35 E5 Udanti *r.* India/Myanmar
33 B3 Udayagiri India
7 M7 Uddevalla Sweden
10 D5 Uddingston U.K.
6 P4 Uddjaure *l.* Sweden
12 D3 Uden Neth.
33 B2 Udgir India
20 H2 Udimskiy Rus. Fed.
18 E1 Udine Italy
59 J2 Udjuktok Bay *b.* Can.
20 E3 Udomlya Rus. Fed.
44 B1 Udon Thani Thai.
36 F1 Udskaya Guba *b.* Rus. Fed.
33 B4 Udumalaipettai India
33 A3 Udupi India
36 F1 Udyl', Ozero *l.* Rus. Fed.
16 G4 Ueckermünde Ger.
41 F6 Ueda Japan
48 C2 Uekuli Indon.
88 C3 Uele *r.* Congo(Zaire)
54 B3 Uelen Rus. Fed.
13 J2 Uelzen Ger.
88 C3 Uere *r.* Congo(Zaire)
13 H1 Uetersen Ger.
13 H5 Uettingen Ger.
13 J2 Uetze Ger.
24 G4 Ufa Rus. Fed.
13 J5 Uffenheim Ger.
89 B6 Ugab *watercourse* Namibia
88 D4 Ugalla *r.* Tanz.
85 G5 Uganda *country* Africa
91 H5 Ugie S. Africa
36 G2 Uglegorsk Rus. Fed.
40 C3 Uglekamensk Rus. Fed.
20 F3 Uglich Rus. Fed.
18 F2 Ugljan *i.* Croatia
20 E3 Uglovka Rus. Fed.
40 C3 Uglovoye Rus. Fed.
25 Q3 Ugol'naya Zyryanka Rus. Fed.
25 T3 Ugol'nyye Kopi Rus. Fed.
20 E4 Ugra Rus. Fed.
16 H6 Uherské Hradiště Czech Rep.
70 C4 Uhrichsville U.S.A.
10 B3 Uig U.K.
88 B4 Uíge Angola
42 D5 Ŭijŏngbu S. Korea
42 C3 Ŭiju N. Korea
6 W5 Uimaharju Fin.
73 F3 Uinkaret Plateau *plat.* U.S.A.
62 E3 Uinta Mts *mts* *UT* U.S.A.
89 B6 Uis Mine Namibia
11 D4 Uisneach *h.* Rep. of Ireland
42 E5 Ŭisŏng S. Korea
91 F6 Uitenhage S. Africa
12 C2 Uithoorn Neth.
12 E1 Uithuizen Neth.
59 H2 Uivak, Cape *hd* Can.
41 D7 Uji Japan
41 A9 Uji-guntō *is* Japan
34 C5 Ujjain India
45 E4 Ujung Pandang Indon.
29 J5 Ukhaydir Iraq
35 H4 Ukhrul India
20 K2 Ukhta Rus. Fed.
20 K2 Ukhta *r.* Rus. Fed.
72 A2 Ukiah *CA* U.S.A.
62 C2 Ukiah *OR* U.S.A.
55 N2 Ukkusissat Greenland
7 T9 Ukmergė Lith.
5 F4 Ukraine *country* Europe
20 J2 Uktym Rus. Fed.
41 A8 Uku-jima *i.* Japan
90 D1 Ukwi Botswana
90 D1 Ukwi Pan *salt pan* Botswana
36 C2 Ulaanbaatar Mongolia
36 B2 Ulaangom Mongolia
50 G2 Ulan Austr.
Ulan Bator *see* Ulaanbaatar
38 C1 Ulan Buh Shamo *des.* China
21 H6 Ulan Erge Rus. Fed.
21 H6 Ulan-Khol Rus. Fed.
38 C1 Ulansuhai Nur *l.* China
38 A1 Ulan Tohoi China
36 C1 Ulan-Ude Rus. Fed.
35 G2 Ulan Ul Hu *l.* China
28 F2 Ulaş Turkey
49 G2 Ulawa I. *i.* Solomon Is
31 E4 Ulāy, Kūh-e *h.* Iran
42 E5 Ulchin S. Korea
7 L7 Ulefoss Norway
7 U7 Ülenurme Estonia
33 A2 Ulhasnagar India
36 B2 Uliastay Mongolia
12 C3 Ulicoten Neth.
6 X2 Ulita *r.* Rus. Fed.
37 F6 Ulithi *i.* Micronesia
50 H3 Ulladulla Austr.

10 C3 Ullapool U.K.
6 S5 Ullava Fin.
8 E3 Ullswater *l.* U.K.
42 F5 Ullŭng-do *i.* S. Korea
16 D6 Ulm Ger.
12 E4 Ulmen Ger.
7 N8 Ulricehamn Sweden
12 E1 Ulrum Neth.
42 E6 Ulsan S. Korea
6 L5 Ulsberg Norway
11 D3 Ulster Canal *canal* Rep. of Ireland/U.K.
50 D3 Ultima Austr.
28 B1 Ulubat Gölü *l.* Turkey
28 C2 Uluborlu Turkey
28 B1 Uludağ *mt* Turkey
44 B5 Ulu Kali, Gunung *mt* Malaysia
28 E3 Ulukışla Turkey
91 J4 Ulundi S. Africa
36 A2 Ulungur Hu *l.* China
44 □ Ulu Pandan Sing.
Uluru *h.* *see* Ayers Rock
28 D1 Ulus Turkey
10 B4 Ulva *i.* U.K.
12 C3 Ulvenhout Neth.
8 D3 Ulverston U.K.
7 O6 Ulvsjön Sweden
31 H1 Ul'yanovo Uzbek.
20 J4 Ul'yanovsk Rus. Fed.
20 H4 Ul'yanovskaya Oblast' *div.* Rus. Fed.
65 C4 Ulysses U.S.A.
21 D5 Uman' Ukr.
31 G4 Umarao Pak.
34 E5 Umaria India
34 D6 Umarkhed India
35 E6 Umarkot India
34 B4 Umarkot Pak.
62 C2 Umatilla U.S.A.
24 E3 Umba Rus. Fed.
71 H2 Umbagog Lake *l.* U.S.A.
48 E2 Umboi *i.* P.N.G.
6 R5 Umeå Sweden
6 Q4 Umeälven *r.* Sweden
91 J4 Umfolozi *r.* S. Africa
29 L7 Umgharah Kuwait
91 J4 Umhlanga S. Africa
54 H3 Umingmaktok Can.
58 E2 Umiujaq Can.
91 J5 Umkomaas S. Africa
91 J4 Umlazi S. Africa
29 K6 Umma Iraq
30 D5 Umm al Qaywayn U.A.E.
30 C5 Umm Bāb Qatar
87 E3 Umm Keddada Sudan
29 L6 Umm Qasr Iraq
87 F3 Umm Ruwaba Sudan
87 E1 Umm Sa'ad Libya
30 C5 Umm Sa'id Qatar
62 A3 Umpqua *r.* U.S.A.
89 B5 Umpulo Angola
34 D5 Umred India
35 C5 Umreth India
91 H5 Umtata S. Africa
91 J5 Umtentweni S. Africa
86 C4 Umuahia Nigeria
82 B3 Umuarama Brazil
91 H5 Umzimkulu S. Africa
91 J5 Umzinto S. Africa
82 E1 Una Brazil
18 G2 Una *r.* Bos.-Herz./Croatia
28 F6 'Unāb, W. al *watercourse* Jordan
82 C2 Unai Brazil
31 H3 Unai Pass Afgh.
54 B3 Unalakleet U.S.A.
10 C2 Unapool U.K.
81 D2 Unare *r.* Venez.
28 E6 'Unayzah Jordan
32 B4 'Unayzah S. Arabia
29 G5 'Unayzah, Jabal *h.* Iraq
63 E4 Uncompahgre Plateau *plat.* U.S.A.
91 H4 Underberg S. Africa
50 C3 Underbool Austr.
64 C2 Underwood U.S.A.
20 E4 Unecha Rus. Fed.
50 F2 Ungarie Austr.
59 G2 Ungava Bay *b.* Can.
58 F1 Ungava, Péninsule d' *pen.* Can.
42 F2 Unggi N. Korea
21 C6 Ungheni Moldova
31 E2 Unguz, Solonchakovyye Vpadiny *salt flat* Turkm.
20 J3 Uni Rus. Fed.
82 B4 União da Vitória Brazil
81 B4 Unilla *r.* Col.
78 F4 Unini *r.* Brazil
82 A4 Unión Para.
71 J2 Union *ME* U.S.A.
67 D5 Union *SC* U.S.A.
70 C6 Union *WV* U.S.A.
68 E5 Union City *OH* U.S.A.
70 D4 Union City *PA* U.S.A.
67 B4 Union City *TN* U.S.A.
90 E6 Uniondale S. Africa
73 F4 Union, Mt *mt* U.S.A.
67 C5 Union Springs U.S.A.
70 D5 Uniontown U.S.A.
69 F4 Unionville U.S.A.
62 E3 Unita Mts. *mts* U.S.A.
23 E7 United Arab Emirates *country* Asia
5 C3 United Kingdom *country* Europe
53 E6 United States of America N. America
57 H4 Unity Can.
71 J2 Unity *ME* U.S.A.
62 C2 Unity *OR* U.S.A.
34 C5 Unjha India
13 F3 Unna Ger.
34 E4 Unnão India
42 C4 Ŭnp'a N. Korea
42 C3 Ŭnsan N. Korea
42 D4 Ŭnsan N. Korea
10 □ Unst *i.* U.K.
13 K3 Unstrut *r.* Ger.
35 G2 Unuli Horog China
35 F5 Upar Ghat *reg.* India
81 E2 Upata Venez.
89 C4 Upemba, Lac *l.* Congo(Zaire)
89 C4 Upemba, Parc National de l' *nat. park* Congo(Zaire)
43 C5 Upi Phil.
81 B3 Upía *r.* Col.
90 D4 Upington S. Africa
34 B5 Upleta India
6 W3 Upoloksha Rus. Fed.
49 J3 Upolu *i.* Western Samoa
70 B4 Upper Arlington U.S.A.
56 F4 Upper Arrow L. *l.* Can.
56 F4 Upper Arrow Lake *B.C.* Can.
51 E4 Upper Hutt N.Z.
68 B4 Upper Iowa *r.* U.S.A.
71 K1 Upper Kent Can.
62 B3 Upper Klamath L. *l.* U.S.A.
62 B3 Upper L. *l.* U.S.A.
72 A2 Upper Lake U.S.A.
56 D2 Upper Liard Can.
11 D3 Upper Lough Erne *l.* U.K.
70 E5 Upper Marlboro U.S.A.
44 □ Upper Peirce Res. *resr* Sing.
59 J4 Upper Salmon Reservoir Can.
70 B4 Upper Sandusky U.S.A.
71 F2 Upper Saranac Lake *l.* U.S.A.
51 D4 Upper Takaka N.Z.
7 P7 Uppsala Sweden
58 B4 Upsala Can.
71 H2 Upton U.S.A.
29 L7 Uqlat al 'Udhaybah *well* Iraq
29 L6 Ur Iraq
81 A2 Urabá, Golfo de *b.* Col.
38 C1 Urad Qianqi China
38 C1 Urad Zhonghou Lianheqi China
30 E4 Ūrāf Iran
40 H3 Urakawa Japan
50 F2 Ural *h.* Austr.
50 H1 Uralla Austr.
4 J2 Ural Mountains *mts* Rus. Fed.
26 D1 Ural'sk Kazak.
Ural'skiy Khrebet *mts* *see* Ural Mountains
88 D4 Urambo Tanz.
50 F3 Urana Austr.
50 F3 Urana, L. *l.* Austr.
82 D1 Urandi Brazil
57 H3 Uranium City Can.
50 F3 Uranquity Austr.
81 E4 Uraricoera Brazil
81 E4 Uraricoera *r.* Brazil
81 E4 Uraricuera *r.* Brazil
81 E3 Uraucaima, Sa *mt* Brazil
73 H2 Uravan U.S.A.
30 B5 'Urayq ad Duḩūl *sand dunes* S. Arabia
21 F5 Urazovo Rus. Fed.
68 C5 Urbana *IL* U.S.A.
70 B4 Urbana *OH* U.S.A.
18 E3 Urbino Italy
78 D6 Urcos Peru
21 H5 Urda Kazak.
20 J2 Urdoma Rus. Fed.
8 F3 Ure *r.* U.K.
20 H3 Uren' Rus. Fed.
24 J3 Urengoy Rus. Fed.
49 G3 Uréparapara *i.* Vanuatu
51 F3 Urewera National Park N.Z.
20 H4 Urga *r.* Rus. Fed.
26 E2 Urgench Uzbek.
28 E2 Ürgüp Turkey
31 G2 Urgut Uzbek.
6 V2 Urho Kekkosen Kansallispuisto *nat. park* Fin.
81 B2 Uribia Col.
7 S6 Urjala Fin.
12 D2 Urk Neth.
21 H7 Urkarakh Rus. Fed.
19 M5 Urla Turkey
11 D5 Urlingford Rep. of Ireland
31 H2 Urmetan Tajik.
Urmia *see* Orūmīyeh
Urmia, Lake *salt l.* *see* Orūmīyeh, Daryācheh-ye
39 □ Urmston Road *chan.* *H.K.* China
19 J3 Uroševac Yugo.
31 H2 Ŭroteppa Tajik.
35 F3 Urru Co *salt l.* China
38 A1 Urt Mongolia
82 C1 Uruaçu Brazil
74 D5 Uruapan Mex.
78 D6 Urubamba *r.* Peru
79 G4 Urucara Brazil
79 K5 Uruçuí Brazil
82 D2 Urucuia *r.* Brazil
79 K5 Uruçuí Preto *r.* Brazil
79 G4 Urucurituba Brazil
80 E3 Uruguaiana Brazil
77 E6 Uruguay *country* S. America
80 E4 Uruguay *r.* Arg./Uru.
Uruk *see* Erech
Urumchi *see* Ürümqi
36 A2 Ürümqi China
21 G6 Urup *r.* Rus. Fed.
36 H2 Urup, O. *i.* Rus. Fed.
21 H7 Urus-Martan Rus. Fed.
21 G5 Uryupinsk Rus. Fed.
20 J3 Urzhum Rus. Fed.
19 M2 Urziceni Romania
41 B8 Usa Japan
20 J4 Usa *r.* Rus. Fed.
28 B2 Uşak Turkey
89 B6 Usakos Namibia
85 B5 Usarp Mts *mts* Ant.
80 E8 Usborne, Mt *h.* Falkland Is
24 J1 Ushakova, O. *i.* Rus. Fed.
30 B5 'Ushayrah S. Arabia
41 B8 Ushibuka Japan
27 F2 Ushtobe Kazak.
80 C8 Ushuaia Arg.
13 G4 Usingen Ger.
24 G3 Usinsk Rus. Fed.
9 E6 Usk U.K.
9 E6 Usk *r.* U.K.
35 E4 Uska India
20 C4 Uskhodni Belarus
13 H3 Uslar Ger.
21 F4 Usman' Rus. Fed.
7 S8 Usmas Ezers *l.* Latvia
20 J2 Usogorsk Rus. Fed.
36 C1 Usol'ye-Sibirskoye Rus. Fed.
14 F4 Ussel France
40 D1 Ussuri *r.* China/Rus. Fed.
36 F2 Ussuriysk Rus. Fed.
20 H3 Usta *r.* Rus. Fed.
25 M4 Ust'-Barguzin Rus. Fed.
21 G5 Ust'-Buzulukskaya Rus. Fed.
21 G6 Ust'-Donetskiy Rus. Fed.
18 E5 Ustica, Isola di *i.* *Sicily* Italy
25 M4 Ust'Ilimsk Rus. Fed.
36 C1 Ust'-Ilimskiy Vdkhr. *resr* Rus. Fed.
24 G3 Ust'-Ilych Rus. Fed.
16 G5 Ústí nad Labem Czech Rep.
Ustinov *see* Izhevsk
16 H3 Ustka Pol.
25 S4 Ust'-Kamchatsk Rus. Fed.
27 G2 Ust'-Kamenogorsk Kazak.
36 C1 Ust'-Kut Rus. Fed.
25 P2 Ust'-Kuyga Rus. Fed.
21 F6 Ust'-Labinsk Rus. Fed.
7 V7 Ust'-Luga Rus. Fed.
25 P3 Ust'-Maya Rus. Fed.
24 G3 Ust'-Nem Rus. Fed.
25 Q3 Ust'-Nera Rus. Fed.
20 J2 Ust'-Ocheya Rus. Fed.
25 N2 Ust'-Olenek Rus. Fed.
25 Q3 Ust'omchug Rus. Fed.
21 C1 Ust'-Ordynskiy Rus. Fed.
25 S3 Ust'-Penzhino Rus. Fed.
24 K3 Ust'-Port Rus. Fed.
20 G2 Ust'-Shonosha Rus. Fed.
24 G3 Ust'-Tsil'ma Rus. Fed.
20 H2 Ust'-Ura Rus. Fed.
20 G2 Ust'-Vayen'ga Rus. Fed.
20 H2 Ust'-Vyyskaya Rus. Fed.
20 G2 Ust'ya *r.* Rus. Fed.
20 F3 Ust'ye Rus. Fed.
20 F3 Ust'ye *r.* Rus. Fed.
24 G5 Ustyurt Plateau *plat.* Kazak./Uzbek.
20 F3 Ustyuzhna Rus. Fed.
41 B8 Usuki Japan
20 D4 Usvyaty Rus. Fed.
73 G2 Utah *div.* U.S.A.
73 G1 Utah Lake *l.* U.S.A.
6 U4 Utajärvi Fin.
30 C5 Utayyiq S. Arabia
7 T9 Utena Lith.
31 G5 Uthal Pak.
44 A2 U Thong Thai.
44 C2 Uthumphon Phisai Thai.
71 F3 Utica U.S.A.
15 F3 Utiel Spain
56 F3 Utikuma Lake *l.* Can.
91 F3 Utlwanang S. Africa
35 E4 Utraula India
12 D2 Utrecht Neth.
91 J3 Utrecht S. Africa
15 D4 Utrera Spain
6 U2 Utsjoki Fin.
41 F6 Utsunomiya Japan
21 H6 Utta Rus. Fed.
44 B1 Uttaradit Thai.
34 D4 Uttar Pradesh *div.* India
9 F5 Uttoxeter U.K.
49 G3 Utupua *i.* Solomon Is
55 M2 Uummannaq Greenland
55 N2 Uummannaq Fjord *in.* Greenland
55 O4 Uummannarsuaq *c.* Greenland
6 T5 Uurainen Fin.
7 R6 Uusikaupunki Fin.
81 C4 Uva *r.* Col.
65 D6 Uvalde U.S.A.
21 G5 Uvarovo Rus. Fed.
88 D4 Uvinza Tanz.
91 J5 Uvongo S. Africa
36 B1 Uvs Nuur *l.* Mongolia
41 C8 Uwajima Japan
87 E2 Uweinat, Jebel *mt* Sudan
9 G6 Uxbridge U.K.
38 C1 Uxin Ju China
38 C2 Uxin Qi China
36 B1 Uyar Rus. Fed.
38 C1 Üydzin Mongolia
25 Q3 Uyega Rus. Fed.
86 C4 Uyo Nigeria
78 E8 Uyuni, Salar de *salt flat* Bol.
20 H4 Uza *r.* Rus. Fed.
29 K4 'Uzaym, Nahr al *r.* Iraq
23 E5 Uzbekistan *country* Asia
14 G4 Uzès France
21 B5 Uzhhorod Ukr.
19 H3 Užice Yugo.
20 F4 Uzlovaya Rus. Fed.
20 G3 Uzola *r.* Rus. Fed.
28 C3 Üzümlü Turkey
31 H2 Uzun Uzbek.
29 L3 Ūzūn Darreh *r.* Iran
21 C7 Uzunköprü Turkey
21 D5 Uzyn Ukr.

# V

7 T5 Vaajakoski Fin.
91 H3 Vaal *r.* S. Africa
6 U4 Vaala Fin.
90 F4 Vaalbos National Park S. Africa
91 H3 Vaal Dam *dam* S. Africa
91 H2 Vaalwater S. Africa
6 R5 Vaasa Fin.
31 G1 Vabkent Uzbek.
17 J7 Vác Hungary
80 F3 Vacaria Brazil
82 A3 Vacaria *r.* *Mato Grosso do Sul* Brazil
82 D2 Vacaria *r.* *Minas Gerais* Brazil
82 A3 Vacaria, Serra *h.* Brazil
72 B2 Vacaville U.S.A.
20 G4 Vad *r.* Rus. Fed.
34 C6 Vada India
7 K7 Vadla Norway
34 C5 Vadodara India
6 V1 Vadsø Norway
16 D7 Vaduz Liechtenstein
6 N3 Værøy *i.* Norway
20 G2 Vaga *r.* Rus. Fed.
7 L6 Vågåmo Norway
18 F2 Vaganski Vrh *mt* Croatia
6 □ Vágar *i.* Faroe Is
6 Q4 Vägsele Sweden
6 □ Vágur Faroe Is
6 S5 Vähäkyrö Fin.
7 T7 Vaida Estonia
33 B4 Vaigai *r.* India
73 G5 Vail U.S.A.
12 B5 Vailly-sur-Aisne France
49 H2 Vaitupu *i.* Tuvalu
31 J2 Vakhan Tajik.
31 H2 Vakhsh Tajik.
33 C5 Valachchenai Sri Lanka
69 K2 Val-Barrette Can.
7 P6 Valbo Sweden
83 C4 Valcheta Arg.
18 D2 Valdagno Italy
20 E3 Valday Rus. Fed.
20 E3 Valdayskaya Vozvyshennost' *reg.* Rus. Fed.
15 D3 Valdecañas, Embalse de *resr* Spain
7 S8 Valdemārpils Latvia
7 P7 Valdemarsvik Sweden
14 G2 Val-de-Meuse France
15 E3 Valdepeñas Spain
14 E2 Val-de-Reuil France
69 K3 Val-des-Bois Can.
83 D4 Valdés, Península *pen.* Arg.
54 D3 Valdez U.S.A.
83 B3 Valdivia Chile
69 J1 Val-d'Or Can.
67 D6 Valdosta U.S.A.
7 L6 Valdres *v.* Norway
29 J1 Vale Georgia
62 C2 Vale U.S.A.
56 F4 Valemount Can.
82 E1 Valença Brazil
14 G4 Valence France
15 F3 Valencia Spain
81 D2 Valencia Venez.
15 F3 Valencia *div.* Spain
15 C3 Valencia de Alcántara Spain
15 D1 Valencia de Don Juan Spain
15 G3 Valencia, Golfo de *g.* Spain
11 A6 Valencia Island *i.* Rep. of Ireland
14 F1 Valenciennes France
40 D3 Valentin Rus. Fed.
73 F4 Valentine *AZ* U.S.A.
64 C3 Valentine *NE* U.S.A.
65 B6 Valentine *TX* U.S.A.
43 B3 Valenzuela Phil.
7 M6 Våler Norway
81 C2 Valera Venez.
19 H2 Valjevo Yugo.
7 U8 Valka Latvia
7 T6 Valkeakoski Fin.
12 D3 Valkenswaard Neth.
21 E5 Valky Ukr.
92 C4 Valkyrjedomen *ice feature* Ant.
74 G4 Valladolid Mex.
15 D2 Valladolid Spain
15 F3 Vall de Uxó Spain
7 K7 Valle Norway
81 D2 Valle de la Pascua Venez.
81 B2 Valledupar Col.
83 C1 Valle Fértil, Sa de *mts* Arg.
78 F7 Valle Grande Bol.
65 D7 Valle Hermoso Mex.
72 A2 Vallejo U.S.A.
18 F7 Valletta Malta
9 C4 Valley U.K.
64 D2 Valley City U.S.A.
62 B3 Valley Falls U.S.A.
70 C5 Valley Head U.S.A.
56 F3 Valleyview Can.
15 G2 Valls Spain
57 H5 Val Marie Can.
7 T8 Valmiera Latvia
15 E1 Valnera *mt* Spain
20 C4 Valozhyn Belarus
58 E4 Val-Paradis Can.
82 B3 Valparaíso Brazil
83 B2 Valparaíso Chile
68 D5 Valparaiso U.S.A.
83 B2 Valparaíso *div.* Chile
14 G4 Valréas France
34 C5 Valsad India
90 F3 Valspan S. Africa
37 F7 Vals, Tanjung *c.* Indon.
20 H1 Val'tevo Rus. Fed.
6 V5 Valtimo Fin.
21 G6 Valuyevka Rus. Fed.
21 F5 Valuyki Rus. Fed.
15 C4 Valverde del Camino Spain
44 C3 Vam Co Tay *r.* Vietnam
7 S6 Vammala Fin.
33 C2 Vamsadhara *r.* India
29 J2 Van Turkey
29 K1 Vanadzor Armenia
65 E5 Van Buren *AR* U.S.A.
71 K1 Van Buren *ME* U.S.A.
44 D2 Vân Canh Vietnam
71 K2 Vanceboro U.S.A.
70 B5 Vanceburg U.S.A.
56 E5 Vancouver Can.
62 B2 Vancouver U.S.A.
56 D5 Vancouver Island *i.* Can.
56 A2 Vancouver, Mt *mt* Can./U.S.A.
66 B4 Vandalia *IL* U.S.A.
70 A5 Vandalia *OH* U.S.A.
91 G3 Vanderbijlpark S. Africa
68 E3 Vanderbilt U.S.A.
70 D4 Vandergrift U.S.A.
56 E4 Vanderhoof Can.
90 F5 Vanderkloof Dam *resr* S. Africa
48 D3 Vanderlin I. *i.* Austr.
73 H4 Vanderwagen U.S.A.
48 D3 Van Diemen Gulf *b.* Austr.
7 T7 Vändra Estonia
7 N7 Vänern *l.* Sweden
7 N7 Vänersborg Sweden
70 E3 Van Etten U.S.A.
89 E6 Vangaindrano Madag.
29 J2 Van Gölü *salt l.* Turkey
65 B6 Van Horn U.S.A.
69 K3 Vanier Can.
49 G3 Vanikoro Is *is* Solomon Is
48 E2 Vanimo P.N.G.
36 G2 Vanino Rus. Fed.
33 B3 Vanivilasa Sagara *resr* India
33 B3 Vaniyambadi India
31 H2 Vanj Tajik.
31 H2 Vanj, Qatorkŭhi *mts* Tajik.
25 V3 Vankarem Rus. Fed.
71 F2 Vankleek Hill Can.
Van, Lake *salt l.* *see* Van Gölü
6 R1 Vanna *i.* Norway
6 Q5 Vännäs Sweden
14 C3 Vannes France
37 F7 Van Rees, Pegunungan *mts* Indon.
90 C5 Vanrhynsdorp S. Africa
7 O6 Vansbro Sweden
7 T6 Vantaa Fin.
49 G3 Vanua Lava *i.* Vanuatu
49 H3 Vanua Levu *i.* Fiji
47 H5 Vanuatu *country* Pac. Oc.
70 A4 Van Wert U.S.A.
90 D5 Vanwyksvlei S. Africa
90 D5 Vanwyksvlei *l.* S. Africa
39 B6 Văn Yên Vietnam
90 E3 Van Zylsrus S. Africa
33 A3 Varada *r.* India
7 U8 Varakļāni Latvia
30 C3 Varāmīn Iran
35 E4 Varanasi India
6 V1 Varangerfjorden *chan.* Norway
6 V1 Varangerhalvøya *pen.* Norway
18 G1 Varaždin Croatia
7 N8 Varberg Sweden
33 B2 Vardannapet India
19 K4 Vardar *r.* Macedonia
7 L9 Varde Denmark
30 B1 Vardenis Armenia
6 W1 Vardø Norway
13 G1 Varel Ger.
83 C2 Varela Arg.
7 T9 Varėna Lith.
18 C2 Varese Italy
40 C2 Varfolomeyevka Rus. Fed.
7 N7 Vårgårda Sweden
82 D3 Varginha Brazil
12 D3 Varik Neth.
6 U5 Varkaus Fin.
19 M3 Varna Bulg.
7 O8 Värnamo Sweden
7 N6 Värnäs Sweden
20 H3 Varnavino Rus. Fed.
28 D4 Varosia Cyprus
6 U5 Varpaisjärvi Fin.
16 J7 Várpalota Hungary
31 H2 Varsaj Afgh.
29 H2 Varto Turkey
35 E4 Varuna *r.* India
70 D3 Varysburg U.S.A.
30 D3 Varzaneh Iran
82 D2 Várzea da Palma Brazil
20 H2 Vashka *r.* Rus. Fed.
Vasht *see* Khāsh
20 H2 Vasilevo Rus. Fed.
7 U7 Vasknarva Estonia
17 N7 Vaslui Romania
69 F4 Vassar U.S.A.
7 P7 Västerås Sweden
7 N6 Västerdalälven *r.* Sweden
6 P3 Västerfjäll Sweden
7 Q7 Vasterhaninge Sweden
7 P8 Västervik Sweden
18 F3 Vasto Italy
21 D5 Vasyl'kiv Ukr.
14 E3 Vatan France
10 A4 Vatersay *i.* U.K.
33 A2 Vathar India
19 M6 Vathy Greece
5 E4 Vatican City *country* Europe
6 E4 Vatnajökull *ice cap* Iceland
17 M7 Vatra Dornei Romania
7 O7 Vättern *l.* Sweden
63 F5 Vaughn U.S.A.
12 B4 Vaulx Belgium
81 C4 Vaupés *r.* Col.
14 G5 Vauvert France
49 J3 Vava'u Group *is* Tonga
86 B4 Vavoua Côte d'Ivoire
33 C4 Vavuniya Sri Lanka
20 C4 Vawkavysk Belarus
7 O8 Växjö Sweden
33 B3 Vāyalpād India
20 H1 Vazhgort Rus. Fed.
89 E5 Vazobe *mt* Madag.
44 B2 Veal Vêng Cambodia
13 G2 Vechta Ger.
12 E2 Vechte *r.* Ger.
13 H3 Veckerhagen (Reinhardshagen) Ger.
33 B4 Vedaranniyam India
7 N8 Veddige Sweden
19 L3 Vedea *r.* Romania
21 H7 Vedeno Rus. Fed.
29 K2 Vedi Armenia
83 E2 Vedia Arg.
20 E2 Vedlozero Rus. Fed.
68 D5 Veedersburg U.S.A.
12 E1 Veendam Neth.
12 D2 Veenendaal Neth.
65 C5 Vega U.S.A.
6 M4 Vega *i.* Norway
57 G4 Vegreville Can.
7 U6 Vehkalahti Fin.
34 B3 Vehoa *r.* Pak.
34 B4 Veirwaro Pak.
13 H5 Veitshöchheim Ger.
15 D4 Vejer de la Frontera Spain
7 L9 Vejle Denmark
81 B1 Vela, Cabo de la *pt* Col.
33 B4 Velanai I. *i.* Sri Lanka
12 F3 Velbert Ger.
19 K3 Velbŭzhdki Prokhod *pass* Macedonia
90 C6 Velddrif S. Africa
18 F2 Velebit *mts* Croatia
12 E3 Velen Ger.
18 F1 Velenje Slovenia
19 J4 Veles Macedonia
81 B3 Vélez Col.
15 D4 Vélez-Málaga Spain
15 E4 Vélez-Rubio Spain
82 D2 Velhas *r.* Brazil
21 H6 Velichayevskoye Rus. Fed.
18 G2 Velika Gorica Croatia
19 J2 Velika Plana Yugo.
20 J3 Velikaya Rus. Fed.
25 T3 Velikaya *r.* Rus. Fed.
20 D3 Velikaya *r.* Rus. Fed.
20 E2 Velikaya Guba Rus. Fed.
40 E2 Velikaya Kema Rus. Fed.
20 D3 Velikiye Luki Rus. Fed.
20 H2 Velikiy Ustyug Rus. Fed.
33 B3 Velikonda Ra. *h.* India
17 Q2 Velikooktyabr'skiy Rus. Fed.
19 L3 Veliko Tŭrnovo Bulg.
20 F3 Velikoye Rus. Fed.
20 F3 Velikoye, Oz. *l.* Rus. Fed.
20 G4 Velikoye, Oz. *l.* Rus. Fed.
18 F2 Veli Lošinj Croatia
86 A3 Vélingara Senegal
17 P3 Velizh Rus. Fed.
16 H7 Veľký Meder Slovakia
49 F2 Vella Lavella *i.* Solomon Is
33 B4 Vellar *r.* India
13 H5 Vellberg Ger.
13 H3 Vellmar Ger.
33 B3 Vellore India
13 J2 Velpke Ger.
20 G2 Vel'sk Rus. Fed.
13 M2 Velten Ger.
12 D2 Veluwe *reg.* Neth.
12 E2 Veluwezoom, Nationaal Park *nat. park* Neth.
57 J5 Velva U.S.A.
96 G5 Vema Fracture *sea feature* Atl. Ocean
93 J4 Vema Trough *sea feature* Ind. Ocean
33 B4 Vembanād L. *l.* India
10 D4 Venachar, Loch *l.* U.K.
83 E2 Venado Tuerto Arg.
18 F4 Venafro Italy
81 E3 Venamo *r.* Guyana/Venez.
81 E3 Venamo, Co *mt* Venez.
82 C3 Venceslau Bráz Brazil
14 E3 Vendôme France
20 F4 Venev Rus. Fed.
Venezia *see* Venice
18 E2 Venezia, Golfo di *g.* Europe
77 D2 Venezuela *country* S. America
81 C2 Venezuela, Golfo de *g.* Venez.
96 E4 Venezuelan Basin *sea feature* Atl. Ocean
33 A3 Vengurla India
18 E2 Venice Italy
67 D7 Venice U.S.A.
14 G4 Vénissieux France
33 B3 Venkatagiri India
33 C2 Venkatapuram India
12 E3 Venlo Neth.
7 K7 Vennesla Norway
12 D3 Venray Neth.
7 S8 Venta Lith.
7 R8 Venta *r.* Latvia/Lith.
83 D3 Ventana, Serra de la *h.* Arg.
91 G4 Ventersburg S. Africa
91 G3 Ventersdorp S. Africa
91 F5 Venterstad S. Africa
9 F7 Ventnor U.K.
14 G4 Ventoux, Mont *mt* France
7 R8 Ventspils Latvia
81 D3 Ventuari *r.* Venez.
72 C4 Ventucopa U.S.A.
72 C4 Ventura U.S.A.
50 E5 Venus B. *b.* Austr.
80 D3 Vera Arg.
15 F4 Vera Spain
74 E5 Veracruz Mex.
34 B5 Veraval India
18 C2 Verbania Italy
18 C2 Vercelli Italy
6 M5 Verdalsøra Norway
83 D4 Verde *r.* Arg.
82 C2 Verde *r.* *Goiás* Brazil
82 B2 Verde *r.* *Goiás* Brazil
82 C2 Verde *r.* *Goiás/Minas Gerais* Brazil
82 B2 Verde *r.* *Mato Grosso do Sul* Brazil
80 E6 Verde *r.* Mex.
80 E2 Verde *r.* Para.
73 G4 Verde *r.* U.S.A.
82 D1 Verde Grande *r.* Brazil
43 B3 Verde Island Pass. *chan.* Phil.
13 H2 Verden (Aller) Ger.
83 D3 Verde, Pen. *pen.* Arg.
65 E4 Verdigris *r.* U.S.A.
14 H5 Verdon *r.* France
14 G2 Verdun France
91 G3 Vereeniging S. Africa
69 J2 Vérendrye, Réserve faunique La *res.* Can.
83 G2 Vergara Uru.
71 G2 Vergennes U.S.A.
15 C2 Verín Spain
21 F6 Verkhnebakanskiy Rus. Fed.
17 Q3 Verkhnedneprovskiy Rus. Fed.
24 K3 Verkhneimbatskoye Rus. Fed.
6 W2 Verkhnetulomskiy Rus. Fed.
25 O3 Verkhnevilyuysk Rus. Fed.

8 D3 Walney, Isle of *i.* U.K.
68 C5 Walnut U.S.A.
73 G4 Walnut Canyon National Monument *res.* U.S.A.
65 F4 Walnut Ridge U.S.A.
35 J3 Walong India
9 F5 Walsall U.K.
63 F4 Walsenburg U.S.A.
13 H2 Walsrode Ger.
33 C2 Waltair India
67 D5 Walterboro U.S.A.
67 C6 Walter F. George Res. *resr* U.S.A.
69 J3 Waltham Can.
66 C4 Walton *KY* U.S.A.
71 F3 Walton *NY* U.S.A.
89 B6 Walvis Bay Namibia
96 K7 Walvis Ridge *sea feature* Atl. Ocean
88 C3 Wamba Congo(Zaire)
34 B2 Wana Pak.
51 B6 Wanaka N.Z.
51 B6 Wanaka, L. *l.* N.Z.
39 E5 Wan'an China
69 G2 Wanapitei Lake *l.* Can.
71 F4 Wanaque Reservoir U.S.A.
50 C3 Wanbi Austr.
51 C6 Wanbrow, Cape *c.* N.Z.
40 C2 Wanda Shan *mts* China
13 J4 Wandersleben Ger.
13 M2 Wandlitz Ger.
42 D6 Wando S. Korea
51 E3 Wanganui N.Z.
51 E3 Wanganui *r.* N.Z.
50 F4 Wangaratta Austr.
38 C3 Wangcang China
39 D4 Wangcheng China
13 F1 Wangerooge Ger.
13 F1 Wangerooge *i.* Ger.
42 A3 Wanghai Shan *h.* China
39 E4 Wangjiang China
39 C5 Wangmo China
42 E2 Wangqing China
34 B5 Wankaner India
88 E3 Wanlaweyn Somalia
13 F1 Wanna Ger.
39 E4 Wannian China
39 D7 Wanning China
38 E1 Wanquan China
12 D3 Wanroij Neth.
39 D6 Wanshan Qundao *is* China
51 F4 Wanstead N.Z.
9 F6 Wantage U.K.
69 G2 Wanup Can.
39 C4 Wanxian China
39 C4 Wan Xian China
38 C3 Wanyuan China
39 E4 Wanzai China
12 D4 Wanze Belgium
70 A4 Wapakoneta U.S.A.
68 B5 Wapello U.S.A.
58 C3 Wapikopa L. *l.* Can.
56 F4 Wapiti *r.* Can.
65 F4 Wappapello, L. *resr* U.S.A.
68 A5 Wapsipinicon *r.* U.S.A.
38 B3 Waqên China
30 C6 Waqr *well* S. Arabia
34 A4 Warah Pak.
33 B2 Warangal India
50 E4 Waranga Reservoir Austr.
34 E5 Waraseoni India
50 F5 Waratah B. *b.* Austr.
13 H3 Warburg Ger.
48 C4 Warburton Austr.
48 D4 Warburton *watercourse* Austr.
57 G2 Warburton Bay *l.* Can.
91 H3 Warden S. Africa
13 G1 Wardenburg Ger.
34 D5 Wardha India
34 D6 Wardha *r.* India
51 A6 Ward, Mt *mt* Southland N.Z.
51 B5 Ward, Mt *mt* West Coast N.Z.
56 D3 Ware Can.
71 G3 Ware U.S.A.
9 E7 Wareham U.K.
71 H4 Wareham U.S.A.
12 D4 Waremme Belgium
13 L1 Waren Ger.
13 F3 Warendorf Ger.
13 K1 Warin Ger.
44 C2 Warin Chamrap Thai.
51 E2 Warkworth N.Z.
8 F2 Warkworth U.K.
12 A4 Warloy-Baillon France
57 H4 Warman Can.
90 C4 Warmbad Namibia
91 H2 Warmbad S. Africa
9 E6 Warminster U.K.
71 F4 Warminster U.S.A.
12 C2 Warmond Neth.
72 D2 Warm Springs *NV* U.S.A.
70 D5 Warm Springs *VA* U.S.A.
90 D6 Warmwaterberg *mts* S. Africa
71 H3 Warner U.S.A.
62 B3 Warner Mts *mts* U.S.A.
67 D5 Warner Robins U.S.A.
78 F7 Warnes Bol.
34 D5 Warora India
50 D4 Warracknabeal Austr.
50 H3 Warragamba Reservoir Austr.
50 E5 Warragul Austr.
48 E4 Warrego *r.* Austr.
50 F1 Warren Austr.
69 G2 Warren Can.
65 E5 Warren *AR* U.S.A.
69 F4 Warren *MI* U.S.A.
64 D1 Warren *MN* U.S.A.
70 C4 Warren *OH* U.S.A.
70 D4 Warren *PA* U.S.A.
70 C4 Warrendale U.S.A.
11 E3 Warrenpoint U.K.
64 E4 Warrensburg *MO* U.S.A.
71 G3 Warrensburg *NY* U.S.A.
90 F4 Warrenton S. Africa
70 E5 Warrenton U.S.A.
86 C4 Warri Nigeria
51 C6 Warrington N.Z.
9 E4 Warrington U.K.
67 C6 Warrington U.S.A.
50 D5 Warrnambool Austr.
64 E1 Warroad U.S.A.
50 G1 Warrumbungle Ra. *mts* Austr.
17 K4 Warsaw Pol.
68 E5 Warsaw *IN* U.S.A.
64 E4 Warsaw *MO* U.S.A.
70 D3 Warsaw *NY* U.S.A.
70 E6 Warsaw *VA* U.S.A.
13 G3 Warstein Ger.
Warszawa *see* Warsaw
16 G4 Warta *r.* Pol.
48 F4 Warwick Austr.
9 F5 Warwick U.K.
71 F4 Warwick *NY* U.S.A.
71 H4 Warwick *RI* U.S.A.
63 E4 Wasatch Range *mts* U.S.A.
91 J4 Wasbank S. Africa
72 C4 Wasco U.S.A.
64 E2 Waseca U.S.A.
31 F5 Washap Pak.
68 C5 Washburn *IL* U.S.A.
71 J1 Washburn *ME* U.S.A.
64 C2 Washburn *ND* U.S.A.
68 B2 Washburn *WI* U.S.A.
34 D5 Wāshīm India
70 E5 Washington *DC* U.S.A.
67 D5 Washington *GA* U.S.A.
68 B5 Washington *IA* U.S.A.
68 C5 Washington *IL* U.S.A.
66 C4 Washington *IN* U.S.A.
64 F4 Washington *MO* U.S.A.
67 E5 Washington *NC* U.S.A.
71 F4 Washington *NJ* U.S.A.
70 C4 Washington *PA* U.S.A.
73 F3 Washington *UT* U.S.A.
62 B2 Washington *div.* U.S.A.
92 B5 Washington, C. *c.* Ant.
70 B5 Washington Court House U.S.A.
68 D3 Washington Island *i.* U.S.A.
55 M1 Washington Land *reg.* Greenland
71 H2 Washington, Mt *mt* U.S.A.
65 D5 Washita *r.* U.S.A.
9 H5 Wash, The *b.* U.K.
31 G5 Washuk Pak.
30 B5 Wasi' S. Arabia
29 L5 Wasit Iraq
58 E3 Waskaganish Can.
57 K3 Waskaiowaka Lake *l.* Can.
12 C2 Wassenaar Neth.
90 C3 Wasser Namibia
13 H4 Wasserkuppe *h.* Ger.
13 J5 Wassertrüdingen Ger.
72 C2 Wassuk Range *mts* U.S.A.
58 E4 Waswanipi, Lac *l.* Can.
37 E7 Watampone Indon.
71 G4 Waterbury *CT* U.S.A.
71 G2 Waterbury *VT* U.S.A.
57 H3 Waterbury Lake *l.* Can.
11 D5 Waterford Rep. of Ireland
70 D4 Waterford U.S.A.
11 E5 Waterford Harbour *harbour* Rep. of Ireland
11 C5 Watergrasshill Rep. of Ireland
12 C4 Waterloo Belgium
69 G4 Waterloo Can.
68 A4 Waterloo *IA* U.S.A.
71 H3 Waterloo *ME* U.S.A.
70 E3 Waterloo *NY* U.S.A.
68 C4 Waterloo *WI* U.S.A.
9 F7 Waterlooville U.K.
91 H1 Waterpoort S. Africa
68 C2 Watersmeet U.S.A.
56 G5 Waterton Lakes Nat. Park Can.
71 E3 Watertown *NY* U.S.A.
64 D2 Watertown *SD* U.S.A.
68 C4 Watertown *WI* U.S.A.
91 J2 Waterval-Boven S. Africa
50 B2 Watervale Austr.
71 J2 Waterville U.S.A.
57 G3 Waterways Can.
69 G4 Watford Can.
9 G6 Watford U.K.
64 C2 Watford City U.S.A.
57 J3 Wathaman *r.* Can.
13 J2 Wathlingen Ger.
70 E3 Watkins Glen U.S.A.
Watling *i. see* San Salvador
65 D5 Watonga U.S.A.
57 H4 Watrous Can.
88 C3 Watsa Congo(Zaire)
68 D5 Watseka U.S.A.
88 C4 Watsi Kengo Congo(Zaire)
57 J4 Watson Can.
56 D2 Watson Lake Can.
72 B3 Watsonville U.S.A.
10 E2 Watten U.K.
10 E2 Watten, Loch *l.* U.K.
57 J2 Watterson Lake *l.* Can.
56 F3 Watt, Mt *h.* Can.
9 H5 Watton U.K.
68 C2 Watton U.S.A.
37 D2 Watubela, Kepulauan *is* Indon.
48 E2 Wau P.N.G.
87 E4 Wau Sudan
68 D3 Waucedah U.S.A.
67 D7 Wauchula U.S.A.
68 D4 Waukegan U.S.A.
68 C4 Waukesha U.S.A.
68 B4 Waukon U.S.A.
68 C3 Waupaca U.S.A.
68 C4 Waupun U.S.A.
65 D5 Waurika U.S.A.
68 C3 Wausau U.S.A.
70 A4 Wauseon U.S.A.
68 C3 Wautoma U.S.A.
68 C4 Wauwatosa U.S.A.
9 J5 Waveney *r.* U.K.
68 A4 Waverly *IA* U.S.A.
70 B5 Waverly *OH* U.S.A.
67 C4 Waverly *TN* U.S.A.
70 E6 Waverly *VA* U.S.A.
12 C4 Wavre Belgium
68 E1 Wawa Can.
86 C4 Wawa Nigeria
68 E5 Wawasee, Lake *l.* U.S.A.
72 C3 Wawona U.S.A.
65 D5 Waxahachie U.S.A.
67 D6 Waycross U.S.A.
70 B6 Wayland *KY* U.S.A.
70 B5 Wayland *MO* U.S.A.
64 D3 Wayne U.S.A.
67 D5 Waynesboro *GA* U.S.A.
65 F6 Waynesboro *MS* U.S.A.
70 E5 Waynesboro *PA* U.S.A.
70 D5 Waynesboro *VA* U.S.A.
70 C5 Waynesburg U.S.A.
65 E4 Waynesville U.S.A.
65 D4 Waynoka U.S.A.
87 D3 Waza, Parc National de *nat. park* Cameroon
34 C2 Wazirabad Pak.
86 C3 W du Niger, Parcs Nationaux du *nat. park* Niger
58 B3 Weagamow L. *l.* Can.
9 H6 Weald, The *reg.* U.K.
8 E3 Wear *r.* U.K.
48 E3 Weary B. *b.* Austr.
65 D5 Weatherford U.S.A.
62 B3 Weaverville U.S.A.
69 G2 Webbwood Can.
58 C3 Webequie Can.
56 D3 Weber, Mt *mt* Can.
88 E3 Webi Shabeelle *r.* Somalia
71 H3 Webster *MA* U.S.A.
64 D2 Webster *SD* U.S.A.
68 A3 Webster *WI* U.S.A.
64 E3 Webster City U.S.A.
70 C5 Webster Springs U.S.A.
80 D8 Weddell I. *i.* Falkland Is
92 B2 Weddell Sea *sea* Ant.
50 D4 Wedderburn Austr.
13 H1 Wedel (Holstein) Ger.
62 B3 Weed U.S.A.
70 D4 Weedville U.S.A.
91 J4 Weenen S. Africa
12 F1 Weener Ger.
12 E2 Weerribben, Nationaal Park De *nat. park* Neth.
12 D3 Weert Neth.
50 F2 Weethalle Austr.
12 E3 Wegberg Ger.
17 K3 Węgorzewo Pol.
38 B2 Wei *r.* *Henan* China
38 D3 Wei *r.* *Shaanxi* China
38 E1 Weichang China
13 L4 Weida Ger.
13 K5 Weidenberg Ger.
13 L5 Weiden in der Oberpfalz Ger.
38 F2 Weifang China
42 B5 Weihai China
42 D2 Weihu Ling *mts* China
13 G4 Weilburg Ger.
13 K4 Weimar Ger.
38 C3 Weinan China
13 G5 Weinheim Ger.
39 B5 Weining China
13 H5 Weinsberg Ger.
48 E3 Weipa Austr.
57 L3 Weir River Can.
70 C4 Weirton U.S.A.
62 C2 Weiser U.S.A.
38 E3 Weishan China
38 E3 Weishan Hu *l.* China
38 E3 Weishi China
13 J5 Weißenburg in Bayern Ger.
13 K3 Weißenfels Ger.
67 C5 Weiss L. *l.* U.S.A.
90 C2 Weissrand Mts *mts* Namibia
13 G5 Weiterstadt Ger.
39 B5 Weixin China
38 B3 Weiyuan *Gansu* China
39 B4 Weiyuan *Sichuan* China
16 G7 Weiz Austria
39 C6 Weizhou Dao *i.* China
42 B3 Weizi China
16 J3 Wejherowo Pol.
57 K4 Wekusko Can.
57 K4 Wekusko Lake *l.* Can.
70 C6 Welch U.S.A.
71 H2 Weld U.S.A.
88 D2 Weldiya Eth.
72 C4 Weldon U.S.A.
88 D3 Welk'īt'ē Eth.
91 G3 Welkom S. Africa
69 H4 Welland Can.
9 G5 Welland *r.* U.K.
69 H4 Welland Canal *canal* Can.
33 C5 Wellawaya Sri Lanka
69 G4 Wellesley Can.
48 D3 Wellesley Is *is* Austr.
56 B2 Wellesley Lake *l.* Can.
71 H4 Wellfleet U.S.A.
12 D4 Wellin Belgium
9 G5 Wellingborough U.K.
50 G2 Wellington *N.S.W.* Austr.
50 B3 Wellington *S.A.* Austr.
51 E4 Wellington N.Z.
90 C6 Wellington S. Africa
9 D7 Wellington *Eng.* U.K.
9 E5 Wellington *Eng.* U.K.
62 F3 Wellington *CO* U.S.A.
65 D4 Wellington *KS* U.S.A.
72 C2 Wellington *NV* U.S.A.
70 B4 Wellington *OH* U.S.A.
65 C5 Wellington *TX* U.S.A.
73 G2 Wellington *UT* U.S.A.
80 A7 Wellington, I. *i.* Chile
50 F5 Wellington, L. *l.* Austr.
68 B5 Wellman U.S.A.
56 E4 Wells Can.
9 E6 Wells U.K.
62 D3 Wells *NV* U.S.A.
71 F3 Wells *NY* U.S.A.
70 E4 Wellsboro U.S.A.
51 E2 Wellsford N.Z.
56 E4 Wells Gray Prov. Park *res.* Can.
48 C4 Wells, L. *salt flat* Austr.
9 H5 Wells-next-the-Sea U.K.
70 B5 Wellston U.S.A.
70 E3 Wellsville U.S.A.
73 E5 Wellton U.S.A.
16 G6 Wels Austria
71 K2 Welshpool Can.
9 D5 Welshpool U.K.
13 M3 Welsickendorf Ger.
9 G6 Welwyn Garden City U.K.
13 H6 Welzheim Ger.
9 E5 Wem U.K.
91 H4 Wembesi S. Africa
56 F3 Wembley Can.
58 E3 Wemindji Can.
67 E7 Wemyss Bight Bahamas
38 F3 Wen *r.* China
62 B2 Wenatchee U.S.A.
39 D7 Wenchang China
39 F5 Wencheng China
86 B4 Wenchi Ghana
38 B4 Wenchuan China
13 K5 Wendelstein Ger.
13 F4 Wenden Ger.
73 F5 Wenden U.S.A.
42 B5 Wendeng China
88 D3 Wendo Eth.
62 D3 Wendover U.S.A.
69 F2 Wenebegon Lake *l.* Can.
39 C5 Weng'an China
39 E5 Wengyuan China
38 B4 Wenjiang China
39 F4 Wenling China
78 □ Wenman, Isla *i. Galapagos Is* Ecuador
68 C5 Wenona U.S.A.
39 B6 Wenshan China
9 H5 Wensum *r.* U.K.
13 J1 Wentorf bei Hamburg Ger.
50 C3 Wentworth Austr.
71 H3 Wentworth U.S.A.
38 B3 Wen Xian China
39 F5 Wenzhou China
13 L2 Wenzlow Ger.
91 G4 Wepener S. Africa
45 A1 We, Pulau *i.* Indon.
13 K2 Werben (Elbe) Ger.
90 E2 Werda Botswana
13 L4 Werdau Ger.
13 L2 Werder Ger.
13 F3 Werdohl Ger.
13 F3 Werl Ger.
13 L5 Wernberg-Köblitz Ger.
12 F3 Werne Ger.
56 C2 Wernecke Mountains Can.
13 J3 Wernigerode Ger.
13 H3 Werra *r.* Ger.
50 E4 Werribee Austr.
50 C3 Werrimull Austr.
50 H1 Werris Creek Austr.
13 H5 Wertheim Ger.
12 B4 Wervik Belgium
12 E3 Wesel Ger.
12 E3 Wesel-Datteln-Kanal *canal* Ger.
13 L1 Wesenberg Ger.
13 J2 Wesendorf Ger.
13 G1 Weser *chan.* Ger.
13 H2 Weser *r.* Ger.
13 G2 Wesergebirge *h.* Ger.
64 C4 Weskan U.S.A.
69 J3 Weslemkoon Lake *l.* Can.
71 K2 Wesley U.S.A.
59 K4 Wesleyville Can.
48 D3 Wessel, C. *c.* Austr.
48 D3 Wessel Is *is* Austr.
91 H3 Wesselton S. Africa
64 D2 Wessington Springs U.S.A.
68 C4 West Allis U.S.A.
92 A4 West Antarctica *reg.* Ant.
93 L5 West Australian Basin *sea feature* Ind. Ocean
93 L6 West Australian Ridge *sea feature* Ind. Ocean
34 B5 West Banas *r.* India
28 E5 West Bank *terr.* Asia
59 J3 West Bay Can.
65 F6 West Bay *b.* U.S.A.
68 C4 West Bend U.S.A.
35 F5 West Bengal *div.* India
69 E3 West Branch U.S.A.
70 D4 West Branch Susquehanna *r.* U.S.A.
9 F5 West Bromwich U.K.
71 H3 Westbrook U.S.A.
10 □ West Burra *i.* U.K.
9 E6 Westbury U.K.
50 F3 Westby Austr.
68 B4 Westby U.S.A.
94 E5 West Caroline Basin *sea feature* Pac. Oc.
71 F5 West Chester U.S.A.
71 G2 West Danville U.S.A.
69 F3 West Duck Island *i.* Can.
67 E7 West End Bahamas
72 D4 Westend U.S.A.
67 E7 West End Pt *pt* Bahamas
13 F4 Westerburg Ger.
12 F1 Westerholt Ger.
16 D3 Westerland Ger.
12 C3 Westerlo Belgium
71 H4 Westerly U.S.A.
57 H1 Western *r.* Can.
48 C4 Western Australia *div.* Austr.
90 D6 Western Cape *div.* S. Africa
87 E2 Western Desert Egypt
33 A2 Western Ghats *mts* India
50 E5 Western Port *b.* Austr.
85 B3 Western Sahara *terr.* Africa
47 K5 Western Samoa *country* Pac. Oc.
12 B3 Westerschelde *est.* Neth.
13 F1 Westerstede Ger.
13 F4 Westerwald *reg.* Ger.
80 D8 West Falkland *i.* Falkland Is
64 D2 West Fargo U.S.A.
68 D5 Westfield *IN* U.S.A.
71 G3 Westfield *MA* U.S.A.
71 K1 Westfield *ME* U.S.A.
70 D3 Westfield *NY* U.S.A.
12 E1 Westgat *chan.* Neth.
71 K2 West Grand Lake *l.* U.S.A.
13 J6 Westhausen Ger.
10 F3 Westhill U.K.
64 C1 Westhope U.S.A.
92 D5 West Ice Shelf *ice feature* Ant.
12 B3 Westkapelle Neth.
39 □ West Lamma Chan. *chan. H.K.* China
70 B5 West Lancaster U.S.A.
51 B5 Westland National Park N.Z.
9 J5 Westleton U.K.
72 B3 Westley U.S.A.
70 B6 West Liberty *KY* U.S.A.
70 B4 West Liberty *OH* U.S.A.
10 E5 West Linton U.K.
10 B2 West Loch Roag *b.* U.K.
56 G4 Westlock Can.
69 G4 West Lorne Can.
12 C3 Westmalle Belgium
65 F5 West Memphis U.S.A.
70 E5 Westminster *MD* U.S.A.
67 D5 Westminster *SC* U.S.A.
70 C5 Weston U.S.A.
9 E6 Weston-super-Mare U.K.
71 F5 Westover U.S.A.
67 D7 West Palm Beach U.S.A.
65 F4 West Plains U.S.A.
65 F5 West Point *MS* U.S.A.
71 F4 West Point *NY* U.S.A.
69 J3 Westport Can.
51 C4 Westport N.Z.
11 B4 Westport Rep. of Ireland
72 A2 Westport U.S.A.
57 J4 Westray Can.
10 E1 Westray *i.* U.K.
69 G2 Westree Can.
12 F5 Westrich *reg.* Ger.
56 E4 West Road *r.* Can.
71 H2 West Stewartstown U.S.A.
12 D1 West-Terschelling Neth.
71 H4 West Tisbury U.S.A.
71 G2 West Topsham U.S.A.
71 G3 West Townshend U.S.A.
68 B4 West Union *IA* U.S.A.
70 B5 West Union *OH* U.S.A.
70 C5 West Union *WV* U.S.A.
68 D5 Westville U.S.A.
70 C5 West Virginia *div.* U.S.A.
72 C2 West Walker *r.* U.S.A.
72 B1 Westwood U.S.A.
50 F2 West Wyalong Austr.
62 E2 West Yellowstone U.S.A.
12 C2 Westzaan Neth.
37 E7 Wetar *i.* Indon.
56 G4 Wetaskiwin Can.
68 D2 Wetmore U.S.A.
13 G4 Wetter *r.* Ger.
13 K3 Wettin Ger.
13 G4 Wetzlar Ger.
48 E2 Wewak P.N.G.
11 E5 Wexford Rep. of Ireland
57 H4 Weyakwin Can.
68 C3 Weyauwega U.S.A.
9 G6 Weybridge U.K.
57 J5 Weyburn Can.
13 G2 Weyhe Ger.
9 E7 Weymouth U.K.
71 H3 Weymouth U.S.A.
12 E2 Wezep Neth.
51 F2 Whakatane N.Z.
51 F3 Whakatane *r.* N.Z.
44 A3 Whale B. *b.* Myanmar
56 B3 Whale B. *b.* U.S.A.
67 E7 Whale Cay *i.* Bahamas
57 L2 Whale Cove Can.
10 □ Whalsay *i.* U.K.
51 E2 Whangamata N.Z.
51 E3 Whangamomona N.Z.
51 E1 Whangarei N.Z.
58 E2 Whapmagoostui Can.
8 F4 Wharfe *r.* U.K.
69 F2 Wharncliffe Can.
57 J2 Wharton Lake *l.* Can.
68 A5 What Cheer U.S.A.
62 F3 Wheatland U.S.A.
68 C5 Wheaton U.S.A.
63 F4 Wheeler Peak *summit NM* U.S.A.
73 E2 Wheeler Peak *summit NV* U.S.A.
70 C4 Wheeling U.S.A.
83 E2 Wheelwright Arg.
8 E3 Whernside *h.* U.K.
62 B3 Whiskeytown-Shasta-Trinity Nat. Recreation Area *res.* U.S.A.
10 E5 Whitburn U.K.
69 H4 Whitby Can.
8 G3 Whitby U.K.
9 E5 Whitchurch U.K.
56 A2 White *r. AK/Y.T.* Can./U.S.A.
65 E4 White *r. AR* U.S.A.
73 G5 White *r. AZ* U.S.A.
62 E3 White *r. CO* U.S.A.
66 C4 White *r. IN* U.S.A.
68 D4 White *r. MI* U.S.A.
73 E2 White *r. NV* U.S.A.
64 C3 White *r. SD* U.S.A.
68 B2 White *r. WI* U.S.A.
59 J3 White Bay *b.* Can.
64 C2 White Butte *mt* U.S.A.
68 E4 White Cloud U.S.A.
56 F4 Whitecourt Can.
68 A2 Whiteface Lake *l.* U.S.A.
71 H2 Whitefield U.S.A.
69 G2 Whitefish Can.
62 D1 Whitefish *MT* U.S.A.
68 D3 Whitefish *r. MI* U.S.A.
57 H2 Whitefish Lake *l.* Can.
68 E2 Whitefish Pt *pt* U.S.A.
11 D5 Whitehall Rep. of Ireland
10 F1 Whitehall U.K.
71 G3 Whitehall *NY* U.S.A.
68 B3 Whitehall *WV* U.S.A.
8 D3 Whitehaven U.K.
11 F3 Whitehead U.K.
9 G6 Whitehill U.K.
56 B2 Whitehorse Can.
73 E1 White Horse Pass U.S.A.
9 F6 White Horse, Vale of *v.* U.K.
92 D4 White I. *i.* Ant.
51 F2 White I. *i.* N.Z.
65 E6 White L. *l. LA* U.S.A.
68 D4 White L. *l. MI* U.S.A.
48 C4 White, L. *salt flat* Austr.
71 H2 White Mountains U.S.A.
72 C3 White Mt Peak *summit* U.S.A.
87 F3 White Nile *r.* Sudan/Uganda
90 C1 White Nossob *watercourse* Namibia
73 E2 White Pine Range *mts* U.S.A.
71 G4 White Plains U.S.A.
58 C4 White River Can.
73 H5 Whiteriver U.S.A.
71 G3 White River Junction U.S.A.
73 E2 White River Valley *v.* U.S.A.
73 E2 White Rock Peak *summit* U.S.A.
63 F5 White Sands Nat. Mon. *res.* U.S.A.
70 B6 Whitesburg U.S.A.
24 E3 White Sea *g.* Rus. Fed.
57 K4 Whiteshell Prov. Park *res.* Can.
62 E2 White Sulphur Springs *MT* U.S.A.
70 C6 White Sulphur Springs *WV* U.S.A.
67 E5 Whiteville U.S.A.
86 B4 White Volta *r.* Ghana
68 C4 Whitewater U.S.A.
58 C3 Whitewater L. *l.* Can.
57 J4 Whitewood Can.
50 F4 Whitfield Austr.
9 J6 Whitfield U.K.
10 D6 Whithorn U.K.
51 E2 Whitianga N.Z.
71 K2 Whiting U.S.A.
9 C6 Whitland U.K.
8 F2 Whitley Bay U.K.
67 D5 Whitmire U.S.A.
69 H3 Whitney Can.
72 C3 Whitney, Mt *mt* U.S.A.
71 K2 Whitneyville U.S.A.
9 J6 Whitstable U.K.
48 E4 Whitsunday I. *i.* Austr.
50 E4 Whittlesea Austr.
9 G5 Whittlesey U.K.
50 F3 Whitton Austr.
57 H2 Wholdaia Lake *l.* Can.
73 F5 Why U.S.A.
50 A2 Whyalla Austr.
44 A1 Wiang Phran Thai.
44 B1 Wiang Sa Thai.
69 G3 Wiarton Can.
12 B3 Wichelen Belgium
65 D4 Wichita U.S.A.
65 D5 Wichita Falls U.S.A.
65 D5 Wichita Mts *mts* U.S.A.
10 E2 Wick U.K.
73 F5 Wickenburg U.S.A.
9 H6 Wickford U.K.
11 E5 Wicklow Rep. of Ireland
11 F5 Wicklow Head *hd* Rep. of Ireland
11 E5 Wicklow Mountains Rep. of Ireland
11 E4 Wicklow Mountains National Park Rep. of Ireland
9 E4 Widnes U.K.
42 D6 Wi-do *i.* S. Korea
13 G2 Wiehengebirge *h.* Ger.
12 F4 Wiehl Ger.
17 J5 Wieluń Pol.
Wien *see* Vienna
16 H7 Wiener Neustadt Austria
12 E2 Wierden Neth.
13 J2 Wieren Ger.
12 C2 Wieringermeer Polder *reclaimed land* Neth.
12 D2 Wieringerwerf Neth.
13 G4 Wiesbaden Ger.
13 L5 Wiesenfelden Ger.
13 J5 Wiesentheid Ger.
13 G5 Wiesloch Ger.
13 F1 Wiesmoor Ger.
13 H2 Wietze Ger.
13 H2 Wietzendorf Ger.
16 J3 Wieżyca *h.* Pol.
8 E4 Wigan U.K.
65 F6 Wiggins U.S.A.
9 F7 Wight, Isle of *i.* U.K.
57 H2 Wignes Lake *l.* Can.
9 F5 Wigston U.K.
8 D3 Wigton U.K.
10 D6 Wigtown U.K.
10 D6 Wigtown Bay *b.* U.K.
12 D3 Wijchen Neth.
12 E2 Wijhe Neth.
12 C3 Wijnegem Belgium
73 F4 Wikieup U.S.A.
69 G3 Wikwemikong Can.
62 C2 Wilbur U.S.A.
50 D1 Wilcannia Austr.
13 L2 Wildberg Ger.
57 J4 Wildcat Hill Wilderness Park *res.* Can.
72 D2 Wildcat Peak *summit* U.S.A.
91 H5 Wild Coast *coastal area* S. Africa
13 G2 Wildeshausen Ger.
68 C1 Wild Goose Can.
56 F4 Wildhay *r.* Can.
68 A2 Wild Rite Lake *l.* U.S.A.
16 E7 Wildspitze *mt* Austria
67 D6 Wildwood *FL* U.S.A.
71 F5 Wildwood *NJ* U.S.A.
91 H3 Wilge *r. Free State* S. Africa
91 H2 Wilge *r. Gauteng/Mpumalanga* S. Africa
92 C5 Wilhelm II Land *reg.* Ant.
70 C4 Wilhelm, Lake *l.* U.S.A.
48 E2 Wilhelm, Mt *mt* P.N.G.
13 G1 Wilhelmshaven Ger.
71 F4 Wilkes-Barre U.S.A.
92 B6 Wilkes Coast *coastal area* Ant.
92 B6 Wilkes Land *reg.* Ant.
57 H4 Wilkie Can.

# ACKNOWLEDGEMENTS

Pages 12-13
Photos : **Pictor International - London**

Pages 24-25
Photos : **Science Photo Library**
Data : **Telegeography Inc, Washington DC**
www.telegeography.com
**Petroleum Economist Ltd., London**
www.petroleum-economist.com
**Network Wizards**
www.nw.com